Civil War America

Gary W. Gallagher, editor

The Life
and Wars of
Gideon J.
Pillow

Nathaniel Cheairs Hughes, Jr.

Roy P. Stonesifer, Jr.

The University of North Carolina Press

Chapel Hill & London

The Life

and Wars of Gideon J.

Pillow

The paper in this book meets the guidelines for permanence and durability of the Committee on Production Guidelines for Book Longevity of the Council on Library Resources.

Library of Congress Cataloging-in-Publication Data

Hughes, Nathaniel Cheairs.
The life and wars of Gideon J. Pillow / Nathaniel Cheairs Hughes, Jr., and Roy P. Stonesifer, Jr.
p.   cm.
Includes bibliographical references (p.) and index.
ISBN 0-8078-2107-1 (cloth : alk. paper)
1. Pillow, Gideon Johnson, 1806–1878.   2. Generals—Confederate States of America—Biography.
3. Generals—United States—Biography.   4. Confederate States of America. Army—Biography.
I. Stonesifer, Roy P.   II. Title.
E467.1.P63H84   1993
973.7'13—dc20
[B]   93-3250
                                          CIP

97 96 95 94 93 5 4 3 2 1

To my great-grandfather,

Pvt. Isaac Swartz,

Company K, 5th Virginia Infantry,

Stonewall Brigade,

who gave a leg for the South,

August 30, 1862,

at Second Manassas

RPS

and

To my kinsman,

Pvt. Edward H. Pointer,

Company G, 11th Tennessee Cavalry,

killed May 7, 1864,

at Lick Creek, Tennessee

NCH

Contents

Maps

Illustrations

Preface

Dispute swirls about many American military figures, but Gideon Johnson Pillow is one of the very few attended by great notoriety in two wars. His role as an aggressive brigade and division commander in Mexico was bathed in controversy and brought the commanding general of the American army into disastrous conflict with the president of the United States. Thirteen years later in the Fort Donelson calamity, Pillow's role was critical, misunderstood then and since.

Pillow, a Middle Tennessee planter-lawyer, had been a civilian success story. His law practice thrived. His land- and slaveholdings expanded and expanded and expanded. Through industry and shrewd investment, Pillow became, in his own words, "rich," one of the wealthiest men in the South. His friendship with James K. Polk led to the Democratic National Convention of 1844, where he was instrumental in Polk's nomination for president. The trust relationship thus developed catapulted Pillow, during the Mexican War, from civilian to major general, second in command to Winfield Scott.

Pillow rendered conspicuous service in Mexico. Afterward, in 1850, he took part in the Nashville Convention, helping defeat southern extremists. He attempted to gain the nomination for himself as vice-president of the United States in 1852 and 1856. On the state level he exercised political power for twenty-five years. In 1860 he walked a tightrope, trying to rally Tennessee behind Stephen A. Douglas in a futile attempt to restore the shattered national Democratic party he loved.

Pillow was Tennessee's best-known soldier in 1861, its senior general officer, its "Hero of Chapultepec." No other living southerner, save Winfield Scott, had held higher rank. With great vigor Pillow and Gov. Isham G. Harris built the military organization that became the Army of Tennessee. Pillow commanded against Grant at Belmont; became ensnared in the fighting and quarreling at Fort Donelson; returned temporarily to field command at Murfreesboro; operated with great success, but again with great controversy, the new Volunteer and Conscript Bureau of the Army of Tennessee; commanded a brigade of cavalry in 1864; and ended the war as commissary general of prisoners, but still brigadier general. Following the war Pillow tried, in every way he could devise, and against terrible odds, to recover his lands, his fortune, and his position in society.

Few individuals have been more fortunately placed. Fame chose Gideon Pillow as her darling and laid opportunities at his feet like golden apples, but he kicked them aside. So she turned her face, pointed her finger at him, and pronounced that in history he would become a caricature of himself, his name always good for a throw-away laugh.

Acknowledgments

No historian works alone. They build upon the work of those scholars who preceded them; they locate and process research material with the guidance of others. Certainly this has been true in the writing of this biography. We are grateful for those who so generously gave of their time and energy to help us.

Linda and John R. Neal graciously opened Clifton Place to us and generously shared Pillow documents they had collected over twenty years. To assist us, they made available the services of historians Paul Cross and Wally A. Hebert, Jr., of JRN, Inc., who helped us with enthusiasm and insight.

To Nathan Lipscomb, Dr. Wayne Cutler, Dr. B. Franklin Cooling, Dr. Paul H. Bergeron, James P. Cole, Douglas C. Purcell, and Charles Spearman go our thanks for reading and commenting on various chapters. They aided substantially by improving the accuracy, the completeness, and the logic of the narrative. The responsibility for errors and judgments, however, remains ours.

Jill K. Garrett, County Historian of Maury County, Tennessee, encouraged us every step of the way and provided indispensable material.

We also wish to thank the following for their assistance, provided either in their capacities as librarians and archivists or as private individuals:

Ann Alley, Tennessee State Archives, Nashville, Tennessee; Anne Armor, University of the South, Sewanee, Tennessee; Louise Arnold-Friend, U.S. Military History Institute, Carlisle, Pennsylvania; Fred Bauman, Library of Congress, Washington, D.C.; Dr. Edwin C. Bearss, National Park Service, Washington, D.C.; Betsy Bishop, University of Chicago Library, Chicago, Illinois; Judy Bolton, Louisiana and Lower Mississippi Valley Collection, Louisiana State University Library, Baton Rouge, Louisiana; Jenny Ann Boyer, Marianna, Arkansas; Stuart L. Butler, National Archives, Washington, D.C.; Virginia J. H. Cain, Emory University Library, Atlanta, Georgia; Andrea E. Cantrell, University of Arkansas, Fayetteville, Arkansas; Dr. James P. Cooper, Harpeth Hall School, Nashville, Tennessee; Neil

Coulter, Lupton Library, University of Tennessee at Chattanooga, Chattanooga, Tennessee; Dr. Charles W. Crawford, Memphis State University, Memphis, Tennessee; Patricia L. Denault, Cambridge, Massachusetts; Al Duke, Chattanooga, Tennessee; John S. D. Eisenhower, Trappe, Maryland; Charles Elliott, Baton Rouge, Louisiana; John L. Ferguson, Arkansas History Commission, Little Rock, Arkansas; Anne G. Fisher, Memphis, Tennessee; Ed Frank, Mississippi Valley Collection, Memphis State University, Memphis, Tennessee; Richard Fraser, New-York Historical Society, New York, New York; John J. Grabowski, Western Reserve Historical Society, Cleveland, Ohio; Todd Groce, East Tennessee Historical Society, Knoxville, Tennessee; Dr. Warren W. Hassler, Jr., Pennsylvania State University, University Park, Pennsylvania; James J. Holmberg, Filson Club, Louisville, Kentucky; Marylin Hughes, Tennessee State Archives, Nashville, Tennessee; Virginia Hughes, Miller and Martin, Attorneys, Chattanooga, Tennessee; Joyce R. Hyde, Chattanooga, Tennessee; Dr. Tim Johnson, David Lipscomb University, Nashville, Tennessee; Louise T. Jones, Historical Society of Pennsylvania, Philadelphia, Pennsylvania; Anita J. Kimball, Decatur, Alabama; Patricia M. LaPointe, Memphis–Shelby County Library, Memphis, Tennessee; Dr. Linda McCurdy, Duke University Library, Durham, North Carolina; June B. Mann, Marianna, Arkansas; W. E. Menery, Howard Tilton Memorial Library, Tulane University, New Orleans, Louisiana; George Miles, Beinecke Rare Book and Manuscript Library, Yale University, New Haven, Connecticut; Dr. Waddy W. Moore, Conway, Arkansas; Paul Morris, Chattanooga, Tennessee; Danette Mullinax, LaFayette, Georgia; Melba Murray, Cleveland, Tennessee; Lt. Col. Clayton R. Newell, Chief, Historical Services Division, Center of Military History, Washington, D.C.; Jim Ogden, Chickamauga and Chattanooga National Military Park, Fort Oglethorpe, Georgia; Joseph H. Parks, Winchester, Tennessee; Mary Lou Pillow, Coronado, California; Mary E. Powell, Phillips County Museum, Helena, Arkansas; Bill Prince, Lupton Library, University of Tennessee at Chattanooga, Chattanooga, Tennessee; Ralph A. Pugh, Chicago Historical Society, Chicago, Illinois; Thomas C. Reed, Marianna, Arkansas; Dr. Harrison D. Riley, Jr., University of Oklahoma Health Sciences Center, Oklahoma City, Oklahoma; Dr. William K. Scarborough, University of Southern Mississippi, Hattiesburg, Mississippi; Peg Shorts, Secretary, History Department, Edinboro University of Pennsylvania, Edinboro, Pennsylvania; Dr. Richard J. Sommers, U.S. Military History Institute, Carlisle, Pennsylvania; Clara Swan, Bicentennial Library, Chattanooga, Tennessee; Dr. Caroline Wallace, Southern Historical Collection, University of North Carolina, Chapel Hill, North Carolina; Edward F. Williams III, Memphis, Tennessee; Galen R. Wilson, Clements Library, University of Michigan, Ann Arbor, Michigan; and the late T. R. Hay, Locust Valley, New York, Stanley F. Horn, Nashville, Tennessee, and Robert M. McBride, Nashville, Tennessee.

For their role in making their material available and for assistance of all sorts, we wish to thank the staffs of the Southern Historical Collection, University of North Carolina; Manuscript Division, William R. Perkins Library, Duke University; Division of Manuscripts, Library of Congress; Lincoln Collection and Manuscript Collection, Illinois State Historical Library; New-York Historical Society; DuPont Library, University of the South; Massachusetts Historical Society; Cartographic and Military History branches, National Archives; Beinecke Library, Yale University; Tennessee State Library and Archives; Mississippi Valley Collection, Memphis State University; Louisiana and Lower Mississippi Valley Collections, Louisiana State University Library; Memphis–Shelby County Public Library; Lupton Library, University of Tennessee at Chattanooga; U.S. Military History Institute, Carlisle, Pennsylvania; Chattanooga–Hamilton County Bicentennial Library; and the Library of the Boston Athenaeum.

The Life
and Wars of
Gideon J.
Pillow

1   A Jacksonian Tradition

One of the Indians saw a baby playing in the dirt, out in front of the log house. No one was home except the mother. Suddenly the Choctaw reached down and scooped up the infant, wrapped him in a blanket, threw him over his shoulder, and vanished into the cane-brake. The boy's mother screamed and ran out into the fields for the father. The man grabbed his rifle and set out through the cane in pursuit. After an hour he caught up with the Indian hunting party and demanded the child. The Choctaws gave him up without a fight.[1]

They would have had a fight. The boy's father, Gideon Pillow, Sr., had killed Indians before. Son and grandson of Revolutionary War veterans, he had accompanied his father, John Pillow, into the wilderness of Tennessee soon after the war.[2] For more than a generation the Pillows and their fellow Middle Tennessee pioneers learned to live day by day with hardship and fear and cruelty. If need be, they "could scalp an Indian . . . behead a criminal."[3] They fought to survive in the middle of a vast common Indian hunting ground. Tranquility was a fanciful dream—for their grandchildren, perhaps. Renegade Cherokees, the Chickamaugas, terrorized the Cumberland settlements. From 1780 to 1794, they killed a settler about every ten days. In 1794 they scalped a young girl at John Pillow's spring just south of Nashville. To retaliate and put a stop to these raids, Gideon Pillow, Sr., his four brothers, and their neighbors joined James Robertson's expedition to destroy the Chickamauga base at Nickajack, a village in the Cumberland Mountains where the Tennessee River slices through.

When they reached the bank of the river opposite the Chickamauga stronghold, Robertson's men placed their rifles and powder aboard hastily constructed rafts of dry cane. Gideon Pillow, Sr., was a good swimmer and pushed one of the rafts before him, with a nonswimmer "holding to the waistband on his drawers." Once across, the Tennesseans formed and attacked. Nickajack became "a slaughter pen" as settlers killed both warriors and women in a "pitiless rage." Then the frontiersmen returned home to their cabins and farms.[4]

Restless, and with boundless energy, Gideon, Sr., surveyed when not farming. He traveled throughout the new state helping lay out townships and set county boundaries. In the fall of 1802, while again on militia duty, he met Annie Payne, the daughter of an officer in the Revolution and a first cousin of Dolley Payne Madison. They married in 1803 and three years later settled on 1,000 acres he had purchased southwest of what soon became the town of Columbia, fifty miles below Nashville. This magnificent Maury County tract would develop into a cluster of three plantations for their sons—Granville, Gideon, and Jerome.[5] In 1806, however, Maury was still part of Williamson County, and there on June 8, 1806, Gideon Johnson Pillow was born in the cedar log family cabin on the west bank of Little Bigby Creek.[6]

Gideon Pillow, Sr., slowly cleared his tract of dense cane and trees and began to plant—corn, wheat, and cotton. Prospects seemed even brighter, however, in neighboring Giles County, just to the south, so in 1812 he moved his family near the town of Pulaski and established another homestead. He was careful, nevertheless, to retain ownership of his Maury tract.[7]

War came in 1812 with the British and the Indians, and Tennessee could not escape. In 1813, at Fort Mims on the Alabama River, Creeks surprised the garrison and the refugees gathered there for protection, killing 250 of them. Always quick to respond, Andrew Jackson gathered three brigades of militia to attack the Creeks. The Pillow brothers, of course, joined in. William commanded the Second Tennessee Volunteer Regiment with his brothers Gideon, Sr., and Abner as enlisted men. It was hard marching and bloody fighting, but Jackson and his men won clear victories at Tallushatchee and Talladega and finally smashed Creek resistance at Horseshoe Bend in March 1814. Col. William Pillow, who had been wounded at Talladega, went on with Jackson to New Orleans and was by his side when he defeated the British in 1815. Jackson could rely on the Pillows.[8]

Young Gideon grew up in Giles County and at age ten began attending a small local school. At sixteen he entered Wurttenburg Academy in Pulaski. Gideon, Sr., housed his son in an abandoned log hut near the school. An old female slave stayed with the boy, cooking and transforming the hut into home. Pillow would attend class, grappling with the challenges of Greek, Latin, and mathematics, and then return to his primitive home to sleep. He made rapid progress and was a good student, it appears, drawing praise from the principal.[9]

In 1822 Gideon, Sr., left Giles County and returned to his farm on the Little Bigby. His family was now complete. Following Granville and Gideon were Jerome Bonaparte, Narcissa, Cynthia, Mordecai, and Amanda. Columbia had grown as well, homes and stores going up on dusty streets which radiated from the courthouse. Young Gideon and Jerome enrolled at Woodward Academy along with other sons of middle-class farmers and townspeople, including Alfred O. P. Nicholson and William P. Martin. Woodward's headmaster, Dr. Simon P. Jordan, presided over a rigorous, classical curriculum typical of nineteenth-century academies. Pillow appears to have excelled, especially in Greek and Latin, so much so that he completed the preparatory program in one year and prepared to enter Cumberland College in Nashville in the fall of 1823.[10]

Nashville was growing too, rapidly developing into an important social, political, and economic center. Its buildings, many of them now in the Georgian style, reflected the transition from pioneer to antebellum South. The evolution of Cumberland College had been stunted, however, from a chronic lack of funds; it struggled along on occasional public subscriptions and a tuition of $25 for a five-month session. Things changed in 1824, Pillow's second year, when Dr. Philip Lindsley took over. He initiated positive reforms and let it be known that he intended to transform the college into a great university. He invited Tennesseans of substance and vision to share his dream. The state legislature responded in 1826 by passing an act incorporating Cumberland College as the new University of Nashville. Andrew Jackson became one of the trustees and involved himself in its affairs. In this capacity and as a family friend, he came to know Pillow and took a liking to him. He would invite the young student out to the Hermitage on Friday nights to spend the weekend. Gideon Pillow adored him.

The Marquis de Lafayette visited Nashville in 1825. There was a great ball, of course, and the undergraduate Pillow asked the dark-haired beauty Georgiana Beck to accompany him. They had a glorious time at the Lafayette ball, and that night, as they danced around the ballroom, Pillow asked Georgiana to marry him. She agreed, but the promises of May faded by fall and the engagement was broken.[11]

Pillow graduated from the University of Nashville in 1827, one of a class of twelve.[12] Among his classmates were Edwin H. Ewing, David W. Dickinson, and Ebenezer J. Shields, all three of whom would become members of Congress. Pillow had made many acquaintances by age twenty-one. He delighted in conversation and social doings, and he was entertaining, with a quick smile and a warm manner. An observer might note that he seemed inordinately careful of fashion and doubtlessly thought very well of himself, but he was charming, gracious, and generous. Pillow was also smart and extremely ambitious, and he knew how to succeed. He worked hard in college, earning distinction in a program including moral, political, and intellectual philosophy, natural philosophy and mathematics, classical languages, and an introduction to chemistry.[13]

Upon graduation, Pillow decided to become a lawyer and began reading law with Judge William E. Kennedy, one of the circuit court judges of Tennessee. After eighteen months with Kennedy, he took further instruction under Judge William L. Brown of the Tennessee Supreme Court. Following another year of study, Pillow passed the bar examination given by Judges John Catron and Hugh L. White of the Tennessee Supreme Court.[14]

One should not assume that Pillow merely read law for nearly three years, however. He had several irons in the fire, as he always would. He cultivated the friendship of his cousin by marriage, Gov. William Carroll, and in turn this merchant-soldier-politician strongly influenced the military and political thought of young Pillow. Carroll, a Pennsylvanian, had moved to Nashville and opened a hardware store in 1811.

A trusted Jackson lieutenant, he succeeded Jackson as major general of the Middle Tennessee militia at the age of twenty-six and quickly justified Jackson's confidence. He proved himself a leader and a fine soldier at Horseshoe Bend and New Orleans. Enterprising and progressive, the debonair, fashionable Carroll fell on hard times during the panic of 1819, losing his business in Nashville and losing a fortune lending money to friends. He could wear being "poor" like a shiny badge, however, and this simple man of the people, as he packaged himself, won the hearts of his adopted Tennesseans.

Billy Carroll parlayed his reputation as a soldier and his friendship with Andrew Jackson into a highly successful political career. He became the energetic reform governor of Tennessee in 1821 and served six terms, more than any other governor before or since. Carroll stood for absolute loyalty to Jackson and the Democracy. His methods, his speech, and his style impressed themselves upon his protégé Gideon Pillow. Carroll's accomplishments as governor—internal improvements, sound fiscal policy, educational development, and constitutional revision—were accepted by Pillow as political constants. A few years later these goals would come to have a Whiggish ring, but that never seemed to bother Pillow.

In the spring of 1830, President Jackson initiated a bill in Congress to remove the southeastern Indian tribes westward. The measure was aimed primarily at the large and powerful Cherokee Nation in northern Georgia and southeastern Tennessee. With his bill still pending, Jackson appointed his friend Billy Carroll a federal commissioner to negotiate with the Cherokees to leave. Governor Carroll hoped to divide Cherokee leadership by bribery. "Success will be found," Carroll said, "in assailing the avarice of the chiefs and principal men. . . . I think I can move among the Cherokees without exciting their suspicion." Carroll appointed twenty-three-year-old Pillow to accompany him as secretary of the mission. Carroll and Pillow failed, however; the Cherokee leaders, with minor exceptions, refused to betray their people. Jackson's bill passed, nevertheless, but removal would wait until 1838–39.[15]

That summer of 1830, after he and Carroll returned from Georgia, Pillow began the practice of law in Columbia. On July 20, 1830, he ran his first advertisement: "Gideon J. Pillow, attorney at law, office on southwest corner [of the square], formerly occupied by Cobbs and Dillihunty."[16] He joined the Columbia bar, which included a group of unusually talented and capable lawyers in the period 1825–40. Among them was Pillow's boyhood friend and frequent rival,

Gov. William Carroll
(courtesy Tennessee State Library and Archives)

Alfred O. P. Nicholson, whose career would include editorship of the Columbia *Western Mercury* and Nashville *Union and American* and service as a state legislator, United States senator, and chief justice of the Tennessee Supreme Court. In October 1831, Pillow made the motion to admit Nicholson to the Columbia bar.[17] Among the other Columbia lawyers were James Knox Polk and Aaron Venable Brown, law partners since 1822. Closely associated in law and politics, both Polk and Brown would play important roles in Pillow's life. Pillow and Brown became associates in a practice, but, contrary to a claim persistent in nineteenth- and twentieth-century accounts, Pillow and Polk were never law partners. Pillow did become a partner of Polk's nephew, J. Knox Walker, although the arrangement was dissolved when Walker went to Washington in 1845 as private secretary to his uncle.[18]

Gideon Pillow was a very good lawyer. He worked hard, with the ceaseless energy he would demonstrate throughout his life. He had a quick mind and a powerful speaking voice and could be incredibly persuasive. His criminal and civil practice blossomed. In 1830 he defended Grant A. Johnson for murder. Pillow handled the case so skillfully that Johnson received an acquittal, and spectators remarked that Felix Grundy, Tennessee's undisputed champion as a criminal lawyer, had a challenger. Indeed, Grundy and Pillow teamed on several cases. During the 1830s, in an active practice, Pillow defended clients against charges of murder, stabbing, gaming, incest, "affray," usury, assault, and perjury. He had the opportunity to observe human nature as closely as anyone.

Grant Johnson tested Pillow's abilities again in 1833. He killed another man with a knife, and Gideon Pillow put up the bond for Johnson's bail. The lawyer stayed with his client and managed with a mix of circumstance, luck, and skill to have the trial postponed year after year until Johnson's death in 1840. In 1841, in another murder case which he lost, Pillow received $500. "This was the largest fee paid to a lawyer up to this time, and it created a great deal of excitement."[19]

The Columbia bar handled most of their routine business before the "farmer-justices" who constituted the county court. The sessions of the superior court, headed at this time by Circuit Judge William P. Martin, frequently drew lawyers to Columbia from surrounding counties. When the circuit judge moved on, a number of Columbia lawyers followed. Pillow, Brown, Polk, and Nicholson, on varying occasions, followed the circuit. The judge would ride along on horseback, accompanied by a "whole host of lawyers." Lawyers who would oppose each other in court the next morning sometimes would share a bed. Crowding into the primitive taverns and rooming houses at the county seat, the men would eat and quarrel and drink and tell stories into the night. They came to know each other well. They also became acquainted with many citizens of neighboring counties, and potential voters in Marshall, Giles, Lincoln, and Lawrence counties got a good look at young lawyer Pillow, constantly on his feet speaking before juries.[20]

Pillow was enjoyable to have along. He could tell a good story and he could laugh. He could be a loyal, generous friend, particularly to the dozens of men and women connected to him by family. No one could question his courage. But he was a young man out to prove something. He took himself far too seriously and cared too much for the opinion of others. He postured, sometimes being transparently pretentious. Quick tempered, sensitive to slight and criticism, he held grudges and made enemies. Impatient and easily frustrated, he would often respond too quickly, sometimes quite imprudently, or he would pick up on a remark when he should have let it pass. His hair-trigger temper was always cocked. In 1834 he was fined for contempt of court, and charges would be brought against him later for "fighting in public" with Andrew J. Donelson, Jackson's nephew and a staunch Democrat.[21]

By age twenty-five Gideon Johnson Pillow had established himself. As a lawyer he had bounded into prominence, and he had acquired an important patron in William Carroll. Pillow had a wide, powerful extended family that would grow even stronger in the years to come. His parents and his ancestors had given him a legacy of service and of willingness to risk. The Pillows would fight, and they stuck together. They loved Tennessee, and they loved Andrew Jackson.

Gov. William Carroll rewarded Pillow in full for accompanying him through the mountains of north Georgia. Appointing him attorney general for the Ninth Solicitorial District in 1831, Carroll brought Pillow's name to the attention of influential Tennessee politicians Dixon T. Allen, David Campbell, and others.[22] Perhaps of greater importance, certainly to the legal community of Tennessee, Carroll in 1830 gave Pillow a grand opportunity, completing the revision of the *Digest and Revision of the Statute Laws of Tennessee*.[23]

In 1825 the General Assembly had passed an act authorizing the *Digest* and assigning Judge John Haywood and Robert L. Cobbs the task. Haywood died early on, but Cobbs continued by himself. Ultimately, he completed the two-volume work and brought it back to the legislature. The reviewing committee complimented Cobbs for his work, but they wanted to add laws passed during the current session, which caused delay. Then the publisher had problems, and the *Digest* had to be referred back to the legislature and a new special legislative committee appointed. Years passed, and reviewing committees had to be appointed for each new legislative session. Cobbs grew weary, and James A. Whiteside took over. More and more hands stirred the soup and still it was not ready. What was needed was push, and Gideon Pillow always could provide that. The project was so near completion that all that remained were appendices for the two volumes.

In 1830 Pillow and Maj. Jacob P. Chase completed the *Digest*.[24] Volume one contained all the statutes of Tennessee and her parent state, North Carolina, from 1715 to 1829, which were still in force in Tennessee. In the forty-page appendix to volume one, Pillow and Chase included the Declaration of Independence, the Articles of Confederation, and the constitutions of the United States and Tennessee.

Pillow and Chase contributed more significantly by adding an excellent collection of forms "as are in general use among justices of the peace, and other officers." Highly practical, the appendices provided samples of wills, marriage contracts, warrants for nuisance, a warrant against a miller for "failure to grind," the proper manner in which to take a legal oath, and advice on how to handle such oaths when dealing with a Quaker. Precedents were carefully included as well, designed to give confidence to officers of the law and to help systemize the legal processes of the state. The appendix to volume two, the "Land Law" of Tennessee, comprised a table of repealed and obsolete laws, treaties with the Indians, boundary treaties with neighboring states, and the like.[25] It appears Pillow and Chase did their work competently and in minimum time, but even so, completion of the *Digest* was not greeted with trumpets. The public never knew, nor cared, but lawyers did.

Carroll wanted more for his protégé. Following their return from the Cherokee mission, he had appointed Pillow aide-de-camp with the rank of colonel in the Tennessee militia. In 1833 Carroll named him adjutant general of the state, with the rank of brigadier general. Twenty-seven-year-old Pillow held this position for four years; he retained the title "General" for life.[26]

Ordinarily an adjutant general did not burrow through tactics manuals, but Pillow contended that he "thoroughly studied all the

Gideon Johnson Pillow as a young man
(courtesy James K. Polk Home, Columbia, Tennessee)

branches of military art of war, with the practical duties in the camp of instruction." Maybe he did, although Pillow later was never known as a commander with well-drilled troops. Indeed, there is no record of his ever having drilled troops; he left that to subordinates. In 1833 he attended and perhaps supervised the militia encampments which were held twice a year in each of the grand divisions of Tennessee. Without question it was a political position, a stepping-stone to the position of major general of militia. Perhaps Carroll saw military promise in his young mission secretary; certainly Pillow learned from close association with this first-rate volunteer soldier. Perhaps from Carroll, and from his uncle William, and maybe from Jackson, Pillow began to form the conviction that intelligent men with common sense and leadership ability could succeed militarily despite a lack of formal military education or training. Observation alone taught him that. He knew he could lead the soldiers of Tennessee.[27]

With a promising career established, the time had come for marriage. Pillow fell in love with Mary Elizabeth Martin, sister of his old classmate, Circuit Judge William P. Martin, and daughter of George M. Martin, schoolmaster and clerk of Maury County. They married on March 24, 1831, at the First Presbyterian Church in Columbia. The marriage proved fortunate for Gideon Pillow. Not only did it ally him with a strong, affluent Middle Tennessee family, but in his letters, in Mary's letters, and in references to them as a couple, they appear to have been devoted to each other. Mary seems to have been extremely capable, managing the household and farm and servants for long periods of time without her husband's presence. She knew how to listen, to advise, to encourage; she knew how to soften the intensity of her husband's personality.

The Pillows set up housekeeping in a home on the corner of Seventh and High streets in Columbia. Their town house and the grand home they built later, Clifton, were known for gracious hospitality. Mary E. Martin Pillow, like her husband, made friends easily and kept them. Caroline Nicholson, a schoolmate and wife of A. O. P. Nicholson, became her friend for life.[28]

Misfortune tested the young couple, however. Their firstborn, William Carroll Pillow, died after living eight months. A second son died soon after birth, and then twin girls, Anne and Margaret, named after their grandmothers, died in infancy. Gideon and Mary Pillow seem to have accepted the loss of their first four children stoically. There was an inner strength about the Pillows, and enormous optimism. Their faith sustained them, it seems. They were both devout Presbyterians before 1850 and probably attended nearby Zion Church along with Pillow's brother Jerome and sister-in-law Elvira Dale Pillow.[29]

Pillow and James K. Polk, eleven years older, appear not to have become close friends until about 1840, although their political association began early in the 1830s. Pillow's first known letter to Congressman Polk was a recommendation written in 1833 supporting the appointment of Judge W. E. Kennedy, under whom Pillow had read law, as federal district judge. Fellow Tennessee congressmen John Bell and Cave Johnson, Pillow advised, "will cooperate" in securing the nomination.[30]

The able and ambitious Polk had established himself in state and national politics during the 1820s. In 1823 he ran for the Tennessee General Assembly and won a narrow election. He worked hard, demonstrated parliamentary and political ability, and soon became a leader of the Carroll faction. In 1825 Polk aimed higher. He defeated Andrew Erwin, the anti-Jackson candidate, for the seat of the Sixth Congressional District. In Congress he joined the forces of Jackson arrayed against the administration of John Quincy Adams. When Jackson captured the presidency in 1828, Polk skillfully marshaled support for "Old Hickory's" policies in the House. He played an active and important role, perhaps an indispensable role, in Jackson's successful struggle against Nicholas Biddle and the supporters of the Second Bank of the United States. Jackson appreciated the support of his fellow Tennessean in this crisis. Polk became a favorite, much to the disappointment of another eager Jackson supporter, Tennessean John Bell.[31]

As Polk rose to prominence in Washington, Pillow became involved in the Tennessee Constitutional Convention. Reform was in the air, and William Carroll and Gideon Pillow wished to be identified with the movement. In December 1833, Pillow suggested to Polk that the latter should allow himself to be nominated as Maury's delegate to the convention. The letter oozed with flattery. Pillow, who underlined words constantly in any letter, depicted Polk as "a man of *talents*, of *experience*, of *correct political principles* and *tried patriotism*." Polk, however, had his hands full in the House, being deeply involved with the maneuvering and machinations of the "War on the Bank." He refused Pillow's plea.

Pillow had been active in Polk's highly successful congressional race in 1833. He became more visible in 1834, helping rally Maury citizens in an expression of their "high regard" for the popular Mr. Polk.[32] A local observer noted to Polk at this time, "Col. G J Pillow has a wonderful itching I think to be brought out."[33] In the spring of 1835, Pillow stood for the Tennessee assembly, but a half-dozen opponents competed with him for the Maury County vote, including the incumbent, his friend Nicholson. Although Pillow had the backing of the Columbia *Observer*, Nicholson was reelected as the representative from Maury.[34]

In 1835 Tennessee's Jackson forces, or the "Democracy," fragmented badly. John Bell had defeated Polk for the speakership of the House the year before, thereby earning the hostility of Jackson. Bell turned against Jackson; although slow to label himself a Whig, Bell had become one at heart. Even greater damage came when the popular, highly respected, and fiercely independent Judge Hugh Lawson White attacked Jackson's choice of Martin Van Buren as presidential successor and began organizing a powerful anti-Jackson combination. The Whig party was emerging in Jackson's Tennessee, and battle lines were drawn for the August 1835 gubernatorial election.

The Jackson-Polk forces, however, had the sure winner William Carroll to run against Newton Cannon, a Whig and longtime enemy of Jackson who had profited from the Bell-White revolt within the Democracy. It proved to be an exciting, hard-fought contest. Pillow was conspicuous. He supported Carroll tirelessly, speaking at rallies, writing newspaper articles, and giving dinners, but Newton Cannon won. Tennessee's Democracy was astonished. Observers believed the unbeatable Carroll had lost because of his declaration of support for Van Buren. More to the point, perhaps, Cannon hung Carroll on the constitutional tenure issue—should a candidate be able to serve as governor for more than six years of any eight? Carroll argued in vain that the new constitution of 1834 rewound the clock. But change was in the air, and the electorate listened to Cannon.[35]

A third candidate, West H. Humphreys, had appeared in the pivotal 1835 gubernatorial race. He, like Cannon, endorsed Judge White. The refined, articulate, thirty-year-old Whig Humphreys gathered more than 8,000 votes and the notice of many. Four years later Humphreys would marry Pillow's younger sister Amanda, switch parties, and quickly become Pillow's devoted friend and political ally.[36]

Jacksonian Tennessee had been torn apart, and the battle between the Van Buren and anti–Van Buren Tennessee Democrats continued. In April 1836, elections were held for county officials and militia officers. Pillow ran for major general of the 3d Division (Middle Tennessee) of the Tennessee militia. Previously Tennessee had elected its major generals by a vote of the militia field-grade officers and the brigadiers. Under the constitution of 1834, however, the major general "would be elected by the *people*," defined as individuals "subject to military service."[37] Pillow liked his chances. He had proved a hardworking, loyal party member, and he could count on Billy Carroll's backing. Of course, Pillow knew that military experience or ability would have little to do with the outcome; popularity and party support were everything. Carroll was writing his followers; Pillow also solicited Polk's help: Would he "*quickly*" write his friends in Lincoln and Bedford counties and get Cave Johnson to do the same in Hickman? Pillow knew the election of militia major general had broader political implications. He had written Van Buren explaining this and asked Polk in Washington to tell Van Buren that "if I should be elected it will afford a *fair test* of the present strength of parties in this part of the state. I am running as you know against a man greatly my *senior* in years [Terry H. Cahal was four years older, born in 1802] & of a more general *acquaintance*, but I will give him the *Camp fever* before I am done with him."[38]

The contest exhilarated Pillow. "My resolve is taken, & I'll *die* in the *ditch* or I will *conquer*." To oppose Pillow, Judge White's forces trotted out Cahal, a citizen of Columbia serving in the General Assembly. Unfortunately for Pillow, Cahal also was a friend and law partner of A. O. P. Nicholson. "We shall have a very *heated contest*," Pillow wrote Polk. "The full strength of the White question shall be pressed upon me. I did not desire to make the contest turn upon this question, but since it is *forced* upon me, I shall meet it *boldly*. If the friends of our cause are true, I fear nothing."[39] Pillow's candidacy may have disturbed the White forces, for Cahal withdrew and was replaced by Brig. Gen. Robert Cannon of Bedford County, Tennessee legislator and younger brother of the governor.[40]

Two weeks before the election, strangely, Pillow left the Columbia area on business. He went to Pontotoc, Mississippi, where he was interested in purchasing land. In his absence, "a report . . . was circulated extensively over the District" that he had withdrawn his candidacy and gone off with a great deal of money to speculate in land. His departure was most ill advised. Upon his return four days before the election, Pillow discovered that another Van Buren supporter, Col. William Moore of Lincoln County, had entered the contest.[41]

Pillow was dismayed and angry. Andrew C. Hays wrote Polk of the gossip "in the strong Van Buren neighborhoods that Pillow had changed his politics and had named a child Hugh L. White."[42] There had been "great efforts by White men," Hays said, to prejudice Pillow against his Van Buren friends and convince him that his allies had acted treacherously.

> I today told Pillow he should be cautious how he believed such reports without conclusive evidence of their truth, that honorable men did not like to be *suspected,* and that he had nothing to gain by listening to slanders upon his friends coming from such a quarter. He said to me that a heavy set had been made to induce him to believe that Nicholson and *myself* particularly had so treated him; that so far as I was concerned he did not believe it, that he knew me to be his friend, and every insinuation from no matter whom, to the contrary, was *false,* but that with the information he had, he was compelled to believe it with regard to Nicholson, and some others (whom he would not mention) until he could get better evidence of their innocence.[43]

Hays knew better. He assured Polk that Nicholson had supported Pillow and even used his influence to keep Moore out of the race. Besides, Hays continued, White partisans in Columbia despised Nicholson.[44]

This confusion contributed to Cannon's victory. Pillow understood that the entry of Moore into the contest divided the Van Buren Democrats and therefore brought about defeat, but he was embarrassed by losing.[45] Defeat followed defeat; reelection of Newton Cannon in 1837 and seizure of both houses of the Tennessee legislature by the White-Bell forces humiliated the Jacksonians. They still could point to Washington, however, where Polk, declaring himself for Van Buren, had been elected Speaker of the House of Representatives on December 7, 1835. He stood strong and confident, accepted now "as the generally acknowledged chieftain of the Tennessee Democracy." James K. Polk and Columbia had replaced Felix Grundy and Nashville.[46]

There had been talk about Pillow running for Congress in the spring of 1838. John H. Dew described the aspirant: "Gen. Pillow wears a suit of *homespun* Janes [jeans], says it is the handy work of the fair hands of old Maury, seems very attentive to the good people, and smiles complacently, and talks loud and much for the democratic principles of Jefferson, Van Burin & Polk. I wonder if Mrs. Polk won't guess that commendable alteration of the manners & dress of the General, don't mean that he wishes to represent the good people of Maury in part in the next General Assembly."[47] But Pillow's aspirations for Congress, or for the General Assembly for that matter, seem to have faded by summer.

That fall an event occurred which appears to have radically changed the relationship between Pillow and Polk. Polk's younger brother, William Hawkins Polk, shot and killed Robert H. Hayes on the streets of Columbia. Hayes, a young Nashville lawyer who had recently become a partner of A. O. P. Nicholson and was living in Columbia, had quarreled violently with the twenty-three-year-old Polk at a table in the Nelson House. Polk insulted Hayes, who in turn threw a tumbler at his tormenter. Polk left, returned with a whip, and lashed him. Hayes fled, armed himself with a derringer, and waited for Polk. When Polk appeared, Hayes fired but missed. Polk then drew his own derringer and killed Hayes.[48]

Pillow became securer for the young man, and the Polk family entrusted him with William's defense.[49] After hearing arguments, the grand jury decided Polk had acted in self-defense but sentenced him to six weeks in jail and fined him $750 for assault; Polk's bride, Belinda, received permission to move into jail with him.[50] Pillow's performance in this case impressed James K. Polk. Prior to the Hayes murder, the relationship between the two appears to have been based on mutual political and business interests, but about this time a close personal friendship began to develop. By 1842 Pillow dropped in frequently at the Polk residence, driving in by carriage from Clifton to Columbia for a leisurely meal.[51]

In 1838 all eyes were turned to Pillow's friend Polk, who had decided to counterattack the victorious Whigs. He returned to Tennessee and let it be known that he would be willing to run for governor in 1839, taking the fight directly to Cannon and the Whigs. To do so, he would abandon his highly successful career in Congress. Originally the Tennessee Democracy had talked of again running Carroll against Newton Cannon, but Carroll wanted to oblige Polk, so he stepped aside and gave Polk his blessing. This, of course, freed Pillow to support Polk. Pillow threw all his energy into the campaign, helping Polk gain a decisive majority in Middle Tennessee and win the gubernatorial race despite being defeated in East and West Tennessee. The Democracy also won control of both houses of the legislature.

The 1839 election, though narrow, was regarded by Polk-Jackson partisans as a "great and glorious triumph."[52]

Pillow's efforts in the gubernatorial campaign, of course, had earned him Polk's ear and a say in patronage. The Democracy knew Pillow to be a highly effective stump speaker and enormously persuasive on a one-to-one basis. Serious thought was given to having him run for the House of Representatives in 1839, and party representatives called on him, but Pillow declined. He had his hands full with private matters.[53]

It helped to have a good friend in the governor's chair. Pillow, his brothers Granville and Jerome, Evan Young, James Walker, and James Hellin got a charter from the state under the Internal Improvements Act to form the Columbia Central Turnpike Company. They proceeded to purchase land and to begin building a macadamized road to Clifton, a little town, formerly named Carrollsville, high on a bluff overlooking the Tennessee River in Wayne County. Granville and Jerome had a cement factory there, and farsighted individuals believed Clifton, with its obvious advantage of being on the Tennessee, would become a second Nashville. Pillow announced that the company intended to continue this grand road farther west and link with Bolivar, Tennessee, and eventually Memphis. The funds with which they financed this project came from bonds issued by the company, half of which were taken by the state under the terms of the Internal Improvements Act. For the actual turnpike construction work, they purchased slaves.

This "pork-barrel" arrangement by which the state aided and enriched certain citizens was monopolized by Polk's Middle Tennessee. Of the twenty-two turnpike companies that qualified to receive state bonds, fourteen were in that wealthy section. Incorporators like Pillow became the contractors. When the subscription books for stock in the Columbia Central Turnpike Company were opened, he and his five partners took all the stock themselves, and when the road was completed, Pillow and his partners took all the profit—they "had the negroes for their own farms. The pike cost them practically nothing."

Polk was not blind to what was happening. Indeed, it was accepted "spoils" practice of the time, but he did become embarrassed and angry when his brother-in-law James Walker spelled out in a letter the benefits of the Columbia Central Turnpike Company for the incorporators—their money was not in it and their profit would be in slaves and the road itself. Although entrepreneurs Walker and Pillow might occasionally don homespun for effect, they were becoming wealthy men, and a contributing factor to their financial success was their special relationship to the man in Nashville.[54]

Conspicuous evidence of prosperity in Maury County could be found in the magnificent homes being constructed. Early in 1838 Pillow contracted with a local citizen, Nathan Vaught, to build "a very fine large brick dwelling-house containing twelve rooms and two large halls." It seems that Pillow himself designed the house "and employed carpenters like Nathan Vaught to construct it." The style he adopted, with its beautiful four-column portico, has been classified as "high vernacular."[55] He built this fine home about four miles west of Columbia on the original Pillow tract. It faced the road to Mount Pleasant, four miles to the west, and to Clifton, on the Tennessee River, sixty miles farther west. Pillow named his home "Clifton" after this road.[56] The stone for the foundation and window trim were quarried from Pillow land, and thousands of brick were made by hand on the site by his slaves. Wild cherry trees were cut from his timber and fashioned into interior trim and furniture; cabinetmakers from Nashville were brought in to work this fine wood.[57]

Vaught and his builders finished the interior of Clifton in 1839. Later that year they added a large two-story brick kitchen and servants' house immediately behind the main house.[58] A granary, smokehouse,[59] and icehouse, all of brick, followed. To the east of the big house Pillow constructed an unusual building—a small brick office, complete with an elaborate columned portico. Beginning behind the office and extending 200 yards to the east were magnificent gardens, grand and formal in the English style. A wide brick walk, bordered by boxwood, led through three sections, "each individually designed and planted." The first garden highlighted shrubs of closely trimmed magnolia, laurel, and spruce. Next came the flower garden, rich with roses and an arbor. The third plot contained vegetables. "Across the end of the third and last garden a line of closely planted cedar trees opened out onto a wide high terrace overlooking the lovely fields below—and here was the greenhouse[60] with glassed conservatory in the rear." Behind Clifton and below the hill on which it stands were the barns and a line of log slave houses, each with fireplace and chimney.[61]

A baronial estate, no doubt, Clifton commanded admiration then and since. Yet, like its owner, Clifton was a dynamo of energy and activity, deceptively disguised. Owners of such plantation ventures sought self-sufficiency, raising their own vegetables and poultry, doing basic blacksmith work, curing their own pork, possessing their own corn mill and often a sawmill. The independent community and enterprise that was Clifton also found itself relatively free from the capricious demands and seasons of money crops, for Pillow emphasized livestock from the beginning. Soon he was producing wool and pork in significant quantity. He had 500 head of Merion sheep in 1839, a large number of Irish grazier hogs, and a growing herd of Durham cattle. Owning only 725 acres, Pillow required most of it for pasture land and to produce the India corn needed to feed his stock. Later Pillow would purchase other farmland in Maury and raise hemp and wheat, but in the early years he gave his attention to livestock. His hogs and sheep won prizes, and the mules he began to raise at Clifton about 1840 came to be known and admired widely.[62]

Mary Pillow had taken a special interest in the development of a dairy on the slope north of Clifton. It featured a pond fed by a spring, the whole bordered by a striking serpentine wall. Connected to the springhouse were "a pantry and a provision store—all hewn in a solid limestone." Water channels cut into the floors allowed for cooling butter and other foods stored there. Knowledgeable Maury County observers declared the dairy "certainly the most handsome establishment in our county."[63]

Pillow experimented with several crops, but he showed particular interest in the cultivation of lucerne (alfalfa). He committed several squares of his garden to this crop. Somewhat later, in the early and mid-1840s, having secured one of the three U.S. Navy hemp contracts, he turned to hemp as a cash crop. He invested in an engine apparatus called a hemp brake to help crack and clean the stalks, which had been allowed to rot in a great vat of brick laid in hydraulic cement mortar.[64] After they had been broken, the stalks were shredded to make fiber. Pillow was interested only in the stalks, although it is thought slaves probably discovered the medicinal effect of the hemp leaves (marijuana).[65]

Gideon Pillow loved farming, and he was a fine farm manager. Not only did he conduct agricultural experimentation, but his animals and crops won prizes. He wrote letters to the *Tennessee Agriculturist*, worked hard to bring trade fairs to Middle Tennessee, and took enormous pride in the success of Clifton. He did not like being away from home, and his private letters are full of concern about the crops, the animals, and the operation of his farm. This aspect of his personality cannot be overemphasized—he loved farming more than law, more than politics, more than soldiering.

Large-scale, profitable farming and raising of cattle, horses, and mules required careful management and much capital. It also required an enormous amount of labor. Slaves, Pillow believed, could best provide this—and there always was the hope of capital appreciation as well. He owned about thirty-five slaves when he built Clifton in 1838.[66] This made him a comparatively large slaveholder.[67] He appears, from his correspondence and from court actions, to have been a liberal master. More than once he was charged with "letting a slave act as a freeman," "letting a slave own a horse," and the like.[68]

Pillow's drive for more land and more slaves would accelerate after the Mexican War.[69] Before the war, however, he showed interest in the newly opened Indian lands in Pontotoc County, Mississippi, in the late 1830s and in the delta land of eastern Arkansas in 1840–42. In 1843 he was dickering with Polk to buy part of the latter's Yalobusha County, Mississippi, tract. How much land he did buy in north Mississippi is not known—and seems not to have been appreciable in any event—but he had land speculation in his blood, as did many of his Maury County contemporaries.[70] For the moment, depressed cotton prices held things in check, dropping from 17½ cents a pound in 1837 to one cent in 1840.[71]

To make Clifton more profitable, Pillow introduced a steam engine, thought to be the first in Maury County. Since cotton had to be baled for shipment, and since the baling and tying was done with hemp rope and bagging, Pillow saw an opportunity. He used his engine to manufacture twine, rope, and bagging.[72] His cotton gin operated lucratively in 1845, and Pillow sought a convenient waterway to ship his cotton and other products, hoping to lessen the nagging transportation costs. In October the Tennessee General Assembly granted him and a half-dozen other incorporators of the Duck River Slack-Water Navigation Company "the exclusive right to navigate Duck River" for fifty years, from Columbia to its mouth at the Tennessee River, with steamboats, barges, and keels.[73] This project would fail ultimately, but it reveals Pillow's enthusiasm for internal improvements, a position he held consistently, though he knew it to be at variance with the Democracy's dogma.

Pillow also took an interest in horses. He raised them and probably entered his mares often at a nearby track, Ashland Park, on Little Bigby Creek. Large crowds flocked to the races. Maury was known for seventy-five years as a center for magnificent racehorses, challenging the best of the South and Midwest. Bright bands would play, elegant ladies would parade, and princely sums would be wagered in the grandstand.[74] Yes, Maury pleased its citizens. As Kate Conyngham observed, "Maury County, (pronounced Murry) you must know, is the gem of Tennessee. It contains the most beautiful hills, the clearest brooks, the prettiest vales, the stateliest trees, the handsomest native parks, the richest farms, the wealthiest planters, the most intelligent population, the best seminaries of learning, and the loveliest ladies of all Tennessee; at least the good people of Maury say so, and who should know so well as they, pray?"[75]

Pillow's brothers busied themselves developing their own plantations on the old family tract. In 1845 Granville contracted with Nathan Vaught to rebuild Rose Hill, his father's home, into a mansion named "Pillow Place." Jerome, too, employed Vaught. In 1855 he built a lovely home about a half-mile west of Clifton.[76] Just west of the Pillow tract on the other side of the Mount Pleasant road was Ashwood Hall, built in 1836–37 by Leonidas Polk, third cousin of James K. Polk. By 1838, however, he was serving in Louisiana as Episcopal missionary bishop of the Southwest. He had come to Maury in 1833 and taken possession of his estate of 1,200 acres, but he lived there himself only a few years. On his visits back to Ashwood Hall, Polk gave his attention to the construction of the small but beautiful St. John's Church on Mount Pleasant Pike. Pillow knew his neighbor, the bishop, casually.[77]

Meanwhile, the political career of Leonidas's cousin, James K. Polk, bobbed uncertainly as Tennessee became for twenty years a Whig-Democratic battlefield watched closely by the rest of the nation. At the Democratic National Convention in 1840, Polk received consideration for the vice-presidential nomination, notably support from George Bancroft of Massachusetts. Party sentiment, however, favored the incumbent ticket of Van Buren and Richard M. Johnson, so Polk quietly withdrew his nomination. It was well that he did. The Whigs swept the national election, including the state of Tennessee, with "Tippecanoe and Tyler too!" The powerful Tennessee Whig party followed up their national victory by challenging Polk for governor in August 1841 with candidate James C. "Lean Jimmy" Jones. Like William Carroll, Jones carefully projected himself as a "common man." His witty, friendly manner proved to be popular with the voters, and he unseated Polk by 3,000 votes.[78] Polk, stung by defeat, returned to Columbia. Money was short, and he reopened his law office. He would "ride the circuit once more—defending murderers and serving litigants for healthy fees."[79] Meanwhile, he prepared carefully to do battle once again with "Lean Jimmy" for the governorship in 1843.

Pillow, with his brother-in-law John W. Saunders, had campaigned hard for Polk in the 1841 race and earned Polk's trust. They had grown closer in 1842, and when Polk declared for the gubernatorial contest in 1843, Pillow plunged in again on his behalf.[80] Working closely with Pillow this time was another brother-in-law, West H. Humphreys, the talented attorney general and former Whig. Pillow chaired meeting after meeting of the Middle Tennessee Democracy and usually became the one designated to draft resolutions and position papers. He was a favorite speaker at the giant barbecues and generally was recognized as the spokesman for the Democracy in powerful Maury County. Polk's wife, Sarah, wrote a glowing letter to her husband praising Pillow for his vigorous campaign speeches around the Columbia district. "The Whigs are dispirited. Genl Pillow & Humphreys has given such a fine account of things in the District that the Democrats are in extacies [sic]. *Pillow* done nothing but talk on Saturday & Monday last, and it has had its effect."[81]

Despite Pillow's efforts in Middle Tennessee, the Whig strongholds in West and East Tennessee held firm. Polk's open support of the New Yorker Van Buren had alienated Tennessee voters. Jones prevailed, defeating Polk by roughly the same margin as before. Politicians of both parties, including Polk himself, pondered whether his political career was doomed.[82]

Pillow may have been discouraged too, but he was never discouraged for long. Already he had begun promoting still another brother-in-law, William Pitt Martin, for circuit court judge. He urged Polk to travel to Nashville and talk to some of his friends on Martin's behalf. "I need not say to you that I feel a deep interest in this matter & that if you will make your feelings known to your particular friends so as to help me out with *this matter*, I shall feel my self under great *personal obligation* to you, and that in my *future* life I will *Seek* an *opportunity of Serving* you in *whatever you may desire*.[83] Pillow's time would come.

2   **A Friend Indeed**

Polk recovered quickly from his second loss to "Lean Jimmy" Jones. Two weeks after the election he was in Nashville, attempting to rebuild the Tennessee Democracy and reestablish control. He found the party divided, numbed by defeat. Facing political oblivion, the twice-beaten Polk sought support once again from his fellow Tennesseans. He wanted his name placed in nomination as vice-president at the 1844 national Democratic convention in Baltimore.[1] He had laid the groundwork that summer, not only campaigning more against Henry Clay than "Lean Jimmy," but writing to Martin Van Buren, assuring him of his availability for second place on the ticket.[2] Polk could always count on Andrew Jackson's support, so he asked Jackson to write to Van Buren also, as well as to influential Amos Kendall, suggesting him as the vice-presidential candidate.[3]

In November 1843, Tennessee Democrats met in Nashville to decide whom they would support at the national convention the following May. Polk worked diligently with two of his closest friends—veteran congressman Cave Johnson and Samuel H. Laughlin, founding editor of the Democratic Nashville *Union*—to guarantee that his name would be put forward for vice-president, and it was. The Tennessee convention did not name a presidential choice, declaring that its delegates would support the selection of the national convention. Polk had engineered this, intending to impress Van Buren that Tennessee was not safely in his column until Polk joined the ticket.[4]

Although the thirteen Tennessee delegates chosen to go to Baltimore were committed to Polk for vice-president, most of them favored Lewis Cass of Michigan rather than Van Buren for president. The delegation included A. J. Donelson, S. H. Laughlin, U.S. senator Alexander Anderson, former congressman John Blair, William Childress (Polk's brother-in-law), Judge Samuel Powell, former governor John Taylor, and five congressmen—Cave Johnson, Andrew Johnson, George Jones, Julius Blackwell, and Alvan Cullom.[5] Gideon Pillow was named head of the Tennessee delegation. This choice seems surprising, considering the experience and reputation of the others, but it demonstrates Polk's clout and the enormous trust he placed in his friend Pillow.

Defeat in 1840 had shaken the national Democracy. The crucial North-South alliance within the party was fragile indeed, and many Democratic leaders, especially Van Buren, went through contortions to "suppress or avoid divisive sectional issues."[6] Things seemed to turn into sectional issues easily—money and banking, the "gag rule," and the tariff.[7] To unify this polyglot political coalition one could only count on the enormous prestige of Andrew Jackson and shared antipathy for England.

Van Buren's opponents displayed little strength. President John Tyler's defection to the Whigs killed his chances.[8] Col. Richard Johnson, hero of the Battle of the Thames in 1813, again sought first or second spot on the ticket, but "Old Dick" was too controversial.[9] James Buchanan of Pennsylvania approached the convention with his state delegation pledged to Van Buren. Levi Woodbury and John C. Calhoun aroused little enthusiasm.[10] Lewis Cass, former governor of the Michigan Territory, secretary of war under Jackson, expansionist, westerner, and free trader, seemed a logical choice for southerners, but, as George Bancroft wrote, "the hatred and jealousy which Van Buren bore him made it absolutely and undisputedly impossible for him to carry the state of New York, and without New York his success would have been desperate or rather impossible."[11]

By January 9, 1844, twelve of eighteen Democratic state conventions had declared for Van Buren.[12] Despite this apparent strength, powerful anti–Van Buren sentiment existed; pragmatists knew he could not carry the South. This was Van Buren's real problem, and almost any issue would cause it to surface. Texas provided the issue. Jackson and Van Buren had nervously pushed aside Sam Houston's proposals for statehood, but in 1843 the threat of intervention by England and France thrust it center stage. Admitting Texas, a slave state, would be bad in the eyes of the North, and many believed it would mean war with Mexico. Expansion, however, was as Democratic as a low tariff.

An anti–Van Buren Tennessean, Aaron V. Brown (Polk's law partner), released a letter he had received from Jackson on March 20, 1844. Jackson stated in strong terms his support for annexation of Texas.[13] Van Buren, who felt compelled to clarify his position on Texas, did so in a letter to William H. Hammet, a Mississippi delegate to the upcoming convention. Van Buren and his trusted adviser, Silas Wright, knew that an anti-annexation stand would endanger chances for the nomination, but they were determined to pursue their convictions.[14] The letter stating Van Buren's opposition to the annexation of Texas appeared April 20, 1844. It was a political blunder of the first order, putting Van Buren in conflict with Jackson's position and in opposition to many northerners, even New Yorkers, who supported annexation for motives ranging from patriotism to land speculation. Van Buren had played into the hands of his enemies. Jackson hastened to heal the situation with a letter to the Nashville *Union* on May 13, but the damage had been done.[15] Jackson wrote another letter May 14 to Benjamin F. Butler, head of the pro–Van Buren New York delegation. "Nothing" he stated flatly, "can restore Mr V. Burren" at the Democratic convention except a reversal of his position. Jackson still hoped for a "democracy again united on Mr. V. B." and immediate annexation.[16]

Polk's strategy was to continue his pledge of support for Van Buren. If Van Buren did carry the nomination, he would be in an excellent position for the vice-presidency. If the "Old Magician" faltered, he could never be accused of political aggrandizement. Perhaps Polk then could ask for and probably receive support for the presidency from Van Buren and his supporters.[17] Another benefit of this strategy was that he could "have telling points made for him that are essentially the same as for a presidential candidate without appearing to compete with others for the higher position."[18]

But promising the vote of the Tennessee delegation and delivering it were two different matters. Of the thirteen delegates, Polk could count on only five to support Van Buren: Cave Johnson, Sam Laughlin, A. J. Donelson, William G. Childress, and Pillow. Since Polk would not be attending the convention, he put his faith in Pillow. In a letter to Cave Johnson he stated: "Whatever is desired to be done, communicate to *Genl Pillow*. He is one of the shrewdest men you ever knew, and can *execute* whatever is resolved on with as much success as any man who will be at Baltimore. Lead him therefore into all of your views. He is perfectly *reliable*, is a warm friend of *V.B.*'s, and is my friend, and you can do so with entire safety."[19]

Pillow had failed Polk in January, however. They had intended to go to the Ohio Democratic convention together; Ohio's role would be crucial in Baltimore, Pillow believed. "He thinks," said Polk, "the result of the contest of 1844, as well as my own political destiny in future life, may depend upon it."[20] But two of Pillow's children became quite ill after Christmas and Pillow would not leave them. Sam Laughlin insisted that he go to Ohio: "We intreat him [Pillow] to lay down the law, and all other personal considerations in the present great emergency." But Pillow refused.[21]

Pillow remained inactive politically during the spring of 1844. He corresponded with Van Buren, however, and received the New Yorker's assurance that he believed, and had so stated, that the national government had no authority to interfere with the institution of slavery.[22] When May arrived, Pillow left Clifton and his Columbia law office. First he went to Nashville, where the Democracy sponsored a mass meeting about Texas that went well. Laughlin earlier had reported to Polk that "we have the enemy in a world of trouble here on the Question."[23] Pillow met with Andrew J. Donelson in Nashville and they agreed to travel to Baltimore together; they took the Louisville stage for Cincinnati. On May 16 in Cincinnati, Pillow had conferences with delegates Nicholas Schoonmaker, Moses Dawson, and James J. Faran. The latter, editor of the Cincinnati *Enquirer* and president of the Ohio senate, introduced him to other Ohio delegates. When he left Cincinnati, Pillow felt "confident of getting the support of the Ohio Delegation." Pillow and his companions departed Cincinnati on the sixteenth and reached Washington on May 21.[24]

Polk was anxious to have Pillow and Laughlin in Washington: "From what Cave Johnson writes—I think the recent occurance [*sic*] on the chess-board—have decidedly improved my prospects. The presence of my friends from Tennessee, at Washington for a few days before the Convention meets is not only vastly important,—but may decide the action of the Convention."[25]

Cave Johnson met Pillow and Laughlin when they arrived the evening of May 21. In a long discussion, he informed Pillow of the meeting held by a large number of annexationist delegates on April 29, the result of the work of Sen. Robert J. Walker of Mississippi, who was acknowledged to be the "brilliant engineer of the Texas scheme" that ensnared Van Buren. Walker had great influence across the Democracy, largely because of his leadership in the Senate and his close connection with George M. Dallas and other powerful Pennsylvanians.[26] Most of the group at Walker's meeting openly declared for Lewis Cass. Cave Johnson, loyal to Van Buren, counseled moderation, but he was worried.[27] Fortunately for Polk, Walker's goal appeared to have been to derail Van Buren's nomination. Beyond that, he seemed to have no special preference.[28]

Pillow found bitterly divided delegates gathering in Washington.[29] He noted in a letter to Polk on May 22 that the northern Democrats were determined to "never yield up their preference for V" and that the delegates of the Southwest and West were "making an extraordinary effort for Cass."[30] Pillow set to work. He showed up everywhere, "making friends with all factions and dropping new hints here and there."[31] On May 22 Pillow, Cave Johnson, and Sam Laughlin assured a Van Buren caucus that the Tennessee delegation would support the New Yorker.[32] At a meeting of the Tennessee delegates that night, however, Pillow found that he had spoken prematurely for his delegation. Only Cave Johnson, Laughlin, Donelson, Childress, and himself voted to support Van Buren.[33] After heated debate the pro–Van Buren and anti–Van Buren factions papered over their differences with a compromise calling for harmony and aloofness from factionalism.[34]

But Pillow's letters to Polk of May 22 and 24 reveal a virtually unmanageable Tennessee delegation. He and Cave Johnson and Laughlin had their hands full just holding their own delegates in line for Polk as vice-president and at the same time winning the support of Van Buren followers for Polk's candidacy. Cave Johnson feared the delegation, with such firebrands as Alexander Anderson, a passionate Calhounite, might soon openly oppose Van Buren or break up, either of which would spoil Polk's chances.[35] Pillow began to meet individually in his room with the Tennessee delegation on the twenty-second. He urged a conciliatory course, but George W. Jones and Anderson, "the worst of agitators," held out stubbornly. They told Pillow bluntly they supported the two-thirds rule and "say they won't go into the Convention" unless it is adopted.[36] Pillow also feared, as did many, that the disaffected might bolt the convention and join the Tyler rump convention.

On the other hand, the Van Buren wing of the party seemed equally resentful and recalcitrant. "I confess myself much surprised at the extent of the *distraction* and the bitterness of feeling which exists," Pillow reported. "I think," he continued in his nightly report to Polk, "it now best to use all our influence and power to *heal the wounds* of the party and re-unite it if possible and until that is done, say but little about the V—— P——."[37] "If we do not unite *all is lost*. If we do unite we will then I feel confident get your nomination. . . . My great effort shall be to *conciliate* and to hold things in attitude to secure your nomination no matter which party may succeed."[38]

Pillow continued meeting delegates and pushing Polk's cause. Since his hands seemed clean of the Van Buren–Cass war, delegates such as Arthur B. Bagby of Alabama and Silas Wright of New York spoke to him in confidence about the problem or impossibility of reuniting the party behind Van Buren. Cass delegates from the South and Southwest told him in despair that the northern Democrats would never yield Van Buren. "If they continue to occupy that ground they will break up *the party* and will leave no hope of reconciliation."[39] On May 23 Pillow held a second full meeting of the Tennessee delegation. It discouraged him. Andrew Johnson and Jones seemed "ready to sacrifice you to get clear of Van. They both profess to be your friends and have been kind enough to say that they are unwilling for your name to go on V——'s ticket. So say Cullom and some others."[40]

By the next day Pillow had given up on having a solid Tennessee delegation. Jones and Anderson are "wholly *rabid* and we do not now consult with them at all." He believed Van Buren would carry 145 votes on the first ballot (he received 146) and feared the two-thirds rule would be adopted, thanks to the Pennsylvanians and "a part of the Tennessee delegations who cant [*sic*] be controuled [*sic*] upon this question. . . . The parties will never meet except upon some other man than Cass. . . . I regard everything as thrown into confusion and uncertainty. I would not still be surprised if a compromise were finally

President James Knox Polk
(courtesy Tennessee State Library and Archives)

made by both parties taking you up, for the P——. This I give you as a *possibility*."[41]

Delegates began buzzing about Pillow, considered now as Polk's "immediate representative." The disaffected from Mississippi and North Carolina told him that "if Polks friends voted for V—— they would not vote for P——." Pillow replied that as the Tennessee delegation had no wish, no intention other than

> to place your name before the Convention, we thought it our duty to be modest and not to *be active* in arraying the parties. . . . When we had determined upon our course, as we would before the convention met, it would be known etc. The object you will easily understand is to *force* me as your friend to commit myself against V—— and to compel all your friends to do so to[o]. . . . I do not think V—— will get the nomination. . . . You have more strength with the Democracy than any man whose name has come before the country. . . . I would not still be surprised if a compromise were finally made by both parties taking you up, for the P——.[42]

Pillow went on, reporting specifically that Samuel Medary and the Ohio people seemed solid, that Gov. Marcus Morton of Massachusetts "is for you," and the Illinois and Indiana are "friendly to you." He could not resist, however, the self-serving observation that "Cave Johnson and all our friends are almost in despair of every thing."[43]

Conspicuously absent from the Tennessee delegation was an important friend, Polk's old law partner Aaron V. Brown. He was supposed to have been in Washington early and to have helped Pillow with the work in Ohio en route, but his wife had become critically ill and he could not leave her. Brown had written Pillow urging him that it was "altogether important" to go on with Laughlin. Meanwhile, he would remain at home in Pulaski and catch up if he could. Sally Burrus Brown died on May 14. Immediately after the funeral, Brown left for Baltimore, arriving there in time to serve as one of Tennessee's delegates.[44]

Cave Johnson was not sitting around wringing his hands. On the contrary, he was actively working with the Van Buren forces on possible alternatives should Van Buren's nomination be blocked by the adoption of the two-thirds rule. The New Yorker had a majority of delegate votes, but clearly lacked two-thirds. Van Buren's enemies, including a number pledged to support him, but ready at the first opportunity to dump him, rallied behind the rule—written by Van Buren himself in 1832, but abandoned in 1840. The critical vote would thus be the one sustaining the two-thirds rule, at the expense of majority preference. If the rule passed, Cave Johnson and others considered Silas Wright as a possible substitute for Van Buren; in fact, Benjamin F. Butler of Massachusetts went to Washington with instructions from Van Buren himself to offer Wright if his own candidacy stalled.[45]

On May 25 Cave Johnson informed the Van Buren leadership that the Tennessee delegation was badly splintered, would probably vote for Cass, and, more importantly, would support the adoption of the two-thirds rule, now certain to be introduced by the annexationist forces of Walker. With Tennessee supporting the two-thirds rule, its adoption was almost assured. Faced with this gloomy conclusion, Cave Johnson, together with Governor Morton, head of the Massachusetts delegation, offered a new version of their earlier alternate plan. If Van Buren was blocked, they would offer a Wright-Polk ticket.[46] This seemed logical, but Wright flatly refused to be considered.[47]

Pillow wrote to Polk on May 25, just before leaving Washington for Baltimore. His tone was more optimistic than before. He told Polk that chances for the vice-presidency looked very good: "I am satisfied you are the choice of ⅔ of the Convention for the Vice." His next statement, however, revealed the outline of his plan to secure Polk's nomination for the presidency, should the opportunity arise: "And almost everyone of your friends say they would prefer you for the Presidency. Things may take that turn yet. We of the South cannot bring *that matter up*. If it should be done by the North it will all work *right*, but if we were to make such a move it would . . . injure your prospects for the Vice." [48] Pillow also reported, "Our delegation[,] that portion of it which we can manage[,] are *still and silent*—urging harmony and peace and abstaining from all active interference in arraying the parties against each other. Powell-Anderson-Jones and Blair and Taylor are all determined to go for Cass." Cave Johnson is "in low spirits about our prospects and seems to have lost his energy." [49]

The Democracy began to assemble at the Egyptian Saloon room on the top story of the Odd Fellows Hall in Baltimore on Monday, May 27, in intense heat. The convention opened at noon. Walker's faction struck quickly: Romulus Saunders of North Carolina walked up to the speaker's podium and swiftly called the meeting to order, nominated Hendrick B. Wright of Pennsylvania as president of the convention, put the question to a voice vote, and declared Wright elected.[50] As Wright took the gavel, Saunders continued his blitz, calling for adoption of the convention rules of 1832 and 1836, which included the two-thirds rule. Had Cave Johnson not suddenly asked that an official roster be drawn up before the vote was taken, the coup would have been completed. Walker, pleased with the progress so far, and not wishing to antagonize the delegates by being too obvious, agreed to Johnson's request.[51] The convention then adjourned until 4:00 P.M. When the delegates reconvened, Walker and Benjamin Butler dueled in a battle of words and passion. Chairman Wright finally ended the exchange by adjourning the buzzing convention.[52] "There is so many rumors, so much excitement," reported Johnson to Polk, "that it seems impossible to come to any conclusions for the future— everything is in doubt."[53]

The Van Buren faction tried desperately on the morning of May 28 to gain approval for a measure that would allow the delegations to vote as state blocs rather than as individual delegates. The defeat of this proposal and the adoption of the two-thirds rule which followed shattered hope for Van Buren's nomination.[54] Walker had done his work well.

Voting for the presidential candidate began in the afternoon. On the first ballot, Van Buren fell short, receiving only 146 of the 177 votes needed. Cass got 83, including Tennessee's 13. As Pillow had predicted, the majority of the Tennessee delegation, which had agreed among themselves to vote as a unit, favored Cass. By the seventh ballot, Van Buren had dropped to 99, and a Cass boom began to develop as his strength increased to 123 votes.[55]

As the Cass drive mounted, Pillow "received a proposition from a leading Delegate of . . . Pennsylvania[56] . . . to bring your name before the Convention for President." Shortly after, George Bancroft approached Pillow with the same idea. In a move replete with irony, Bancroft, author of an in-progress biography of Van Buren, had already lined up the New Hampshire and Massachusetts delegations for Polk. Pillow saw that the plan that he had outlined to Polk in his letter of May 25 was materializing.[57] Consistent with this strategy, he hedged, first with the Pennsylvanian, then with Bancroft. He told them that he would "not at present bring it [Polk's name] before the Convention. That if it was the will of the Convention the name should be brought out by the North."[58] Pillow accurately gauged the momentum of the convention. "I do not think it prudent to move forward in *that* matter now. I want the North to bring you forward as a *Compromise* of all interests."[59] Although he delayed at this time, Pillow realized that Polk's name must be submitted soon. He told Bancroft that if New England would nominate Polk the following morning, he would work during the night to swing the Tennessee, Mississippi, and Alabama delegations into line.[60]

The convention was out of control, "wholly ungovernable by the chair." Pledged delegates now openly talked of switching their votes; New Yorkers and southerners traded insults. At last, mercifully, the chaotic political proceedings adjourned. As they left the hall, delegates like Henry J. Seibert thought it inescapable that "Lewis Cass will be the Candidate for president and Johnson Vice president."[61]

But a long night lay ahead. Bancroft and Pillow went to the house where the New York and Ohio delegates stayed. Benjamin Butler was asleep, but the two men went from delegate to delegate, seeking support for Polk. Many of the disheartened Van Buren supporters were sympathetic. Pillow and Bancroft won promises from Medary of Ohio and G. R. Kemble of New York to support Polk the next day if Van Buren's name were withdrawn. They believed, as did others persuaded by Bancroft, that they would see a Silas Wright–Polk ticket or perhaps a Polk-Wright ticket. What they did not know was that Wright had already refused by letter, and in the strongest terms, being considered for the presidential nomination.

About midnight Bancroft, perhaps accompanied by Pillow, left and went to the Massachusetts headquarters. Bancroft pressed Marcus Morton. The governor fell in line. He would try to swing the delegation toward Polk if Van Buren withdrew from the race. Bancroft felt confident enough to get some sleep, but Pillow, brimming with excitement and sensing victory, went searching for disaffected southern delegates and talked into the night. Alabama and Louisiana appeared cooperative, but Mississippi wavered, apparently unwilling to desert Cass.[62]

Excitedly, Pillow reported, "It was all done last night after my letter was written. . . . I was at it nearly all night. I entered into no Combination. I used *no improper* or *dishonourable* means. It was the *result* and *force* and *power* of *circumstances* which I seized hold of and wielded, as I think with *no little skill* and *judgment*."[63] Unable to avoid a conspiratorial tone, Pillow added that he received "no help last night from our home people. . . . They had *no faith* in the *thing* and so expressed themselves. . . . The fatal blow was given, but it was not *seen* nor known what produced such a result—nor where the blow came from."[64]

The next morning most of the delegates awoke early. New York met at 8:00 A.M., and Chairman Butler proposed that Van Buren's name be withdrawn and Silas Wright's substituted. A friend of Wright's, however, produced his letter refusing to be on the ticket without Van

Buren. The confused delegation adjourned and rejoined the convention. Bancroft and Pillow conferred. With New York wavering, it appeared Polk's chances looked excellent if only the ball would start to roll.[65]

New Hampshire gave the initial push—six votes for Polk. Then Bancroft announced the support of Massachusetts. Votes came from Tennessee, Alabama, Louisiana, and a smattering from Pennsylvania and Maryland. Polk had forty-four! Small though it was, this support coming from both southern and northern delegates jarred the convention. Could Polk of Tennessee bring the broken wings of the party together? Reah Frazer of Pennsylvania stood and gave a strong endorsement, reminding the convention that Polk was the "born friend of Old Hickory." Pillow asked for the floor himself and held his friend Polk out to the convention as "the *Olive Branch of Peace*."

The Democracy agreed. After a flurry of other speeches, the climactic ninth ballot began. In succession Maine, New Hampshire, and Massachusetts went for Polk. Virginia delegates, noting the drift, caucused and cast their votes for Polk. Butler now freed the New York delegates from their commitment to Van Buren and all of their votes—except one—went to Polk. The shift of the New York delegation tipped the scales. Delegates hastened to cast their ballots; "all parties ran to you as to *an arc of safety*." The convention had its man.[66] Pillow noted, "I never saw such enthusiasm—such exultation—such shouting for joy."[67] Quickly and without proper consultation, Silas Wright was chosen as the vice-presidential nominee. Pillow was euphoric: "What a ticket. How *pure*, and *elevated* and Herculian in intellects."[68] A cloud appeared, however, marring Pillow's beautiful sunrise. Wright, as some had expected, declined the vice-presidential nomination, and the Democracy turned to George M. Dallas of Pennsylvania, a relative of Robert J. Walker.[69]

Gideon Pillow always claimed credit for Polk's nomination, but others did too. George Bancroft wrote Isham G. Harris forty years later, "Polk owed his nomination by the Democratic Convention to me."[70] Bancroft did not minimize Pillow's role, however, and said on his behalf that he "conducted himself throughout with the modesty and firmness, which deserved highest commendation."[71] Ira A. Eastman of New Hampshire put in his claim, as did Reah Frazer. Despite discounting by Pillow, Cave Johnson also appears to have contributed significantly.

James K. Polk became the "dark horse" nominee because of the

Texas issue and a skillfully orchestrated campaign by Robert J. Walker to ensnare Van Buren. The Democracy actually rewarded Polk because of his loyalty to Van Buren and to the party, and because of his faithful work in Congress and his special relationship with Andrew Jackson. Polk's campaign to secure the nomination was masterful in design: doing careful preliminary work in pivotal Ohio and having Pillow and Johnson, heading a broken delegation, lobby hard within the convention for second spot on the ticket. They asked for everyone's vote, all the while distancing themselves from the suicidal Van Buren–Cass infighting. The objective was a deadlocked convention, leading to the moment when North and South would wear themselves out and turn to an acceptable westerner. Pillow played this role better than Johnson, who had a broader national party agenda. Without Gideon Pillow in Washington and Baltimore, keeping his name enthusiastically and constantly before the delegates, Polk might well have gone unrewarded. He certainly thought so.

So did Cave Johnson. In his excitement and astonishment over the outcome, Johnson flattered Pillow, telling him that he was "a *great General* and that the first war we have I [Pillow] shall command the Malitia of Tennessee *By God.*"[72] Pillow would remember that. He also would remember delegates flocking about him: "You cannot know how much pains they take to give in to me *their adhesion* to you, and to impress me with the *great merits* of their *conduct.* I am almost ready to conclude that *your success* has made *me a great man.* Every body wants *my 'address,'* and desires me to present *them* and their *services* in the proper point of view to *you.*"[73]

Gideon Pillow loved every minute. He is "the happiest man I ever saw," said Sam Laughlin. "He is a *friend indeed.*"[74] Rather than return home, however, Pillow thought he could best serve Polk by proceeding north to Philadelphia and New York. Andrew J. Donelson noted that "Pillow is admirably suited to the task of responding to the applause which every where welcomes your nomination. He does so in fine style and is happy and joyous. Last night the masses hurrahed around him for half an hour before he could proceed to speak."[75] The occasion was a mass meeting of the Democracy in Philadelphia; Pillow estimated their numbers at 12,000 to 15,000. "I was literally dragged to a large gathering of the Democracy & forced to address the people giving them an account of your life—purity of character, public services &c and if I were allowed to form my opinion of the speech from the applause, I should say I had made a distinguished popular effect, but it was the very popular *theme* which drew forth such bursts of applause." Pillow also noted for Polk's benefit that the New York delegation participated enthusiastically.[76]

While in Philadelphia, Pillow called on George M. Dallas, just nominated by the Democracy to replace the unwilling Wright. They had a long conference, and Pillow took care to assure Dallas that Polk, generally known as a low tariff man, would campaign with a moderate tariff policy.[77] Dallas impressed Pillow. "He is very talented and popular and most captivating in his address."[78] Pillow listened to Dallas, just as he had listened to Sam Medary of Ohio about making expansion truly an issue—not just the annexation of Texas, but Great Britain's interference in Oregon as well. Pillow urged Polk to be cautious, indeed, to say nothing publicly, until he came home. "I think I have acquired a knowledge of the *feeling* and conditions of parties in this country."[79]

Pillow returned to Columbia about June 15, tired from travel but exhilarated, ready to do battle with Whigs. "I had no knowledge of Pillow's worth," said Sam Laughlin, "his moral worth, feelings, and energy, and whole-soul'd devotion to his friends, til I traveled and served with him."[80] Pillow, like Polk himself, remained in Tennessee during the presidential campaign, but that was strenuous enough. From June to November, Pillow met with Polk regularly and advised him; he corresponded with Democrats in Pennsylvania, Ohio, and New York and across the South; he published letters in the eastern press; he supplied guides, information, and material to Polk speakers, within and without the state, particularly aiding electors like Levin H. Coe who had to debate Clay's highly effective elector, Gustavus A. Henry. He put out political fires in Middle Tennessee, and he took to the stump himself. In Tennessee certainly, and to a large extent across the nation, party members looked upon Gideon Pillow as Polk's spokesman and campaign manager.[81]

Pillow carefully fed the press Polk's position resisting British "aggression" in Oregon.[82] The powerful and emotional question of expansion, said Pillow over and over again, is a national concern, "not a sectional issue at all."[83] The United States demands positive action on Texas. In a major speech in Columbia on July 13, Pillow defended the annexation of Texas. "Texas constitutes the great issue. Henry Clay is dead wrong in his contention that the Republic is not a de jure government." Pillow went to great lengths, in the closely spaced sixteen-page speech, to argue that Texas was both a de facto and a de jure government. He invoked international law and recent history as justification for annexation. He cited paragraphs of evidence to "establish *fully, clearly and conclusively* the existence of the *plot* or *conspiracy* between the abolitionists of England and America, for the abolition of slavery in the United States, and of the active co-operation of the British Government."[84] Pillow's interminable Texas speech in Columbia is a marvel of political bombast and legal hairsplitting, with an echo of Jacksonian jingoism—a prototype Pillow delivery.

Polk loved it. He yanked a letter Sam Laughlin had prepared for publication and set it aside, stressing the importance of getting Pillow's Texas speech published as soon as possible. He insisted the speech be circulated widely, not only in Tennessee, but across the nation, so it was printed in pamphlet form.[85] "The Southwest is in a *blaze of enthusiasm*," Pillow wrote Democrats in Pennsylvania. "We now entertain *no doubt* of carrying Tennessee by a large majority. . . . The excitement on the Texas question is carrying and sweeping down every resistance."[86]

Pillow struck Whigs time and time again with the badly worn, but still highly effective "corrupt bargain" between Clay and John Quincy Adams.[87] He wrote letters to the North and went to Nashville for special conferences to help Polk dance around the very delicate tariff issue. When Clement C. Clay, Gen. George S. Houston, and Col. Nathaniel Terry of Alabama came to Tennessee to campaign for Polk, they gathered at Clifton. Polk joined them there for strategy sessions.[88] When challenged to answer interrogatories of a public meeting in Giles County, Tennessee, and Pulaski Whigs came to Columbia with resolutions, Pillow received them at his office and seems to have parried the attack.[89] When a question arose about the patriotism of Polk's ancestor Ezekiel Polk, Pillow formed a committee of prominent Maury County citizens to examine and authenticate Ezekiel's commission as an American officer in the Revolution.[90] When the *Albany Argus* exposed an account written by an English tourist mentioning Polk's slaves, Pillow joined in the defense of his friend, ripping the author for exaggeration and irresponsibility. Polk inherited his slaves, wrote Pillow, and "in my life I have only known him to buy two, and one of those mine to keep a family from being separated."[91]

President John Tyler made Polk nervous. His friends had nominated him for president in a rump convention held simultaneously with the Baltimore Democratic convention. Tyler remained in the race, stubbornly demanding that the Democracy's newspapers stop assailing him. Furthermore, he wanted assurances "on reliable authority" that his followers would be respected "as entitled to trust and confidence," which, translated into nonpolitical language, meant that his appointees hoped to keep their preferments. Robert J. Walker, to whom Tyler had complained, suggested Polk write a private letter and Jackson a public one, providing the guarantees. Polk sent Pillow to the Hermitage to meet with Jackson and secure his assistance. Jackson, however, balked, feeling such a letter "imprudent." By giving assurances to Tyler in such a manner, they would play into the hands of the Whigs and their action "be seized upon as a bargain and intrigue for the Presidency. Just as Adams and Clay bargain." The conference with Jackson, Pillow, Gen. Robert Armstrong, and Major Donelson continued, and they finally resolved upon a letter from Jackson to Maj. William Lewis, an old ally who now held a position in the Tyler administration. "If Tyler withdrew," said Jackson in his message, his friends would be "received as brethren . . . all former differences forgotten."[92]

James K. Polk won the election of 1844 with a minority victory, gaining a plurality of 36,725 out of 2,700,061 votes cast. Tennessee was another matter. Consistently Whig in national elections, it had been lost by the Democrats in 1840 by a margin of 12,000. The 1844 campaign was furious, "a most exciting and violent contest," according to Polk. Whig William B. Campbell wrote his uncle David Campbell that the week before last there had been three "barbacues" in Smith County. At each there had been "not less than five thousand persons." It was the same in other counties across the state. "Politics absorbs every thing else here no business is doing at the law."[93] A. O. P. Nicholson, who had quarreled with Polk when the latter supported Van Buren in the spring, pitched in to help defeat the Whigs, as did Andrew Johnson. Unified, the Tennessee Democracy gave battle: Aaron V. Brown, Landon C. Haynes, Cave Johnson, and Hopkins L. Turney debated Whigs William T. Haskell, Neill S. Brown, Gustavus A. Henry, and John Bell. If Clay wins the presidency, said Pillow in a ruined voice, it means the return of federalism—traitorous, aristocratic, tory federalism. Tennessee should support its own son and Texas![94]

Henry Clay nevertheless carried Whig Tennessee by a whisker, 113 votes. East and West Tennessee supported Clay; Middle Tennessee went to Polk. The wide swing to Polk in Maury and her neighboring counties was conspicuous.[95] "Our contest was the closest—the most terrific in the world," wrote Pillow, "& Tennessee has been the hard fought battlefield in the Union."[96]

3   Tennessee's Own Son

James K. Polk wrote his friend Gideon Pillow from Washington shortly after the election. He would be meeting Congress in his new capacity as president. He was excited, exuberant. "I hope you may be satisfied with what I may say to them."[1] Pillow wrote back that he would be in Washington for the festivities, but he cautioned Polk that his first problem as president would be "how to get rid of Calhoun" as secretary of state.[2] Indeed, Calhoun would be the first of many problems. Each cabinet appointment Polk made seemed to rip and tear at the fabric of the Democracy. The Van Buren faction was furious, irreconcilable. Polk, attempting to cloak himself in disinterest, announced that he would not seek reelection and would require his cabinet appointees to pledge that they did not seek the presidency themselves.[3]

Among the many appointments made to good Democrats was the lucrative consulship at Liverpool, which went to Polk's faithful and valuable ally, General Armstrong of Nashville. Pillow would have liked this position himself, but he tried to be patient, knowing Polk would find something suitable.[4] In January 1845, it appeared that a new federal court would be created in the Southwest, and Pillow believed the boundary of the circuit would be drawn to include Alabama and Mississippi. He wrote Polk at once that he wanted the new judgeship. Granted he was a Tennessean, but he did hold property in Mississippi, "identifying me with its interests," and thus would be considered legally a "floating resident."

> I prefer *that*, over any *earthly station*. I am now about 40 years old— have been at my profession about 18 years of that time. Long habit and a natural taste for my profession, have united to make my happiness dependent very much upon the mental excitement of the *Law* in the one way or the other. . . . I trust I could become eminent upon the bench.
>
> That I have been your warm personal & political Friend from my earliest manhood—that I have freely devoted my time, my talents, my energies and my money to your elevation, & that I have *gone farther* in my devotion to you, than I *have, or ever will* again to any man living, you are well apprized. But for *these considerations*, I claim nothing at your hands.[5]

In a carefully and kindly constructed response, Polk declined Pillow's request. He stated with finality that the "judge selected should be a resident citizen of the Circuit from which he is appointed."[6]

So Pillow, the trusting lieutenant, turned his eyes elsewhere and focused his energies on opportunities at home. In the spring of 1845, Pillow sought from his friend George Bancroft, the new secretary of the navy, a three-year contract from the Navy Department to provide thirty tons of hemp annually. Bancroft gladly obliged and Pillow immediately began to construct the required buildings at Clifton and to purchase additional slaves necessary for hemp production. His capital venture of building Maury County's first steam engine had been justified by this navy contract.[7]

Pillow also kept his hand in Tennessee politics. He helped his brother-in-law West Humphreys in a "hard struggle" to be reelected attorney general, and he went about Middle Tennessee trying to smooth the political feathers of Polk's army of disappointed office seekers. He reported to Polk that in the race for the Senate won by Hopkins L. Turney, he believed Turney had sought the support of Gustavus Henry and the Whigs. In reality, Turney had defected, joining the ranks of the "traitors." "I have never had much confidence in his *devotion* to *principle* or his political integrity. . . . He will doubtless oppose your administration."[8]

Polk would need support. Diplomatic relations with Mexico deteriorated quickly in 1846 and the president ordered Gen. Zachary Taylor to advance his army of 4,000 regulars to the Rio Grande. The Mexicans crossed this border on April 25 and attacked an American detachment. On Sunday, May 10, 1846, Polk prepared his war message for Congress. He found time to explain his action to Pillow: "No alternative was left—when she shed American blood East of the Del Norte, but to recognize the war which she had made." Congress, despite stalling maneuvers by Calhoun and the Whigs, passed Polk's war bill on May 13. To provide the necessary manpower, Secretary of War William L. Marcy called for 20,000 volunteers to serve twelve months.[9] Two new major generals and six brigadiers, all loyal Democrats, would lead them. Since Tennessee was asked to provide three regiments—two infantry and one cavalry—surely she would receive one of the brigadiers.

Pillow and his new brother-in-law, Gov. Aaron V. Brown, wrote Polk, and apparently both let him know that Pillow wished to be appointed brigadier.[10] Cave Johnson on June 27 wrote William B. Campbell, a popular and highly regarded Whig who commanded the 1st Tennessee Regiment, that the Tennesseans and Kentuckians would be placed in the division of Maj. Gen. William O. Butler of Kentucky, and that the Tennessee brigadier would "probably be Pillow of Maury or Trousdale of Sumner."[11]

Polk decided to reward Pillow and sought the support of Tennessee senators Hopkins Turney and Spencer Jarnagin. When he had secured their approval, Polk submitted Pillow's name to the Senate on June 29; confirmation came July 1. By luck of the draw Pillow ranked second in seniority behind Thomas Marshall of Kentucky, and ahead of Thomas L. Hamer of Ohio, Joseph Lane of Indiana, John A. Quitman of Mississippi, and James Shields of Illinois.[12] Polk believed he had done the right thing when he appointed his friend. "I have great confidence in Pillow but he is young in the service and the country does not know his merits as well as I do."[13]

The Whigs, if not the country itself, were aghast at this blatant display of partisanship. Qualified West Point graduates had to seek commissions through state appointments. Men such as Albert Sidney Johnston, whose brother was a close friend of Clay's, simply were ignored.[14] William B. Campbell, although a Whig, seemed a certain choice to many within and without Tennessee. When he was bypassed, Gov. David Campbell of Virginia wrote his disappointed nephew: "I know his [Pillow's] character and pretensions. . . . A personal disrespect has been offered to you by the president in appointing Pillow over you. . . . You are in continual danger if you have over you an unprincipled General Officer—and he too taken from the sinks of party corruption . . . a low demagogue . . . a man politically hostile. . . . I see now that this Mexican war is to sink down into a miserable party affair. You whigs will compose a large portion of the rank & file, but you are to be kept there." [15]

Pillow received his commission, dated July 6, on the evening of July 13, 1846, along with orders to proceed immediately to Gen. Taylor's headquarters at Camargo, Mexico.[16] The War Department further ordered Pillow to take command of the brigade of Tennessee volunteers, consisting of the 1st Tennessee Infantry (under Col. Campbell), the 2d Tennessee Infantry (under Col. William Haskell), and the regiment of Tennessee Mounted Volunteers (under Col. Jonas E. Thomas). The two infantry regiments had already been ordered to New Orleans by boat, and thence by ship to the Rio Grande. The cavalry regiment was at Memphis, awaiting Pillow's orders to go overland through Arkansas and Texas to Matamoras, the brigade rendezvous.[17]

Pillow left Clifton at once, accompanied by two servants, Alfred and Ben, and arrived in Memphis July 18. Already fretting about plantation operations at home, he wrote Mary that "my contracts for hemp must be fulfilled." Brother Jerome would see to that, and he had Pillow's confidence, but Pillow worried and sent back detailed instructions. He added, "I have been very prudent in eating. Have not touched tobacco since I left home. . . . I shall come home perfectly content to live at home the ballance [sic] of my life in the enjoyment of the society of my dear wife (the sweetest of women) and our sweet and interesting children." [18]

In Memphis the officers of the brigade rushed to pay their calls. Among them was Capt. William R. Caswell, "an old college mate of mine . . . who I used to love very much & who is a gallant officer and a Gentleman of high standing and character from east Tennessee." Caswell commanded the Knoxville Dragoons.[19] He was a fellow lawyer and Presbyterian and attorney general for the Twelfth Solicitorial District. Unfortunately, Caswell was also a Whig, but Pillow brushed that aside and made him his aide-de-camp. "As far as the comfort of the service is concerned I shall be in clover," Caswell confided to his wife.[20]

Pillow's worries about being accepted by the Tennessee volunteers all but vanished. "My appointment is well received by the Troops," Pillow wrote Mary. "They have given me a warm and hearty reception. . . . I am sure I shall have no difficulty in making my Troops all like me." The Nashville *Union* published a letter from Memphis commenting on the favorable reaction by the soldiers. "No doubt is now entertained in camp as to the propriety of Gen. Pillow's appointment."[21] The Memphis *Daily Eagle* disagreed. West Tennesseans, particularly in Haskell's regiment, had wanted state Inspector General L. H. Coe to command the brigade. They were "greatly disappointed."[22]

While in Memphis, Pillow became fast friends with Kentucky's General Butler, and they traveled together to New Orleans aboard the steamboat *Champion*.[23] They and their staffs lodged at the fashionable St. Charles Hotel in New Orleans along with Shields, Quitman, and Gen. John E. Wool of the regular army. "I started out on horse," wrote Caswell, "with Genl. Pillow (who is a rigid Presbyterian)" to see the sights. "The General especially wished to visit Congo Square and watch the Negroes dancing." Later he and Caswell set about purchasing camp furniture—mess chests, small tables, silver, and all sorts of items—placing it upon "a carry-all on springs" which they also purchased. It would be drawn by six mules brought from Clifton. So far Caswell had not been paid and his situation embarrassed him, but Pillow "offers me his purse." "We live on the best of the world—the best fruits & choicest wines."[24]

The delights of New Orleans were left behind as the steamer *New York* started down the Mississippi. Crammed aboard were five generals, their staff officers, servants, saddle horses, and two companies of Illinois volunteers. As they passed the old New Orleans battle site, General Butler, who had been there as a young captain with Jackson and Pillow's uncle William, clustered officers about him and pointed out American and British positions and the progress of the English attack. When they neared the mouth of the Mississippi, Pillow noted the land had become "overgrown with rank grass—too soft for cultivation." Soon after the steamer entered the Gulf of Mexico a school of porpoise followed the boat, "jumping and rolling." Four days' sail took them past the sand isle of Brazos Santiago into a "lagune" separating it from the mainland. Pillow was glad to see Point Isabel off in the distance. "I was never sicker in my life than I was for the 2 first days. . . . The vessel . . . rocks and pitches and tosses so much I can scarcely write at all."[25]

As quickly as he could, Pillow unloaded his troops and began moving them to the Rio Grande, where they boarded river steamers to Camargo.[26] The journey 100 miles upriver proved slow and difficult. "The Rio Grande is certainly the crookedest River in the world," Pillow complained. General Taylor's river steamers kept going aground and slamming against the banks. "If I ever succeed in getting them together so that my whole command would be under my eye, I should feel greatly relieved."[27]

Camargo stood at the head of navigation, on the bank of the San Juan River close to its confluence with the Rio Grande. The San Juan had overflowed recently, causing brick in the "dilapidated village" to dissolve. Much of Camargo simply had washed away.[28] The only water available to the troops was from the brackish San Juan. Within two weeks Pillow's Tennessee brigade seemed to be washing away itself: measles, typhoid, and dysentery tore through the camps. Pillow was appalled. In Camargo, he wrote, he had "seen more human suffering than I ever saw in all my life before."[29] Colonel Campbell reported that the muffled drum of the funeral dirge could be heard almost every day; by August 24 one-fourth of his 1st Tennessee Regiment were unfit for duty.[30] Pillow had rubbed Campbell raw: "Genl Pillow is one of the smallest caliber that has ever been elevated to so high a command and, although he professes to be very friendly to me and is tolerably agreeable yet he seems not to know what to do & is often directing & interfering in matters which he properly has nothing to do with, but I will bear with him."[31]

On August 17 Pillow met with Zachary Taylor at Camargo. He found Taylor a "frank and manly old gentleman about the size of myself," he wrote Mary, "except that he is quite fat—not so fat as your Brother William, but more so than your father." Taylor invited Pillow to dine, and they shared ham and bread. "Ham and bread is all we have & but little of that," Pillow reported. Taylor agreed with his subordinate that if the Mexicans did not quickly surrender, the true course would be to land an expeditionary force near Vera Cruz and march inland against the City of Mexico. In the meantime, however, Taylor intended to march into the interior on September 1 and seize Monterrey, although he did not expect a fight. "Taylor does not want to take many volunteers with him," Pillow wrote Mary. "I shall of course be very unwilling to stay behind and will not if I can avoid it. I came to fight and if any is done I want to have a hand in it."[32]

Everything seemed discouraging. "Oh my Dear wife, how strong my feelings this morning turn towards home—home, my sweet home where all on this earth that is dear to me is to be found. What would I not give to be with my Dear sweet wife & children. But I must not indulge this strain of feeling. Duty to my country calls me here and that duty must be met and will require your Husband to subject his feelings to great *Privation*—so long an absence from his truly interesting family."[33]

Taylor marched toward Monterrey the first week in September 1846. In addition to two divisions of regulars, he took Butler's division of volunteers, which included the brigades of Hamer and Quitman. Campbell's 1st Tennessee, reduced to 500 picked men, were taken from Pillow's brigade and placed under Taylor's friend Quitman.[34] This pleased Campbell, who wrote to his uncle that Quitman "is far superior to Pillow in every point of view both as a man and as a military man."[35] To Pillow, however, the Whig Campbell expressed himself differently, writing that he and his men regretted very much being placed temporarily under Quitman. They appreciated all of Pillow's efforts to relieve the sick and "your efforts to introduce and carry into effect a proper system of discipline and to fit your command for the active duties of the field." "If it be our fortune to participate in the conflicts with the Enemy," Campbell continued, they would wish to "be led into the field of Battle by Tennessee's own Son."[36]

But Taylor wanted veteran officers along, and Quitman possessed combat experience from the Texas War for Independence, while Pillow did not.[37] The loss of the 1st Tennessee left Pillow mortified and resentful: "This does not please me. It was *unlooked for*. . . . My troops are very much excited and displeased at being taken from under my command. . . . I will not be ordered forward at all."[38] "Our Genl Pillow," Campbell wrote, "does not go on but is ordered to remain here with the balance of his command. He has been greatly dissatisfied. He is a very weak, light man, but is so far very agreeable to me & I say nothing and wish my friends to be silent as yet in relation to him."[39]

Butler's division of volunteers left Camargo on September 6. The remaining volunteers, nearly 10,000 of them, were loosely strung out from Camargo to Brazos Santiago under Maj. Gen. Robert Patterson;

Pillow and Marshall commanded mixed brigades under him. So many troops were sick and disabled, however, that Pillow had to borrow "men from the Alabama regiment to bury the dead" of Campbell's regiment.[40]

Pillow, burning with anger, characteristically set to work with great energy. Ordered by Patterson to see to the training of the volunteers, he established a regular system "of instruction in the school of the soldier, company and battalion." He moved the brigade camp from the riverbank to a site nearer Camargo, and then into the town itself. He established his headquarters in an open square in the upper end of town, five walled tents in a line: the kitchen tent; the tent of Bvt. Capt. Oscar F. Winship, Pillow's newly appointed assistant adjutant general, a West Pointer from New York who had distinguished himself at Resaca de la Palma; Pillow's own tent; Captain Caswell's tent; and that of Capt. Robert B. Reynolds, the highly political East Tennessee quartermaster.[41] Pillow's tent was "furnished with a table, a rude desk for his papers, his cot, a water jar sunk partly in the ground & his tent carpeted with empty corn sacks." One observer noted that Pillow's "Bible is constantly found in his tent, and its pages are perused as often as camp duties will permit."[42]

Caswell had become despondent. Captain Winship had taken over his staff duties, he had no prospect of joining in the fight at Monterrey, he worried about the "terrible" sickness that prevailed, and he had begun to borrow heavily from Pillow. "Gen. Pillow is very rich, being worth perhaps 200,000$. He is a good financier and says he will put me in a way to make some money but I do not depend on this, for I know of no way he can do so, by any means I could accept."[43]

Evidently Pillow's servant Alfred needed to be perked up as well. "I told Alfred yesterday," wrote Pillow, "I would give him his freedom if he wanted to stay *here* & that he could gather a Mexican wife. . . . He said he didn't want a Mexican wife, nor his freedom either, that he preferred to go home with his master & see his mistress & his own wife."[44]

Flies, bad water, and lack of shade made the soldiers miserable. Pillow watched men die about him in September. Fifteen hundred Americans perished because of bad sanitation and diseases against which they had no immunity. Haskell's 2d Tennessee at one point had 317 ill out of 588 on the rolls.[45] Pillow himself, however, "never enjoyed better health in my life" and developed a deep tan from the scorching sun. He prayed every morning and evening, giving thanks that he had been spared, and he made a special point to do what he could to relieve the suffering of others.[46] Caswell acknowledged in the Nashville *Whig* that Pillow had endeared himself to his troops by his attention and kindness to the sick at Camargo.[47] "I am of course exceedingly anxious to go forward with my Brigade," Pillow wrote Mary, to get out of "this sickly place and get into the pure mountain air."[48]

Sometime early in October, Pillow's luck ran out. For sixty days he suffered from two attacks of typhoid followed by a serious occurrence of "bloody dysantary." He regained his feet early in November but was forced back to his sickbed and confined to quarters. The tone of his letters home changed. He spoke often of his "utter unworthiness" and a "stronger sense of my dependence upon the mercy of God." "Surely under such blessings of providence we ought to be grateful & good Christians & should love him and worship with devoted hearts."[49]

Meanwhile, in late September the 1st Tennessee had seen action at the Battle of Monterrey. Colonel Campbell performed very well, as did the company of Nashville Blues led by Capt. Frank Cheatham. The regiment, however, lost heavily. Pillow congratulated them from his sickbed with unconcealed bitterness: "If anything could compensate me for the *injustice* done me, in not being permitted in person, to have led *forward* and *onward*, the Regiment, in its gallant charge, it would be the high gratification afforded me by the *noble daring* of the regiment in that charge."[50]

While Campbell's Tennesseans were distinguishing themselves, a ditch was being constructed at Camargo that would become perhaps the most celebrated in American military history. Pillow's detractors, to the end of his life, told and retold the story of the ditch. Customarily such a ditch was dug at the front base of the wall to heighten the face of the parapet. Pillow, however, came up with the "happy idea of placing the ditch inside the breastwork." Regular officers roared with delight, and to demonstrate the folly of Pillow's fortification, Lt. Jimmy Stuart of the regulars is supposed to have jumped it "in one easy bound" with a "stunted Texas mustang." Pillow defended himself, of course, stating that the ditch was one of several cut across the streets of Camargo, intended not as breastworks but as obstacles for "mounted rancheros who might make a sudden attack on the town at night." Majors Charles J. Williams and Robert Farquharson supported Pillow after the war, claiming that the ditches were Patterson's idea and that Pillow only supplied work details. Years later, *Confederate*

Veteran editor S. A. Cunningham would bend truth to the point where he could maintain that Pillow actually had been innovative, using a method "adopted by both armies during the Confederate war."[51]

By the fall of 1846, Pillow had thus become the visible symbol of the Jacksonian volunteer officer that the regular army despised—an enemy of West Point, an incompetent, insubordinate spy of the Democracy's president, who held a general's commission because of political patronage. Ridicule and distrust of Pillow became part of the creed of the professional soldier. The officer corps, particularly the professional officer corps of the army in Mexico, was riddled through with Whigs, from Taylor to William Caswell. Polk knew this, and it was one of the reasons for Pillow's appointment: just as at Baltimore in 1844, Pillow went to Mexico as Polk's representative and confidant, this time to keep an eye on the military establishment. Pillow would suffer from the boundless sarcasm and animosity of the Whigs and the military establishment for the rest of his life. He would be a common joke that would bind enemies on the battlefield fifteen years later in common cause.

Pillow focused his frustration and wrath on Taylor. He believed Taylor had wronged him by taking away the 1st Tennessee and denying him the opportunity to gain a reputation at Monterrey. Prolonged illness at Camargo deepened his resentment, and he determined on revenge. For three months his confidential letters back to Washington contained criticism of his commander: Taylor was actually the political dupe of Polk's antagonist, the Whig Balie Peyton; the army was greatly dissatisfied with its commander; the armistice he allowed at Monterrey was "ruinous to the public service." Quartermaster Reynolds echoed Pillow's thoughts in additional private letters to the president. The atmosphere at Pillow's headquarters became poisonous, and a disgusted William Caswell asked to return to his cavalry company on November 1.

Meanwhile, Pillow wrote Mary:

> The war is miserably managed by Genl. Taylor. He is exceedingly *indolent* & *slow* in his movements—is very obstinate & will not be advised—is displeased at the Govt. . . . I would not be surprized that he should be superceded in the command of the army. The President will bear with him as long as he can, but if he proves too obstinate & refuses to carry out the orders of the Govt. he will be knocked into a *cocked-hat.*[52]

You need not my Dear feel any uneasiness about my talking too freely of Genl. Taylor. *I am cautious.* I do not talk upon that subject here. I have now paid him in full for his *injustice* to me. He is a Tyrant in disposition & undertook at an early day, to crush me because I was known to be the President's bosom friend, but he did not know me. . . . I think he will *now respect me.* I understand he has a strong suspicion of the source from whence the heavy blows have come.[53]

Taylor regarded Pillow as "that contemptible fellow."[54] "He is I consider a very small man in every respect, but I apprehend has the ear of the President. . . . It is no doubt more advisable to treat him and others of similar character with courtesy and politeness without committing oneself with them, in any way."[55]

While Taylor's army fought in the streets of Monterrey, Polk proposed on September 22 "an expedition to Tampico and eastern province of Tamaulipas . . . under Patterson . . . accompanied . . . by Pillow and Shields." Polk clearly intended to inject some Democratic generalship into the war.[56] "We must possess it [Tampico]," Polk confided to Pillow, and Patterson has been "instructed to consult with you."[57] Taylor blocked Patterson's overland march from Camargo to Tampico in October. But by mid-October Polk had decided to extend the Tampico movement into an expedition against Vera Cruz and ultimately against the City of Mexico itself. The concept was to make the port of Tampico a staging area for the attack on Vera Cruz. The subsequent thrust inland would draw the Mexicans out to defend the capital, whereupon they could be defeated totally. Pillow much admired this "present purpose of the Govt. to attack Mexico near the *heart.*"[58] Polk sent Maj. Robert M. McLane to Taylor with dispatches, informing him of the plan to seize Vera Cruz by way of Tampico. McLane, who "knows the views of the govt. and possesses the confidence of the secretary of war and the president," was authorized to communicate the plans to Pillow.[59]

General-in-Chief Winfield Scott would lead the Vera Cruz expedition. He would detach the best troops from Taylor's army, leaving Taylor to suffer Pillow's fate and "stand on the defensive with the remainder."[60] Colonel Campbell surmised that "General Taylor's fault may be that he has been too successful & may be superceded by Mr. Polk because he is jealous of his growing reputation. . . . Mr. Polk may direct Gen Taylor to stay here or march to Saltillo where there is nothing to do and order some Democrat General to march at the head of the army to Tampico, that he may be immortalized by a successful fight."[61] Pillow wrote Mary, when it was certain Scott would be in charge:

> I have kept the President regularly informed of Taylor's movements. Scott Succeeds Taylor: *It is my work* & I am proud to have been able thus to serve my country in getting the service clear . . . of a man who has no respect for the rights of others and who has adopted a system of proscription & persecution towards the President's friends which was calculated and intended to drive them in disgrace from the service. My advice is that Scott is now on the way and that he is made fully aware by the President that I must & shall be held foremost in his estimation.[62]

Pillow was sick again. He was told by the surgeon that "he would certainly die if he remained in that place," and the doctor recommended that he be sent down to the seacoast. Patterson also insisted he leave Camargo, and Pillow did so on November 30, remaining a week aboard a government transport at the mouth of the Rio Grande. The change worked miraculously, and he returned on December 8, ready for the march to Victoria and Tampico.[63] Patterson gave Pillow command of four volunteer regiments at Matamoras, the 3d and 4th Illinois, the 2d Tennessee, and the 3d Tennessee Cavalry, while he retained overall command of the force. Pillow left Matamoras on December 14 and advanced twenty-five miles; he then waited for Patterson and the rest of the column to come up.[64] Pillow was still so weak the first few days of the march that he had to be placed on and taken off his horse by his servants Alfred and Ben. The exercise of the march, however, began to agree with him, and he felt renewed and excited.[65] "We will be passing over a country almost entirely unknown to any American."[66]

The column continued on. They marched to San Fernando and spent Christmas nearby. A Pillow critic reported that "the low morale of the plodding volunteers was not raised by the exhibition of [Pillow] eating and drinking a plentiful Christmas dinner in sight of his weary and famished men."[67] Tempers became frayed. Two days after Christmas, Pillow pounced on a volunteer officer who argued with him. Pillow even drew his revolver. Later he accepted an apology from the officer and dropped the matter.[68]

The volunteers reached Santander on December 29 and Victoria on January 4.[69] Patterson and Pillow were surprised to find Victoria

Col. William Bowen Campbell
(courtesy Tennessee State Library and Archives)

already occupied by some of Taylor's forces, specifically, Quitman's brigade—including Campbell's 1st Tennessee.[70] Campbell maintained he was glad to see Pillow arrive and to serve under him once again: Pillow "tries to make himself agreeable to me."[71] So the 1st Tennessee returned to Pillow's command, while Quitman received the 4th

Illinois in exchange.[72] Pillow's brigade now consisted of Haskell's and Campbell's Tennessee regiments, the regiment of Tennessee cavalry, Lt. Augustus A. Gibson's battery, and the 3d Illinois.[73]

On January 15, 1847, the march for Tampico resumed. Twenty-six-year-old William G. McAdoo of Haskell's regiment observed the beautiful country, the "open rolling prairies, covered with luxuriant grass on which fed thousands of cattle and horses."[74] On the second day out, the column stirred before dawn; in the darkness, Patterson fell and severely sprained his ankle.[75] He relinquished command of the division to Pillow.

As commander, Pillow continued to enforce, with a fury, the "rigid system of discipline," said Caswell, now a company commander in the cavalry regiment, "despite the odium which it excites . . . and the loud and uncontrolled murmuring approaching sometimes almost to insubordination."[76] He and Campbell clashed when Pillow "prescribed too harsh discipline for cutting sugar cane." "Neither Patterson nor Pillow appreciate the character of Citizen soldiers," contended Caswell. "Pillow would have made an excellent waggon master." Yet, illustrating the incredible ambivalence in many minds about Pillow, Caswell was quoted two weeks later as defending his old classmate for his industry, energy, and firmness.[77]

A member of Capt. Robert C. Foster's company in the 1st Tennessee left the column without permission and fired his musket, presumably at game, but the ball struck in the midst of a group of officers. The ranking officer took action, but Pillow intervened and ordered the man tied to a wagon wheel and placed under guard. Foster, upon hearing of the matter, cut the soldier loose. Pillow waited two days, expecting an explanation and an apology from Foster. When he received none, Pillow ordered Foster arrested for insubordination. Pillow appears to have relented, however. Foster, the son of influential Whig congressman Ephriam H. Foster, got word to Maj. Gen. David Twiggs, who apparently took an interest in Foster's situation, requesting to see him in person. The incident was dropped without court-martial.[78]

Word got around that Pillow was a severe disciplinarian and had a bad temper. He could be unjust. Among the Tennesseans arrested and punished were eighteen-year-old John Vines Wright and a young lawyer from Giles County, Preston Smith. Pillow let Wright off easy, however, not because he did not deserve punishment, but because of the general's high regard for Wright's father. Another young officer who made Pillow's acquaintance on this march and who learned about Pillow's justice was Lt. Bushrod Johnson. Even the rank and file turned against him. A Tennessean wrote, "Our Brigadier General I am sorry to say is universally unpopular." Another confided, "It is his misfortune to be cursed with unalloyed selfishness."[79]

During the march, in accordance with instructions from Polk, Pillow examined major terrain features which might be used as a national boundary. He recommended two: the Sierra Madre, with passes at Saltillo, Santa Barbara, and Victoria, and the Pánuco River, which emptied into the Atlantic at Tampico. Pillow loved this country, "the richest & most beautiful country I ever saw."[80] He worked hard: "I scarcely ever sleep more than 5 hours out of 24 hours. My usual bed time is 11 oclock and I rise between 3 & 4 in the morning & have my whole column consisting of nearly 2,000 men . . . & nearly 300 wagons in motion by 5 oclock in the morning which is about 2½ hours before sun rise." The division reached Tampico "much fatigued," but safe and ready for action. Colonel Campbell gave Pillow credit, as did General Patterson.[81]

The head of Pillow's column arrived on January 23 and encamped "on a beautiful open plain" ten miles out from town. Morale was high. "We are in perennial summer," Pillow's confidant, Capt. Robert B. Reynolds, happily reported. The volunteers were proud of their march and liked their camp at Laguna de la Puerta.[82] The regulars sulked, however. Capt. William H. T. Walker found himself and his company of regulars attached to Pillow's brigade. "I am surrounded by volunteers. . . . Tis disgusting in the extreme & such contemptible appointments make me feel like quitting my country in disgust. . . . All these citizen political soldiers imagine they are great Jackson men and that they must have his soldierly qualities."[83]

Scott was due any day, and Pillow worried they might not get along. The great storms at sea kept delaying his arrival, thus postponing the day when the Tennesseans would embark for the attack on Vera Cruz. If and when they became established in Vera Cruz, they could expect more sickness—the "vomits" and yellow fever. After commanding the division for most of the march, being reduced to brigade command again was a letdown for Pillow. So were letters from Mary, for that matter. She was anxious about the approach of the "sickly season" and kept asking him to resign his commission and come home. Pillow responded that "it . . . would be regarded by the world as *a cowardly desertion* of my post and would reflect upon a *name* which is, as to *courage & bravery*, without a stain, although the family have had active participation in the war of the Revolution, the war of 1812 and all the

Indian wars."[84] Pillow's answer to worry was activity. He filled the brigade's days with drill and instruction—company and battalion drill in the morning, regimental and brigade drill in the afternoon, climaxed by parade at 5:00 P.M. For diversion, he dispatched squads down the riverbanks to capture Mexican cattle and mules.[85]

Winfield Scott arrived on February 19. Pillow conspicuously lined three Tennessee regiments on the riverbank and fired a salute. "Not withstanding the distance we could distinguish on the deck the majestic form and uncovered head of the old hero, towering, as he did, above the throng around him, in body as well as mind."[86] When he came ashore, Scott captivated Pillow. "He has treated me with great kindness & consideration. He granted every request I made of him." He assigned Lt. Edward J. Steptoe's battery to Pillow—"the largest & finest battery of Artillery in the army." One of Scott's staff came to Pillow and reported that the general had directed him

> to say to me that he wished to be upon terms of personal & confidential relationship with me. I have now rode down all obstacles, and feel that I am, by the army, esteemed the *first officer* of all the recent appointments by the President. Indeed I have been recently so much flattered, & have received so much attention, and so many marks of respect & consideration, that I might well *be vain* of my present standing in the army & of the prospects *ahead*, but I am prudent enough to conceal my great satisfaction and devote myself . . . to the duties of my command without seeming to be at all conscious of my rapid and growing reputation.[87]

Scott remained in Tampico for twenty-four hours. He inspected the units, issued embarkation orders on February 19, and sailed February 20 for Lobos Island, the expedition rendezvous, about sixty-five miles south. The troops were to strike their tents and march the five miles to the mouth of the river to board the transports. Pillow's brigade would lead the volunteers aboard the steamer *Virginia*.[88]

Scott's orders prohibited officers from taking their horses because of the lack of space. This would not do at all, Pillow reasoned. He complained to his division chief, Patterson, that recent illness made him "too feeble for service on shore without his horses." Patterson declined to send his request on to Scott, replying, "Sir, I warn you that the consequences of violating the orders of the General-in-Chief will be your arrest when the army is disembarked at Vera Cruz." Pillow began to load his horses anyway; Scott would understand.[89]

Maj. Gen. Winfield Scott
(painting by Miner K. Kellogg; courtesy New-York Historical Society, New York City)

4   **Hurra for Pa**

Pillow's Tennessee volunteers reached Lobos Island, a coral patch in the Gulf of Mexico 100 miles above Vera Cruz. There they waited for the remainder of the fleet to join them and then sailed to the shelter of Anton Lizardo Bay, twelve miles below Vera Cruz. By the afternoon of March 5, all transports had arrived and anchored. Fortunately, the sea was "smooth as a mill pond."[1]

Scott made a reconnaissance on March 6 aboard the small steamer *Petrita*. Accompanying him were Generals William J. Worth, Patterson, and Pillow and Commodore David Conner. They examined the defenses of Vera Cruz and searched for a suitable landing site. "The white bastion and towers of San Juan d'Ulúa, the spires and domes of the broad city of Vera Cruz burst upon the sight presenting a scene of strength, magnificence and beauty rarely paralleled—a scene to which ten fold interest was imparted by the anticipation of the conflict." Pillow and the reconnaissance party saw flashes from the castle and then from the city. Scott, nevertheless, ordered the *Petrita* even closer. Enemy fire increased, but no rounds struck the vessel. Mission accomplished, the *Petrita* sailed away jauntily.[2]

Pillow's brigade swapped their transports for Conner's warships on March 9. Buffered from the sea by Sacrificios Island, they transferred again to surfboats and headed ashore at Collada Beach, two miles south of Vera Cruz. Approaching shore, they worried about the line of sand hills in the distance, running along behind the beach. Comdr. Josiah Tatnall's "Mosquito Fleet" of gunboats stood close in, however, ready to shell any enemy who might appear. Worth's regulars landed first, and then Patterson's volunteers, who cheered as they passed Tatnall's line of light-draft craft. "We landed in great confusion" but quickly formed into regiments and rushed forward to secure the line of sand hills. The unopposed amphibious assault was a glorious success; by 11:00 P.M. Scott's 8,600 men were ashore.[3]

The Tennesseans slept on the beach, "coughing all night and our Division seemed to be composed rather of consumptive invalids than of soldiers."[4] The next morning Patterson's division, with the two Tennessee regiments in advance, passed through Worth's division and pushed inland and northward to extend the investing lines. Patterson detached Pillow's brigade, which consisted of the 1st and 2d Tennessee, the 1st Pennsylvania under Col. Francis M. Wynkoop, and the 2d Pennsylvania under Col. Benjamin Roberts. Pillow led them across sand dunes or hills rising to 250 feet in height, interlaced by "almost impassable" forests of thorny chaparral. He insisted on dragging along Steptoe's battery, detailing Major Farquharson and a company of the 1st Tennessee to "open a road" for the guns. About 2:00 P.M. the brigade reached the ruins of the hacienda St. Malibran near a large pond of shallow water known as Laguna Malibran. The Mexicans used the buildings as a magazine.

Pillow quickly attacked with both Tennessee regiments, leading their charge himself.[5] Patterson supported the attack through the chaparral with a six-pounder cannon. After a sharp exchange of fire, in which the Mexicans lost one officer and three men, Pillow easily dislodged the light forces defending the magazine. Leaving Campbell and the 1st Tennessee to hold the objective, Pillow pushed on with Haskell and Wynkoop to occupy the intersection of an unfinished railroad and the Medellin road. Mexican cavalry and infantry in small numbers opposed him, but he drove them off. The enemy retreated to a high sand hill, where they regrouped and opened fire.

Pillow reacted at once, calling up Haskell's 2d Tennessee. Haskell deployed, his men moving by twos up a narrow road. At the bottom of the hill they found themselves fired upon from both sides. Quite calmly Haskell's men turned "back to back" and returned the fire. "Gen. Pillow who was in our midst, ordered a charge up the hill which was so steep that he had to dismount to get up. We have one 'Yell' and up we went, while the balls, fired at random from . . . the cavalry on the hill whizzed over our heads. . . . We had to pull up by the bushes. On we went and at last perfectly exhausted, reached the top of the hill where we saw that our foes were 'vamoosing.'" Pillow led the attack, placing himself "at the head of his men." In less than fifteen minutes Pillow's men had captured the lightly held heights and planted their flag.[6] "We held these heights all evening and until morning," Lt. Wiley Hale, 2d Tennessee, reported, "the artillery playing upon us until dark. Each man with his bayonet scratched himself a little ditch and slept secure while the balls whizzed over our heads." Quitman's Mississippians relieved them, and Pillow's men returned to a position near the St. Malibran ruins.[7]

Pillow and his volunteers had done very well. Their movements on the tenth resulted in the capture of the magazine and cut "the Alvarado road and gave the Americans control of the city's water supply." A great deal of the success could be attributed to Pillow's personal leadership. Patterson and Scott freely praised him. Col. Joseph G. Totten, a professional highly regarded by the military establishment, would report to the president that Pillow had "made much character with the army." Not so, however, with regulars W. H. T. Walker and Lt. Daniel H. Hill, neither of whom were engaged. Walker watched from a distance, disdainfully "amusing himself" at the antics of the volunteers, while Hill dismissed any action of "that fool Genl. Pillow."[8]

The investment of the walled city of Vera Cruz continued with the divisions of Worth positioned on the right, Patterson in the center, and Twiggs on the left. The Americans held a range of large sand hills "forming an irregular semicircle, at the distance of about two miles around the city." On March 13, with the enemy skirmishers driven within the walls, Scott's men set about with great energy laying trenches and planting batteries. Time was critical. Vera Cruz had to be reduced before "the vomito" (yellow fever) infected the army. Northers kept scattering the fleet and handicapping landing of siege ordnance. "The eyes of the soldiers were blinded by clouds of sand continually beating in their faces, the open trenches were filled almost as fast as the efforts of the men could clear them."[9]

For two weeks Pillow's brigade worked hard, digging trenches, "acting as guard for the working parties, or on duty moving artillery & military stores." Lieutenant Hale wrote his mother that the men were "sleeping . . . upon the sand without tents and having a shower of rain upon us every night."[10] Pillow himself stayed at division headquarters, set up in the ruins of St. Malibran. Although magnificent, and "in the spanish regime must have been one of the most princely residences on this continent," it was damp and cold, and Pillow became chilled. When he had a free moment he admired what remained of an extensive garden and the walls enclosing fifteen or twenty acres. On a clear day he could see Mount Orizaba, a silent, snowcapped witness to the west.[11] Enemy cavalry kept annoying the rear of his brigade, and on March 16 Pillow led his men in a brisk reconnaissance in force, easily brushing the enemy back into the chaparral. A regular officer, Capt. John P. McCown, guided Pillow's lead elements.[12]

Vera Cruz refused to surrender. Each American shot seemed to be answered by two or three from within the city and from the great castle Ulúa. So the Americans continued to dig. By March 22 advanced works had been completed in Worth's sector, so that seven ten-inch mortars went into operation; soon they were joined by four more large guns.[13] "The terrible work was continued day & night & such whistling & bursting of shot & shell around, above & on all sides of us was sublimer than comfortable."[14]

It was not enough; Vera Cruz still held out. Scott asked the navy for help. In advance of Pillow's lines Colonel Totten had selected a position for these navy guns, and the two Tennessee regiments set to work constructing emplacements on March 19, "exposed to an almost incessant shower of missils [sic] from both city and castle."[15] Supervising their work were Captains McClellan and Robert E. Lee and Maj. John Sanders. They masked the position and its construction so well that the Mexicans were unaware of its presence. Here, 700 yards from the city walls, were to be positioned two thirty-two pounders, three eight-inch Paixhans, and a sixty-four-pound shell-gun, all manned by navy gunners, their fire directed by naval officers.[16]

The Tennesseans dug by day; during the night the brigade, assisted by sailors and engineer troops, would move up the big naval guns from the beach. Mounted on extremely heavy ship-carriages, the guns sank deep into the sand, and Pillow's men, using long drag ropes, struggled to drag the dead weight (three guns weighed over three tons each) two miles over sand hills, through thorny chaparral, and through the water and mud of the Laguna Malibran.[17]

In the early morning of March 24, three heavy naval guns were in position, and the last three pieces were being hauled up in the darkness. The men had been at it all night, their difficult work aggravated by yet another norther, "beating directly in the faces of the men." Scott had ordered that the guns be moved only at night and that the naval battery should not open fire until all six cannon were emplaced. The guns had to be brought across the unfinished railroad bed, a position swept by Mexican batteries. By dawn of March 24, five of the guns were in position, but the sixth and last piece had not been brought across the railroad. Colonel Campbell, supervising the work crews, refused to bring the last piece over, declaring that to do so would violate an order by Scott not to move any of the pieces in broad daylight. Realizing that failure to move the cannon might delay the firing of the naval battery for a full day, Pillow took it upon himself to set aside Scott's orders. He directed his Tennesseans to move the piece into position.[18] Again Pillow had displayed his willingness to indulge in the dangerous practice of setting aside a superior's instructions. This time his gamble proved productive, but he was establishing a disturbing pattern of insubordination.

The naval battery opened fire at 10:00 A.M., and the weight of its shot quickly began to breach the walls of Vera Cruz and to disable enemy cannon. The Mexicans concentrated their fire on the position, but the American sailors kept at their guns. At 4:00 P.M. a white flag appeared from the city. The truce was temporary, however, and firing resumed at 1:00 A.M. "with redoubled energy."[19]

As the firing continued on March 25, a party of the 1st Tennessee went inland to kill beef and were attacked by a small party of Mexicans. The alarm was sounded, and Pillow went out with Haskell's 2d Tennessee and a company of the 1st toward the village of Boca del Rio. The enemy chose to defend a stone bridge across the Morena River. Led by Capt. Frank Cheatham's Nashville Blues, "our boys raised the Tennessee yell and charged the bridge." Into the fight roared Col. William Harney and the 2d Dragoons. It was a short, "smartly successful" engagement with the enemy put to flight. The Tennesseans distinguished themselves, as did a young dragoon captain, William J. Hardee.[20]

American gunfire began to tear the city's walls apart. Shells rained on the city; rockets were unleashed. Maj. Edmund Kirby observed the

Maj. Gen. Gideon Johnson Pillow, 1848
(engraving by Henry S. Sadd; courtesy John R. Neal)

bombardment: "A horrid business, the shower of iron falling upon the . . . city from the 22nd to the 26th March was incessantly being kept up day and night. At night the spectacle was grand. The air being filled with shells crossing each other in every direction. The havoc was terrible; the crash of buildings, the shrieks and moans of the poor creatures within the walls could be plainly heard at night within our lines."[21]

By the morning of March 26, the Mexican commander, Gen. Juan Morales, had had enough. He turned over command to Gen. José Landero, who sent out a flag of truce that afternoon. Firing was suspended. Scott honored Pillow by appointing him as one of the American team of commissioners to negotiate the surrender, along with Major General Worth, Colonel Totten, and Capt. John H. Aulick of the navy. William Campbell noted, "Scott is paying Polk for letting him come here in his notice of and putting forward Pillow on all occasions."[22]

The commissioners began their negotiations at a lime kiln on the beach during yet another great norther. Scott's terms were offered by Worth, and the Mexicans countered with demands of their own. The talks nearly broke down and were adjourned to the morning of the twenty-seventh. Following concessions by both sides, an agreement was settled by midnight of March 27 calling for the surrender of Vera Cruz and Ulúa. The Mexican garrison was to be paraded, disarmed, and then paroled.[23] Accordingly, on March 29 Scott stationed Patterson's division on the left and Worth's division on the right to form an arch.[24] Patterson's left flank and Worth's right rested on the city walls. The line, more than three miles long, curved gently away from the walls with Scott, immaculate in full dress uniform, sitting his horse at the apex. A white flag stood in the center of the ground.

Following the surrender, soldiers ventured inside the city and marveled at the strength of the fortifications they had reduced. Most felt compassion for the "few miserable looking beings extricating themselves, as it were, from the ruins." Pillow's brigade camped outside the walls, comfortably situated on a grassy plain south of Vera Cruz. He made a point of holding parades every morning at 8:00 A.M., but duty was light and pleasant as the army waited for sufficient wagons to arrive by sea so they could begin the advance inland.[25]

The news of the brilliant victory at Vera Cruz quickly reached home. In Nashville, 200 cannon were fired. Fifty miles south in Columbia, "our little six pounder sent forth its thunder, a caution to all anti-war men."[26] They heard the cannon at Clifton. Pillow's daughter Amanda, according to Mary, "was almost run mad with excitement. I think I saw her jump as high as the back of a chair one dozen times at least, and shout hurra for Pa." Amanda had her brother Gid "load your shotgun and fire it, notwithstanding Amanda's great aversion to hearing a gun fire. When she would hear it she would shout and hollow that is the way Pa shot the old mexicans."[27]

Pillow told Mary he expected to complete soldiering in sixty days and leave for home about June 1, the time when the enlistments of his Tennesseans would expire. He loved the idea of being home. He enjoyed and valued his immediate family as well as his extended family, and Clifton needed him. (Indeed, that winter the facilities he had erected for hemp production had burned, along with the hemp itself.) Quite contradictorily, he strongly hoped—and this he did not confide to Mary—to remain with Scott's army in Mexico, but in command of a division, not a brigade.[28] He had prepared Mary for such an eventuality by qualifying his intent to return, using the innocent phrase "unless the army shall have active duties before it which make it my duty to stay. I cannot shrink from duty, or run off while the public service requires me to remain. Such a course would *forfeit* all the character which I have won—which I think is a good deal."[29]

Meanwhile, in December 1846, Secretary of War William Marcy in Washington had recommended raising ten new regiments of regulars. The authorization bill ground slowly through Congress and passed in mid-February. Ten regiments meant two additional major generals, and the scramble was on. Thomas Hart Benton, miffed because he could not replace Scott, declined. So did William Cummings of Georgia and Robert Armstrong.[30]

Pillow knew what was happening, of course, and determined to inject himself. He sent his East Tennessee quartermaster, Reynolds, to Washington to see the president, instructing Reynolds in a most indiscreet letter. First of all, Pillow wrote, Gen. Robert Patterson had notions of becoming one of the major generals of regulars. That would not do:

Patterson is, as you know, not only *without character* as a military man here, but is exceedingly odious not only to his own command, but to almost the whole army.

The President will injure himself very much indeed by giving

Mary Elizabeth Martin Pillow and George M. Pillow
(courtesy James K. Polk Home, Columbia, Tennessee)

him any other place. Of this fact you have personal knowledge & can & ought in justice to the P——t so to say. He can attribute to you no possible motives now, but the right ones.[31]

Pillow continued at length:

I believe moreover that if the P——t were correctly informed, & from a reliable source, of the character of my services and of my standing & character here, that he would confer upon me one or the other of these appointments by way of promotion, and that being done, our party would in *future demand* that I should be retained in the service, as it at present has no officers in the service of rank, but Twiggs, & he is as you know without much character . . . and without any popularity. The party might well *demand* of the Govt. to retain *one* of the *Majr Generals* of the party & might well expect in *that officer* to build up in the army a power to counter-act that . . . which is exclusively whig.

So my Dear Sir, these are reasons and things which I cannot say to any one else but yourself. This position & the prospect of getting it *wins* its way directly to my *heart*, and my object is to lay these views before you, and to urge you, as you *love me* & by the love which I bear you (almost unequalled by that I feel for any other man)—to go first to my home and thence *directly* to *Washington* City & press this matter directly upon the President's attentions. You can tell him a thousand things relative to myself, & men & things here which I could not say; & which it is your duty to your country to do, and I feel sure you can procure for me the appointment.

I know I need not hold forth to you any considerations conducing to your own *future elevation.* You *know* you have already had the most indisputable evidence of my friendship & of my readiness— even in advance of your own wishes & expectations & voluntarily & and [*sic*] unsolicited, to serve you & procure your advancement. This I have done because I love you and the same considerations will prompt me in future to promote your views; but give me that place, and make it permanent—as it most probably will be & my power would be such as to secure your permanent advancement to almost any position you might desire.

I have today written a long letter to the P——t.; but I have not mentioned that subject to him, although it is written with the view to promote that result.

. . . Since the fall of this place the appointment may well be *claimed* as justly due to *my character* & service of 12 months in the actual field in the next rank below it and the *opinion of th*—— *of my Gallantry*, all which you can better explain than any one else. . . . *Time* is *precious*, & *pregnant* with *danger*. I will pay the expense of your trip, but you must go directly there & return by your home.

I pledge myself to *sink* or *to swim* with you if you will go it with me. Report . . . fully & fairly to my friends & kin at Nashville & contradict any lies . . . about me if any such should be in circulation. An article from your pen at Nashville for the Union would do a great deal *of good*.

Farewell,
Gid. J. Pillow [32]

Self-promoting in the extreme, this letter to Reynolds reveals a man with an inflated sense of self who saw himself highly and warmly regarded by those around him—in effect, mirroring his own distorted perceptions. Through a fractured prism he viewed the American army in Mexico as a powerful political entity, dangerous to the interests of the president. Pillow, Polk's loyal fighting lieutenant, intended to do battle for his chief and the Democracy to secure control of that army. His comments to Reynolds that he wished relayed to the president are destructive of the work and reputation of his superior Robert Patterson as well as of David Twiggs, not to speak of the Whig general officers.

Pillow himself paid the expenses of Reynolds's political trip and offered him the debasing bribe—"my power would be such as to secure your permanent advancement to almost any position you might desire." Loosely and cynically employed by Pillow, the terms love, pledge, friendship, and gallantry are turned inside-out. His admission to Reynolds that he has a hidden personal agenda in his communications with his trusting friend Polk is stunning—but consistent ethically with the document's transparent flattery and triumphant self-interest.

With Vera Cruz established as base of operations, Scott rushed to gather sufficient supplies and transportation. His objective was first Jalapa, sixty miles inland, and then Puebla, sixty miles farther. Twiggs advanced on April 9, followed by Patterson's division; Pillow's and Shields's brigades started the following day. With Patterson ill, Pillow held division command once again. He did not expect serious resistance until they reached the City of Mexico, and not much then. Once they had seized the capital, "I shall certainly get leave of absence & return home with the Tennessee troops."[33]

The 1st and 2d Tennessee and the 1st and 2d Pennsylvania marched out escorted by Capt. William R. Caswell's company of cavalry and another company of Kentucky cavalry. Pillow pushed his men hard, just as he had on the march from Tampico. He worried about straggling and enforced march discipline almost with a vengeance. Rumors ran through the column that the rear guard was jabbing laggards with bayonets or dragging them behind wagons. Stories of the general's cruelty and hardheartedness quickly circulated, and gossip spread that volunteers threatened to shoot Pillow at the first opportunity.[34]

On April 11 Twiggs reached the Rio del Plan and encamped. Pillow came up with Patterson's division the following day; they were exhausted. They were also surprised to discover Mexicans prepared to defend Cerro Gordo Pass. Twiggs wished to make a frontal attack immediately, but Pillow, because of the condition of his men, persuaded him to delay until the fourteenth.[35]

Scott arrived at noon on April 14 with Worth's division. The Mexican position appeared formidable. The National Road leading to Jalapa curved across the Rio del Plan, rising sharply through a mile-long ravine or pass commanded on either side by towering hills. The hill to the north, El Telégrafo, rose over 500 feet. In every direction, it seemed, one saw sharp cliffs and broken ground covered with chaparral. The Mexican commander, Gen. Antonio Lopez de Santa Anna, had placed his batteries carefully, completely dominating the National Road. He had every reason to believe the position impregnable. Yet imaginative and thorough reconnaissance work by American engineers, conducted over four days, discovered a feasible approach around the Mexican left flank. Scott decided that Twiggs's division would conduct a difficult and dangerous enveloping maneuver around the enemy left, breaking into the rear of Santa Anna's position, seizing El Telégrafo, and driving forward until they snapped the escape route to Jalapa. He issued his orders on April 17. Twiggs's division, reinforced by Shields's brigade, would move against the enemy left and rear before daylight on April 18. Worth's division would support.[36]

On April 13, 15, and 16 Pillow had accompanied Lt. Zealous B. Tower of the engineers on daily reconnaissances of three promontories on the Mexican right. It had been risky; Pillow reported they were "repeatedly shot at," and once "hotly pursued." Tower recom-

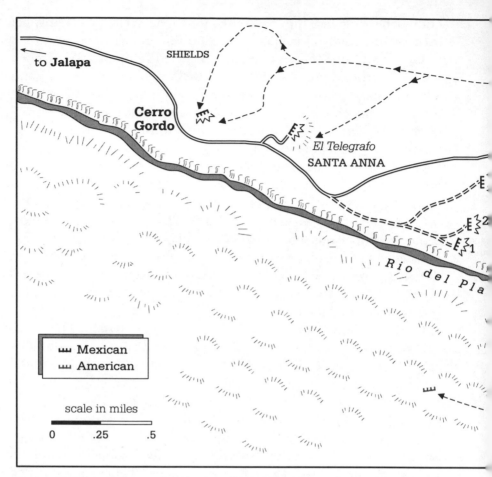

Map 1. Battle of Cerro Gordo, April 17–18, 1847 (adapted from Vincent J. Esposito, *West Point Atlas of American Wars* [New York, 1962], © 1959, 1962 by Frederick A. Praeger, Inc., by permission of Henry Holt and Co., Inc.)

mended to Scott, apparently with Pillow's consent, a sound plan for an approach march and assault on Santa Anna's right. Pillow's brigade would take the National Road for three miles. At the proper point, sheltered from the fire of Mexican batteries near the road, the brigade would exit to the left and continue on a protected line of march. As they approached the river, the column would turn right into a position from which they could storm the fieldworks closest to the river. During the attack, Tower and Pillow believed, the brigade would receive only moderate fire from the center battery, and even less from the one closest to the road.[37]

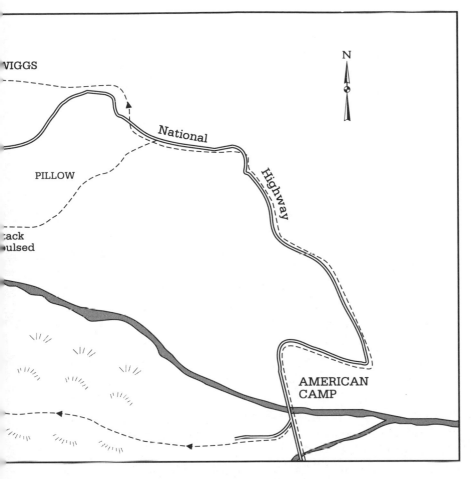

Scott saw merit in this plan. At the least it promised a strong diversion from the main American flanking column. Accordingly, he included it in his general order. He called a council of war on the morning of the seventeenth to explain the plan of attack and to be certain each commander understood his mission.[38] Pillow would conduct the secondary attack, engaging Santa Anna's right—reinforced batteries on three fingers of high ground between the National Road and the river. "Pillow's brigade will march at six o'clock tomorrow morning, along the route he has carefully reconnoitered, and stand ready, as soon as he hears the report of arms on our right, or sooner, if circumstances should favor him, to pierce the enemies line of batteries at such point—the nearer to the river the better—as he may select. Once in the rear of that line, he will turn to the right or left, or both, and attack the batteries in reverse, or, if abandoned, he will pursue the enemy with vigor until further orders."[39]

Pillow's troops arose before daybreak of April 18, had breakfast, and moved out from their camp on the Rio del Plan. Wynkoop's Pennsylvanians led. Tower, together with Lt. George B. McClellan and a small detachment of engineers, guided the brigade up the National Road.[40] When they reached the point where the brigade would turn off to the left, McClellan and his men paused, waiting for Pillow, who rode up at the head of the column. On the spot, Pillow impulsively altered the route selected by Tower and McClellan, ordering the brigade off the National Road into a defile leading southwest. He gave no reason.[41] Tower cautioned Pillow, but the general insisted and the lieutenant fell silent. McClellan felt that Tower, as senior engineer with the column, should "have taken a firm stand and forced . . . Pillow to have pursued the proper path.[42] Pillow, in his official report, said that he and Tower had agreed to change the route and thereby the angle of attack.[43]

Pillow ordered Wynkoop's 1st Pennsylvania to proceed down the narrow trail, turn to the right flank, deploy into tactical formation, and attack No. 1, the Mexican battery nearest the river. Wynkoop would be supported by Campbell's 1st Tennessee. Haskell meanwhile would attack No. 2, supported by Roberts's 2d Pennsylvania. To give greater weight to Haskell's assault, Pillow attached Williams's Kentucky cavalry company and a company of the 2d Pennsylvania. Caswell's Knoxville Dragoons would stand ready in the rear to "dash upon the enemy whenever the storming party should have obtained possession of the breastwork."[44]

Pillow's four regiments left the National Road in "almost single file": Wynkoop, Haskell, Campbell, Roberts. The narrow path over broken ground, guarded by chaparral, caused unevenness, separation of units, and nervousness. With the brigade stretched thin as a rubber band, it would be difficult for Campbell and Roberts to funnel their troops forward and form them to support the assault regiments.[45] Sounds of Twiggs's attack, off to the north, could be heard by Pillow's men and bolstered resolve. After two-thirds of a mile, Wynkoop's advance reached a crest bordering upon a ravine. Ahead, in front of the Mexican batteries, a "strong picket" of the enemy could be seen. Tower advised Pillow to "incline his Brigade well to the right in order to cross the ravine lower down and out of view."[46] Pillow agreed, but this maneuver required a countermarch by Wynkoop's regiment and, of course, took time.

Wynkoop's Pennsylvanians moved off. Now Haskell, who had been following Wynkoop, turned his regiment off the path by the flank and began deploying them for the attack on No. 2. His men had straggled badly, and more time was lost getting the Tennesseans positioned. In fact, Pillow had changed plans, so that Haskell came between Wynkoop and Campbell. This meant that when Haskell left the path, Campbell, who had the responsibility of supporting Wynkoop, suddenly confronted a great gap between his regiment and Wynkoop's assaulting force. Campbell would have to race to catch up, a difficult feat over this narrow, broken path.

Pillow knew the Mexicans had strong positions ahead; how strong, he did not know. Nevertheless, he believed in his heart that nothing could resist the coordinated attack of his volunteers, and he meant to demonstrate that. To Haskell's front, unfortunately, was No. 2, with eight guns and 1,000 troops, behind continuous breastworks of stone. No. 1 waited for Wynkoop with six guns and 500 men.[47]

It was almost 9:00 A.M. Ahead, voices of Mexican officers on No. 2 could be heard distinctly. Haskell had deployed just two companies when Pillow noticed Wynkoop's regiment. He shouted loudly, "Why the Hell don't Colonel Wynkoop file to the right?" This alerted the enemy, according to Lieutenant McClellan, although, so close to fortified enemy positions, anything could have triggered the reaction. A Mexican bugle sounded the alarm, and within minutes, Mexican cannon opened fire.[48]

Pillow ordered Haskell to attack, despite incomplete deployment. What was Haskell to do? Should he "fall back under cover, without executing his orders, or rush forward unsupported and unorganized. He gallantly, but unwisely, chose the latter alternative." The chaparral had been cut down and pitched in front of the breastworks, waist high, "constituting a thorny brush entanglement."[49] Other companies of the 2d Tennessee never formed. They simply abandoned the trail and rushed with a great shout into the chaparral behind their general and colonel.[50] Twenty-eight-year-old William T. Haskell—lawyer, poet, songwriter, Whig, veteran of the Seminole War—wanted revenge. Mexicans had murdered his brother Charles at Goliad.[51] "We charged for about 400 yards, up a considerable ascent, over the roughest rocks I ever saw," wrote Private McAdoo, "and through thick brush and cacti cut and uncut—all the time exposed to cross fires of grape and canister from about 20 pieces of artillery, and to the incessant fire of some thousands of muskets. By the time we had approached to within sixty yards of the front of the work, nearly 100 of the 350 men we started with were killed or wounded."[52]

Less than 100 yards from No. 2, Haskell's men broke into the open, in full view of the totally concealed enemy. Small-arms fire and direct fire from seven cannon wreaked chaos. Some of Haskell's men, however, refused to stop; Lt. Thomas Ewell, a Virginia regular, dashed to the earthworks and was killed as he leaped on top. No. 1 opened up on one flank, and No. 3 on the other. Haskell, shaken and angry, his hat shot from his head by canister, knew he could not take the earthworks; there was no sign of Roberts's 2d Pennsylvania coming to support.[53] He ended the madness by yelling, "Retreat! Retreat!" The 2d Tennessee fell back in confusion; some broke to the rear, some took cover, and some did not stop running until they reached the National Road.[54]

Pillow, after ordering Haskell to charge, had sent his acting aide-de-camp, regular Lt. Samuel Smith Anderson, with orders to Wynkoop to hurry his attack on No. 1; he sent another aide, Lt. George W. Rains, off to hurry Roberts's 2d Pennsylvania.[55] Delayed, apparently, by intense enemy fire, Anderson did not deliver the order.[56] Just before Haskell's repulse, McClellan approached Pillow, who was squatting on the ground with his back to No. 2, some 450 yards off. The lieutenant was asking for orders when a canister shot struck the general above his right elbow, breaking the arm and cutting under the main muscle. Pillow and Lieutenant Rains withdrew to the rear. Recovering from the shock of his wound, Pillow headed off to find Wynkoop himself. Passing Campbell's regiment, however, he became faint. He stopped, and when Campbell came up to him, he told Campbell to take command of the brigade and complete the assault on No. 1.[57]

Campbell pushed on to join Wynkoop. Haskell, with his hair "streaming wildly in the wind," came up to Pillow, and a "very warm conversation" took place. Pillow accused Haskell of misconduct and deserting his men. Haskell angrily denied these charges and reported his regiment "cut to pieces."[58] Pillow ordered Haskell to return to his command, reform them, and prepare for an assault on No 1. Haskell stomped off. Pillow, furious himself, frustrated and suffering from his wound, turned on the Pennsylvanians, accusing them of having "waved." Colonel Roberts, "not the man to contradict him," stood by silently. Pillow then sent McClellan off on a futile jaunt to find Scott and secure regulars to help in the attack on No. 1.[59]

Pillow rode back to Campbell and resumed command. Campbell had the 1st Tennessee moving forward and had ordered the Pennsylvanians to the attack.[60] At this moment a messenger rode up from Scott and informed Pillow that the Mexicans had surrendered, thanks to Twiggs's successful flank attack. At least Pillow's abortive frontal assault had fastened Santa Anna's attention to the right. Once he had repulsed Pillow, Santa Anna hastened back to Cerro Gordo, but it was too late. His troops were broken and he could not restore the situation.[61]

The performance of Pillow and his brigade "mortified" the army and detracted from Scott's otherwise stunning victory.[62] Haskell's 2d Tennessee had been humiliated despite a frontal assault that cost sixteen lives and forty wounded. All the field-grade officers except Haskell went down, including Major Farquharson on loan from the 1st Tennessee, and so did four company commanders. The 2d Tennessee blamed Pillow. Campbell's regiment did little to add to its reputation and suffered casualties itself passing behind Haskell to support the Pennsylvania attack on No. 1, an attack which was never made. Wynkoop and Roberts claimed they never received orders to do anything once Pillow and Haskell decided to charge.

Pillow had failed in his first major combat action. "Craving of distinction," he disregarded the plan and the advice of engineers Tower and McClellan, opting for a shorter but exposed line of approach. He changed the objective of attack from the river battery to the middle battery, which resulted in having to withstand not only frontal fire from one battery, but enfilade fire from two others. Such an impulsive shift of objective also resulted in having to realign units on the trail in the face of enemy fire, thus separating supporting units from those attacking. Pillow did not make use of an eight-inch howitzer which was positioned on a ridge south of the Rio del Plan to provide fire support for the brigade. He failed to do so because he had neglected to arrange a code of signals for its use. During the action, the piece fired only seven times, most ineffectually.[63]

The reconnaissances Pillow made, or is supposed to have made, evidently were of no value. However much he emphasized the strength of the Mexican position in his battle reports, he seems to have underrated them before the attack. He appears to have been surprised and off-balance at every turn. Incredible lack of coordination and poor timing may have resulted from faulty staff work, but even excellent staff performance could hardly have undone the damage wrought by amateurish command decisions. The most that can be said is that Pillow demonstrated aggressiveness.

Scott was generous, however. In his official report he praised Pillow for his "daring" assaults and concluded by saying, quite rightly, that the attacks had "contributed much to distract and dismay" the enemy.[64] Ulysses S. Grant, never a Pillow admirer, declared Pillow had "contributed to the victory" with his "formidable demonstration."[65] Campbell's evaluation of Pillow shortly after the battle was blunt: "He is no Genl. and on the field of action, has no decision or judgment."[66] W. H. T. Walker was inclined to be charitable: "I am sorry for Pillow. He is a gallant, grand fellow but no soldier. When he saw his command deserting him he wished for regulars to lead."[67] McClellan disagreed, speaking of Pillow's failed assault—euphemistically being called a "diversion" by Scott—as "folly, his worse than puerile imbecility."[68] D. H. Hill was objective: Pillow at Cerro Gordo "got badly whipped."[69]

Scott pursued the shattered Mexican army and occupied Jalapa on April 19; then things grew quiet. Fortunately, the Mexicans demonstrated little enthusiasm for renewing hostilities. Enlistments of the volunteers were up, and they prepared to go home. Pillow applied for sick leave, which was granted. He had been in bed ten days and was "wholly unable" to use his right arm; he also was "very sick" with recurring chills and fever he attributed to exposure during the siege of Vera Cruz. He left for home on May 4, leaving Campbell in command of the brigade.[70]

Campbell was happy to see him go: "[Scott] is mightily taken with Genl Pillow who is a light vain man & can flatter Scott to his hearts content, but is very deceitful and cares nothing for Scott only so far as he can use him—being a hand plant of Mr Polk and ready to do at any time any dirty work for him. Pillow has tried hard to demean himself properly towards me and as to personal treatment I could not complain, yet he is no part of a Genl or military man & as light as a feather & is always making himself ridiculous by his foolishness."[71] The disgusted Campbell would march the "Old Volunteers" back to Vera Cruz and then sail with them for New Orleans.[72]

Navy Lt. Raphael Semmes met Pillow as he returned to Vera Cruz with a small escort: "He was just from the army, and gave us many items of intelligence. . . . He had been wounded slightly at the battle of Cerro Gordo, and was returning home on temporary leave. I had the pleasure of being the first to inform him of his having been promoted to the rank of Major-General. I was struck with the youthful appearance of this gentleman, he not being over thirty-five. He was of the middle size, with a light and agile figure, handsome countenance, with expressive black eyes, and conversed with ease and fluency."[73] Pillow made his way to Point Isabel and there secured passage on the old sidewheeler *James L. Day* for New Orleans. As was his habit, Pillow engaged in conversation with a wounded lieutenant, Samuel G. French, who was also on board, captivating the young man.[74]

Pillow reached Columbia on the evening of May 19, via New Orleans, Memphis, and Nashville. A large number of admirers and friends had escorted him home from Nashville, including his mother, Annie Payne Pillow, whom he adored, and his brother-in-law Gov. Aaron V. Brown. In Columbia crowds turned out to greet him. He addressed his neighbors, telling them "of the perils and pains through which he passed in (the) enemy's country." He consulted with Jerome and Granville about farming matters at Clifton and examined the hemp works which had burned during his absence. He paid careful attention to the progress of construction on the three-story kitchen and servants' quarters connected to Clifton. Pillow remained home a fortnight, leaving Clifton to return to Mexico on May 28.[75]

The 2d Tennessee was mustered out in New Orleans on May 25. Colonel Haskell, 11 officers, and 170 "sick and wounded" went immediately to Memphis. Haskell made a speech at their welcoming reception at the Gayoso Hotel and displayed trophies of the war, including "a brass six pounder which had been captured at Cerro Gordo."[76] The veterans quickly sought to settle old scores. Haskell and seventeen of his officers charged Pillow with incompetence and cowardice at Cerro Gordo in a lengthy attack appearing in the New Orleans *Daily Picayune*. The Whig press joined in, republishing the charges. The Memphis *Daily Eagle* blamed Pillow for the "terrible carnage among the Tennessee troops."

Pillow countered these charges with biting attacks on Haskell. Granville and Jerome placed notices in newspapers seeking statements concerning Haskell's conduct and appearance in that action. Replies came in quickly from members of Campbell's 1st Tennessee, just home upon completion of their enlistments. Their comments, screened by the Pillow brothers, were generally critical of Haskell. Socrates Martin wrote that Haskell "was precipitately retreating bareheaded . . . and in my opinion . . . very much confused. His appearance was the subject of laughter and mirth." J. B. Cook and B. F. Luna commented on the confrontation between Pillow and Haskell after the repulse of the 2d Tennessee. They pictured Haskell as "apparently greatly excited . . . gesticulating most vehemently, and occasionally running his hand through his hair." Their opinion of Pillow was that he had been cool and collected, and that he encouraged their regiment as it passed him with "go ahead my brave boys and give them your bayonets." Pillow himself blasted Haskell in a "Statement to the Public" published in the friendly New Orleans *Daily Picayune*.[77]

Haskell's criticisms of Pillow soon reached Polk. Pillow defended himself to the president by writing: "Haskell's assault upon me was wholly unprovoked, and though it made statements which unexplained would have been prejudicial to my reputation, yet I have so completely turned the tables upon him as to have floored him. His own friends admit that he is so badly used up that his military reputation, if any he had, is completely gone."[78] Pillow miscalculated. Haskell and the Whigs carried the 1847 elections handily. Veteran Democrat John P. Heise, in a letter to Thomas Ritchie, laid the disastrous Democratic defeat squarely on the doorstep of Gideon Pillow.[79] When Pillow left Columbia to return to Mexico, it was his own military reputation, more than Haskell's, that hung in the balance. Partisan swords, he found, are always double-edged.

At New Orleans, where Pillow busied himself forwarding troops to Vera Cruz, several letters caught up with him. The first, from Polk, contained official notice of his promotion to major general in the regular army. Pillow would rank second to Scott himself. "In conferring on you this high command I have taken it for granted that it was your desire—to continue in the service during the war." Polk would receive another round of criticism for his promotion of Pillow to major general. Among those unhappy this time was Joseph Davis, who complained directly to his younger brother, Col. Jefferson Davis.[80]

Pillow also received a letter in New Orleans from Knox Walker, Polk's private secretary and nephew and Pillow's former law partner. It contained the latest news on the mission of Nicholas P. Trist. A Democrat and chief clerk at the State Department, Trist was in charge of its affairs when Secretary of State Buchanan was away. He had attended West Point but dropped out to read law with Thomas Jefferson. He had even served as Andrew Jackson's secretary for a while, an unimpeachable qualification for Pillow. Buchanan had recommended Trist to "set out on a mission to the headquarters of the (Scott's) Army . . . with full powers to treat with the authorities of Mexico for Peace." Polk seemed impressed with Trist. He "is a gentleman of high character and possesses my closest confidence. . . . I have said to him that you were my personal friend and that he could confer freely and confidentially with you." But Pillow saw the arrangement somewhat differently: "Mr. Trist was the *ostensible* commissioner, I was, in fact, the confidential officer of the Government, upon whom the President relied to guard and protect the honor of the country."[81] Knox Walker also informed Pillow of trouble between Trist and Scott. Pillow, however, had already learned the details from his friend, Paymaster Archibald W. Burns, who had just arrived in New Orleans from Jalapa. Pillow promised to work closely with Trist "to accomplish your [Polk's] wishes."[82]

Scott was angry; he resented being bypassed by the administration. Indeed, he had been ordered by Marcy "to yield to Trist the right to decide upon the suspension of military operations. . . . It is doubtful if a more astounding order was ever sent to a commanding officer in the field."[83] Unknown to Pillow, however, Scott and Trist reconciled their differences at Puebla during June 1847 and came to trust each other. Polk, meanwhile, had become impatient and convinced himself that a "golden opportunity to conclude peace" had been missed following the victory at Cerro Gordo. He considered recalling both Trist and Scott and found himself inclined to depend more and more on Pillow.[84]

Scott did not need more problems. His army was melting away—from sickness, volunteers going home, and troops being shipped north to help Taylor. He needed troops to garrison the towns in his rear and protect his communications, as well as sufficient manpower to break into the Valley of Mexico. Fortunately, reinforcements were on their way.

5   Hero of Chapultepec

When Pillow arrived at Vera Cruz from New Orleans, he began pushing reinforcements inland toward Puebla. First went Col. James S. McIntosh on June 4 with 600 men and Scott's treasury—$350,000. Guerrillas heard of the silver and began to swarm. The debonair Pennsylvanian, Brig. Gen. George Cadwalader, rushed out from Vera Cruz to McIntosh's aid. They joined forces on June 8 and moved on together toward Jalapa, which they reached on the sixteenth, beating off repeated guerrilla attacks.[1]

Pillow himself followed on June 18 with 2,000 men. He struggled to keep the column closed up, but his wagon train, hindered by hundreds of "unbroke & broke down animals," slowed to a crawl. Guerrillas boldly approached the column, capturing many of his mules. Without cavalry, Pillow felt vulnerable: "I have quite my hands full." Worried about straggling, he enforced march discipline; the recruits suffered intensely. They were loaded down: "Four days' provisions in their haversacks, besides knapsacks, their clothing, and forty rounds of ammunition, and this under a hot tropical sun, and over a road deep with burning sand." Eight men died from sunstroke; 150 fell out. A reporter quipped, "The poor soldiers had less chance than even Haskell's command at Cerro Gordo enjoyed." [2]

Pillow entered Jalapa June 28 but found Cadwalader gone. This seems to have surprised him. Scott, anxious for troops and money, had ordered Cadwalader to abandon Jalapa and hurry on. An annoyed Pillow wrote Polk on June 28 expressing displeasure at Scott's action. Jalapa, said Pillow, anchored the army's line of communications. He recommended Polk send more reinforcements quickly if Jalapa were to be held and communications secured. He also sent word forward for Cadwalader at Perote to halt and wait for him. [3]

Pillow reached Perote on July 1, added Cadwalader to his column, and moved on toward Puebla. [4] A soldier in the 2d Pennsylvania observed the "rich and fertile country," with fields of corn "which must contain at least 1000 acres." [5] Pillow kept his guard up in this magnificent setting, throwing out a "strong advance" which dispersed small groups of the enemy from natural defensive positions; flanking parties labored alongside the main column for additional security.

On July 8 Major General Pillow rode into Puebla; behind him trailed 4,000 troops, a train of 500 wagons, and a line of pack mules extending for miles. The column marched in at 1:00 P.M., and Pillow had them parade up and down the wide streets. Puebla, "City of the Angels," was truly beautiful. The "great curiosity" was the cathedral, with spires, "full of bells," rising over 200 feet; "the gilding, carving and ornamental work inside is truly magnificent." General Scott welcomed his new men, galloping along the column, "followed by ringing cheers." Pillow had each regimental band play "Hail to the Chief" as he passed; Scott was delighted. [6]

Pillow quickly established contact with Nicholas Trist, put him up in his quarters, and invited him to join his mess. Trist informed Pillow of a move under way to bribe Santa Anna. Trist confided that he, of course, had been repulsed by the thought initially but, after discussion with the helpful secretary of the British legation, Edward Thornton, had reconciled himself to the concept. He noted that the Polk administration knew nothing of this, but that he considered this course the only alternative to a bloody campaign against the City of Mexico.[7]

On July 15 Trist informed Scott of the scheme, and Scott told Trist that secret service funds might be used. Acutely aware of the controversial and serious nature of such action, Scott withheld final approval until he could seek the counsel of his generals. He called them together on the evening of July 17: Quitman, Pillow, Shields, Cadwalader, and Twiggs. Quitman sensed that Pillow had been informed previously, indeed, had been involved in the development of the scheme. It is likely that Scott, like Trist, had discussed the bribery scheme with Pillow. Scott needed Pillow's support. Without it, and certainly without the approval of the largely Democratic council of generals, he would have had to abandon the plan. With Pillow's backing, Scott planned to defuse criticism by the administration— the wrath of Polk that one might anticipate for engaging in such a questionable, though not unique, American diplomatic practice.[8]

Scott's idea worked to perfection. Pillow not only approved, he spoke first, "very fully and eloquently," when Scott broached the idea to his generals. Pillow stipulated, however, "as a condition, that the United States should have such a treaty as was desired." Quitman dissented; Cadwalader and Shields expressed doubts. Twiggs declared it to be a political question and would not give an opinion. Scott decided to go ahead, nevertheless, and sent the Mexicans $10,000, with $1 million to come when the treaty of peace was concluded.[9]

Bribery talk was put aside in July, however. It seemed rather irrelevant once Scott learned that the Mexican Congress refused to rescind its decree of April 20 prohibiting any negotiations for peace. So Scott set about organizing his army: a cavalry brigade under Col. William Harney and four infantry divisions under Worth, Twiggs, Pillow, and Quitman. Pillow's 3d Division, about 2,500 troops, had two brigades; the first, under newly arrived Brig. Gen. Franklin Pierce, included the 9th, 12th, and 15th Infantry regiments, with Capt. John B. Magruder's light battery. The second brigade, commanded by Brig. Gen. George Cadwalader, the fashionable Philadelphia Democrat, contained the 11th and 14th Infantry and a regiment of Voltigeurs (once light infantry used for skirmishing, but now simply riflemen). Although Pillow's troops were designated as regulars, they were raw recruits for the most part, commanded by the "utterly ignorant," according to regular Lt. D. H. Hill. "Mr. Polk seems studiously to have selected the most worthless and inefficient men that he could find." [10]

Scott advanced his army from Puebla on August 7, led by the large, hard-looking, hard-swearing regular Davy Twiggs. Pillow's division left last on August 10. Their route into the Valley of Mexico wound around Lake Chalco, a body of water which gave a "singular maritime appearance in that elevated mountain region." Pillow's column moved cautiously. Mexicans killed one of his soldiers who wandered off foraging, and Pillow issued "severe orders" to prevent straggling. Capt. Joseph Hooker, Pillow's chief of staff, rode ahead and reported to Scott at Ayotla that Pillow was meeting with no resistance and that he would stop at the village of Chalco on the thirteenth.[11]

Santa Anna expected Scott to come along the National Highway and thus positioned his National Guard troops to block them at the hill of El Peñón, ten miles from the City of Mexico. The reconnaissances of Captain Lee and Lt. Col. James Duncan on August 12 and 13 convinced Scott that the Mexican defenses at El Peñón and the village of Mexicalzingo were too strong. So he reversed the army's marching order, leaving Twiggs's division at Ayotla to hold the attention of the enemy by threatening an attack on El Peñón, while he took the other three divisions around Lake Chalco and Lake Xochimilco to approach Mexico City from the south. Worth and Scott disagreed about the route around Lake Chalco. Pillow, according to Worth, supported his arguments privately and appears to have encouraged him to disagree with the commander in chief.[12]

They marched on August 15, with Worth in the lead, covered by Harney's cavalry. Behind Worth came Pillow and Quitman. They advanced with great care, feeling for the enemy, expecting a fight. The road was narrow, "very bad."[13] On the eighteenth, the column experienced a "piercing cold rain." The road became "truly horrible. If a man made the least false step he was sure to be plunged over his hips in mud."[14] That day Pillow reached the village of San Augustín. Worth, two miles up ahead, approached the hacienda of San Antonio but found it heavily defended. The main road north to the City of Mexico, however, ran through San Antonio on to Churubusco, three miles farther north. Once again it seemed Santa Anna had placed his army directly across Scott's path.

Reconnaissance by "the daring engineers" determined that Santa Anna's defenses at San Antonio could not be flanked from the east because of marshy ground, easily swept by enemy cannon. The alternative was a footpath leading west across the southern edge of the Pedregal (a three-by-five-mile lava bed west of San Antonio). Scott sent Lee to determine if infantry and particularly artillery could use the path. Would it be possible to cross the southern edge of the Pedregal and reach the San Angel wagon road? It ran north to Coyoacán, where it divided. One road led south into the rear of San Antonio; the other led north, intersecting the main road through Churubusco to the City of Mexico.[15]

Lee found the trail suitable for infantry, but in need of improvement for the passage of field guns. He had observed the terrain along the San Angel road from Zacatepec, a prominent hill dominating the southern portion of the Pedregal. Due west of Zacatepec stood the village of Padierna, commonly mistaken by Americans as Contreras, which actually lay farther south. Lee also observed a large force of Mexicans busily entrenching on a small hill just west of Padierna.[16] These were the troops of Gen. Gabriel Valencia, 5,500 men and twenty-two guns.

In a council of war on the night of the eighteenth, Scott listened to the reports of the engineers and the advice of his generals. The following morning he decided the army would advance west to the San Angel road, using the path Lee had reconnoitered across the volcanic field. If everything worked out, this route would bypass Santa Anna's defenses at San Antonio and promised the opportunity for attacking San Antonio and Churubusco in reverse.

The next morning, August 19, while American artillery blasted away at San Antonio, holding Santa Anna's attention, Pillow moved west with his division. Scott had assigned him the task of transforming Lee's footpath into a road suitable for field pieces; Twiggs's division would offer security for Pillow's working parties. Scott expected little Mexican resistance. Worth's division, meanwhile, would be coming up behind Pillow and Twiggs, while Quitman remained in San Augustín guarding the trains and attempting to deceive Santa Anna.[17]

Pillow rode with the construction detail two miles out from San Augustín. So far, little had to be done to the road. Twiggs was nowhere in sight, but Pillow pressed on. As they neared the hill Zacatepec, the trail narrowed; Captain Lee put his engineers and 500 of Pillow's soldiers to work, tearing at the sharp, tangled rock. The work progressed, but Pillow kept receiving word of the enemy ahead, waiting in strength and positioning artillery. Then a staff officer arrived from Scott, who, from the roof of his quarters at San Augustín, could observe Valencia's forces fortifying Padierna. He cautioned Pillow. Pillow sent Hooker back to tell Scott his wish was "to push on with the infantry and dislodge the enemy before his heavy guns were in position." He wanted Scott's approval.[18]

Meanwhile, Twiggs, who was supposed to be screening Pillow's road construction, was only now arriving in San Augustín from the east. Scott hurried Twiggs forward and sent a reply to Pillow by Hooker. Pillow was to finish the road as far as possible without bringing on a fight. Twiggs would join him and take the advance as in the original order. Twiggs was to "brush away the enemy in case he became impertinent." If enemy resistance became serious, Pillow was to "support Twiggs with his whole division and assume the command."[19]

When Twiggs had reported to Scott, the general-in-chief had told him Pillow would command the column. This was difficult for Twiggs to accept. He was fifteen years Pillow's senior and a veteran officer, distinguished by gallant service in the War of 1812 and at Monterrey. A disciplinarian "who could outswear any one," he was a good soldier, "rough of manner and speech," but reliable. To many he personified the frontier regular army. Twiggs "expressed some dissatisfaction" about the arrangement, but Scott would not listen, pointing out that Pillow was senior major general and "the law must be obeyed." Twiggs rejoined his troops and led them into the Pedregal.[20]

Scott's order reached Pillow before Twiggs came up. To protect the work details, Pillow already had advanced some of his troops, and he climbed Zacatepec to observe. As he watched from that point, the road was completed to the base of the hill. Twiggs arrived and moved his division to the front. Suddenly, around 1:00 P.M., the Mexicans opened fire with heavy cannon at a range of about a mile.[21]

Pillow decided to fight. From Zacatepec he sent orders down to Twiggs to deploy Brig. Gen. Persifor F. Smith's brigade[22] down the trail to his front and send his other brigade, that of Brig. Gen. Bennet Riley, around the Mexican left to hit them in flank and rear "and check any reinforcements of the enemy that might be thrown out from the city." He also called up both his batteries, Magruder's light battery and Lt. Franklin D. Callendar's mountain howitzers, plus a section of rockets, and placed them at Twiggs's disposal. This pleased Twiggs.[23]

Twiggs, in executing Pillow's order, directed Smith's brigade to move directly against Valencia's fortifications. Magruder's light guns were "picking their way close in the rear of the infantry."[24] The Mexicans gave ground initially. Twiggs seized Padierna and pushed west toward the main enemy fortifications. A deep ravine, covered by Mexican fire, halted his advance, however.[25]

Magruder found a position 1,000 yards away from the enemy earthworks and opened fire in support of Smith's probing action. Valencia's massed heavy guns located Magruder quickly and began to pound

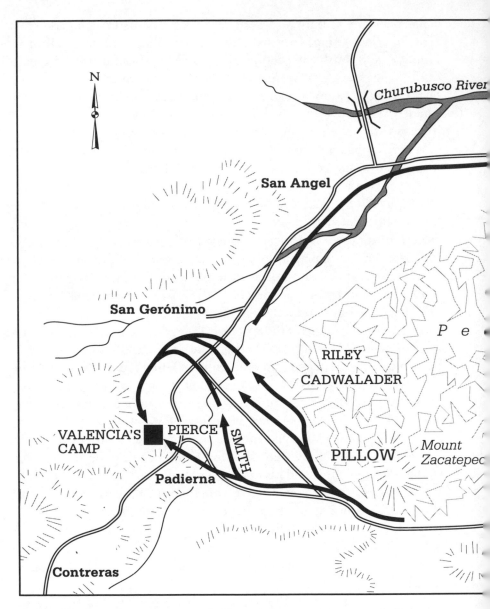

Map 2. Battles of Contreras and Churubusco, August 20, 1847 (adapted from a map by Arnold Holeywell in John S. D. Eisenhower, *So Far from God: The U.S. War with Mexico* [New York, 1989] by permission of John S. D. Eisenhower and Random House, Inc.)

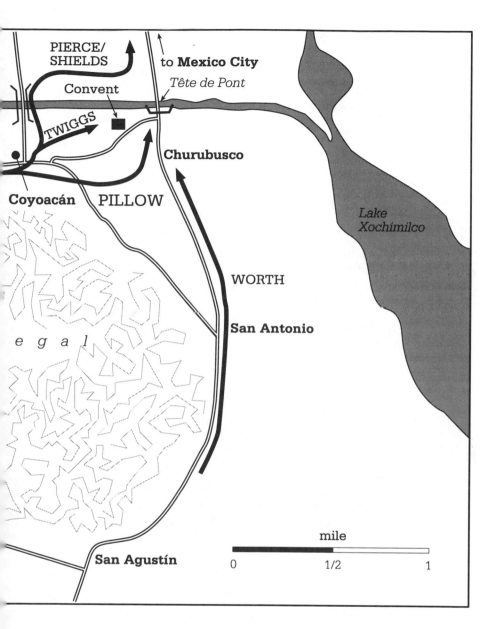

PIERCE/
SHIELDS

to **Mexico City**

Tête de Pont

Convent

TWIGGS

Churubusco

Coyoacán   PILLOW

*Lake
Xochimilco*

WORTH

San Antonio

e g a l

mile

San Agustín   0   1/2   1

his position. Magruder held on stubbornly. Pillow had given him discretionary orders to withdraw out of range when necessary, but he decided to remain despite heavy losses and the deadly fire from the enemy.[26]

From Zacatepec Pillow could observe enemy forces gathering at San Angel. They looked as though they would continue south to reinforce Valencia and smash into Riley's enveloping force. At this point

Pillow committed his own division, dividing it. He sent Cadwalader's brigade to follow Riley; Pierce would support Persifor Smith.[27]

The Americans retained momentum. Smith, halted by the ravine and Valencia's cannon, realized the futility of continuing the attack along that line and asked Pillow's permission to try a flanking movement to the right. He left some infantry behind to support Magruder and asked the battery commander to do his best to divert Valencia's attention.

Magruder resumed firing. Lt. Thomas J. Jackson now commanded one section of guns. The match was frightfully uneven—Magruder's cannoneers at one point even tried "falling flat at each Mexican discharge." Magruder remained in action until after nightfall, when, "with the greatest difficulty," he pulled his guns back close to Zacatepec. Lt. D. H. Hill reported: "Certainly, of all the absurd things that the ass Pillow has ever done this was the most silly. Human stupidity can go no farther than this, the ordering of six and twelve pounders to batter a fort furnished with long sixteen, twenty-fours and heavy mortars!! Sage general, the Army appreciates you if the Country does not."[28]

Persifor Smith's infantry struggled north through the Pedregal, groping for a way to strike the enemy left flank. As he neared the western edge, Smith saw enemy soldiers marching south to Valencia's support. He swung his brigade forward across the San Angel road to block them. Pillow, who could see everything from Zacatepec, became alarmed for Smith. He instructed Riley's column to go to his aid.[29]

Riley had his hands full, however. He had emerged from the Pedregal, crossed the San Angel road, and pushed on beyond San Gerónimo. There he received attack from a heavy column of Mexican lancers, three regiments of them, but he drove them off handily. These lancers were the leading edge of 7,000 troops Santa Anna was pushing south from Coyoacán to San Angel. Had Santa Anna struck with greater force or had he and Valencia coordinated an attack against Riley's column, the result probably would have been disastrous for Pillow's flanking movement. But Santa Anna grew cautious at the moment when the Americans were in jeopardy.[30]

Riley fell back to San Gerónimo and found Cadwalader, who had been following him, under attack himself by Mexican skirmishers from Santa Anna's leading units at San Angel. They decided to make a stand together at San Gerónimo and, as night began to fall, welcomed the sight of Persifor Smith's brigade coming to join them from

Brig. Gen. George Cadwalader
(courtesy Free Library of Philadelphia)

the San Angel road. Smith took command of the combined force and set to work to establish a defensive position.

The perilous adventures of Riley, Smith, and Cadwalader had been aided greatly, of course, by another attack against Valencia from the east. Pillow, responding to a request from Smith, had sent Pierce's brigade to the Padierna ravine to command Valencia's attention and to pin down his infantry. There Pierce's men fought a bitter, inconclusive action, and Pierce himself was badly injured.[31]

Pillow took another measure to strengthen his endangered flanking force. He committed his reserve, sending Hooker to rush Col. G. W. Morgan's 15th Infantry to support Riley and Cadwalader. About 3:00 P.M., as Morgan started out, Scott arrived at Zacatepec. He approved what Pillow had done and ordered up more help—Shields's brigade from San Augustín. When Shields came up, Pillow immediately sent him to stiffen the force at San Gerónimo. As Pillow and Scott observed the action, the volume of Valencia's fire increased. Even the American command post was struck, and Scott received a slight wound.[32]

But Santa Anna hesitated. He did not advance south in force from San Angel, crush Persifor Smith's blocking force at San Gerónimo, and unite with Valencia. Then darkness and a terrible rainstorm ended hostilities for the day.[33] Both Scott and Santa Anna had reason to feel anxious that night. Santa Anna, cautious when he should have been aggressive, ordered Valencia to abandon his position at Padierna and retire to San Angel. But the insubordinate Valencia replied that he would stay where he was.[34]

At San Gerónimo, Smith concluded on the basis of a reconnaissance by Lieutenant Tower that a ravine could be followed to reach the rear of Valencia's position. Using superb initiative, Smith decided to attack. Cadwalader and Riley agreed. Captain Lee volunteered to recross the Pedregal, find Scott, and explain Smith's plan. Smith asked Lee to request a diversionary attack; he would attack at daylight if Lee did not return.[35]

Persifor Smith did not realize how close he came to being replaced in command. While watching developments from Zacatepec, Scott felt Pillow should go to San Gerónimo and take charge. It would be fair; Pillow had been directing the fighting at Contreras all day and deserved the opportunity to complete his initial plan of flanking Valencia. With the light gone and "rain pouring in torrents," the commanding general left Zacatepec and returned to San Augustín. Pillow and Twiggs set out across the Pedregal for San Gerónimo but quickly became disoriented in the jumble of sharp lava. It was a terrible night, cold and dark, raining continually. Twiggs fell heavily among the rocks and injured his foot. Finally, about 9:00 P.M., the two generals emerged from the Pedregal, but not at San Gerónimo. They were back at San Augustín![36]

Meanwhile, Lee had reached San Augustín and reported.[37] Scott agreed with Persifor Smith's proposed assault. He alerted Worth's division in San Augustín and ordered the newly arrived Twiggs to collect troops for a "powerful diversion" to be launched along the Padierna ravine at 5:00 A.M. on the twentieth. Scott decided against another attempt by Pillow to reach San Gerónimo and told him to stay put at headquarters until morning.[38]

At 3:00 A.M., August 20, Persifor Smith began to move three brigades from his blocking position at San Gerónimo against Valencia's rear at Padierna. Smith left Shields behind to maintain numerous fires around San Gerónimo, hoping this would deceive Valencia and add to his chance of surprise. Shields's defensive position at San Gerónimo could also protect against an enemy advance from San Angel and trap Valencia's force if Smith's attack were successful.

Smith's flank attack succeeded brilliantly. Simultaneously, Twiggs assaulted from the front, and it was over in seventeen minutes. Valencia was struck from virtually every direction, "shot down in front and rear." Most Mexicans surrendered. Many hid in gullies and ravines; many more fled toward San Angel and found themselves intercepted by Shields; others tried to reach the Pedregal. Valencia escaped, but four of his generals were captured, along with over 800 prisoners and twenty-two pieces of artillery. Seven hundred Mexicans, killed or wounded, lay about the works and along the San Angel road. American casualties in the final attack were sixty killed and wounded.[39]

Euphoria seized the rain-soaked Americans as they realized they had wrested a complete victory on this forbidding terrain. Pillow heard their shouts as he was recrossing the Pedregal about dawn. He caught up with Twiggs and Smith north of Padierna and joined them in pursuing Valencia's fleeing troops. He sent a message back to Scott that the pursuit must be pressed, through San Angel to the rear of the Mexican force defending San Antonio.[40]

The American pursuit continued to San Angel, where Pillow caught up with his men and resumed command of the division. On the road past San Angel, Pillow saw Colonel Riley. In the presence of Scott, Pillow rode forward and shouted to Riley, "You have earned the Yellow sash, Sir, and *you shall have it.*" The yellow sash marked the general officer, and, as Nicholas Trist noted, it seemed now that Pillow had become the "dispenser in Mexico, of those rewards and honours."[41]

Valencia was finished, but not Santa Anna. Furious and full of fight, he gathered the survivors of Contreras and led them back past San Angel through Coyoacán to Churubusco. There he took up a defensive position and hurriedly concentrated his forces, ordering the withdrawal of those he had stationed at San Antonio and Mexicalzingo.

Meanwhile, Pillow had taken command of the American troops (his own along with Twiggs's divisions and Shields's brigade) and was advancing north with caution from San Angel to Coyoacán. Once they arrived in Coyoacán, Scott came up. He observed great activity in Churubusco; it appeared Santa Anna's army was disintegrating. Retreating forces from San Angel and San Antonio seemed to be mixed together in confusion as they rushed into the little town. Obviously they were frantic to escape across the Churubusco River and retire within the walls of Mexico City. A quick, hard blow at Churubusco would destroy Santa Anna's army; it should be easy.

The key bridge across the Churubusco River was just north of the town. Santa Anna, however, had protected the bridge with two positions, the fortified bridgehead itself (tête de pont) and the convent of San Mateo, several hundred yards away within easy supporting distance. Scott, unaware of the strength of the bridge defenses, decided upon immediate attack. He would throw every unit he had into one great effort; he would keep no reserve. Furthermore, in his rush to attack, he would forgo his practice of careful reconnaissance. He sent Shields, supported by Pierce's brigade, north across the Churubusco River to cut the road leading back to the City of Mexico.[42] While Shields snapped the route of retreat, Twiggs would storm the convent.

Scott dispatched Pillow with Cadwalader's brigade from Coyoacán across open country to sever the San Antonio–Churubusco road, hoping either to strike San Antonio in the rear or to trap some of its garrison as they retreated north. Worth, in the meantime, had already moved against San Antonio and through it, sending the enemy reeling back in disorder toward Churubusco. Pillow was to cooperate with Worth, advancing north from San Antonio. Together the two divisions would move up the San Antonio road and attack Churubusco from the south, drive through the town, and assault the tête de pont.[43]

Pillow's troops had difficulty reaching the San Antonio–Churubusco road. They found themselves slowed by marshy ground that was slashed by deep ditches filled with mud and water. When they finally reached the road, they saw the welcome sight of Worth marching north with the advance of his division.[44] Pillow and Worth, in accordance with Scott's orders, joined forces for the attack on the tête de pont. Their objective was a "powerful, scientifically constructed work with four feet of water in the ditch and three heavy cannon." Members of the infamous San Patricio battalion served these thirty-two pounders.[45]

When they reached the outskirts of Churubusco, Pillow and Worth deployed. Col. John Garland's brigade with Lt. Col. C. F. Smith's light infantry battalion formed on the right of the Pillow-Worth line. They would engage the left face of the bridgehead. In the center, just to the right of the San Antonio road, was Col. Newman S. Clarke's brigade. Across the road, forming the left of the American attacking force, was Cadwalader's brigade, the 11th and 14th Infantries on line, the Voltigeurs in reserve. Cadwalader's left flank rested close to the convent, but the Mexicans in that building were so occupied with Twiggs's attack, fortunately, that they did not open an enfilade fire. Pillow would direct Cadwalader's deployment through his chief of staff, Hooker. The combined attack by Pillow and Worth would be supported by Lt. Col. James Duncan's battery.[46]

The Mexicans at the tête de pont opened a heavy and effective fire when the Americans approached within range. Worth responded, ordering his best regiment, the 6th Infantry, to assault the bridgehead frontally. Intense cannon and musket fire broke up the charge, however, creating "dreadful havoc." The 6th fell back in some disorder. Again they charged, but with the same result. The engagement became general. Garland's attacks tended to stall, while Cadwalader's attacks in column on the left became disorganized and disoriented as dense cornfields, crisscrossed with troublesome ditches, broke up formations.[47] The enemy cannon fire was most effective. Pillow was horrified at the slaughter: "In the very column with which I was moving the men were mowed down with cannon shot at a terrible rate—scattering their limbs & heads in every direction."[48] Pillow and Cadwalader had no artillery support. Marshy ground on either side of the road prevented Duncan's battery from replying to the Mexican guns; to emplace the battery on the road itself would have been suicide. Worth and Pillow kept up the pressure despite heavy loss. A shell exploded near Pillow, and the concussion threw him to the ground.

Help came presently as Shields's envelopment north of the river began to take effect. Reinforcements were required to meet Shields's threat, so Santa Anna withdrew units from the bridgehead, thus shortening and weakening that line. This enabled the flank of the tête de pont to be turned. Elements of Worth's division worked their way to the right, crossed the Churubusco River under fire, and turned the Mexican left. Meanwhile, Cadwalader and the remainder of Worth's command edged closer and closer to the bridgehead in the center and on the left.[49]

Clarke's 8th Infantry reached the edge of the twenty-foot ditch. Supported by the 5th and Cadwalader's two regiments, they waded across under fire, rushed the parapet, and crashed over. The hand-to-hand fight was fierce, but short. The tête de pont fell with 192 prisoners, three cannon, and two colors; the remainder of the defenders fled across the bridge. Conspicuous during the fighting was a major in the 9th Infantry from Connecticut, Thomas H. Seymour. A portion of the San Patricio battalion with its colors was captured by Tennessean Col. William Trousdale and his 14th regiment.[50]

During the initial phase of the assault at Churubusco, as Worth and Pillow closed in, Pillow himself supposedly engaged in close combat with a Mexican officer and killed him. The episode, highly publicized later in newspapers by "Leonidas," began when one of Pillow's staff saw a Mexican officer leave the lines of the tête de pont and advance in the open toward the Americans. When told of this "impudent rashness," Pillow "put spurs to his charger and galloped at full speed toward him." The Mexican called out in Spanish,

"Let the honor and prowess of our respective countries be determined by the issue of this combat." Straightway the Mexican drew his sword with one hand and balanced his lance with the other, and rushed towards our general, who, with a revolver in one hand and his sabre in the other, waited the onset of the Mexican. The combat was a long and severe one. The Mexican was a large, muscular man, and handled his arms with great vigor and skill, but our general was his superior in dexterity and coolness. At last the Mexican made one terrible charge at our general with his lance, which the latter evaded with great promptitude and avidity, using his sword, tossed the weapon of the Mexican high into the air, and then quietly blew his brains out with his revolver. Both the American and Mexican armies witnessed this splendid effort.[51]

Pillow had dispatched the Mexican; his troops had helped capture the tête de pont. The bridge across the Churubusco belonged to the Americans, and the cannon had been captured. This enabled Duncan to place his guns on the San Antonio road in direct, decisive support of Twiggs's bloody attack against the convent, now isolated. Meanwhile, Shields's and Pierce's troops, across the Churubusco River, had successfully enveloped Santa Anna's forces from the west and reached their rear. Pillow and Worth pushed through to link up. Mexican resistance collapsed, and their broken army fled toward the City of Mexico; Churubusco was over.[52]

The fighting of August 19 and 20 at Contreras and Churubusco destroyed one-third of the Mexican army. Santa Anna's casualties approached 10,000. Scott also lost heavily: of 8,000 engaged, about 12 percent were killed or wounded. Ahead now lay the gates of the City of Mexico, as American dragoons pursued Santa Anna's fleeing soldiers to the walls. Scott halted his tired and hungry army, however. He determined not to exploit his success by attacking the city immediately, "lest by wantonly driving away the government and others—dishonoured—we might scatter the elements of peace, excite a spirit of national desperation, and thus indefinitely postpone the hope of accommodation."[53]

Pillow had done well at Contreras and performed creditably at Churubusco. Scott complimented his work, while Pillow's new friend, Maj. Gen. William Worth, a Whig and close friend of Scott's, commented on the "gallant bearing of Major General Pillow . . . with whom he had the gratification of concert and cooperation at various critical periods of the conflict."[54] Pillow was at his best here. His decision to commit Riley to a flank attack at Contreras demonstrated initiative and flexibility and was basic to victory. Allowing Smith to break off his frontal attack against Valencia and begin an uncertain enveloping movement to the right demonstrated at least an open mind and willingness to trust a subordinate. Critics contended it only showed ignorance and recklessness, exposing Riley, Cadwalader, and Morgan at San Gerónimo, where they were vulnerable to attack from above and below by larger enemy forces, not to speak of the folly of sending Smith off to join them in their plight.

Certainly Pillow took risks at Contreras, but he got away with it. The success of his boldness boosted his belief in himself. Indeed, in his own mind, Pillow not only thought he had won the battle at Contreras, he came to think he had commanded the army. And he had, at least in the initial stages on August 19, when he directed the engagement from Zacatepec through Hooker, Theodore O'Hara, and the rest of his staff. He did so until Scott arrived in mid-afternoon, and even then he continued to offer tactical advice which Scott heeded.

Brig. Gen. Franklin Pierce
(courtesy Chattanooga–Hamilton County Bicentennial Library)

Scott seemed well satisfied with Pillow's performance, and certainly Pillow, not Scott, provided basic shape to the battle. Persifor Smith, of course, must be credited also, for he seized the moment, organizing and carrying out the decisive thrust on the morning of the twentieth. Pillow, however, provided Smith his opportunity, and he gave Twiggs opportunities also.

At Churubusco, Pillow fulfilled his mission. He coordinated well with General Worth, and he demonstrated personal leadership and courage in the continued attacks against the tête de pont. All in all, Thursday and Friday, August 19–20, had been very good days. "I can only say," Pillow reflected correctly, "my part was far more brilliant & *conspicuous* than I myself, in my most sanguine moments ever hoped for."[55]

Both armies sought a respite after Contreras and Churubusco. In the City of Mexico, Santa Anna had to deal with panic and demoralization. He required time to regroup and prepare his defenses. Meanwhile, in Coyoacán, Scott's army, cocky and full of fight, wanted to be done with the task, but they too needed rest and food. Their commander and his friend Trist were quite aware of the precarious position of a depleted army of 7,000 deep within the Valley of Mexico, one defeat away from disaster. But they needed a peace treaty and were willing to try patience.[56]

Gen. Ignacio Mora y Villamil, Santa Anna's chief of engineers, appeared at Coyoacán on August 21, 1847, with a truce proposal. Scott, with Trist by his side, replied that he would agree to an armistice if negotiations for a comprehensive peace treaty were begun; as a precaution, he reserved the right to reposition his troops. Scott, Trist, the dragoons, and Worth's division moved up to Tacubaya. Pillow's division occupied Mixcoac, two miles south of Tacubaya; Twiggs at San Angel and Quitman at San Augustín remained in easy supporting range. The armistice proposed by Scott was ratified and went into effect on August 24.

Pillow and Worth openly opposed the armistice. Pillow not only objected verbally but wrote a letter to Scott in protest. He thought that with the Americans holding the upper hand, no armistice should be allowed unless the fortress of Chapultepec were "surrendered as a guarantee of good faith." When he found Scott adamant, Pillow wrote Polk, giving him a full account of these "measures so disreputable to the Government."[57]

Trist entered negotiations, but they abruptly ended on September 6 when the Mexicans, having recovered their confidence, submitted counterdemands, clearly unacceptable to Trist. Scott, his patience exhausted, and furious at what he regarded as treachery on the part of Santa Anna, prepared to attack.[58]

To avoid the fortress of Chapultepec, the Americans originally wanted to attack the city from the south. This plan changed, however, when Scott decided to capture El Molino del Rey (The Mill of the King), a group of low stone buildings just north of Tacubaya which Scott suspected were being used by the enemy as a cannon foundry. Worth's division would attack El Molino. Cadwalader's brigade would act as his reserve, while Pillow, with the remainder of his division, and Twiggs would feint against the city's southern gate. Worth's assaults on September 8 encountered heavy resistance but carried the enemy strong point. His loss was severe.[59]

Pillow had disagreed with the attack on El Molino. He reported to Scott on September 7 at 10:00 P.M. that the "machinery for casting and boring cannon was removed from the foundry on Aug. 21 to the City of Mexico." He also told Scott how the water power operating the machinery might be cut off. There was just no need to attack and seize El Molino. According to Pillow, Scott could not be dissuaded from ordering Worth's attack. Pillow watched the fight develop but became concerned about the progress of the attack. Without orders, he advanced two brigades to Worth's support. Just as Pillow's troops arrived to help, the enemy resistance against Worth collapsed.[60]

The following day, September 9, Pillow's division pushed forward and occupied La Piedad. Elements of Riley's regiment under D. H. Hill were thrown out from La Piedad as "piquets" toward the Niño Perdido causeway. Hill commanded what he thought to be a reconnaissance probe and watched the enemy fall back on an "immense force" positioned between the Niño Perdido and San Lazardo causeways. At that point an order reached him from Riley to withdraw back to the regiment. In the meantime, a staff officer from Pillow rode up and ordered Hill to remain until another company relieved him. Hill, unaware that Pillow now controlled Riley's brigade, "of course obeyed the orders of the veteran Riley rather than those of an ignorant puppy. Gen. Pillow used harsh and insulting language to me for disobeying his orders and I thereupon shook my sword at him and peremptorily forbade him to use such language again. He then arrested me and I immediately reported the fact to Col. Riley who interested himself about me and the Genl. *magnanimously* released me and retracted his offensive language."[61]

The fierceness of the Mexican defense of El Molino del Rey worried the Americans. Scott became more anxious to fight his way into the capital and end the campaign as quickly as possible. His immediate problem was where to strike. The choices were limited; six causeways, each about 1,000 yards long, ran across fields, "some marsh, some inundated," terrain difficult for infantry and impossible for artillery. He could attack west from El Molino del Rey against massive Chapultepec and then continue north and west along the Belén, Verónica, and San Cosmé causeways into the city, or he could attack due north up the fortified Niño Perdido, Piedad, and San Antonio causeways.[62] "Each of these routes (an elevated causeway) presents a double roadway on the sides of an aqueduct of strong masonry, and great height, resting on open arches and massive pillars, which together, afford fine points for attack and defense. The sideways of both aqueducts are, moreover, defended by many strong breastworks at the gates, and before reaching them."[63]

Scott, as usual, sent out his engineers to reconnoiter, searching for weak points in the city's defenses and firm ground over which he might launch a general attack. Then he gathered his engineers and general officers on the night of September 11 in the church of Piedad to weigh alternatives. Scott opened the council by telling them that he favored the Chapultepec route. Pillow followed with an eloquent argument for the southern route. The engineers, including Lee and Tower, favored the Niño Perdido and San Antonio, or southern, approach that Pillow advocated. If they could break into the capital from this point, the mighty Chapultepec would "fall of its own weight." The other generals, except Twiggs and Riley, agreed. Then engineer P. G. T. Beauregard arose and took exception. He presented a long argument for a demonstration before the San Antonio gate (garita) and then an assault on Chapultepec. When Beauregard had finished, Pierce announced that he was changing his vote. Scott then gave his decision: "Gentlemen, we will attack by the western gates." It would be Chapultepec.[64]

Earlier on September 11, Pillow had been startled when Santa Anna and a host of cavalry emerged from the San Antonio garita and began moving toward his position at Piedad. Magruder opened up with his battery on the intruders and in turn was fired on by Mexican cannon near the garita. Pillow advanced Riley's brigade to Magruder's position and summoned Pierce's brigade. The Mexicans continued to advance. Pillow now rushed a staff officer to bring up Cadwalader. Have Cadwalader, Pillow instructed him, try to cut behind the advancing enemy. The fire from Magruder's guns and from Riley's infantry, however, created disorder in Santa Anna's advancing force and they retired, evading the flanking movement by Cadwalader.[65]

Scott had brought Quitman up from Coyoacán to join Pillow at Piedad on September 11. The two divisions made a feint toward the San Antonio garita. When night fell, Quitman and Pillow slipped back west to Tacubaya. All during the twelfth, Scott's siege guns fired on Chapultepec. The Mexican position appeared formidable. The height of the 200-foot hill was increased dramatically by the sharp brick walls of buildings housing the military college. The heavy guns, however, tore great holes through the masonry and sapped the morale of the garrison. They also disabled important cannon in the fortress. By nightfall, nevertheless, it was clear to Scott that artillery alone would not reduce the position. It must be stormed.[66]

Scott ordered Pillow up from Tacubaya to occupy the captured buildings of El Molino, while Quitman moved out of Tacubaya to an assault position just southeast of Chapultepec. Worth's division was placed west of El Molino to support Pillow; Twiggs would hold Piedad with Riley's brigade and demonstrate, while Persifor Smith would come up from reserve at San Angel and aid Twiggs.[67]

Early on September 12, Pillow moved a brigade and Lt. Jesse L. Reno's mountain howitzers to El Molino and occupied it. Their presence drew fire immediately. Skirmishing continued during the day between El Molino and the grove of cypress at the foot of the Chapultepec fortifications. Reno's guns would drive off the Mexicans each time they appeared in force from the grove. After nightfall on the twelfth, Pillow moved the rest of his division up to assault positions.[68] The next morning they would attack.

Scott called in division commanders Pillow, Worth, and Quitman for detailed orders the night of the twelfth. Pillow and Worth were not pleased. Undoubtedly, the fresh memory of the bloody attack on El Molino haunted them. Pillow offered a "peculiar plan" of his own which none of the participants seem to have bothered to record. Whatever it entailed, it apparently gave a supporting role to his division. Scott listened in "polite and patient amazement" to Pillow and then issued his "orders with an exactitude not to be misunderstood."[69]

Pillow's division would strike due east from El Molino, while Quitman advanced north on the Tacubaya road over the steeper slope. Worth's and Twiggs's divisions would be in support. Pillow and Quitman each were assigned a storming party of 260 regulars equipped with ladders. Capt. Samuel McKenzie of the 2d Artillery from Worth's division would command the party advancing with Pillow. Pillow left the conference in low spirits. His friend Worth muttered, "We shall be defeated." Even Scott had his personal misgivings about the assault, and D. H. Hill confided in his diary that night that the army was in a "deep depression."[70]

Pillow had reason for concern. His volunteers would be leading the assault, and the Mexican position at Chapultepec looked most formidable. The terrain sloped up from El Molino for about three-fourths of a mile to a knob of ground 200 feet high, the fabled Aztec Hill of the Grasshoppers. Atop it stood the masonry walls of the Mexican military academy. Surrounding the castle on the east and south was a high stone wall. Cliffs protected the north and east sides. The approach from El Molino, which Pillow would use, began with a cornfield and continued through uncultivated but well-drained fields with "high tangled grass." Across this ground ran seven or eight ditches, most ten to twelve feet wide with "water waist deep and mud to depth of 1–2 feet." The approach ran on to a large swamp, across a deep irrigation ditch, through a grove of ancient cypress, "many of a great size," to the foot of the steep hill on which the castle stood. Halfway up the hill was another ditch, "ten feet deep and twelve feet wide," covered by musket fire from the windows above. An assortment of breastworks and a mine field strengthened these obstacles.[71] Despite its obvious strength, however, the Mexican defense had serious flaws. The garrison was understrength—only 900 defenders. The walls of the academy, although partially strengthened by sandbags, were vulnerable to American artillery.[72]

At dawn on September 13, 1847, bombardment of Chapultepec resumed. Pillow, busy deploying men and guns, began to regain enthusiasm. Scott's guns had once again silenced the Mexican batteries, and American shells now blasted the castle. Pillow turned his attention first to his own artillery. He had had Lieutenants Beauregard and Roswell S. Ripley work through the night repairing batteries at El Molino that had been firing all during the twelfth. Now Pillow tended to his field guns, placing a section of Magruder's battery and Reno's mountain howitzers where their supporting fire would be most effective for the rush across the swamp to the grove. Their first targets would be a redan to the front and the breastworks along the grove. Next, he turned to the deployment of the assault formations. The Voltigeurs would lead the way, divided into two columns of four companies each. On the right of Pillow's line, a Voltigeur battalion would be led by Lt. Col. Joseph E. Johnston, followed by McKenzie's storming party. Johnston's mission was to force a gate in the southern part of the outer wall. In the center, Col. T. P. Andrews with the remaining Voltigeur battalion and Pierce's 9th and 15th Infantries would attack frontally. On the left, Tennessee's Colonel Trousdale, commanding the 11th and 14th Infantries and Jackson's section of Magruder's battery, was to advance along the Anzures causeway. Pillow himself elected to go forward with Andrews's force.[73]

At 7:30 A.M. the American artillery shifted their fire from the castle itself to the cypress swamp and grove at the base of the hill that sheltered Mexican light troops. At 8:00 A.M. the firing stopped suddenly. This was the signal for the infantry to advance. Pillow ordered the attack. Johnston's Voltigeurs rushed forward along the outside of the outer wall of the castle, captured the redan, passed through the gate in the outer wall, and stormed a circular redoubt and nearby entrenchments. They then linked the left of their line to Pierce's, took cover, and laid a heavy fire on the southern face of the academy.

In the center came the main attack. Andrews's Voltigeurs started off, followed closely by Pierce's brigade of the 9th and 15th Infantries and Reno's howitzers. Pillow, on horseback, led the advance. They charged across the open meadow, and the going was easy at first. Then boggy ground and high grass slowed them. Units became "mixed up, the strong and active having the advantage over the weak." As they waded through the soft mud into the grove, Mexican fire increased. The enemy depressed their heavy cannon and "sent showers of grape and cannister crashing through the cypress tops, the limbs crashing and falling with every discharge."[74] Pillow's central attack splintered in the cypress grove at the foot of the slope. "He was gallantly leading us to the charge on Chapultepec," wrote E. S. Parker of the 9th Infantry. He last saw Pillow "among the leaders on the level ground whilst we was giving 'Them Hell' (Gen. Pillow's own words the night before) under the walls of their far famed castle."[75]

Fighting became confused. Close to the base of the hill, as he emerged from the grove, Pillow was struck by a ricocheting grapeshot that broke his left ankle and tore apart "the leaders [tendons] of the top of the foot." Lee, who was with Pillow, directed soldiers to carry the general to a place of safety. They propped him against a large cypress and Pillow leaned back, continuing to shout commands. A staff officer from Worth appeared, and Pillow sent him hurrying back to his commander with a call for reinforcements. Then Pillow turned over command to Cadwalader. Word raced through the division that Pillow had been killed, compounding confusion and uncertainty.[76]

When Andrews and his Voltigeurs and Reno's howitzers bore to the right and linked with Johnston, a clear path of attack was opened for Ransom's 9th and Lt. Col. Joshua Howard's 15th infantries. They moved into the face of a heavy and effective Mexican fire but charged on, nevertheless, capturing a breastwork. As they approached the walls of the military academy, Ransom shouted, "Forward the Ninth!" Then a bullet struck him in the head and he fell dead; the attack stalled.[77] McKenzie and his storming party with their heavy ladders had not kept up. The troops scattered for cover, firing at Mexicans high on the walls. Cadwalader, aided by Hooker and the rest of Pillow's staff, struggled to keep the division in place. Pillow asked Worth to send a brigade to his relief.

After a delay of over fifteen minutes, Clarke's brigade of Worth's division arrived, and finally McKenzie's party came up. Help also came from the right. Quitman's parallel attack, supported by fresh troops from Twiggs and Worth, made headway and kept the assault moving to the base of the walls. Scaling ladders were placed against the walls, and troops of Pillow, Quitman, and Worth mingled as they fought desperately to seize the parapets above them. Soon fifty men at a time were going up the walls. The surviving defenders melted away. Their commander, Gen. Nicholás Bravo, came forward and surrendered his sword to Cadwalader. Capt. Moses Barnard planted Johnston's Voltigeur colors above the east wall.[78]

As the fighting subsided, Pillow had his soldiers carry him in a blanket up the hill into the academy, where he saw the Mexican tricolor flutter down and Maj. Thomas Seymour of the 9th Infantry hand it to Cadwalader. Then the American flag was raised above the walls. Pillow looked about with great pride and listened to Cadwalader make a speech to the division from a balcony. Pillow saw some American troops and asked a sergeant standing nearby who they were. "Sir," the sergeant replied, "this is the 2nd Pa. Regt., the men who you said waved at Cerro Gordo." Pillow opened his mouth to respond something about always having held the 2d in esteem, but he thought better of it. He became angry and turned on the sergeant. "I think you have a damn sight of impudence for a sergeant."[79]

Scott pushed on. He had Worth attack along the San Cosmé highway with his division and Pillow's 11th and 14th Infantries under Trousdale. In this hard fight, Trousdale's arm was shattered by two musket balls. Jackson's section of guns, operating in front of the army, "was dreadfully cut up."[80] By evening, however, Worth had secured the San Cosmé garita and Quitman had smashed the defenses along the Belén causeway and at the garita. That night the Americans lay on

The storming of Chapultepec
(lithograph by James C. Walker, #48.74, courtesy Amon Carter Museum, Fort Worth, Texas)

their arms, expecting to renew the fight the following morning. But at dawn they discovered Santa Anna had evacuated his capital and retreated to Guadeloupe-Hidalgo. There was the "wildest enthusiasm," and Scott entered the city triumphantly at noon on September 14.[81]

A month later Pillow would write Mary about Chapultepec:

Instead therefore of having a one legged Husband, you have for your Husband—a gentleman, who has now the name in the army of the *"Hero of Chapultepec."*

I have won this by the *glorious charge upon that powerful fortification*. It was *daring & glorious* charge, *unequalled* in the history of the American arms. I promised you my Dear, when I left home, not unnecessarily to expose myself. I did not do so *unnecessarily*. Our artillery had been so cut to pieces by the many bloody battles we had fought, that it had now become necessary to *carry the place* to save *us all* from *slaughter*. I was selected to do the work, & I threw myself at the head of *my command* & led the way, driving every thing before my *invincible* boys, to the very Cannon's mouth, where I was cut down. Then my men picked me up & carried me forward under my orders & with a shout of exultation & triumph, scaled the ditch & wall upon ladders, gloriously carrying the day & saving the army . . .

Don't censure me therefore my Dear good wife; but rejoice & praise God, that while your husband did his duty in such way as to call forth the admiration of the whole army, his life was spared & he permitted to enjoy the proud satisfaction of this brilliant triumph & glorious achievement. I know you will think a great deal more of him, than if he had acted a less distinguished part & had *skulked behind* his men *from fear*. Oh my Dear that day's work was *the proudest* of my life. I know I am not mistaken when I say it will give my name a place in History which will *live* while our *Republic stands*. But of this I have said enough, I am apprehensive you will consider me *vain* and *egotistical*.[82]

6   Leonidas

The fall of the City of Mexico ended major hostilities. Some fighting would continue as Scott sought to extend the zone of American occupation and to secure his lines of communication, but mostly it would be guerrilla and counterguerrilla activity. Gideon Pillow remained in his quarters almost a month, "hopping about my room *with crutches*," waiting impatiently for his broken ankle to mend and venturing out only by carriage. Like his fellow Americans, he marveled at the city, "gorgeous beyond description," "the most remarkable City in the New World." As he had done at Camargo, Pillow made a point to visit and revisit the wounded of his division, who welcomed him warmly.

Suffering from his own wound, Pillow cut a lock of his hair and wove it into a clasp which he mailed to Mary in October. *"While you live never part with it. If I should return to the bosom of my tenderly loved family* as I confidently believe I will under God's providence, be allowed to do, I shall be grateful to see it clasp the arm of my angelic wife, whom I will then *clasp* to my bosom. If (Oh God how painful the thought!) I should be denied this *happiness, then wear this token, in remembrance of him* who *never loved any other."* By mid-November Pillow had put away his crutches and began using a cane. The break healed slowly, however, and his lameness depressed him. It was not until the following February that he could report he no longer walked with a limp. He was overly optimistic, however. His limp and pain would return.[1]

Meanwhile, Pillow had his minion Reynolds in Vera Cruz watching for official dispatches and procuring brandy and indispensable American newspapers. Pillow took time to write home, not only to Mary, but to his children and friends. He wrote twelve-year-old Gideon, Jr., admonishing him to work hard and to behave himself. This extraordinarily competitive father instructed his wife to tell young Gideon "his Papa has a deep interest in his beating all the boys of his age and class at school in every thing. Tell him that his Pa hopes he will live to constitute his pride and to emulate his Deeds in the field."[2]

Sometime in October, Pillow learned of the Englishman James Walker. This young man, a teacher of drawing at the Mexican Military College in Tampico, found himself in the City of Mexico, recuperating from yellow fever, when Scott invaded. He got away from the city somehow and joined Worth's staff as an interpreter. As the Americans advanced inland, Walker found time to sketch battle scenes, and when the capital fell he set up a studio, intending to enlarge his sketches into paintings. Quitman got to Walker first, and Walker's painting of the storming of Chapultepec featured Quitman's division and the general himself.

This would not do at all. According to Quitman's staff officer, George T. M. Davis, Pillow came by Walker's studio and offered him $100 for the painting, "conditioned upon its being remodeled to meet the representations made by General Pillow as to that battle."[3] Quitman's version triumphed, but the enterprising Pillow found a way. He had Walker paint another version of Chapultepec, this one featuring Pillow and his division. He was delighted with the result and sent it off immediately to Polk. "It is a beautiful painting which I sent to

Washington City for the present that it may be seen by the *world* which will be congregated at that place this winter, after which, I will take it home & present it to my good wife. I am placed in my proper position in the painting. It is quite large & will make a splendid ornament for your parlors."[4]

In late August, shortly after the Battle of Churubusco, Pillow had sent for James L. Freaner, correspondent for the New Orleans *Daily Delta*. He pressed Freaner to accept an account of Contreras and Churubusco which he had prepared. Pillow's version gave himself the credit for the planning and execution of both battles, minimized the roles of officers such as Persifor Smith, and practically ignored Scott. Freaner glanced over the report and noted its inaccuracies. He pocketed the document and forgot about it.[5]

A few days later, Pillow's division paymaster, Maj. Archibald W. Burns, according to Pillow, happened to be in Pillow's quarters, where he discovered the account shown to Freaner. He picked up the document and took it with him. Then, using Pillow's narrative as a basis, Burns wrote the story of Contreras and Churubusco himself. Burns signed it "Leonidas" and mailed it directly to Alexander Werth, editor of the *Daily Delta*. Burns's account employed almost the same language that Pillow had used in the report given to Freaner. Werth printed the Leonidas letter in the September 10, 1847, issue of the *Daily Delta*. Another version of the letter, with certain elaborations, appeared in the New Orleans *Daily Picayune* on September 16.

Although moderated somewhat by editor Werth, Leonidas's version of the battles was outrageous. "During this great battle, which lasted two days, Gen. Pillow was in command of all the forces engaged. . . . Gen. Scott gave but one order, and that was to reinforce Gen. Cadwalader's brigade." Pillow's plan of battle was "judicious and successful," demonstrating "masterly genius and profound knowledge of the science of war which has astonished so much the mere martinets of the profession." "Nothing could have been better planned than this battle." Leonidas compared Pillow to Napoleon at Ulm and, to further heighten the effect, provided the American public with the Homeric version of Pillow's slaying of the Mexican officer at Churubusco.[6]

Pillow, meanwhile, had submitted his official reports of Contreras, Churubusco, and Chapultepec to Scott. These documents made representations similar to the account given to Freaner and those made by Leonidas. All three documents were written in a similar style. Still ignorant of the "Leonidas Letter," Scott, on October 2, requested

Pillow to alter his Contreras-Churubusco report and, in addition, to moderate exaggerations within his Chapultepec report.[7] Specifically, Scott, in tactful terms, insisted that he, not Pillow, ordered Morgan and the 15th Infantry to support Cadwalader at Contreras, and he challenged Pillow's assuming credit for Smith's and Riley's successful attacks. Regarding the Chapultepec report, Scott criticized Pillow for suggesting that the latter "ordered all batteries silenced" and gave the command for the general advance. He also made it clear that he, not Pillow, ordered Clarke's and Cadwalader's brigades to support Worth. Scott concluded with irony that he perceived an intent by Pillow "to leave General Scott entirely out of the operations of September 13."[8]

Pillow replied in a letter to Scott on October 3. His tone was conciliatory. "You have been my friend, you have given me your confidence and have placed me in positions of great responsibility. . . . For your uniform kindness. . . . I shall ever feel . . . a proper sense of gratitude." Pillow ended his letter by asking Scott to visit him (because of his painful wound) so that he could give a personal explanation, and to return his reports so that they could be corrected.[9]

Scott, however, was too busy. Furthermore, he had come to disapprove of Pillow and said so to Trist: "From the moment he first joined the army, it has been the studious endeavor of Genl Pillow to impress . . . that *his* influence, the surest of all passports to the favor of the Executive, at Washington was unbounded." So Scott and Pillow exchanged polite letters. Pillow gave in on all but one point, continuing to claim credit for Smith's and Riley's flanking movement at Contreras. Scott, weary of the matter, accepted the reports, commenting that "the discrepancies between your memory and mine, respecting those operations, are so many and so material . . . I shall forward them to the War Department." He concluded, "Here, I suppose, all further correspondence between us on the subject ought to cease." Pillow thought Scott overreacted. Everyone understood, did they not, that in politics stretching truth was like stretching taffy? Scott simply did not understand. "Our only offence consisted in having indiscreet friends, whose partiality betrayed them into the folly of giving us more credit, than it was *pleasant* to the General-in-chief, any of his *juniors* in rank should have." Pillow tended to blame the strained relationship not only on Scott's jealousy, but on his "pimps," Trist and Hitchcock, who "hatched the difficulties and provoked the rupture."[10]

All seemed well enough, and when copies of New Orleans papers containing the Leonidas letter arrived in the City of Mexico, Scott may have been seething, but he took no official notice. To the army, the exaggerations that appeared in the *Daily Delta* and *Daily Pica-yune* made Pillow appear comic. Lt. John D. Wilkins wrote his mother that anyone "will at once, from reading the letters, see the sycophantic manner in which everything is told. Genl P. is a brave man & is always foremost in battle but there are others equally so and entitled to small part of the credit. The General is strongly suspected of being the author of the letters himself." Knowledge of the Leonidas letters spread rapidly throughout the army; officers decided for themselves about loyalties and proprieties.[11]

Then the issue of the howitzers surfaced. On September 13, after Chapultepec had been secured, Lt. Justin Hodge, 9th Infantry quartermaster, and Mr. Welsh, "a follower of the army," took two small Mexican howitzers, removed them from their carriages, and placed them in Pillow's baggage wagon. They did this, according to Pillow, without his knowledge or consent. That evening, Midshipman R. C. Rogers came to Pillow and told him about the howitzers. He also told him that Lt. Col. Joshua Howard, new post commander of Chapultepec, knew about them.[12]

Perhaps Pillow intended the howitzers as trophies for Clifton. After all, had not Haskell and the 2d Tennessee brought captured cannon home to Memphis? In any event, such was out of the question now. So, on the evening of September 14, Pillow maintained, he ordered staff officers Ripley and Rains to remove the guns from his wagon and place them back on their proper mounts. In the darkness, however, the staff officers could not find the gun carriages. Accordingly, they did nothing. The following day, September 15, Pillow's wagon, with the guns still in it, was driven into Mexico City along with the other wagons of his division. Once within the city, one of the howitzers was carried away by Welsh, apparently for his own use, and another was claimed by Rogers and taken to his quarters.[13]

Pillow, nursing his ankle, claimed he forgot about the matter until October 8, when he happened to ask his staff about the howitzers. They told him that the guns had not been removed from his baggage wagon. Pillow, accordingly, wrote Scott on October 9 informing him that the cannon had been moved without his knowledge; he appended statements from Ripley, Rains, Rogers, and Welsh. Scott, however, believed Pillow's explanation too thin and refused to accept it. Pillow, embarrassed and indignant, demanded a court of inquiry.[14]

Relations between the two men deteriorated rapidly. Indeed, Pillow's relations with the army seem to have changed. When the Aztec Club, composed of officers of all ranks and branches of service, was organized on October 13, Pillow apparently was the only senior officer other than Winfield Scott who did not choose to become an active or honorary member. Perhaps because it was composed primarily of regular officers, or perhaps because Quitman headed the club, Pillow wanted no part of it.[15] Pillow also avoided an important farewell banquet Scott gave for Twiggs, but then, his relations with the tough old regular, never good, seem to have worsened also. Perhaps he was not invited.[16]

Scott had bitten his tongue over the Leonidas affront, but he remembered well the distortions and inaccuracies in Pillow's battle reports and no doubt had become highly suspicious of Pillow's motives. It did seem like a conspiracy to deride him. Pillow sensed the change:

> Notwithstanding Genl. Scott selected me to storm Chapultepec & to do all the *hard jobs* & *dangerous work*, and notwithstanding I served him with so much felicity and with such distinguished success, he has become my enemy & without the slightest provocation. His reports will be found, I understand, to speak of me in the highest terms of consideration, (because the facts & my conduct are so well known in the army that he was obliged to do so). Still he is beyond all question dissatisfied with himself & is envious of my distinction. I have however got a *start now* & have got above his reach.[17]

The court of inquiry regarding Pillow's howitzers, convened by Scott and presided over by Worth, met on October 23 and completed its deliberations on November 2. In its findings the court ruled that Rains and Ripley had made an "error in judgment": "Such an appropriation was in violation of the accepted premise that such booty was government property."[18] The court cleared Pillow, with one exception: based on Colonel Howard's testimony, the court concluded that Rains and Ripley had reported to Pillow that the guns had not been removed from his wagon.[19]

Word got around the army that the court had found Pillow "guilty of ungentlemanly conduct." Most believed Pillow had not intended returning the howitzer and slipped the charge by shifting blame to his young staff officers. Capt. Richard S. Ewell wrote on November 25: "I suppose you have seen some of the strictures upon General Pillow, but they are nothing to what would be written could an accurate account of his follies and absurdities be got at in the United States. There was a Court of Inquiry lately in reference to some howitzers taken at Chapultepec which he tried to appropriate. The Whole proceedings convict him very plainly of falsehood and other little weaknesses, such as trying to throw the responsibility on his aide."[20] Pillow, stung by talk of alleged impropriety, blamed Scott. "He is a most vindictive man," Pillow wrote Mary. "I gave him no provocation whatever." Scott was angry "because of the letter which has appeared in the newspapers speaking in terms of high commendation of my services . . . but I am not, thank God, dependent upon him now."[21]

Pillow deeply resented personally and politically being bypassed by Scott and Trist regarding negotiations with the Mexican government. He had expected Trist to consult him at every stage, but Trist had drawn away, working closely with Scott. Pillow had trusted Trist the Democrat, confided in him, and told him how politically charged the treaty-making process was, how it related directly to "upcoming elections." Trist, however, was compulsive in his eagerness to secure a treaty, and he had become disgusted with Pillow and the underhanded situation. He had tired of Pillow's continued reference to himself as " 'the President's *other self*, a pretension which I have reason to believe but too well founded.' " In a letter to Buchanan, Trist referred to Pillow and Santa Anna as " 'twin phenomena' in 'moral obliquity.' "[22]

Pillow did two things to retaliate. First, on October 28, he wrote Polk disclosing the attempted bribe of Santa Anna in July. He knew Polk would disapprove strongly. Since he was implicating himself as well, Pillow confessed that initially he had given "reluctant assent" to the bribe, but then, upon reflection, he had protested against it.[23] Next Pillow fired back "an insulting letter to Scott's adjutant" asking the commanding general for redress. Scott refused. Pillow now appealed officially to Secretary of War Marcy, skipping past his superior in an arrogant disregard of regulations. In a parallel and unofficial letter to Polk, he complained that Scott would have him "branded with the attempt to '*embezzle the public property*,' if that record does not receive your attention & action."[24]

Scott was infuriated by Pillow's appeal to Marcy. He regarded it as rank insubordination, and on November 22 he ordered Pillow to consider himself "in a state of arrest confined to the limits of the city." A general court-martial would be convened. Going over his head to Marcy was the last straw.[25]

Scott was also enraged about the appearance of yet another article. On November 10 a newspaper arrived from Tampico containing a letter which had first appeared in the *Pittsburgh Post* signed "Veritas." The letter lavished praise on Worth for the critical decision to take the approach around Lake Chalco.[26] On November 12 Scott issued General Orders No. 349, reminding officers of an ancient general regulation prohibiting publication of "any private letters or reports, relative to military marches and operations." Scott included in the order a blast at Leonidas and Veritas. "False credit may, no doubt, be obtained at home by such despicable self-puffings, and malignant exclusion of others; but at the expense of the just esteem and consideration of all honorable officers who love their country, their profession, and the truth of history."[27]

Worth, stung by the veiled accusation and looking for a fight, asked for details from Scott. When Scott refused, Worth appealed to Polk, charging his old friend and colleague Scott with conduct unbecoming an officer and gentleman. Scott retaliated by relieving Worth of his command and placing him in arrest. To further muddy the situation, Lt. Col. James Duncan, Worth's chief of artillery, announced himself in the *North American* as author of the "Tampico Letter." He too was placed under arrest. Doubtless Pillow encouraged both officers in their insubordination.[28]

Pillow wrote Polk notifying him of the arrests and of Scott's General Order No. 349, further evidence of Scott's "*assassin-like* tactics." Both Pillow and Polk knew the enormous importance of such public letters. They remembered the Charles Cassady letter of 1835, from which John Bell of Tennessee never recovered politically, and certainly Van Buren's disastrous Texas letter of 1844. The practice "is a great nuisance as all admit," wrote Pillow, "and if Genl. Scott had issued an order at Vera Cruz and notified the army of his purpose, it would have been well enough . . . but it so happened that all the letters at that time, & for some time afterwards, *praised* and *glorified* Scott himself. As long as that was the case, he did *not see its evils*." Pillow appealed for Polk to immediately intervene and "protect me against unlawful arrest" and expressed the wish that "you will order us both home at once."[29]

The following day, November 25, Pillow wrote Mary a letter revealing that he welcomed the confrontation with Scott and believed events could work so as to bring unexpected rewards. He thought Scott was bluffing, not intending to have a court-martial, expecting the charges to go "unanswered by his victim."

My offence consisted in an official letter of mine to the Government [to Marcy] in which he professes to think my language was not *respectful* towards him. My letter. I know made the *blood fly*. It was however true as I am prepared to show. He has violated the Law & outraged my principle of justice in regard to myself & I feel very confident of *flooring him*. . . . He is offended with me for opposing his views in connection with the *fatal armistice* [following Churubusco] & that hostility is the real motive under which he has acted, though he seizes hold of this letter of mine as a *pretext*.[30]

By requesting the War Department to hold the courts-martial in the United States, Pillow believed the president might recall him, Worth, and Duncan, as well as Scott, replacing the latter with General Butler. He wrote Mary:

I will blow him [Scott] higher & kill him deader than did the "*hasty plate of soup*" letter or "*the fire in front & fire in rear.*" You need not have the least *uneasiness.* The whole affair will produce much excitement & newspaper discussion at home, but it will prove ultimately great to *my advantage.* My enemies seem determined to make me a *great man* whether *I will* or not. If I have any knowledge of the American people & of the signs of *the times*—the affect of this proceeding will be [*sic*] place me more *prominently* and more favorably before the nation, and will result even more to my advantage than do my successes in this valley, but when coming as it does immediately upon the news of my brilliant successes, it will startle the public and as soon as the facts come to light will show a degree of *malignity* in Scott, as *black* and *atrocious* as ever *disgraced* a fiend.[31]

Since Worth was a prominent Whig and Scott's protégé, Pillow believed public reaction in the United States would be to view the conflict as an "*issue between Two Whigs* and will therefore prevent the matter assuming a party character at home & will relieve the Govt from all embarrassment as between myself & Scott. The Taylor Whigs, who constitute at least two thirds of the party will aid in crushing Scott. . . . He had to take not one more step to plunge into the bottomless abyss of deep public condemnation. That Step *he has taken.* This now gives me joy *inexpressible.*"[32]

Pillow attended the reopened opera house in the City of Mexico on November 26, and his reception confirmed hopes for support from the army. "My presence produced such a sensation that I was loudly and *enthusiastically cheered* by almost the whole audience."[33] Pillow misled himself. Reaction within the army to the conflict between the commanding general and two of his division commanders was one of disgust. D. H. Hill, by habit a Pillow-basher, nevertheless seems to sum up the feeling of most responsible officers: "The infamous sycophant who wrote the false, fulsome letter in praise of Genl Pillow has not yet been discovered though suspected to be Paymaster Burns. Genls Pillow and Worth have both been arrested in this connexion, though I do not know the exact ground. Genl Scott has lowered himself very much in the Army by his jealousies of the reputation of his subalterns. He is in many respects a very small man."[34] General Shields reported to Polk that the Leonidas letter "had done injustice to other officers, & had done Genl Pillow an injury in the estimation of the army; but . . . no one doubts his bravery & gallantry, and that he was a good officer."[35]

About this time, Pillow's letter to Polk informing him of Scott's attempted bribe of Santa Anna arrived in Washington. Polk's fury knew no bounds. "This subject has given me great pain, but it must be investigated," wrote Polk, "and the censure fall where it is due, whatever may be the consequences to the officers concerned."[36] He pitched into Pillow first: "Your great error consists in having given an opinion, or yielded your reluctant assent . . . when you were consulted by others. I am gratified that you afterwards took a different and a correct view of the matter, and protested against it."[37] As for Scott, Polk and his cabinet discussed recalling him, and Polk took the matter up with influential Democratic leaders. In the meantime, he had his private secretary, Knox Walker, write Pillow to "*keep quiet* and be not *too anxious* to put down your prosecutors and to do justice to yourself, let your military achievements speak for themselves."[38] When he received Scott's charges against Pillow, Worth, and Duncan from Marcy on December 30, Polk concluded this further demonstrated "the vanity and tyrannical temper of General Scott" and his unfitness for command.[39]

On January 13, 1848, Secretary of War Marcy issued the order removing Scott from command of the army and replacing him with Maj. Gen. William O. Butler. Marcy's letter arrived in the City of Mexico on February 18. It further stipulated that Worth, Pillow, and Duncan were to be released from arrest and that the charges brought against them by Scott were to be investigated by a court of inquiry. Scott was infuriated by Marcy's action and saw himself as the victim in yet another in the "series of the greatest wrongs . . . in continuation of the [Andrew] Jackson persecution."[40]

The army was shocked. Colonel Hitchcock, who believed Pillow to be "a brave and competent but vain commander and a pet of President Polk," spoke for most of the officers when he wrote: "There is in the army a feeling of unmitigated condemnation of the late change except among the immediate partisans of Pillow, etc. We all see the enormity of the conduct of the President—deplore and abhor it." Lt. Edmund Bradford reported that "the course the President has pursued has met the disapprobation of almost all the officers of the old Army and I have heard many of them say that if it were in their power, they would send in their resignation immediately." Characteristically, D. H. Hill reacted violently, but this time his feelings seemed to reflect those of the officer corps. "The recall of Genl. Scott is owing to the intrigues of that arch-scoundrel Pillow. He has very great influence with our weak, childish President, and boasted when Genl. Scott arrested him that he would get the General recalled. That an idiot monkey could cause the greatest Captain of the age to be disgraced upon the very theatre of his glory will not be credited by posterity. The whole Army is indignant." Perceptive Helen B. Chapman, a veteran army wife stationed at Matamoras, summed it up in a letter to her mother: "All seem to think he [Scott] has been shamefully treated by the Government. General Pillow will find that his petty little attorney tricks for notoriety are out of place with Army men."[41]

Pillow, on the other hand, wrote Mary that the government's orders were "entirely *satisfactory*. . . . He has released us all from arrest—suspended Scott from command and ordered his conduct to be investigated also."[42] He continued to keep Polk abreast of the diplomatic work of Trist and Scott, criticizing them at every turn. Trist he repudiated as a "traitor to friendship," who "betrays all conversations of mine to Scott." He again urged Polk to conclude the war while he was still president and suggested Polk reconsider seeking another term. Once again Pillow recommended to Polk establishing the Pánuco River as the natural boundary between Mexico and the United States.[43] He also wrote Reynolds in Vera Cruz to "give the enemy *hot shells*. . . . The columns of the Nashville Union—The Ohio Statesman—and the Washington Union, are all open to you as I am persuaded, & the enemy will quail under your vigorous pen."[44]

Polk and Marcy, meanwhile, chose the court carefully. Brig. Gen. Nathan Towson, paymaster-general of the army, would sit as president. He would join Brig. Gen. Caleb Cushing and Col. Edward G. W. Butler, two proven Democrats of Massachusetts and Louisiana.[45] The court of inquiry convened on March 13, 1848, at Puebla, organized itself, and adjourned to the City of Mexico. Pillow, naturally, made no challenge to the membership of the court. Scott, however, was angered by the lack of rank, an obvious slight.[46]

With the opening of the court, Worth withdrew his charges against Scott. Scott's case against him and Duncan was eventually dropped. Captain Lee hoped the court might adjourn. "But I fear the desire of Some in the Army to bring Genl P. to Judgement will have opened the whole question again . . . While these Genls were under his [Scott's] command, it was his duty to maintain the discipline & honour of the Army, but having them now suspended their prosecution is no matter of his."[47] The stage had been cleared for the showdown between Pillow and Scott.

Pillow now attempted to draw closer to Duncan, perhaps to strengthen his own position. He apparently "offered to marry the Colonel to a rich and handsome widow" and told him that he would ask Polk to name him inspector general of the army. Pillow did make this later request, but not until January 1, 1849.[48] In his letter to Polk, Pillow commented that he had known Duncan "intimately in Mexico and [knew] not his like in the American Army."[49] Pillow, however, made a general practice of recommending accommodating friends for higher positions. Among a number of requests, he sought a position in the navy pay office for Burns, a four months' extension of leave for Ripley, and an extra brevet promotion for Hooker. "I have never had a truer or better friend than Hooker," he wrote Polk. "My arm should *wither*, before I would request you to do what was inconsistent with your duty to the public," but he reminded Polk of his promise that "you would grant me any thing for myself or my friends which I asked." If Hooker failed to get his second brevet, it would be a "secret triumph & exultation of Scott and his *coterie*."[50]

Historian Justin Smith offered an opinion about Pillow's motives. "Without a particle of real military ability . . . , he now stood second in our army, and hence logically enough saw no reason why he might not, by some devious path, arrive at the first position and even at the Presidency."[51] Without doubt, Pillow intended to use the coming court of inquiry to serve the Democracy by discrediting a formidable Whig. He believed the court would be a showcase, a magnificent political opportunity for the Democracy and for himself. He had known of Worth's political ambitions—a wild dream of the presidency itself— and doubtless had encouraged Worth in his defiance of his old friend Scott and in his mounting opposition to Henry Clay and the Whig party. "I suppose every body," Pillow confided to Mary, "is now busy intriguing for the Presidency."[52]

The court met again in the hall of the Supreme Court of Justice in the National Palace in Mexico City on March 16, 1848.[53] Pillow conducted his own defense, although he flattered Maj. John C. Breckinridge, Kentucky protégé of General Butler, by asking him to serve as defense counsel. Breckinridge agreed and did examine some witnesses, but he seems to have had "little influence on the outcome." Pillow quickly made it clear that in a courtroom he was the master and professional soldiers were now the amateurs.[54]

Pillow faced two charges. The first accused him of violating paragraph 292 of the General Regulations of the Army in having written or procured to be written a letter signed "Leonidas" published in the New Orleans *Daily Picayune* of September 16, 1847.[55] The second accused him of conduct unbecoming an officer and a gentleman and listed eight specifications. Pillow immediately counterattacked, charging that Captain Lee, Scott's staff officer and favorite, was also guilty of violating paragraph 292. A letter of Lee's dated August 22, 1847, had appeared in the Washington *Union*. The letter, containing a straightforward account of Contreras and Churubusco, was sent to Mrs. J. G. Totten, wife of the chief of engineers. She took the letter to the engineers' office, where Capt. George Welcker thought it of interest to the public and passed a copy to the *Union*. Lee had sent the letter to keep his bureau chief, Colonel Totten, informed and had had nothing to do with its publication. Pillow worked hard to make the point that an officer of Scott's staff could violate the same regulation without any action being taken against him. Lee was obviously innocent but greatly embarrassed. Disgusted, Lee sent a transcript of the proceedings to his father-in-law. "You will see what a person Genl. Pillow is, & for whom Gen. Scott has been sacrificed."[56] As for Lee's writing the letter in the first place, it was a common practice for officers of a particular branch, such as the engineers, to keep their bureau chiefs informed.[57]

Pillow next tore into Col. Ethan A. Hitchcock and skillfully wrung an admission that Hitchcock had "written a long and abusive attack on myself and Worth" and placed it in the New York *Courier and Inquirer*. "I have *convicted* him [Scott] of the very offense with which he charges me while I have proved myself entirely innocent," wrote Pillow. Scott "has raved with passion & tried to *bully the court* and *brow-beat* me; but he is now so thoroughly whipt that he is *quiet as a lamb*."[58]

Scott came under attack from a different direction when the court received instructions from Marcy to investigate the attempt to bribe Santa Anna back at Puebla in July 1847. Pillow testified at length, as did other participants in Scott's council of generals, but Scott refused to give evidence about the incident and the court eventually aban-

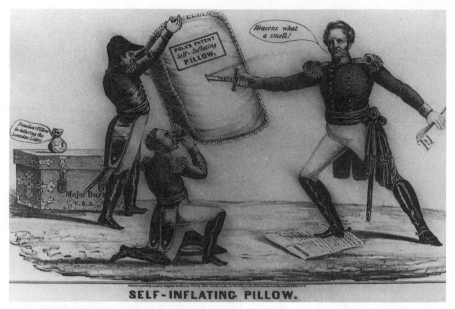

SELF-INFLATING PILLOW.

Political cartoon about Pillow, 1848
(courtesy John R. Neal)

doned the issue. On April 21 the court adjourned. It would reconvene
at Frederick, Maryland.[59]

Pillow took a fast and comfortable ship to New Orleans, traveling
with members of the court. They had a pleasant, friendly trip, in the
manner of old circuit court days. Pillow stopped by Clifton for a few
days and persuaded Mary to join him for the trip north. He was enormously complimented when a Democratic organ, the Nashville *Daily
Centre–State American*, began publication in April 1848 and placed on
its masthead "Cass for President, Pillow for governor." Pillow appears
to have done little to encourage the effort, however. By June 5, 1848,
he was in Frederick, refreshed and confident.[60]

The parade of witnesses began, including the secretary of war.
Some, like Quitman, looked over their shoulders at the Democratic
convention in Baltimore and wanted this dreary affair finished.
Nicholas Trist was horrified at the conduct of the court. He regarded
Pillow as an "intriguer . . . of incomprehensible baseness of character" and watched with amazement as Pillow skillfully reduced Scott's
charges to pulp. While Pillow cross-examined Scott, Trist saw General Cushing "furtively communicating with and giving advice to"
Pillow. Then he witnessed all manner of shenanigans regarding the
admission of documents into evidence. As Hitchcock presented his

testimony, Pillow reached over and picked up Hitchcock's "personal and private" notebook, which he had used to corroborate the time of an event, and thumbed through it knowingly. Enraged but helpless, Hitchcock twisted in the witness box.[61]

Since Paymaster Burns assumed all responsibility for the Leonidas letter, the principal charge against Pillow was nullified. Pillow explained to Polk that "in his anxiety to serve me, he [Burns] involved himself, as well as myself in much embarrassments," though "all statements of facts" in his letter "proved to be true."[62] With the authorship of the Leonidas letter set aside, Scott's case unraveled, and the court of inquiry deteriorated into pulling apart minor specifications to determine whether Pillow had overstated his role in his official reports.[63] Pillow summed up his defense on June 20. His presentation was superior—even his critics admitted that—and it would be published in pamphlet form and distributed widely. He took full advantage of the poorly worded and repetitious specifications. Scott, on the other hand, was ill and exhausted, as his closing statement reflected.[64]

In its judgments, the court undoubtedly weighed the politics and realities of the matter. Pillow's critics, then and since, have written off the findings as a "whitewash." This may have validity with regard to the Leonidas letter, but the court demonstrated considerable patience and judgment in untangling the charges, statements, and claims of Scott and Pillow in the minor specifications. The court concluded that "no further proceedings against General Pillow . . . are called for."[65]

Polk examined the findings of the court and agreed "that no further military proceedings in the case were required." As Scott noted with sarcasm in his memoirs, Polk promoted Towson to brevet major general and Col. William G. Belknap (who had replaced Butler on the court) to brigadier "for their acceptable services in shielding Pillow." Polk, however, did not concur with the court in all their conclusions and inferences from them: "They do not, I think, do him [Pillow] full justice." Polk, however, "did not deem it necessary to say any thing in relation to the findings." Polk also spoke to Marcy about the "small howitzers" and directed him to find that Pillow "did nothing for which he deserves the slightest censure."[66] "Gen'l Pillow is a gallant and highly meritorious officer, and has been greatly persecuted by Gen'l Scott, for no other reason than that he is a Democrat in his politics and was supposed to be my personal & political friend."[67]

Thus the matter died officially. The wounds, however, would not heal. The majority of the West Point officer corps did not forgive nor forget; neither did Whigs. Reasonable people of good will looked upon the episode as shameful. Winfield Scott's reputation as the foremost American military figure of his age, rather than being burnished in Mexico, as merited, had been blemished. He also had been damaged as a Whig presidential aspirant. But his opponent had been hurt as well. Despite the appearance of winning, Gideon Pillow lost credibility with the American public, even among partisan Democrats, in a way he never would understand. This Tennessee volunteer soldier, of the classic Andrew Jackson mold, had come home from the Mexican War not as the hero he believed he had become, but as a caricature of the very image he set out to create. Considering the service he rendered, he deserved a kinder fate, one might argue, but it is difficult to deny that he received justice in its purest form.

Pillow left Frederick and the United States Army and returned to Washington. He and Polk talked for hours; then he and Mary had dinner with the Polks in the White House and he presented Sarah Polk a lovely fan he had brought from Mexico.[68] Pillow had written Cadwalader when he and Mary first arrived and invited him and his wife to visit them in Washington. Cadwalader came down from Philadelphia in July, and he and Pillow managed to get Polk stirred up about the Senate's lack of willingness to confirm the general officers the president had appointed in 1847. R. B. Reynolds earlier had warned Polk that Scott intended to see that Pillow's confirmation was defeated, and Polk had come to fear what the Whigs might do. Therefore he dallied in sending the general's name up to the Senate. Pillow and Cadwalader, however, pressed him to submit all the names together now, for Pillow wished to be "relieved from any imputation." Polk met with the cabinet and changed his mind three times. Finally, he submitted the names of all the general officers at one time as Pillow had suggested. To Polk's joy the Senate confirmed them. Thus Gideon Pillow became major general of the Army of the United States on July 17, 1848. "Gen'l Pillow has now been fully vindicated & his triumph is complete," Polk wrote happily.[69]

On July 10 Pillow appeared at the White House unexpectedly; Polk excused himself from a meeting to speak privately with his friend. It seemed that the Whig Alexander Stephens had "abused Pillow personally" in the House of Representatives. He had applied the term "infamous," or so it had been reported to Pillow. Twice that day Pillow had been to Stephens's boardinghouse looking for him; "he was determined to flog him on sight." Polk calmed Pillow down, counseling him to exercise caution and to avoid a situation where the Whigs might make political hay out of "an officer of the army attempting to browbeat Congress."[70]

Before leaving Washington for Clifton, Pillow urged Polk to reward the faithful for their services: Col. James Duncan to be appointed inspector general of the army and second brevet promotions for Hooker and Ripley. The president complied.[71] Pillow and Mary then put the northers of the capital behind them and headed home, accompanied by Duncan as far as Philadelphia, where they enjoyed the hospitality of the Cadwaladers. They reached Clifton in early August. Pillow wrote Cadwalader from "my own *sweet home*" that once again he was settled in the midst of "our little flock of children (only 7 you know)."[72] He did not resume the practice of law for a while, choosing instead to concentrate his time and effort on Clifton and the development of Mound Plantation near Helena, Arkansas. Always interested in internal improvements, he found time to serve as a delegate to the Tennessee Railroad convention in Memphis in July 1849. He also became involved in rebuilding the Presbyterian church in Columbia and gave to it generously.[73]

Pillow intended to escape the campaign or canvass for the 1848 presidential election. Polk, however, wanted very much for Lewis Cass to be elected over Whig military hero Zachary Taylor. Polk regarded the election of Cass as a vindication of his administration, and the support of Tennessee would be particularly gratifying. So Polk appealed to Pillow in the strongest terms to make speeches and have them published and to get his friends involved in the canvass as well. Cave Johnson and Sam Laughlin followed up: "Do, my dear General, buckle on your armor, and bestir yourself in the great and good cause up to the day of election."[74] Pillow, however, had become "no account." He refused his friends, excusing himself from campaigning because of his long absence in Mexico and the consequent neglect of his business interests. He added, with finality, "I have been all the summer, suffering much from the effects of my last wound." To Duncan he wrote in September, "I labor under constant pain—the limb is much weaker & I cannot walk any distance—nor ride on horseback without much suffering."[75]

7   **Making Good Democratic Music**

Before Pillow packed away his uniform and stepped into civilian life, he commissioned Washington Bogart Cooper, a painter of prominent Middle Tennesseans, to do his Mexican War portrait. Cooper had done a portrait of Gov. Billy Carroll earlier, and Pillow admired that work very much. It was also about this time that Henry S. Sadd, an English mezzotint engraver, did the engraving of Pillow (see Chapter 4) that appeared in contemporary books about the Mexican War.[1]

One of these books, a correct version of the Mexican War—"a work of *high authority*"—was being prepared under Pillow's supervision at Clifton by Capt. Roswell Ripley, his former staff officer. Ripley worked fast, but still Pillow fretted. He had secured a leave of absence for Ripley in May 1848, and then an extension, but time was running out. Polk would be out of office soon, and Ripley would be ordered back to his regiment, so Pillow pushed Ripley to hurry. Pillow had managed to keep knowledge of Ripley's whereabouts from Secretary of War Marcy, and he instructed Knox Walker to tell anyone in Washington who got nosy that Ripley was in Maury County "engaged in an interesting *negotiation* with a *young lady*."[2]

By the end of April 1849, Ripley had completed his history and set off to New York to have it published. Pillow liked the final draft, and doubtless much of the work came from his pen, if not his mind. Gideon Pillow understood very well the political importance of getting in print quickly and creating the proper public image. He wrote his friend Cadwalader that the Pennsylvanian's role in the fighting around the City of Mexico had been done reliably and appreciatively. He contended with his inveterate exaggeration that Ripley's *The War with Mexico* "will in general style, & accuracy of narrative rank with Prescott & Bancroft's works, which in military criticism and description of Battles it is clearly superior to either, & will compare favourably with Napier's." He confided to Duncan cynically that Ripley's work was "just & impartial in its deductions" and thus would "*skin Scott* not *ill-naturedly*, nor *captiously* but upon his *conduct* as evidenced by the *documents*."[3]

Pillow was busy at Clifton, which required careful attention. He inspected every inch of the rear portico and the three-story kitchen that had been constructed while he was off in Mexico. Clifton required greater elegance, he thought, a new face, something in which he might see himself. So he added a "Greek Revival portico and cornice" facing north across Clifton Pike. This meant, among other things, extensive roof realignment and required that workmen construct a second roof several feet above the cedar shake original.[4]

The president came to visit on April 5. Polk had left office on March 4, 1849, and made his way home touring a number of southern cities. In Columbia he was received by a huge turnout, replete with a military company from Jackson College, a brass band, and of course his old friend Pillow, who gave a long and warm welcoming speech at the Maury County Court House. The *Maury Intelligencer*, however, ominously noted that Polk "looks fifteen years older than when he left here four years ago. He . . . has the appearance of one worn down by care and anxiety." Polk would die in Nashville two months later, one of the victims of a devastating cholera epidemic. Gen. William Worth would die in Texas in May, and in July Col. James Duncan would die in Mobile. These deaths struck Pillow hard. He wrote his confidant Reynolds: "These two [Polk and Duncan] were my most devoted & best friends. I have never been more pained by the loss of any friends than by theirs. It is a personal affliction which I deeply feel."[5]

Earlier in 1849, after he had returned from an inspection of his Mound Plantation in Arkansas, Pillow had been urged by his brothers-in-law West Humphreys and Aaron V. Brown to let his name be placed in nomination for governor. Other Tennessee Democratic leaders agreed and added their voices. Pillow, the heir of James K. Polk, the "Hero of Chapultepec," seemed an obvious choice. He could have had the nomination, it was commonly believed; the timing seemed perfect. Word of Pillow's candidacy even reached Joe Hooker in New York City. Pillow considered the opportunity carefully, but finally declined, excusing himself on the basis of the "deranged condition in which I found my private affairs after so long an absence in Mexico. I always believed I could carry the State and I now have no doubt but that I would have done so & I may have failed to adopt the wisest course, but the Truth is I did not want to be Governor." He confirmed his action in letters to James Duncan in May and June. "I have, I think modestly, declined a canvass for Governor of Tennessee much against the wishes of my political friends. I am satisfied that I did right."[6]

Pillow seemed content enough to see his former subordinate, Col. William Trousdale, receive the gubernatorial nomination and go on to defeat Whig Neill S. Brown. Meanwhile, following Polk's death, Pillow and Aaron V. Brown grew closer each year as personal friends and political allies. Pillow lent him money, as he had Polk, and Brown kept Pillow closely informed about political and financial doings within the state and sought his advice in business dealings. Together, they offered financial and political support to E. G. Eastman, former editor of the Democratic Nashville *Union*, in his attempt to secure the ownership of the Nashville *American*.[7] In 1849 Pillow went north to secure $100,000 in venture capital, some to complete his obligations with the Duck River Company, but most to purchase still more slaves and Arkansas land. To help raise this capital he also sold lots in the town of Clifton, the terminus of the turnpike in Middle Tennessee he had helped construct in the early 1840s.[8]

National events, however, began to intrude on Pillow and Tennessee. Beginning with the Wilmot Proviso in 1846, the struggle over regulation of slavery in the territory acquired from Mexico heightened sectional tensions and seemed to defy solution. Slavery remained

Gov. Aaron Venable Brown
(courtesy Tennessee State Library and Archives)

an open wound for Americans, and by 1850 the nation had reached a crisis. In January Henry Clay came forward and offered his Omnibus Bill, a bundle of compromises, each strongly opposed by some interest and strongly supported by some other. In March a dying John C. Calhoun attacked Clay's attempt at compromise and warned that if the South did not receive justice she would leave the Union.[9]

Calhoun had recommended convening a southern convention. So

had other southern leaders, though many of them, like Beverley Tucker, were suspicious of Calhoun and "his perverse ingenuity."[10] It took a bipartisan convention in Mississippi in October 1849 to issue the call. Mississippi asked representatives of the southern states to meet in Nashville the following June. Nashville was selected because Tennessee, although excited and upset over interference with slavery in the territories, seemed to lack extreme southern views, and Governor Trousdale appeared receptive. Still, the Nashville Convention was a dangerous, radical undertaking in the eyes of many southerners. There was talk of constitutional change, disunion, a confederacy between southern states. It would "try the strength of the southern states to see what course they will have to pursue to save their slaves." Rumor had it in South Carolina that President Taylor would "send down the regular army on them" if they attempted to hold the meeting.[11]

Only nine southern states were represented in Nashville. Tennessee was wary about being included, indeed, about being the site of the meeting. Tennessee Whigs would have no part of the convention and boycotted it. Tennessee Democrats knew they must be careful. Of the 101 Tennessee delegates, half came from Maury and Davidson counties; only one was from East Tennessee.[12]

The delegates began to arrive in Nashville on June 2. Their numbers overwhelmed Odd Fellows Hall, so they adjourned to McKendree Methodist Church, which could accommodate 1,500. Aaron V. Brown opened the meeting on June 3, and the convention quickly organized itself, with Judge William L. Sharkey of Mississippi as chairman. Pillow served as chairman of the Tennessee delegation, chairman of the credentials committee, and chairman of the committee on elections. E. G. Eastman, Pillow's friend and editor of the Nashville *Union*, was secretary of the convention. Only delegates and women were admitted to the first floor; the pews on either side were reserved for the women, "like borders of flowers."[13]

One of these women, "a Yankee girl," a governess using the assumed name of Kate Conyngham, recorded her observations. Judge Sharkey, a "Jackson looking man," seemed impressive. Over in the Tennessee delegation, to the left of the pulpit, she noticed the bearded William H. Polk, brother of the former president, and General Pillow in his "military white vest"—the next governor of Tennessee, someone whispered. The general lives in "elegant and opulent retirement," they added. "He is in the prime of life," Conyngham declared, "decidedly a handsome man, with a marked military air. There is a smile in his eyes and which generally plays about his finely shaped firm mouth, that renders the expression of his countenance singularly pleasing. He looks like a gallant and chivalrous gentleman, and his speeches were all patriotic and to the point. This distinguished man has been called vain, because some suppose he wrote a self-commending account of the battle in which he fought so well." [14]

Nashville opened her doors to her visitors. "Brilliant parties" were the order every day and night. Perhaps the most splendid was the one given by Brown and Pillow. Pillow toasted his guests, remarking that in five days the hesitant Tennessee delegation had been "brought into line." [15] This, of course, was only talk. Pillow knew better.

The Tennessee delegation stood for conciliation, for compromise, and was determined to have a moderating effect on the Nashville Convention. Give Congress time, they argued. Let them act on the issues dividing the sections. Let this convention, demonstrating the influence of a South united, act as a lever to pry redress and justice from Washington. The leaders of the Tennessee Democracy—Brown, Nicholson, Pillow, and A. J. Donelson—worked for this throughout. Nevertheless, resolutions and speeches abounded—urging protection for southern rights, castigating abolitionists, and condemning northern attempts to seize the territory of Texas. All the while, "the galleries thundered applause, and the ladies smiled approbation."

Direction steadily emerged. On Monday, June 10, thirteen resolutions were adopted, and then an additional fifteen. Pillow took the lead in amending the address, written by R. B. Rhett and more radical in tone than the resolutions. He wanted the "sting and venom" removed; he wanted to delete that portion of the address attacking Clay's packet of compromises; he wanted "unanimity among all the southern states." His amendments to the address, though hotly debated, carried unanimously as the states voted on June 12, the last day of the convention. Some of the delegates, however, individually registered their opposition to the softened address.[16]

The Tennessee delegates seemed pleased with themselves. They had fought for flexibility and virtually alone advocated acquiescence in the decisions of Congress. "Fire and brimstone" had not prevailed. There had been no ultimatum regarding the Missouri Compromise line, as some had feared, only a recommendation that it be extended to the Pacific. The convention was not, certainly, a disunionist assembly, yet it was hardly a satisfactory undertaking. Its outcome, a proposal which in effect went back to the 36°30′ line, was "impractical and its constitutionality was questionable." Ironically, Tennessee, led by Pillow, in its successful amending of Rhett's address and subsequent support of it, had contorted itself into an unintended alliance with the "hotspurs against Clay's compromise."[17]

But no explosion had occurred. June and July 1850 saw great excitement in some areas of the South. President Taylor died in July. What would the South do? Choose the 36°30′ line proposed by the Nashville Convention or accept compromise measures if and when they were passed by Congress? Pillow wanted the solution to be the extension of the Missouri Compromise line, but he accepted political reality and believed that the South's best hope lay in the responsible cooperation of the northern wing of the Democratic party. With their help, he wrote Cushing, "we should have all the distracting questions now agitating the public mind, and distracting the deliberations of Congress settled *fairly & honourably* to both sections of the country." Pillow stayed informed about political conditions in the North, and he kept in touch with his many northern friends. As ever, he worked hard to keep the national Democracy vibrant.[18]

The second act of the Nashville Convention occurred November 11, 1850. Clay's conciliatory acts, collectively labeled the Compromise of 1850, had been passed by Congress, but the recommendations of the June Nashville Convention had not been accepted. Dissatisfied southerners felt the convention should be reconvened. The overwhelming majority of Tennesseans, on the other hand, felt accounts had been squared and rejoiced in the Compromise of 1850. Many felt a second session of the Nashville Convention not only was unnecessary, but might be viewed nationally as an act of bad faith.[19] Thus when the convention reassembled in Nashville in November, Tennesseans gave it "the cold shoulder." There were no receptions, no elegant dinner parties. Indeed, many Democrats had thought of not participating at all. It seems, however, that Pillow influenced them to attend. But instead of 100 delegates, Tennessee would provide only fourteen, all from Maury and Davidson counties.[20]

The convention met this time in the smaller Christian Church. Any church would have been large enough for the fifty-seven delegates, however. To critics—to Whigs—it seemed the convention was composed "of fire and water, out and out secessionists."[21] The convention, reduced in number of states represented as well as participants, was called to order by Pillow. He again would serve as the head of Tennessee's delegation and chair the credentials committee.[22] Now, however, the delegates were in no mood for Tennessee's gestures of compromise and conciliation. Hard, frightening declarations immediately boiled over from the resolutions committee. They spoke openly of state sovereignty, resistance, economic warfare, and secession. The Tennessee delegates caucused at J. J. B. Southall's office and designated Brown and Nicholson to draw up a set of their own resolutions, which were adopted by the group two days later. Pillow, as chairman, would present them.[23]

The Tennessee resolutions contrasted sharply with the radical resolutions being presented, a number of which supported the proposal by South Carolina's Langdon Cheves for immediate secession. Tennessee would accept the Compromise of 1850, although acknowledging that it failed to meet the needs of the South completely. The North must live up to her part of the agreement and faithfully and fully carry out her obligations; otherwise, the South "should boycott the North commercially." If Congress itself failed to comply with the compromise and passed measures conflicting with it, another convention should be held with delegates authorized by their respective states to take whatever action necessary to protect the interests and rights of the South. The Compromise of 1850 should be regarded as final. "The resolutions of the other states look to secession and the ultimate dissolution of the Union," wrote Eastman of the *Union*. "The Tennessee resolutions are for the perpetuity of the Union."[24]

The Tennessee resolutions failed, however. The convention received them in a hostile mood. Tennessee spokesmen Brown and Nicholson were denied the floor. When A. J. Donelson attempted to speak for the resolutions and for moderation, he too was silenced by parliamentary tactic, infuriating the packed galleries, and the convention ended in pandemonium.[25] The Tennessee resolutions, nevertheless, were printed and widely circulated. They apparently had substantial influence, representing a responsible, moderate southern voice. Brown and Nicholson also had the speeches they intended to deliver printed and distributed.[26] Pillow's Tennessee delegation found themselves isolated, voting against the final report of the resolutions committee. Tennessee Democrats wondered why they had become involved in the first place and regretted the damage done the party. Even the Nashville *Union* limply admitted the convention "to have been a complete failure."[27]

Afterward the Whig press joyfully lambasted the whole affair. Its "failure," remarked the Memphis *Daily Eagle*, "would weaken the cause of the South by creating an appearance of conflict and dissension." Parson William G. Brownlow scorned Pillow, Brown, and the Democrats for hypocrisy: "They went into this second edition of the

Hartford Convention, knowing what its objects were. They knew, as did the whole country, that they must be there to resolve themselves out of the Union and to rebel against the General Government."[28]

Pillow and Aaron V. Brown might argue that their participation frustrated the ambitions of the southern extremists and perhaps averted secession. It remains true, however, that they unwittingly identified themselves with the Beverley Tuckers, defending slavery, aristocratic government, and disunion. They played into the hands of the Whigs, who would win victories in Tennessee in 1851 and 1852, and they played into the hands of Andrew Johnson, the dissident Democrat.

Gideon Pillow probably intended to enhance his national image by actively participating in both Nashville conventions. His voice was one of moderation. He spoke for the Union, for patriotism, and, like the devoted Jacksonian that he was, he fought all attempts to promote the idea of secession. On the other hand, he recognized the threat to the institution of slavery and displayed a distinct prosouthern spirit. In this he reflected Tennessee, caught in the middle—Unionist at heart, but troubled deeply by "Northern encroachment."

In the summer of 1851 Gideon Pillow took a rather unusual vacation. He went east, in the company of fellow Democrats Jefferson Davis, John A. Quitman, and Thomas L. Clingman of North Carolina. They traveled to Boston, where they met their Mexican War comrade Caleb Cushing. Talks began in a promising manner, so Cushing invited his southern friends home to Newburyport, close to the New Hampshire border, and sent word to Franklin Pierce over in Concord to join them. After a few days as Cushing's guests at Newburyport, the five men journeyed on together, sampling a string of New England mountain and beach resorts, talking politics all the while. They ended their holiday with a week together at Little Boar's Head, New Hampshire, where Pierce had a summer place on the ocean. Here they separated, but only to come together again in October 1851 in Concord, at the close of the vacation season. They had agreed, it appears, to work together in the nomination process in 1852, although they seem not to have decided on any candidate. They also shared the conviction that the Democracy should avoid identification or involvement with the Free Soil movement. Their candidate would be a man who would "support the Compromise of 1850 and the preservation of the Union."[29]

While Pillow enjoyed the luxury of New England's favorite watering places, things were not going well at home. The summer of 1851 brought defeat after defeat to the Democracy in Tennessee. Prospects looked so gloomy that the party was actually drawn closer together. A. O. P. Nicholson reported to John P. Heiss, "We are in better tune for making good democratic music than we have been for many years."[30] Lewis Cass looked fine as a national candidate for 1852, but so did Stephen A. Douglas, James Buchanan, and William L. Marcy. Even Sam Houston should not be ignored, for some knowledgeable Democrats thought he well might carry Tennessee. The "indifference" over whom to support for vice-president in 1852 seemed to be fading. Now that Whigs talked of Winfield Scott for president, Tennesseans began to talk of Gideon Pillow almost as a reflex. "I returned home from Nashville yesterday," Nicholson continued, "and after mingling for a week with the democratic members of the Legislature I became thoroughly satisfied that the vote of the state will be given to Pillow for Vice President in the Baltimore Convention."[31]

Pillow had lobbied hard for nomination by the Tennessee Democracy. Aaron V. Brown and Knox Walker promoted him actively and effectively in Nashville; West Humphreys also helped. Pillow wanted to re-create the conditions that had led to Polk's nomination in 1844— only this time he would be the principal player. His first goal would be to gain control of the state Democratic convention and have Tennessee nominate him for the vice-presidency. This would give him a base which he could seek to enlarge. As insurance he would seek the nomination of the Democracy in Arkansas as well. He had spent time cultivating Democrats there and believed he could count on their support. He would begin a public relations campaign, particularly in the newspapers, presenting a favorable image of himself and his career. If all went well, this bloc of Arkansas and Tennessee convention votes would give him strong leverage in Baltimore in June 1852.

Pillow initially linked his candidacy to that of Stephen A. Douglas of Illinois, advocate of sectional compromise, who led the "Young America" wing of the Democracy. This tactical move seemed to project the Jacksonian nationalistic posture Pillow had taken at the Nashville Convention, underlining his willingness to compromise, to put party and nation above narrow sectional concerns. The Douglas-Pillow alliance, of which little is known, was an obvious political convenience for both candidates. It backfired for Pillow, however, because it frustrated the work of politically powerful Cave Johnson, Buchanan's longtime Tennessee ally.[32]

When the Tennessee Democratic convention opened in January

1852, it was primarily Cave Johnson who prompted Alfred Balch to put forward the name of William Trousdale for vice-president "for Buchanan's benefit by killing off Pillow who wanted to unite with Douglas and create strife in Tennessee." Governor Trousdale was popular, a serious and most unwelcome threat to Pillow's hopes. Trousdale may have cared "not a straw about a nomination," but his entry split the Democracy. A. O. P. Nicholson also appears to have been interested in the nomination, and he and his friend Andrew Johnson joined in against Pillow. After a hard struggle in the state convention, Nicholson lost out, while the Pillow and Trousdale forces reached an unsatisfactory compromise. Both were deemed "suitable" for the vice-presidency. Once again, as in the days of Polk, Tennessee's delegation would go to Baltimore in June 1852 uninstructed. A disappointed Pillow appears to have reacted to defeat by breaking or loosening ties between himself and Douglas.[33]

Pillow should not have been surprised. As Polk had found, winning the nomination of the Tennessee Democracy could be more difficult than winning nomination by the national party. But Pillow was prepared to try. He was not discouraged; he wanted Winfield Scott defeated. Perhaps that was his primary objective all along, but he also intended to hold national office himself, and he believed he knew how to achieve both objectives, Tennessee notwithstanding.[34] He felt that 1852 would be his opportunity. Scott was thought to be the Whigs' best prospect, but Whigs seemed nervous with their tarnished war hero. William B. Campbell acknowledged that Tennessee Whigs did not want Scott. But loyal to the end, Campbell expected "to go to the devil with the Whigs."[35] Pillow welcomed the chance to compete against Scott. He had defeated him soundly at Frederick, Maryland; the second time would be easy. "I would be willing to be a *slave* & work in the *mines* of Mexico, the ballance of my life, for the pleasure of *beating him*." First, however, Pillow must secure the nomination. If Tennessee could not provide the springboard, he knew where to turn.[36]

In April 1852, Pillow journeyed to Washington, D.C., ostensibly to vacation again. He had laid the groundwork for his trip, corresponding with his court of inquiry friend, Caleb Cushing. He suggested that they might travel together to New England, "presumably to organize the Mexican War officers in support of a ticket of Pillow and Pierce or vice versa." Cushing met Pillow in Washington and they talked. Cushing had with him another New England Democratic politician, Edmund Burke of New Hampshire. Pillow knew Burke from Polk administration days, and Pillow, who closely followed Burke's work with

Gov. William Trousdale
(courtesy Tennessee State Library and Archives)

the Washington *Union*, respected him as an able newspaperman and
political strategist. Burke and Cushing proposed that they unite to
advance the political fortunes of Franklin Pierce, Pillow's comrade of
Contreras and the City of Mexico. Talk soon turned to a Pierce-Pillow
or Pillow-Pierce ticket. Pillow found all this quite heady.[37]

After a letter from Pierce arrived on April 13, stating he would place himself "in the hands of his friends," the issue was settled. Burke, Cushing, and Pillow set to work to gather support. Cushing and Pillow left Washington and proceeded to New York City, where they held encouraging talks with Marcy representatives.[38] They met Gov. Thomas L. Seymour in Connecticut and talked of Mexico, the glories of the 9th Infantry, and national politics. Then they continued on to Boston, where Gov. George S. Boutwell received them. They revealed to Boutwell not only the plan to nominate Pierce, but a grandiose aspiration: a blueprint for control of the national Democracy! Pillow eloquently outlined it for Boutwell, but it probably was the brainchild of Cushing and the Mexican War generals who vacationed together in 1851. There would be a national steering committee, "self-constituted." On the state level, there would be assistants, few in number, who would supervise the work of "confidential agents in the counties, cities and large towns." By use of this network and the coordination of "other expedient means" (newspapers), party nominations and policy could be controlled at the state and national level. The Democracy's presidential candidates, in effect, would be decided by the steering committee. Boutwell listened carefully but wanted no part of the scheme.[39]

Others, however, including Benjamin F. Butler of Massachusetts, Charles G. Atherton of New Hampshire, and Sen. James W. Bradbury of Maine, gave Cushing and Pillow their support, if not for visionary grand strategy, then for the candidacy of Franklin Pierce. So Pillow and Cushing went on to Concord, New Hampshire, where their friend Pierce received them on April 30. During a reception in their honor they took Pierce aside, reported what they had accomplished, and told him of the enthusiasm of their Mexican War comrades. Pierce heard them out and rather passively assented. Their mission was no secret by now, and the good citizens of Concord at the reception were most interested by the whole affair, though according to one observer, Paul R. George, they warmed more easily to Cushing than to the smooth Tennessean.[40]

After spending the night with Pierce, Pillow and Cushing left Concord and set out for Cushing's home in Newburyport, where Pillow remained for a few days outlining strategy with his host. They envisioned a deadlock in the convention. They and their allies would encourage division by working initially for Marcy, Cass, or Buchanan. They would attempt to secure a simple majority for this or that candidate, but never enough to carry him to the necessary two-thirds. As the convention tired and wilted in the heat, they would bring forward Pierce's name and carry the day, just as with Polk in 1844.[41]

For Pillow, politics and business were inseparable, the best political cement, so amid these strategy sessions he and Cushing worked out a land deal. Cushing would arrange the funding, Pierce would serve as agent for the owner, and Pillow would guide the transaction. Pillow left Cushing in Newburyport early in May 1852 and went back to Washington, where he remained almost a month as the guest of his old friend Knox Walker. En route he appears to have dropped off in New York a lengthy, flattering, and timely biographical sketch of himself which appeared in the *New York Herald* on May 8, 1852. As might have been expected, Pillow's Mexican War service was inflated and Scott's flattened.[42] From Washington Pillow made one trip to Philadelphia to visit Cadwalader and while in the city made a point to emphasize that the two-thirds rule, the basis of all their planning, must be enforced in the coming Democratic convention.

Having laid the groundwork for an exciting convention in Baltimore, Pillow waited in Washington with Knox Walker, lobbying for Pierce among the gathering delegates. He was in high spirits. The plan of the Mexican War generals had gone well to this point. The newspapers all but ignored the Pierce-Pillow ticket; attention was focused on the front-runners, just as Pillow had hoped.[43]

When Pillow arrived in Baltimore, he may have been struck by the similarities with the convention of 1844. Delegates were crowded into hot, stuffy hotels. Great buffets of food were available, but the quantities of liquor attracted more attention. The convention was a scramble of noise and chaos, while wonderful intrigues and counterplots went on without end.

Benjamin F. Hallett of Massachusetts, chairman of the Democratic National Committee, called the convention to order at noon on Monday, June 1, 1852. That day and Tuesday were spent in organization. Members of the Pierce-Pillow group were strategically placed—Cushing on the committee to nominate convention officers, Burke chairman of the credentials committee, and Aaron V. Brown chairman of the platform committee. An early attempt to dispense with the crucial two-thirds rule was easily defeated. With 288 official delegates, the magic number for nomination became 192.[44] Brown played an important role in shaping the platform, which emphasized states' rights and supported the Compromise of 1850. Cushing and Burke kept buttonholing delegates. Things seemed to be going very well.[45]

Nomination for president began on Wednesday morning. During

the first eight ballots, Cass jumped to an early lead with 119 votes, which he never exceeded. Buchanan peaked at 95, and Douglas remained in the 20–34 range, followed by Marcy with 23 votes. The Massachusetts and New Hampshire votes fragmented according to plan. On the first ballot, the Massachusetts votes were scattered: nine for Cass, two for Marcy, one for Douglas, and one for Sam Houston. During the day Cushing visited Henry A. Wise, a key member of the Virginia delegation, and implanted the idea that Pierce should and would be brought forward. Would Virginia do its part?[46]

More balloting on Wednesday produced little change. On Thursday Cass began to slip, Buchanan remained steady, and young Stephen Douglas came on with his spurt, gathering 51 votes. Buchanan made his move on Friday, reaching 104 on the twenty-second ballot. The Marcy forces refused to join the Buchanan rush, however, effectively containing him in the afternoon ballots. Cass came on again, rising to 123, but that was all.[47]

The moment of crisis predicted by the Pierce managers had arrived. On Friday evening, the delegates of six important Buchanan states caucused. Henry Wise brought forward a proposition to the exhausted delegations of Pennsylvania, Virginia, North Carolina, Alabama, Mississippi, and Georgia. He suggested that they experiment with some fresh choices—Pierce, Marcy, and Butler. Cushing's hand is evident in the all-important order of these names.[48]

The plan of Cushing and Burke and Pillow could have gone up in smoke, however, when the balloting resumed. The Virginia delegation, despite Wise's proposal, decided to cast their votes for native son, former senator Daniel S. Dickinson. This unexpected entrance of a new name at such a critical moment could have preempted the introduction of Pierce's name. Dickinson, however, declined the nomination in deference to Cass, and the crisis passed. Cass peaked on the thirty-fifth ballot, and the Pierce steamroller began with fifteen votes from Virginia. The thirty-sixth ballot brought forth most of the hard-core Pierce votes—eight from Maine, two from Tennessee, and five from New Hampshire. Cushing withheld the Massachusetts ballots from Pierce, waiting for the breakthrough. On Saturday morning, the end came on the forty-ninth ballot when Pennsylvania shifted to Pierce. By the end of the tally, Pierce had 282 out of 288 votes and the nomination.[49]

When the convention reconvened that afternoon to nominate the vice-presidential candidate, Pillow received a shock. Political expediency ruled the day as the Cushing-Burke team showed themselves perfectly willing to dump him and nominate Sen. William R. King of Alabama.[50] Burke explained the shift in a letter to Pierce on June 6. "I think we are right in picking King as Vice President. You know he is Buchanan's bosom friend, and a great and powerful architect of conciliation. . . . If Scott is nominated, his great battle probably will be in New York and Pennsylvania. These choice states will fall into our cap like ripe apples." Pierce-Buchanan unity in preparation for the November election was clearly the predominant factor. Burke and Cushing undoubtedly were also grateful for the Buchanan support that had carried Pierce to victory.[51]

Pillow managed to ripple the waters of the convention, gathering twenty-five votes for vice-president on the first ballot—all of Tennessee's, those of faithful Arkansas, and nine from New York and Illinois—but the effort was doomed. He had been dumped. He rationalized: "As Pierce went *up*, I, of course, went *down*. The Politicians would not, of course, submit to a ticket *wholly military*." Saucy as ever, Pillow told his friend Pierce, immediately after his nomination, that "if you had not received the nomination, I should have received the nomination for the V-P-y, by a ⅔ vote, upon the first ballot. I am however content, as my past life proves, that I have no love for place and that my love of the Democracy & its principles does not find its origin [in] a love of office." Pillow told Cushing that he was "well pleased" with Pierce's nomination, "& I am therefore satisfied in the certain prospect of Defeating Scott & the Whig Party." A disgruntled and eternally suspicious Andrew Johnson believed Sam Houston still could have been nominated for president if it had not been for "Genl. Pillow and Aron [sic]" and their ambitions for the vice-presidency. "A Tennessee man could have been put upon the ticket for the V. P. if our delegation had been disposed to have cut loose from Pillow."[52]

Loyal Democrat to the end, Pillow worked hard for Pierce in Tennessee during the summer and early fall of 1852. He wrote a flattering "Opinion of Franklin Pierce" and had it run in the Nashville *Union* in July. Another letter in support of Pierce was republished by the entire Democratic press. Writing to a New England friend, Pillow hoped his letter "meets with the approval of my friends of the Ninth." He urged Maine to join Massachusetts in solid support of Pierce. "She must not prove a *defaulter*, when one of New England's gallant sons are before the nation. . . . I have never seen the defection from the Whig Party so great as it is now." Pillow's Mexican War staff officer, Theodore O'Hara, now editor of the Louisville *Times*, joined in the attacks, scoring Scott as "no friend" to the Catholic church or the Irish.[53]

Pillow took great pleasure at Scott's defeat in the November elections. Pierce demolished Scott in the electoral vote, 254 to 42. Tennessee's Democracy had rallied behind Pierce, but once again it was not enough. The Tennessee electorate "defaulted," going Whig as they had since Andrew Jackson left office.

Following Pierce's triumph, Pillow's New England associates seemed to have forgotten him. He was not offered a cabinet position or a diplomatic post, although brother-in-law West Humphreys did receive appointment as federal judge for the West Tennessee District. Pillow had pushed hard for Humphrey's appointment. He wrote the president in support of other individuals, but with Scott defeated he seemed content, for the moment at least, to mind his farming interests. January 1853 found Pillow "at home, quietly seeing after his wife—his children—his mules & his cotton bales. 'Biding his time' & not wanting any office under the administration & so I think Pierce understands it."[54]

For the next few years Pillow managed to keep in the public eye, although concentrating his energies on private affairs. In September 1853, Democrats held a dinner in Washington honoring him and Tennessee congressman Fred P. Stanton. Pillow addressed his friends on the subject of Cuba, the "weeping child of the seas." He strongly urged annexation by force, expressing the fear that Spain might follow the example of England and free the slaves.[55] A. O. P. Nicholson, who was in the audience along with Maj. J. D. B. DeBow and Cushing, confided to Cushing that Pillow seemed to be identifying himself with "the States Rights wing of the party." It seems that about this time Pillow's friendship and partnership with Isham G. Harris began. This young West Tennessee congressman already was noted for his strict constructionist views.[56]

Pillow interested himself in his alma mater, the University of Nashville. In April 1855, an agreement was reached whereby Western Military Institute of Georgetown, Kentucky, would move to Nashville and become the collegiate department of the university. With the merger would come WMI's northern, antislavery superintendent and professor of civil engineering, Col. Bushrod Johnson. Pillow, as a trustee of the university, heartily supported the merger and helped raise money for the venture. He enrolled his second son, George M., and his nephew and ward, John E. Saunders. The reinvigorated university proved a great success, and the trustees insisted on a military orien-

Alfred O. P. Nicholson
(Tennessee State Library and Archives)

tation. West Point–style uniforms gave evidence of budding southern
nationalism.

Pillow spoke to the university's literary societies in June 1856. His
speech, typical Gideon Pillow, displayed the civilian patriot militant.
"No matter what your country's cause or quarrel, it is enough for the
patriot to know she is in a war. Be her cause right or wrong, it is your

Making Good Democratic Music : **139**

duty to espouse it, and if she calls on you to command her armies, to lead them to victory or to death." He continued on, warning the students about the evil of drink, pleading with them not to become "educated drunkards" who "spend their days and nights in Bacchanalian orgies, in blasphemous revelry, and in a wild delirium of lust." Despite the heavy-handed moralizing, the students loved the speech and had it printed at their expense.[57]

When the Kansas question crashed upon the national scene in the mid-1850s, Pillow became involved. He shared the platform with Barclay Martin, Washington C. Whitthorne, and Randal McGavock, pleading for good sense to triumph.[58] Emotions ran high. Pillow and his old associate, Maj. Andrew J. Donelson, clashed at a political rally in Columbia in July 1855. Donelson charged that the members of the Nashville Convention were traitors to the United States. A disgraceful scene then occurred where Pillow cracked Donelson over the head with his cane. After subduing his opponent physically, Pillow "finished his remarks, which were followed by deafening applause."[59]

Pillow also served as a delegate to the middle division of the state fair representing Maury County, and he spoke to the people of Maury in terms of economic nationalism: "Let the people of Tennessee change their system—resuscitate their lands—adopt labor-saving machinery—build up manufacturing. . . . The impulses of self-interest should prompt this course; but the instincts of self-preservation may soon demand it."[60]

8   Palace of Fire

Pillow involved himself more and more in the life and politics of Arkansas. As a conduit to the Pierce administration, he was appealed to by Democrats across the state for endorsements. He appeared at Democratic rallies in eastern Arkansas, often on the platform in Helena with Jacob Thompson and Gov. Joseph Mathews of Mississippi, J. R. McClanahan, editor of the Memphis *Daily Appeal*, Sen. William K. Sebastian of Arkansas, and two younger political aspirants, Thomas C. Hindman and Patrick R. Cleburne. Indeed, Cleburne credited Pillow with having intervened at his request in a threatened duel between Hindman and a Whig lawyer. Pillow left his

Mound Plantation, came into Helena and managed to "have the duel called off without damage to the honor of either lawyer."[1]

Pillow owned a small empire in eastern Arkansas, primarily five plantations in Phillips County, with smaller holdings to the southwest in Drew County. In St. Francis County he had "three unimproved tracts," mostly swamp land that yielded great quantities of choice, marketable cypress. He had begun purchasing Arkansas land about 1840, and following his return from Mexico, he and his brother Jerome continued to invest heavily there. Pillow himself liked Arkansas and believed in its future. During the 1850s he spent three or four months a year in the state. All the while he continued to buy more land and slaves. He wrote George Cadwalader in 1855, "My plantations in Arkansas . . . at fair market prices, would be estimated at about $500,000."[2]

As in Maury, intervention by state government greatly aided Pillow's efforts. Beginning in 1849, federal enactments gave Arkansas over eight million acres of swamp and overflow land near the Mississippi to assist the state in the development of its resources. The sale of this land supplied Arkansas with money which it used to issue scrip for the construction of levees. Pillow benefited from these laws, as did railroad companies, using these inducements to acquire land. He himself spent thousands of dollars building miles of levees which, of course, enhanced the value of Mound Plantation on the St. Francis River and his other holdings acquired under the Swamp Lands Acts.[3]

By 1855 Pillow owned 3,825 acres and 120 slaves in Phillips County alone. Most of his land was in cotton, although he had fields of corn and orchards and perhaps had planted some rice. Boom times continued as cotton prices surged in the late 1850s. Phillips had become the leading slave county in Arkansas; more slaves lived in the county than whites. Slave owners prospered enormously as their slaves and land rapidly increased in value. Four years later, in 1859, the year of the bumper cotton crop, Pillow owned 6,788 acres in Phillips, with 160 slaves assessed for tax purposes at $750 each. By 1860 the number of slaves had grown to 221. It has been estimated that Pillow spent $18,900 during this period to purchase new slaves for Mound Plantation—a sizable outlay for the time. By late 1860 Pillow was buying slaves in great numbers. In December of that year he purchased eighty-five slaves from John A. Pointer in Tennessee for $109,200. They were to be taken to his plantations in Arkansas.[4] Even before purchasing these slaves from Pointer, however, Pillow was becoming conspicuous for the number of slaves he owned. In his study of the slaveholding elite, historian William K. Scarborough finds that Pillow in 1860 ranks third among the slaveholders of Tennessee and was the sixth largest slaveholder in Arkansas.[5]

A visitor to Mound Plantation in the spring of 1857 found the overseer to be very pleasant; 450 acres of cotton were under cultivation, as well as much corn. "The plantation seemed to be very well ordered and is supplied with all the modern conveniences. There is a sewing-machine for making up the clothing for the hands, which a negress was using." In contrast with Clifton, however, one might have remarked critically about overcrowding in the slave cabins. Pillow housed 139 slaves in sixteen cabins in 1857; at over eight slaves to a cabin, this was well above the slave housing average for Arkansas of 5.72 and for the South as a whole in 1860 of 5.2.[6]

Pillow kept raising capital. On his yearly trips east he seems to have been constantly hunting backers. He sought loans from wealthy friends like Cadwalader. One endorser wrote a potential investor that Pillow had an "untarnished name" financially. "The property he holds wholly unencumbered could not upon any fair valuation, be estimated as worth less than a million of dollars. He is one of those men that in general estimation never touches anything without turning it to gold." Aaron V. Brown wrote Caleb Cushing in 1859 that Pillow was heading to New England looking for a loan of $100,000–$200,000 after his usual stops in Washington and Philadelphia:

> Few men can be found so punctual in meeting his arrangements & still fewer whose property could be more readily cashed. . . .
>
> On & near the Mississippi river in the county of Phillips near Helena . . . , he has three of the best organized plantations I ever saw. They are already in a high state of cultivation, with every year large accessions to the improvements. In the three tracts there are something more than 4,000 acres of deep rich alluvial soil, now worth forty dollars per acre. On these lands he is working about 200 effective hands, which with the smaller negroes about 50 in number worth about 240 or $250,000. Besides these, he is the owner of some seven or eight thousand acres of river land, lying some 15 or 20 miles from his plantation which are already valuable & must very soon be saleable at from 10 to $20 or more per acre. . . .
>
> He has lately purchased some hundred & fifty or sixty thousand acres more of Mississippi River land, which I think has given rise to the wish to make this negotiation for money.[7]

Clifton was home, however, despite Pillow's growing interest in Mound Plantation and his rapidly increasing Arkansas holdings. "I am staying at home," he wrote to Reynolds in 1853, "attending to my own *little Patriarchal Government*. Above all else, I did not wish to be *mixed up* in the *stew* at Washington. If I have done nothing to be remembered by the country, I am content to be forgotten."[8] Aaron V. Brown described Clifton as having about 700 acres "elegantly improved & in a State of high cultivation & could command at least $50,000. On this place there are between 80 & 90 negroes, remarkably likely and healthy which are worth from sixty five to seventy thousand dollars."[9]

Pillow had built model slave quarters. He selected a ridge several hundred yards from the main house. The cabins were usually sixteen by twenty feet and housed one family. They were spaced fifty yards apart for privacy and sanitation and were raised two feet from the ground for ventilation. Brick chimneys and large fireplaces provided adequate warmth. The cabins were described as "neat but not costly." Pillow provided bedding and plenty of blankets in winter. For clothing, male slaves received two cotton suits for spring and summer, two wool suits for winter, four pairs of shoes, and three hats. The food ration, given out on a certain designated evening, for each male slave, was five pounds of bacon, one quart of molasses, and a supply of bread, coffee, and sugar. The slaves were encouraged to use liberal amounts of red pepper in their food, supposedly to stimulate the system and prevent illness.[10]

The value of Pillow's Tennessee real estate and personal property increased dramatically in the 1850s. The 1860 tax list for Maury County sets his real estate value at $571,000 and his personal property worth at $500,000. When compared with what Pillow owned in 1837—four slaves, thirty acres, six town lots, and one carriage—his accumulation of wealth is striking.[11]

One day a Maury constable, R. C. Wells, passed by Clifton on the turnpike. Pillow rode out on a "fine horse, gayly caparisoned," and asked the constable if he were related to Capt. Thomas Wells. "Yes, sir, he is my father." "Glad to make your acquaintance," Pillow replied. "I am acquainted with your father. He was a captain in the army that was with Gen. Jackson in the Creek war and the battle of New Orleans and besides, sir, your father is a good democrat." Nothing would do but Wells must stay for dinner at Clifton. He first declined, but when Pillow insisted, Wells agreed.

Clifton Place
(courtesy John R. Neal)

His horse was taken, stabled and fed, he was ushered into the house, his hat taken off and hung on the rack, escorted into the parlor— well furnished with settees, divans and sofas and mirrors . . . that made him feel that he was in a charmed palace. . . . He was then invited to have a wash; when the water was poured into silver pans on wash stands of marble and towels of bright linen hung on rollers of gold and yet being abashed he would take hold the wrong way and before a mirror of polished steel he combed his hair with an ivory comb which made him feel he was committing a trespass and into the dining room he was ushered. . . .

He managed to get through and as the General sat back waiting on the rest of the family, he sat back. The General picked up a knife and a fork that had a spring tooth pick attached and touching the spring the pick was ready for use. He . . . thought he would try it and . . . he cut his mouth. He got through, however, and before he left the General invited him in to take a drink. He went to the sideboard and in turning up the decanter he caught a view of himself in one of those distorting mirrors. . . . All seemed topsyturvy. . . .

After a while he was ready to go and being at a big man's house, he thought he would be a big man too and gave the negro boy 50 cents for holding his horse, all the money he had made that day as constable and had no money left to pay his pikage home.[12]

Gideon Pillow was more than a rich man living in a grand Greek Revival manor house. He was a splendid, progressive farmer. In this sector of his life he invariably excelled. He understood and advocated crop rotation, yet he knew rotation itself was not enough; he urged other farmers to use the discoveries of science to increase crop yield, all the while "preserving and enriching their soil." He would speak at length of agricultural chemistry, of nitrogen and magnesia and alkaline bases. He read agricultural periodicals avidly and corresponded with men like J. D. B. DeBow and Felix Zollicoffer about farming practices across the South and in Maryland and New Jersey. He experimented with different types of fertilizers to renew "the power of the soil."

He advocated, rather ironically, that Tennesseans abandon their dependence upon cotton production. "The staple products of Middle Tennessee should be corn, wheat, oats grass and live stock. . . . Let the people of Tennessee change their system—resuscitate their lands—adopt labor saving machinery—build up manufactures, and apply thereto our fine water power, and, with their surplus labor, manufacture their own clothing and implements of husbandry; let them extend their railroad system and develop their mineral resources. . . . Push forward with energy and courage."[13]

Pillow seems to have been flexible enough, and farsighted enough, to have seen the advantage of railroads. He believed they offered more reliable and efficient means of communication and distribution, and he used his influence to redirect the energy and capital invested in his Duck River improvement project into backing efforts to hurry construction of the Mobile and Ohio railway. He was happy to promote rail construction in Tennessee and across the South and favored government subsidies and inducements to speed their growth.[14]

He imported the finest stock he could purchase in Europe and developed prize-winning herds. His Ayrshire cattle were celebrated, and he not only had the finest mules in Maury, but he had twice as many as any other farmer. In 1860 he raised 12,500 bushels of Indian corn, 40 tons of hay, and 500 bushels of sweet potatoes at Clifton. He produced crops of rye, wheat, oats, peas, orchard products, clover, and grass seed. From Clifton's dairy came 3,650 pounds of butter.[15]

Gideon Johnson Pillow, about 1855

(courtesy National Archives)

Jefferson would have appreciated Pillow's love of the land and his restless search to reconcile common agricultural practices with the "truths of nature." Yet it must be borne in mind that although Pillow used Jeffersonian rhetoric regarding farming—"hardy sons of the soil," "dignified and ennobling pursuit of those who cultivate the earth"—he was a nineteenth-century entrepreneur at heart, progressive no doubt, but just as interested in the mechanic as the husbandman. He was enraptured with inventions and contraptions and advocated the development of natural resources for the benefit of industry. Pillow wanted Tennessee to have a diversified economy like the state of Pennsylvania he so admired. Let loose of cotton and raise cattle and grain. Remain a land of gracious farms, surely, but married to manufacturing—a land of machine shops and mines and textiles and railroads. He challenged his fellow Tennesseans to make greater use of steam power and to explore ways to harness the miracle of electricity. Furthermore, palatial Clifton with its silver doorknobs and carefully selected eastern wallpaper notwithstanding, Pillow appears to have had little interest in objects of beauty; aesthetics simply did not concern him. Ultimately, Gideon Pillow was no Jeffersonian.[16]

Andrew Johnson was sure Pillow or Aaron V. Brown, or both, wanted the vice-presidency in 1856. To Johnson it appeared likely they might abandon Franklin Pierce, and perhaps join forces with Cave Johnson in support of James Buchanan. Johnson seems to have misread Pillow's intent, however. Pillow was interested in this presidential election, but not to the extent nor with the same spirit as before. He appears to have been working for Brown rather than himself, and in March 1856, after the state convention failed once again to agree upon a candidate, Pillow left Tennessee for Arkansas to tend to business affairs. He thought this year it might be interesting to participate in the Arkansas state convention being held in Little Rock in May. He believed he would skip the Democratic national convention in Cincinnati; it appeared the Democracy would be deadlocked again, and he had played that game too often. He also knew that Brown, still peeved over being ignored for a cabinet position by Pierce, might throw his support to Buchanan. Pillow, though invariably sympathetic to Brown, disagreed privately, believing Tennessee and the South should remain behind Pierce. "His Administration has been *eminently Democratic & Patriotic.*"[17]

So in 1856 Pillow remained on the sidelines while Aaron V. Brown worked hard for Buchanan. Brown was rewarded this time, however, and went to Washington in 1857 as postmaster general. He filled that post capably while his wife, Cynthia, and stepdaughter, Narcissa Pillow Saunders, became vital to the administration's social scene. His family's success and obvious enjoyment of Washington seemed to have whetted Pillow's political appetite once again. In the summer of 1857, Pillow set out to make himself attractive to Tennesseans as a candidate for the Senate that fall.

The timing seemed right. Both of Tennessee's senators in 1857, "Lean Jimmy" Jones and John Bell, Whigs or former Whigs, were finished politically in the state and would be relinquishing their seats. Andrew Johnson looked very strong, despite his antagonism toward the "Pillow and Brown regency" and Cave Johnson, not to speak of his old quarrels with James K. Polk. Johnson received the endorsement of the Nashville *Union* in February 1857, and when the Tennessee Democracy met in convention that April they complimented Johnson's work as governor, deeming him "entitled to the thanks of the people of the state." Johnson wanted to go to Washington as senator, and he began a campaign to that effect, "a tactic unique to Tennessee Senate seat battles." Popular among the people, especially the small farmers of East Tennessee, Johnson struck at the patronizing Middle Tennessee Democrats. "Brown, Pillow and Humphreys Seem to think they are the State and there Can be nothing done unless they are in it somewhere. As to their democracy their [*sic*] is no reliance to be placed in it further than it promotes there [*sic*] interest." [18]

Smashing Democratic victories in August 1857 brought Isham G. Harris to the governor's chair in Tennessee and further boosted Andrew Johnson's chances for the Senate. Pillow set to work. He conceded Johnson might take one Senate seat, but there were two up for grabs. So he began writing letters to friends and articles to the press. His "Address to the People of Tennessee," published widely that summer, attempted to clarify issues between Whigs and Democrats, lashed out at that old whipping boy, President John Tyler, and reminded voters of Pillow's record as a loyal Democrat and patriot, once again gratuitously at the expense of Winfield Scott.[19] On July 30 Pillow showed up in Winchester, Tennessee, when the circuit court was in session, "with a view of feeling the popular pulse in regards to his prospects for the US Senate." Randal McGavock noted that, characteristically, Pillow "distributed his likenesses through the country."

Pillow's political stance seemed to be changing. Advocacy of a low tariff was nothing new, but now he openly styled himself as a "strict constructionist." He warned his listeners of the dangers of the "Abolitionist Fanaticism" and became vehement when speaking of the influence of the "Black Republicans." John Bell, he noted caustically, had deserted Andrew Jackson entirely and now voted with the abolitionists.[20]

In early August Pillow traveled to Knoxville to attend the Southern Commercial Convention. He used the opportunity, of course, for "making Senitorial [sic] capital." Then, on September 4, 1857, Pillow announced his candidacy in the Nashville *Union*. He would be opposed by his old schoolmate and associate, A. O. P. Nicholson, and by veteran Democrat Andrew Ewing of Nashville. Buchanan, probably because of Brown's influence, let it be known that he favored Pillow; Nicholson was perceived as too close to Pierce. Another old Pillow associate, William H. Polk, showed interest in one of the Senate seats as well.[21]

On October 2, in the Nashville *Republican Banner*, Winfield Scott fired back at Pillow with a most untimely rebuttal of Pillow's Mexican War claims and charges. Whig Randal McGavock took delight in the article, which "places Pillow in a very unenviable position." In reply Pillow published a caustic, accusatory attack which did nothing to help his cause.[22] The Tennessee legislature met in convention less than a week later, on October 8. They chose Andrew Johnson as senator quickly. Then the Tennessee Democracy, having control of both houses of the legislature, had the happy problem of deciding who would get John Bell's seat. Whig observers believed Pillow would triumph. Yet the combination of Johnson and Pillow in the Senate perplexed William B. Campbell: "Our state has fallen into strange times and the election of such men as Johnson & Pillow astonishes all conservative men of all parties."[23] Nicholson worried that he might not be considered seriously because he had identified too closely with the Pierce administration and thus antagonized Buchanan's supporters. But Nicholson had the support this time of Andrew Johnson, who despised Pillow, and when the Democrats caucused on the evening of October 26, the "hand of Andrew Johnson could be discerned."[24] "His [Pillow's] Claims consist in nothing but his inordinate vanity and arrogance," Johnson confided to a political ally. "I trust the time will never come when the State is to be controlled by a little upstart *democratic aristocracy* that does not entertain one single sentiment or feeling [sic] in common with the great mass of the people."[25] When the balloting opened, Pillow received 25 votes, Nicholson 21, and Ewing 6, but Pillow could not capitalize on his lead. On the sixteenth ballot the caucus chose Nicholson as their nominee. Pillow quite rightly blamed Johnson.[26]

Pillow's enemies were not through. On October 28, 1857, there appeared in the Nashville *Republican Banner* a "long and scathing communication" responding to Pillow's attacks on Winfield Scott that summer. The author this time was not Scott, but a younger man—a Kentuckian, a former officer in the regular army, and a West Pointer, Simon Bolivar Buckner. A businessman now, and new to Nashville, Buckner felt obligated to come to Scott's defense. He signed the *Banner* article "Citizen" but, with careful propriety, informed Pillow that he was the author. Three days later, on October 31, another article by "Citizen" caused sidewalk and dinner party conversation. Buckner had hit hard again, reopening the matter of the two lost howitzers being found in Pillow's wagon. The articles were "masterpieces of gibes, ridicule, irony, and sarcasm," delighting not only Whigs, but all who loved to see the pretensions of the prominent exposed. They contained verse which hardly befit Pillow's carefully cultivated Mexican War image:

> He fought and fit, and gouged and bit,
> And struggled in the mud,
> Till all the ground for miles around,
> Was covered with his blood.[27]

> On many a bloody field of death
> Where warriors' hearts are tried,
> He braved the deadly cannon's breath,
> At least *he says he did*.

> Then go it to the Senate chair,
> O, Gideon, Gideon, Gideon Pillow!
> And when I see you safely there,
> *I'll hang my harp upon the willow*.[28]

Buckner's articles (still another would appear in February 1858) appeared too late to influence the choice of Tennessee's senator, and therefore must have appeared all the more malicious to Pillow. He was embarrassed, angered, and resentful. Some in Nashville expected a duel. Instead of a duel with this man Buckner, however, whom he hardly knew, Pillow kept quiet and bided his time. And his time would come, five years later, with disastrous consequences.[29]

The year 1859 brought personal anguish to Gideon Pillow. His faithful friend, confidant, and political and business associate Aaron V. Brown died. Brown, an older man, had replaced James K. Polk in Pillow's life when the former died in 1849. He provided guidance for Pillow, and they delighted in each other's company. Brown also was devoted to his wife, Pillow's sister Cynthia, and to Pillow's mother, Annie Payne Pillow, who made her home with the Browns at "Melrose" in Nashville, and whom the general seems to have worshiped. The loss of this talented Tennessee lawyer and political leader deprived Pillow of a personal and political anchor.

Another painful blow came in April 1859. Gideon, Jr., who had graduated from the University of North Carolina and had been given several months in Washington, D.C., society by his adoring father, took passage on the steamboat *St. Nicholas* from Memphis, probably heading for Mound Plantation. About eleven o'clock that night, Leonard H. Mangum was writing a letter at his home in Helena when flashes of light came through his window. He looked out and "beheld the magnificent Steam boat St. Nicholas in full blaze drifting—down about the middle of the River. She was indeed a floating palace of fire." He heard horrible screams for help and watched the steamer drift slowly out of sight. Gideon, Jr., and sixty others perished. His body was never recovered.[30]

The nation itself seemed a floating palace of fire in 1860. Talk of disunion abounded in the South. Sectional differences seemed irreconcilable. Tennessee's Democracy reflected the general division, disaffection, and confusion, as did Gideon Pillow. In the state convention of the Democracy which met January 17, 1860, Pillow threw his support once again behind Stephen A. Douglas. Douglas had broken with Buchanan over the Lecompton Constitution, which he regarded as incompatible with, if not a violation of, the doctrine of popular sovereignty. If Aaron V. Brown had lived, it is doubtful Pillow would have taken such a strong position backing Douglas, but in 1860 Pillow thought he heard in Douglas the voice of union, of sectional compromise. This is what Andrew Jackson would have wanted, he thought, as well as Polk and Carroll. Douglas was popular in Tennessee initially, with pockets of followers in the southeast corner, the remnants of the Pillow-Brown faction in the middle of the state, and great strength in

Memphis and throughout West Tennessee. Pillow was very hopeful of sending a Douglas delegation from Tennessee to the 1860 convention in Charleston. He well knew, however, that Andrew Johnson "since his days in the House had shown a distaste for Douglas." This antagonism appealed to the perverse side of Pillow, making Douglas all the more attractive.[31]

The state convention in January started off well enough. Pillow, aided by Knox Walker, whom Johnson also detested, was asked to draft the slavery planks in the state platform. Pillow and Walker carefully constructed a moderate statement for the party, one that accommodated Douglas's position on popular sovereignty. It was "*so shaped*," Pillow explained to Douglas, "as not to conflict with *your position*—nor to compromise your friends." The document blasted the Republican party for its "hostility to slavery" and supported the Dred Scott decision. In essence, the platform proposed adoption of the "Tennessee Resolutions"—a return to Tennessee's middle ground of the Nashville Convention. Douglas supporters who stood by the "Tennessee Resolutions" were regarded by many Tennesseans as Unionists. They were regarded by others, including Andrew Johnson, as ambitious, out-of-power, political opportunists who hoped to recapture "influence and prominence" within the party.[32]

Pillow turned to Douglas (as he had before) because Douglas stood closest to his own position of conciliation, compromise, and union. He told Douglas that they disagreed "upon the subject of the powers of the People of the Territories (previously [*sic*] to the adoption of a state constitution)." Pillow believed there was a bright prospect for a Tennessee-Illinois axis, a chance to flank the extremists, an opportunity to mend the national Democracy and halt the drift toward polarization. As a slaveholding Jacksonian Democrat, Pillow believed backing Douglas to be consistent with principle and eminently practical. That he wished to regain political power and position himself goes without saying. Not surprisingly, Pillow reconciled both impulses within himself and found them hardly contradictory.[33]

Pillow's hopes for Douglas were dashed, however, when Johnson's son, who managed his interests in the state convention, brought to the resolutions committee ("thrust upon the committee") a resolution presenting Johnson as Tennessee's choice for president. Pillow spoke strongly against it and closed his statement of "*bitter opposition*" with the announcement that he would not go to Charleston, even if elected a delegate, if Johnson were recommended as the "choice of the people of Tennessee." In a pivotal vote demonstrating the political power of Johnson, the committee turned its back on Pillow, voting 12 to 10 to recommend Johnson. Pillow was not finished, however. Before the convention closed, he managed to work a compromise: Tennessee would support Johnson at Charleston but would "come to Douglas if and when Johnson dropped out."[34]

So Pillow, true to his word, washed his hands of the affair and remained at Clifton while the Democracy assembled at Charleston, South Carolina. If Douglas were nominated there by the Democrats, and Pillow believed this possible, he felt that "Douglas could carry every Southern state." He regretted very much the failure of the northern Democrats to yield to requests from moderates to provide safeguards in the party platform for slavery in the territories. He deplored even more the irrational attacks on Douglas by southern extremists and by the press of Tennessee, but he believed this "campaign of calumny" would abate.[35] Pillow, however, grossly underestimated the powerful forces, not only political, but economic and social, tearing at the fabric of the nation and the South. In this he was not alone.

Douglas did possess a small majority of delegates when the national convention opened, but his support was unstable and ineffective in the face of uncompromising and well-organized extremists. Tennessee's delegation remained in their seats when other southerners walked out. They even switched from Andrew Johnson to neutral James Guthrie of Kentucky after thirty-six ballots, but the damage had been done. No one was nominated in Charleston. The Democracy had exploded.[36]

Pillow, bitterly disappointed by the calamity at Charleston, attempted in May 1860 to retrieve Douglas's fortunes by appealing to disaffected factions of the party. "Pointing out that the Supreme Court had denied the national government the power to regulate slavery in the territories, Pillow argued that consequently the people of potential states might determine whether they wished to be free or slave; therefore Douglas's policy was not in conflict with Taney's decision."[37] It was futile to argue: no one was listening. Pillow realized this in the early summer of 1860. When the Democrats reassembled in Baltimore on June 18, "the Douglas men refused to make any overtures whatsoever to the Southerners" and nominated Douglas. Five of Tennessee's delegates remained in their seats, but nineteen bolted. On to Richmond they went, swallowing fears of creating a sectional party, joining Isham G. Harris and mainline Tennessee Democrats in support of Buchanan's vice-president, John C. Breckinridge.[38]

The presidential election of 1860 in Tennessee was exciting. Douglas still had a strong political base in Memphis, and he visited there, as well as Nashville and Chattanooga, and spoke. John Bell and his Constitutional Union party also had great strength in West Tennessee and appealed directly to the many who opposed secession. Harris, leading the Democrats, fought back. Andrew Johnson was not enthusiastic about the Breckinridge ticket and chafed under Harris's leadership, but he stayed within the party. Nicholson and Pillow campaigned hard for Breckinridge. During this struggle Pillow worked with John C. Burch, the new editor of the Nashville *Union and American*, and won him over. Previously Burch had been a "close friend and supporter of Johnson." This Chattanooga lawyer and journalist, armed with what Henry Watterson characterized as "infallible" political judgment, would become Pillow's friend and staff officer, remaining with him through most of the Civil War.[39]

When Abraham Lincoln was elected on November 6, 1860, Pillow's world turned topsy-turvy. On November 12 he wrote a long letter to the editor of the Nashville *Patriot*. Although the election had placed the government of the United States "in the hands of the enemies of the South," he plead in Jacksonian terms for the South to remain within the Union and work for her rights. As a safeguard, however, he advocated a special convention with delegates duly appointed by state legislatures. These delegates should investigate the appropriateness of taxing, "to the point of prohibition," all northern goods, of raising and equipping 20,000–50,000 volunteers, and of demanding the amendment of the Constitution so that slavery would be guaranteed in the territories. If these actions evoked no positive response from the North, secession would be justified.[40]

9   **The Provisional Army**
         of Tennessee

Pillow's plan for a "General Convention of the Slave States" was doomed, however. The mood of the South was to secede first, then talk. But Tennessee was different; she stood by as southern states withdrew one by one. Unionist sentiment was too strong in all three grand divisions of the state. A special referendum held on February 9, 1861, resulted in a massive turnout of bewildered, emotional voters who convincingly defeated the secessionists.[1]

Gideon Pillow had cast his lot with Governor Harris and the southern Confederacy following the 1860 election. Reflecting the sentiments of many Tennesseans, Pillow was truly alarmed and threatened by the election of Lincoln; as a man of action, the thought of delay or awaiting further developments repelled him. By mid-January 1861, certainly, he had become a Harris lieutenant, a passionate secessionist, a self-styled revolutionary, believing that Tennessee's future lay outside the Union.[2]

The spring of 1861 seemed like an extension of the violent political campaign of 1860, except now more and more people openly talked of war. Tennessee wavered, uncertain. Its direction would be determined by the most energetic, Pillow believed. So in February and March of 1861, he worked hard to unify public opinion behind Isham G. Harris and the idea of secession. He also seems to have been busy, quite unofficially, organizing a military force within the state. Harris stationed Pillow in Memphis in March, and from there Pillow activated a company of West Tennessee militia at Grand Junction, Tennessee, on the fifteenth.[3] Later in March, John L. T. Sneed, a Mexican War comrade and state attorney general, assembled another force at Randolph, about sixty miles above Memphis, a point where the Mississippi River might be interdicted easily. Sneed and the troops in Grand Junction awaited Pillow's orders.[4] Pillow's political enemies in West Tennessee, however, and there were more than a few, wasted little time in voicing their complaints. William S. Walker wrote Jefferson Davis on March 17 that Pillow's active role had caused "wide spread and decided dissatisfaction." This lament would continue through the spring and into the middle of summer.[5]

In early April 1861, Pillow went to Montgomery to tender his services to Jefferson Davis. He offered Davis a regiment of Tennessee volunteers, presumably including the troops assembling at Grand Junction and Randolph.[6] Nothing came of his trip, except, perhaps, alienating or at least distancing himself from Davis and Davis's powerful "closet" general, Samuel Cooper. About the same time, back in Tennessee, some wag taunted Parson William Brownlow about this regiment of Pillow's (it was rumored Pillow intended to recruit him as chaplain). Brownlow predictably stormed, "When I shall have made up my mind to go to hell, I will cut my throat, and go *direct*, and not travel round by way of the Southern Confederacy."[7]

To Brownlow and other East Tennesseans, Pillow represented the haughty, corrupt, and controlling element of the Democracy in Middle Tennessee. They felt that Pillow, Samuel R. Anderson, and William McNish, the "Post Office clique" in Nashville, had conspired with Governor Harris to accomplish his goal of splitting Tennessee from the Union.[8] Pillow, on the other hand, despised Brownlow and his fellow demagogue and obstructionist, Andrew Johnson. Johnson, now distributing patronage for the Lincoln government in Tennessee, also opposed Harris and Pillow and the idea of the southern Confederacy at every turn. When Johnson left Middle Tennessee in late April, Pillow happily reported to Confederate Secretary of War Leroy Pope Walker that his old enemy "had at last returned to East Tennessee and had his nose pulled on the way; was hissed and hooted at all along on his route. . . . His power is gone and henceforth there will be nothing left but the stench of a traitor."[9]

While distancing themselves from Johnson, Pillow and Harris turned to their new Whig allies and tried to include as many as possible in the military organization they were forming. Harris was particularly anxious to do this. Pillow wrote the popular and able William B. Campbell on April 22 asking him if he would take command of a brigade. "If I should take the Field I want you along."[10] Former governor Campbell, a Unionist at heart and deeply distrustful of Pillow from his Mexican War experience, hesitated and ultimately declined in mid-May. This caused great disappointment; Whig Memphis wanted Campbell. Memories of Haskell and the plight of the 2d Tennessee at Cerro Gordo lingered. "There are many objections to Pillow," a Campbell friend wrote. "I fear it is too duplicated to be eradicated. A false move, or an unwise policy would precipitate upon him a fatal obloquy—a want of confidence from which he could not recover. But let us hope for the best."[11]

In mid-April Pillow had 500 men and a battery of artillery ready near Memphis. He planned to move at once with this force to Fort Smith, Arkansas, and seize government munitions stored there, but a discouraged Gov. Henry M. Rector of Arkansas informed Pillow that the weapons in question had been whisked away to the federal arsenal in St. Louis. Impatient for Tennessee's secession, Pillow reported to the Confederate secretary of war that "we have now no longer any elements of strength in the State opposed to the union of Tennessee with the Confederate States. The actions of tyrant Lincoln and the cries of war have stifled the voice of Union shriekers, and we are now ready and anxious to place Tennessee under the protecting aegis of the Confederate Constitution."[12]

Pillow hurried from Nashville to Memphis and back again, meeting with members of the General Assembly and urging them to support the army bill and to appropriate $2 million for public use. Next he was off to Louisville, Kentucky, as Harris's and Tennessee's representative

Gov. Isham Green Harris
(courtesy Library of Congress)

extraordinary, to confer secretly with Gov. Beriah Magoffin and discuss common military defensive arrangements. Pillow met with the governor, his 1857 political enemy Simon B. Buckner (commander of Kentucky's state guard), and Roger Hanson at the Galt House on April 23. He found Magoffin pro-Confederate in sympathy but insistent on a policy of armed neutrality for his state.[13] Also in Kentucky at this time were John C. Burch, Pillow's new political friend, and Nathan B. Forrest. Both were in Louisville, Forrest buying horses and supplies for a Tennessee cavalry company, Burch gathering intelligence.[14] On April 20 Pillow had directed Burch to undertake another mission, this time to St. Louis, to meet with Gov. Claiborne Jackson and urge him to seize the federal arsenal in St. Louis at once. In the meantime, Pillow rushed back to Nashville to help Harris draft the bill creating the Provisional Army of Tennessee.[15]

On April 19 two trains met in Grand Junction, and the passengers got off to rest. Word passed quickly that Pillow was in one of the cars, and a dozen or so people cheered him until he came out and addressed them. A "considerable crowd" gathered, and Pillow took advantage of the opportunity. He climbed atop a cotton bale and urged his fellow Tennesseans to arm themselves. "Every thing dear to you, fellow-citizens," he shouted, "is in peril." He exhorted them to support the "holy Southern cause," to repel the northern Goths and Vandals who intend to "liberate your slaves or incite them to insurrection, to ravish your daughters, to sack your cities." "Never! Never!" cried the crowd. "I too, say Never," shouted Pillow. He informed them that Lincoln had already seized the arms from the St. Louis arsenal and shipped them into northern Kentucky. Disaster to the South could only be averted by the "will and muscle of Tennesseans."[16]

Pillow again offered his services to Jefferson Davis on April 20, through Secretary of War Leroy P. Walker. "He can employ me any where and in any position he may indicate. I am content to serve my country in her perilous moment in any position he may put me."[17] To underline his intent he hoisted the Confederate flag atop his headquarters at the Gayoso Hotel in Memphis.[18] Two days later Pillow told Walker that 25,000 men had "tendered me their services." He could put 50,000 Tennesseans into the field "if you can furnish arms." Walker responded by shipping several thousand small arms and four heavy cannon to Pillow in Memphis.[19] Pillow in turn forwarded the ordnance to Randolph, where troops were gathering. On April 24 Lt. Col. Marcus J. Wright of the 154th Senior Tennessee regiment arrived at Randolph. He and his men set to work at once constructing

Col. John C. Burch
(courtesy Chattanooga–Hamilton County Bicentennial Library)

a large fort on the Mississippi bluffs ten miles above Randolph which they named Fort Wright.[20]

An Arkansas regiment commanded by Pillow's Helena friend Cleburne was also at Randolph. General Sneed thought Cleburne's troops "too close to entrenchments for their health," so he had Cleburne move his men further upriver. There Cleburne established an advanced post on the highest of three Chickasaw bluffs above the intersection of the Hatchie River and the Mississippi, just south of Coal Creek. "The steamboat channel runs right under the bluff and brings every boat as it passes within musket-shot of the shore." Eventually these works, initially named Fort Cleburne, would extend from the Coal Creek bottoms on the north to the Mississippi on the south, forming what would become Fort Pillow. Chugging and clanking its way below the fort was the Confederate steamer *General Pillow*.[21]

The Tennessee General Assembly passed the law creating the Provisional Army of Tennessee on May 6, 1861. The act called for a force of 55,000 Tennessee troops and a supporting appropriation of $5 million. The army would consist of 25,000 men enlisted for twelve months and organized into regiments, brigades, and divisions. Thirty thousand militia would be in reserve. The governor would be commander-in-chief, with two major generals to assist him. The following day, May 7, Tennessee ratified a military league with the Confederacy, which placed her army under Confederate control in the event of war.[22]

On May 9, 1861, Governor Harris named Gideon Pillow commander of the Provisional Army of Tennessee with the rank of major general, a logical appointment. Pillow was "Tennessee's outstanding military figure" and since the fall of 1860 had been the governor's closest ally and strongest supporter. Nevertheless, the selection of Pillow was unpopular in West Tennessee, traditionally a stronghold of Whigs. "His appointment gives unbounded dissatisfaction," wrote Kentucky observer L. P. Yandell, Jr. "He is generally considered wholly wanting in military knowledge, wanting in discretion and common sense, and he has the reputation of being tyrannical and even cruel to soldiers . . . unfortunate appointment of this ditch digger . . . I fear it will dampen the military ardor of West Tennessee."[23]

Harris appointed Nashville postmaster and Mexican War veteran Samuel R. Anderson as Tennessee's other major general, but Anderson would be subordinate to Pillow. With two Democrats in place as major generals, Harris, acutely conscious of the political nature of the army, turned to former Whigs for four brigadiers—Felix Zollicoffer, Robert C. Foster III (the young officer with whom Pillow had quarreled in Mexico), John L. T. Sneed, and Pillow's old classmate and Mexican War friend, William R. Caswell. The fifth brigadier, Frank Cheatham, was a Democrat, as was adjutant general Daniel S. Donelson.[24]

Pillow came to Memphis to organize the Provisional Army of Tennessee. Although he brought with him $25,000 from the state military board, all requisitions had to be made on Nashville. This financial arrangement proved inadequate and inefficient for Pillow. He finally resorted to drafts on his own funds and used his personal credit to secure needed supplies and equipment while awaiting authorization and reimbursement from the Military and Financial Board. Although Governor Harris chaired the four-man board, Pillow chafed under its control.[25]

Early on, Pillow thought the board would be supplying the needs for his army, and he sent them appeals for arms, ordnance, and supplies.[26] He learned very quickly, however, that he must rely on other means. Purchase of arms, especially heavy cannon, quickly exhausted the thin ordnance department account. Vouchers presented to the military board were honored slowly. Memphis banks balked at extended credit, and Pillow found himself at odds with his friend Harris over monetary policy and the uneven and inadequate flow of funds. Impatiently, he dipped deeper into his personal credit line and then pushed the military board for reimbursement. The process was intolerably slow for Pillow. Ultimately, he claimed, $300,000 of his own money was spent.[27]

He took an adversarial stance with the board about reimbursing soldiers when their horses died on duty. Pillow and the board also disagreed about furnishing swords to officers and providing them with rations at cost. He thought that giving tobacco and whiskey to the troops who labored building the earthworks was a capital idea and did so, but the board disagreed and disallowed the expenditures. Pillow countered by going over their heads, sending a memorial to the General Assembly.[28] He became furious when the board then demanded bonds from staff officers before they purchased supplies or gave vouchers in the name of the state. Pillow angrily complained to the board and to Harris that he was being "crippled in my energies, cramped at every point by mere matters of form." "I cannot *create* the means of defending the country," Pillow continued. "I owe it to myself to retire from the Service. I would be glad to see you and have a full conference with you before I take the step, but my mind is made up to take that course unless matters are differently arranged at Nashville." Pillow ended the letter to the governor by stating: "I know you have arduous public duties to perform but I cannot leave here & I suppose you would prefer coming down to my leaving my position at present."[29] Harris came to Memphis, heard Pillow out, and settled matters. He worked out a procedure for strict accountability on the part of staff officers but allowed Pillow a separate contingency military fund upon which he might draw.[30]

One solution Pillow proposed to Harris during this conference over the embarrassing shortage of funds was to confiscate stock "held by our enemies in Union and Planters bank and sequestering the same for the use of the state." (He had already issued a general order to that effect on June 21.) "It is a clear right," Pillow contended. "In such a struggle any and every thing recognized as a proper means of weakening the enemy and of strengthening ones self is justifiable by the Laws of nations."[31] Heretofore, Harris had reluctantly stood by as Pillow blockaded the Mississippi, seized steamers headed for Cincinnati and Pittsburgh, and ordered their cargoes sold. The Clarksville *Weekly Chronicle* reported the capture of yet another steamer, the *Prince of Wales*, on June 21, 1861.[32] Pillow would sell a cargo of sugar or tobacco, for instance, and then use the proceeds to purchase arms.[33] Harris, however, opposed the confiscation of assets in Memphis banks. He believed such action beyond the proper bounds of the executive branch and rescinded Pillow's order. Only the legislature properly possessed such power, Harris maintained. To quiet Pillow, Harris wisely secured the support of Judge West Humphreys for his position opposing confiscation.[34]

Pillow understood as well as anyone the bite of economic warfare. He did not hesitate to regulate commerce, believing if he cut sources of supply and opportunities for export, it would weaken the enemy and shorten the war. He carefully enforced the policy of prohibiting shipment of cotton except through southern ports. As military commander, he also arrested those disrupting the war effort. In June he jailed a civilian whom he found waving a United States flag and recruiting men to oppose the Confederacy.[35]

The Gayoso Hotel in Memphis suited him just fine as headquarters, and Pillow and his ever enlarging staff settled in. A visitor found him "in his bedroom, fitted up as his office, littered with plans and papers." "General Pillow is a small compact, clear-complexioned man, with short grey whiskers, cut in the English fashion, a quick eye and a pompous manner of speech; and I had not been long in his company before I heard of Chapultepec and his wound, which causes him to limp a little in his walk, and gives him inconvenience in the saddle. He wore a round black hat, plain blue frock coat, dark trousers, and brass spurs on his boots; but no signs of military rank."[36]

Pillow found recruiting for the Provisional Army of Tennessee ridiculously easy, but providing recruits with serviceable firearms was another matter. Maj. Gen. Samuel R. Anderson, commanding at Nashville, wrote Secretary of War Walker on May 12 that the supply of muskets or rifled muskets stood at 5,000 percussion muskets at Memphis, 2,000 muskets and 1,000 rifled muskets at Nashville. Four thousand old flintlock muskets were stored at the Nashville armory; these had to be repaired before being distributed. Most of the troops were armed with long-barreled civilian shotguns.[37]

The shortage of firearms was desperate. If possible, Pillow wanted Enfield rifles, 10,000–15,000 of them. He and Governor Harris were assisted in locating and purchasing rifles by Sam Tate, president of the Memphis and Charleston Railroad, and others. They went to Augusta, Georgia, and Baton Rouge, Louisiana, among other places in their search.[38] To add to his problems, Pillow had to compete with the Confederacy for arms. When he learned of 3,200 muskets being shipped through Memphis, Pillow wired Harris for permission to seize them. Richmond had taken some of the Mississippi regiments Pillow had counted on and shipped them east. To arm them properly, other regiments in and around Corinth had to give up their own weapons. The Confederate officials "leave me utterly unable to meet the immense force gathering at Cairo. This is my only *resource*. Do you disapprove?" Pillow also urged Harris to intercept arms coming into East Tennessee from Kentucky at night by wagon. "Lose no time."[39]

The lack of cannon for the Provisional Army of Tennessee was just as serious. On May 9 Pillow did not have "a single battery of field artillery"; indeed, by June 1 Col. John P. McCown, who commanded the army's artillery, had organized several field batteries but still had no guns. Forts had priority, and Pillow sought heavy cannon everywhere. He was quite successful in securing them with the indispensable assistance of Secretary of War Walker.[40] Yet, as the big cannon began to arrive and to be mounted in the forts, the acute shortage of powder compelled him to stop firing practice for what seemed an interminable interval. To help meet the crisis, Pillow wrote Anderson in Nashville to have the powder mills there shift immediately from the production of musket powder to cannon powder. Pillow begged for trained artillery officers to handle these heavy guns, even appealing to Secretary of the Navy Stephen R. Mallory. He also asked Mallory for naval craft at New Orleans to be brought to Memphis. With these gunboats, "we will arrest this *invading column*."[41]

Memphis itself supplied many of Pillow's needs. The Quinby and Robinson foundry quickly converted to casting cannon; cannonballs were made in Sam Tate's railroad shops. The Memphis Novelty Works turned to producing sabers and soon reached a production rate of fifty per day. Other shops produced gun carriages and rifle cartridges.[42]

Pillow excelled at such a massive, urgent organizational job. It exhilarated him to issue flurries of orders and oversee many men, all the while performing an endless variety of tasks. No detail was too small. He involved himself in procuring musical instruments as well as cannon. He was magnificent at pushing subordinates, cutting through red tape, and shaking the collars of bureaucrats. He would approach and reproach governors, generals, and high government officials as quickly as he would a company commander, always taking time to speak to a solitary private, however. For the common soldier, like the common voter, seemed to warm his spirits and impress him just as much as those of elevated station. He delighted in proclamations and edicts and convoluted legalities. He would make a speech to troops or citizens instantaneously. It would be stuffy and self-serving, for sure, but invariably upbeat. Pillow seemed to approach the whole affair of being "Commander in Chief of the Army of Tennessee," as he styled himself, as a responsibility for which he had been training all his life. He believed—and had demonstrated in Mexico—that a lack of professional background could be made up for by intense activity.[43]

The concoction of personal traits that was Gideon Pillow—at once naive, at once the master of misrepresentation and misconstruction—confused friend and foe alike. He never seemed troubled about consistency. He could write Gen. John L. T. Sneed at Fort Randolph and censure him for lack of military courtesy in communicating directly with Governor Harris, while he himself would fire a letter past Harris or any superior without a blink. He would not tolerate insubordination in others, but it came as naturally to him as changing shirts, as naturally as transforming reality through rhetoric.[44]

Of course Pillow, with his preoccupation with posturing and image-building, was a spy's delight. To his headquarters at the Gayoso came Allan Pinkerton. The forty-one-year-old detective had worked with George B. McClellan when the latter had been vice-president of the Illinois Central Railroad, and thus he thought it unremarkable to receive an assignment from McClellan to go to Memphis to gather military intelligence. So Mr. E. J. Allen, as Pinkerton called himself, appeared at the Gayoso. Pillow and his staff found him charming. "He [Pillow] little dreamed when on one occasion he quietly sipped his brandy and water with me, that he was giving valuable information to his sworn foe." Pillow strolled about the streets of Memphis with this stranger and decided to show him the strength of the river fortifications. A Confederate agent, fresh from a spy mission to Cincinnati, had seen the so-called E. J. Allen that spring in the company of McClellan. He informed Pillow, who, furious at being deceived, ordered Allen's arrest. It was too late. A Gayoso porter tipped off the spy, and Pinkerton slipped off into Mississippi while Pillow's men madly searched the streets of Memphis.[45]

For purposes of command, Pillow divided the state into its three traditional parts. By the end of May 1861, Caswell commanded the forces in East Tennessee and Anderson those in Middle Tennessee, while Pillow retained control in West Tennessee. Foster commanded the infantry gathering at Camp Cheatham in Robertson County, Zollicoffer those at Camp Trousdale in Sumner County, Cheatham those at Union City in upper West Tennessee, and Sneed those at Randolph. Among the very many other appointments made or approved by Pillow was Bushrod Johnson, who was named chief of engineers. Johnson, however, seems to have spent most of May 1861 as Pillow's mustering officer.[46]

A glaring contrast between the Provisional Army of Tennessee and the Confederate army gathering in Virginia was in the number of West Pointers. Pillow had only a handful, and this deficiency of course damaged organizational and training efforts—to what extent will never be known. Pillow's prejudice against professional soldiers, especially those trained at Whiggish West Point, was common knowledge, and this serious weakness in the officer corps can be attributed directly to him. Pillow's Provisional Army was to reflect the army of Andrew Jackson and Billy Carroll, not the encrusted, by-the-book soldiers of Winfield Scott.

From his first day in command, Pillow eyed the Mississippi River as the enemy's most likely avenue of approach and set to work with a fury to strengthen its defenses. Harris supported him fully. It has been carefully pointed out by historians Thomas L. Connelly and Richard McMurry that Harris allowed Pillow to create an "unbalanced defensive line in Tennessee that was heavily slanted toward the western border." The two leaders neglected the defenses of Middle Tennessee and placed only "a token force" in East Tennessee, thus putting "exaggerated emphasis on the supposed threat from up the Mississippi." Together with Harris's conviction that Kentucky would remain neutral and thus buffer Tennessee's northern border, this course of action would prove fatal to the state in the snow and sleet of 1862.[47]

In the heat and dust of May 1861, however, Pillow and Harris, if they thought linearly at all, thought in terms of the perpendicular. They were not alone. Most military and civil leaders of the time believed the invasion of the South would come down the Mississippi from the Federal forces gathering at Cairo, Illinois, using the fleet being rapidly constructed far upstream. Pillow must be credited, in all fairness, with realizing the strategic weakness of stacking defenses along the most likely avenue of approach, the Mississippi. He wrote Secretary of War Walker on May 9 warning that "the character of the land is such that a land army could march down behind the river defenses. Forces to stop this are not adequate. Under the circumstances would it not be wise to discontinue moving Tennessee troops to Virginia?" "Our system of railroads invites this approach," he added.[48]

Pillow believed from the outset that Columbus, Kentucky, was the key to the defense of the Mississippi. Its high bluffs dominated the river in a manner unmatched by any other position above Memphis. Moreover, its possession, he thought, would stop any enemy invasion of West Tennessee with the objective of taking the Mississippi River defenses in reverse. Pillow had broached the subject of Columbus with Governor Magoffin in the spring, and he pressed the point with Harris continually. Harris, however, emphasized political realities. He cautioned Pillow on May 7 that Magoffin could not hand over the natural fortress and that its seizure by the Pillow would only invite "Federal troops to similar invasion." Harris, believing the true defense of Tennessee depended upon the neutrality of Kentucky, directed that a concentration of troops at Union City, Tennessee, would be the most appropriate response. From Union City, help could be rushed to Kentucky if requested; a counterattack could be launched against Columbus if the enemy were suddenly to occupy it. Such caution did not satisfy Pillow at all. With his singular understanding of the proper role of a subordinate, he circumvented Harris and sent a special messenger to Magoffin "asking his authority to fortify Columbus."[49] He followed this with direct appeals to Secretary of War Walker on May 15 and President Davis on May 16 for permission to take Columbus with or without Magoffin's consent. Pillow felt perfectly justified.

If the South dallied, the enemy would seize the initiative and the natural fortress.[50]

Day-by-day perplexities, however, kept yanking Pillow from the heady dilemmas of grand strategy. He must build an army quickly. He ordered the many companies of volunteers heading for Memphis into camps of instruction; by May 9 he already had 5,000 men to train, feed, clothe, and arm. He grouped them into regiments, generally on a county basis. As true patriots, these men agreed to confine themselves in inhuman conditions, overcrowded and confused, subject to deadly camp diseases. Illness soon reached epidemic proportions.[51] Complaints poured in: Pillow and Harris had to respond to angry letters about the shocking number and the "great neglect" of the sick, the mismanagement of the commissaries, and the camps themselves, in such "filthy condition that it is dangerous for men to remain there." Sneed's Camp Randolph became known as Camp Yellow Jacket.[52]

Pillow could hardly manage the crowds of recruits he already commanded, but he hungered for more, especially coveting the thousands of Mississippians gathering in Holly Springs and Corinth just south of Memphis. He worked with Gov. John J. Pettus directly, agreeing that Tennessee would provide subsistence and pay for the Mississippi troops if they would come north and be placed under his command. These regiments belonged to the Confederacy, however. So Pillow wrote Walker, requesting that the two Mississippi regiments already organized under Gen. Charles Clark be ordered to join him. They would be the "supporting force" he required to open the new line at Union City and Columbus. "*Say at once,*" he demanded of the Secretary of War.[53] Pillow provided even greater urgency on May 21 when he informed Pettus, quite incorrectly, that "no doubt" existed "but that the enemy has taken possession of Paducah." Pillow got his way. He ordered Clark to move toward Union City and told Pettus he wanted the artillery company of Holly Springs sent along as well. Two Mississippi cavalry companies should go promptly to Memphis.[54]

Troops came to Memphis from everywhere: Mississippi, Missouri, Kentucky, southern Illinois, Indiana. Congressman Thomas C. Hindman of Arkansas chose Memphis as the place to recruit and organize his legion; Daniel C. Govan and John D. Martin came there to raise and equip their Arkansas regiments, as did John S. Bowen with his Missouri regiment.[55] Pillow was doing his work very well. By the end of May, Tennessee itself had twenty-one regiments organized under his command, with three others mustered into the Confederate army and dispatched to Virginia. Pillow, however, wanted even more troops in the Provisional Army of Tennessee. Disingenuously, he wrote Col. Patrick Cleburne on June 1 that the governor of Arkansas had put him "in the unfortunate position" of having to "temporarily take command of your forces and direct your operations. This I have no wish to do—nor will I do so, unless it be the wish of the volunteers under your command." [56]

Pillow not only succeeded in gathering a large number of troops, he managed quite well in having them rapidly forwarded through Jackson, Tennessee, to Union City. The last week of May 1861, Pillow worked in a frenzy. He placed Zollicoffer in charge of Camp Trousdale near the Kentucky line and ordered Cheatham, who had been assisting Sneed at Fort Pillow, forward to Union City to take command of the troops arriving there.[57] Cheatham could report by May 28 that he had found the 13th Mississippi in Union City, the 12th "will be here tonight," Col. William H. Stephens's 6th Tennessee had just arrived, Col. William E. Travis's 5th Tennessee would be "here tomorrow night," and the "new regiment at Jackson" (Col. Robert M. Russell's 12th Tennessee) would arrive by the end of the week.[58] Pillow hurried the process, closely coordinating the rail movement and supply of these troops being shipped north to Union City.[59]

Construction of the Mississippi River defenses proceeded rapidly. Building earthworks was not glamorous, however, nor popular. Pillow promised the men at Randolph that he would relieve them from the pick and spade as soon as he could, and he did try, with circulars and direct appeals, but his fellow planters proved reticent in providing slave labor: "The agricultural exigency is just now very pressing." Pillow pushed on nevertheless, ordering the soldiers to rush completion of the river batteries and field fortifications. He would gather his men together after an inspection and give them a speech. English correspondent William H. Russell listened to one and called it a "harangue" in which Pillow "expatiated on their patriotism, on their courage, and the atrocity of the enemy, in an odd farrago of military and political subjects." The men did not appear interested, according to Russell, even when Pillow "wound up with florid peroration by assuring them, 'When the hour of danger comes I will be with you.'" Russell was wrong, however; the men did listen to Pillow. His speeches had a positive effect on many of his soldiers. Through them and through conversations with individual soldiers he transmitted a sense of purpose and urgency. "If we can only have ten days," Pvt. Val W. Wynne wrote home, "we can resist 40,000." [60]

Pillow first looked to the defenses of Memphis itself, placing two batteries there with the aid of engineers sent by Walker. Pillow personally supervised the construction of the works and was pleased. By June 20 he had emplaced six batteries, mounting some thirty heavy guns.[61] His enthusiasm was not shared by observer Russell, however, who thought one of Pillow's forts high on the bluff not only inadequate but ridiculous—a parapet of cotton bales covered with tarp, "so placed that a well directed shell into the bank below it would tumble it all into the water."[62] The other battery, with a "fine command of the river," met with Russell's approval, and Pillow confided that this earthen position would be extended and sixteen more guns added.[63]

Pillow took Russell with him to inspect the fortifications at Randolph. These were "rudely erected" emplacements, Russell reported. "A more extraordinary maze could not be conceived, even in the dreams of a sick engineer. . . . They were so ingeniously made as to prevent the troops engaged in their defence from resisting the enemy's attacks, or getting away from them when the enemy had got inside." Pillow had gun drill for Russell's benefit. The demonstration, worthy of Gilbert and Sullivan, convinced the British visitor that Pillow, his Mexican War reputation notwithstanding, knew little of the science of artillery. One old piece continued to misfire; another fired, "but where the ball went no one could say"; yet another fired, "but off went the gun, too, and with a frantic leap it jumped, carriage and all, clean off the platform."[64]

As summer passed, however, a string of formidable installations developed, stretching upriver from Memphis to Fort Harris (six miles above) and on to Fort Randolph, Fort Pillow, Fort Wright (opposite Osceola, Arkansas), and Island No. 10. To further control all river traffic, Pillow strung a ship-cable chain across the Mississippi at Randolph. Its weight was supported by rafts and buoys. In the event the enemy fleet attacked at night, illumination was provided by great barrels of tar. Pillow specified that these be put in five piles to be lighted successively as enemy vessels made their way downriver, thus keeping the enemy ships silhouetted between the guns and the flaming barrels. Pillow also experimented with the "Drummond Light" and "Calcium Light" to aid night firing.[65]

These elaborate river defenses, however, came at the expense of properly fortifying other points within the state. Initial work had begun on the Cumberland and Tennessee river forts, and Daniel Donelson had clearly stated the needs to Pillow, but Pillow gave priority to the defenses of the Mississippi. Work on the river forts lagged badly throughout the summer. "Middle Tennessee," Neill S. Brown complained to Davis, "is very much exposed through the Tennessee and Cumberland rivers to incursions by the enemy, & will be more so when those rivers are swollen by the Autumnal or winter rains." Of the ten artillery companies in the Provisional Army of Tennessee, all but one had been removed from Nashville by Pillow, without notice to Anderson, and ordered to the western portion of the state, thus further weakening the defensive strength of the center. Middle Tennessee had not been stripped of organized units, however. On June 12 Anderson reported eleven regiments of infantry along the northern border. Pillow, of course, opposed shifting manpower from the Mississippi to East Tennessee; there was "not the least danger of Invasion. . . . Lincoln is too hard *pressed*." [66]

Pillow continued to worry about the Federal buildup at Cairo and the possible loss of Columbus. The mayor of Columbus, B. W. Sharp, wrote Pillow that the enemy at Cairo would embark within the next few days for an attack on Memphis. Pillow received similar messages "from so many sources" that "no doubt of their purpose" existed in his mind. The "only uncertainty is the time." [67] Cheatham's scouts and pickets from Union City saw and brushed close to Federals on the Kentucky side of the river near Columbus, and Cheatham posted a company on the Kentucky border in accordance with Pillow's order.[68] The Provisional Army of Tennessee breathed their commander's aggressiveness. The Pillow Guards, "sworn in for the purpose of guarding the person of our gallant Genl Pillow," wrote their counterparts, the Prentiss Guards, in Cairo. "We challenge you to meet us at any time, at any place, in any number, and with any arms or equipment you may select." Unchivalrously, the response came back: "We accept no challenge from traitors, but hang them." [69]

As June closed, so did Pillow's role as commander in chief. On June 29, 1861, the Tennessee General Assembly passed a joint resolution directing the governor to offer the army Harris and Pillow had built to the Confederate States of America. It was an impressive force: twenty-two regiments of infantry, two of cavalry, and ten artillery companies.[70] Davis hesitated a few days before replying to Harris. In the meantime, on July 2, Tennessee officially became a Confederate state. President Davis gladly accepted the Tennessee troops, but to the surprise of Isham G. Harris and to the astonishment of Gideon J. Pillow, he did not accept the slate of Tennessee general officers. Pillow, Anderson, and Donelson were made generals, but only brigadiers. Harris pointed out to Davis that he had failed to appoint any Whigs. "It is a political necessity, as well as strict justice that the whig element be fully recognized." Davis relented somewhat in July, appointing Democrat Cheatham and Whig Zollicoffer as Confederate brigadiers, but he ignored Foster, Sneed, and Caswell.[71]

Harris argued with Davis about Pillow. He deserved to be a major general: "In view of his ability, experience and past service in that position during the Mexican War, I feel that he is entitled to the appointment."[72] Congressman John V. Wright and other prominent Democrats echoed Harris's objection.[73] But Davis would have none of it. Pillow became a brigadier on July 9, assigned to command of the first division of the Western Department, consisting of Knox Walker's and Robert M. Russell's brigades.[74]

Even J. B. Jones in the War Department was surprised at the demotion of Pillow. He knew the Tennessee general "was exceedingly unpopular in the Adjutant-Gen. Cooper's office. I presume this arose solely from mistrust of his military abilities; for he had certainly manifested much enthusiasm in the cause, and was constantly urging the propriety of aggressive movements with his command. All his proposed advances were countermanded."[75]

The demotion from major general to brigadier humiliated Pillow. Bitterly he appealed to Harris. He would accept the commission and do his duty, but he would just as soon serve the cause as a private.[76]

And the question remained—if not Pillow, then who, in the infinite wisdom of the president and the War Department, had the experience, the knowledge, and the ability to command the Western Department?

10   To Aid Our Friends in Missouri

The news stretched belief. Richmond had appointed Leonidas Polk to command the Western Department. Pillow knew Polk, of course, but, although the same age and born of families so much alike, their paths had diverged in boyhood. When Pillow had gone to Pulaski and the University of Nashville for his education, Polk, who spent his boyhood in North Carolina, had attended the University of North Carolina for a short time and then entered West Point, where he was much admired and made a number of close friends, among them his roommate, Albert Sidney Johnston, and underclassman Jefferson Davis. Polk had undergone a dramatic religious conversion at West Point, and upon graduation he resigned his commission and entered the Episcopal priesthood. He was well educated, well traveled, and propertied by the time he came to Maury County in the early 1830s to manage lands he had inherited. He established his home, Ashwood, and developed his plantation on the Columbia–Mount Pleasant Pike close to the site where Pillow's Clifton would be built. In 1838, however, the General Convention of the Episcopal church chose him to be missionary bishop of the Southwest. Henceforward Polk's activities and interests would be tied to Louisiana and the Mississippi Valley as he built a wide network of friends and acquaintances and a reputation for energy and effectiveness.

Davis pressed the popular bishop in June 1861 to accept responsibility for the defense of the Mississippi Valley and a commission in the Confederate army. Other friends and Confederate leaders supported Davis's appeal. Polk hesitated and only after great reflection agreed. On June 25 he accepted appointment as major general commanding northern Alabama and Mississippi, northeastern Arkansas, and western Tennessee. His primary responsibility was defense of the upper Mississippi.[1]

Polk and Pillow saw things differently. On his way to Memphis to assume command, Polk surveyed conditions in East Tennessee and reported to Davis, "No time is to be lost." He advocated enlarging the Confederate presence there from 2,000 to 10,000 troops and placing Felix Zollicoffer in command. Isham G. Harris agreed. He worried more each month about that section. His policy of conciliation and caution had failed, it seemed; troops should be stationed there. Pillow, however, felt Harris and Polk overestimated the problem. East Tennessee "only sulked."[2] Perhaps Pillow was blinded by economic self-interest. Quick punches down the Mississippi by the Union army and fleet gathering at Cairo, however, would have been disastrous to the Confederate cause, as Pillow quite rightly understood. He also disagreed with Polk and Harris over East Tennessee because it meant the transfer of manpower from the Mississippi, from his command.

Pillow had a plan, and to implement it would require every Confederate soldier available. M. Jeff Thompson seems to have been the catalyst. This personable and persuasive Missourian had come to Memphis June 15 and had several meetings with Pillow and his staff at the Gayoso Hotel. These two visionaries seem to have fed upon each other's enthusiasm, as a result of which Pillow ordered all Missourians who had enlisted in his army discharged so that they could join Thompson.[3] Of wider import was the idea to invade Missouri, which Thompson appears to have generated.[4] There had been some apprehension on the part of Harris that the Federals might attempt to attack Memphis unexpectedly by moving from Cairo across the Mississippi to Bird's Point, Missouri, and then south along the river through the Missouri boot heel into Arkansas, being supplied and supported all the while by their river fleet.[5] Anxious to assume the offensive and retain independent command, Pillow saw opportunity. Gen. Sterling Price held Cowskin Prairie, Missouri, with 6,000–8,000 troops, while Gen. Ben McCulloch had 6,000 additional troops ready within easy supporting distance just across the Arkansas border at Bentonville. Pillow envisioned a grand, strategic Confederate counterstroke, sweeping up through southern Missouri with the Army of Tennessee in conjunction with McCulloch and Price, seizing St. Louis and its great arsenal, then turning east and taking Cairo in reverse.[6]

On June 20 Pillow wrote Harris asking permission for "a forward movement for the relief of Missouri."[7] On the same day he wired Secretary of War Walker: "There is great anxiety here to aid Missouri. I can gather in hand for that purpose, of Tennessee, Mississippi and Arkansas Troops, Twenty Thousand men and with that force I can place Missouri on her feet. It requires only the order of the President. I can place myself in communication with McCulla [sic] and Governor Jackson. My governor approves, you need not wait for formal action of Tennessee. She will turn over her Army right away but you can act at once as time is important."[8]

Harris had agreed to "send a force to aid our friends in Missouri." He believed the proper line for offensive operations should be along the west bank of the Mississippi, thus avoiding violation of Kentucky's neutrality. But such "must be delayed till the policy of the Union men of East Tennessee is fully developed." Harris meant what he said. When Pillow proceeded to push ahead with the plan, an alarmed Harris countermanded his preparations, suspending any expedition to Bird's Point and Cairo. Troops were needed in East Tennessee.[9] Discouraged but determined, Pillow continued to hammer away. He wrote Secretary of the Navy Stephen Mallory on July 4, his last official day in command at Memphis, urging the seizure of New Madrid, Missouri. He considered it the "entrance into Missouri, . . . the key . . . to future operations," adding the caveat that the Federals, he had been informed, were "about to seize that place."[10]

Maj. Gen. Leonidas Polk came to Memphis to assume command on July 13. Although Memphis welcomed him enthusiastically, he found he succeeded an angry and unreconciled Pillow—reduced in rank, deprived of station, and denied an opportunity for glory in Missouri.

Polk at once attempted to console his subordinate and, as many before him, appears to have fallen victim to Pillow's charm, enthusiasm, and persuasiveness. On July 20, a week after being in command, Polk wrote the War Department recommending that Pillow be made his second in command and promoted to major general.[11]

Pillow then received support for his Missouri initiative from an unexpected quarter. A professional soldier, Brig. Gen. William J. Hardee, a Davis favorite, had arrived in Memphis en route to organize Confederate forces defending Arkansas. He realized the importance of New Madrid, Missouri, and urged Polk and Pillow to occupy it. Hardee strongly supported the occupation of New Madrid for his own purposes, as a defensive measure to "block one of the logical routes into Arkansas."[12] The governor of Missouri, Claiborne Jackson, arrived in Memphis about this time, accompanied by former United States senator David R. Atchison, and added his voice in support of the Missouri expedition.[13]

Polk was convinced. On June 23, 1861, ten days after assuming command, he ordered Pillow to detach 6,000 men from the Army of Tennessee, cross the Mississippi, occupy New Madrid, and advance into Missouri. Polk modified Pillow and Thompson's plan somewhat. Pillow would advance northwest from New Madrid toward Ironton, where Hardee would join him with a column of 7,000. From Ironton Pillow and Hardee "are directed to pass in behind Lyon's force by land, or to proceed to Saint Louis, seize it, and, taking possession of the boats at that point, to proceed up the river Missouri, raising the Missourians as they go." Polk also hoped Pillow's force could "enter Illinois and take Cairo from the rear."[14]

Pillow's vision, however, was based on faulty information. To his dismay, Hardee encountered Arkansas leaders determined not to allow their troops to be transferred into the Confederate army. Instead of 7,000 men at Pitman's Ferry, Hardee discovered about 2,300, "poorly organized, badly equipped and wanting in discipline and instruction." They also lacked transportation. McCulloch's and Price's numbers had been equally exaggerated by Governor Jackson.[15]

Pillow, unaware of Hardee's plight, issued marching orders to the troops at Fort Randolph on July 26. That night excitement ruled the camp as the men built a "brilliant bonfire of boxes and barrels."[16] Inevitable delays ensued. The troops waited for hours on the riverbank and finally embarked at sunset on the twenty-seventh. As they steamed up river the next day, they were "heartily cheered from both the Missouri and Kentucky shores." To Pillow, the fleet of eight cargo

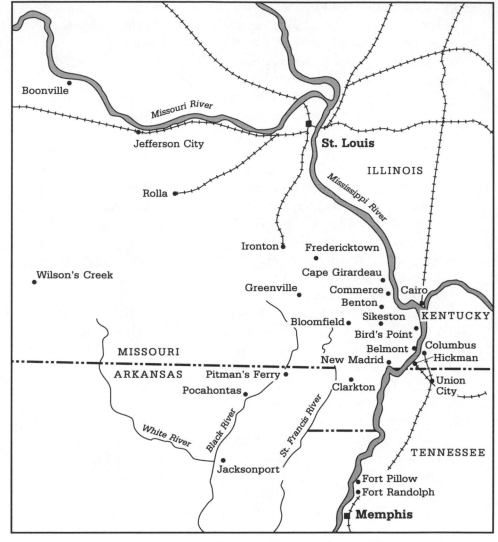

Map 3. Upper Mississippi Valley, April–December, 1861

steamers was "a beautiful sight." The troops' spirits were high. They landed at New Madrid about 4:00 P.M. and found it "a pretty place," with streets "wide and level. The houses are all painted white, and have an air of comfort and neatness." The "whole population" of New Madrid welcomed them with open arms, and Pillow did not disappoint them. He had his Tennesseans give a dress parade in their honor, and the citizens marveled at the military elegance, the lively bands with drum and fife. Pillow inevitably said too much, issuing a proclamation to the people of Missouri that Tennesseans had come to "protect you from tyranny and oppression." He promised to drive the enemy from Missouri in short order. He styled his army the "Army of Liberation" and let it be known that he and his men were eager for the "Dutch hunt." [17]

A soldier remembered Pillow at New Madrid as having a "mild pleasant expression when not excited. . . . He is fond of the good opinion of his men," although he quickly added that Pillow carried the reputation of being a "strict disciplinarian." [18] Pillow administered the oath himself to many new recruits who had joined up in Union City and found themselves a week later at New Madrid. One private "had seen him when a boy. . . . He was a fine looking man. He asked me if I would take the yanks." Pillow made speeches to his troops and had them at fever pitch. Pvt. Val Wynne wrote his brother about the projected campaign from New Madrid—a march of 150 miles to a point in central Missouri where Pillow's ranks would be swelled by 10,000 men and 2,400 Indian warriors. "General Pillow is mad . . . and he is determined to have a desperate campaign. We don't expect any thing in Missouri but the hottest of conflicts. . . . Gen. Pillow enters the state to lead us to St. Louis and we confidently believe that ere November, the Confederate flag will wave over the ruins of that city. . . . You never saw men so anxious to get off. When we received orders to get ready for a march, the boys were in a perfect delirium of joy." [19]

Jeff Thompson, near Bloomfield, heard Pillow had landed in New Madrid; he rode fast, crossing Nigger Wool Swamp, to call upon the Tennesseans. He found that Pillow had "camped in the Park and had the Logwood Cavalry for a Guard. Among the gay and brilliant uniforms that surrounded Headquarters, I must have looked rather strange in my wild and uncouth dress." [20] The Tennesseans did take notice. One remembered Thompson's milk-white stallion with black spots. This wild Missourian had a long bowie knife stuck in his belt, a red sash, and a white plume in his hat. His Indian orderly, Ajax, followed him every step. [21] Thompson held a quick conference with Pillow and Governor Jackson; it was decided to send Thompson back to assist Hardee's move against Ironton from Pitman's Ferry. [22]

Meanwhile, Union Gen. Benjamin Prentiss had heard of Pillow's arrival. He fully expected an attack on Cairo; if not, he surmised quite correctly, the Rebels would advance either upon Ironton or Cape Girardeau. The latter points needed immediate reinforcement. [23]

Unfortunately, Pillow had been yoked with two of the most cautious and conservative generals in the West. Polk had gone along with the advice of others and authorized the seizure of New Madrid. He had adopted as his own Pillow's monumental invasion scheme, but he worried about the risks. Being so new in command and a novice at military affairs, he committed the characteristic error of the cautious—he temporized, sending across the river to Missouri only a portion of the Army of Tennessee. As Polk learned more about the exaggerated numbers of Price and McCulloch and Hardee, he paused. "I shall proceed to fortify my position at New Madrid," Polk wrote the War Department, "with the view of making it a base of operations, and will move forward as circumstances will allow." [24]

Hardee's enthusiasm had waned as well. He began to reflect Jefferson Davis's fear of snarling his small force of Arkansas Confederates in the Missouri political thicket. Hardee was wary of Price and Jackson and Thompson. When Sterling Price welcomed him to the front and asked him to cooperate in a combined attack on Lyon at Springfield, Hardee refused. "I do not wish to march to your assistance with less than 5,000 men, well appointed, and a full complement of artillery." [25] As a conservative man, the quintessence of the professional soldier, Hardee kept paramount his assignment—to build rapidly a Confederate force capable of defending Arkansas. He thought in terms of mission and immediate objectives. He left grand strategy to superiors. To Hardee, the occupation of New Madrid made good sense defensively. He seriously questioned the feasibility of the attack on Ironton by his and Pillow's combined force and wanted the impulsive Pillow restrained "until I am in readiness to support him." Nevertheless, he did assure Polk on July 29 that "I shall strain every nerve to move in a week with 3,000 men, and as many more as practicable. I agree with you that now is the proper time to move into Missouri." [26]

Hardee was as good as his word. He learned of Pillow's arrival in New Madrid on July 29, and scouts reported a Union advance south from Ironton upon his screening force of Missouri cavalry, so he immediately issued orders for his command to advance north toward Ironton. They did so on July 31. By August 4, Hardee had reached Greenville, Missouri, occupied it, and taken a defensive position. He ordered the Missouri cavalry with him to cut the railroad between Ironton and St. Louis. The attack had begun. [27]

Hardee's precipitate invasion of Missouri took Pillow and Polk by surprise. Relying on Hardee's past communications, neither believed he would be able to advance for at least another week. Just as suddenly, however, on July 30 Pillow independently and inexplicably changed the objective of the joint expedition. He wrote Polk that he intended to advance not upon Ironton but directly north upon Cape Girardeau. He would require heavy reinforcement unless Hardee would march east from Pitman's Ferry and unite with him closer to the river. He had decided against marching to Ironton, or at least deferred such a move, until he could reduce Cape Girardeau. The enemy force there "is too large to leave in my rear. The route across the country to Ironton does not furnish subsistence." Pillow requested that Knox Walker's regiment be sent to him from Randolph. "I could then advance and sweep the enemy from my way."[28]

Pillow reiterated his plans to Polk on August 1. He had learned that the route from New Madrid to Ironton would be "*impassable all the way to Jackson except on the plank road.*" "I beg you to press Hardee to move and join me here."[29] The following day Pillow learned Hardee was advancing toward Greenville. He was not pleased. Rather, this meant to him that Hardee would not be coming to assist in the capture of Cape Girardeau. Pillow therefore believed it imperative to engage the enemy at Cape Girardeau at once. "As I cannot have the cooperation of Hardee's force, I wish you to send me two or three more regiments as promptly as practicable." With Neely's and Walker's regiments in New Madrid, he wrote Polk, "I will move in three days after their arrival, and I will cut my way through to Ironton, and there form a union with Hardee." Two sentences later in this confused letter, Pillow contradicted himself. "The swamps make it impossible to form a union with Hardee, as he has taken the Greenville route."[30]

Polk had heard enough. On August 3 he responded to Pillow, cautioning him against attacking Cape Girardeau. To do so would leave an open flank, inviting attack from the enemy at Bird's Point. It "is a matter you should debate very seriously before attempting." Polk advised Pillow instead to strengthen the defenses of New Madrid.[31]

Hardee, meanwhile, moved deeper into Missouri, unaware of Pillow's switch of objectives. His force was small, only 1,500 infantry, but so far he had met with success, and if the Missourians cut the railroad as he had directed, he intended to continue on and attack Ironton. His Missouri cavalry detachment failed, however, so Hardee ordered M. Jeff Thompson to break the railroad with a force from Bloomfield. As Thompson attempted to carry out Hardee's order, he received a peremptory dispatch from his commander, Governor Jackson, ordering him back to New Madrid to support Pillow. It seems

Pillow's intelligence sources had alarmed him with news of a Federal fleet bearing down upon New Madrid, so Pillow had prevailed upon Jackson, who was with him in New Madrid, to divert Thompson. Hardee was disgusted. "Pillow and Jackson destroyed all my plans, for Thompson would have executed my orders and the road would have been broken. *Now* a force of 900 is guarding [the railroad]." Using his prerogative as an independent commander, Hardee also wrote President Davis directly, complaining that Jackson and Pillow had "broken up" his expedition against Ironton.[32]

Confederate plans were in shambles. Delay in receiving communications had led to misinterpretation not only of information, but of motives. Pillow misconstrued Polk's letter of August 3 discouraging attack upon Cape Girardeau to mean abandoning any forward movement. Pillow wanted no part of holding New Madrid for defensive purposes. "If we are to await [the enemy's] pleasure and the accumulations of his forces, then this is not the proper place to meet him. . . . If I am not to go forward it is certainly a very unfortunate movement. . . . You promised me the cooperation of Hardee's force. He is clear out of reach."[33]

Frustrated by Polk, who only restrained him and would not send him the support he required, Pillow decided to ignore him. He appealed directly to Hardee, urging him to unite with him at Benton for a joint attack on Cape Girardeau.[34] Hardee, consistent in his misgivings of Pillow, did not improve matters when he responded somewhat condescendingly that it would be impossible for him to march to Benton even if he had his full force up at Greenville. "It is doubtful if I would be justified in exposing my communications by moving in the direction proposed." He urged Pillow instead to change his base west to Pitman's Ferry, close to the Arkansas-Missouri border.[35]

Pillow responded by writing Polk a letter at once peevish, insubordinate, and threatening. "Before I agreed to come on this duty you assured me I should have the support of Hardee's and Thompson's forces, and you said you would give me a *carte blanche*. In all these assurances I am disappointed. It is painful to be under the necessity of thus complaining, but I am left without support, in an exposed condition, and with inadequate supporting force. . . . Controlled by these circumstances, my convictions of duty compel me to inform you that, unless assured of support, I shall take my whole force, abandon this place, and strike into the interior as the only course left. If the result should prove disastrous to my command or the country below, the responsibility will not rest on me."[36]

Polk, in the meanwhile, had become concerned that the enemy might now send down a flotilla to attack either New Madrid or Island No. 10. Therefore he reacted precipitously himself on August 8, sending ten boats upriver to New Madrid and ordering Pillow to abandon the base and fall back upon Fort Randolph and Fort Pillow immediately.[37] Then just as suddenly, on August 10, elated from preliminary news of Price's victory over Nathaniel Lyon at Wilson's Creek, Polk reversed himself. He ordered Pillow not to return to Tennessee but to join Hardee at Greenville, using the plank road leading inland from the river landing at Pt. Pleasant, just south of New Madrid. He further directed Pillow to abandon his base at New Madrid and re-establish it at Pitman's Ferry or Pocahontas. This was precisely what Hardee had wanted and what Pillow did not wish to hear.[38]

These shifts in direction understandably threw Pillow's command into confusion. Upon receipt of Polk's order of August 8, Pillow had moved with dispatch. He broke camp and began transferring his troops to Tennessee. "Your order to fall back casts a deep gloom over this army, and caused me the most anxious and painful day I ever experienced, but still I promptly complied with it."[39] When Polk countermanded the order, the "Army of Liberation" had already embarked, so Pillow had to dispatch a steamer to stop the fleet and turn it around. Pillow now, and apparently only now, learned the plank road from Pt. Pleasant to the interior was unusable.[40] He informed Polk he was returning his Tennesseans to New Madrid and would do what he had intended all along—take another road to the interior, a "fine road" leading north, running close to Cape Girardeau. Pillow reassured his commander that he would take care to avoid the enemy as he passed them on his flank. He further reassured Polk that he would fulfill his role as subordinate. "You know I understand the work before me; my prompt obedience to your order to evacuate was the proof of my submission to orders as a soldier." This was precisely what Leonidas Polk did not wish to hear.[41]

Pillow reported to Polk on August 12 that he was back in New Madrid and ready to advance, "only detained for want of transportation." Once again he had assumed command of Jeff Thompson's Missouri force and had positioned him in advance at Sikeston. Pillow wanted one more regiment from Tennessee, however, before he marched. "You ought to give me the strength necessary to make my movement a brilliant success."[42]

Meanwhile, Hardee had ordered Fredericktown, forty miles north of Greenville, occupied and railroad communications with St. Louis snapped. He would soon discover he had acted on faulty information. When he learned Polk had ordered Pillow to abandon New Madrid and "march out and join me," making Pitman's Ferry his base, he wrote Hindman: "This puts a new phase on affairs above. . . . We shall certainly have much hard fighting, and soon." He ordered another Arkansas infantry regiment forward to Greenville and made plans to rush others up as soon as they had been organized. Hardee thought the situation looked very good.[43]

On August 13, when Polk received Pillow's letter of August 11 and learned that his subordinate planned to reoccupy New Madrid and crash ahead to the north past Cape Girardeau, he was clearly provoked but failed to take action other than to express his disappointment. He would come to New Madrid himself.[44]

Thompson's force of 1,500 Missourians, reinforced by some of Pillow's Tennessee cavalry, took position at Sikeston and began to range about the countryside raiding and serving for a screening force for the advance of Pillow's infantry from New Madrid. Thompson demonstrated before the river town of Commerce, Missouri, on August 18. He found the town lightly defended, seized it, and from the riverbank fired into passing steamboats and across the river into Illinois. Flushed with success, Thompson believed if the Confederates acted promptly they could capture Cape Girardeau, a primary objective of Pillow's all along. Col. John P. McCown commanded the column coming up from New Madrid composed of the 4th, 13th, and 154th Senior Tennessee regiments. They advanced within four miles of Benton, Missouri, linked up with Thompson, and halted awaiting further orders.[45]

Polk came up to New Madrid on August 15 to confer with Pillow and a council of his senior officers. He explained his worries about the movement north to Benton, and his frustration over Pillow abandoning the plan to change his base of operations inland to Pitman's Ferry. Pillow, however, appears to have been utterly persuasive and somehow convinced Polk of the feasibility of his own design. Even though Hardee operated on a different set of assumptions, Polk vacillated, seemingly unwilling or unable to impose his own concept of operations. Polk and Pillow still differed over the importance of the defenses at Island No. 10. Polk considered it vital to the security of the Mississippi. He wanted it fortified and had taken steps to reinforce it. Pillow disagreed, believing the times called for offensive action, and discounted the enemy's ability and will to attack so far downriver.[46]

Uncertain of his own judgment, Polk left the conference still worried about the security of the river fortifications and Pillow's exposed position. On his return to Memphis he received information confirming his fears: a Federal attack by water seemed imminent against Island No. 10. Resolved on a course of action, he at once dispatched three steamers to ferry Pillow's troops to Tennessee. "My opinion therefore is, I repeat, *that you cross the river forthwith and make Union City your base.*"[47] To emphasize his order, which he unfortunately framed as a suggestion, and to make certain it would be carried out, Polk wrote again on August 16 that the enemy threatened Island No. 10 and that he wanted it held with Pillow's troops; Colonel McCown's brigade would occupy it and fortify. Polk had also received a dispatch from Richmond "ordering the immediate removal" of two regiments at Union City for East Tennessee. These considerations demanded that Pillow delay "any movement contemplated by you in Missouri." Polk, however, added a last paragraph, fatal in dealing with a subordinate like Gideon Pillow: "In regard to compliance with this order, you are left to conform your action to the exigencies of the case."[48]

What was Pillow to do? Abandon his expedition? He wrote Polk that the enemy gunboats that had landed in the vicinity of Island No. 10 were not there to seize the place but were only chasing after the annoying Confederate gunboat *Grampus.* Pillow had new information that the enemy had no intent to seize the island. They were preoccupied instead with the defense of St. Louis. Federal newspapers made it clear how demoralized Missouri had become since Lyon's defeat at Wilson's Creek. "If you will only order me up one more regiment, and push up my transportation, . . . I will drive everything out of my way, join Hardee in five days, and push on to Saint Louis, destroying the railroad; but for God's sake don't hold me back or cripple me for a *want* which will wait on you until the work of emancipating Missouri is completed." Therefore, Pillow continued, he felt justified, based on "the *new light* we now have," in suspending Polk's order regarding Island No. 10. Most indiscreetly, he informed Jeff Thompson of Polk's order and that he intended to disobey it.[49]

Pillow was fortunate. Polk received information on August 17 that troops were being sent him from Mississippi to offset those removed to East Tennessee. He now felt secure enough to allow Pillow to proceed with his expedition into Missouri; he was sending him the additional regiment he needed (Knox Walker's 2d Tennessee) and fifty wagons with teams.[50] Polk also agreed to release experienced Colonel McCown to command Pillow's advance brigade. Col. R. P. Neely's 4th Tennessee, which he was forwarding, could tend to the defenses of

Island No. 10. Polk enclosed a dispatch to Hardee, which he wanted Pillow to read and forward. It explained the change in plans.[51]

Pillow, however, wanted more. He decided to keep McCown and Walker and Neely's regiment, too. He wrote Polk that the engineering officer assigned to Island No. 10, Capt. A. B. Gray, "does not want Neely's regiment."[52] When Neely arrived at New Madrid en route to Island No. 10, one of Pillow's staff directed the colonel to take his troops off the boat and march toward Benton. This clearly contradicted Neely's explicit orders from Polk, so he refused and went to Pillow's headquarters, where the general gave him a "more peremptory [*sic*] order." After Captain Gray told him he was not needed on Island No. 10, Neely yielded and set off inland. Neely's second in command, Lt. Col. Otho F. Strahl, wrote Polk himself, however: "Why do we have to *obey* Gen. Pillow and Col. Neely's orders to march on shore immediately for the interior when this conflicts with your orders?"[53]

Polk took action, ordering Pillow to return Neely's 4th Tennessee to Island No. 10 "immediately."[54] Pillow fired back two angry letters; insubordination bubbled close to the surface of both. In the first, he openly disobeyed Polk and refused to recall Neely. But Polk's staff officer, Lieutenant Colonel McGehee, who delivered the order, surprised Pillow. He went forward and ordered Neely back himself.

Pillow then wrote a second letter to Polk. This letter followed a pattern common in Pillow's communications with superior officers. There was disbelief that such instructions could have been issued in the first place. Obstacles were revealed, rendering compliance contradictory to previous orders, incomprehensible, or suicidal: "If Neely should return under the order, which I cannot suppose you would have given had you known all the circumstances and the condition of things, it will greatly imperil the forces already 40 miles from me." There was the usual blame shifting ("I only know that I had no idea you would be offended at my agreeing to what your engineer requested"); the usual declaration of purity of intent ("I have no motive to gratify but to serve the country; and it seems to me that you ought to be disposed to strengthen the force all you could"); the lament of the injured innocent ("If I have not your confidence, and if I am to be tied down and allowed no *discretion*, I certainly cannot but regard it unfortunate that I yielded to your wishes and accepted a command my feeling so strongly prompted me to decline"); and, ultimately, the justification for insubordination: "If I should shrink from the responsibility of acting upon my own clear convictions in a case involving the safety of the forces under my command, even though in doing so

I disobeyed your orders, I would then, indeed, be unworthy of your confidence."[55]

Pillow struck again the following day, August 21. He wrote Secretary of War Walker, ostensibly to submit a list of his staff, but actually to update Walker on affairs in east Missouri and the expectation of linking up with Hardee. "When we meet," Pillow told Walker about Hardee, "from his rank, he will take command of the whole unless in Courtesy, he allows me to command which is not probable." Pillow reminded Walker of how he had worked and spent his personal resources to build the Tennessee army at New Madrid: "You can judge with what reluctance I yield the command to an officer who was a captain under me in the Mexican war—while I was a Major General. Why is it that I have been placed in position & ranked by nearly every General officer of the Confederate Army when it is known that I ranked every officer now in that army in my long term of service." Pillow closed with an attack on his commander: "I would have been off some time since but for my shortness of transportation and for General Polk's orders and varying views and countermanding orders, repeatedly made, thus crippling my operations and movements."[56]

Polk responded sternly to Pillow's insubordination. "You have usurped an authority not properly your own, by which you have thwarted and embarrassed his [Polk's] arrangements and operations for the general defense." Pillow's behavior, therefore, would be referred to the War Department. When he received Pillow's second letter and learned the latter had agreed to return Neely, Polk softened somewhat. He would not report Pillow, and so far as curtailing his discretion, Polk assured his subordinate that he would never limit him within the "sphere embraced by your command," unless "there seems to be a disposition manifested to exceed your lawful authority."[57]

The enemy had not remained idle waiting for Pillow, Polk, and Hardee to decide a common course of action. Maj. Gen. John C. Frémont, commander of forces in Missouri, had sent a tough-minded brigadier, Ulysses S. Grant, to take over the 3,000 Federals at Ironton on August 8. He would take special care to post heavy guards to keep the railroad open to St. Louis. With energy and skill Grant quickly prepared his troops not only to repel Hardee's threat from Greenville, but to take the offensive themselves. A week later, as Grant prepared to strike against Hardee, Frémont appointed General Prentiss to the command, strongly reinforced him, and ordered him to secure the railroad and to seize Fredericktown.

Hardee was concerned about this buildup to his front and discouraged by the Pillow-Polk confusion. He wrote Hindman to report with his troops to McCulloch and informed him that he had sent Col. Solon Borland to Pillow to explain his views.[58] Borland arrived at Pillow's headquarters in New Madrid and told him that Hardee did "not see much prospect at present for striking a blow against Ironton. . . . I apprehend that if Pillow should unite his forces with mine, that we are too weak, combined, to march on Saint Louis."[59] Pillow interpreted Hardee's feelings more closely: "Hardee thinks he cannot advance to Jackson (one of the proposed points of rendezvous), Cape Girardeau, or any other point. In other words, he thinks himself unable to co-operate at all, but proposes that we shall occupy our positions and await the maturity of the growing crop and the arrival of reinforcements." Pillow disagreed completely: "This is against my judgment. My opinion is that we should move promptly on the enemy's positions, and dislodge him before he has time to gather his forces and send them down upon us. I regard the success of everything as depending upon our immediate advance. . . . To fall back is to give up the cause of Missouri." He expressed himself the same way to Hardee. Pillow sent Borland downriver on the *Grampus* to confer with Polk and to secure a decision on the course of action to be taken.[60]

It appears Pillow thought twice about having Borland alone with Polk and decided to accompany him. The three held a conference at Fort Pillow, probably on August 23. A grandiose plan emerged, on which Pillow's imprint is clear. Pillow would go ahead with his attack on Cape Girardeau. Once he had captured it, Thompson's force would remain there while Pillow crossed the Mississippi north of Cairo, turned south, and took the Federal staging point in reverse. "In anticipation" of success, Pillow wrote Polk to alert General Clark and the Mississippi forces to be ready to move to Union City and advance through Columbus to meet him at or near Cairo. "If I can take Cairo and hold it, it will put an end to the idea of a descent on the river, and of course there will be no use of force at Union City." When he returned to New Madrid, Pillow issued the necessary orders to implement this military fantasy.[61]

Sam Tate in Memphis was appalled. The influential railroad president urged Confederate Congressman David M. Currin to speak to President Davis and tell him about Pillow "acting on this own hook" and his lack of cooperation with Polk. Pillow "says he intends to fight his own fight first before he joins commands with Hardee or any one else," Tate reported. "Insist upon their sending a practical military leader here to take charge of our army in the field or put Hardee on this line of defenses."[62] Missouri Lt. Gov. Thomas C. Reynolds echoed Tate's remarks. He found Polk willing to listen to suggestions, "but General Pillow's pecularities forbid my taking such a liberty with him." Reynolds advocated to "let him go ahead to find out, occasionally by knocking his head against a wall, that he is on the wrong path."[63]

It is incredible that Pillow, with Borland present, won Polk's approval of his plan to attack Cape Girardeau. Then, with an astonishing somersault of logic and purpose, on August 25 Pillow reversed himself completely and countermanded his own orders. He explained in a long letter to Polk that he had talked again with Borland and had reconsidered. "Hardee is an old officer, of large experience," wrote Pillow, "and I have thought that with this positive expression of opinion by him, knowing, as he must, his exact position and resources, it is perhaps not prudent for us to constrain him by your decision to act against his positively expressed opinion in a matter involving the safety of the force under his command." So Pillow told Polk that he would hold his force near Benton until he had heard Hardee's reaction to the decision for Hardee to advance east and unite at Benton, and then to march on Cape Girardeau and Cairo.

In fact, what chilled Pillow's plans for the grand attack was not his talk with Borland nor his reliance on the judgment of Hardee. It was Frank Cheatham. He had come forward in New Madrid and appealed to the elated Pillow at the moment he was about to plunge forward. Perhaps the plain-spoken Cheatham—the good Democrat—was the only man capable of dissuading him. Cheatham told Pillow that he was "strongly opposed" to the attack on Cape Girardeau, as were his regimental commanders Preston Smith and John V. Wright. "Without the co-operation of Hardee's force, my judgment has been all the while against the movement," Pillow continued. In an opinion now "well matured and settled," Pillow advised Polk to let Hardee "decide what he can do," and if he still resists the idea of attacking Cape Girardeau, "I think his force should be brought over to the river front and occupy this place and fortify it in conjunction with your works at No. 10, while your own force [Pillow and the Army of Tennessee] could be disposed the more effectually to protect the river and interior of Tennessee, and after strongly fortifying Island No. 10 you may see the way open to fortify Columbus."[64]

The reaction to Pillow's decision to abandon the attempt on Cape Girardeau was mixed. Lieutenant Governor Reynolds of Missouri, bitterly disappointed, wrote Hardee asking for a meeting of Hardee,

Thompson, Reynolds, and Pillow. He was openly critical of Pillow's management of the operation, claiming that he "disposed his own army so unskillfully as almost to invite attack."[65] Jeff Thompson was "really grieved to know his conclusions, after being so encouraged by his letters of last night, which assured me that he would advance this morning [August 25]. . . . We never had any business this side of the swamp, and it has only been a Memphis fear that prompted such a move."[66]

Hardee, on August 27, felt sure that the final decision had been made against a joint campaign on Cape Girardeau when he received Pillow's letter informing him that he had suspended the attack until he could hear that Hardee would join him. Hardee wrote privately to Pillow, expressing "my unfeigned satisfaction at your determination. I shall go to bed tonight with a lighter heart." The campaign to capture Cape Girardeau and move across the river to seize Cairo was, Hardee continued,

> without precedent in history. It must inevitably have led to disaster. Who ever heard of such a flank march in the presence of such an enemy or whoever heard of marching such a distance with so small a force, with the ability of the enemy to concentrate such an overwhelming force against him at the point of contact. When Colo. Borland returned and told me the result of his mission, I exclaimed, Pillow and Polk are crazy. . . . As I said in a previous letter a retrograde movement is dispiriting, but better than disaster. If you had lost your army it might have cost us untold men and treasure to have regained our prestige. Rest assured you have done the wisest act of your life.[67]

When Pillow reported his misgivings to Polk, Polk at once accepted his reluctance as the end of the operation. He had agreed to the attack against his better judgment at the Fort Pillow conference. He told Pillow to post Thompson on the Missouri side of the river and to divide the "Army of Liberation" between Island No. 10 and Union City.[68] None of this sat well with Pillow. Doubtless Hardee's patronizing letter angered him, and he in turn would use Hardee as his scapegoat. Pillow wrote Polk on August 28 acknowledging the end of the Cape Girardeau operation and stating that now he "would turn my face . . . upon other duty, without an apparent abandonment of a forward movement."[69] He argued that Island No. 10 was "greatly overrated" and that the true defense of the Mississippi depended upon the occupation of Columbus, adding a statement from Captain Gray, Polk's pliable engineer, strongly supporting this position. He closed his letter with a poisoned pen: "Hardee did not wait until he received my dispatch, which followed Borland, and of which I gave you the substance, before he decided. He has acted in the face of his agreement, by Borland, to abide your decision."[70] Pillow also blasted Hardee in a letter to his friend, Secretary of War Walker. The operation had failed because of "Hardee's falling back and failing to cooperate with me." Pillow added with accurate insight that the abortive joint expedition nevertheless had distracted Frémont and kept reinforcements from Lyon, thus enabling him to be defeated at Wilson's Creek.[71]

So the grand Missouri campaign of the summer of 1861 ended ingloriously. Staff officer John F. Henry[72] wrote his father on August 31 from Sikeston, where Pillow had left a brigade of Tennesseans dangling, not knowing whether the next order would be to advance or retreat: "Somehow or other our officers here in this part of the state don't work together at all. Between Polk, Pillow & Cheatham I don't know who is in command, they are all pulling in opposite directions, one will give an order and the other will countermand it." General Pillow "is not popular with the men & officers and never will be I believe. I never did see a man with as few admirers in my life & so many enemies. He is a vain man and does some foolish things, but he is the hardest worker I ever saw & is no doubt a good general, but some how he can't get up that impression."[73]

It would be a mistake, however, to view Pillow's New Madrid adventure as folly. His sometime critic, Lieutenant Governor Reynolds, wrote him on October 10 that Missouri was grateful:

One of the earliest and most ardent of our friends in our struggle for independence, you led your brave countrymen to our aid when almost our entire territory had been overrun by foes, and internal sedition, insolently claiming the right to abolish the regular government of the State. Although circumstances prevented you from seeking the enemy in the strongholds in which his timid caution held him, yet the presence of your army at New Madrid powerfully contributed to the success of the common cause by diverting forces which might otherwise have been used against us in the South West.[74]

Another notable development during the Missouri campaign was Pillow's opening negotiations with Union Col. W. H. L. Wallace at Bird's Point regarding the exchange of prisoners. It was a cat-and-mouse game on the part of the Federal officials, who did not wish by their action to recognize the legitimacy of the Confederate forces. Pillow succeeded in having three members of the Missouri state guard (Thompson's men) swapped for three Union soldiers. This exchange apparently was the first instance of formal exchange of prisoners in the war.[75]

Polk, who had failed so badly in attempting to coordinate the Missouri enterprise, wrote Davis on August 29 that experience had shown the need for unified command. The War Department complied at once, on September 2, extending Polk's command to include Arkansas and operations in Missouri. But it was too late. Davis added in a note to Polk that he must have "cordial cooperation" to succeed, and that anyone "who disturbs the harmony of joint action" should be kept "near to your Hd. Qrs. and under your immediate supervision." He suggested that perhaps Cheatham, who "could cooperate," should head the army in the field.[76]

11   A Plunge into the Forest

Restless for anything positive to divert public attention
from the failure in Missouri, Pillow returned to the idea of seizing
Columbus, Kentucky. That is what "induced me to establish the force
at Union City," he wrote Polk, "looking with certainty to the time I
could occupy Columbus." The compelling reason, Pillow argued, was
that "its possession is a military necessity, involving the ultimate safety
of Tennessee from devastating invasion." Unionists in Kentucky were
organizing rapidly, "and as soon as it is possible for Lincoln to raise
forces to meet other pressing wants he will take possession of this
place, and from it, as a *point d'appui*, he will direct his column upon
Tennessee." "If you do not intend to let the enemy take possession of

that gateway, you must take it *first*." He had made the same argument months earlier to Governors Harris and Magoffin.[1]

Pillow, obsessed by the desire to initiate action, disregarded the enormous political consequences in the name of *"paramount military necessity."* For a man who talked, from time to time, in terms of the "law of nations," this insistence on invading Kentucky, violating her fragile neutrality, seems not only impulsive, but irrationally contradictory. On the other hand, the willingness to choose expediency at the sake of principle marks the political realist. Startling success, Pillow believed, paints over blemishes and makes all bright and new. "I am willing to be saddled with all the responsibility," he wrote to Polk, the man who would, of course, be responsible. Pillow hoped to shape Confederate strategy with his hammering persistence. Championing an idea with energy and determination, despite odds, despite logic, could result not only in the adoption of that idea, but in its success; motivation counted for everything. Pillow believed this with all his heart.

Polk decided to go along. Again and again, from mid-August to early September 1861, Polk seems to have put his own judgment aside, deferring to Pillow. This time the critical factor leading him to yield to Pillow's persuasion was the occupation of Belmont, Missouri, across from Columbus, on September 2 by a reinforced regiment of Federals. It seems to have "pulled the trigger in Polk's mind." As Pillow had suggested, Polk ordered the troops assembling at Union City up to the Kentucky border. On the night of September 3, Pillow's forces left New Madrid, Missouri, crossed the Mississippi, and captured Hickman, Kentucky. Enemy gunboats attempted to interfere, but Frank Cheatham provided cover. He tied the side-wheeler *Jackson* to the shore, banked the fires, and let the steam go down; then he ran out guns on deck and opened fire on the enemy, who withdrew up river. Columbus fell September 4 as Confederates raced in from Hickman and Union City.[2]

The backlash was immediate. Responsible Confederate leaders were horrified. Harris asked Pillow to withdraw his troops from Kentucky immediately; Davis ordered Pillow out of Columbus and demanded an explanation from Polk. The credibility of Polk, not Pillow, was damaged badly.[3] Polk would spend the balance of September unsuccessfully explaining and defending his action, as would the president of the Confederacy. Grant's seizure of Paducah on September 6 put most discussion of principle aside and justified, in Pillow's mind at least, Confederate aggression. As he had thought all along, prizes go to the bold.[4]

Pillow intended to use the towering bluffs of Columbus as a mighty bastion blocking the Mississippi and protecting West Tennessee from invasion, but he also wished to use it as a springboard for the control of Kentucky, certainly that portion of the state west of the Tennessee River. Once Columbus had been occupied, he urged Polk to push a column north to attack Paducah. Nothing came of this, but Pillow did succeed in having Cheatham, with two brigades, advance east to Mayfield and seize it.[5]

The second week in September, Jeff Thompson had the first of several fights with the Federals on the west side of the river. It was an uneven match since the ever-present gunboats joined in and shelled Thompson's camp. Pillow decided to intervene and took the 4th Tennessee and a field battery to Thompson's assistance. They crossed the Mississippi and raced along the Missouri shore several miles, but the enemy withdrew and Pillow's Tennesseans had to sleep on the riverbank without blankets or rations. They raged in disappointment: the Yankees would not fight.[6]

Sidney Johnston took command of the Department of the West on September 15, 1861. Polk was assigned the 1st Division, Western Department, which included Columbus and the upper Mississippi River defenses. Pillow was second in command to Polk. Johnston came to Columbus on the nineteenth, met with Polk and Pillow, and surveyed the situation. The Confederates would remain on the defensive, stretched paper-thin from Cumberland Gap across the Mississippi to the Indian Territory. Heavily fortified positions at Columbus and Bowling Green would anchor the line.[7]

Thus Pillow sheathed his sword and spent the balance of September and October 1861 at Columbus. Actually, he served as commandant of the town, immersing himself in the details of scheduling massive working parties to rush the construction of the miles of complicated fortifications. He appointed courts, supervised the provost marshal, provided security arrangements, settled disputes in regimental elections, calmed protesting citizens molested by chicken- and corn-stealing soldiers, appointed a medical board to help battle widespread camp diseases, inspected living quarters, and sent details out to secure provisions and wood and Kentucky recruits. As he had in Memphis, he kept a tight rein on river commerce and all traffic entering and leaving Columbus by road or rail. Once again he constructed a huge chain across the Mississippi which blocked all river traffic for a while.[8] He waged a war against liquor and had offenders publicly flogged. Pillow ran Columbus like a fiefdom, and he did a very good job. Observers, even his critics, acknowledged his effectiveness. He was "a hard-working man."[9]

Jealousy of Polk and painful awareness of status ate at Pillow, however, taking the form of complaints, squabbles, and threats.[10] Aggressive leadership was needed at Columbus, and Pillow believed he had to suffer fools. An English observer noted that Pillow openly expressed himself as being better suited for command than his superior. His "vanity," wrote the Englishman, "is not less conspicuous than it was in Mexico, and he is eternally carping at 'the bishop,' as he terms Polk."[11] Pillow commanded a division under Polk. Cheatham, Bowen, and McCown also had divisions, each about 3,000 in strength. Pillow's 1st Division, however, contained 6,862 men in three brigades. His old comrade, Col. Knox Walker, commanded the 1st Brigade, Col. Robert M. Russell, a West Pointer, commanded the 2d, and Col. William E. Travis the 3d.[12]

By mid-October the Confederate defensive line through Kentucky protruded at the strong points, Bowling Green and Columbus. The area between lay open and vulnerable. The neglected river forts, Donelson and Henry, supported by a "vital position" at Clarksville, were the keys to its defense. To strengthen this undermanned sector, Johnston wanted to shift 5,000 men from Columbus. Specifically, he wanted Pillow's division. Polk protested politely that the loss of these troops would seriously weaken his army in the face of the numerically superior foe at Cairo. It is easy to imagine Pillow standing behind Polk's shoulder as he wrote to Johnston. Of course Pillow fed his superior's innate caution. Pillow had no desire to leave Columbus and the Tennessee troops he had organized and commanded; he had no desire to be just another brigadier in Bowling Green, subordinate to Major General Hardee, not to speak of having to serve alongside his nemesis, division commander Buckner. So Polk, probably at Pillow's insistence, sent him to Bowling Green in person to explain to Johnston more fully. Pillow met with Johnston on November 4 and returned to Columbus the following day. Johnston had listened patiently, but he remained unconvinced. Pillow's division would move to Clarksville immediately.[13]

Pillow's troops prepared for the march November 6, breaking camp and cooking extra rations. At dawn on the seventh they formed on the road leading to Clarksville; after being fed they began moving east.

Already their tents, baggage, and some ammunition had been loaded into wagons. The men themselves carried only essentials and a minimum of cartridges. A staff officer from Polk suddenly appeared. He rode up to Pillow and ordered him to halt the column and proceed immediately to headquarters. When Pillow arrived, Polk gave him welcome news. Federal gunboats had appeared at Lucas Bend, several miles upriver. They were escorting transports which appeared to be disembarking troops, a "considerable force," on the Missouri side, above the Confederate camp at Belmont. Polk told Pillow to reverse his column, cross the Mississippi at once with four regiments, and take charge of the forces on the west bank at Belmont.[14] Pillow sent a staff officer to rush the Clarksville column back to the riverbank. Clanking and jangling at the double-quick, they came down the steep cliffs to the landing. Pillow's men would remember the hurry, and they would recall how little ammunition they had: "I had only 7 cartridges and Polk Dillon just one." Many had only three. At the riverbank the *Charm*, *Prince*, and *Harry W. R. Hill* waited with steam up.[15]

First across was the 12th Tennessee. At their head rode Lt. Col. Tyree H. Bell, a native Kentuckian but recently a Sumner County, Tennessee, farmer. The colonel of the 12th was Pillow's best-trained regimental commander, Robert M. Russell. Russell had brigade responsibilities that day, so Bell marched the 12th out from the Belmont steamboat landing and formed them, awaiting Pillow's instructions.

Stationed at Belmont was another of Pillow's regiments, the 13th Arkansas, commanded by Col. James C. Tappan of Phillips County. Tappan had married a niece of Aaron V. Brown. He was a strong Democrat, well educated, refined, and wealthy—"a perfect Chesterfield."[16] Tappan had his men out chopping timber that morning, dropping trees randomly, to form a crude abatis about their tent camp, called "Camp Johnston" in honor of their new chief. Inside Camp Johnston was a splendid battery of field artillery, the Louisiana Watson Battery, commanded by Lt. Col. Daniel Beltzhoover, an experienced professional.

Tappan and Beltzhoover established a defensive position before Pillow arrived, throwing two companies of cavalry well forward and placing a two-gun section and a company of infantry to cover a road leading into the rear of Camp Johnston. The remainder of the Watson Battery commanded a road coming into Belmont from the west. Most of Tappan's infantry was deployed to the right of these guns in front of the abatis. "Good idea," thought Pvt. Phil Stephenson of the 13th, "for the intention was for our men to use the fallen timber as bulwarks in case of having to fall back." Tappan completed his deployment by 8:45 A.M. and waited.[17]

Pillow crossed with Bell's 12th Tennessee about nine o'clock. "I had no choice of position, nor time to make any reconnaissance," Pillow reported. He took a company from each of three regiments and sent them out as skirmishers to retard the advance of the enemy from Hunter's Farm. Then he called out his regiments from the riverbank and placed them. "We were soon marched in double quick something less than a mile and formed into line of battle."[18] Instead of accepting Tappan's line and extending it, however, Pillow pulled Tappan back forty yards, which meant that, when extended, the Confederate line no longer ran inside the edge of the woods. Instead of having the cover of the woods, most of Pillow's troops, almost three full regiments, would be out in the field itself.[19]

Bell's 12th Tennessee went in the woods to Tappan's right. Bell had a strong position, as did Tappan. To Tappan's left, in an open field, Pillow placed Thomas J. Freeman's 22d Tennessee, then Ed Pickett's 21st, and finally John V. Wright's 13th, bent back at an angle about thirty degrees to the left. The 21st had its left and left center tucked behind the Watson Battery, while the left of Tappan and right of Freeman overlapped clumsily. At the left center of his line Pillow concentrated Beltzhoover's guns on the road from Hunter's Farm. The result was a short, cramped line of battle about 400 yards in length, running generally north to south across a wide cornfield. The axis lay parallel to the river and some one-half mile west of Camp Johnston.[20]

Pillow's plan of defense appears passive: to block the road from Hunter's Farm, stand and receive the enemy's attack, and then, perhaps in the back of Pillow's mind, countercharge with bayonets. It seems he placed Wright on the extreme left as a precaution—a potential flanking force and reserve. To replace the Watson Battery at the rear of Camp Johnston and to close the interval between the 13th and the river, Pillow detached one of Wright's companies.[21]

Pillow's deployment gave the Confederates the advantage of "good lateral and rear communications." The right flank was well positioned, but the left (Wright's 13th Tennessee) was dangerously exposed and overextended, and the center lay in an open cornfield, facing heavy woods forty to eighty yards to its front. A soldier in the 22d remarked it was like "fighting a duel with his enemy behind a tree and he in the open field."[22] Pillow did not take advantage of the abatis; he ignored the defensive potential of the ravines running perpendicular to the enemy's line of advance; he allowed the enemy the heavy woods and took the open field. One of his critics, Colonel Freeman, felt "it would be very difficult to place our troops in a position where they would be more exposed to the fire of the enemy." Others agreed that Pillow's choice of position was unfortunate.[23]

After deploying his five regiments, Pillow, contrary to his official report, went forward to reconnoiter. He returned and found Maj. Henry Winslow of Polk's staff. Evidently worried about the size of the enemy force advancing upon him, Pillow asked Winslow to send over another regiment and another battery.

Ulysses S. Grant, an untested and untrusted Illinois brigadier, commanded the Federals. He struck hard at the Confederate right and center about 11:00 A.M. The fight was inconclusive on the right with foiled envelopments, charges, and countercharges. The exposed regiments of Pillow's center, however, came under heavier and heavier fire from an unseen enemy. Frustration mounted as ammunition ran out. Meanwhile, the Watson Battery fired away ineffectually, tearing trees to splinters above the heads of the Federal infantry; all the while, those same infantrymen hidden in the forest fired back, wounding and killing Watson gunners.

Soon two sections of Union artillery fought their way through the woods and opened up on the Watsons. The fight was short and unequal. Dan Beltzhoover had a terrible time: his horse was killed under him, his coat and hat were "literally riddled," and his sword had been "knocked all to pieces with minie balls." Then it seems the Watson Battery ran out of ammunition. Pillow ordered Beltzhoover to pull back to Camp Johnston, and the battery retired in some disorder under heavy fire. One of the prized cannon was abandoned.

Reports came in to Pillow from the right and center that ammunition was exhausted and casualties were mounting.[24] Grant seemed determined to remain in the woods and pick the Confederates off one by one. When word came that the left flank regiment, John V. Wright's reliable 13th, had one battalion without ammunition, Pillow decided upon a bayonet charge. He sent his staff up and down the regiments with the order. Unfortunately, "half our men had left their bayonets back in camp," as a Confederate reported.[25] The bayonet charge was poorly coordinated, regiments and sometimes companies executing the order on their own. Men in Pickett's and Freeman's regiments raced across the open field; a rail fence broke their formations. From the woods in front came a "withering volley," musket balls "whistling like the north wind." Most units penetrated the woods, but no deeper than seventy-five yards. The only breakthrough (in the Union right center) was quickly plugged by counterattack.[26]

While his men charged, Pillow remained conspicuously in the open, cheering and observing. Surrounded by staff, he made a choice target, as he had throughout the fight. His display of courage, of "daring, personal bravery," won admiration by those who observed it. Staff officer Gustavus A. Henry, Jr., watched a Yankee take aim at Pillow. Henry shouted "to the Genl & he spurred his horse & the fellow fired & down went my horse." Two members of Pillow's staff fell (Q.M. Maj. John G. Finnie and aide Capt. "Red" Jackson). Everyone, even Pillow's orderly, had a mount killed or wounded.[27]

The grand bayonet charge failed. Pillow's troops were caught in the fringe of the woods; they could not hold for long. Colonel Freeman was furious. It "was more like a plunge into the forest to ferret the enemy out and then drive him back. . . . I think the charge was ill-judged and almost impossible to have been executed with success." The 13th Tennessee, for instance, got the order to charge too late, and its adjoining regiment, the 22d, attacked unsupported. It was a costly failure for the Confederates, in casualties and in morale. They pulled back piecemeal, some to the shelter of a slight ridge in the cornfield, others into the deep woods to the right rear of the line. Many abandoned the fight altogether.

Pillow watched the bayonet charge fizzle and realized his only hope was to reach Camp Johnston and re-form. But at this time he began to hear ominous sounds of musket fire from the left rear, from the back road where he had placed the security company. Pillow ordered retreat at once. To leave their position in the line, however, entailed great danger. Many of his men who had held and fought till their ammunition ran out now had to cross open ground, making prime targets for Yankee marksmen. When the Union artillery opened on them, Pillow's line crumbled.[28]

Meanwhile, on the far right of the Union line, an unengaged regiment of Federals under Col. Napoleon B. Buford and Grant's cavalry on the extreme right were blocked from advancing by a water-filled slough. Buford led them south, away from the battle, on a road that skirted the obstacle. Unfortunately for the Confederates, Buford, while marching, discovered yet another road, which led the column behind the enemy into Camp Johnston itself. Pillow had placed Company A of the 13th Tennessee there as security, and it fought hard but was overwhelmed, and Buford drove into Camp Johnston from the south, into the rear and flank of Pillow's retreating troops.

Ammunition gone, artillery gone, assailed from front, flank, and rear, Pillow's command fled to the riverbank. Here and there an officer would rally a company and make a stand. Attempts were made to re-form the regiments in Camp Johnston, but the fast-moving Yankee field artillery would unlimber and blast away at any organized body of men. The Federals chased Pillow and his troops through the streets of the tent camp a few hundred yards up the riverbank. "General Pillow and his whole suit partook of the general panic & rushed madly to the water's edge." [29] The abatis—and the disorganization of the attack itself—began to take its toll on the Federals, too. Pursuit, such as it was, became more like a mob chasing a mob. Pillow shouted and begged his men to stand and fight, but nothing seemed to avail. They sought the shelter of the high riverbank and hid, utterly demoralized.

At this terrible moment, as if in answer to a prayer, Pillow saw the *Harry W. R. Hill*, loaded with troops, appear at the Belmont landing. Before the steamboat could tie up, men began to leap from the decks into the water and swim for shore. They were Knox Walker's wild Irishmen, the 2d Tennessee. Pillow met Walker on the bank and urged him to buy time by attacking at once. Walker complied. He formed a line of battle on the riverbank, adding to his regiment a number of men from the shattered 13th and 21st. Then Walker's reinforced 2d counterattacked with the bayonet "at the full run." [30] The fighting grew savage, with big knives flashing and rifles being used for clubs in hand-to-hand fighting. Some of Grant's Iowa troops were "overpowered and threw down their arms." The Yankee pursuit had been stopped cold. [31]

Pillow used this miraculous opportunity to reorganize. Aided by Russell, Tappan, and others, he tried to develop a defensive line between the abatis and the levee. But again the Union artillery proved Pillow's undoing. Up came a section of guns, and then an enterprising Yankee officer got infantrymen to turn four of the abandoned Watson guns on the Confederates. This artillery fire was "murderous"; to stand and shoot back invited death. Walker's regiment was smashed. Panic fed upon itself, and Pillow's makeshift force began to tumble over the riverbank. They dared not look up. "I felt no human power could save us & our whole command from capture or death," one man said. Pillow did his best to stem the tide. "We saw the old hero stand exposed to grape and bullet and beg his men to stand when hope was gone and hundreds of our brave boys had fallen. He rode in front all day at Belmont and the raging thunder of artillery did not alarm him." [32]

The energy had gone out of the Federal pursuit, however, and although Grant's guns continued to blast away, infantry activity on the riverbank degenerated into squad-level skirmishing. Thousands of Confederates watching the battle from the Kentucky shore stared in disbelief. They saw the enemy in Camp Johnston and Pillow's routed troops scattered and fleeing upstream.[33] About 2:00 P.M. firing ceased. An eerie lull, "a perfect quiet," came over the battlefield. Incredibly, it would last almost thirty minutes. Grant's army was celebrating.[34] Meanwhile, Pillow's soldiers worked their way north along the river, away from their burning camp and the Federal artillery. The Mississippi was low, fortunately, creating a narrow shelf of deep mud that hid them.

Leonidas Polk had watched Walker's 2d Tennessee swallowed up in the fighting on the Missouri shore and had to decide whether to commit more troops. How many enemy confronted Pillow over there? Pillow had reported an attacking force with three times his own numbers.[35] Could this Missouri attack be a diversion for a main attack down the east bank of the Mississippi against Columbus itself? Polk "with great reluctance" decided to commit his reserve. Over went Col. Samuel Marks with the 11th Louisiana and the 15th Tennessee. Polk ordered Marks to land upriver from Camp Johnston, near Belmont Point, use the woods there to cover his movements, and strike the enemy in the flank.

Once across, however, Marks's reinforcements were mobbed as they attempted to disembark. "We found the landing obstructed by our disorganized forces, who endeavored to board and take possession of our boat, and at the same time crying: 'Don't land!' 'We are whipped!' 'Go back!' " [36] Although Marks managed to force his way ashore with most of his troops, the rest were diverted farther upstream. When all his men were ashore at last, Pillow's staff officers met them, begging "us 'for God's sake' to hurry up." Pillow himself appeared and gave Marks the same order Polk had, "to lead the advance in double-quick time through the woods and to the enemy's rear, and to attack him with vigor." Pillow would support this attack on Grant's rear, he assured Marks, with another attack using the fragments of regiments now rallying on the riverbank under Colonel Russell. Capt. "Red" Jackson would guide Marks through the woods. Jackson's battery had not been able to cross the river, but he had made it across himself earlier in the day and served Pillow as a volunteer aide.[37]

For about fifteen minutes, "Red" Jackson led the 11th and 15th west into the forest. They traveled almost a mile, far enough to avoid those enemy cannon on the riverbank and to be parallel with Camp Johnston. Then they flanked south toward Belmont. Ironically, they had assumed almost the identical position and angle of attack used by Grant's 31st Illinois four hours earlier.[38]

As Marks's column maneuvered into position, Frank Cheatham brought his brigade down to the Columbus landing. Polk ordered him across ahead of his brigade with instructions "to rally and take command of the portions of regiments within sight on the shore, and to support the flank movement ordered through Colonel Marks."[39] As Cheatham and his staff crossed, the Confederate heavy artillery on the bluffs opened fire. At last they could be certain of their targets— Camp Johnston had been set afire by the enemy. Cheatham did not wait for the steamer to touch shore. "He stuck spurs in his horse and jumped him out of the boat before it had landed." A shout was raised when the Tennesseans caught sight of him; as Cheatham rode up the bank they gathered to him in hundreds. He told them "to follow him, and he would lead them to h–ll or to victory."[40]

Pillow welcomed Cheatham eagerly. He had already assembled a mixed bag of troops, men from three or four of the original regiments, about 600 in number. He and Cheatham, Tappan, and Knox Walker continued to gather and form the disorganized mass. Presently they had a force of about 1,000–1,500. Cheatham formed them into column and led them directly inland through the woods.

The Yankees, meanwhile, had ended their celebration at Camp Johnston as projectiles from the "Lady Polk" and other heavy Confederate guns began to strike dangerously close. Grant formed his men and they began their march back to their transports. But they smacked headlong into Marks's column. After a short fight, Col. John Logan and his 31st Illinois punched through Marks's line. The Confederates did not run away, however. They retired to the cover of the trees and opened a murderous fire on the retreating Federals. Then Cheatham's makeshift column came up and immediately, with a great shout, attacked the rear of the Union column. "We are flanked," rang out along Grant's line. "They're surrounding us," others began to cry. The Federal retreat turned into a rout.[41]

In the meantime, Polk had come ashore himself, bringing with him

Cheatham's brigade as well as the 154th Senior Tennessee and Blythe's 1st Mississippi Battalion, both now commanded by Col. Preston Smith. On the shore Polk met Pillow and Cheatham. The latter, flushed with the success of his counterattack, had halted pursuit and ridden back to the landing to receive Polk's instructions. Without hesitation Polk directed Cheatham to continue "to press the enemy to his boats," using not only Smith's brigade, but "the whole force."[42]

The Confederates pursued cautiously, stopping to regroup at the Federal hospital. Polk knew that the head of the column already had advanced within range of Grant's gunboats, and he expected Grant, despite evidence of a precipitate retreat, to have taken a defensive position. As they approached the landing at Hunter's Farm, the Confederates spread out and conducted a rather elaborate envelopment, using every unit available. They saw the two "black monsters" out in the river belching smoke and Yankees on the bank hurrying aboard steamers. Three hundred yards from the landing, the Confederates charged. Their fire "was so hot and destructive," Pillow reported, that the Yankees "rushed to the opposite side of the boats and had to be forced back by the bayonet to prevent capsizing."

The attack came too late, however. The Union transports backed out of range, covered by blistering fire from the gunboats. The Confederates hugged the riverbank, firing prone. In the fight at the Hunter's Farm landing, Pillow directed the fire and maneuver of company-size groups of soldiers, whomever he could find to command. Contrary to Pillow's statement in his report, it does not appear that he managed the attack at the landing, although he may have thought he did.[43]

Belmont was a sharp, bloody engagement. Both sides lost about 600 men. In the initial fight between Grant and Pillow, the sides were roughly equal—about 2,500 Federals and fewer than 3,000 Confederates. Pillow always believed he was greatly outnumbered ("three times the strength of my own") and that he had been driven from the field because Polk failed to support him promptly. Following the battle Pillow telegraphed Mary: "I fought 4 regts against 9 for 4 hours without help. . . . We drove the enemy back three times; his greatly superior numbers overpowered my command. I rallied it repeatedly, and ultimately got reinforcements, drove them from the field and pursued them five miles into their boats."[44]

The Confederate Congress rushed through a resolution congratulating Polk, Pillow, and Cheatham for having "converted what at first threatened so much disaster into a triumphant victory." Belmont was swept from the headlines quickly, however, by two major events the following day: the capture of Port Royal and the "Trent Affair."[45]

Belmont should have been Pillow's kind of fight. He had the advantage of position, had he chosen to remain on the defensive behind the sloughs crisscrossing the battlefield. He might have used the abatis or the heavy woods to his advantage; he did neither. He might have accepted the hasty dispositions of Tappan, secured the roads with cannon, and rested his flanks upon the abatis. Certainly he should have picketed the road leading into Belmont from the south and west.

On the other hand, had he chosen to be more aggressive, he might have groped for the enemy in the woods with his five regiments, confident in the knowledge of a fallback position at Camp Johnston. Instead, Pillow chose to deploy his troops in the cornfield, receive Grant's attack, and then launch an all-or-nothing bayonet charge against an enemy concealed and protected by timber. Such reckless tactics threw away lives and defied the common sense of the men he commanded.

Pillow should be credited with attempts to rally his men at Camp Johnston, only to have his formations blown away by Federal artillery and Buford's flank attack. He tried again at the riverbank and, assisted by Cheatham, succeeded in organizing remnants of his force into a group capable of counterattack. Pillow fought bravely himself and set a conspicuous example. Nevertheless, he was beaten soundly by Grant with an equal force.

Four days following the Battle of Belmont, on November 11, the monster gun "Lady Polk" exploded, killing her crew and several observing officers. Leonidas Polk, who was present, escaped, but he was so severely stunned that he could not carry out his duties. He turned command over to Pillow, who immediately rang the fire bell. On November 13, his second day in charge of Polk's 1st Division, Western Department, Pillow began sending out reports of a threatening enemy buildup to his front. On the seventeenth he sent dispatches to Harris, the governors of Alabama and Mississippi, and the military commander at Memphis stating that the enemy numbers before Columbus were enormous: "I anticipate being entirely surrounded." These alarming reports were issued almost daily for two weeks. Harris dutifully called out the Tennessee militia.[46]

Something close to hysteria gripped Columbus. The movement of Pillow's division to Clarksville, repeatedly ordered by Johnston, was countermanded.[47] At least once, 10,000 Confederates turned out in line of battle to receive a Yankee attack that never came. Despite skepticism on the part of some of Pillow's men who suspected this was "another of the Genl's *blows*," work on fortress Columbus proceeded "day and night."[48] Pillow announced to the South, "We will hold this place and fight to the end." To Johnston, Pillow reported on November 22 that Polk "is still very unwell. . . . His system is greatly shocked, and there are strong indications of more serious results from it than was at first supposed. I doubt if he will be able to resume command at an early day."[49]

A distraught Sam Tate wrote from Memphis on November 30: "His [Pillow's] daily sensational dispatches keep the country in alarm and commotion. . . . No one here has the slightest confidence in Pillow's judgment or ability, and if the important command of defending this river is to be left to him, we feel perfectly in the enemy's power. . . . [Belmont] has not in the least changed public opinion about Pillow."[50]

Polk returned to command the first week in December. With their forces strengthened, alarm transformed itself into aggressiveness. Pillow now pushed Polk hard for permission to conduct a combined operation, a daring, large-scale attack on Cairo, Bird's Point, and Fort Holt. Perhaps, if considered as a limited raid, such as Grant's at Belmont, and with the element of surprise, the proposal had merit, but Pillow saw it as a major operation and asked Polk to "allow me to exercise my own judgment." The proposal was scuttled quickly, however, when Cheatham, McCown, and two regimental commanders protested (as they had at New Madrid) that the plan was vague and visionary. Even if they succeeded in seizing Bird's Point or Cairo, they argued, with their insufficient numbers they could not hold what they captured. Besides, such a campaign would jeopardize Columbus and surely stir up the people of southern Illinois, whom Tennesseans counted on for sympathy, if not support.[51]

Pillow found himself reduced to a garrison subordinate once again, under a man he considered unqualified. He fretted. According to Polk, Pillow complained "publicly and privately" about the major general commanding and

that the President did not appreciate him, and had intentionally and systematically slighted and overshadowed him; that his removal to another field would furnish no relief, as he would everywhere find himself ranked by men whom he had commanded; that he had let himself down by accepting the commission of brigadier-general in the first place; that no argument against his resignation was of any avail with him now, and that he would be "sunk into the bottom of the sea" before he would continue to hold his commission any longer. In this temper it was he left Columbus, having first arranged for getting up expressions of sympathy among the troops.[52]

The controversy did make interesting camp talk. Surgeon Lunsford P. Yandell, Jr., wrote home on December 29: "The general sympathy seems to be with Pillow, and I believe that notwithstanding the poor estimation in which Pillow is held as a General, Polk is considered a poorer one. Polk is respected for his integrity, and polished manners & goodness only. Pillow is respected for his indomitable energy, his wonderful dispatch in business affairs, his extraordinary rapidity in supplying the necessities of the army, and for his unflinching bravery."[53]

Shortly after Christmas, Pillow resigned. Polk accepted his resignation, and Pillow went home to Clifton.[54] Secretary of War Judah Benjamin wanted an explanation. Pillow responded at once, using the opportunity to charge Polk with negligence at Belmont, by failing "to re-enforce me promptly and send me ammunition."[55] He blasted Polk as an administrator at Columbus, for interfering with his staff, "*centralizing* the powers of the whole Army in himself," and inattention to duty, harshness, and violence of temper. "I felt I was reduced to the position of a *cipher*, and was valueless to the service. . . . I felt it was my duty to *silently retire.*"[56]

"Since I reached my residence," Pillow wrote on January 16, 1862, "I am informed that the army, deeply distressed at my departure, were engaged addressing a respectful petition to the President, expressive of their confidence in me, and requesting him to order me back, when Major-General Polk issued an order intended to suppress this respectful appeal to the President, thus stifling the honest conviction of the army and the sympathy so naturally arising from his injustice to me."[57]

In his official reply to the War Department, Polk stated:

Having known him [Pillow] well for many years, and received from him frequently the most earnest protestations of personal esteem and regard, I was, nevertheless, not surprised upon my taking command at Memphis to find him exhibiting petty jealousies, indulging in disingenuous criticism, and conducting himself generally as towards a rival, to be undermined and supplanted, rather than towards a brother officer in the commission of the Government, to whom a manly patriotism required he should give a generous support.[58]

Thus 1861 closed for Gideon Pillow. He had done much for his cause, creating and equipping an army, only to see the thousands of men he had gathered slip under the control of others. He, more than any other individual, had set the strategy for the defense of the upper Mississippi Valley and seen to the establishment of an elaborate system of fortifications. Consistently, his had been the voice for aggressive action in the valley, both in eastern Missouri and western Kentucky. In this, his thinking might well have been more realistic than is usually believed. Considering his incredible persuasive powers, his visions might have triumphed had they not been larded with overstatement. The good service he did render was spoiled by arrogant willfulness and malignant insubordination.

12   **I Will Die First**

Pillow could not tolerate waiting in the wings at Clifton. Throughout January 1862 he looked for an opportunity to return to the army without loss of face. He knew he had won sympathy, at least among Tennesseans, for his role at Columbus. Pvt. Val Wynne believed "Tennesseans ought to beg him to go back and take command. . . . [He is] a brave and chivalrous man, cool and sober and ever watchful of his country's interests." There was even a rally of officers in Columbus, organized by Pillow's subordinates and friends, to pass resolutions "regretting Pillow's absence." It was unevenly attended, however, and nothing came of it. Many, including James J. Neely, a young captain of the Hardeman Avengers, believed it to be improper.

Elizabeth Cheatham wrote her son, Frank, on January 7, "I hope you have had time to dry your eyes since the crying at Pillow's parting from the army."[1]

It appears that the killing of Pillow's friend Felix Zollicoffer and the demoralizing defeat Tennessee Confederates suffered at Mill Springs, Kentucky, on January 19–20, prompted Pillow's return, although it may have been at Sidney Johnston's request. In any event, on February 2 Pillow withdrew his resignation and took himself to Bowling Green, not Columbus. His return, Surgeon L. P. Yandell wrote, "will be a good thing too. He is held in much higher estimation by the soldiers than formerly—and is a most capital Brigadier." One soldier entered in his diary, "The men were all glad to hear this for he was loved by all officers and men under him." There was thought, in this time of crisis, of assigning him the Tennessee militia; let him "bring out the militia and fight them." One citizen wrote Davis after Mill Springs that "if you have not yet accepted the resignation of Pillow he will be able to restore order out of this chaos" and advised the president that Pillow might be placed in charge of Confederate forces in East Tennessee.[2]

Almost overnight, however, attention shifted to the troublesome seam between the Bowling Green and Columbus sectors. In late January Grant made demonstrations up the Tennessee River that revealed the vulnerability of the defenses. The Federals determined to attack and open the river, and they did so, suddenly and decisively, with a fleet and two divisions of infantry. Fort Henry on the Tennessee River, undermanned and inadequately prepared, fell on February 6. The strategic results were enormous. The loss of Fort Henry broke Johnston's already crumbling defense line, cutting communications between his two wings at Columbus and Bowling Green. It gave Federal gunboats control of the Tennessee River up to Muscle Shoals, Alabama, and it demonstrated, with startling force, the might of ironclads. The momentum of reverses begun at Mill Springs continued. Unless Johnston reacted swiftly by concentrating to protect Fort Donelson, he might have to abandon not only Donelson itself, but Columbus, Bowling Green, and even Nashville.[3]

Johnston, shaken by Grant's success at Fort Henry, immediately sent Pillow to Clarksville, where he would gather troops and take a defensive position. Charles Clark's Mississippi brigade was on its way from Hopkinsville and would serve as the nucleus. Why did Johnston chose Pillow? Because he was in Bowling Green; because he was without a command and anxious to redeem himself; and because, other than Hardee, he was the most experienced general officer available. Johnston "had a high opinion" of Pillow's "talents as a military man" and had so expressed himself to Confederate senator Gustavus A. Henry in Bowling Green in January.[4]

Pillow arrived on the night of February 5, and, according to his welcome by the Clarksville *Weekly Chronicle*, his presence was "a source of gratification to everyone." He made a hurried inspection and the next day wired Johnston alarming news: none of the defensive works at Clarksville had been completed and, of the four heavy guns there, "not one ready for use." Furthermore, he had no artillerists. Pillow asked Johnston for a field battery, preferably "Red" Jackson's, and for more troops, from his division of Tennesseans at Columbus if possible. He also suggested, "If Donelson should be overcome, we can make no successful stand [at Clarksville] without larger force."[5]

Johnston quickly responded. He sent a field battery and dispatched the divisions of Brig. Gen. John B. Floyd and Brig. Gen. Simon B. Buckner from Russellville. This meant, however, that once Floyd arrived in Clarksville, he would outrank Pillow. Johnston sent Floyd on his way with authority to "make the dispositions for the defense of Clarksville, Fort Donelson and the Cumberland river at his own discretion." "You had better keep yourself informed of the State of affairs in Clarksville," Johnston further advised Floyd, "through Genl. Pillow."[6]

As usual, Pillow displayed great industry at Clarksville and miraculously "transformed that post into a well-functioning distribution point, especially for forwarding men and supplies downriver" to Fort Donelson. Not surprisingly, indeed, almost overnight, he wired Johnston that he felt he could take the offensive once Clark and his Mississippians arrived. Pillow advocated marching north and, with the assistance of Floyd's and Buckner's divisions, falling upon Grant's force.[7]

Pillow's plan had merit; it was not a mindless offensive reflex. Grant's force was vulnerable. The plan foundered, however, when Clark's brigade stalled on its way from Hopkinsville. Pillow and Clark quarreled, and the latter refused to recognize Pillow's authority. Johnston had to intervene. He backed Pillow, which caused Clark to obey reluctantly. The opportunity to implement Pillow's plan to strike boldly was lost.[8]

On February 7 Pillow received orders from Johnston to move his force to Donelson, following Bushrod Johnson, who had just gone forward to take charge of the Fort Henry survivors gathered there. Johnston, displaying great confidence in Pillow, telegraphed him later

Brig. Gen. Simon Bolivar Buckner
(courtesy National Archives)

in the day: "If your services or Buckner's or both are most important at Donelson, go there."[9]

Pillow sensed opportunity and a chance for independent command. He wired Bushrod Johnson at Donelson, the same faithful, brow-beaten, insecure Johnson who had worked under Pillow's direction for so long, to take charge of the four Tennessee regiments there and assume command of the fort. In the meantime, Pillow began to forward troops and supplies to Donelson as quickly as they arrived. He dashed off a dispatch to Floyd: "I shall stand in great need of Genl. Buckner at Donaldson & I hope you will send him down at the earliest possible moment." Pillow promised to keep Floyd advised by a line of couriers, and he came up with the novel idea of having Floyd continue to stockpile supplies at Donelson "in the event the enemy gunboats run past." When Floyd came to Clarksville later on February 8, he found Pillow had already sent two of his Virginia regiments to Donelson, and when Buckner's 2d Kentucky under Col. Roger Hanson arrived by rail, Pillow stopped a steamer heading downriver and loaded them aboard too. As he left Clarksville himself, Pillow, in typical fashion, had managed to cajole Clark, whom he had deposed, into lending him one of his horses as a personal mount.[10]

Floyd did not like the idea of strengthening Fort Donelson; he regarded it as a trap. Instead of Donelson, he advocated concentration at Cumberland City, where, "in case of danger, a road for withdrawal would be open."[11] Pillow, however, had arrived at Donelson and taken charge; henceforward it would be the focus. Floyd's deliberative niceties of concentrations and combinations would have to wait. Pillow brought with him to Fort Donelson 2,800 men, once the brigade of Clark, now commanded by Col. T. J. Davidson of Kentucky. Pillow made speeches before leaving Clarksville and upon arriving at Dover. In both he announced the "watchword" for Donelson, "Liberty or Death," and struck at conduct that led to the surrender of Fort Henry. "He [Pillow] never had seen a time," a listener reported, "that he felt disposed to surrender and he never expected to. This has greatly enhanced our opinion of him and we feel some hope that the time is not far ahead when we shall wipe out (if necessary with our own blood) the disgrace which now rests upon the Confederate Army in this region." Lt. Col. Randal McGavock, who had heard Pillow speeches before, was not so sure. "I regret very much that Gen. Pillow has been placed in command, as I have no faith or confidence in him as an officer."[12]

Pillow surveyed the Donelson defenses accompanied by Maj. Jeremy F. Gilmer, a West Pointer and chief engineering officer. Certainly their present lines could not withstand a land attack. Along irregular ridges ran works three miles long, primarily shallow rifle pits, only a fraction of which had been completed. This extended line guarded the fort and the village of Dover. Three creeks swollen with water and the Cumberland River itself tended to isolate the fort. The position looked dangerous, and Pillow so confided to Floyd. Publicly, however, and to Johnston himself, Pillow maintained the fortifications were "very strong." [13]

Pillow set to work. Although his men lacked sufficient tools, he ordered them to dig. They worked day and night; trenches took shape, and log parapets appeared along the lines Gilmer had laid out. Using "the natural energy of his character," Pillow imparted a sense of urgency, driving the men, motivating them. Sheer activity itself, as Pillow well knew, seemed to restore "the confidence of the troops, sadly shaken by the Fort Henry surrender and the legend of the terrible invincibility . . . of the gunboats." As fresh regiments, ten of them, went into line and began work, spirits lifted. Pillow and his shadow, Bushrod Johnson, saw instant progress. In the logic of Pillow's mind, cleared fields of fire, crude abatis, newly created battery positions, and troops growing more enthusiastic by the day all translated into the conviction that Fort Donelson could be defended successfully. Pillow wired his friend Harris in Nashville: "Upon one thing you may rest assured. I will never surrender the position, and with God's help I mean to maintain it." [14]

Col. Nathan B. Forrest's 3d Tennessee Cavalry arrived on the east bank of the Cumberland and encamped late on February 10. The next morning they crossed and reported to Pillow, who immediately ordered them to reconnoiter toward Fort Henry. In a short time Forrest encountered Federal patrols and presently a heavy infantry force advancing east. He fell back to Fort Donelson, informing Pillow that Grant's army was on the march.[15]

Preparing to meet Grant once again, and finding himself short of artillerymen, Pillow turned to McGavock's 10th Tennessee Infantry; he ordered a company into the fort as heavy artillerists. When the troops balked, their captain sent for the general, who hurried over and ordered the captain to form the company. Then Pillow addressed them: "'You are Irishmen and I know you will prove true to your adopted South. I come here to drive the Hessians from this neck of land between the rivers, and to replant the stars and bars upon the battlements of Fort Henry. I will never Surrender! The word is not in

Brig. Gen. Bushrod Johnson
(courtesy Roy Morris, Jr.)

my vocabulary! I had Irishmen with me in the Mexican War—and at
Belmont where they proved themselves equal to any of our soldiers.
Many of you know me personally, *certainly all of you by reputation* and I
want you to go now when I command you.' " [16] The Irishmen did go to
the fort, but evidently Pillow had misgivings; later in the day he sent
McGavock's Irishmen back and turned to his Maury County neigh-

bors, Capt. Reuben R. Ross's field artillery battery. He needed them, he explained, to man the "half moon battery," consisting of the rifled gun, two carronades, and the eight-inch howitzers; Pillow promised to be with his neighbors when the fighting came. So the men from Maury went to their "post of honor," relieving the Irishmen.[17]

Pillow and Bushrod Johnson formed the infantry regiments and brigades into two divisions, or wings, the left under Johnson and the right to be commanded by Buckner when he came downriver. Buckner arrived on February 11 with the last of his division; he had been in no hurry, it seems. He had met in Clarksville with Floyd, and they, without Pillow's knowledge, had agreed the Confederate concentration should not be at Donelson. To implement their plan, Buckner had brought orders from Floyd to Pillow to vacate Donelson, leaving no more than a rear guard in the fort. The two divisions presently occupying the trenches would fall back to Cumberland City; there the Confederates would concentrate. The plan was conservative and cautious, but it was flexible and husbanded Floyd's limited manpower. Cumberland City, moreover, was located on the railroad, promising ease of movement—either to combine with Johnston's retreating forces or to have Johnston bring some or all of the Army of Central Kentucky to Cumberland City.[18]

But Pillow wanted no part of the Floyd-Buckner plan. It meant retrograde, and he had had a stomach full of that in Missouri. It meant abandoning a position he believed could be held, and it meant, it seemed to him, the sacrifice of at least a token garrison. Abruptly, he suspended Floyd's order. On the spot, he refused to allow Buckner to remove his troops from Fort Donelson, and he told the wide-eyed Buckner to wait in Dover while he took a steamer upriver to see Floyd himself. Before he left, Pillow wired Sidney Johnston to allow him to keep Buckner's division, and he sent Forrest out to probe again.[19] Pillow got as far as Cumberland City, but whether he met with Floyd or not is unknown. He probably did not. In a situation reminiscent of the Pillow-Polk push-pulls of August 1861, he wired Floyd that he had just heard ten heavy discharges of artillery from Donelson. Therefore he was turning back to the scene of the action, and, as a tail on the kite, Floyd must "suspend the order for Buckner to fall back at present." The telegraph operator repeated the message to Johnston and Harris.[20]

When he returned to Donelson, Pillow watched a demonstration by Federal gunboats, firing more than a dozen shells into the fort, testing defenses. Pillow ordered the Confederate gunners not to reply.

Simultaneously, skirmishing occurred in front of the rifle pits, but most Confederates kept at their business, digging and piling up logs, readying for the attack they knew was to come. One had to be careful about exercising too much initiative, however. When Bushrod Johnson, who should have known better, selected a position for the Goochland Battery without consulting his superior, an angered Pillow took him to task.[21]

Pillow reported to Floyd that the enemy were all about, "within distance to close in with me in ten minutes march. . . . We shall have a battle in the morning, I think certainly, and an attack by gunboats." He was ready, though. "I have done all that it was possible to do, and think I will drive back the enemy." To further strengthen his force, Pillow had ordered up William E. Baldwin's brigade from Cumberland City.[22]

It was now, with Donelson under imminent attack, that Pillow chose to make his strongest argument. He wired Johnston: "If I can retain my present force, I can hold my position. Let me retain Buckner for the present. If now withdrawn, will invite an attack. Enemy cannot pass this place without exposing himself to flank attack. If I am strong enough to take field, he cannot ever reach here; nor is it possible for him to subsist in the country to pass over, nor can he possibly bring his subsistence with him. With Buckner's force, I can hold my position. Without it, cannot long."[23]

The night of February 12, Grant's infantry, having pushed aside Forrest's dismounted cavalry, closed in on Pillow's line of defense. The Union line was not continuous; gaps of several hundred yards separated the six brigades. After dark it became bitterly cold, with a high piercing wind. Men on both sides tried to sleep, out in the open, without fires, afraid of enemy attack, shivering violently, waiting and hoping for the sun.[24]

Dawn brought Brig. Gen. John Floyd. He and Pillow knew each other as Democrats, and for a time in the 1840s, Floyd had matched Pillow's enthusiasm for land speculation in Arkansas. But while Pillow made Arkansas a bonanza, Floyd failed badly. The two generals had breakfast together, and Floyd then toured the field fortifications. Pillow, instead of accompanying his new chief, directed McCausland's Virginia brigade, which Floyd had brought with him, to its place in the line, displacing Baldwin's brigade, which then moved to the extreme Confederate left. Floyd's inspection caused him to express worry over the placement of the outer line of trenches, but for the most part he seemed oddly detached and diffident, apparently relying on Pillow.[25]

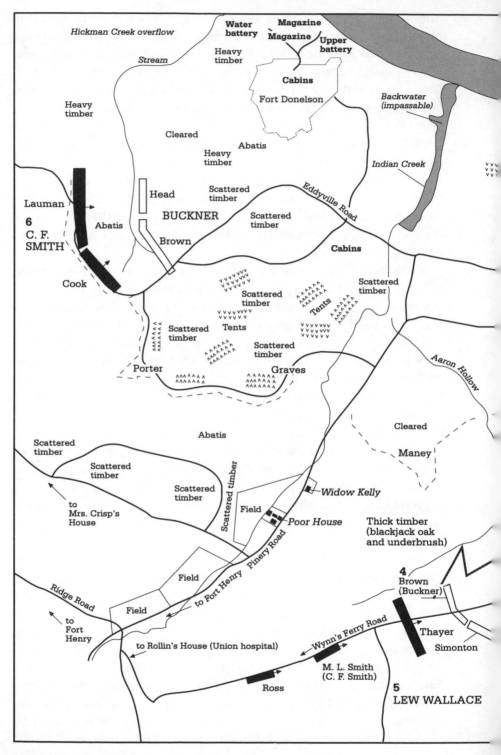

Map 4. Battle of Fort Donelson, February 15, 1862

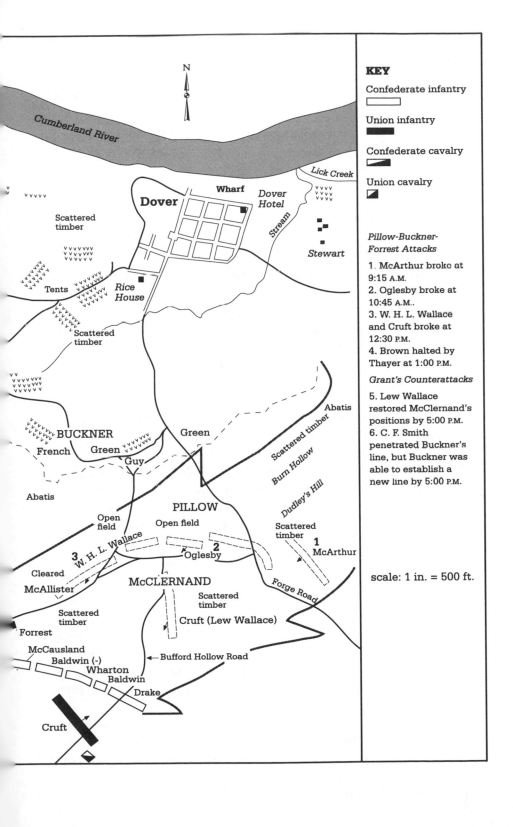

KEY

Confederate infantry

Union infantry

Confederate cavalry

Union cavalry

Pillow-Buckner-Forrest Attacks

1. McArthur broke at 9:15 A.M.
2. Oglesby broke at 10:45 A.M..
3. W. H. L. Wallace and Cruft broke at 12:30 P.M.
4. Brown halted by Thayer at 1:00 P.M.

Grant's Counterattacks

5. Lew Wallace restored McClernand's positions by 5:00 P.M.
6. C. F. Smith penetrated Buckner's line, but Buckner was able to establish a new line by 5:00 P.M.

scale: 1 in. = 500 ft.

N

Cumberland River

Lick Creek

Wharf

Dover

Dover Hotel

Stream

Scattered timber

Stewart

Tents

Rice House

Scattered timber

BUCKNER

French

Green

Green

Guy

Abatis

Scattered timber

Burn Hollow

Dudley's Hill

Abatis

Open field

PILLOW

Open field

Scattered timber

1 McArthur

3

W. H. L. Wallace

2

Oglesby

Cleared

McAllister

McCLERNAND

Scattered timber

Forge Road

Forrest

Scattered timber

Cruft (Lew Wallace)

McCausland

Baldwin (-)

Wharton

Baldwin

Drake

← Bufford Hollow Road

Cruft

The right flank of the Confederate line was protected by the flooded Hickman Creek. This impassable obstacle allowed the Confederates to concentrate their strength on the left. Running south of Hickman Creek were the rifle pits of Hanson's 2d Kentucky. Next were the trenches of John C. Brown's brigade, with Capt. T. K. Porter's Tennessee battery jutting out in a salient on the highest point in the immediate area. South of Porter's guns the line turned east and was held by more of Brown's troops. Capt. Rice E. Graves's Kentucky battery was emplaced on the slope leading into the valley of Indian Creek. This valley, about 500 yards wide, divided the right wing of Buckner and the left of Bushrod Johnson.[26]

To the east, across the valley, rose the hill held by Adolphus Heiman's brigade and Frank Maney's battery. Only a few pickets were posted in the valley itself because of the excellent fields of fire. East of Maney's redoubt was Erin (Aaron) Hollow, about 250 yards wide. Heiman and Col. Joseph Drake's brigades held this sector. Capt. D. A. French's battery came next, supported by Drake's men. About 300 yards east of French's redoubt, the Wynn's Ferry road passed through the line of rifle pits toward Dover. A section of Green's Kentucky battery was on the west side of the road, while Capt. J. H. Guy's Goochland Battery was on the east. Col. Gabriel Wharton's infantry supported both. About 350 yards east of the Wynn's Ferry road was the Forge road leading north to Dover. Another section of Green's Kentucky battery commanded this road, supported by Davidson's brigade. John McCausland's and then William Baldwin's brigades completed the forces occupying the outer works. Forrest's cavalry was positioned behind Baldwin on the Charlotte road, east of Dover. Jackson's Virginia battery was held in reserve behind Buckner, while Col. John W. Head's brigade held Fort Donelson itself.[27]

Skirmishing began all along the line as Floyd ended his inspection tour. On the Confederate right, Buckner's men spent the day repelling probes by Gen. C. F. Smith's division. Buckner's position seemed very strong. On the river, the gunboat *Carondelet*, hiding behind a wooded bend, would advance and shell Fort Donelson at long range and then retire, as was done at Belmont. The Yankee gunboats were effective at long range, but Captain Ross fired back and projectiles flew up and down the river—an inconclusive engagement that greatly boosted Confederate confidence.[28]

Meanwhile, John A. McClernand's brigades kept shifting east, extending Grant's investment. McClernand attempted to locate and turn the Confederate left flank, pushing cavalry out to Dudley's Hill.

This ridge now became the extreme right of the Federal line. Maney's battery bothered McClernand's envelopment. To silence this worrisome battery, McClernand ordered repeated infantry attacks against the position held by Maney and Heiman. The main attack in the early afternoon pushed through heavy brush to an abatis fifty yards from the southern breastworks. Joint artillery fire from Maney's, Graves's, and French's batteries tore into the Federal ranks. Three attacks were made against the strong Confederate position on the left; all were successfully repulsed. Floyd, in a restrained telegram to Johnston, reported, "The day is closed, and we have maintained ourselves fully by land and water."[29]

That night it snowed and rained; troops on both sides suffered. Many Confederates worked all night. "Men were so exhausted that they actually slept in their position while shells were exploding around them."[30] Captain Ross, in the upper battery of the fort, sent random shells screeching downriver toward spots where he thought Yankee gunboats might be lurking. He may have kept his enemies awake, but he also bothered Pillow, who was comfortably situated in Dover at the home of his aide, Maj. John E. Rice. Pillow sent a staff officer over to the fort to stop the firing. To soften his order to the enthusiastic Ross, who had performed so well that day, Pillow had the order delivered along with a bottle of peach brandy.[31]

Pillow was busy that night of February 13. He and Floyd and Buckner met in Rice's home and discussed reports of enemy transports landing troops (6,000 men, who would form Cruft's and Thayer's brigades of Lew Wallace's division). The reports had been coming in since afternoon, "suggesting 15,000 to 20,000" reinforcements. But no action had been taken, no decisions made, until the three generals could confer. They were also told that night that McClernand's brigades had taken position astride the Wynn's Ferry and Forge roads south of Dover. Floyd believed the enemy now numbered about 40,000, and he informed Bowling Green to that effect.[32]

The three generals decided to break out. According to Buckner, they agreed to attack at once, before fresh Federal troops could be placed in position. Pillow would mass his troops and attack the enemy right; Buckner's division would be the rear guard. Once the opening had been forced, the entire command would march southeast toward Charlotte, about forty miles away, and then to Nashville.[33]

Pulling troops out of the line went slowly on the morning of the fourteenth. It was a delicate movement, withdrawing thousands of soldiers from their trenches in the presence of the enemy. Conflicting orders, crippling cold, inexperience, exposure to Yankee sharp-shooters—a hundred excuses accumulated to slow the Confederate pullout until afternoon. Maj. Peter Otey, a member of Floyd's staff, rode with Pillow at the head of the breakout column when it finally got under way. According to Otey, writing two decades later, Pillow became alarmed when a sharpshooter fired and hit "one of the front men in our column." "'Captain, our movement is discovered,'" Pillow exclaimed. "'It will not do to move out of our trenches under the circumstances.'" He sent Otey at once to notify Floyd and to tell him that the flank movement must be aborted. They would try again the next morning. A disappointed and angry Floyd sent back the message, "Tell General Pillow he has lost the opportunity not by being discovered, but by the delay in sending the message and the consequent delay in getting a message back to him at this late hour."[34]

Otey contended this was "the fatal mistake at Fort Donelson." Perhaps it was. It is true that the Confederates would find the Union right stronger the next morning, but whether the attack would have succeeded with darkness only a few hours away is questionable. For victory, under any conditions, the Confederates would have needed an energetic and resolute commander leading the breakout. They lacked such a general officer on February 14.

So the Confederates went back to their trenches and turned their attention to the terrible racket on the river. Six Yankee gunboats had attacked Fort Donelson. They moved into "point blank" range and for two hours blasted away at the Confederate water batteries. Shells from the ironclads occasionally sailed over the works and crashed into the Confederate lines. Confederate cannoneers returned the fire stubbornly; they had the advantage at close range. It resulted in a grand repulse of the dreaded Yankee monsters. The *Carondelet*, *Pittsburgh*, *St. Louis*, and *Louisville* were damaged to varying degrees, with a loss of 54 men, flag officer Andrew Foote among them. As the battered Federals withdrew downstream, cheers went up from the weary gunners in the fort; frozen soldiers in the trenches echoed their shouts of joy.[35]

Pillow appears to have been more interested in the gunboat fight than the attempted breakout; perhaps the noise of cannon fire on the river caused him to stop the flanking movement. He certainly dashed back to the fort quickly to be among his Maury County cannoneers, cheering them on, sometimes directing their fire, and congratulating them on their fine shooting. In his elation over smashing the gunboats, he sent a message to Johnston himself, describing it as "the fiercest fight on record." Typically, he signed the telegram "Commander." (Technically, of course, he did take command of the fight at the fort.)[36]

Later in the night of February 14, Floyd called a council of war at the Dover Hotel. He did so in response to a strange message from Sidney Johnston: "If you lose the fort, bring your troops to Nashville, if possible."[37] Floyd saw no reason why the plan to evacuate Fort Donelson should be changed, despite victory at the river. Grant would surely continue the investment, and with the 40,000 men they estimated he commanded, each day's delay would be to the Confederates' disadvantage. Against Grant's force they could muster only about 15,000 effective troops. Choices seemed limited to an immediate attack on Grant's right, creating an opening through which to "pass our people into the open country lying southward toward Nashville," or to staying in the works, fighting off attack, and waiting for the total investment that promised to swallow them.[38]

Pillow saw the situation somewhat differently. He acknowledged the overwhelming strength of the enemy, his control of the roads by cannon, and the presence of two large forces of infantry. One sat astride the Wynn's Ferry road; the other, even larger, massed "in front of the extreme left of our position," blocking the overland route to Nashville. Pillow advocated that the attack they had attempted that morning be carried out now. He should lead the attack on the extreme left, Buckner should strike down the Wynn's Ferry road, and Heiman should remain in position, guarding Buckner's right flank. Only a token force should man the vacant trenches. If this massed attack succeeded, the enemy defeated by Pillow on the extreme left near Lick Creek would retreat west into the teeth of Buckner's attack and be routed. Buckner disagreed with Pillow in the matter of detaching some of his division (Hanson's 2d Kentucky) to bolster the flanking force, but otherwise he supported Pillow's plan. They would attack at 5:00 A.M.

Floyd, Pillow, and Buckner assembled the brigade commanders at 11:00 P.M. and informed them. Pillow conducted the briefing, describing the plan and assigning specific missions; it concluded at 1:00 A.M. Officers would later recall crucial points that were not covered: "how and when the retreat should commence," the marching order for the escape, and whether "rations and blankets [were] to be carried." Pillow's emphasis seemed to be on the breakout assault itself and the folding back of the opposing Union forces. Every officer, it seems, left "the meeting with a different notion as to what would happen after the successful attack."[39]

Six months later Pillow would argue forcefully that the object of the planned attack was

> to cut up the investing force before the fresh force of 20,000, which arrived at the gunboat landing on the evening of the 14th, could be got into position. . . . We knew we should have a desperate fight; but we made no preparation before going into the battle for retreating from the battlefield. . . . We could not have gone into such a fight with the men loaded down with blankets, knapsacks, and six days' rations, and without these the march over 60 miles of extremely broken and poor country, covered with snow and sleet 4 inches deep, could not have been made. We had left all of our field artillery within our works, because we could not use it on a battle-field covered over with a thick undergrowth of black-jack bushes. We could not have commenced a retreat before the enemy's large force of cavalry and artillery, without artillery to protect our rear.[40]

Although the prevailing sentiment among the Confederate officers at the briefing was that Donelson was being invested by a strong force that ultimately would cut off their escape and capture them, the manner in which the meeting was conducted—the instructions provided in the presence of Buckner and Floyd—leads to the conclusion that the meeting, as Pillow contended, was held for the purpose of planning an attack, not the extrication of the garrison. Buckner, John C. Brown, and others in Buckner's division, however, thought that once the breach in the Union line had been effected, they would not return to their works but would strike out for Nashville; thus Brown's brigade attacked the following morning carrying three days' rations and blankets.[41] Thousands of trusting Confederate privates would pay, either with their lives or with months of imprisonment, for this command muddle that defies belief. Pillow, as the briefing officer, must be held accountable for the resulting confusion.

Things went well at first in the early hours of February 15. The wind picked up, helping to muffle sounds of Confederate units moving to the rear of the trench line. The temperature dropped even lower, decreasing the vigilance of the Yankees out in the blackjack, trying to keep from freezing, trying to snatch a few moments of sleep. So in the dark, shortly after 4:00 A.M., Pillow's men pulled out of their trenches and rifle pits and began to assemble on the Charlotte road. It had snowed again, and the ground was covered with snow and ice. The road itself was slippery, and a man could get frostbite. But spirits were high; it was good to be going to the attack.[42]

Pillow arranged his flanking force in a column of brigades, with Baldwin's Mississippians in front, screened by Forrest's cavalry. Reminiscent of the tortured column at Cerro Gordo, each brigade had its backup, its reserve. McCausland's Virginians, for instance, would second Baldwin's attack. To Pillow's consternation, however, he found Davidson's brigade missing. So Pillow sent Bushrod Johnson hurrying back to the rifle pits, where he found the brigade still bivouacked, their commander "prostrate with illness." Inexcusably, Davidson had taken to his bed after the briefing, not bothering to inform his regimental commanders of the attack plan. Pillow replaced Davidson with Col. John M. Simonton of the 1st Mississippi, but by the time Simonton got his men formed and into position an hour had been lost.[43]

About 6:00 A.M., Pillow's assault column of 9,000 struck out for Dudley's Hill, an identifiable terrain feature and potential strong point on the Federal right. As Baldwin's men approached the hill, they encountered skirmisher fire and then stiff resistance from a single Federal regiment atop the hill. When a surprise Yankee bayonet charge scattered the lead Confederate regiment, the 26th Mississippi, Pillow reacted quickly. He pushed up McCausland's and Simonton's brigades on Baldwin's right. The engagement became general.[44]

Pillow's line of battle struck determined resistance by McClernand's Federals. Two dozen fights took place between brigades, regiments, and clumps of soldiers over the broken terrain. The Confederates kept moving, however, Baldwin's and McCausland's brigades progressively bending McClernand's right flank back toward the Wynn's Ferry road. Dudley's Hill was behind them now, and advance units entered the valley of Lick Creek. About 8:00 A.M. John McArthur's Union brigade was flanked, attacked by three Confederate brigades. When McArthur's ammunition began to run low, he could maintain his front no longer and the brigade broke, exposing the right of Richard Oglesby's Illinois brigade. McClernand sent for help.[45]

Pillow and Bushrod Johnson pressed the attack, throwing in brigade after brigade. Wharton took position to the left of Baldwin; then Drake went in on Wharton's left, further extending the flanking force. McCausland and Simonton on Baldwin's right kept pounding Oglesby's brigade, strongly positioned on a ridge. At one point Wharton's attack stalled. Pillow rode up to the 56th Virginia and threw out his arm toward their regimental colors. "'I trust to old Virginia my safety and my honor.' The effect was electrical." The Virginians reformed and went back to the attack.[46]

Grant's skillful brigade commander, W. H. L. Wallace, now came to Oglesby's assistance with a sharp counterattack that sent Simonton reeling. Pillow, observing Simonton's repulse, sent a messenger to Buckner to launch his attack now, if possible. What was keeping Buckner? Brown's brigade responded, moving forward through the abatis, and attacked a hill held by Wallace and two batteries. After hard fighting Brown was driven back; he succeeded, however, in occupying Wallace and depriving Oglesby of badly needed help.[47]

Confederate artillery joined in all along the line. For the most part they remained in fixed positions, immobile as at Belmont. Green's Kentucky battery, however, did displace forward at Pillow's direction and became "hotly engaged."[48] Its good work was offset, however, by bungling artillerists behind Brown's attacking regiments. They dropped short shells into their own men, helping to defeat the attack on W. H. L. Wallace's position.

Pillow's men attacked in columns for the most part that morning. Although often a clumsy tactical formation, the column tended to keep troops massed effectively and usually made for rapid movement. When a column reached the desired point, it would, through precise drill movements, change the formation into line of battle. The brigades of Pillow's division were all committed, all on line, some still in column formation, some in line of battle. Although attacks by these brigades were sometimes delivered piecemeal and poorly coordinated, the assault was continuous over a wide front. Commands became jumbled as the distance covered by the advance increased, but the initiative was maintained as Confederate soldiers drove the enemy from one position to another and another. The beleaguered Union right flank anchored by Oglesby finally collapsed when a Federal Kentucky regiment mistook Illinois troops for Confederates and opened fire from the rear.

McClernand was saved from disaster that snowy morning by Gen. Lew Wallace, who responded to his call for help. Wallace sent the brigade of Charles Cruft, which took position on the Wynn's Ferry road and helped slow Pillow's advance. A second brigade, a much larger one, was started on its way. Fortunately for Oglesby, the Confederates did not press their advantage after his line collapsed. This gave him and Cruft time to organize a new position on a ridge just east of the Bufford Hollow Road.[49]

Pillow was everywhere. Constantly on the move, he prodded and pushed, "berating laggardly field officers to move up, and urging the weary foot-soldiers to greater effort." He made tactical decisions on the spot, changed the direction of regimental and brigade attacks, and helped deploy units as they came up. Frequently he overstepped himself, meddling in subordinates' business, but always he led by example, exposing himself to fire. This was Pillow at his best, a fire-breathing mass of human energy. Men liked fighting beside him.[50]

Among his admirers was Bedford Forrest. They were together a great deal that morning, moving from hot spot to hot spot. Pillow had reclaimed Forrest from the Lick Creek bottoms on the right flank, where he and his men were being wasted, floundering about, fighting terrain more than enemy. At one point, when Forrest was being driven back by a superior force, he turned to Pillow and asked permission to counterattack. "'We can't hold them,'" he told Pillow, "'but we can run over them.'" Pillow threw Forrest against a knot in the Union defenses on the Forge road. Roger Hanson's 2d Kentucky was close by, and Hanson agreed to support Forrest. Together they attacked and carried the position.[51]

A round from an enemy gun struck in the middle of a section of Green's Kentucky battery, killing one and wounding several. The gun crews fled. Pillow saw what happened and could not halt those who ran away. But he needed the fire of that section, so he rode over to the Goochland Battery. He assembled a group of men, faced them, and yelled, "'Will you follow me?' We replied we were not afraid to follow him anywhere. He said, 'Come on!'" The Virginians followed him at a run across an open field, with "bullets flying thick and fast." When they reached the abandoned gun, Pillow took charge and directed the fire himself. After a few rounds they disabled the piece that had done the damage to Green's battery. "This was a consummation devoutly wished for."[52]

Federals under W. H. L. Wallace fought on stubbornly, holding out against repeated Confederate attacks. Wallace added to his command fragments of McClernand's division, stragglers from here and there. It was now about 11:00 A.M. Wearily, Wallace's regiments fell back west along the Wynn's Ferry road to a fixed position held by McAllister's two guns and made a stand. The Union line was bent back badly at a right angle, but not broken.[53]

Noting that Buckner's sector was quiet, Pillow "asked Forrest where Buckner was, and said that he had not heard any firing from his side yet. He asserted it was time Buckner was moving."[54] To rush things up, Pillow, accompanied by Gilmer, the engineer, rode up to the

Confederate breastworks. He found, to his disgust, Buckner's troops lounging about in the trenches. Pillow, furious at what appeared to be complete lack of spirit, morale, and leadership in this division, ordered Col. Edward Cook's 32d Tennessee to leave the entrenchment, march down to the right, and attack the Union (McAllister's) works. This action, without clearance with Buckner, was irregular, but Pillow was not in the mood for military proprieties—he intended to keep the assault moving.

Buckner and Brown noted Cook's movement and came up to find out what was going on. Cook told them of Pillow's order, and Buckner promised to support the attack with the 18th Tennessee.[55] Shortly after, Pillow met Buckner. Considering the prickly relations between the two, both appeared to hold their tempers. Pillow asked for an explanation of the inactivity and tardiness; Buckner explained that he had sent in one assault and was now trying to rally his troops.[56] Buckner undoubtedly felt Pillow's presence an intrusion and was embarrassed by his presence and his usurping ways. Nevertheless, the two generals and their staffs rode together to a point overlooking Aaron Hollow. Pillow revised the attack plan and told Buckner to use the hollow for cover and to maneuver to the west of the redan and strike it in flank and rear. Pillow ordered Forrest to attack the redan from the east and started back to Maney's battery position to view the assaults.[57]

Forrest drew up his men into a column of squadrons for the attack, and Hanson's 2d Kentucky came up again to support the cavalry charge. Buckner ordered Maney's, Green's, and Graves's batteries to concentrate their fire on the Union redan, and Brown deployed his brigade for the attack.[58] At noon Brown, Forrest, and Hanson converged on the redan, which was supported by the 45th and 48th Illinois.[59] The Union infantry directed their fire at Forrest and Hanson, while McAllister's guns opened on Brown's advancing line. Forrest charged the Federal infantry, taking heavy casualties as he came, but he broke through, regrouped, and attacked McAllister's battery in reverse.[60] McAllister attempted to wheel his guns about to meet Forrest's charge, but it was too late. Northern gunners defended their pieces desperately for a few minutes but were forced to abandon them.[61]

The design and supervision of this particular attack displayed sound, aggressive generalship by Pillow. One might properly ask, however, what he was doing playing wing commander, division commander, and battery commander simultaneously. In an emergency, or at the climactic moment, this might be fine, but what about conducting a battle through one's subordinates? What was the point of having a Bushrod Johnson on the field unless he was to have a responsible role? Was Pillow sufficiently detached to observe and direct as he had from the hill at Contreras in 1847? Of course not. Gideon Pillow was very much a "hands on" general officer.

The story persists that at the turning point in the battle, while Pillow was off to the right tending to Buckner's troops, Forrest rode up to Bushrod Johnson, then in command of the left, and urged him to unleash Pillow's five brigades for a general charge on the retreating Yankees. Johnson hesitated, "unwilling to assume direction in Pillow's absence." This story, repeated by Forrest and Johnson biographers, seems unlikely. Pillow's brigades were fought out, at least offensively, by noon. To have reformed them and led them once more in the attack would have required extraordinary generalship.[62]

As Brown's brigade wheeled to the right at approximately 12:30 P.M. and pursued W. H. L. Wallace's two regiments west along the Wynn's Ferry road, the Confederate line now curved in a continuous line one mile long, reaching from the Wynn's Ferry road south to Drake's brigade on the road leading to Buford Hollow. The object of the attack had certainly been achieved. Pillow had breached the Union line, driving their right back upon the center in confusion. Escape was possible: the passage to Nashville lay open. Pillow sent a staff officer galloping off to Dover, carrying a message to be sent to Bowling Green ecstatically proclaiming to Johnston (and the world) a great victory, concluding with "on the honor of a soldier, the day is ours!"[63]

Brown's brigade continued the attack against Wallace, but again the Federals stiffened. Unknown to the Confederates, another brigade from Lew Wallace's division, John Thayer's, had moved up through fleeing Union soldiers to take a very strong position along Wynn's Ferry Road. From this point Thayer's reinforced brigade, almost twice ordinary size, successfully repulsed, with heavy loss, determined charges by Brown and Forrest.[64] The defeat of Brown's attack ended the Confederate offensive. Exhausted Confederates milled around on the battlefield. Some units attempted to regroup; others busied themselves with the wounded, hunted for trophies, or tried to stay warm. Pillow, acting on his own, without consulting Floyd or Buckner, halted the battle and ordered all the Confederates back to their works about 1:30 P.M.[65]

It was an extraordinary order. Buckner was astonished and angry; Floyd perplexed and angry. The two generals conferred, and Floyd, rather than rescinding Pillow's order on the spot, set off across the battlefield to find him. One account, written forty years later, has Floyd confronting Pillow: " 'In the name of God, General Pillow, what have we been fighting all day for? Certainly not to show our powers, but solely to secure the Wynn's Ferry Road, and now after securing it, you order it to be given up.' "[66] As the two men talked, Pillow explained with an air of confidence why he had ordered the men back to the trenches: "worn-out troops, the need for food and ammunition replenishment, the character of the snow-covered terrain which hampered re-supply, the totality of battlefield victory, and the inhumanity of leaving the wounded on the field without medical treatment and in freezing temperatures." "The weather was the coldest I ever saw," he said. Furthermore, Pillow told Floyd that the withdrawal back to the lines was nearing completion; it was irreversible.[67]

Another factor entered their consideration—news of 20,000 fresh Union troops approaching the battlefield. Alarming firing was heard coming from the thinly held trenches on the right of the Confederate line of works. In another telegram sent during the day, Pillow reported victory, but he mentioned that the enemy was being reinforced "and is probable may make another attack." In any event, Pillow persuaded Floyd, or the two generals persuaded themselves, that the proper course of action was to allow the withdrawal to the trenches to continue.[68]

One Pillow partisan has argued that Pillow made the "soldier's decision," although he "took an unmilitary liberty" when he acted without his commander's knowledge. "To rush out [to Nashville] had never been contemplated or prepared for. So say Floyd, Pillow, Johnson, Gilmer, Forrest and others. Buckner stands alone as having thought the plan decided on or even possible. He had his men go to battle with knapsacks, haversacks, and food. He had assumed he was to be the rear guard, a point never discussed."[69] A lieutenant in Graves's Kentucky battery put it bluntly, however. Pillow's "head was turned with the victory just gained, and he was too short sighted, to see that it was entirely thrown away, unless we used it to escape."[70]

Pillow must have concluded that he had won a victory of adequate proportions. The beaten and disorganized Union army could not prevent Confederate escape. The Confederates had inflicted about 2,100 casualties and captured 5,000 small arms and seven cannon. They had routed four Union brigades and come close to smashing Grant's army.[71] The opportunity to evacuate Fort Donelson had arrived, and it was early enough in the day to execute the original plan, regroup the entire army, and march out together that afternoon if they wished, or otherwise in the morning. But there was no need, Pillow felt, to abandon the fort precipitously. Indeed, considering the battered state of the Confederate army, it would have been done at high risk. Besides, he did not wish to leave behind the wounded or the garrison or the artillery, and the soldiers of his division had not brought their equipment or extra rations. The Wynn's Ferry road had not been cleared of Federals, although the Charlotte and Forge roads were open.[72]

To disengage and retire within the lines, however, risked all. Who would keep the escape route to Nashville open? What if the Yankees were to reoccupy their blocking position? Voluntarily to abandon the battlefield to the enemy from whom it had been seized at great price, to surrender a newly acquired line of communications, and to retreat into a blind corner, commanded by enemy field guns and gunboats, staggers the imagination—unless Pillow believed the enemy too battered and discouraged to attempt to block escape. No other logic seems to work.[73]

The Confederates returned to their original positions over "ice covered hills." When the order came, Maj. N. F. Cheairs, commanding the 3d Tennessee, received it from Pillow himself. The general rode up with his escort and beckoned Cheairs to him. He wanted the 3d and Hanson's 2d Kentucky to go at "the double quick to our former positions upon our right." Buckner, however, had ordered Cheairs to wait on the Wynn's Ferry road, aiding Forrest in covering the retirement and gathering small arms. When Cheairs told Pillow of the conflict in orders, "Pillow rose in his stirrups & said 'I am Genl in command of the forces of Donalson. Obey my order.'" Cheairs told Pillow that his men were "broken down & almost frozen," but he would carry out the order.

Cheairs and Hanson marched their regiments back to the right wing, where they found to their dismay that Federals, under C. F. Smith, had seized their thinly held positions. The 3d Tennessee and 2d Kentucky counterattacked at once but were repulsed. Buckner arrived with more troops, and the fighting continued until dark. It was bitter, discouraging fighting, with the Confederates throwing in more and more troops against increasing numbers of the enemy. Important sections of the trenches were never recovered. The Confederates were able, however, to establish a formidable new line, fully manned.[74]

Meanwhile, as the sun set on the Confederate left, Union troops led by Lew Wallace pressed forward with determination, recovering and reoccupying the terrain and the roads lost that morning. They reached Wynn's Ferry Road and extended their line to the right as far as Forge Road; thus there were no Federal troops on Dudley's Hill. Union forces did not block Charlotte Road or keep it under observation. Everything was almost back where it had started.

Lt. Col. Randal W. McGavock, the popular former mayor of Nashville, felt perfectly comfortable in paying a call at headquarters after the firing had ceased, having known "Gens Floyd and Pillow intimately for years." He sat with the two generals and discussed the battle. Pillow complained that Buckner's performance that morning had robbed them of a perfect victory: "If Buckner had have been up in time according to his promise, the enemy would have routed." Later Buckner himself showed up, back from the front lines, and came into headquarters. McGavock excused himself, confident that "the battle would be renewed tomorrow with greater vigor."[75]

That night, as the generals sat at headquarters, Confederates loaded their wounded and prisoners aboard steamers, the last leaving about midnight for Clarksville and Nashville.[76] An hour later a council of war assembled at Pillow's headquarters in the Rice house. The meeting became progressively more tense as couriers kept coming in and handing messages to Buckner. Large forces were reported forming to Buckner's front, and others were moving laterally across the entire line toward the Confederate left. Floyd informed the council that Grant continued to receive reinforcements. The best estimate now was that the enemy had some eighty-three regiments on the field.[77]

There was little or no talk of a making a stand within the Donelson perimeter. Floyd simply ordered the retreat to Nashville, the movement that had been agreed upon the previous day. It would begin at 4:00 A.M. on the sixteenth. Units would pull out of their defensive positions and assemble behind the left of the Confederate line as they had done Saturday morning, February 15. This time the retreat would be for real—stores would be burned at dawn and all artillery would be spiked. The council adjourned, and officers returned to their commands.[78]

Floyd, Buckner, Forrest, Pillow, and the latter's staff remained behind in Pillow's private room. Messages continued to come in. Two scouts reported campfires in front of the left. It could only be assumed that the enemy had reoccupied their former positions. The generals turned to Major Rice, their host, and asked him about the condition of the road to Charlotte. Rice replied that the roads were most unfavorable. Rice then asked Dr. J. W. Smith, another resident, to join them. Under close questioning, particularly by Pillow, Smith testified that "though exceedingly difficult, it was possible to pass the roads with light baggage trains." About this time another scout appeared and reported the enemy had indeed reoccupied the positions from which they had been driven. Pillow doubted this and sent out still another scout to confirm the information. Forrest, who had ridden across the terrain to the left of the Confederate lines that night, believed the enemy had not occupied it, but he agreed that additional scouts should be sent out immediately. To him it appeared the fires had been made by good samaritans, neighbors in the area tending to the wounded freezing out on the battlefield.

In the meantime, Pillow took his friend and aide, John C. Burch, aside and told him and Gustavus A. Henry, Jr., to start packing headquarters books and records. To his commissary officers, Haynes and Nicholson, Pillow issued instructions to burn all stores about daybreak, consistent with Floyd's order for evacuation.

Gloom settled in; nerves were frayed. Pillow and Buckner no longer minced words. Their hostility, simmering, on Pillow's part, since 1857, had flared when Buckner arrived at Donelson and again that morning when Buckner failed to press down Wynn's Ferry Road at dawn as planned.[79] The two generals began a desperately serious debate about the fate of the army. Floyd listened.

Buckner sat at an angle to the fireplace. Pillow sat next to him facing directly into the fire. "I am confident that the enemy will attack my lines by light," said Buckner, in no mood for Pillow's optimism. "I cannot hold my position half an hour after the attack." "Why can't you?" demanded Pillow. Buckner countered that he had only 4,000 effective troops, who had been "demoralized by long and uninterrupted exposure and fighting." Buckner continued with a litany of what sounded like excuses to Pillow: the presence of Federal gunboats, overwhelming numbers of the enemy, shortages of this and that. Pillow would have none of it. "I think you can hold your position; I think you can sir," he fired back.

"No," responded Buckner, with great emphasis. "I know my position, and I know that the lines cannot be held with my troops in the present condition." Pillow shook his head again. "I do not think so; at any rate, we can cut our way out." Buckner countered dejectedly, "To cut our way out would cost three-fourths of our men, and I do not think any commander has a right to sacrifice three-fourths of his command to save one-fourth."[80] And then General Floyd spoke up. "Certainly not."[81]

Buckner continued, saying that the "principal object of the defense of Donelson [was] to be to cover the movement of General A. S. Johnston's army from Bowling Green to Nashville," and that resistance should continue if Johnston's movement had not been completed. Floyd, agreeing with Buckner, as he had throughout, remarked that Johnston's army had already reached Nashville, as if to say that the Donelson command had fulfilled its mission and could now surrender.[82]

More scouts came into headquarters. "Two reliable men" had been sent by Forrest to Smith's ford. They substantiated what Smith had said earlier: backwater blocked the road, "just high enough to reach the saddle-skirts on a horse of medium size." No Federals were in sight, only campfires, burning at the Union positions of February 14–15. Forrest believed that these were old fires, fanned by the wind, which still blew hard. The scouts also reported mud in Smith's ford about "half-leg deep" and that the width of the flooded ford was about 100 yards.[83]

Decision time had come. Pillow and Buckner continued to wrangle, old wounds being scratched open by looks, attitudes, and words. Buckner grew stubborn in his insistence that surrender was the proper course. They could not hold their lines, and if they attempted to break out, the pursuing Federals would chop them to pieces. There was no alternative. Forrest entered the argument, siding heatedly with Pillow; they could fight their way out. Pillow offered another alternative: hold out a day, allowing time for the steamers to return, and then begin ferrying the army not to Clarksville, but simply across the river to the east bank to safety—a Dunkirk solution.

This was the crucial moment. Pillow had offered a constructive way to save the command. The gunboats had been neutralized, the Confederate positions were strong, and the troops were rested and in high spirits. His proposals to stand and fight or to evacuate the fort by stages, however, seem to have received scant consideration. Curiously, the highly persuasive Pillow appeared overmatched that night by his adversary. Their old animosity seemed to have returned with a vengeance, blurring eyes, blocking ears. Buckner grew more emphatic. He could not hold the right against C. F. Smith the next morning. "My right was already turned, a portion of my entrenchments in the enemy's possession—they were in position successfully to assail my position and the water batteries." In his mind everything boiled down to that hopeless certainty. Floyd agreed with Buckner. "We will have to capitulate," he said.

Pillow acquiesced. He was tired, and he had doubts himself—at least about the prospects for a successful defense against a heavy attack on the right. Scouting reports made it appear that to extricate the army toward Charlotte would mean punching a hole in the Union line once again, and maintaining that opening until all units passed through, probably under fire. At best, it would be very difficult and dangerous. They had done so less than twenty-four hours earlier, but Pillow had felt the weight of Grant's reinforcements during the fighting that afternoon. He now believed there were 40,000 out there. The very argument he would employ months later justifying his decision to abort the attack on the fifteenth applied. Without field artillery—and orders had been given to spike it—a breakthrough, even if successful initially, would have been only the beginning of a chase. Confederate infantry without support of cannon would not be capable of effective rear guard stands. The Donelson force would degenerate into a fleeing mob. Pillow had seen that before, on November 7. Without the cooperation of Buckner and Floyd, a breakout would have failed anyway, and surely there would have been unacceptably high casualties.

Pillow failed himself, his army, and his cause, however, by not strongly pushing for an evacuation. Rather than loading the two available steamers with Floyd's troops and shipping them to Nashville, ferrying just to the east side of the river as many infantry as could be crammed aboard would have salvaged, under the worst of conditions, a goodly portion of the army, considerably more than the two regiments that were saved. To have withdrawn the army from the trenches in the teeth of enemy pressure was a perilous tactic, but at least it offered an alternative.

Buckner's assessment of the military situation should be questioned seriously. It is sufficient to note that contemporary letters and diaries, as well as postwar memoirs, seem to contradict him. Confederate morale was high. Whether they could have successfully defended their long line of works is uncertain. Whether Grant's green troops could have successfully conducted the required assault is also uncertain, but Buckner thought his friend Grant could smash through. Besides, Buckner wanted no part of a life and death fight chained to that fool Pillow. Buckner had lost his confidence; he had set his mind on surrender.

And Gideon Pillow had lost his conviction. A general officer with determination could have defended the trench line, could have undertaken the desperate breakout around Grant's right, or could have evacuated by boat much of the Donelson command. What was needed was a true "Hero of Chapultepec." It was a dangerous, brilliant moment offered to few military leaders. But Pillow the politician triumphed that early morning of February 16. The deep cynicism that had hollowed out a spot within him led Pillow to a fatal error of judgment. He had at Donelson a story that would sell—the gallant Tennesseans had shown they could fight, and they had done so effectively on the fifteenth under his personal leadership. Everyone knew that. This fearless Donelson army that had fought so well had been tricked by the unforeseen, overwhelmed, after fulfilling its mission of buying time, by an enemy at least three times as large, well equipped, with a fleet of battered but serviceable gunboats at its command. Pillow wished to fight on to the death and would have done so with his loyal Tennesseans but for Buckner, who quit, and Floyd, the commander of them all, who caved in. That is squarely where the public would place the blame. Pillow himself had served his country very well by escaping to fight another day; he had saved his honor by refusing to surrender; he had justified his cause for promotion to major command by being responsible for the success of this army, yet not responsible for its base surrender.

So to cleanse himself, Pillow shrewdly announced to his fellow generals, in the presence of his own staff and his friend Forrest: "As for myself, I will never surrender the command or myself; I will die first." "Nor will I," seconded Floyd.[84]

Buckner at this point agreed to take upon himself the repulsive task. "Then I suppose the duty of surrendering the command will devolve on me." Floyd, his superior and commander of the Confederates at Donelson, answered him obliquely, "How will you proceed?" Buckner told him he intended to send a flag of truce to Grant and ask for "an armistice of six hours to arrange terms." Then he continued, "Am I to consider the command as turned over to me?" Floyd responded, "Certainly, I turn over the command." Pillow "replied quickly, 'I pass it; I will not surrender.'" And the fraudulent, irresponsible conveyance was done.

Compounding damage, Floyd and Pillow ignored the military implications of surrender. No plan was adopted to guide Buckner. Thus when white flags went up later Sunday morning, the Confederates themselves, not Grant, made the surrender unconditional. There would be no paroling of men and officers on the spot as Buckner and Pillow doubtless expected.[85]

Reacting with fury at this startling turnabout, this opéra bouffe, Forrest turned to Pillow. "What shall I do?" Pillow replied, "Cut your way out."[86]

Then Pillow proceeded on his self-destructive course, compounding his fatal error in judgment. He left the room and began to gather his staff and servants and make preparations to escape. An afterthought prompted him to return in a few minutes. In the presence of his aide Lt. Hunter Nicholson, he said to Floyd and Buckner: "Gentlemen, in order that we may understand each other, let me state what is my position; I differ with you as to the cost of cutting our way out, but if it were ascertained that it would cost three-fourths of the command, I agree that it would be wrong to sacrifice them for the remaining fourth."[87] Floyd and Buckner responded, "We understand you, general, and you understand us."[88]

Following their meeting, Floyd and Pillow went to the river landing. They were standing near a blacksmith shop and talking. A young Tennessee lieutenant overheard Floyd having second thoughts about Pillow's idea of ferrying troops across the river. Pillow, angry and petulant, responded, "This thing began at that court martial in Mexico."[89] He washed his hands of the business.

Truly the troops had been forsaken. At 4:00 A.M. that morning, February 16, following the plan and order of the council of war, they gathered their rations and weapons and belongings and marched to the designated assembly points behind the lines. There they waited to repeat the enveloping movement they had made the morning before, around the left of their army, breaking Grant's right flank again if need be. And there that Sunday morning, they would wait and continue to wait for over two hours, standing in ranks in the terrible cold, in ankle-deep mud, until they saw to their astonishment, not their commanding officers coming to lead them, but white flags of surrender sprouting on the battlements like ghastly flowers of winter.

But how would Pillow escape? "There was no means of crossing the river." Resourceful Major Rice came to the rescue and conveniently discovered a small flatboat somewhere on the other side of the river. He and Gilmer and Pillow crossed the Cumberland shortly before dawn. When Pillow looked back over the river he saw the steamer *Anderson* and another little boat coming down the river. He hoped his staff could find a place aboard.[90]

Floyd saw to that. He removed 400 unfortunate recruits who happened to be aboard the *Anderson*, replaced them with McCausland's Virginia regiment and Pillow's staff and horses, and had them ferried to the east side of the river immediately. The remainder of Pillow's staff, and some who claimed to belong to his staff, his servants, and his baggage would come later with Floyd and Wharton's Virginians aboard the *Anderson* and would steam not to the east bank, but all the way to Nashville. A private belonging to the 3d Tennessee made every appeal to get aboard one of the steamers, but was refused. Then, enraged, he watched "3 horses & 2 negroes with baggage taken on." Confederate officers beat off other would-be boarders with their swords.[91]

Meanwhile, Pillow turned away from the chaos and terror at the Dover landing and set his face toward Nashville. He and his staff rode overland, crossed the bridge at Clarksville back to the west bank, found a steamer, got aboard, and continued on to Nashville, arriving there at 7:00 A.M., Monday morning, February 17. While on board the steamer, Pillow made his first public attempt to justify what had happened. Taking the magic wand of rhetoric and waving it over the wad of reality, he attempted to create out of disaster a diverting illusion of something noble. To a group of Virginia soldiers he spoke of the "upwards of 40,000" Yankees who had closed in upon them at Donelson, making it suicidal for the 13,000 gallant Confederate defenders to repel them.[92]

The barometer of confidence in Nashville had dropped from "almost unbounded confidence" before church on Sunday to "perfect tumult" as news of the surrender leaked out. When Pillow arrived in Nashville, welcomed by steady rain and sleet, he found the streets "a complete jam of citizens and soldiers." Sidney Johnston, fresh from Bowling Green, called a council of war in which Pillow, Floyd, Hardee, and prominent citizens of Nashville participated. Should they fight to defend the capital? The city's fathers begged the generals not to, so it was decided to abandon Nashville—and all that that implied. Floyd would take command of the city itself in the interim, while Johnston and Hardee took the army south through Murfreesboro. To calm the panicked populace, the council agreed that Pillow and Floyd should address them that evening. A handbill was quickly printed and circulated.[93]

Long before 7:00 P.M., the time scheduled for Pillow to speak, a "very large crowd assembled" on the Public Square. Pillow made one of the shortest speeches of his life. He informed the people that the army would not make a stand at Nashville and that the civil, not military, authorities would actually surrender the city. He advised and implored citizens to remain "quiet and orderly" in their homes. "The Federals," he said, "will be with you only for a time, and I pledge to you my honor that this war will not end until they are driven across the Ohio river. The officers who will come among you are gentlemen, and, of course, will behave as such towards you." He praised the Tennesseans' fight at Donelson and told of the awful carnage there. His speech took five minutes. Floyd followed, confirming what Pillow had said about Donelson and what to expect in Nashville.

While Floyd was speaking, Pillow slipped away from the crowd and made his way down to the depot, where he climbed aboard a waiting train car for Columbia. He would look back, down the rails, to the capital of Tennessee, abandoned to violence and "wildest confusion." "Such a disgusting scene of brawling, quarreling, horror struck, cowardly crowds I pray God we may never see again."[94]

13   **Is This Right?**

A badly shaken Gideon Pillow arrived at Clifton early on February 18, 1862. He set to work preparing his report of Donelson, although he kept in touch with Johnston and the army in Murfreesboro by telegraph. He also prepared a circular, a call to arms for Tennesseans, which explained the sacrifices at Donelson and laid out the course of action required to restore their fortunes. John C. Burch had the circular published in the *Union and American* shortly before Nashville fell.[1]

Sidney Johnston reorganized his fragmented Confederate commands on February 23, pooling survivors of the Mill Springs debacle, miscellaneous commands he had picked up in Nashville, and his own Bowling Green troops into an army of three divisions and a reserve, commanded by Hardee, George B. Crittenden, Pillow, and Breckinridge. Johnston's confidence in Pillow never wavered, despite Donelson. Hardee wrote Pillow for Johnston, "Your presence here is much needed." Your division "in the meantime will be under command of Genl [Sterling A. M.] Wood."[2]

Division commander Pillow, however, had another agenda. He left Clifton and was on his way to Memphis, arriving on February 25. He gave his Donelson report to the Memphis *Daily Appeal*, which published it the following day. General Johnston had agreed unofficially that "the facts should be communicated to the public through some friend. . . . The mode of doing this in the least objectionable manner is left to your discretion."[3] This was highly irregular, of course, infuriating to Samuel Cooper, to Jefferson Davis, to military professionals who took the proprieties of their profession seriously. Who should have known this better than Gideon Pillow, who still carried his "Leonidas" scar. Would the man never learn?

Yet Pillow deliberately gave the *Appeal* his report for publication. He justified his action to the War Department, arguing that he had done so "to correct misapprehension & explain the necessity which compelled capitulation at Donelson."[4] The Atlanta *Daily Southern Confederacy* pounced immediately: "Gen. Pillow is a wire working politician and has been all his life; and the publication of his report before sending it to the War Department is entirely characteristic of such a man." A friend of Floyd's wrote from Richmond that news of Donelson had evoked "some feeling of despondency here," and "the manner of publication of Genl Pillow's report, excites surprise and remarks."[5]

Pillow also attracted attention in Memphis. He spoke to a large crowd gathered in the lobby of the Gayoso. He told them about Donelson, not a tale of despair and of hopes betrayed, but a thrilling story of a "terrible and hard-contested battle" which, though sad in outcome, demonstrated once again the "invincibility of the hero of Chapultepec" and "reflect[ed] new luster upon the well-earned fame of Southern valor."[6] Pillow appealed to his fellow Tennesseans to dispel the gloom of the present, redouble their efforts, and rush to arms.[7] From Memphis he wrote the secretary of war, advising that the "one remedy for the existing condition of things" was to abandon all the coast defenses except New Orleans, "concentrate all the forces in

Tennessee, drive the Enemy north of the Ohio River & press invasion of Ohio and Indiana." The South must regain "control of the interior rivers."[8]

After calming the people of Memphis and trying to give them a sense of deeper determination, Pillow returned to Clifton and packed "such articles of furniture as are necessary for the comfort of my Family." He had their belongings loaded into two army freight cars which he asked Johnston to have set aside for the purpose.[9] Unfortunately, in the frantic rush and crush of retreat, "my furniture was all mashed up today in cars except one car load."[10] Then he and Mary and the rest of the family left Clifton. He situated them safely in north Alabama, while he and his staff took their posts at Decatur, Alabama, supervising the army's crossing of the Tennessee River.[11]

At Decatur Pillow received the shock of his life. On March 16, 1862, Johnston issued an order relieving Pillow and Floyd from command. He did so in accordance with a directive from Jefferson Davis. "The reports of Brig. Genls. Floyd and Pillow of the defense and fall of Fort Donelson are unsatisfactory," Davis wrote, and he angrily demanded to know why there had been failure "to give timely notice of the insufficiency of the garrison to repel attack." Why did they not evacuate the garrison? Why had his two senior generals abandoned the command and by what means did they themselves escape? How were the units selected (the Virginia regiments of Floyd) that did manage to escape?[12]

Pillow, mortified and without a command, moved his family to Oxford, Mississippi, and remained there himself throughout the spring and summer of 1862. He slipped away for a while in April, at the request of Sidney Johnston, who telegraphed him to join the army at Corinth. They discussed Pillow's resuming command of "my division," and, according to Pillow, he refused, believing President Davis might suspend Johnston himself for offering him the command. Accompanied by Governor Harris, Pillow visited Johnston the night before the Battle of Shiloh, and the gloomy army commander confided that the following day he would either lead his army to victory or leave his body upon the field. No record exists of Pillow's participation in the battle, however, beyond this talk with Johnston and the fact that one of Pillow's slaves was captured on the field.[13]

A week after Shiloh, Pillow turned up in Helena, Arkansas. He made a mock sale—all his slaves, all his Arkansas land, all his buildings and equipment to Henry P. Coolidge, a citizen of Phillips County, for $575,000. Pillow and Coolidge then executed a second agree-

Brig. Gen. Gideon Johnson Pillow, 1862
(courtesy Valentine Museum, Richmond, Virginia)

ment, a secret one, that showed "in point of fact no sale of this property was intended, but the real object of the pretended sale was to create in Coolidge an agency for the management of Pillow's estate and to supply the wants of Pillow's large slave population." [14]

Meanwhile, Clifton had attracted the fancy of Federal Gen. William "Bull" Nelson, who used it as temporary headquarters. Many of Nelson's men "gaped in amazement as they wandered the beautiful grounds," entered Pillow's magnificent greenhouses, and examined the stonework of the "dairy." Nelson passed through, but Gen. James S. Negley remained in the area, ruling it "with an iron hand." Negley, fortunately, was one of Pillow's Mexican War Pennsylvanians, and he took care not only to post guards at Clifton, but to protect Pillow's property, justifying his action because 400 "broken-down" horses were pastured there. [15] Negley had become a great friend of Jerome Pillow, who, about this time, had seen fit to take the loyalty oath. In July 1862 Jerome attempted to use his favor with Federal authorities to get his brother Gideon's wife and children back to Clifton. His friend Negley did not object to repatriating the family, but for permission he had to refer Jerome to Gen. Don Carlos Buell, who saw things differently. Buell refused to allow Gideon Pillow's family safe conduct back home "until your brother can himself return to Tennessee under that protection which all loyal citizens of the United States are entitled." [16]

After the fall of Memphis on June 6, 1862, Pillow had great difficulty reaching Mound Plantation in Arkansas, and more and more he came to depend upon Coolidge. Even this inconvenient arrangement ended in July 1862, when Helena fell. Pillow saw his fortune, the work of a lifetime, in jeopardy. He tried to take steps in anticipation of the Federals adopting a policy of "seizing our negro men" and placing them in the army, where they "will be lost to us forever." From Oxford he wrote Jerome a letter which he attempted to slip into Maury by his slave boy Sol, who hid it under the skirt of his mule's saddle. Pillow confided to Jerome that he intended, as soon as Gen. Samuel R. Curtis "gets out of the way," to bring his slaves "to this region of the country." Unless property owners like the Pillows took great care and were most fortunate, he wrote, "we will accomplish our independence but we will lose one Thousand Million Dollars worth of Negroes." [17]

But Curtis did not get out of the way. Instead, he took Mound Plantation and transformed it into a refugee camp for thousands of slaves. The U.S. Army issued rations to those who gathered there, and Curtis issued letters of manumission to many who claimed they had been used as "property to carry on war." With the cotton crop of 1862 still in the fields waiting to be picked, the Federal government went into partnership with contractors who agreed to harvest it on a sharecrop basis. The slaves were organized into companies and put to work. Word got to Pillow that Curtis had taken his slaves by force, "sweeping" not only Mound Plantation, but Phillips County of slaves, livestock, corn, and meat. Slaves who resisted or tried to escape were threatened with being chained or shot.

On August 2, 1862, Pillow wrote his friend Sam P. Walker (Knox Walker's brother) in occupied Memphis and asked him to get a letter complaining of the atrocities into the hands of Sherman or Grant. Pillow maintained in his letter that armed bodies of men had taken off all his slaves, some 400 of them, "and destroyed everything else I have." They had killed an overseer and had jailed three others. His slaves, even the women and children, now wandered the streets of Memphis hungry; eighty-five of them had been locked in a cotton warehouse. The Yankees, he complained, had also taken the slaves of his brother Jerome, his staff officer Lemuel Long, and Thomas J. Brown, his young Alabama son-in-law. Pillow argued that "the law of confiscation does not take effect for some time to come, and my negroes were in no legal sense liable to seizure." In hope that the letter would reach its destination, he reminded Sherman and Grant that he had protected property of Union men in Kentucky and Missouri, especially that of Gen. Thomas L. Crittenden, whose slaves and plantation below Columbus he had "kept from being interrupted." Pillow had wired a similar message to Jefferson Davis, informing him of the Federal depredations against property and the slave population, but in this telegram he added the clipped ending, "Can no retaliatory measures be adopted?" [18]

Davis responded to Pillow by telegram July 31, expressing regret over the "wholesale devastation and robbery which you report." [19] Sherman also responded promptly, but privately, through Sam Walker. He had investigated and conferred with General Curtis. The latter denied killing or imprisoning any overseers. No slaves had been taken by armed force except when Curtis had proof that "such slaves had been used in war against him." The damage to Pillow's property "was only such as will attend the armies, such as marked the progress of your and A. Sidney Johnston's columns a year ago in Kentucky." Sherman did not believe Pillow's slaves wandered the streets of Memphis "in want and destitution"; rather, turning the knife a bit, he related that Curtis had expressed surprise at "your solicitude for these negroes. He says you had sold them all or had transferred them by some instrument of writing for a record to a gentleman near the plantation [Coolidge] who is a loyal citizen of the United States."[20]

Pillow had suffered severely. By March 1863 he estimated he had lost over $1 million in slaves (409 taken in Arkansas), 4 gin houses valued at $10,000 each, 10,000 pounds of bacon, 2,000 hogs, 500 head of cattle, and 2,100 bales of cotton. Mound Plantation was wrecked, and homes and facilities on his other properties had been destroyed. To further deepen Pillow's troubles, and make him abandon any thought of giving up the fight and taking the loyalty oath, he was indicted for treason in June 1862 by the grand jury of the Federal Circuit Court for the Middle District of Tennessee, ironically the former jurisdiction of his brother-in-law West Humphreys.[21]

The southern press indicted Pillow as well. With few exceptions, such as the Memphis *Daily Appeal*, they appeared to disbelieve his account of Donelson. The Augusta, Georgia, *Daily Constitutionalist* said: "Two facts, may in part, explain Gen. Pillow's conduct. One is that he is a remarkable conceited, selfish, and inconsequential man. The other is that he cordially hates Buckner."[22]

At Fort Warren, Massachusetts, another court indicted and tried Pillow in absentia. There Confederate general and field-grade officers, the imprisoned victims of the Donelson debacle, closed ranks and agreed upon a common story and a common verdict. Pillow's brigade commander, Adolphus Heiman, rendered it in biting verse.[23] These officers, penned up and festering at Fort Warren, itched for the opportunity to repay Pillow and Floyd. As brigade commander and former Whig, Col. John C. Brown, expressed it to his friend, Col. Joseph B. Palmer, "We fought on the same field and were fellow-victims of the fatal blunder of that Ditch-digging General, and we are now inmates of the same prison. We never bargained for this."[24] They could never forgive Pillow for deserting them, for robbing them of a victory they had paid blood to win, for staining their honor with disgraceful surrender. Gen. Lloyd Tilghman, whom Pillow had castigated at Clarksville in February, seethed with fury, and when he had the opportunity to address three regiments of Tennesseans in September 1862, "he pitched into Gen Pillow pretty severely—and charged him with having caused all our misfortunes at Ft Donelson."[25] Fellow Maury Countian, Capt. Robert N. Moore, repeated the chant in his Bible: "Fort Donelson was surrendered . . . after a hard fight and a brilliant victory on Saturday, Febry 15, 1862, by a cowardly general, to wit, Gen. Pillow, who deserted us Saturday night."[26]

Even Ulysses S. Grant cooperated. When he met with Buckner following the surrender, according to Buckner, he asked about Pillow. "Gone," Buckner responded. "He thought you'd rather get hold of him than any other man in the Southern Confederacy." "Oh," replied Grant, "if I had got him I'd let him go again. He will do us more good commanding you fellows." "This made us both laugh," thought Buckner, "for we remembered Pillow in the Mexican War."[27]

Tennessee had honored Pillow "in days gone by," said Col. Edward C. Cook of the 32d Tennessee, "but his course is ruined and he will go down unwept, unhonored and unsung." Col. Roger Hanson, who fought under Pillow at Cerro Gordo and who commanded the 2d Kentucky, the regiment Pillow tried so hard to get from Buckner on February 15, declared, "To be under the command of Pillow once in a life time is misfortune indeed but to be under his command twice— the first time whipped and the second time surrendered is more than human nature can bear—if it should be my good fortune to be in another battle for the cause of liberty all I ask of Providence is not to be under Gen. Pillow." Maj. N. F. Cheairs, 3d Tennessee, another Maury citizen, wrote his sister Nancy on May 7, 1862. He had heard that Pillow was sitting out the war in Oxford. "I would not exchange conditions with him, if I knew I had to remain here for 50 years."[28]

Thus the myth, the grand excuse, of Fort Donelson was created: the Confederate army, full of fight, could have successfully continued their defense or could have escaped; they were surrendered because of delusion, cowardice, and betrayal. Buckner became the martyr and Pillow, with the deaths of Johnston in 1862 and Floyd in 1863, the scapegoat, the target of ridicule and revulsion then and ever since.[29] A harassed Jefferson Davis also succumbed to the temptation, partly from his love of Sidney Johnston, partly from Secretary of War Randolph's whispers in his ear, partly from his distrust of Pillow, and partly because it offered an expedient explanation.

So Gideon Pillow prepared to do battle to defend his good name. When he learned on March 16 that he had been suspended from command, he drew up a supplemental Donelson report including sworn testimony from Burch, Forrest, Henry, Haynes, and Nicholson. Randolph replied on March 26 that the "Government still keeps its judgment suspended" because the report of General Johnston had not been received, and Floyd and Bushrod Johnson "have not yet been heard from." Weeks dragged by. Receiving no reply, an impatient Pillow prodded the War Department on May 15, pointing out that he had answered each of Davis's interrogatories promptly, that

Floyd's report had been made public, and "that I should continue patient under indefinite suspension could hardly be expected. If the Government does not need nor does not want my services, it is my duty to retire. I have no wish to be in the way."[30]

Still with no response, Pillow wrote again on June 21, 1862, this time from Bragg's headquarters at Tupelo, where he had turned up to visit old friends.[31] (Bragg was not exactly pleased when the controversial general came by to pay his respects and would write later, "Our acquaintance commenced, general, not without prejudice in my mind adverse to you.")[32] It had been nearly four months, Pillow reminded the government, since he had been suspended from command, and still no charges had been preferred against him. He pointed out that the Confederate House committee investigating Donelson had summoned him to appear and asked him to respond in writing to certain questions about the disaster. Pillow had refused, "from motives of delicacy." He also declined to furnish Congress with copies of his supplemental report, "upon the ground that proper respect for the Government forbade it while the Government had the subject under consideration." Pillow himself could indulge in such irritating behavior, but when he learned that the president also refused to furnish copies of this information, he exclaimed, "The public are denied the means of judging how or in what I have been derelict in duty. Is this right?"[33]

Pillow brought up once again the telegram from Floyd to Johnston of February 16 informing the commanding general that the command had been passed to Buckner. It had never devolved upon him. "How could I have attempted to defeat the execution of that purpose (viz, to surrender the command) without a violation of all discipline and subjecting myself to arrest for insubordination. Certainly I saw no alternative, but acquiesced in what I could not avert."

"If I am to continue in the service," Pillow continued, "I respectfully submit that such treatment is not likely to increase my efficiency for command or my usefulness as an officer. . . . I feel that proper self-respect and personal dignity leave me no alternative but to retire from the service. If, therefore, no action is deemed proper in response to this communication, I respectfully tender this as my resignation." Braxton Bragg, as commander of the Army of Tennessee, forwarded Pillow's letter with an endorsement supporting Pillow's appeal for an official investigation, "as due to himself and the Government."[34]

Randolph responded on July 5, 1862, informing Pillow that the release of Buckner and the other Fort Donelson participants was expected soon. At that time a thorough investigation would be possible. Meanwhile, Pillow should know "that your suspension has never been considered an accusation, but as preliminary to an investigation."[35] Pillow protested on July 20. "I have never regarded the order itself an accusation, but I did then and do yet consider it as implying censure and displeasure of the President, and the country so understands it."[36]

When Buckner's report came in, Davis studied it and had the following special order issued on August 22: "It is impossible to acquit Brig. Gen. G. J. Pillow of grave errors of judgment in the military operations which resulted in the surrender of the army, but there being no reason to question his courage and loyalty, his suspension from duty is removed, and he will report to General B. Bragg for orders."[37]

This was not good enough. Pillow wired back, "Is the order of suspension simply removed, without anything being said relieving me from censure?"[38] But there was no reply. To whom was Pillow to report anyway? Bragg and the Army of Tennessee had left Mississippi, going by way of Chattanooga into Kentucky. Buckner had returned, been promoted, and had assumed command of the division that had been Pillow's. With irony, Pillow later wrote, "But if he was promoted for advocating the surrender it would seem as a matter of logic, looking at matters upon their face, that General Pillow was suspended for opposing the surrender; or, if not for that, for not surrendering himself. . . . This suspension, perhaps, caused him more pain than any event of his life."[39]

No course was left, Pillow believed, but to go to Richmond and seek not only an explanation, but restitution. He met with Davis and Randolph in mid-September, and the two officials took care to clarify what they meant by "grave errors of judgment." The first was that Pillow should have remained with the army, "to have taken command and fought it out" or to have "surrendered the command and myself with it." Pillow accepted this.

He rejected flatly, however, the government's claim that his second error was breaking off the attack on the fifteenth and ordering the army back into the trenches, thus losing the chance of escape. "We made no preparation before going into the battle for retreating from the battlefield. No suggestion or proposition was ever made that we should do so, and all that was determined upon in the conference on the night of February 14 was that we would give the investing force battle next morning." Buckner, Pillow contended, was the guilty party, "and yet I am made to bear all the odium of that measure, while he who caused it is held blameless and uncensured." "Against such injustice I solemnly protest."[40]

Pillow protested in vain; the matter was closed. On October 10, in one last effort, he wrote Randolph asking that the government reconsider its position. Van Dorn had given him nothing to do in Mississippi, "and believing that I can render the country no service, I am forced to the conclusion that it is my duty to retire from the service." "I need not say that the promotion of my juniors in rank, who, when promoted had fought no battle, had no experience in high command and little of any sort, taken from the very forces organized by myself as a part of the Army of Tennessee, of which I was the commander—promotions made over me while I was suspended under an unjust order—adds additional poignancy to other acts of injustice I have sustained." Yet he hesitated to retire, Pillow said, because "my whole fortune, large as it was, has been swept away by the enemy." His cotton had been burned, he faced $5,000 in taxes which "I have no means of paying," and "I am reduced to poverty, with a large and dependent family of grown-up and unmarried daughters on my hands." He would return to Tennessee and there await the action of the government.[41]

Randolph brushed aside Pillow's arguments and interpreted his letter of October 10, 1862, as an offer of resignation, which he accepted on October 21. Astonished, Pillow wrote back on November 8 from Bragg's headquarters at Murfreesboro, "I have not resigned." With this letter he submitted a brief defending his position and requesting Davis to have Randolph's decision reversed. He took the letter to Richmond himself and appealed directly to the president. Davis promised him, according to Pillow, "that he would take up the case on his return from his western trip, and explain it himself, and assured me, that he would do me justice."[42] When Davis returned from Tennessee, he did agree to have the order accepting Pillow's resignation rescinded, effective December 10, 1862. Pillow was to report to Gen. Joseph Johnston for duty.[43]

Persistence might win him another command in the Army of Tennessee, but Davis remained silent about Pillow being censured for "grave errors of judgment." Pillow had lost out. Over time he shifted blame from Davis to Randolph for his misfortune; he wrote Davis in October 1863, informing him that George W. Randolph "was my *personal enemy*, growing out of my controversy with General Scott, in which Mr. N. P. Trist (Mr. Randolph's brother-in-law) was a chief witness." He asked once more for redress and submitted still more proof, not believing Davis "capable of intentional injustice." Davis did not respond.[44]

The return of Pillow to the army in September 1862 brought predictable response. The Jackson *Daily Mississippian* lamented, "We look for disasters where Pillow goes. We had hoped that the war was falling into the hands of the fighting men of the country. . . . Another splendid army will have to be sacrificed to gratify his vanity and glaring incapacity."[45]

Van Dorn had no units he was willing to turn over to Pillow. Bragg was out of reach. "I have nothing to do," Pillow complained. Perhaps he could organize a command for himself from the Donelson prisoners now in the process of being exchanged. Since Van Dorn "thinks he can make no order about it," Pillow decided to take matters into his own hands. He wrote the War Department proposing that he be given ten of the thirteen skeleton Tennessee regiments returning from prison. He would return with them to Middle Tennessee and fill their ranks with volunteers. All this came to nothing. Randolph believed recruiting in Tennessee would conflict with the conscript law; besides, the Tennessee regiments had been promised to Tilghman.[46]

Pillow pestered everyone about a command. He turned up in Murfreesboro, remaining there most of November.[47] Unsuccessful with Bragg, he went to Richmond, met with Davis about December 10, and secured reassignment to the Army of Tennessee. He then headed west, passing through Chattanooga. When word came down the line that a great battle was in progress, Pillow hurried on toward Murfreesboro.[48]

He arrived at Bragg's headquarters in Murfreesboro late on the morning of January 2, 1863. It was an awkward, inconvenient time. A major battle had begun there two days earlier. Rosecrans's Army of the Cumberland had marched out from Nashville to confront Bragg, who had struck across Stone's River suddenly on December 31. Fighting had been desperate, with initial success going to the Confederates.

Bragg had decided to attack again on the afternoon of January 2, determined to oust a Federal division lodged on a hill east of Stone's River, near McFadden's Ford. He thought the enemy artillery posted there threatened Polk's corps, the right of the Confederate line. Conversely, once Bragg took this high ground and positioned guns there,

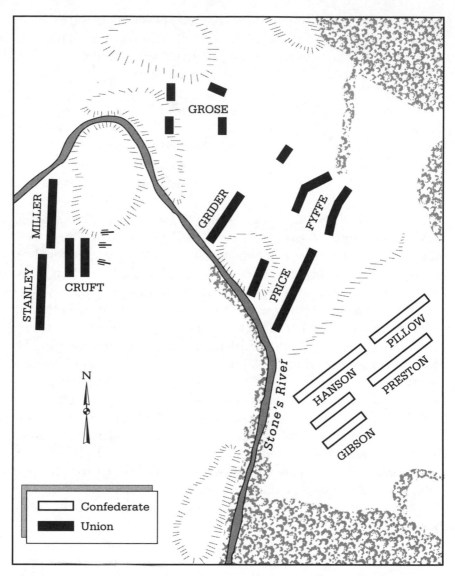

Map 5. Battle of Murfreesboro, January 2, 1863 (adapted from Peter Cozzens, *No Better Place to Die: The Battle of Stones River* [Urbana, Ill., 1990], by permission of the University of Illinois Press)

the Union line west of the river would be enfiladed. Actually, only one Union battery was across the river at that time; the threat was more potential than immediate.[49]

Bragg assigned division commander John C. Breckinridge the job of conducting the assault using four brigades.[50] But Breckinridge wanted none of this attack. He believed the high ground on the west side of Stone's River commanded the objective. Thus, once Confederate troops seized the hill, they would be under fire themselves from the enemy on a higher elevation. Furthermore, the terrain would tend to channel Breckinridge's advancing troops into a great open field within view and easy range of enemy gunners.[51]

When Pillow showed up, Bragg knew very well how badly he wanted a command, a chance to vindicate himself on the battlefield. So Bragg assigned Pillow to Breckinridge and told the latter to give him a command. The only available unit suitable for a general officer was a brigade of Tennesseans, formerly John C. Brown's, now commanded by Col. Joseph B. Palmer. When Pillow reported to Breckinridge, the latter scarcely concealed his displeasure. He ordered Palmer to turn over the brigade to Pillow at once and gave the popular Palmer the option of "honorably retiring from the field." Palmer, however, decided to remain and lead his old regiment, the 18th Tennessee, into the fight.[52]

Pillow rode up to his new command just as they had begun to form in a skirt of woods for the attack; with him was staff officer John E. Saunders, his nephew and ward. A drizzle that had begun about 1:00 P.M. had turned to a cold, driving rain; the troops were shivering. It was almost 4:00 P.M., the time designated for attack. Pillow's skirmishers began to advance almost immediately upon his arrival, breaking down the rail fences to their front.[53]

Breckinridge had given Pillow a good brigade: Palmer's 18th Tennessee, Col. John M. Lillard's 26th, Col. Preston D. Cunningham's 28th, and Col. Anderson Searcy's 45th. The 18th and 26th had been at Donelson, captured, exchanged, and rebuilt. Palmer's 18th would be the right of the brigade and the extreme right of Breckinridge's division. Attached to Pillow's brigade was Moses's Georgia battery, commanded by Lt. R. W. Anderson.[54] The brigade totaled approximately 1,750 men.[55] It had been only lightly engaged in the bloody fight on December 31 and thus was rested and in high spirits.[56]

Breckinridge deployed his division of 4,500 men in two lines. Roger Hanson's Kentucky brigade was on the left up front; Pillow's was to his right. Col. Randall L. Gibson's Louisiana brigade supported Hanson, while Brig. Gen. William Preston's Florida/North Carolina/Tennessee brigade backed Pillow. Gibson's and Preston's second line followed the Pillow-Hanson line by 150–200 yards, an unusually close interval. Four field batteries supported the attack, and Breckinridge told Pillow there was cavalry under John Pegram and John A. Wharton to his right, supporting the flank. Pillow asked Breckinridge if he were in communication with the cavalry leaders. When Breckinridge replied, "No," Pillow asked that it be done. "It was not only proper, but important."[57]

At 4:00 P.M., a cannon shot signaled the Confederate advance. Pillow's and Hanson's troops moved forward with rifles loaded and bayonets fixed. Breckinridge had ordered them to close with the enemy, fire one volley, and then charge and rout the Federals with the bayonet. Emerging from the cover of the timber, Pillow's brigade pushed into an open cornfield, nearly 1,000 yards wide, scattering enemy skirmishers as they advanced. The sky cleared. The scene was truly grand as the Confederates advanced with steady step, in "admirable" order. The Federals could hear them cheering before they came into view. It all seemed like a glorious parade until Breckinridge's first line reached the middle of the field. Ominously, at that point, Federal artillery on both sides of the river began to fire into the advancing lines of gray.[58]

Breckinridge would later claim that, at this crucial moment in the attack, he saw Pillow hiding behind a large tree, screening himself, as the second line of the division went by, and that Pillow hid there until Breckinridge himself ordered him to come out and rejoin his brigade. This terrible accusation by Breckinridge has been repeated through the years and accepted by historians of Murfreesboro. Feelings ran high between the two men, and Breckinridge, openly angry with Bragg, certainly did not welcome Pillow's intrusive appearance on January 2. Breckinridge failed to mention the incident in his report, however, nor is it mentioned elsewhere, officially. A charge of cowardice was prepared against Pillow by Maj. Rice Graves, Breckinridge's chief of artillery and a Donelson captive; Lieutenants Darrah and W. D. Gilman were listed as witnesses. It appears, though, that Breckinridge rethought the incident and decided to drop the matter. Surviving evidence consists of a single sheet of paper with one charge and one specification.[59]

Something about this matter does not ring true. Pillow's reputation for bravery had been well established; he took enormous and careful pride in it. He wanted command on this day desperately, and no man was more aware of the importance of battlefield deportment. Yet where is mention of Pillow personally in any of the official reports of other Confederate officers, except to note he commanded the Tennessee brigade? It is as if Breckinridge seemed determined to ignore his performance. That could be explained, but what about Pillow's regimental commanders or reporting officers in the three other brigades? That they mentioned no instances of leadership, commands issued, or troop movements is most unusual; Pillow always made his presence known. Cowardice at Murfreesboro is understandable, but puzzling. Would it not seem more likely to have occurred at the height of the fighting, at a moment when cannon and rifle fire blew apart Confederate lines and brave men looked to their own safety, rather than at the moment the division stepped into the open field, confident and eager?

As the brigade broke free of the woods and marched forward, Pillow took care to insure Hanson's brigade dressed upon his left and "directed" Hanson to that effect. The front line of Pillow and Hanson advanced some 300 yards, angling steadily toward the hill using a left oblique maneuver. Hanson struck the enemy—troops of Col. Samuel W. Price's brigade. Despite heavy direct fire, the Kentucky brigade charged on, smashing Price's first line, and throwing it back on reserve regiments which quickly collapsed.

From Pillow's left front, the 35th Indiana, part of Price's line facing Hanson, fired a volley into his ranks and caused him to face the brigade even more to the left to confront this troublesome regiment. Hanson's men helped when they flanked the 35th Indiana. The withdrawal of the 35th, badly battered, uncovered the flank of its neighboring Union regiment; they in turn gave way. With Price's brigade routed, Col. James P. Fyffe's brigade on its left crumbled also and fell back in disorder to the area of the Hoover house, where they joined Groses's brigade, which had been held in reserve. Thus the enemy confronting Pillow and Hanson were swept back, with Confederate infantry in hot and uncontrolled pursuit. Pillow collected 200 prisoners and the colors of the Federal 9th Kentucky Infantry.

Not long after they had begun to receive fire from Price's position on the hill, the right of Pillow's brigade under Palmer also was hit. Heavy firing came from a large body of enemy, two infantry regiments and the 3d Wisconsin battery, posted in thick woods and partially concealed. Pillow's line of infantry halted. Neither Pegram nor Wharton were in sight, so Pillow took steps himself to deal with this threat. He ordered up Anderson's guns and directed their fire against the enemy battery in the woods. Anderson's shooting was most effective, and the enemy in the thicket began to waver.[60] Breckinridge, realizing the danger to his right, reinforced Anderson's Georgia battery with three more guns. This artillery fire, when combined with an attack by Palmer's infantry, proved too much for the defenders on the flank, and they fled west to the riverbank. The delay, however, had been costly, giving the enemy time to concentrate more guns and infantry on the opposite bank of Stone's River.[61]

This cannon fire from the west bank helped wreck the alignment of the Confederate attack formation. Preston's men, too closely following Pillow's, became confused. They could not lie down and remain there as ordered because they were helpless, receiving deadly fire from the enemy. So they rose and rushed ahead, many of them firing into Pillow's ranks in front. These men of Preston's soon mingled with Pillow's troops, destroying order. Furthermore, confusion occurred at the crest of the hill as the oblique attack culminated. The right flank of Hanson's brigade and the left of Pillow's overlapped badly, the regiments of Hanson tending to be jammed against Stone's River.[62]

The assault had succeeded, but the Confederate lines had lost all order, and men found themselves crammed into a small space. They also had advanced into point-blank range of one of the largest artillery concentrations of the war. Fifty-eight Yankee guns poured a storm of fire at the rate of 100 shots a minute at the Confederate infantry as they reached the crest of the hill and "swarmed down the slope toward the river."[63] In addition to the artillery, four, and perhaps more, Union infantry brigades joined in with heavy rifle fire.[64] Hanson fell mortally wounded, and the Confederates recoiled from the cannon fire—canister, and shells filled with balls. Almost instantaneously, it seemed, they went from wild assault to wild retreat.

Pillow, facing this destructive artillery fire to his front, also found his brigade under fire from the right flank and rear as the enemy rushed up reinforcements. The Tennesseans, now hopelessly mingled with Preston's brigade, began to retire across the hill, but they were exposed to enemy artillery fire the entire distance back to their original positions. They broke and ran; Federal infantry crossed Stone's River in pursuit, and Pillow directed Anderson's Georgia battery to cover his retreat, to somehow hold off these pursuers. Anderson's quick, decisive work probably saved the brigade from even heavier casualties.[65]

This bloody engagement of January 2 shattered Breckinridge's division: 4,500 had attacked, with 1,300 casualties. Pillow lost 425, one-fourth of his command. Palmer's 18th Tennessee lost nine color-bearers.[66]

To assess Pillow's generalship at Murfreesboro is difficult. Reports are skimpy, and the omissions glaring. To reconstruct his performance one must rely too heavily upon his own report; hardly any of his individual actions can be corroborated. It must be pointed out, however, that details about the Breckinridge assault itself are not plentiful. Confederates tended to hurry over this painful, blurred episode, perhaps the most memorable of the Battle of Murfreesboro.

Pillow had taken over the brigade as it prepared to move into action and did not have time even to familiarize himself with his regimental commanders. He seems, however, to have made the correct decisions at the proper times. With his flank in air and under attack, he took appropriate measures. Later in the action, he again called for artillery support when the advance was held up by the stubborn Indiana regiment, and he overcame its resistance. He shielded his retreat, once more by timely employment of Anderson's battery. His command decisions, particularly his management of artillery, are quite in contrast with the Pillow of Belmont who allowed his Watson Battery to remain immobile.

There is no evidence that Pillow played an inspirational role at Murfreesboro, although this had always been his strength as an infantry commander. He seemed distanced from his troops, which was not his style. But then Palmer, their familiar leader, seems to have been resentful at his assuming command of the brigade, undoubtedly harboring the Donelson grudge, perhaps simply disgruntled at being superseded. Pillow apparently acted in high-handed fashion, giving orders to his old subordinate Hanson and even trying to instruct Breckinridge. Such actions on the part of a commander appointed only hours before would certainly have led to greater hostility. If Pillow stopped briefly at a tree, unfriendly eyes might have been eager to misinterpret such an act by this unwelcome intruder. Nevertheless, Pillow's troops captured their objective and drove the enemy off the high ground in confusion. Normally one should credit the commander when this occurs, and in fairness, Pillow deserves at least some acknowledgment for the Tennessee brigade's good performance at Murfreesboro.

John C. Breckinridge's charge of cowardice, however, blights examination of Pillow's leadership at Murfreesboro. Pillow, in all probability, never knew about Breckinridge's accusation. Certainly he could not have imagined that this battle, in which he thought he had performed well, would destroy, in the eyes of posterity, not only what was left of his military reputation, but his honor as a soldier. It seems a cruel injustice that, a century later, the man cannot be defended.

14 A Place He So Exactly Fits

The Army of Tennessee retreated south from Murfreesboro, leaving behind a bitterly contested field, littered with dead
dreams. Officers of the highest rank pointed fingers. Braxton Bragg,
blamed by nearly everyone himself, criticized John C. Breckinridge
heavily and began to collect evidence. Bragg turned to Pillow, about
the only friend he had now among the general officers, and Pillow,
in a supplementary battle report, willingly supplied evidence against
Breckinridge's conduct of the fight on January 2. Pillow even went
beyond this to earn Bragg's favor. He turned against his old subordinate, Gen. John C. McCown, and provided Bragg's staff and a
court-martial with accounts of private conversations he had had with

McCown in which the latter had denounced Bragg. Thus he played a direct role in the complicity that led to McCown's removal from active Confederate service. It paid to stay on the good side of General Bragg, and Pillow knew the general was not immune to flattery. But then, who else could Pillow have turned to? Surely not Polk; surely not Hardee.[1]

The former commander of Pillow's Tennessee brigade, Gen. John C. Brown, returned to the army from convalescent leave the second week in January and wanted his command back. Pillow knew he must relinquish command and told Bragg on January 12 that he wanted a "respectable division or brigade." He probably realized there was slight chance of that and, as an afterthought, added, "I could do much to bring back those improperly absent." So Bragg gave Brown his Tennessee brigade back and told Pillow to come to headquarters.[2] Pillow had given his chief a good idea for redeeming him.

The Army of Tennessee needed troops desperately. The Conscription Bureau, directed from Richmond, had produced only a trickle of men. So, when Adj. and Insp. Gen. Samuel Cooper issued a circular on January 8 encouraging armies to attempt "field recruitment" of conscripts, Bragg saw an opportunity. He brought Pillow to headquarters; they talked and fed each other's excitement. Pillow assured an attentive Bragg that if given proper backing he could fill up the Army of Tennessee. The result was the creation on January 16, 1863, of the Volunteer and Conscript Bureau of the Army of Tennessee. It would be headed by Pillow.[3]

Bragg generously provided manpower: three field officers and two companies of cavalry from each corps, a captain and six lieutenants from each regiment, and surgeons to examine recruits and conscripts. Officers who had been displaced by the consolidation of regiments (supernumeraries, as they were called) were also assigned.[4] Pillow and his men would be guided in their mission by the conscript laws of April and October 1862 respecting all exemptions from service. Pillow began work immediately. He established headquarters at Fayetteville, Tennessee, on January 17 and published a proclamation to the people of Tennessee the next day, appealing for their cooperation, urging them to volunteer for the army and report to Fayetteville and Shelbyville.[5]

Out went supernumerary officers to the counties where their regiments had been raised. Pillow admonished these hardened veterans, many of them disabled from wounds, to appeal to "the patriotism and sense of duty of citizens to induce them to enter the service of their Country." Pillow also ordered them to arrest and return "all stragglers and absentees without leave from this army who may come within your reach."[6] So much for patriotic appeal. Pillow's real plan was to "rake" each Tennessee county with cavalry for stragglers. He decided to strike Bedford County first and so deployed his command. He believed he would find 1,500 men in Bedford, either deserters or subject to conscription, and he was "anxious to clean out that county by one movement, and doing it at once to avoid giving alarm," thus allowing the "conscripts to scatter and hide out."[7]

The Bedford County strike was successful, so Pillow widened his sweep. Aided by an enthusiastic Bedford Forrest and three veteran cavalry regiments hungry to turn up deserters and skulkers, Pillow charged into Maury and Marshall counties. Meanwhile, he had his principal assistant, Alexander W. Campbell, former political leader and presently the wounded and furloughed colonel of the 33d Tennessee, supervise the work of still another regiment in Lincoln County and along the Tennessee-Alabama line. Pillow shifted his headquarters to Columbia, then to Shelbyville, and, about February 1, to Huntsville, Alabama. "The selection of Huntsville, which was, according to Sen. C. C. Clay, the citadel of Union sentiment, for headquarters illustrates the audacity of the man."[8]

Pillow knew Alabama was swimming with deserters and believed almost a third of those liable for conscription had been granted exemptions. He instructed his officers to examine a man's papers carefully. Some of the "disabled" citizens were as fit as their examiners; some exempted men carried forged papers. Just as Pillow and Bragg had suspected, there had been flagrant abuse of the system. So Pillow had his officers collar hundreds, even thousands, of men, many of whom had been excused formally by local conscript officers and examining boards. In most cases, when doubt existed, individuals were hauled in to army headquarters.[9]

Of course, such heavy-handed tactics brought a chorus of complaint. The War Department in Richmond was flooded with telegrams and letters. The director of the rival Bureau of Conscription, Gen. Gabriel J. Rains, protested vigorously. On February 7 Cooper took action. He issued General Order No. 16, noting that Pillow's officers "have been practically setting aside the authority of the commandants of conscripts." They were ordered by Cooper to "refrain from interference with conscripts already in the custody of the officers regularly on conscription duty." The War Department hoped Pillow's eager subordinates would concentrate on recruiting volunteers and searching out absentees and not meddle with conscription. They were to supplement, not replace, the Bureau of Conscription.[10]

Pillow probably would have ignored Cooper, but Bragg insisted that he operate within the limits of Cooper's directive. Pillow wished very much to please his exacting superior, so on February 16 he clarified instructions to his officers, explaining that the Confederate Congress had deliberately established many exemptions, and they were to be honored. He further directed his officers not to interfere with the camps of instruction operated by the Conscription Bureau. Characteristically, however, he included a clause encouraging and empowering his officers to continue their hunt: "Exemptions which have been allowed by enrolling officers and others are liable to re-examination, and if found to have been granted in violation of the law will be set aside and the parties placed in the Army."[11]

Annoyed by Cooper's criticism, and setting the stage for what was to come, Pillow on February 17 petulantly explained to Bragg his reluctance in taking the responsibility of heading the bureau, an assignment "most distasteful and repugnant to my feelings." He reminded his superior that this new job had been "pressed" upon him—with an urgent appeal by Bragg to find more troops or "he could not hold Tennessee." "I will in the future," Pillow promised, "carefully avoid doing anything that can give you cause of reprimand."[12]

It appears Pillow had no such intention. General orders he issued on January 27 mentioned the "rigid enforcement of the Conscript Law" and slapped at the Richmond bureau. "This Bureau [Pillow's own] grows out of the failure to properly execute the law, by the agencies heretofore employed for this purpose."[13] His recruiting organization continued to ride over the established conscription network. Col. J. W. Echols, for instance, formerly of the 34th Alabama, now a Pillow subordinate, set up his headquarters in Montgomery, representing himself as chief of the Volunteer and Conscript Bureau. A local official complained that "his constant disregard of all details, exemptions, and discharges" has produced "much confusion and dissatisfaction."[14] Pillow himself "made bold to give orders" to Rains's officers, including the commandant of conscripts for the state of Tennessee. He detailed some of his officers to return to South and North Carolina to recruit and enroll conscripts.[15] Even hospitals harbored malingerers. "There is around every hospital I have seen," said Pillow, "a large number of men, capable of nursing and cooking, whose time is occupied around drinking shops."[16] Public officials were not exempt from Pillow's rake; he instructed his officers to enroll all justices of the peace, constables, and deputy sheriffs of the proper ages. They were permitted to remain at their residences if there was no "emergency of the service," providing they would search out and bring in conscripts and deserters in their respective districts.[17]

Pillow felt perfectly justified. The number of absentees from the armies of Bragg, Lee, and Pemberton approached 100,000 and was growing. The hemorrhage must be stopped. In this, military men throughout the Confederacy were in perfect accord. The Conscript Act, a reaction to the despair of Fort Donelson, even though amended, strengthened, and expanded, was ineffective and, in the minds of many, unjust. In the West, in the territory that supplied men for the Army of Tennessee, it was largely ignored or, at best, enforced laxly.[18]

Troops began to pour into Tullahoma, headquarters of the Army of Tennessee: volunteers, arrested deserters, conscripts, absentees. The army received them with open arms, and Bragg wired Davis joyfully that he could now put an army of 40,000 in the field. "Stragglers and conscripts come in so rapidly under General Pillow's active measures that we are at a loss for arms. You must give me credit for being the first to find a place fit for him, and a place that he so exactly fits." [19]

Pillow popped up everywhere. His staff officers, particularly John C. Burch, wrote hundreds of letters creating and coordinating a network of officials throughout occupied and unoccupied Tennessee and most of Alabama. He established two dozen rendezvous in Alabama alone, ten in Mississippi, and others, all commanded by field officers, from Asheville, North Carolina, to Marianna, Florida, Natchitoches, Louisiana, central Arkansas, and east Texas.[20] The Knoxville *Register* reported the chief of the conscripts as "no respecter of persons," "tireless, sleepless," with "energy beyond all precedent." He gladly attacked loungers on the streets and yanked them into service. "Would to God he had charge of the Conscript Bureau of the Confederate States." A single rendezvous, Selma, Alabama, reported 344 men secured in August, with 1,344 added by late fall.[21]

Pillow gathered and forwarded intelligence to Bragg. He also gathered and forwarded bacon, flour, and wheat and dozens of wagon loads of commissary stores; he located hundreds of army weapons taken off by stragglers, confiscated them, and sent them back; he rounded up laborers for Sam Tate to use in repairing the Memphis and Charleston Railroad; and he twisted the arms of fellow planters, securing slaves to use as teamsters. Substituting black slaves for white teamsters would immediately release 2,000 soldiers for frontline duty. Pillow set the example himself; two of his slaves were used as teamsters for the army, while another drove the general's baggage wagon. One critic, who protested conscription and impressment of blacks "without authority," admitted privately that "surely the Gen. has very enticing ways."[22]

Even at the height of his search for manpower, Pillow never gave up the fight to clear his name. He and his friend Governor Harris continued to write Secretary of War Seddon and Davis about Donelson. Pillow submitted sworn testimony of officers who had been present at the disaster, officers who backed his argument that his action at Donelson on February 15 was anything but "a grave error of judgment." All Pillow received from Richmond was silence.[23]

Though deeply resentful, Pillow restrained himself admirably in public. The Chattanooga *Rebel* recorded a speech he made late in February to his fellow slaveholders. After urging them to allow their slaves to be used as teamsters, he encouraged them about the war effort. Jefferson Davis, he told them, was the "very man for the position." "If he could not conduct us safely through this revolution, no man could." Davis, said Pillow, "was a man of delicate form, but of large brain and patriotic heart." Although, he admitted, the president had not done him justice insofar as removing the unfair and erroneous charges arising from Donelson, he preferred Davis "for President to any other man."[24]

As for the enemy, their war aims were now clear. They intended to destroy the South, Pillow said, and "make slaves of white men." He urged that every man "use his property to strengthen our army." "The slave power of the South was an element of strength if we would use it properly, but an element of weakness if we did not." He told his Huntsville audience of his correspondence with Sherman in the summer of 1862, bending the truth badly. Sherman, Pillow reported, had offered to indemnify him for his property losses in Arkansas if he would abandon the Confederacy. Pillow told his loudly cheering audience that he had replied, "General, while I thank you for your courteous letter, let me say to you the property your Government has taken from me was my own. Your Government has the power to rob me of it, but it is too poor to buy me."[25]

The obvious increase in strength of the Army of Tennessee brought many compliments to Pillow, and the news traveled. Gen. Richard Ewell wrote Gen. Jubal Early of Pillow's effective work, which was "sending in crowds every day. It is well they can find something for him to do besides mischief."[26] Generals Joseph Johnston and Bragg were lavish in their praise, the latter estimating that Pillow had sent in 10,000 men since mid-January, while the enrolling officers of the Conscription Bureau had managed to obtain only nineteen.[27]

Pillow's very effectiveness, however, was his undoing. The Bureau of Conscription in Richmond became defensive. Gabriel Rains had the ear of Seddon, and he pointed to Pillow's disregard of repeated warnings by the secretary of war to stop interfering with the work of the bureau. He reminded the secretary of the incessant complaints: Pillow's force "not infrequently is compared to the press gang, sweeping through the country with little deference either to law or the regulations designed to temper its unavoidable rigor." "Its personnel was self-sure, energetic, impatient, and arrogant. It seemed utterly unable to accommodate itself to the fact that the Richmond Bureau had 'exclusive control of the whole subject of conscription,' and that it was to act in a supplementary way only."[28]

By March 2 Seddon had had enough. He ordered Pillow to stop all conscripting work. He could keep chasing deserters, but "no interference in the conscription service can be permitted."[29] Pillow was hurt and angered. He accepted the War Department's directive but wrote Bragg a long letter justifying the actions of his subordinates as they went about the country reexamining certificates of exemption. He ended the letter requesting to be relieved. The War Department had "cut up by the root" his power to enforce the conscript law. Bragg forwarded his letter to the War Department with biting sarcasm: "General Pillow has acted most zealously and efficiently in strict conformity with the orders of the Department and his instructions from these headquarters. In six weeks he has done ten times as much to strengthen this army as all the conscript officers. . . . He but feebly portrays the abuses known to exist in our conscript camps. As requested, he will be relieved and this army will again decrease."[30]

The wooden-headedness of the War Department, the touchiness of Bragg, and the cavalier attitude of Pillow all obscured an elemental debate over philosophy. Pillow represented, ironically, the point of view of the military, and Seddon and Rains the civilian. While Pillow's methods of rounding up men may have received "a sort of justification from their apparent immediate good effects," Rains argued, they upset the public, "engendering a spirit of hatred and resistance to the very name of conscription." "After all conscription has nothing in it dishonoring, but is the most equal and justly discriminating mode in which a country can summon to the field its proper defenders." Conscripts could become the "best soldiers in the world" if treated as equals to the volunteers.[31]

To this Pillow responded with icy realism. Conscripts could never be equals of volunteers; Mexico had proved that. In any case, the volunteer system had exhausted itself early in the war. The compulsory system, which by necessity succeeded it, had been "based upon the supposition that the moral obligation created by the law will be sufficient to bring into the Army the great mass of men liable to duty under the law." That assumption was wrong, Pillow emphasized, fallacious, disproven conclusively by experience. In dealing with a reluctant population, "no organization will be successful which does not rest on the exercise of force."[32]

Pillow appealed to the government to give him backing, to let him combine the two rival recruiting organizations, and he would "throw into the Army 100,000 men in a short time." The War Department disagreed. Officers fresh from the firing line should not be allowed to serve as interpreters of the law. Richmond refused to allow conscription to be broken down by Pillow's aggressive, extralegal activities.[33] Davis, however, did ask Col. William P. Johnston to make inquiries when he went west to inspect the Army of Tennessee. Colonel Johnston reported back to Davis that not only Bragg and Joseph Johnston, but the army generally gave Pillow full credit for the "great increase in strength." The army felt that Pillow's bureau, instead of being abolished, "should have been given absolute jurisdiction over conscription throughout the Confederacy."[34]

The months of April, May, and June 1863 passed with Pillow supervising his network of officers recruiting volunteers. Resentfully, he wrote Bragg, "I have been so crippled by orders of the Secretary of War suspending enforcement of the Conscript Act that I am at a loss what to do with the great number of officers ordered to report to me. I cannot keep them properly engaged." He found a way though, keeping them busy chasing deserters. He asked Polk and Hardee for lists of absentees in their corps and made efforts to run them down. He continued to send intelligence to Bragg and Johnston, advised them on strategy, and kept appealing for a field command.[35]

He accompanied Joe Wheeler on a raid close to Murfreesboro in April, taking along some of his cavalry. It was a demanding effort physically, serving to remind Pillow that he was rapidly approaching sixty. He and Forrest had a talk soon after, about the time Maj. Gen. Earl Van Dorn was murdered (May 7, 1863). Pillow reported to Harris that Forrest and "Red" Jackson had asked him "to get command of the cavalry." They wanted to serve under him. To Pillow's disappointment, however, Bragg saw fit to promote Forrest to Van Dorn's cavalry command. Forrest took the assignment and promotion to major general, although he told Bragg "he preferred promotion of another officer, whom he suggested, as having more capacity for the functions which properly belonged to the rank of major-general." Pillow probably was the officer to whom Forrest alluded. Pillow greeted the news of the latter's appointment lamely: "Forrest is assigned to the command, I am gratified at the result. He deserves the position, though I had not thought he would be assigned to it." Despite Pillow's gnawing jealousy, the two always got along well, and on at least one occasion, in June 1863, Pillow appears to have gone to West Tennessee with Forrest to help recruit cavalry.[36]

Everything turned topsy-turvy in mid-July 1863. Vicksburg fell, and with it Pemberton's army; Rosecrans skillfully and with slight loss maneuvered Bragg's Army of Tennessee out of Middle Tennessee; desertions kept rising startlingly; and tories now openly defied the government in Alabama. Rains had managed to have Pillow's wings clipped, but the timid and ineffective ways of his bureau led to his own demise. General Johnston, exasperated by the failure of the Richmond bureau and faced with a critical shortage of manpower, applied to Seddon: "The Conscript law is not enforced in Tennessee, Alabama, and Mississippi. I ask authority to enforce it."[37]

The War Department, desperate for success, reacted swiftly, granting Johnston complete control over conscription in Alabama, Mississippi, Tennessee, and Florida. He could delegate that authority if he wished. Johnston immediately put Pillow in charge of the conscript organization within Department No. 2 and gave him three regiments of cavalry as muscle. Pillow also inherited what remained of his old Volunteer and Conscript Bureau of the Army of Tennessee. He rushed to set up his headquarters, first in Chattanooga and then, when that city fell, in Marietta, Georgia.[38] Knowing the source of his trouble in the spring, Pillow took great care to have Johnston place officers of the Richmond Conscription Bureau operating in Department No. 2 under his command. "If they are not . . . conflicts are again likely to arise . . . and misrepresentations made to the War Department."[39]

Pillow wrote Bragg that he had resumed his work. "I performed great labor and added vastly to the strength of the Army of Tennessee, and instead of receiving commendation I was visited by the censures of the Government. Under circumstances so discouraging I could hardly be expected again to go willingly into the work, but as my sole object has been to be useful to the country in this great struggle, I will again resume that work if allowed the supporting force so essential to success." Bragg responded by assigning Pillow the 4th Alabama Cavalry.[40]

Pillow cracked down hard in August 1863. Some men fled his enrolling officers to the mountains of north Alabama, where they joined thousands of dissidents—exchanged prisoners who did not wish to return to the army, deserters, Unionists, and those who simply wished to sit out the war. Southern mountain people, "miserable, ignorant, poor, ragged devils," became their unwitting allies. They resisted by tradition any form of government, distrusted outsiders, and despised rich slave owners. Many of these disaffected were dangerous, armed, and operating in quasi-military bands. They drove off the small conscription detachments and then, becoming bolder with greater numbers, began to raid into the valleys, making off with food and valuables. They pillaged and murdered, spreading a reign of terror as far south as Talladega and as far west as north Mississippi. Loyal folk, their soldiers paid in depreciated currency, their taxes having to be paid in kind, their farms devastated by neglect and inflation and raids, cried out to the Confederate government for help.

The Peace Society made the situation even more serious. This organization, centered in Alabama, wanted peace; it also wanted the Confederate army defeated. Feeding on discontent, it changed philosophies to suit any locale in which it operated. Using secret signs, passwords, and all the devices of a fifth column, members set up an underground railroad for deserters. They spread dissension and encouraged resistance to authority; they intimidated; they infiltrated military organizations and even the Conscription Bureau itself. They were blamed for provoking mutiny in the brigade of Gen. James Clanton at Pollard, Alabama. The commandant in Blount County was a Peace Society member, as was the enrolling officer in Winston County. When a group of the Peace Society felt strong enough, it would attack a Confederate unit.[41]

The situation called for force. Pillow estimated there were 8,000–10,000 deserters and tory conscripts in north Alabama, "as vicious as copperheads. . . . They hide and dodge in the thickets and swamps and mountains, and when hard pressed they run into the enemy's lines to elude capture by my officers."[42] When he did manage to round them up and ship them to the Army of Tennessee, they would desert and return to the mountains. Pillow recommended they be shipped to the Army of Northern Virginia.

As the summer progressed Pillow organized some twenty companies of cavalry and posted local defense forces in each county, in response to citizens "constantly" appealing to him for protection against bodies of armed deserters. His officers worked very well with the local authorities and invoked the aid of every citizen. He directed his men to report and take evidence against any who harbored deserters or aided them in any way. "The evil of desertion must cease." By late October he had succeeded in restoring order and confidence, meeting force with force, using conscripts themselves, at least those with horses, as patrols to keep the peace.[43] The Talladega *Democratic Watchtower* acknowledged in December 1863 the effectiveness of the military arm of the Conscription Bureau. "Outrages have ceased and quiet prevails." For this Pillow won the full support and admiration of Alabama's governor, John G. Shorter, and the state legislature.[44]

All went well for a while, so well, in fact, that Leonidas Polk in Mississippi pushed for Pillow to be placed in charge of conscription for the Confederacy. He deserves to be promoted to major general, Polk suggested. "No officer could have proved himself more capable, faithful and efficient." This is an urgent and powerful statement when one remembers the difficulties Polk had experienced with Pillow in the summer and fall of 1861.[45]

In late summer Pillow concentrated his attention on Mississippi. Vicksburg parolees, the wreckage of Pemberton's army, wandered the state, hundreds resisting reorganization. Governor Pettus, however, did not like the idea of Pillow's bureau sweeping through the state. He much preferred the concept of organizing men into state units under his control, and in this he found sympathy from Jefferson Davis. Pillow disagreed. Mississippi is "full of floating companies," Pillow declared, "without having been mustered or received by the state authorities, all claiming to be part of the State force." The program Pettus had set up, according to Pillow, was "deliberately designed for the purpose of taking shelter from conscription."[46]

Pillow's objective was strictly, aggressively, to enforce the Conscript Law, arresting evaders and those illegally exempted. Precious few were exempted—269 under his bureau, compared to 7,993 under the old system.[47] Much like the comprehensive political organization Pillow had foreseen at Newburyport, Massachusetts, in 1852, his Conscription Bureau "spread like a map all over those portions of the States in our possession, and with an active corps of officers with supporting forces of cavalry."[48] For dispatch he returned deserters directly to their regiments and shipped off conscripts directly to the army without passing through camps of instruction; volunteers could choose their regiment. Within weeks Pillow built up and armed almost thirty companies of cavalry, containing mostly conscripts. These were the troops he used to suppress tories.[49]

He pushed his men hard, exhorting them to extend themselves. "The hopes of the country depend upon the labors of this bureau in strengthening the armies of Tennessee and Mississippi. No higher motive to exertion could be presented to the patriot soldier. We have the population required for this purpose, and it is our duty to put it in these armies."[50] Officers by the dozens showed up to help, many from consolidated regiments, others from units decimated at Chickamauga. Many regimental commanders gladly released wounded officers to help chase down conscripts. Pillow tried to funnel manpower into the infantry, but this was resisted; every man seemed to want a horse, a chance to ride with Forrest or Morgan or Wheeler. Seddon and Cooper wanted troops for the Army of Northern Virginia; the Tennessee and Alabama regiments there had been reduced to "skeletons." Pillow and Johnston were more than willing to send them arrested deserters, but Seddon resisted making "a Botany Bay of General Lee's Army," so they squabbled over volunteers and conscripts.[51]

Pillow sent many recruiters into West Tennessee, a popular hiding place for Confederates. Isham G. Harris knew the area well and provided Pillow invaluable assistance and encouragement, as did Bedford Forrest. Pillow particularly liked the device (which Forrest employed) of sending in entire units, regiments if possible, and having them return to Mississippi fattened with volunteers and conscripts. They would be armed and equipped and then sent back to West Tennessee to bring out even more men. In 1863 this seemed to work with ridiculous ease.[52]

Throughout the late summer and fall of 1863, Pillow moved about —Columbus, Meridian, Montgomery—although he located his headquarters generally at Marietta, a curious site considering that the focus of his operations was in Johnston's department. Marietta provided at least one benefit, however: Pillow made a strong ally of Gov. Joseph Brown of Georgia. The two were strange bedfellows, but Brown, sympathetic with one who had received injustice at the hands of Davis and the Richmond government, liked Pillow and his ideas. Georgia, especially north Georgia, was full of refugees, deserters, and men fleeing the conscript laws, not to speak of driftwood from Pemberton's army. Pillow's methods for enforcing conscription would reach and affect elements of Georgia's population secure in occupations providing exemption, doing work "well attended to by persons not subject to conscript." Uncharacteristically, Brown was drawn to Pillow's more objective military enforcement, which would substitute agents from outside, men "not subject to local influences that often control local enrolling officers." Brown urged Richmond to place Georgia under Pillow's jurisdiction. This was not what Richmond wanted to hear.[53]

Seddon and the new chief of the Conscription Bureau, Col. John S. Preston, knew Pillow was marshaling support: "Gen. Pillow has applied to have Georgia in the jurisdiction of his Bureau of Conscription, and the Governors of Georgia, Alabama, and Tennessee unite in the request; also Generals Johnston and Bragg. Gen. Pillow already has Mississippi, Tennessee, Alabama, etc.—a much larger jurisdiction than the bureau here. Col. Preston, of course, protests against all this, and I believe the Secretary sympathises [sic] with him."[54] In a letter to Johnston, Seddon acknowledged the strong support for extending Pillow's command but reminded Johnston that the establishment of his bureau had been only a temporary measure, indicating that he was being cautious in placing power directly in the hands of Pillow, and that Georgia was out of the question, for "political reasons."[55]

Pillow became more ambitious by the month. He set about incorporating the standing Bureau of Conscription into his command; he abolished a line drawn by Pemberton and Pettus in north Mississippi and began enlisting conscripts above it; he sent Col. E. D. Blake to Richmond to explain why West Virginia and North Carolina, west of the Blue Ridge, ought to be added to his territory; and he suggested, not very discreetly, that since his system had pleased the generals and governors concerned, it should be extended to embrace the entire Confederacy.[56]

Results were impressive. In the first month, with partial reporting, Pillow returned 7,336 men to the armies. In early October, an average of 500 men came in per day, with a hard figure of 8,811 for the month. It is reasonable to credit Pillow with having placed about 25,000 men in the Confederate army in the late summer and fall of 1863. Some believed he had worked a miracle. A Nashville visionary recommended to Seddon that inland fisheries throughout the South could feed the armies, thus alleviating that dreadful problem. Put Pillow in charge of the fisheries, he advocated. "He will put the whole plan into operation sooner than any man in the Confederate States. He is practical and of untiring energy and industry. . . . He can direct matters in the Conscript Bureau and attend to this meat supply also."[57]

Seddon was sick of Pillow. In the very beginning, he had cautioned him to "execute the law in the fullness of its spirit and intent." "You have been substituted almost entirely for the authority exercised heretofore by the Bureau."[58] Johnston himself had reminded Pillow to go through proper channels in the War Department.[59] But Pillow had blasted ahead. Ignoring advice of Conscription Bureau veterans, Pillow used the term "to arrest" when he meant "to enroll" conscripts. A matter of semantics, perhaps, but it reflected Pillow's attitude—hard-nosed, haughty, heedless. As though possessed, driven by the need to put men in the Army of Tennessee, he stripped the bureau's camps of any instruction of conscripts and sent them straight to the army or enrolled them in cavalry units to fight bands of deserters. This made perfect sense, of course, but in the process he earned the wrath of the commandants, who had employed conscripts on their own special projects like building blockhouses and defenses. He crashed into Governor Pettus's state units, regarding them as "asylums for deserters" and conscript dodgers.[60]

The South rejected conscription. In the minds of many, if not most, southerners, it violated the principles for which the war was being waged. Citizens were being coerced, their liberties set aside by some pompous martinet who used press gang methods. It turned citizens against the cause, against the government. This inevitable discontent, abetted by undermining efforts of the Richmond bureau and the quiet opposition of Samuel Cooper, dogged Pillow's steps. "Only his superior energy and determination allowed Pillow to accomplish as much as he did in the face of these overwhelming obstacles."[61]

Pillow's letterbook reveals that he tried hard initially to get along with Richmond and avoid conflicts in authority. It was only a matter of time, however. A crisis came on September 23, 1863, when Seddon wired Pillow that all doubtful exemption cases should be referred to Richmond, not handled by him in the field. Peeved and hurt, Pillow wrote back, "My authority is cut down." He agreed reluctantly that henceforward all applications for exemptions would go to Richmond. "The immediate effect of this will be to throw all the work of this bureau into your office," said Pillow, "and to suspend the operations of my functions as superintending officer of this bureau."[62]

The whole system unraveled on October 7 when Cooper wired Pillow: "In assigning you to conscription duties in Alabama and Mississippi it was not designed you should control or in any way interfere with the officers who are on that duty under the Bureau of Conscription in this city. The Secretary of War desires to see you here, and you will consider this an order to come."[63] Pillow saw all this as destructive, small-minded, and contradictory to the orders that established his bureau. So he threw the business into Johnston's lap: "Under the instructions, as I understand them, I can decide nothing finally, not even such questions as the enrolling lieutenants were empowered. . . . If the general should concur with me the construction of these letters, I respectfully ask if it is not my duty to myself to ask to be retired from all further connection with the bureau."[64]

This embroiled Johnston with the War Department, and Seddon backed off, insisting only that the right of hearing appeals must rest in Richmond. "Authority to enforce the conscript law, heretofore reposed in General J. E. Johnston, within the limits of Mississippi, Alabama, and Tennessee is continued." Victory, however, was momentary, and Pillow knew it. Seddon, assistant secretary of war Judge John A. Campbell, Preston, and Cooper remained unimpressed, convinced that Pillow was taking the cheap route, "press gangs sweeping through the country with little deference to law or the regulations designed to temper it unavoidable rigor." They only waited for the right opportunity to unhorse him.[65]

Pillow wanted out, but on his terms, while he still had the flush of success and bargaining power. He wrote Cooper on October 23, requesting to organize a division of cavalry composed of troops he had raised in West Tennessee. "I am not content with my present position. I have applied to Generals Johnston and Bragg to relieve me. This they declined upon the ground that my services in my present position are so important that I cannot be spared. . . . I make this appeal to your sense of justice."[66]

Pillow tried again on November 27. He had exhausted the conscript population in the area, he wrote Cooper. Quiet prevailed, and the companies of cavalry backing up the enrolling officers were no longer required. Could he organize them as a cavalry command and operate on the enemy flank? Samuel Cooper, with fine cynicism, endorsed Pillow's request: "I think this letter affords a convenient opportunity" to relieve Pillow and close his bureau. Rather than giving Pillow an independent cavalry command, however, Cooper suggested he be sent to Hardee, who was commanding the Army of Tennessee.[67] So, on December 16, 1863, Pillow was relieved of command and ordered to Hardee at Dalton, Georgia. General Preston would assume Pillow's command and reincorporate his command into the Richmond bureau.[68]

Pillow was stung:

I decidedly prefer going to the front if I am placed in command of a respectable force. If I am not to have such command, I would prefer my present service, and that was what I meant to say. . . . If I am to be forever overlooked (notwithstanding my sacrifices, sufferings, and labors for the cause I have so much at heart) I cannot but feel myself deeply aggrieved. As a soldier I know it is my duty to submit to the judgment of the President without murmuring, and I do not wish to be considered now as doing so; but I should be less than a mortal or more than a mortal if I could be always indifferent to the treatment I receive from my own Government.[69]

Leonidas Polk, who assumed command of Johnston's department in late December, protested to Davis. He wanted the conscript function and its units reporting directly to him; thus he sided with Johnston, Bragg, and Pillow. But it was in vain.[70] Preston would write Robert E. Lee a year later, scoffing at the idea of using a single national military organization or bureau to enforce conscription. "The one proposed by General Pillow was full tried under auspices of the highest authority and failed almost ridiculously."[71]

Had Pillow failed? Not according to Governors Brown and Harris. Not according to Gov. John G. Shorter. The Alabama legislature presented a joint resolution to the Confederate Congress, complimenting Pillow and endorsing his methods. They recommended his bureau be enlarged. Representing the Military Committee, powerful Edward Sparrow reported that the committee was "deeply impressed with the vigor and usefulness of General Pillow as conscript officer," but that before the receipt of the Alabama resolution, he had been ordered to a field command.[72]

The army also praised Pillow. Johnston and Bragg, even Polk, strongly recommended Pillow's promotion to major general. Frank Cheatham, as representative of the army as any general officer could be, wrote: "Having served under Gen. Pillow in the Mexican War as well as in the present Revolution, I may crave your pardon when I say that I know of no officer more deserving promotion than General Pillow, although he has not been on duty in the field for the past twelve months, I consider that he has done more for the Army of Tennessee during that time than any one officer."[73]

Seddon, speaking for Davis and the Confederate government, disagreed. Pillow had failed.

That officer, with characteristic energy and zeal, but with numbers of supernumerary officers and in an irregular manner, proceeded to change the old system of administration previously adopted by the Conscript Bureau, and to enforce a sort of general impressment of all the conscript classes. . . . Numberless complaints of irregularities, or disregard of the exemptions and restrictions of law, and of the employment of military coercion besieged the Department. . . .

The substitution . . . of mere military authority and employment of coercion when there was really no resistance was believed and has proved mischievous and productive of great discontent.[74]

One might suggest, with all the advantages of over a century of hindsight and with the subsequent examples of mobilized nations, that Pillow had faced the issue squarely, as had Cleburne when he advocated placing slaves in the Confederate army. Lack of manpower would destroy the ability of the Confederacy to defend itself. Pillow rejuvenated Bragg's army in the spring of 1863 with the great net he cast over the men of the mid-South who had other things to do than serve in the army. Using battle-tried veterans, he combed the area for soldiers again in the late summer and fall. Without this effort, Johnston's strong 1864 Army of Tennessee, which rose from the ashes of Missionary Ridge, would have remained but a dream.[75] Pillow pointed the way, but the Confederacy insisted on confronting the twentieth-century issue of conscription with nineteenth-century niceties.

15 **I Only Want a Respectable Command**

Grant smashed the Army of Tennessee at Missionary Ridge on November 25, 1863, and drove it into north Georgia. Bragg left the army, discredited as a field commander. Hardee wanted no part of the command of the army, so Davis most reluctantly turned to Joseph E. Johnston. When Johnston came to Dalton in December 1863 to take charge of the army, Leonidas Polk succeeded him as departmental commander in Mississippi and Alabama.

Pillow wrote a kind, complimentary letter to his banished friend Bragg, and a grateful Bragg responded on January 10: "No influence, no power, and no clamor can ever the suppress the admiration with which I have witnessed the intense labor and patriotic zeal with which you have served, and successfully served, our cause since you joined me more than a year ago." Bragg continued, "I have learned, too, to admire and view in their true light your unrequited sacrifices."[1]

With this flip-flop of commanding officers, Pillow saw opportunity. First he appealed to Johnston for a place in the Army of Tennessee, but Johnston replied on January 4, 1864, that he had "no command suitable to your rank vacant." He offered instead command of the city of Atlanta, an assignment Pillow evidently rejected out of hand.[2] Pillow had a better idea. He wrote Polk suggesting that he become the link between two departments. Stationing himself at Tuscumbia, Alabama, Pillow would protect Polk's right flank and Johnston's left, all the while throwing a shield before the vulnerable Alabama iron and coal complex and the government facilities at Talladega, Tuscaloosa, and Selma. All he would require would be two brigades of cavalry. The boundaries of the departments might have to be changed, but that was incidental.

Polk liked the idea and "believed he [Pillow] could give good service there," so he wired Pillow to come to his headquarters, where they could have a frank, face to face discussion. When they had met and talked, Polk agreed to support Pillow's concept. Polk's wife, Frances, recorded the meeting in a letter to her daughter. It had been described to her by Polk's staff officer and kinsman, Henry C. Yeatman, who was present:

Your father met him as if they had parted as ordinary acquaintances a few hours before. "Good morning, Gen.—take a seat. I received your dispatches," etc. When they had gotten through the business, Gen. Pillow laid his hand on your father's arm & said "Now Gen.—you must permit me to explain the past, & tell you that I regret having acted from misconception," etc. etc. That Pope Walker had told him he was entirely mistaken, & that he found so— far from having stood in his way, your father had recommended him for promotion & finished by saying that his mind was sore & "*I think Gen. in my place you would have acted as I did.*"

"There we differ," was your father's reply—but said he was willing to let bygones be bygones. They were both working for their country & he would do all he could to further his views. He, your father, came out & told us we must be very civil.[3]

Polk was as good as his word. He wrote to Johnston and to Forrest, enthusiastically endorsing Pillow's proposal. Simultaneously, a group of Alabama citizens picked up the idea and appealed to Johnston. It all seemed sound enough to Johnston, so he recommended the plan in a letter to General Cooper on January 22. Pillow was fully qualified for the task, Johnston maintained, because of his "knowledge of the country, activity, courage and capacity." He did hedge a bit, however. "I had rather see him in command of a division of infantry, a position for which he was recommended by General Bragg and myself." Furthermore, Johnston thought Polk should provide the two cavalry brigades; he wished to have Phil Roddey's brigade, which operated in the area, thrown forward into East Tennessee against the enemy's communications.

Pillow capped the arguments of the two senior officers with his own appeal to the War Department: "If placed in this position, I would be content to work on, giving to the country what ever of talent and energy I possess. Occupying the line that connects the two armies and departments and protecting a flank of each, I would yield an implicit obedience to the commands of both."[4]

Jefferson Davis knew about Pillow and "implicit obedience." So, at the end of January 1864, Pillow was summoned to Richmond. Armed with a first-rate concept, strongly backed by Johnston, Polk, and Gov. Thomas H. Watts of Alabama, Pillow conferred, first with Cooper, then with Seddon, then with Davis. Gen. Josiah Gorgas watched Pillow operate and perceptively entered in his diary: "He is a man of energy and ability, and, were he content to serve, would, I think, be very useful; but his great ambition leads him to seek commands to which his military status is hardly equal. To a General by whom he would be controlled he would be very useful."[5]

The president gave Pillow half a loaf. He would not be independent but would report to Polk. Within that department he would take command of Robert V. Richardson's brigade, four loosely organized, understrength, partially armed regiments in West Tennessee. For the second brigade, in what Pillow intended to be a division, he could have such companies as he had raised for conscript service "so far as they may not be needed by Colonel Preston, Head of the Conscription Bureau."[6] Pillow was not at all happy. He notified both Polk and Johnston that "I am not allowed to take the command you proposed." Yet he accepted Davis's offer and set off to Alabama to round up troops.[7]

While Pillow was in Richmond, 1,000 miles away in Phillips County,

Arkansas, the United States Treasury Department sponsored a meeting in Helena of loyal citizens, "gentlemen from various northern states," to deal with leasing abandoned plantations. These citizens would relieve the Freedmen's Bureau, which had been operating a very large camp or "home" at Mound Plantation for some 2,000 former slaves. They would stake out and lease land in sections, privately employing the freedmen as hands to "learn them to subsist upon their own skill and Labor." Pillow's Swan Lake Plantation (650 acres), five miles south of Helena, was leased to George W. Perry of Wisconsin and Washington Warwick of Iowa. Perry and Warwick would pay the United States government one cent per pound for cotton they produced, and they agreed to employ one freedman for each twelve acres, setting aside one acre for the employee's benefit.[8]

Pillow had dismissed thoughts of recovering his Arkansas lands. The only remedy, the only hope, was victory by the Confederate forces, so, with the aid of the faithful John C. Burch, he focused his attention and efforts on gathering troops. His command of the Northern District of Alabama existed only on paper. Armed with orders from the secretary of war, he summoned all the conscript companies he could locate, informing them and the citizens of Alabama that he was forming a cavalry division. He placed advertisements in newspapers urging men to recruit companies and join him. He sent for conscription support units he had organized in 1863 in Florida and Mississippi. He also sent for the cadets at the University of Alabama. This group, all being under eighteen, would be formed into a regiment, and just for them Pillow resurrected the term "Voltiguers." One company of these boys would be set aside as Pillow's "body guard." Pillow also sought a battery for his semi-independent cavalry division.[9]

He met resistance at every turn. Beauregard would not part with his Florida cavalry. Pillow's former subordinate in the conscripting effort, the effective Lt. Col. Harrison C. Lockhart, protested that Pillow intended to strip to the bone his conscript and defense force in Talladega and, further, that "the chaotic state in which the conscription service was left by Brigadier General Pillow has seriously embarrassed the action of the Bureau of Conscription in Alabama since it has attempted to restore order and system." When Lockhart failed to cooperate fully with Pillow, turning over only thirteen of twenty-five companies under his command, Pillow became upset. Lockhart reported to Polk that Pillow "seems to think that I am not disposed to assist him in obtaining a command in the field."[10]

Polk sided with Lockhart and refused to allow Pillow to take a squadron of cavalry he coveted. He must look elsewhere. Governor Watts reported rising resistance to using the cadets at the university, and one father wrote Pillow to excuse his son. How could the fifteen-year-old be an effective soldier? He "hasn't worked a day in his life." [11] Exasperated, Pillow complained to Johnston, "I have as yet no command, General Polk having failed to give me any command as yet, except a small force, less than two regiments." Four regiments that he had counted on (Richardson's brigade) had been incorporated into Forrest's command by Polk. He substituted James H. Clanton's ragged brigade of sixteen companies which had mutinied six months earlier and an "unarmed" regiment. [12]

Pillow wrote to Bragg on April 5 that he had only been able to collect twenty-seven companies out of the eighty to which he felt entitled. "The Government has the right to expect me to take the field with a command capable of performing important service. . . . In consequence of my former unpleasant relations with Genl Polk, I have felt it was best to make no *official complaints* believing that it would exasperate him and do no good. . . . I have been so long neglected & have been the object of such marked injustice at Richmond." [13]

Polk, contrary to Pillow's belief, had been working to secure troops for him, but the cupboard was bare, and he hesitated to rip them from other commands, such as Forrest's. [14] In late April, Maj. Gen. Stephen D. Lee assumed command of the cavalry in Polk's department, and Polk ordered Pillow to report to thirty-year-old Lee for duty. Pillow "has assigned to him certain regiments," Polk wrote Lee, "to constitute a brigade. . . . I concur with you in thinking that he merits a division, and shall be pleased to see him in command of one." Lee thought perhaps Roddey's command could be placed under Pillow. Added to his brigade, it would give him a division. [15]

That plan never materialized, so Pillow spent April and May 1864 recruiting any men he could find and attempted to arm them as best he could. Lee assisted him, hoping to position Pillow near Montevallo, Alabama, as support for Roddey. This would stabilize northern Alabama, thus freeing Forrest for a raid into Tennessee. Lee wrote Pillow to situate his four regiments so that he could block any sudden Federal thrust through north Alabama toward Selma. "I desire to give you a command such as your service and experience entitles you to. . . . It is my intention to give you a division, to be composed of the new regiments and Roddey's or a part of Forrest's cavalry." Forrest, said Lee, is also "anxious to see you have a command and will aid me in forming it, and rest assured, general, as early as practicable you shall have a division." [16]

For a month Pillow pressured Lee to provide the troops he had promised. Apprehensive of a raid on Selma, Lee ordered Pillow there about May 15 to inspect its defenses, as well as those of Montgomery, and to take command of forces in the area. At Selma Pillow found some 1,500 men, including civilians, and a line of defenses two-and-a-half miles long, "unfavorably located." Lee sent Pillow the cavalry regiments of Charles G. Armistead and Charles P. Ball to augment his force at Selma and moved James R. Chalmers's division to Montevallo as a blocking force.[17]

Once the scare about a raid on Selma had subsided, Lee placed Pillow in charge of the cavalry for the defense of the Alabama iron and coal complex. He would take position at Blue Mountain, Alabama, near the Georgia state line. The Confederacy had turned Blue Mountain into a supply dump and staging area by running a spur of track from Oxford, Alabama. Pillow would operate from there with his own and Clanton's brigades. The brigade of James J. Neely of Chalmers's division of Forrest's cavalry was also started for Blue Mountain from Montevallo. Chalmers, who had lost communication with Neely as he moved east, asked Pillow to send Neely back because of a threat in Mississippi. Although Pillow reported to Lee that he had relayed Chalmers's order to Neely, the latter "felt obliged by previous order" to journey on to join Pillow at Blue Mountain.

Pillow himself remained nearby at Oxford, Alabama, while his troops assembled. On June 10, the day Forrest defeated the Federals at Brice's Cross Roads, Pillow saw fit to write Lee again, demanding that he retrieve four West Tennessee regiments from Forrest. He enclosed orders from the secretary of war "dictated by the President himself in the presence of the Tennessee senators." He challenged Forrest's right to these regiments, which Forrest had organized in a brigade under Tyree Bell. "General Polk recognized my right to these troops, but said he would give me others in their place. But he did not do so. I believe General Forrest to be my friend, and do not think he would do me an intentional injustice. . . . I am not disposed to be captious about this particular brigade. I only want a respectable command. . . . I have only three small regiments: Armistead's, Ball's and Thomas'." Forrest, consistently deferential to Pillow, responded in restrained language that Bell, though expressing high regard for General Pillow, preferred to remain under his command.

Map 6. Northern Alabama and Georgia, Spring 1864

Since Chalmers was ill, Forrest suggested that Pillow temporarily join him and assume command of Chalmers's division. Nothing came of it, however, as Chalmers recovered.[18]

Pillow's opportunity came two weeks later. Johnston and Polk had written Richmond for help. The tremendous pressure being exerted against the Army of Tennessee by Sherman might be relieved if Forrest were ordered to operate between the rear of Sherman's army and Dalton.[19] The War Department responded by dispatching Pillow to "interrupt the enemy's line of communications." Sherman was aware of his vulnerability, however. In fact, on June 10, 1864, he had created the District of Etowah under Gen. James B. Steedman, charging him with the specific mission of protecting the Federal supply line from Chattanooga to the front.[20]

With Neely now in Blue Mountain, Pillow had two brigades with which to make the raid. James J. Neely was a daring, experienced officer, a good fighter, and a trusted subordinate of Forrest. Pillow had known him and his older brother, Col. Rufus Neely, at Columbus, Kentucky. The younger Neely, however, had refused in December 1861 to join a group of officers petitioning for Pillow's restoration because of what he regarded as an injustice at Pillow's hands. On May 10, 1864, Neely took command of Richardson's brigade, described during an inspection of June 10 as "the debris of Richardson's Brigade and many other partisan and irregular organizations and commands" raised behind the lines in West Tennessee.[21] Neely's brigade was tired from the "dreary monotonous ride" from Grenada to Oxford to Blue Mountain; a number of men were sick from eating spoiled corn along the way. Pillow allowed them nearly a week to rest. Rain continued, as it had throughout June, tending to make everyone restless. Neely's Tennesseans began to bait Armistead's Alabama troops with insulting imitations of the birdcall of the yellow-hammer. Quarrels broke out between the units, but that was a good sign; it was time to move on.[22]

On June 18 Pillow alerted his command. He ordered Neely to prepare four days' cooked rations and to issue forty rounds of ammunition. To keep the column lean, Pillow ordered Neely on the nineteenth to choose 600 men, sending his wagons and disabled horses to the rear. They set out on the twentieth, Armistead's Alabama brigade in front, Neely's Tennesseans following—a minidivision of 1,200 men. From Blue Mountain they went to Jacksonville, Alabama, where they attempted to cross the swollen Coosa River. Armistead experienced difficulty but got across. Neely tried at several places and finally had to take his brigade to Gadsden, where it took all night on June 21–22 to ferry horses and men over.

Pillow wrote Lee from Gadsden on the twenty-first. "The rain continues to pour and I find myself more delayed than anticipated." Every stream stopped the march, and every halt consumed more rations. The column was running out of food rapidly, and Pillow knew that by the time he reached Blue Pond, Alabama, he would have to send back not only his train, but a number of men. He would "sift and retain the best mounted and most effective." Apparently as an afterthought, Pillow wired Lee requesting that a diversion be made upon Rome, Georgia.[23]

On the twenty-second Pillow moved the column to Blue Pond, where they camped and waited. Ferrying wagons across the Coosa had been slow and cost them a day; the fiery Neely chafed at the delay and sniped at Pillow. At Blue Pond Pillow issued rations and sent back all vehicles except two ambulances. He again inspected the command, weeding out suspicious horses and "invalids," who went back to Blue Mountain with the wagons. A wheat field was discovered nearby, so Pillow had each man ride among the shocks of wheat and get "a bundle or two" for his mount.[24]

His column trimmed to about 1,000 troopers, Pillow left Blue Pond but almost immediately encountered still another water obstacle— Little River, a tributary of the Coosa. Even without wagons he found he had to ferry the two brigades across. Hours flew by. Once past Little River, however, Pillow made excellent time, moving east to Gaylesville, Alabama, then turning north for Alpine, Georgia, and then east to Summerville. They arrived there about nightfall on the twenty-third, dead weary.[25]

The objective of the raid, never precisely designated by Lee or Johnston, and never stated by Pillow, may have been one of the great wooden trestles between Bridgeport, Alabama, and Chattanooga or the vital bridge across the Tennessee at Bridgeport. Considering Pillow's route, however, and the comments by one of his privates, breaking the railroad or destroying a bridge or tunnel between Ringgold and Dalton seems a more likely objective.[26]

As his men began to unsaddle at Summerville, scouts brought word that there was a garrison of 400 Federals at LaFayette, Georgia, twenty miles north—a tempting prize, if they could be surprised and overpowered, and a danger if bypassed. Pillow decided to engage.[27] So Armistead and Neely had their tired troopers remount and set out into the night. "Orders were given to keep perfect silence. We were stopped from singing and loud talking." Again Armistead took the lead. Seven miles from LaFayette, the road split. Pillow sent Armistead left, to the west; Neely, "under the personal supervision of Pillow," took the right fork.[28] The plan was for both columns to strike the sleeping LaFayette garrison simultaneously at dawn—Armistead from the west and north, charging in on the Dug Gap road and swinging north to sever the Chattanooga road, Neely from the south on the Summerville road. The signal for attack, if one was designated, would be Neely's opening volleys, since he seemed to have the more direct route.[29]

Most unfortunately for Pillow and his men, two unlikely things occurred. A Yankee soldier, one of the garrison at LaFayette, happened to be fishing that night south of town. He heard enemy cavalry coming and ducked under a bridge. The Confederates chanced to halt there, and within hearing of the Yankee private, Pillow apparently gave instructions to his columns. The Confederates moved on, the soldier remaining under the bridge trying to count their horses. When they had passed, he sprang out and took a shortcut through fields to LaFayette. He dashed into the hotel and alerted Col. Louis D. Watkins, the Union commander.[30]

In another unlucky circumstance for the Confederates, Watkins, as well as many of his officers, happened to be up and dressed before dawn. It seems that not long before, the vigilant commandant of Nashville had raided the gambling houses there and confiscated vast heaps of poker chips. An alert officer in Watkins's command, however, was at headquarters at the time and made off with a supply, which he brought to LaFayette. Some old southern farmers in the area heard about the poker chips and knew about Yankee hard money, so a game of draw developed, the farmers putting up five-pound packages of "fine smoking tobacco," just "as good as gold." The breathless fisherman-trooper had rushed in just as the game was breaking up.[31]

LaFayette was a typical southern county seat, laid off in a square, with the two-story brick courthouse, finished in white stucco, in the center; the jail, which faced it, was also brick. LaFayette had been occupied on June 19 by about 400 Federals, detachments from the 4th, 6th, and 7th Kentucky cavalry regiments of the brigade of Colonel Watkins.[32] He had been ordered to LaFayette to scout west of the town to the Alabama line, a "vicinity infested by guerrillas." The men were quartered in frame houses on or near the square, with a large number of the 7th Kentucky camped at a seminary about a quarter of a mile north of town on the Chattanooga road.[33]

About 3:00 A.M. Armistead approached LaFayette from the west along the Dug Gap road. He had made good time, except that Maj. Thomas H. Lewis's battalion, to the rear somewhere, had been left behind when a bridge collapsed. Armistead was unsure of the distance remaining, so he cautiously dismounted about half his men, sending ahead a small detachment to capture the enemy pickets. He placed the dismounted men, primarily the 8th Alabama, under Colonel Ball and had them deploy. Ball's objective was to reach the Chattanooga road leading north from town. Behind Ball's men, Armistead formed the mounted troops into columns and prepared to dash directly into town. It was almost dawn when Armistead heard firing far ahead from the picket line. This surprised him; the distance to town was much greater than anticipated. The heavy fog covering the ground gave everything an eerie feeling.[34]

Ball's dismounted men rushed toward LaFayette at the double-quick, but distance itself almost defeated them. They reached the back streets of the town exhausted. Then Armistead's mounted troops came thundering down the Dug Gap road. They swung north, by-passing Ball's weary troops, to a point almost on the Chattanooga road, where they encountered light resistance that was broken after a sharp fight. More Federal troops, led by Colonel Watkins himself, then galloped out from town to confront Armistead, who mistook them for friendly forces and found himself a prisoner. But he was able to escape and rejoined Ball and Lewis, who had come up at last with his Alabama battalion. Together they drove Watkins back into town, pursuing him to the square. Once in town, however, they were jolted by terrible volleys from the jail, the courthouse, and frame buildings on and near the square. Major Lewis was killed, and a number of officers were wounded, including Armistead. The brigade recoiled and withdrew from the square; command passed to Ball.[35]

Meanwhile, Neely advanced from the south. Pillow had kept Neely under close rein during the approach, which annoyed the free-wheeling cavalryman. Even the officer in charge of Neely's advance guard of forty men of the 15th Tennessee "received his orders from the brigadier-general commanding." Close to the picket line, Pillow had Neely halt the brigade. The general himself proceeded to conduct a reconnaissance in a fog so thick one could scarcely see forty yards ahead. "After some delay of a half hour, I suppose,"[36] Pillow returned and directed Neely to move off the Summerville road through some fields to the west and attack the town. Pillow and the advance guard would remain on the road and engage the pickets guarding it once he heard the sound of Neely's attack.

As Neely entered the field he heard the sound of Armistead's struggle with the enemy north of town. At the same time, the pickets Pillow was to have attacked opened fire; surprise was gone. Neely tore down the fences of the field and pushed forward a line of skirmishers, followed closely by Col. Francis M. Stewart and the 15th Tennessee. They advanced past light resistance from enemy sharpshooters in outlying houses and gained the "houses in the suburbs of the town." Neely deployed Col. R. R. White's 14th Tennessee to Stewart's left and the advance continued, with the 12th Tennessee held in reserve. Neely's brigade continued to move ahead, although his line swung farther and farther to the left, "driving the enemy from the houses back toward the center of the town."[37] In effect, as Neely swung left, he crossed the front of Armistead's (Ball's) brigade, which had been repulsed and fallen back. Thus, as Pillow's total force prepared to assault the town, Neely's line ran "nearly parallel with the west side of the square." Most of Armistead's brigade were behind and to the left of Neely.

Pillow ordered Neely to direct the assault on the courthouse, and the latter sent a staff officer to bring up Ball's brigade, but the Alabama troops were in confusion. Command had changed, and the lieutenant colonel of Ball's 8th Alabama had been wounded. Ball was off reconnoitering, Neely's staff officer was told, so he himself ordered the Alabama regiments forward. They refused to budge without an order from Ball, however, so Neely had to send for Pillow, who intervened with one of his staff and got Ball's units moving. All this caused further delay. Finally Ball appeared, and the two brigades moved forward together into the center of town. They seized a number of houses and buildings on the side streets, but the effort was piecemeal, with many of Ball's Alabama brigade hanging back.

The fire from the courthouse was intense. The enemy had barricaded the doors and blocked the windows with sacks of corn. Again, the Federals had been lucky; a big shipment of grain had arrived on the twenty-third and been placed in the courthouse, making it easy to fortify. Inside were jammed Watkins, some 200 Kentucky cavalrymen, a number of their best horses, and a company of captured Confederates. If Pillow had had even one field piece, he could have bagged the lot.[38]

At this point in the fight, about 7:00 A.M., Pillow sent a flag of truce to Watkins: "Sir: To prevent an unnecessary shedding of blood I demand of you an immediate surrender of this post and your forces. I have the force to take the place and am determined to do it. If necessary I will resort to the torch as well as to shot and shell to drive you from your present position. An immediate answer is required." Watkins refused Pillow's demand out of hand; the "fight resumed with great fury."[39]

Three attacks were made against the square. Individual buildings were captured, even the bottom floor of the jail. Ball, showing great courage, managed to reach the door of the courthouse accompanied by a first sergeant and a single private, but they found they could not force the door.[40] Although the Confederates had made little headway breaking into the courthouse, Watkins and his men were surrounded, ammunition was running low inside, and there was no water. "Thousands of bullets . . . pitted and marked the stucco, until, looked at from a little distance, each of the walls suggested a human face badly marked by recent smallpox." Pillow later would contend that at this time, considering his losses and the strength of the enemy position, he decided to abandon the attack. Without artillery to reduce the courthouse, continued attack would have been futile. He had sent almost 100 prisoners back toward Summerville, as well as a number of horses, and Neely had the flag of the 3d Kentucky as a trophy.

Accounts conflict, however. It appears Pillow had decided to burn the courthouse and was preparing for this when, suddenly, down the Chattanooga road crashed the 4th Kentucky Mounted Infantry led by Col. John T. Croxton and Lt. Col. R. M. Kelly, armed with Spencer carbines and Ballard breech-loaders. They struck hard and on a broad front, surprising Pillow's Confederates and routing them. "We left that place much quicker than we went there," reported Pvt. Charles G. Joy, Company C, 14th Tennessee. "How many Yankees there were I never knew, but they stampeded us." Confederates lucky enough to have their horses at hand fled down the Summerville road, across fields, "through an old tanyard, our horses jumping the vats."[41]

Pvt. John Johnston, while trying to locate and save a wounded comrade, got separated from his regiment, the 14th Tennessee. He wandered off onto an "old deserted-looking road through the woods." There, to his surprise, he discovered Pillow and his staff. He asked Pillow where the 14th was, and Pillow replied, "We do not know. We are lost ourselves." Johnston rode on, leaving Pillow and his staff "standing in the middle of the road. It struck me as something very remarkable that the commander of a division of cavalry on so important an occasion should have been thus lost in the woods."[42]

The Alabama troops were not so lucky; many of their horses were being held a good distance away. When they hurried back for their mounts, they found Pillow had ordered them moved. Then a large number of horses stampeded, and the men panicked. Ball attempted to rally his troops, but it was useless; his brigade disintegrated. Fortunately, the Federal pursuit lacked sufficient force. Neely had the 14th Tennessee form a rear guard, and they were able to protect the fleeing Alabama troops, who passed through their lines to safety.[43]

The retreat south through Summerville back to Blue Pond hardly could be described as orderly. Perhaps the Tennessee regiments and some of Alabama troops maintained march integrity, but frightened Confederates—officers and men—fled directly to Talladega and spread word of disaster. A furious Pillow later would denounce them and their "most exaggerated and false reports," promising these miscreants a speedy court-martial. It could not be denied, however, that many wounded were abandoned, and many prisoners who had left LaFayette under guard escaped and returned to LaFayette. One asserted "Pillow ran fifty miles the day of the fight, and was still going towards Blue Mountain."[44]

LaFayette cost Pillow twenty-four killed, fifty-three wounded, and seventy-seven captured; the Federals lost four killed, seven wounded, and sixty-four captured. Most Confederate losses came in the Alabama brigade (Ball's 8th Alabama and Armistead's 12th Mississippi).[45] It was disheartening. Pillow blamed Armistead for attacking prematurely and carped at Lee for not having provided him with artillery. "Before leaving I made known my extreme reluctance to move without this arm of the service. . . . These remarks are not made in complaint, but as an explanation of my failure to accomplish all that was expected."[46]

Pillow recrossed the Coosa River on June 27 and, safe from pursuit, rested his command. There, sitting down by the river, Private Johnston and General Pillow had a talk. Pillow explained to the private why the attack had been made and why it had failed. "The soldiers all liked Gen. Pillow personally," Johnston believed, "although they did not have any great confidence in his military ability. . . . He was always pleasant and approachable and indeed seemed to be fond of talking to the private soldiers, and he was withal a gallant, old fellow, but had a good deal of egotism of an inoffensive sort. He loved to talk of himself and the great things he would do or had done, but was not arrogant or unkind to other people."[47]

Pillow's LaFayette raid had accomplished nothing. No bridges were destroyed; no tunnels blown; no railroads cut. It wore out two Confederate cavalry brigades needed elsewhere. It seems to have broken the spirit of Armistead's inexperienced and largely conscript Alabama brigade, which would bolt again in their next fight. It alerted Sherman to the ease with which a raiding party could strike his communications. "You cannot be too vigilant," he wired Steedman. The raid would lead Sherman, on July 10, to unleash a daring and highly effective counterraid to Opelika. "This move will check a repetition of Pillow's attempt."[48]

LaFayette destroyed what remained of Pillow's reputation as a general officer. Although Stephen Lee initially viewed the raid as partially successful, word got around that it had been a bungled, bloody exercise. The enemy laughed. A poem written about LaFayette, "The Psalm of Life," taunted Pillow about his "boastful twaddle." "Let the Yankees bury our dead! Run! Run!"[49]

Fundamentally, Pillow lost sight of his mission. The instant gratification of a quick showy victory enticed him to engage at LaFayette, and to engage prematurely. He rationalized his decision, blaming it on his reluctance to leave a dangerous enemy on his flank. Thus his lean, mobile column entangled itself in confused street fighting, ultimately destroying its offensive capability and opportunity. The march itself, at least from Blue Mountain to Summerville, and despite the problem of high water, seems to have been sloppily handled, particularly the river crossings and the logistics. Pillow seemed preoccupied with his wagon train, a rock tied about the neck of the column until it crossed Little River.

The decision at Summerville to race weary troops through the night to attack LaFayette can be justified. Most bold commanders, fearing the loss of surprise, would have agreed, although prudence might have suggested reducing the distance traveled on June 23. But the attack on LaFayette, while sound in concept, demonstrated poor coordination and terrible control. Pillow attached himself to the brigade of Neely, leaving the much less experienced Armistead the more difficult task of maneuver. No attempt to capture the pickets on the Chattanooga road seems to have been made, unlike the efforts south and west of town. These pickets fled and reached Croxton, who was camped ten miles north at Rock Spring Church; they brought back reinforcement and counterattack.

Up to the assault phase, Pillow had kept J. J. Neely under tight control, but then, instead of leading Neely's brigade into town, he held it inactive while he indulged in small unit action and reconnaissance, losing time, perspective, and control. Once the attack commenced, Pillow should have provided strong security on the north side of town, a precaution against interference from Chattanooga. He should not have moved the Alabama mounts without notification of proper subordinates. In the reports and accounts of the Battle of LaFayette, the lack of effective, personal battlefield leadership by Gideon Pillow is glaring.

He had been given a magnificent opportunity with this north Georgia raid of June 1864. If he had been able to snap Sherman's line of communications, even for a few days, or if he had won a smart little victory at LaFayette, the consequences for Pillow would have been dramatic. So much could have been redeemed.

Pillow led his troops back to the Blue Mountain–Oxford area. He urged Lee to allow him to try again. He had artillery now and felt confident he could successfully attack gunboats on the Tennessee or conduct another raid against Sherman's communications. Lee responded by detaching Neely from Pillow, moving him west to Mississippi on forced marches to rejoin Chalmers and Forrest, who were threatened by an impending advance of Federal forces under A. J. Smith. As a precaution, Lee pulled Pillow back to Montevallo, leaving a small force at Blue Mountain and scouting parties out toward Rome.[50]

On July 6, a week after seeking the offensive, Pillow reversed himself, writing that his command could not move before July 8 because of the "jaded condition" of his horses.[51] This was most unfortunate. Federal commander Maj. Gen. Lowell H. Rousseau, though not an experienced cavalry officer, led a raid into Pillow's domain on July 11, while Pillow was away in Tuscaloosa. His objective was to break the railroad between Montgomery and Opelika, but Pillow never caught on. Confused, he returned to Montevallo trying to determine Rousseau's direction and intentions, exercising extreme caution and virtually no control over his subordinate Clanton, who lay in Rousseau's path.

Lee, preoccupied with Smith's penetration of north Mississippi, sent infantry to reinforce Pillow, but he himself had a battle on his hands at Tupelo. Bragg intervened. From Richmond he urged Pillow to pursue Rousseau's raiders vigorously "in whatever direction they go. . . . Move with all possible expedition." Pillow informed Bragg that he was moving his brigade to Selma, but that Lee had ordered him (quite correctly) to Montgomery and West Point, Georgia. Pillow believed Rousseau's objective was the release of the Andersonville prisoners. As late as July 16, Pillow wired his beleaguered subordinate Clanton that he could not help him or unite with him. Yet he "expects to take the field" and advance in the direction of Blue Mountain. He did take the field on the seventeenth, not toward Blue Mountain, where he had a chance of cutting off Rousseau, but toward Selma.[52]

Even as Pillow got his brigade in motion south from Montevallo to Selma, Rousseau had begun his return march. The raid was over, the damage done. Losing less than fifty men, Rousseau had broken the railroad, destroyed a vast amount of supplies, and demonstrated that Pillow's shield protecting the heart of Alabama was glass.[53] As a further embarrassment, while Rousseau was wrecking his department, Pillow had spent time trying to reach Lee, who was advancing to engage Smith in the Battle of Tupelo. He wished to explain how his son, George, and one of Lee's staff officers had lost a confidential dispatch on the streets of Demopolis.[54]

Pillow was through as a field commander. The inability to deal with Rousseau's raid, coupled with the LaFayette debacle, discredited him completely. Richmond relieved him about July 20, 1864, replacing him with Gen. Daniel W. Adams. Pillow's staff scattered, some to Adams, and others, like Burch, reporting to different commands.[55]

In Montgomery, Alabama, a distraught Pillow wrote Confederate Secretary of the Treasury George A. Trenholm:

> I am without a command. I contemplate retiring from the army. When this war commenced I possessed a large estate. I am now reduced to poverty and my large Family (Six unmarried Daughters, a wife & a small son) are living in destitution within the Enemies lines. My residence & all else that I had in Tennessee having been confiscated & sold. I seek employment in which I can be useful & provide a living for my family. I am satisfied I can combine Agencies which will enable me to ship large amounts of Government cotton if it is the wish of the Gov't to do so. If you consider it a matter worthy of attention & will have me ordered to Richmond I think I can satisfy you of my success.[56]

Pillow remained in Montgomery, apparently totally inactive, while the great struggles around Atlanta took place in the late summer. In October one of his former brigades, Armistead's, was smashed in a small skirmish near Rome while attempting to mask the movements of Hood's Army of Tennessee.[57]

Simultaneously, Pillow, now in Tuscumbia, learned that Clifton had been "sold" and "that my family are to be turned out of House & Home." Clifton had been confiscated by the Freedmen's Bureau and leased to C. C. Bean.[58] An informant, H. G. Smith, who shared ownership of the Bean lease, accused George G. Moulton and Jerome B. Pillow of "maltreating" blacks at Clifton; they had also "aided guerrillas" and involved themselves in the smuggling of cotton. Smith urged that they be arrested. Moulton, a friend of the Pillow family, was made prisoner in mid-October, and this apparently convinced Gideon Pillow that something must be done to safeguard his family. He wrote Rousseau, commander of the Tennessee district, and Col. W. B. Sipes, commandant of Columbia, asking if he might come to Clifton to bring out his family, accompanied by an escort of twenty-five men to protect against bushwhackers.[59]

Receiving no answer to his incredible request, Pillow appealed to Sherman on November 2, having his friend Gen. "Red" Jackson deliver the message through the lines. He told Sherman he had received no response to his inquiry of Sipes and Rousseau, and again he asked if he, a combatant and Confederate general officer, might enter Tennessee and bring his family out. He also wanted to retrieve wagon loads of furniture and as many servants as might wish to accompany them. "If the application is not allowed in the form presented," Pillow continued, "you will confer a favor on me to allow a personal interview with yourself."[60]

A letter from Mary the following day, however, relieved Pillow's distress. She reported calmly that things were fairly normal at Clifton. "Our present lessees say if it is rented they will rent it & we shall remain as long as they hold the place. They have alway [sic] acted in the most gentlemanly manner towards all the family & have been a protection to us." Furthermore, Jerome had been very attentive, and he and General Rousseau were getting along famously. A guard had been assigned to protect Clifton. "I was a good deal annoyed at first while losing everything I had but have long since become accustomed to doing without many things that we all ways had heretofore."[61] These were dangerous times. Caroline Nicholson, Mary Pillow's special friend, had been robbed by a group of men dressed in Federal uniforms in the spring. They afterwards "paid Mrs. Gen. Pillow a call" but were chased off by a relative, Mark Pillow. It undoubtedly helped that Rousseau's aide, Capt. Thomas C. Williams, and Gideon Pillow's niece Cynthia Saunders delighted in each other's company.[62]

Pillow's world had been transformed, as had his attitudes. Less than a year before, when his old friends Cleburne and Hindman had petitioned the Confederate Congress to enroll former slaves in the army, Pillow indignantly had recommended that both officers be relieved from duty "instantly." The fall of Atlanta and the exhaustion of the South's manpower pool, however, convinced Pillow. He urgently advocated conscription of "all able bodied negro men between the ages of 18 and 45."[63]

Maj. Gen. Lovell Harrison Rousseau
(courtesy Tennessee State Library and Archives)

In November 1864, Hood's army swung west toward Tuscumbia, preparing to invade Tennessee. Pillow wanted to be part of the action, so he wrote Gen. Richard Taylor requesting to be placed on duty once again. "If it be the wish and purpose of the President to place me on duty in Tennessee to organize the reserves, allow me." The Army of Tennessee needed additional strength desperately. If such an assignment materialized, added Pillow, it would help greatly to have John C. Burch back. A commission as major general would be even more helpful, "that I might carry with me the prestige which promotion would give me."[64]

When Hood began crossing the Tennessee River near Florence, Alabama, Pillow joined the army. Unfortunately, at a party for the leaders of the army at the home of a prominent Florence resident, Robert M. Patton, Pillow tripped over the large ornate fountain on the front walk and fell in, breaking his arm. This gave rise to nasty gossip about his being drunk.[65] But nothing, it seemed, could stop Pillow's reentry into Tennessee with the army. Broken arm strapped tightly against his body, he joined Hood's column, riding along over the frozen ground as they crossed the state line and entered Wayne County. The column kept closed up because of swarming bushwhackers; Pillow rode with Chaplain Charles T. Quintard. When they reached Clifton, Quintard stopped to visit, as did Stephen Lee (now a lieutenant general) and, on November 27, Maj. Gen. Edward Johnson. Spread about the grounds were D. C. Govan's veteran Arkansas troops of Cleburne's division.[66]

Pillow did not take part in the Battle of Franklin on November 30, but on the day before the Battle of Nashville (December 15–16), General Hood asked him to resume recruiting duty in Tennessee, raising and organizing as many companies as possible. Pillow got the indispensable Burch back and immediately started to work. A citizen of Maury wrote on December 16 that Pillow was out to take every man; even employing substitutes "is no excuse for the Southern Confederacy." Men fled Maury in droves.[67]

Meanwhile, Hood's broken army retreated south from Nashville, a long column of defeated men, struggling over the ice and snow, ditching rifles, wagons, and cannon alongside the road. Hope for a stand at Columbia was forgotten. On Christmas Day, 1864, the army recrossed the Tennessee at Florence, intent upon reaching warmth and safety at Corinth and Tupelo.

Pillow left Tennessee with the army. He made his way to Macon, Georgia, where he and his daughter, Mary Amanda Brown, wife of sometime staff officer Thomas J. Brown, were refugee guests in the home of the James C. Cook family.[68] In early February 1865, Pillow apparently slipped back through enemy lines to Maury. He and Mary, accompanied by their six unmarried daughters and their youngest child, Robert Granville, appeared at St. Peter's Episcopal Church in Columbia, where they were baptized.[69]

Six days later Pillow was in Montgomery for a conference with Gen. Pierre G. T. Beauregard about how to rebuild the Army of Tennessee. Pillow offered his services, and the two generals evidently reached an agreement similar to the arrangement Pillow had with Johnston in the summer of 1863. All this ended abruptly on February 10, however, when Pillow received an unexpected telegram from the War Department.

Samuel Cooper announced that Pillow had been "constituted Commissary General of Prisoners, and will enter at once upon his duties." It seemed that Gen. John H. Winder, longtime provost marshal of Richmond and, since November 1864, commissary general of prisoners, had died suddenly on February 7. Pillow wired back, telling Cooper of the plans he and Beauregard had developed. He made it plain that he preferred being returned to the duty of chasing stragglers. "Which does the President prefer I should do?" Davis preferred he take over Winder's responsibilities, so Pillow returned to Macon, where he established temporary headquarters.

He inherited an impossible situation. Confederate military prisons "were overflowing" as a result of the nonexchange policy of the Federals. Most of the prisoners from the fighting in Virginia had been transferred to prisons in Georgia and Alabama. Conditions were deplorable—there were acute shortages of food, medicine, shelter, clothing, and guards. In desperation, General Winder had suggested in mid-January the radical expedient of releasing Union prisoners, paroling them, and sending them home.[70] Winder's assistant was Gen. John D. Imboden, a conspicuously successful officer in the Army of Northern Virginia until he had been struck down by malaria. In Augusta, Georgia, Imboden read a newspaper account of Winder's death and Pillow's appointment, so he set off for Macon to report to his new commanding officer.[71]

In the meantime, Pillow prepared to leave Macon and go to Richmond to meet with Cooper and the new secretary of war, John C. Breckinridge. However, he chanced upon Capt. John C. Rutherford of the prison bureau, who told him "prisoners were being rapidly paroled for exchange." This meant an important change of policy and coincided with what Pillow had been reading in the newspapers.[72] So Pillow postponed his trip and waited in Macon for Imboden. When Imboden arrived, he and Pillow held a long conference, joined by the commander of all Georgia state troops, Gen. Howell Cobb, who was responsible for providing prison guards. Pillow, according to Imboden, led the discussions and focused attention on the newspaper accounts that revealed Grant had reached an agreement with Richmond that "either side might deliver to the other on parole, but without exchange, any prisoners they chose, taking simply a receipt for them." Of course, this account was highly unofficial, perhaps incorrect; they had heard nothing from Richmond. But it sounded "probably true, and we decided to act upon it." They agreed to send all prisoners at Andersonville and Eufaula to the closest Federal garrison. They would do so unconditionally, "simply taking a receipt." Of course, the released prisoners would be on parole until formally exchanged.[73]

Pillow knew how to handle this. He sent Captain Rutherford under a flag of truce with a message for Gen. E. P. Scammon, commander of Federal forces at Jacksonville, Florida. Pillow informed Scammon of the reported agreement between Grant and authorities of the Confederate government, "which is now being rapidly carried into effect in the eastern portions of the States." He proposed, therefore, to send to Jacksonville a portion of the prisoners at Andersonville. "Will you receive them, and receipt for them as paroled prisoners for exchange?"[74] Pillow had chosen Jacksonville as the most likely depot because all railroad connections with Savannah had been cut by Sherman in December. From Andersonville, prisoners could be moved by rail to Chattahoochie, then downriver to Quincy, Florida, and then by rail to Jacksonville. Using this "less fatiguing" route, they could be moved securely and rapidly, much to the benefit of the Confederates. Earlier, 1,500 prisoners had been put aboard cars and shipped across Alabama through Jackson, Mississippi, to Vicksburg. Pillow had planned to continue at the rate of 800 prisoners a day. Gen. Richard Taylor, however, had stopped further shipments to Jackson, believing such movements constituted a security risk.[75]

Settling into his new position, Pillow had other ideas. He ordered that former slaves recently captured in a battle in Florida be sent to Andersonville as laborers. On March 26 he wrote to his Federal counterpart (whose name he did not know) with a sweeping proposal for a cartel to select healthy locations for prisons, to issue the same rations in kind and quantity and clothing "corresponding as nearly as practicable with the uniform," and to forbid maneuvering armies from molesting or interfering with the other party's prisons. Pillow, still unable to resist testing limits of authority, appended a provision empowering the Confederate commissary general of prisoners to ship cotton, free of duties, "to markets of the United States or foreign governments." The proceeds would be used to pay for medicine, food, and clothing for the "exclusive benefit" of Federal prisoners.[76]

While his commander dreamed bold dreams, Captain Rutherford had arrived in Jacksonville and wired back wonderful news: "Send on the prisoners." General Scammon confirmed acceptance of the arrangement by wire on March 29. So Pillow had rations cooked and started 6,000 Federals on their way with minimum security. He cautioned Rutherford to see that they were treated with kindness. Just at that time, Federal raider James H. Wilson came tearing through the defenses of north Alabama, heading straight for Andersonville, or so Pillow thought. Imboden, Cobb, and Pillow met once again and agreed they could do nothing to stop Wilson. They decided, therefore, to withdraw the remaining prisoners from Andersonville and send them all to Jacksonville.[77] But the arrangement exploded as March drew to a close. First, Scammon's superior, Gen. Quincy A. Gillmore, countermanded the agreement between Scammon and Pillow. "No prisoners will be received in your district," Gillmore ordered, until official approval is received from Grant, which meant a delay of at least two weeks. So the Federal prisoners en route to Jacksonville had to turn around and return to Andersonville.[78]

Pillow would not be responsible for dealing with this turn of events, however. On March 30, 1865, he was relieved as commissary general of prisoners, and Gen. Daniel Ruggles was assigned to the post. Pillow would report to Johnston as "chief of the recruiting service of my army west of the Savannah River."[79]

As the Confederacy neared collapse, confusion reigned in Richmond. As early as February 27, the order of February 14 naming Pillow as commissary general of prisoners had been revoked, and Pillow was ordered to report to Johnston for assignment "to duty of collecting and forwarding . . . all absentees." Learning that Johnston already had assigned Gen. W. W. Mackall, Richmond had changed its mind and allowed Pillow to remain until Ruggles was appointed.[80]

The Conscription Bureau was under enormous pressure. On March 3 the Confederate House passed a heavily supported resolution accusing bureau chief John S. Preston of "laxity and culpable neglect." Congress wanted Pillow back, and this time they would hold

Davis himself, rather than Pillow, responsible for proper execution of the law. This was fine vindication, although it is doubtful Pillow knew of it.[81]

Pillow never resumed his work collecting absentees. With Federal units appearing everywhere, communication and control broke down. On April 20, Wilson and his raiders stormed into Macon; Pillow fled the James Cook home in such a hurry that he left his sword.[82] It appears he made his way to Montgomery, leaving his daughter Mary Amanda Brown behind. In Montgomery he joined Beauregard and Governor Watts, and they prepared to head west in seven wagons.[83] Illinois cavalry, however, intercepted them at Union Springs, about thirty-five miles southeast of Montgomery. There Pillow surrendered. Dressed in a dusty uniform, he went to Brig. Gen. Thomas J. Lucas at Union Springs, told him that he had no command and was waiting in Union Springs for his daughter, and asked if the two of them might be permitted to return to their home in Columbia. Since the "terms of the armistice (between Sherman and Johnston of April 26) are so vague," Lucas allowed Pillow to go.

The Federal officers treated Pillow "with kindness, courtesy and respect." Some, who recognized their old Mexican war commander, saluted him and offered to lend him money. "I accepted no money, not one dollar." He was allowed to keep his personal property; the provost marshal noted that "the headquarters effects of Major Gen. Pillow consisted of a dingy old chest such as emigrants used to bring over, a pair of badly worn boots, and old U.S. Army blanket and a small blank book." The 2d Illinois Cavalry escorted the celebrated prisoners back to Montgomery to be paroled.[84]

Montgomery, commanded by Federal Gen. Frederick Steele, was peaceful. Black troops were coming across the Alabama River to occupy the city, and "the Citizens are considerably 'ground' by the operation." On May 5, 1865, an "excessively hot" day, Pillow arrived. A Federal soldier noted that the fifty-nine-year-old brigadier was 5'8", with gray hair, gray eyes, and fair complexion. "He was without money to travel with." When he had received his parole, Pillow set out for Columbia accompanied by Mary Amanda, her two children, and four servants.[85] He arrived back home at Clifton on May 20, 1865.[86]

16   **A Bitter Cup**

Pillow's first objective was to regain control of his property. It had been confiscated by the United States Treasury Department under Federal laws of March 12, 1863, and July 2, 1864, empowering agents to do so because the "lawful owner was voluntarily absent therefrom, and engaged either in arms or otherwise in aiding or encouraging the rebellion." Pillow immediately wrote U.S. Secretary of the Treasury Hugh McCulloch, asking that Clifton be restored to him. McCulloch refused.[1] Curtis C. Bean, who leased Clifton from the Treasury Department in 1864, had planted some 350 acres of corn and put in a small meadow of hay in front of the main house. Pillow, however, saw only mismanagement and incredible waste. Hands began eating the corn before it had become good roasting ears; boldly, they would take it to town to sell as if it were their own. Bean apparently left gates open and did not bother to repair fences, thus allowing hogs and stock to destroy much of the crop.[2]

Pillow brought back to Clifton nine mules, several horses, and eight freedmen. When he tried housing the freedmen in the slave quarters, Bean threw them out—his own hands occupied these. So an angry Pillow brought the freedmen to the top of the hill and found space for them in buildings where only house servants once lived. Poor Curtis Bean did not know with whom he dealt. Pillow set to work to dislodge him and, from the beginning, Bean said, "evinced a disposition to give me trouble." Pillow and his family and hands spread out from the main house, occupying or making use of the large stable, the springhouse, the gardens, the orchard, and the smokehouse. He ran off Bean's stock by constructing a large hog pen close to their drinking water. "This," said Bean, "so befouled and nasticd the stream my stock would not drink there." Pillow interfered with the work of Bean's hands "most unwarrantably." When they threatened Pillow, Bean had to step in "to secure peace and harmony among all concerned."[3]

Yankee correspondents discovered Pillow at Clifton that summer. "He greeted us very affably, and is quite communicative, indeed exceedingly talkative." One observer from Milwaukee found him "not imposing," yet he "would pass for an intelligent and genial farmer of the old school." Of course Pillow applied lard: "You Yankees are our masters; we give it up; we are at your mercy." Expecting to receive a pardon, Pillow declared he was not guilty of treason and was willing, at any time, to be tried by a jury of Federal general officers, "except that Gen. Curtis."[4]

Once he received his pardon, Pillow, through the good offices of his new friend, Gen. Clinton B. Fisk of the Freedmen's Bureau, negotiated a fresh lease with Curtis Bean; he was required by law to allow Bean to remain until his government lease terminated in 1866. The Pillow-Bean lease was only legal wallpaper, however. Bean knew he was unwelcome; he knew Pillow would try to drive him off. When Bean's lease expired February 1, 1866, he was gone. Pillow stalked him, however, as far as the Arizona Territory and sued him in 1869 for full payment of rent corn.[5]

Obtaining a pardon was humiliating for most Confederates. For Pillow, however, it seems to have been easier. Legend has the once rich man, in the early summer of 1865, borrowing money from a former slave to go to Nashville. There Pillow asked Governor Brownlow's help and that of Gen. George H. Thomas, military commander of Tennessee. Would they both write President Johnson on his behalf? He had lost much of his vast property, he reminded them. Now he found himself heavily in debt—land would have to be sold for back taxes and to satisfy creditors. "Is this not enough suffering and punishment for one error?" Using classic Pillow misdirection, he explained his political position in 1861: "That I clung to the *Union*, and exercised all my influence to hold it together as long as there was hope of a peaceful adjustment . . . all intelligent men in Tennessee can testify. It was not until *war actually existed*, that I determined my course of action." "How deeply I have had cause to regret the course, I then felt it my duty to pursue."

Pillow's sister Cynthia Saunders Brown, a Unionist to her bones, reminded Brownlow that throughout the war, even with her son (John E. Saunders) and brother as Confederate officers, she "threw all my energies, resources and moral support on the Federal side." She urged support of Pillow's pardon request, telling of his financial needs, his six unmarried daughters, his opposition to secession, and his work as commissary general of prisoners to "ameliorate the condition of Federal prisoners." Jerome, in a startling letter to President Johnson, told of a trip he had made to Nashville in March 1864. He went there, he said, to make known to Federal authorities Gideon Pillow's "anxiety to return to his allegiance to the United States." Jerome had asked them, at the height of the war, if his brother could "be allowed to return to his home near Columbia . . . , give bond for the strict observance of the same and become a loyal and law-abiding citizen."

On June 29, 1865, two weeks after his talks in Nashville, Pillow took the loyalty oath in Phillips County, Arkansas, and forwarded it that day to his old enemy Johnson. He pledged to be a loyal citizen and to use his influence "in favor of the restoration of the authority of the Government." Johnson pardoned him on August 28, 1865. Pillow's pardon, it should be noted, was opposed by George R. Riddle of Pittsburgh, Pennsylvania. Pillow had seized Riddle's coal at Memphis in the summer of 1861, and Riddle was intent on revenge.[6]

Maury County was very tense during 1865. Federal authorities had seen fit to station a black regiment in Columbia. Dangerous incidents occurred; tempers were as short as money. On July 31 congressional candidates spoke in Columbia. They supported the disenfranchisement of Confederates; they "would rather let the Negroes vote than the Rebels." The crowd listened sullenly. Then, somehow, Gideon Pillow got a chance to speak. "He made himself out now the best of Union Men." Employing the ancient Jacksonian tactic of saber rattling, he declared his willingness to take the field once more, this time against the French. As he spoke, listeners melted away. His remarks did not seem "very appropriate for the time."[7]

Even more inappropriately, on July 15 Pillow had Mary agree to release her dower to him. In return he deeded Mound Place Plantation to Jerome, thus giving Mary an estate—a trust—in the plantation equal to her dower, which he estimated at $60,000. About the same time, John Pointer sued Pillow to foreclose on the mortgage he held on forty-three slaves and two plantations. Pillow responded vigorously that emancipation had changed all. "Slavery," he argued, "violates the Declaration of Independence." The suit would drag on.[8]

To get on his feet financially, Pillow needed capital and labor. Once he had his pardon and could hold property again, Pillow set out for Washington. On September 20 he met with Gen. Oliver O. Howard, head of the Freedmen's Bureau, and obtained a letter from Howard to his subordinates restoring to Pillow "as much of his property formerly owned as you now hold as abandoned or confiscable." The rents on these lands were transferred to him also, as in the case of Curtis Bean.[9]

From Washington, Pillow journeyed on to New York City, where a group of prominent southern planters gathered in the Anson House on September 28, 1865. Pillow opened the meeting and called for the formation of an organization for "united action and mutual support" in raising capital. "We lost our peculiar institution," he said, "and all the capital invested in it." He went on to compliment President Johnson and advocate accepting emancipation as "an irrevocable fact, and deal with it accordingly." His former slaves, he told the group, had formed a committee to visit him, "begging him to employ them." He had promised to do so, "but unless we can borrow money, we cannot pay the negro his wages."[10]

At the end of Pillow's speech, Gen. Robert V. Richardson, an old friend from Mexican War days, a fellow lawyer, and one of Forrest's brigade commanders, got to his feet. Speaking as a large Arkansas landowner himself, Richardson seconded Pillow's ideas and moved that the American Cotton Planters Association be formed, that Pillow be named president, and that an executive committee, named by

Pillow, be authorized. Thus the association was created with Richardson, Gen. James R. Chalmers, C. G. Baylor of Georgia, Frederick Woodson of Alabama, J. P. Beasley of Arkansas, and Pillow as the executive committee. Pillow's propertied son-in-law, Thomas J. Brown, however, soon replaced Woodson and Beasley on the executive committee.[11]

These planters had ambitious goals and a wide range of membership. They had rounded up an eye-catching group of "patrons," including governors across the South, Parson Brownlow among them; authentic northerners such as Gen. Benjamin F. Butler; railroad men such as Sam Tate; and Confederate household names such as Hood and Bragg. These eminent men, in the words of Pillow, stood as "a moral guaranty." However—and Pillow wished to make this clear to the public and potential creditors—they took "no pecuniary liability in the affairs of the Association." The ACPA's solicitor, Gen. John C. Brown, would "investigate the titles of Planters proposing to borrow money" from the association; authorized agents would then "examine the plantations and verify values and productiveness."

The executive committee set up headquarters in New York and contracted with the house of Marcus M. Walker of New York as their representative in Europe and America to sell the securities of the ACPA. Pillow and his associates cast their net wide. They sought loans in New York, Washington, Boston, Delaware, Virginia, and especially in France. Richardson and Monsieur E. Bellot of Menieres Brothers worked hard in Paris seeking money, including negotiations with the Crédit Mobilier. The idea was to pledge, by bonds and three-to-ten-year mortgages to a trustee, the property of the planters at about one-half of its present value, as well as the crops, the stock, and the implements to be purchased. Although they met resistance and refusal at many points, Pillow and Brown, at least, succeeded in borrowing $125,000 and $150,000 respectively from Watts, Given and Company of New York. It appears that Pillow may have abandoned the ACPA once he had secured his own loan. He abruptly left New York for home in October, causing Baylor to complain, "Your sudden departure has embarrassed me and our mutual friends." [12]

So far Pillow had been quite successful. He had his pardon, his property had been turned back to him, he had obtained a significant loan, and he had established a good relationship with Howard and Fisk. He decided to push for more. He learned the Federal quartermaster might sell surplus wagons, so he made a proposal, substantially lower than others might bid, reminding the quartermaster that General Curtis had taken twelve excellent wagons from him in 1862. His bid was turned down flat. It was considered, in the words of the Yankee quartermaster, "down right impudence." [13]

Next Pillow sought his 200 prized mules that Curtis had taken. Acquaintances informed him in November 1865 that the mules were in St. Louis. Pillow made a trip there immediately and identified some of his animals. He went to Sherman and asked to have them returned, arguing that since his citizenship had been restored, he still had a right to his mules. They had not been confiscated technically, since he had never received a decree of confiscation as such. Sherman apparently agreed Pillow could reclaim his mules but referred him to the quartermaster in St. Louis, who also yielded; before releasing the mules, however, they wired Washington for permission. Unfortunately for Pillow, the request reached the desk of Secretary of War Edwin M. Stanton, who squashed it. "I submitted to their decision without a murmur," Pillow lamented.[14]

Pillow always made good copy—he saw to it himself. When he reported his progress to Howard, for instance, he would make sure that a duplicate made its way into a Memphis newspaper, knowing that often it would be republished in other cities. He considered his work "successful beyond my most sanguine expectations." By December 1865 he had engaged about 400 freedmen; he gave them part of the cotton and set aside land for them to grow vegetables and corn for their own use. He placed one of his Arkansas plantations "under white laborers from the North upon precisely the same terms I engaged the freedman. I feel anxious to try the system of white labor of that character." [15] The *New York Times* commented, "There seems to be no prominent man in the Southern States who is doing more for the solution of the industrial problem. . . . The whole country will profit by hearing from time to time the industrial reports of Gen. Pillow." [16]

Pillow put his borrowed capital to work, investing primarily in his Arkansas properties. He repaired buildings and constructed new ones; he rebuilt fences and levees; he bought dry goods, food, crockery, and tools for his hands. He purchased new steam-powered gins and the most efficient farm equipment available. Positive, pragmatic, and enthusiastic as ever, he made "conciliatory" speeches whenever possible, supporting Johnson and the efforts of the Freedmen's Bureau. In June 1866 he wrote Howard, "*Freed Labour is proving a success. . . .* In bringing about this great result, I have been, as you are well aware, an earnest believer & co-worker." He went so far as to apply to the Treasury Department for permission to organize a national bank in Columbia.[17]

Indeed, Gideon Pillow was a beacon of light in these troubled times. Disease, violence, hunger, and fear stalked eastern Arkansas and Maury County. Andrew Johnson's lenient Reconstruction policies were under attack by the Radicals. When Tennessee's representatives were denied their seats in Congress, demonstrations and mass meetings occurred. Pillow appeared and spoke in favor of Johnson, urging Tennesseans to continue their support of the president and his policies. Parson Brownlow, however, had broken with Johnson and saw such conciliatory statements by conservatives as the self-serving rhetoric of the wealthy.[18]

Clouds appeared in the late spring of 1866.[19] Pillow became unwell, and creditors began to crowd around. John Pointer died, and his executor vigorously pressed claims against Pillow's Arkansas property. The Planters Bank of Nashville sued and won a judgment for $56,753. Other old debts surfaced in this suit—$42,000 to Jerome and $18,000 to Pillow's ward, Cynthia P. Saunders. A lien was placed against Clifton itself to satisfy these creditors.[20]

Even more frightening was a suit filed against Pillow in 1867. Riddle, Coleman & Company of Pittsburgh and Wisconsin brought suit in the Sixth Judicial Circuit, District of West Tennessee, for $125,000 in damages for his seizure in 1861 of eleven coal barges and 29,249 barrels of Pittsburgh coal. Pillow retained Landon C. Haynes, the former prominent East Tennessee political leader, who now practiced law in Memphis, to represent him.[21] Pillow lost the suit, and a judgment was rendered against him for $38,000. Haynes and Pillow appealed and won a new trial. This time Pillow argued strenuously that he only acted as the agent of a belligerent. Seizing coal in time of war, he maintained, was like killing during wartime—not murder, but an honorable act. Responsibility, if it must be placed, should be assigned to the State of Tennessee. The court, however, did not agree; the judgment stood. Pillow petitioned the Tennessee General Assembly for help, but they turned a deaf ear. In 1870 he appealed to Gov. John C. Brown, and in 1874 to his former staff officer, Gov. James D. Porter, but to no avail. "Being then abandoned by the State . . . I must submit to the judgment of the courts . . . and take my fate."[22]

Debts continued to mount: a note to the Manchester and Alabama Railroad for $50,000, interest on the large Watts, Given loan, tuition, taxes, fees of every description. Even Bushrod Johnson joined in, being named special commissioner by the Maury chancery court in yet another suit against Pillow. About this time, late 1867–68, as Pillow was becoming desperate, his old friend Isham G. Harris returned to Memphis. Harris had fled the country after the war when Tennessee placed a bounty on his head. Brownlow relented in 1868 and did away with the reward, thus making it possible for Harris to come home. Harris and Pillow became law partners at once, establishing their practice in Memphis. Mary Pillow would stay at Clifton, however, and Harris's wife would live in Paris, Tennessee.[23]

Pillow turned his attention to the law, working hard to build up a profitable practice with Harris. Harris maintained he "never saw a man he thought could live under the amount of work Gen. Pillow performed." He had no more money to dump into farm operations, and this lack of capital investment would eventually prove self-destructive. Pillow became an absentee landlord, leaving farm operations in the hands of his sons-in-law John D. Mitchell and Wilbur F. Johnson, on the Arkansas plantations, and Melville Williams at Clifton. The labor situation soured; complaints against Pillow's overseers increased, and hearings were held before civil magistrates. Planting on shares meant enforcing rents and attaching the black tenants' cotton. Unstable cotton prices worried Pillow as he watched them drop to seven cents a pound in 1869. Flooding was another worry; his land lay dangerously close to the St. Francis and the Mississippi, and more than once he would write, "How much of my cotton has gone under?"[24]

Politically, during 1867 Pillow appears to have worked to recruit blacks away from the Radical Republicans, encouraging them to abandon the Union League. He and Gen. T. C. Hindman held joint rallies of blacks and whites in Arkansas, appealing to them to unite and work together, accepting the Reconstruction Acts. Conservative southerners disagreed. Most rejected the acts outright and refused to cooperate in their enforcement. Pillow's critics pointed out that he curried the favor of the northern wing of the Democratic party—Horace Greeley "and his tribe." Pillow "seems to like," reported the Memphis *Avalanche*, "writing letters filled with matter well-suited to the taste of those who, for the present, are the disposers of glory and greenbacks."[25]

A crisis developed in Tennessee in 1868. That spring the Ku Klux Klan became very active, attempting to suppress or drive out particular Radicals in Middle and West Tennessee. They also intimidated certain freedmen, with the aim of disarming them and separating them from the Union League. An angered Governor Brownlow called the General Assembly into extra session and sought to create a state military force of loyal Union men to deal with the Klan. "Let the white and colored Radicals meet them promptly," wrote Brownlow, "and in the spirit of their own lawless mission, and disperse them, and if need require this in dispersing them, exterminate them." Brownlow's sentiments and action caused deep and widespread resentment; there was talk of violence, of civil war.

On July 31 Generals Cheatham, George Maney, and Bushrod Johnson asked to meet with the military affairs committee of the legislature to see what might be done to alleviate the situation. The following day in Nashville these generals met with ten other Confederate generals, including Pillow and Forrest. They drafted a memorial to the governor and General Assembly and had John C. Brown present it. Conciliatory and responsible in tone, the petition sought to "avert the precipitation of the crisis which is acknowledged to be imminent." They assured the assembly they did not seek to overthrow the state government and "do not believe there is an organization in Tennessee with such a purpose." If it did exist, it would receive "no sympathy or affiliation" from the generals. They expressed the opinion that it was "unwise for the legislature to organize a military force." They promised to use their influence to support the law but reminded the assembly that when "the large mass of white men in Tennessee are denied the right to vote or hold office, it is not wonderful or unnatural there should exist more or less dissatisfaction among them." They urged that disenfranchisement be removed to "heal all the wounds of our State."

The General Assembly responded. It was glad to receive the pledge of cooperation from Pillow and his fellow generals for the maintenance of peace. Yet the assembly and the governor, they emphasized, stood fast in their conviction to protect by whatever means necessary the loyal people of both races in Middle and West Tennessee. Gen. George Thomas, a key figure in the volatile situation, seemed sufficiently encouraged by the action of the Confederate leaders to leave the state and serve on a court-martial in Washington. Nevertheless, the Tennessee legislature, despite the gesture of the Confederate generals, went ahead and passed a law providing for the raising of troops to suppress the Klan and another to fine and imprison individuals belonging to or aiding the Klan. Although the gulf between the factions would widen even further, the days of Brownlow's power were drawing to an end. The attempt to recruit the necessary militia companies brought a disappointing number of volunteers. The people of Tennessee seemed to be saying they wanted peace and an end to Radical rule.[26]

Brownlow departed Tennessee for Washington in 1869 to take a quiet seat in the Senate. That year also saw the capture of Tennessee's legislature by conservatives. One of their first acts was the incorporation of the Mississippi Valley Immigration Company. Pillow was behind this, aided by his friends Harris and Forrest. On July 13, 1869, the Chinese Labor Convention, called by the Memphis Chamber of Commerce, had assembled at the Greenlaw Opera House in Memphis. Nearly 500 delegates attended; the Memphis *Daily Appeal* enthusiastically backed it. Pillow dominated the convention from the start and pushed through formation of a Chinese immigration corporation to be capitalized at $1 million ($2 million if circumstances allowed). Pillow reported that $100,000 was required initially, and he used the convention floor to promote the sale of shares. They sold slowly the first two days, until Pillow played his high card, placing before the convention a letter from Forrest stating that he intended to employ 1,000 Chinese workers and pay them in cash. Furthermore, the Selma, Meridian, and Memphis Railroad, of which Forrest was president, would subscribe $5,000 toward the stock company. Pillow then announced that a northern investor was putting up another $5,000. Before the convention adjourned the total had reached $60,000 pledged. The project was not popular, however, even though it promised the South a cheap source of dependable labor. Opposition quickly developed. New Orleans papers and the New York *Tribune* attacked the company on nativist grounds. Funding lagged badly. Finally, the Mississippi Valley Immigration Company was poisoned by the Tennessee General Assembly when it passed the enabling act with a fatal rider attached: "Nothing in the Act shall be so construed as to authorize the importation of Chinese into Tennessee, by said company."[27]

Earlier in 1869 Pillow had involved himself in a dangerous situation in Arkansas. According to refugees who sought protection in Memphis, the militia of the military district across the river were terrorizing residents. The militia commander refused to withdraw his men. The refugees wired President-elect Grant, but he replied that he would support state authority fully. They considered driving out the militia by force but decided instead to attempt negotiation and requested Arkansas Gov. Powell Clayton to turn over citizens being held by military authority in Crittenden County to local courts for trial. They went a step further and engaged Pillow to represent them. Pillow reacted with vigor. He appealed to Clayton, asking permission to hold a "law and order" meeting in the county. To allay the governor's fear of violence, he offered himself as a "personal hostage"; this prompted Clayton to go to Crittenden County himself. He did send most of the militia home but refused to lift martial law in the county.[28]

During this time the activist Pillow and his partner Harris helped to revive the moribund Confederate Historical Association in Memphis, which had been founded in 1866. With Harris as president and Pillow soliciting members, the society grew to 225 members and in 1870 was granted a charter by the state. Pillow corresponded widely with individuals attempting to write biographies or campaign accounts; he was most interested, of course, in documents and writings touching on Donelson and the Army of Tennessee. A member of the society observed that Pillow "was a man of unquestioned courage, fine address and high culture, a charming conversationalist, and in all respects a typical chivalric Southern gentleman of the best school." [29]

Pillow also encouraged the formation of St. Lazarus Episcopal Church in Memphis. Former Confederates, including Jefferson Davis, wanted a parish of their own and created St. Lazarus, with a former chaplain of the Army of Tennessee as rector. Pillow served St. Lazarus as vestryman, being first elected in 1869.[30]

Memphis may have been a fine setting for the frenetic Pillow, but things were not going well back home in Maury. In January 1869, the Merchants Bank filed suit against Pillow, as did W. J. Dale and others in a separate suit; meanwhile, the old Planters Bank case dragged on in chancery court at Columbia. His son George, who had been drinking heavily, frightened the family with his continued suicide attempts; Gideon Pillow suggested to Mary that the time had come to commit George to an asylum.

Then, suddenly, like a terrible, blinding bolt of lightning, Mary died. She had been at church on Sunday, October 4, 1869, and came home for lunch; she collapsed during the meal and died that evening, at the age of fifty-seven. When Pillow returned home from Memphis, he buried her at neighboring St. John's Church.[31] An adoring, totally uncritical wife, Mary had provided essential stability in the life of her husband. She was the mistress of Clifton in the fullest sense, remaining there with her children for almost twenty years while Gideon Pillow engaged in public affairs and developed his Arkansas empire. She bore him fourteen children, four of whom had died in infancy; Gideon, Jr., had perished in the steamboat accident. A quiet woman, she made and kept good friends and seemed to be universally well liked and respected. Her friend from girlhood, Caroline O'Reilly

Gideon Johnson Pillow, about 1870
(courtesy John R. Neal)

Nicholson, wrote, "No purer type of womanhood blessed the earth." The *Lincoln County News* remarked, "She always carried her religion with her . . . but not of the Puritanical order." From Pillow's correspondence and actions, it appears clear he was devoted to her until the day he died.[32]

Pillow kept his family at Clifton for a year after Mary's death and then moved with his three unmarried daughters and son Robert to Memphis. Before the Pillows left Maury, they had the grandest wedding of the season at St. John's in September 1870, when Margaret married Capt. Daniel Fountain Wade. "Miles of buggies could be seen headed for the little church."[33]

Pillow always held hopes for something to turn up on the national scene. He felt he uniquely represented the South and could interpret the South for national leaders. The election of Ulysses S. Grant in 1868 had given him hope, prompting a letter expressing gratitude for Grant's attitude toward the South and for "resisting Mr. Johnson's wish to have the Govt prosecute Genl Lee and others in violation of the Honor of your trust to his army." He referred to his own "*quiet* and submission to the authority of the Government," closing the letter by assuring Grant that he had no ulterior motives in writing him. Pillow carefully kept channels open. Grant's appointment of Pillow's friend Henry S. Foote as superintendent of the New Orleans mint was observed and noted.[34]

Yet Pillow's unhappy relations with Jefferson Davis worsened in 1870. Following a reception in Memphis, Davis wrote Pillow, "Your remarks of last evening suggested that you had accusations to make in regard to me, which were suppressed for the occasion; I therefore invite you to the full expression of whatever you have to say against me." Pillow replied immediately in his usual bold but equivocal manner: "I decline to enter upon any discussion of past events. . . . You certainly misapprehended me. . . . You ought to be sensible of the injustice done me, in your manifestation of temper. Whenever you are sensible of that fact, its acknowledgement, is all that is necessary to a restoration of our past relations." It is doubtful if their relations were ever restored, although they would appear together publicly from time to time.[35]

Memphis was booming. Brick buildings seemed to go up by the day; trade increased quickly, as did the population. Pillow wrote John D. Mitchell that his law practice was "increasing so fast" that he must rely on Mitchell to manage his Swan Lake Plantation. "It is impossible for me to be here and there at the same time." He warned Mitchell that the next cotton crop would be crucial. "I shall lose my homes if you fail to make a successful year's work."[36] The firm of Harris and Pillow prospered, however, "doing the big business of Memphis," although there were some 300 lawyers struggling to earn dollars in the city.[37] Pillow had become chairman of the West Tennessee Bar and there was talk, editorials even, of his qualifications for the Supreme Court of Tennessee. He was further complimented in 1871 by Col. Benjamin Thomas of the Arkansas Committee of Public Works, who asked him to prepare an opinion of the constitutionality of the Arkansas levee tax law of 1871. In an opinion that was printed and distributed, Pillow strongly supported the law, calling it a "wise, liberal and safe system of reclamation for the State and its people. . . . I entertain not a doubt about the constitutionality of the Act of 1871." To its opponents, the levee tax law clearly was "*beneficent* to the planter" and paid an extra premium to the railroads, already receiving heavy state subsidies for each mile constructed.[38]

In the summer of 1872, Pillow attended the Democratic National Convention in Baltimore. What, if any, role he played there is unclear, but he openly expressed himself "in unyielding opposition to Horace Greeley, no matter in what shape he appears." He told reporters the black vote would be "solid" for Grant. On this trip Pillow appears to have approached either Grant or one of his lieutenants. His aim, other than securing an appointment, seems to have been a trade-off: his support for Grant in return for reimbursement for his 235 treasured mules, "mules so fine they commanded popular attention when seen on the road." To Grant's aide, Horace Porter, he wrote: "I cannot live without these means. If I advocate his [Grant's] election I *literally cut my own throat*, and defeat my only hope in the future. If I am paid for my mules I can then act independently of this *duress* . . . and would make my *strength* & *influence* felt for Genl Grant. . . . Nearly the entire Southern press are upon me & many—very many of my personal & Political friends." Grant would have none of the Pillow accommodation, and soon word of Pillow's claims provided attractive copy. "His wonderful impudence," said the *New York Times*, "will lead to payment for slaves and then leave the government impoverished." He will "henceforth hear the ceaseless tramping of his lost mules haunting his dreams." This man has "exhibited decidedly more cheek than falls to the usual lot of a dozen ordinary pillows."[39]

Pillow continued his financial juggling with great skill. Holding creditors at bay, he managed to pay off some here, some there. He sold Arkansas land to pay taxes; he managed to compromise the

Pointer suit and relieve his friend William E. Woodruff and others from their bonds as his security, at least in that suit; he had to give new bonds in regard to the pressing Pittsburgh coal case. For a while in the fall of 1871 it appeared all claims against him might be settled successfully, and he might end up with a significant portion of his property. "These mountains are thrown off my shoulders. I feel that I am a man again. I thank God for his goodness and mercy towards me in these great *deliverances.*" Nevertheless, the strain told. He became sharp with his son-in-law Mitchell, who quarreled with him over money and demanded a salary for managing his Arkansas properties. "You should show a little respect for me, my interests or judgments."[40]

Pillow had his sons George and Robert with him in early 1872, but George did not enjoy life in Memphis. He moved down to Mound Plantation to join the colony of Pillow children—Narcissa and John Mitchell and Lizzie (Martha Elizabeth) and Capt. W. F. Johnson. There they worried with their father about "cotton, *always cotton.*" Could they gin enough to keep the Arkansas tax collectors from their door? To satisfy this demand for back taxes, in November 1872 Pillow authorized his agent Woodruff to sell all of his Drew County land.

George evidently did not like the solitude of Arkansas plantation life either, so he returned to Maury, where he died August 26, 1872, at age thirty-three. The Columbia *Herald*, with startling nineteenth-century candor, described George M. Pillow as a "man of powerful intellect and much learning, and he might have made his name even more famous than his illustrious father, but for a total lack of ambition."[41]

Pillow cut his ties with Maury County. He conveyed Clifton to his daughter Sallie Polk and her husband, Melville Williams, who had been married at Clifton the year before. In Memphis he purchased a large Greek Revival home of 6,000 square feet, set back on a hill, high above unpaved Adams Street. He would live there the rest of his life.[42]

Pillow would need a large, elegant home, well suited for entertaining and an active social life, for he had decided to marry again. He had met and fallen in love with a twenty-eight-year-old widow, Maria Eliza Dickson Trigg, daughter of a wealthy cotton planter, Michael Dickson, of Bossier Parish, Louisiana, and his wife, Hannah Palmer.[43] During the war Mary Eliza Dickson had married, at age thirteen, James B. Trigg. They lived on a Red River plantation in Louisiana until Trigg, whom Mary Eliza described as a "profligate young man," died in June 1866. Trigg bequeathed his wife and their infant daughter "a stack of debts and an estate from his father that lunged into red figures when the Trigg creditors emerged after the war."[44] By 1872 Mrs. Trigg's resources were dwindling dangerously.

Gideon Pillow apparently did not know this. He saw a fashionable, highly attractive young woman of "queenly presence, daring, wit and polish." She needed help, a champion. The Federal government had seized a great amount of Mrs. Trigg's Louisiana cotton during the war, at a time when she was still a minor. Pillow believed Mary Eliza had a good claim, and he offered his services. Who had more experience than Pillow in fighting off creditors and attempting to reclaim property lost in the war? They understood each other, or thought they did. So they returned to Louisiana and on November 29, 1872, were married in New Orleans by Archbishop Napoleon J. Perché. Then Pillow and his young Catholic bride dashed back to Memphis in time for him to give away his youngest daughter Alice in marriage to a Memphian, Daniel P. Fargason. It all made for a grand and exciting 1872 Christmas season.[45]

The new Mrs. Pillow pleased her husband very much. She knew how he revered the memory of his first wife and, probably because of this, began to refer to herself also as Mary E. Pillow,[46] a practice confounding to latter day genealogists. In a demonstration of unusual practicality she had consented to a prenuptial contract. They agreed to keep their estates separate, and Pillow went so far as to acknowledge notes payable to his daughter, Mary Amanda Brown.[47]

After Christmas Pillow and "his handsome young bride" took a long wedding trip. First they traveled to Maury and met many of the family. Friends thought he "never looked handsomer or in better health." Then they journeyed on to Washington. They stayed at the Arlington Hotel, and nothing would do but for Pillow to introduce Mary Eliza to the president. Pillow, it seems, fully intended not only to impress his bride, but to throw her impeccable cotton claims before the highest authority. To Pillow's mortification, however, the audience with Grant was short, stiff, and probably curt. Afterward Grant recanted and wrote Pillow a note inviting the couple to pay a social call upon him and his wife.

Pillow used the opportunity to write back a letter from Memphis effusive in thanks for the invitation, dismissing the incident at the White House as due more to "your pressing engagements, than to intentional indifference." The couple had intended to pay their respects, Pillow went on, to express their "*steadfast* and *immoveable*" support of Grant's administration and joy at his election. "I was known

Mary Eliza Dickson Pillow
(courtesy John R. Neal)

all over the country" to be for you over Greeley, despite "strong appeals made to me through the press and letters." And Pillow went on, for nine more pages, lecturing Grant on the proper policy toward the southern people: "If your Policy as the Chief executive of the Nation should be as wise, as was your talants [*sic*] skill and success as a General in the Field," Grant will "rank with Washington in greatness and glory." Pillow spoke of the South's "misguided *political teachings*" and suggested that the president needed "some sensible & prudent southern Friend of your own (not *politician*) as your agent." With disarming modesty, Pillow added, "I seek no place," but he closed his letter urging Grant to give his attention to a matter (the cotton claims) about which his wife had written him.[48]

Two months later Pillow wrote Grant again, without the slightest indirection. "I should feel most grateful for the appointment of Judge on the Supreme Court of the U.S. I suppose it would be deemed *indelicate in me*, to say that I suppose there is no Southern lawyer, who would be more acceptable to the Southern people."[49]

Throughout 1873–74 Pillow worked hard building a case for Mary Eliza Dickson Pillow's cotton claims. He traveled to Louisiana taking depositions and seeking "proof" of the seizure of the Dickson cotton, a wedding gift to Mary Eliza from her father at the time of her marriage to Trigg. The Pillows also sued for recovery of other confiscated cotton bought by Trigg using his wife's money. Mary Eliza welcomed Pillow's help. She had sued as a minor in 1865 for recovery of her property but was unsuccessful, the government arguing that half of the cotton she claimed to own had been sold previously to the Confederate government by her father, and that she had been fully reimbursed for the remainder. Pillow, like a bulldog, saw an opportunity under an act of 1872 which instructed the Treasury Department to restore to the rightful owners proceeds of cotton seized unlawfully. Pillow gathered scores of depositions, bills of lading, warehouse receipts, and the like. He used the testimony of former Dickson slaves, one of whom, Samuel Thomas, had been a "house boy" but was now a member of the Louisiana legislature. He even went to the trouble of having his brief printed. His efforts failed, however, and the Pillows' claim for $90,000 was dismissed finally on the grounds, as in 1865, that the cotton was "Confederate cotton" and not the property of Mrs. Trigg/Pillow.[50]

To Pillow's surprise, Mary Eliza's debts surfaced with embarrassing regularity. Then Olympe Boisse, a New Orleans dressmaker, sued her for about $4,000, mostly for dresses and ladies' apparel purchased by her in the late 1860s.[51] Mary Eliza, at the advice of her husband, who represented her, answered Boisse's bill in the chancery court of Shelby County in May 1875, listing debts of $53,000 (including $20,000 to Gideon Pillow for legal services) and declaring bankruptcy.[52]

In 1874 Granville Pillow's daughter Susan and his wife, Olive, became involved in a lawsuit over a note Granville had given his brother Gideon to collect. The knotty case was settled out of court, but it alienated family members, with Susan and Olive charging Gideon Pillow with having collected Granville's note and "appropriated monies to his own use" and Pillow objecting to the competency of Olive.[53]

Publicly, Pillow kept up a good front; as always, he faced adversity with contempt and frenzied activity. He carefully maintained his contacts in the legal profession. He attended the decoration of the graves of Union soldiers at the National Cemetery near Memphis as a spectator. Out of courtesy he was called upon to speak and did so eloquently: "All around us lie buried in this cemetery those who died for their country." In the presence of his law partner Harris and Bedford Forrest, who also attended, he told of the "great pain" it gave him to take up arms against the United States. Then, lightening his tone, he brought laughter and applause with the statement, "Even the dread of the gallows did not scare me away from treason." With seriousness, he concluded, "Still we can claim the honor that we are all Americans. . . . It is my government and I would not live under any other." After all the speechmaking came a grand mixing of Federals and Confederates.[54]

More mixing came on July 5. Pillow and Forrest were invited to speak at the annual celebration of the Independent Order of Polebearers at the Memphis Fairgrounds. Five thousand blacks attended this gala, honoring the oldest and most prestigious of black fraternal orders. Hezekiah Henley, a blacksmith and founder of the Polebearers, presided. A man "of vision, a patriot," who wanted "to see black children in schools competing with whites in the race for knowledge and in the professions," Henley held out his hand. Forrest responded graciously. Pillow, knowing Memphis blacks had wavered in their support of the Republican party since the collapse of the Freedman's Savings and Trust in September 1873, spoke pointedly: "You and I are equal before the law. . . . No power on earth could re-enslave you." No government "can place you in ease and wealth. . . . You need most the means of education. . . . The two races have a common interest in each other's welfare." Then the years of frustration began to break through, the pain of indifference from Grant and the Republicans. "Discard all partisan views . . . , disband all colored political organizations," he urged them, raising the banner of southern Democrats. The Yankees "have ruled and ruined the country since the war, and by your support. . . . My colored friends give up politics as a pursuit."[55]

Pillow's ruin came in 1876. The joint practice with Harris had ended in 1874, very probably with animosity. All that remained was an unresolved suit (Williams v. Whitmore) in which Harris had to account for Pillow's having taken the payments of Williams and Whitmore and "appropriated to his own use." Pillow's action, though not illegal, left him indebted financially to Harris.[56] Throughout 1875 Pillow's other creditors—the Planters Bank of Nashville, the Merchants Bank of Kentucky, the Bank of Tennessee, and the Pittsburgh coal company—kept up the pressure. "Step by step they track me up, and hound after me as their victim." Finally, Gideon Pillow filed for bankruptcy, listing as assets Mound Plantation (1,100 acres) and Brown Plantation (710 acres) in Lee County, Arkansas, and his residence on Adams Street in Memphis. Among the thirty-seven claimants were his old Arkansas friend of convenience, H. P. Coolidge (for $1,000), his sons-in-law Daniel Fargason and Melville Williams, his daughter Mary A. Brown, Isham G. Harris (for $2,200), Mrs. W. S. Pickett (Knox Walker's sister), and Bushrod Johnson (for the education of his son Robert).[57] The home on Adams Street was auctioned on February 14, 1876. There was no competition in the bidding, and the house and Pillow's fine library were sold separately. An unidentified gentleman (believed to be a family friend, Col. H. Clay King) stepped forward and bought both and presented them to Mrs. Pillow. King also appears to have purchased Mound Plantation.[58]

Utter desperation led Pillow to write the New York *Tribune* on February 24 explaining his status, fighting back with thinly disguised irony against their "*kind sympathetic* notice of my Bankruptcy." He debased himself in this pathetic letter: "I am without hope for the future . . . *homeless* . . . family without means . . . with *gaunt poverty* staring me in the face, at my advanced age." The New York editors heartlessly interpolated phrasing in Pillow's letter and published it under the title, "The Pillow Mules: The General not a Willing Belligerent in the Civil War."[59]

Turning and twisting in the wind, Pillow applied for a disability pension because of his Mexican War wounds. He lashed out against

Surviving children of Gideon Johnson Pillow; *left to right*: **Lizzie, Narcissa, Annie, Robert, Alice, Gertrude, and Sally** (*courtesy John R. Neal*)

his children and their husbands in suits against Narcissa and John Mitchell and in a larger suit (Pillow v. Wade) against the Mitchells, the Wades, the Williamses, and his brother Jerome over Mary Martin Pillow's dower and his debt to her of $60,000. The court ruled against Pillow in the latter suit, contending that the contract between Mary Martin Pillow and her husband was a nullity since "husband and wife are incapable of contracting with each other."[60]

He wrote Narcissa, bitterly complaining of her and her sisters. "I have felt very *deeply* their *silence* & apparent *forgetfulness* of their Father. That you all had cause to remember in *love*, him who had given you being, and who had supplied your wants in infancy." Pillow spoke of his "bitter cup of alienation," and when he made his will in April 1876, it would spell out the deep resentment he felt toward three of his daughters and their husbands. The little he owned would go to Mary Eliza Dickson Pillow and their three children: Mary Eliza, Annie Payne, and Gideon Johnson, Jr. He hoped his wife could do something for Robert and Gertrude, "for whom as yet I have done nothing."[61]

The disputed election of 1876, which brought Republican Rutherford B. Hayes to the presidency, revived Pillow somewhat. He sought and received support from General Sherman for a "mid level office," although nothing came of it. As self-styled spokesman for a group of southerners, he wrote Hayes in March 1877 supporting the appointments of David M. Key of Tennessee as postmaster general and W. M. Waldron as U.S. marshal and attacking the "carpet bag & bourbon democratic parties . . . that have held our Southern Country down since the war."[62] Pillow went to Washington in the late spring of 1877 and there applied "through others" for appointment as circuit judge. The New York *Sun* learned of it and blasted the notion of a "carpet bagger from the South" succeeding Judge Halmer H. Emmons of the Sixth District (Michigan, Ohio, Kentucky, and Tennessee). Pillow broke into print again with his response, acknowledging that he had voted for Tilden and had thought the election of Hayes "a misfortune for the South." He had changed his mind, of course, and "in my long and eventful life, this is my first application for any position in the Federal Government."[63]

The judgeship did not work out, but Pillow, still in Washington, wrote Hayes thanking him for his attitude and actions toward the South, which he felt reversed the "unfriendly treatment" of Grant. He proceeded in a very long letter to advise Hayes to acquire the boundary with Mexico he had recommended to Polk thirty years earlier. He called on Hayes before he left for Memphis and offered his services in defense of his policies and administration.[64]

Pillow spent his remaining days close to poverty. He and his son Robert maintained a law office in Memphis, but his practice was sadly reduced. He tried vainly to rent land to plant, made spasmodic efforts to revive Mary Eliza's cotton claims, and accepted invitations to speak on ceremonial occasions.[65]

On August 13, 1878, Mrs. Kate Bionda, who ran a small store for river men in Memphis, died of yellow fever. An "overly cautious" city board of health did not declare an epidemic until ten days later. Death swept through the town in late August and early September, claiming as many as 200 a day. Terrified citizens raced to escape; trains were filled and platforms "packed to suffocation." The Pillows fled also, crossing the Mississippi to seek refuge on the St. Francis River.

Yellow fever stalked its victim, however. At Mound Plantation in Lee County, Pillow died a slow, agonizing death on October 8, 1878.[66] The *New York Times* reported that he died of congestion of the brain, dismissing the life and death of this "man of suave manners" who had made good copy for their editors for thirty years. "His most notable military achievement was the digging of a trench in the wrong place at Saltillo."[67]

Gideon Pillow was buried at Mound Plantation, in an "Arkansas swamp." Later, Mary Eliza's friend, Col. H. Clay King, would pay for having the body reinterred at Elmwood Cemetery in Memphis. It would be 100 years before a monument would mark the grave.[68]

Epilogue

Gideon Pillow ended his days embattled. His will, prepared at age seventy, is a rambling argument, a lawyer's brief, laden with cross bills, assignees, and bills of revivor. He pointed a finger at those who had held him personally responsible for his actions as a Confederate officer and bankrupted him. He complimented his new wife Mary Eliza for her "*unselfish* and *generous nature*" and then snapped about and censured "some of my daughters and their husbands" for having "greatly added to my troubles and embarrassments." "For this wrong I hope God will forgive them," he wrote, although he himself would not. This curious, contradictory document also contains a personal profession of faith, for Pillow lived and died a religious man:

"My confidence in the goodness of God and my faith in the merits of the atoning blood of his son the Lord, our Savior, to wash me of my sins, has accompanied me and sustained me through all the trials of my long and eventful life. I *know* my *spirit* is of *God*, and I willingly commit it to him who gave it relying upon his mercy and the atoning blood of his son as the rock of my faith."[1]

Repentant yet unforgiving, Pillow, the master equivocator, exasperates those who would be sympathetic. One can overlook, as did many of his soldiers, his posturing, his bombast, his pretense, his whining, his grand mistakes, but he inevitably provokes students of his life and career with his total and foolish lack of self-examination. Why could he not step back from himself and admit an error? Did he not wonder why men of good will flinched in his presence? Angry and puzzled by those who "have not been *just* to *me*," Pillow remained, in his own eyes, an injured innocent, a victim who blamed others—those who doubted his motives and would not play by the rules, as he understood them. But he was quick to bend or break the rules himself. Eventually this habit of oblivious self-justification and the ready alibi maimed him far worse than the Mexican ball that ruined his leg.

Yet one is attracted to him. A bright, spinning engine of a man, Pillow could make humdrum paper shuffling in some remote headquarters tent exciting and important. People had to notice him; this celebrity made grand entrances and good copy. The little southeastern Missouri villages in 1861 must have thought Napoleon himself had arrived to liberate them from the Hessians. Was he playacting? No one knew for sure. He loved the Union and he loved Tennessee, and yet these passions in him were hopelessly mixed with self-interest and could be set aside conveniently. If one could only whirl contradictions and values fast enough they could be reconciled and new truth emerge. Thus one could ride off to fight another day and leave fellow Tennesseans to their fate in the snow. Thus, in his "anxiety to return to his allegiance," one might entertain thoughts of giving up and withdrawing to idyllic Clifton while war raged. Honor went only so far, after all.

This prince of pretense had every advantage and could have become a significant figure in American history. Industrious, intelligent, charming, highly persuasive, he was a promoter and organizer of the first order, and he usually thought on a grand scale. He was a man of promise—and always thought of himself as such. James K. Polk agreed; he was drawn to the man and trusted him. So did Billy Carroll; so did Franklin Pierce; so did Isham G. Harris, Braxton Bragg, and the Johnstons. And so, for a while, did his enemy Winfield Scott, who offered this choice insight: "An anomaly," this Gideon Pillow, "without the least malignity in his nature—amiable and possessed of some acuteness, but the only person I have ever known who was wholly indifferent in the choice between truth and falsehood, honesty and dishonesty."[2]

Truth for Pillow was refracted through a political prism. Reality could be manipulated, and it should be. Transcendent causes should be supported and fought for but never allowed to become a mainspring of behavior. Thus it follows that one wrote battle reports, newspaper articles, and wills like legal briefs, stuffed with selected evidence, basted with overstatement and understatement. One was justified in paying painter James Walker to position the right men in the right places at the storming of Chapultepec. Certainly one should provide sanctuary, good food, and elegant surroundings for an impressionable Roswell Ripley—and sit by his elbow as he prepared the definitive history of the Mexican War.

Pillow invented himself as well; he spent a lifetime defining and defending the character. The story about the Indian and the young child that opened this biography is apocryphal, probably, as much so as the account of Gideon slaying the Mexican officer at Churubusco's tête de pont. To dismiss these tales entirely, however, would be as wrongheaded as to include them uncritically. There is a basis of truth in each, and, as Pillow undoubtedly knew, biographies of classical heroes often open with mysterious occurrences and divine touchings. While Pillow's attempt to create the legend of Gideon Johnson Pillow is not singular, it failed, it seems, because he collected enemies faster than he could friends, and he made friends quite easily.

The dark side of Pillow lies not so much in his remorseless pursuit of recognition, which he tempered with irrepressible displays of cheerfulness, optimism, generosity, enthusiasm, and good will, but in his infatuation with secretiveness. He gloried in having an opponent, be he a Martin Van Buren, a Zachary Taylor, or a Winfield Scott, brought down by a blow from an unseen assailant. Pillow would conceal, or attempt to conceal, his most self-interested maneuvers even from his beloved Mary or his devoted friend Polk.

As a friend, Pillow was demanding and emotionally expensive. He used people. He tended to look upon colleagues, and certainly immediate superiors, as rivals, to be undermined, to be deposed. Jealousy ate him alive. His life, therefore, is a long, painful trail of broken relationships and bitter recriminations. He seemed to take joy in revenge, and he imputed this tendency within himself into the actions of others. Why else, thought Pillow, would Jefferson Davis refuse to retract his statement of "grave errors of judgment" regarding his behavior at Donelson?

To define him as a soldier is not difficult. His concept of the citizen soldier had been formed for him by Andrew Jackson and Billy Carroll and his uncle William, yet their dogma led him to despise what he most needed—professionalism. It is doubtful if he ever read a tactics manual—he had staff officers for that. It is doubtful if he ever learned to drill a regiment, not to mention a brigade. But he knew how to conduct an inspection, and he knew the value of parades. He gave little evidence of being able to use intelligence gained from reconnaissance; he had little appreciation of terrain from a military perspective. He fought one battle that demonstrated military skill and promise—Contreras. There his holding action with Twiggs, coupled with a bold but risky flanking march by Riley and Cadwalader, won the day and merits admiration. In his other battles—Cerro Gordo, Churubusco, Chapultepec, Belmont, Donelson, Murfreesboro, Lafayette— he always attacked, usually in a mindless manner, usually with high casualties. One can hardly imagine a more aggressive field tactician. Joseph Johnston seems to have been correct in his view that Pillow would have made a good infantry division commander.

But who would have commanded him? Leonidas Polk tried and failed, as did many others. Pillow required constant praise, recognition, and tender loving care. He wore his skin inside out, and when offended, he would strike back like a copperhead. He made quarrels with almost everyone with whom he served, seemingly unable to work within any system. His attitude of self-entitlement annoyed the fair-minded. His military counsel tended to be flawed, as superiors who wilted before his powerful personality or who made the mistake of trusting him discovered. He cost the Confederacy precious momentum in Missouri in 1861; he sowed distrust and discord within the leadership of the Army of Tennessee; while at Columbus he sabotaged Sidney Johnston's attempts to strengthen the river forts; and his reckless insistence on offensive action placed enthusiastic Tennessee volunteers at Donelson where they were abandoned shamelessly.

To dismiss him as a military buffoon, however, is simplistic and wrong, although a very large cabal of professional soldiers, including two dozen of the most renowned names in American military history, worked to create and sustain this image. Sherman is typical, viewing Pillow as "a mass of vanity, conceit, ignorance, ambition, and want of truth." In their eyes, Pillow's sin was not so much being a bungling amateur—there were many of those indulged by the professionals—but in being powerful enough politically to rattle the military establishment and to bring down the greatest soldier of pre–Civil War America, Winfield Scott.

Pillow could fight, and he could get others to fight with him, as Chapultepec and the first day at Donelson demonstrate. But his talents lay elsewhere; his feats in mobilizing the Army of Tennessee in 1861 and helping to revive it in the winter of 1863–64 are evidence of that. In 1861, however, Pillow thought and acted in the short term, as did Harris and so many Confederates. Preparing for a long war of attrition and developing the economic sinews of war were beyond his vision. He intended to put an army of Tennesseans into the field as quickly as Jackson could have called out Uncle William and his militia. Pillow required guidance and control; Jefferson Davis, however, showed little imagination in properly directing these powerful energies and abilities. Abraham Lincoln did far better with Pillow's mirror image in Illinois, John McClernand.

Politically, Pillow was handicapped by the notoriety fastened on him by the Mexican War; it is doubtful if he ever understood this. He believed the image he created of "the hero of Chapultepec" authentic. Perhaps it was, but not in the perception of Americans at large. Pillow maneuvered carefully for years, cultivating support in New England, Pennsylvania, and New York; no politician of the Democracy save Douglas stood in a better position for the presidency in the 1850s than this Jacksonian, Unionist war hero. He opposed secession and stood for compromise and moderation in a time of extremists, but he was tainted by his aggressive defense of slavery and expansion and by snickers behind his back about the ditch at Camargo. Did they see, this Democracy that he so loved and seemed to understand so well, a man without real substance, driven by powerful hungers—a dangerous man?

Gideon Pillow's dream of becoming a second Andrew Jackson, a James K. Polk with sword in hand, perished along with his material wealth. His beloved Clifton passed to others, and he died across the river.

Appendix 1.
And Afterward

BROWN, THOMAS JAMES, would return to Maury with his wife, Mary Amanda Pillow, after ten years in Giles County, and die near Columbia in January 1878, mourned by Gideon Pillow.

BUCKNER, SIMON BOLIVAR, would become a newspaper editor, governor of Kentucky, and, in 1896, a vice-presidential nominee of the Democratic party. The mention of Donelson, however, would cut him like a whip and, when he was an older man, bring tears to his eyes. He died at ninety-one in 1914.

BURCH, JOHN CHRISTOPHER, would purchase controlling interest in the Nashville *Union and American* in 1869 and again become its chief editor. He would move on in 1873 to become state comptroller and in 1879 would be elected secretary of the U.S. Senate. He died in Washington in 1881.

CADWALADER, GEORGE, would rise to major general in the Union army, although he would sit out the war in the Philadelphia area, suspected by many of having southern sympathies. A "don't-give-a-damn sportsman and bonviveur," he would die wealthy and beloved in Philadelphia in 1879.

CAMPBELL, WILLIAM BOWEN, would accept a brigadier general's commission in the Union army but grow dispirited and resign in 1863. He would become a close ally of Andrew Johnson and work hard to have Tennessee restored "on a conservative basis." His reelection to Congress in 1865 would be opposed by Radical Republicans, and he would die in 1867.

CASWELL, WILLIAM RICHARD, would attempt to serve the Confederacy loyally in East Tennessee and for his trouble have his throat cut in 1862.

CLIFTON PLACE would be swapped by Melville and Sallie Polk Pillow Williams to Col. J. W. S. Ridley (son-in-law of Jerome Pillow) for another Maury farm and cash in March 1876. The Ridleys would retain possession until 1972, when it passed into the loving hands of Linda and John R. Neal, who set about patiently and meticulously restoring Clifton.

CUSHING, CALEB, would chair the 1860 Democratic convention at Baltimore and draw close to Andrew Johnson after the war. Grant would appoint him to negotiate a treaty for a ship canal across the Isthmus of Panama in 1872, and he would represent the United States in the arbitration of the *Alabama* claims. He almost became chief justice of the Supreme Court in 1874 and did become envoy extraordinary to Spain. He died in Newburyport in 1879.

HARRIS, ISHAM GREEN, would practice law successfully following his separation from Pillow, return to political life, and be elected U.S. Senator in 1877. He would serve until his death in 1897.

HASKELL, WILLIAM TURNER, would go to Congress as a Whig in March 1847 for one term, practice law for a while, and die in an asylum in 1859.

HOOKER, JOSEPH, would rise to fame as a soldier and fall even more rapidly. By 1864 he appeared a "used up man." Controversial until his death in 1879, he had himself immortalized, like Pillow, by James Walker in a giant painting of the battle of Lookout Mountain.

HUMPHREYS, WEST HUGHES, would never resign his federal judgeship, although he became Confederate district judge for Tennessee. He would enter private practice after the war and become active in the temperance movement. He died in 1882.

JOHNSON, CAVE, would become president of the Bank of Tennessee and, although elected as a Unionist, refuse to serve in the Tennessee senate. He died in 1866 at age seventy-three.

LAUGHLIN, SAMUEL HERVEY, would continue to reside in Washington and die there in 1850, after losing the job in the Land Office which he held during the Polk administration.

LEE, STEPHEN DILL, would assume command of Leonidas Polk's corps and rise to lieutenant general. He became the first president of Mississippi State College after the war and died in 1908.

LOCKHART, HARRISON CLAIBORNE, would return to Stewart County, Tennessee, and practice law until his death in 1878.

MOUND PLANTATION would burn February 22, 1881, "the work of incendiaries." Mrs. Pillow was in Memphis, and it was believed the caretaker and his family "had been chloroformed." Not long before, the cotton house had been destroyed and the gin set on fire. The twentieth century has seen the plantation slide into the Mississippi. A Corps of Engineers map for Latour, Arkansas, notes Mound Place Landing on a sandbar.

NEELY, JAMES J., would run afoul of Forrest in September 1864, protesting the elevation of Edmund W. Rucker to brigade command. Neely and several compatriots were charged with mutiny and cashiered.

NICHOLSON, ALFRED OSBORNE POPE, would serve as chief justice of the Tennessee Supreme Court from 1870 until his death in Maury in 1876. His son Hunter (Pillow's staff officer) would live into the twentieth century and become editor of the Washington *Union*.

PIERCE, FRANKLIN, would shout into the wind his fears of Republican extremists and his pleas for national unity and reconciliation. He would die unpopular and without honor in 1869.

PILLOW, ANNIE PAYNE (GROSS), would, for years, sell reproductions of the great seal of the Confederacy for $1 apiece to raise funds to erect a "modest monument" to her father. Unsuccessful, she would go to work for the War Department and die after 1935.

PILLOW, JEROME BONAPARTE, would die at age eighty-two on September 16, 1891, at the Maury home of his son-in-law (and former Gideon Pillow staff officer) Lemuel Long.

PILLOW, MARIE (MARY) ELIZA DICKSON TRIGG, would live on the edge of poverty the rest of her life, her only income the last thirty years being a

Mexican War widow's pension of $8 a month, which began in 1887 and was raised to $30 by a special act of Congress in 1904. She lived in Arkansas and Alabama until about 1890, when she moved to Washington, D.C. Her involvement with Col. H. Clay King (a Kentuckian who raised the Pillow Guards No. 2 in 1861) would end in monumental scandal, murder, litigation, and wide publicity. She would be struck by a streetcar in Washington and die on May 4, 1913, at the age of sixty-nine. As the widow of Gideon Pillow, hero of Chapultepec, she would be buried in Arlington National Cemetery.

PILLOW, ROBERT GIDEON, would die in Little Rock in 1918.

PILLOW, COL. WILLIAM, energetic Jacksonian to the end, would die in Maury in May 1868 at age eighty-seven.

POLK, WILLIAM HAWKINS, would oppose Isham G. Harris for governor in 1861 and lose. He formed a Confederate cavalry company called the Polk Guards, but when the guards did not elect him captain, he became a Unionist.

RAINS, GEORGE WASHINGTON, Mexican War staff officer of Pillow's, would become a first-rate scientist, the heart and soul of the Confederate munitions effort. Following the war he would distinguish himself as professor of chemistry at the medical school of the University of Georgia and die in 1898, seventeen years after his brother Gabriel, the Confederate land mine expert and Pillow's nemesis in the Conscript Department.

REYNOLDS, ROBERT BANNON, would disappear into the folds of the regular army paymaster corps and then surface at New Orleans between 1855 and 1860. April 1861 would find him at Fort Fillmore, New Mexico Territory, a post he resigned July 1. Refusing a commission as Confederate paymaster, he would become an East Tennessee commissioner under West Humphreys, jail Brownlow, and lose his Knoxville home and property as a result.

RICHARDSON, ROBERT VINKLER, would journey to Clarkton, Missouri, in 1870, promoting a railroad in which he and Forrest were interested. As he stopped for the night, from behind a wagon parked at his lodging would come a deadly load of buckshot from an unknown assassin.

RIPLEY, ROSWELL SABINE, after chasing Seminoles for a while, would join the Confederacy but, like the general he formerly served, would be "forever at odds with both his superiors and subordinates," including Lee, Cooper, and Pemberton. He would die in New York City in 1887 after failing in an English manufacturing venture.

ROGERS, ROBERT C., would rise from passed midshipman to acting master following the Mexican War, resign in 1854, and drop from sight.

TRIST, NICHOLAS PHILIP, too slippery for Gideon Pillow to handle, would remain loyal to Pillow's sometime antagonist, A. J. Donelson. The Mexican experience would finish him as a diplomat, so Trist would turn to the practice of law, at which he also proved unsuccessful. He would publicly denounce states' righters, vote for Lincoln, and become postmaster of Alexandria, Virginia, dying there in 1874.

WALKER, J. KNOX, would never recover from the guilt of watching his nephew Jimmie, Sam Walker's boy, perish at Belmont. He would die in occupied Memphis less than two years later.

WINSHIP, OSCAR F., would go west to fight against the Sioux in the early 1850s, translate Jomini's *Précis de l'Art de la Guerre* in 1853, and die at age thirty-eight in 1855.

Appendix 2.
Some of Gideon J. Pillow's
Staff Officers

Abernathy, John T., ADC,
November 1861, volunteer
commissary

Alison, Pvt. B. G., orderly

Anderson, Lt. Samuel S.,
ADC, 1846

Armstrong, William J.,
surgeon, 1863

Avent, B. W., surgeon, June 1861

Avery, Lt. Col. Isaac W., Conscript
Bureau, 1863

Ball, Maj. Charles G., P&CS,
March 1864

Barbee, Capt. Samuel E., ACS,
August 1861

Barber, Capt. James E., ACS, 1861

Bell, W. S., surgeon, August 1861

Bethel, Capt. William D., ADC,
Fall 1861

Blake, Capt. E. D., AAAG,
November 1861

Bradford, Hiram S., AAG, 1861

Brandon, Lt. Col. Nathan, ADC,
February 1862

Brown, Capt. Thomas James, ACS,
May 1863

Burch, Col. John C., ADC, AAG,
1861–64

Burns, Maj. Archibald W.,
paymaster, 1847

Cabler, Capt. L. F., AQM,
August 1861

Caldwell, Maj. George A., ADC,
AAAG, June 1847

Campbell, Maj. Alex W., A&IG,
August 1861; Conscript
Bureau, 1863

Carnes, W. W., ADC, drillmaster,
June 1861

Caswell, Capt. William R.,
AAAG, 1846

Cheatham, Edward, ADC,
September 1862

Cheatham, Maj. Munroe, AAQM,
February 1863

Coltart, Col. J. G., Conscript
Bureau, 1863

Conway, George W., surgeon, 1861

Deas, Bvt. Capt. George,
AAG, 1847

Derrick, Capt. Clarence, AAG,
February 1862

Dickson, William, QM,
November 1861

Echols, Lt. Col. J. W., Conscript
Bureau, 1863

Edwards, Capt. Owen H.,
AQM, 1861

Fackler, Maj. Calvin M., AQM,
August 1861

Fairly, Lt. John S., ADC,
February 1865

Finnie, Maj. John G., AQM,
August 1861

Gilmer, Maj. Jeremy F.,
February 1862

Glass, Maj. Presley T., AQM, June
1861–June 1864

Guy, Maj. William Wallace, AACS,
August 1861

Hammond, Maj. R. H.,
paymaster, 1846

Haynes, Maj. W. H., ACS,
February 1862

Henry, Capt. Gustavus A., Jr., AAG,
August 1861–February 1862
Hill, Capt. John S., AQM,
August 1861
Hooker, Capt. Joseph, chief of staff,
Mexican War
Humphries, J. Pillow, ADC,
May 1864
Jackson, Capt. William H., AADC,
November 1861
Johnson, Lt. William F., Spring 1864
Jones, Maj. J. Wyatt, AQM,
February 1862
Keller, J. M., surgeon, 1861
Key, Maj. William O., QM,
May 1864
Lay, Lt. Col. G. W., Conscript
Bureau, 1863
Lee, Henry B., ADC, June 1864
Lee, Pollock B., AAG, May 1861
Lockhart, Lt. Col. Harrison C.,
AAG, July 1861; Conscript
Bureau, 1863–64
Long, Lt. Lemuel, ADC,
June–November 1861, May 1864
Lovell, Lt. Mansfield, ADC,
Mexican War
McCormack, Charles, assistant
surgeon, 1861
McIver, Capt. E. J., AQM,
Spring 1863
Martin, Lt. Charles F., private
secretary, October
1861–February 1862
Martin, Lt. George S., ADC,
August 1861
Mason, Maj. Richard M., AQM,
August 1861
Moorman, George, ADC, 1861
Nicholson, Lt. Hunter, ADC,
February 1862, September 1862
O'Hara, Capt. Theodore, QM,
August 1847

Parker, Capt. J. P. (D), ordnance,
November 1861–February 1862
Perrin, E. B., surgeon
Peters, Maj. Thomas, AQM,
May 1862
Pickett, Capt. William D.,
engineering officer, 1861
Pillow, Capt. George M., ADC,
August–November 1861,
September 1862,
May–October 1864
Porter, Capt. John Davis, Jr., AAG,
Summer 1861
Portis, Capt. Thomas J., AAG,
August 1863
Rains, Lt. George Washington,
ADC, Mexican War
Reynolds, Capt. Robert B.,
QM, 1846
Rice, Maj. John E., ADC,
February 1862
Ripley, Lt. Roswell S., ADC,
Summer 1847–Spring 1848
Rogers, Passed Midshipman Robert
C., ADC, Summer 1847
Saunders, Capt. John E.,
December 1863
Stephenson, Vernon K., QM,
June 1861
Thompson, Capt. W. Vance, AAAG,
Fall 1863
Tyler, Maj. Robert C., AQM,
August 1861
Weakley, S. D. (probably Samuel
Morford W.), ADC,
November 1861
Wiggs, Capt. James A., AQM,
August 1861
Winship, Capt. Oscar F., AAAG,
1846–47

Notes

ABBREVIATIONS

BY   Beinecke Rare Book Library, Yale University, New Haven, Conn.
CV   *Confederate Veteran*
DU   Duke University, William R. Perkins Library, Durham, N.C.
GJP   Gideon Johnson Pillow
HLH   Houghton Library, Harvard University, Boston, Mass.
HSP   Historical Society of Pennsylvania, Philadelphia, Pa.
HUL   Huntington Library, San Marino, Calif.
JKP   James K. Polk
JRN   John R. Neal, Columbia, Tenn.
LOC   Library of Congress, Washington, D.C.
MEP   Mary Elizabeth Martin Pillow
MHS   Massachusetts Historical Society, Boston, Mass.
MOHS   Missouri Historical Society, St. Louis, Mo.
MSPL   Memphis–Shelby County Public Library, Memphis, Tenn.
NARS   National Archives and Record Service, Washington, D.C.
NOR   U.S. Government, *Official Records of the Union and Confederate Navies in the War of the Rebellion*, 31 vols., Washington, D.C., 1894–1919.
NYHS   New-York Historical Society, New York, N.Y.
OR   U.S. Government, *The War of the Rebellion: A Compilation of the Official Records of the Union and Confederate Armies*, 128 vols., Washington, D.C., 1880–1901. (Unless otherwise indicated, all volumes cited throughout notes are from series 1.)
PMSR   Gideon Johnson Pillow Military Service Record, RG 109, National Archives and Record Service, Washington, D.C.
SHC   Southern Historical Collection, University of North Carolina, Chapel Hill, N.C.
SHSP   *Southern Historical Society Papers*
TSLA   Tennessee State Library and Archives, Nashville, Tenn.
UMI   University of Michigan, William L. Clements Library, Ann Arbor, Mich.
UVA   University of Virginia Library, Charlottesville, Va.

1. C. M. Polk, *Colonial Families*, pp. 108–9; "The Birth, Parentage, Family and Ancestry of General Gideon J. Pillow, His Early Life, Education and Selection of a Profession." This document, now in the possession of Brig. Gen. and Mrs. William P. Campbell, Searcy, Ark. (hereafter cited as Campbell manuscript), and its supplement, "Gen. G. J. Pillow's Military Service in the Mexican War," JRN, have been passed down through Pillow's daughter Narcissa Mitchell and are believed to be the work of Pillow himself. Phraseology, references to certain incidents, and the general tone have led the authors to this conclusion.

2. The Pillow family in America originates with Jasper Pillew, an Englishman, who settled in Amelia County, Virginia, in 1740. Jasper, a yeoman farmer, and his wife had three sons: John (1750–94), Jasper, and William. The family moved to Prince Edward County, Virginia, and, prior to the Revolution, to Guilford County, North Carolina. John married Mary Ursula Johnson, the daughter of Gideon Johnson, Sr. Gideon Johnson Pillow's great-grandfather is thought to have been Gideon Macon. Through Macon, Mary Johnson Pillow was the second cousin of Martha (Dandridge) Custis Washington and the niece of Nathaniel Macon of North Carolina. The name Gideon probably originated with the Macon ancestor. Livingston, *Eminent American Lawyers*, pp. 651–52; C. M. Polk, *Colonial Families*, p. 112; Campbell manuscript; Robert M. McBride, "The Gideon J. Pillow Everybody Knows," in possession of Jill K. Garrett, Columbia, Tenn.; Conrad, *General Scott and His Staff*, p. 83.

3. Abernathy, *From Frontier to Plantation*, p. 161.

4. Nashville *American*, Nov. 3, 1878; Abernathy, *Frontier to Plantation*, pp. 130–31, 195; Guild, *Old Times*, p. 27; Campbell manuscript; Phelan, *Making of a State*, pp. 149, 161; Ramsey, *Annals of Tennessee*, p. 615.

5. James Roper, "The Founding of Memphis," *West Tennessee Historical Quarterly* 23 (1969): 20, 24; C. M. Polk, *Colonial Families*, p. 43; McBride, "Pillow"; Maury County, Tenn., Deed Book A, p. 30 (deed to Gideon Pillow from John Johnston for $2,000, dated May 20, 1806).

6. F. H. Smith, *History of Maury County*, p. 2; Campbell manuscript; C. M. Polk, *Colonial Families*, p. 115; Nathan Vaught, "Youth and Old Age," in possession of Jill K. Garrett, Columbia, Tenn.

7. Campbell manuscript; Garrett, "General Pillow"; Census of Giles County, Tenn., 1820.

8. Uncle William Pillow's recovery was miraculous. A ball passed through his body, and a surgeon had a silk handkerchief drawn through the wound. Somehow, he survived; credit was given to the short rations upon which they had subsisted. Tebbel, *Compact History of the Indian Wars*, pp. 117–22; James, *Andrew Jackson*, pp. 161–63, 181–84, 235–70; Bassett, *Life of Andrew Jackson*, p. 96; Garrett, "General Pillow"; Columbia *Herald and Mail*, Sept. 21, 1877.

9. Campbell manuscript; McCallum, *Early History of Giles County*, pp. 16, 105.

10. Goodspeed, *History of Tennessee*, p. 778; Columbia *Herald and Mail*, Feb. 18, 1876; Garrett, "General Pillow"; C. M. Polk, *Colonial Families*, p. 126; Campbell manuscript; Highsaw, "History of Zion Community," p. 115. Woodward Academy was located on North Glade Street between East Eighth and Ninth streets.

11. Kelley, *Children of Nashville*, pp. 82–83.

12. Pillow was a well-educated man, "retaining a thorough knowledge of Greek and Latin." He read widely the remainder of his life and took great pride in his splendid personal library.

13. W. B. Turner, *History of Maury County*, p. 268; Speer, *Prominent Tennesseans*, p. 138; Campbell manuscript; Abernathy, *From Frontier to Plantation*, pp. 204, 284; Crew, *History of Nashville*, pp. 387, 392; Nashville *Clarion*, Mar. 30, 1813.

14. Nashville *American*, Nov. 3, 1878; Campbell manuscript; C. M. Polk, *Colonial Families*, pp. 115–16; Garrett, "General Pillow."

15. Folmsbee, Corlew, and Mitchell, *Tennessee*, pp. 139–40, 142, 163; Abernathy, *From Plantation to Frontier*, pp. 231–35; William Carroll to John M. Eaton, Aug. 16, 21, 1829, Carroll Papers, TSLA; James, *Andrew Jackson*, pp. 178, 213, 227–68; Golden, "William Carroll and His Administration," pp. 28–29. Pillow cast his first vote for John Bell, then a staunch Jacksonian. GJP to the Democracy of Lawrence County, Tennessee, n.d. [ca. 1857], JRN.

16. Columbia *Western Mercury*, July 20, 1830. Edmund Dillihunty would become Pillow's political enemy. Another Columbia lawyer who would present a problem was Terry H. Cahal.

17. J. W. Caldwell, *Bench and Bar*, pp. 228–31; Garrett, "General Pillow."

18. It appears that Knox Walker read law under Pillow before becoming his partner. Sellers, *Polk: Jacksonian*, pp. 59–60, 62; Columbia *Herald*, Mar. 29, 1872; Garrett, "General Pillow"; Columbia *Tennessee Democrat*, June 3, 1841; Crist, McIntosh, and Monroe, *Papers of Jefferson Davis*, 7:403.

19. Garrett, "General Pillow"; State Docket Book, 1828–37, Maury County Court; N. W. Jones, *History of Mount Pleasant*, p. 64.

20. Sellers, *Polk: Jacksonian*, pp. 61–78; R. F. Nichols, *Franklin Pierce*, p. 28.

21. Circuit Court Minute Book, Maury County, Tenn., Nov. 20, 1834; Summons, State v. A. J. Donelson and G. J. Pillow, Aug. 1, 1855, Maury County Superior Court.

22. GJP to Dixon T. Allen, Aug. 5, 1831, with endorsement from Allen to David Campbell, Campbell Family Papers, DU.

23. Justice William L. Brown, Pillow's legal mentor, probably assisted Carroll in securing this assignment for the young man.

24. Little is known of Jacob Chase. An early settler of Tuckertown (now New Market), Tennessee, Chase held various offices in Jefferson County during the 1820s. Following his work on the *Digest*, he became a member of the General Assembly representing Jefferson, Campbell, Claiborne, and

Grainger counties. McBride and Robison, *Biographical Directory*, p. 136.

25. Haywood and Cobbs, *Statute Laws of the State of Tennessee*.

26. Nashville *American*, Nov. 3, 1878; Conrad, *General Scott and His Staff*, p. 83; Campbell manuscript.

27. "Pillow's Military Service," JRN.

28. Mary E. Martin Pillow was born April 2, 1812. Garrett, "General Pillow"; Conrad, *General Scott and His Staff*, p. 83; C. M. Polk, *Colonial Families*, p. 46; Columbia *Herald*, Nov. 5, 1869; Vaught, "Youth and Old Age"; Nicholson, "Reminiscences of an Octogenarian," SHC.

29. McBride, "Pillow"; Garrett, "General Pillow"; Columbia *Herald*, Nov. 5, 1869.

30. GJP to JKP, Jan. 6, 1833, JKP Papers, LOC.

31. Sellers, *Polk: Jacksonian*, pp. 76–78, 85, 95–100; McCormac, *Polk*, pp. 25–26, 29–30.

32. GJP to JKP, Dec. 19, 1833, JKP Papers, LOC; Sellers, *Polk: Jacksonian*, pp. 214–22; Columbia *Observer*, Aug. 8, 1834.

33. Adlai O. Harris to JKP, Jan. 3, 1834, JKP Papers, LOC.

34. Nashville *Union*, Mar. 30, Apr. 13, 27, 1835; Clark, "Nicholson," p. 20.

35. Columbia *Observer*, Apr. 17, 1835; Folmsbee, Corlew, and Mitchell, *Tennessee*, pp. 184–85.

36. Garrett, "General Pillow"; Nashville *Union*, Jan. 2, 1839; Robinson, *Justice in Grey*, pp. 21–23.

37. GJP to JKP, Mar. 4, 1836, JKP Papers, LOC.

38. W. R. Rucker to JKP, Mar. 29, 1836; GJP to JKP, Mar. 2, 4, 1836, JKP Papers, LOC.

39. GJP to JKP, Mar. 2, 1836, JKP Papers, LOC; Clark, "Nicholson," p. 35.

40. James Walker to JKP, Mar. 3, 1836, JKP Papers, LOC.

41. GJP to JKP, May 31, 1836, JKP Papers, LOC.

42. Andrew C. Hays to JKP, Apr. 26, 1836, JKP Papers, LOC. Of course it was Gideon J. Pillow, Jr., who was born during the political tumult.

43. Andrew C. Hays to JKP, Apr. 26, 1836, JKP Papers, LOC.

44. One wonders. Nicholson was a Calhounite nullifier who very well might have been working against Pillow. Then there was Cahal, the disappointed aspirant and law partner. Andrew C. Hays to Polk, Apr. 26, 1836, JKP Papers, LOC; Wayne Cutler to author, Apr. 5, 1991.

45. The Columbia militia company, named the "White Guards," undoubtedly voted heavily for Cannon. Pillow must have been distressed by the membership of Anthony Pillow, his first cousin, in this company. GJP to JKP, May 31, 1836, JKP Papers, LOC; Columbia *Observer*, Apr. 14, 1836; James Walker to Polk, May 31, 1836, JKP Papers, LOC. Walker, Polk's brother-in-law, was one of a carefully constructed network of observers who kept the congressman informed about political, business, and social events in Columbia and the District.

46. Sellers, *Polk: Jacksonian*, pp. 267–83, 295, 341, 355; S. H. Laughlin to JKP, Apr. 17, 1835, JKP Papers, LOC; Columbia *Observer*, Apr. 17, 1835.

47. John H. Dew to JKP, Feb. 23, May 16, 1838, JKP Papers, LOC.

48. John B. Hays to JKP, Dec. 4, 1838, JKP Papers, LOC; Garrett, "General Pillow."

49. Samuel D. Frierson of Columbia may also have helped with the defense. He and Pillow took depositions from witnesses. Weaver et al., *Correspondence of Polk*, 5:5n.

50. Garrett, "General Pillow"; Sellers, *Polk: Jacksonian*, p. 331.

51. GJP to JKP, May 6, 1842, JKP Papers, LOC; Parker, Cross, and Hebert, *Friendship of Polk and Pillow*, pp. 4–5.

52. John H. Dew to JKP, May 16, 1838, JKP Papers, LOC; Folmsbee, Corlew, and Mitchell, *Tennessee*, pp. 199–200.

53. West H. Humphreys to JKP, Sept. 25, 1839; Hillary Langtry to JKP, Jan. 24, 1839, JKP Papers, LOC.

54. GJP to JKP, Nov. 20, 1839, Jan. 10, 25, Feb. 13, 20, 1840, JKP Papers, LOC; Folmsbee, *Sectionalism and Internal Improvements*, pp. 247–49; Columbia *Observer*, Dec. 1, 1842; interview of Col. Nat W. Jones, Aug. 6, 1907, Garrett, "General Pillow"; State of Tennessee, *House Journal, 1847–1848*, *Appendix*, pp. 74–75; author's interview with Wayne Cutler, Nov. 30, 1990; Bryan, *Southern Kinsmen*, p. 116; F. H. Smith, *History of Maury County*, p. 147.

55. Patrick, *Architecture in Tennessee*, p. 171.

56. One wonders if a connection existed with Clifton Place, the home of Tyree Rodes in Giles County. Mrs. Rodes was Cynthia Holland of Maury, and Pillow's younger sister who married Aaron V. Brown was Cynthia Holland Pillow. Gideon Pillow represented Cynthia Holland Rodes in 1838 and helped her settle the estate of her second husband, Peter R. Booker. See memoir of the Holland family by Mrs. S. S. L. P. Cochrane, "Memorabilia of Her Family," in TSLA, and Cynthia Rivers Carter, "Tyree Rodes and Cynthia Holland," SHC.

57. As cherry was in limited supply, some of the back rooms of Clifton had baseboards, probably of oak, painted carefully so the grain resembled cherry. Cross, *Clifton Place Plantation*; Patrick, *Architecture in Tennessee*, p. 171; Brandau, *History of Homes*, pp. 226–27; R. Smith, *Majestic Middle Tennessee*, pp. 12–13.

58. Vaught, "Youth and Old Age," p. 26.

59. This impressive three-story building still exists today, sufficiently large to cure 2,000 country hams.

60. Probably the only greenhouse in progressive Maury County at the time, it was connected to the manor house and extended across to the plantation office. It had an underground heating system complete with furnace and flue. A second, larger greenhouse existed at the upper (east) limit of the garden. It was also of glass with a brick base. Although some compartments in the greenhouse were probably used for experimentation, it is thought that the greenhouse next to the plantation office was used primarily for flowers.

61. In 1837 Pillow owned four slaves valued at $2,500, several town lots, and thirty acres. By 1840 he owned thirty-five slaves. Tax lists, Maury County, Tenn., 1837, 1840; Cross, *Clifton Place Plantation*, n.p.; Brandau, *History of Homes*, pp. 226–27.

62. By the late 1850s Pillow would become a large cotton grower, but for this crop he would use his Arkansas lands. India corn remained the principal crop at Clifton, demonstrating Pillow's consistent emphasis on livestock. Columbia *Southern Cultivator and Journal of Science and General Improvement*, Oct. 11, 1839; author's interviews with Paul Cross, Clifton Place farm manager, May 22, June 20, 1991, Jan. 28, 1993.

63. Columbia *Southern Cultivator and Journal of Science and General Improvement*, Oct. 11, 1839; Cross, *Clifton Place Plantation*.

64. It is believed that Pillow was the first to make use of hydraulic cement in Middle Tennessee.

65. Officials in the Boston Navy Yard publicly praised Pillow's hemp. One superintendent of the largest rope factory in Philadelphia testified that Pillow's hemp was "the best Hemp I have ever seen foreign or domestic." Author's conversations with Paul Cross, farm manager of Clifton Place. Columbia *Southern Cultivator and Journal of Science and General Improvement*, Oct. 11, 1839; Nashville, Tenn., *Agriculturist*, 2:187.

66. Garrett, "General Pillow"; Census of Maury County, Tenn., 1840.

67. Patterson, *Negro in Tennessee*, p. 61.

68. Garrett, "General Pillow"; State of Tennessee v. GJP, Jan. 20, 1842. Mexican War correspondence between MEP and GJP substantiates this belief.

69. Pillow's law practice remained active, although it appears he may have been tiring of it, "practicing when he had to." Certainly he devoted greater attention to farming and to the purchase of lands to the west.

70. In a letter to Polk of January 22, 1846, Pillow speaks of "my planting interests in Mississippi." R. Patterson to GJP, July 18, 1843, Miscellaneous Collection, UMI; Rt. Rev. James H. Otey to GJP, June 7, 1841, Dreer Collection, HSP; GJP to William McKissack, June 15, 1842, in possession of author; GJP to William Trousdale, May 3, 1838, Nov. 17, 1839, Trousdale Papers, TSLA; Livingston, *Eminent American Lawyers*, pp. 651–52; Weaver et al., *Correspondence of Polk*, 6:352.

71. Highsaw, "History of Zion Community," pp. 224, 226; Patterson, *Negro in Tennessee*, p. 67; F. H. Smith, *History of Maury County*, p. 147.

72. F. H. Smith, *History of Maury County*, p. 336. Pillow later shipped his steam engine to the big plantation he developed in the 1850s near Helena, Arkansas.

73. Columbia *Tennessee Democrat*, Jan. 18, 1844; F. H. Smith, *History of Maury County*, p. 147.

74. F. H. Smith, *History of Maury County*, p. 109.

75. Conyngham, *Sunny South*, p. 194.

76. Jerome's home was known as "Bethel Place" after the Civil War. Brandau, *History of Homes*, pp. 223, 225; Garrett, "General Pillow"; R. Smith, *Majestic Middle Tennessee*, pp. 14–19.

77. Parks, *Leonidas Polk*, pp. 7, 41, 54, 74–76, 88, 94, 98–99.

78. Nicholson, "Reminiscences of an Octogenarian," SHC; Sellers, *Polk: Jacksonian*, pp. 373, 409, 415–17, 426, 444.

79. Sellers, *Polk: Jacksonian*, p. 459.

80. In the fall of 1842, Pillow chaired the meeting of the Democracy of Maury County in a rousing anti-Clay rally. Daniel Gordon to JKP, June 12, 1841; GJP to JKP, May 6, 1842, JKP Papers, LOC.

81. Sarah C. Polk to JKP, May 3, 1843, JKP Papers, LOC; Columbia *Tennessee Democrat*, Oct. 20, 1842, Sept. 7, 1843.

82. Sellers, *Polk: Jacksonian*, pp. 488, 491–92.

83. GJP to JKP, Oct. 9, 1843, JKP Papers, LOC.

CHAPTER TWO

1. Sellers, *Polk: Continentalist*, pp. 3–11.

2. JKP to Van Buren, Aug. 18, 1843, Van Buren Papers, LOC.

3. Andrew Jackson to Amos Kendall, Sept. 20, 1843, newspaper clipping, Jackson Papers, LOC; Jackson to Van Buren, Sept. 22, 1843, Van Buren Papers, LOC.

4. GJP to JKP, May 25, 1844; J. G. M. Ramsey to JKP, Oct. 12, 1843; S. H. Laughlin to JKP, Oct. 12, 1843, JKP Papers, LOC; Reeves, "Letters of Pillow to Polk," p. 832; Sioussat, "Diaries of S. H. Laughlin," Oct. 18, 22, 1843, entries.

5. Nashville *Union*, Nov. 25, 1843.

6. Holt, "The Democratic Party," p. 497.

7. Sellers, *Polk: Continentalist*, pp. 14–18, 40–45. Southerners generally favored a tolerance for paper money and private banks, continuation of the "gag rule," which banned discussion of slavery issues in Congress, and downward revision of the tariff of 1842.

8. McCormac, *Polk*, p. 212.

9. Sellers, *Polk: Continentalist*, pp. 21–22; Garraty, *Silas Wright*, pp. 257–58.

10. Klein, *President James Buchanan*, pp. 156–59; Garraty, *Silas Wright*, pp. 245–46; Wiltse, *Calhoun*, pp. 134–49.

11. Sellers, *Polk: Continentalist*, p. 22; Garraty, *Silas Wright*, p. 259; George Bancroft to Isham G. Harris, Aug. 30, 1887, Bancroft Papers, MHS.

12. Sellers, *Polk: Continentalist*, p. 3.

13. Ibid., p. 47; Bassett, *Life of Andrew Jackson*, 2:735–36.

14. Clay and Van Buren thought they could avoid the issue if both leading candidates opposed *immediate* annexation. Both went public at the same time on the Texas issue. Wright to Van Buren, Apr. 6, 8, 1844, Van Buren Papers, LOC; Wayne Cutler to author, Apr. 3, 1991.

15. Mushkat, *Tammany*, pp. 211–12; Reeves, "Letters of Pillow to Polk," p. 832.

16. Reeves, "Letters of Pillow to Polk," pp. 833–35.

17. Sellers, *Polk: Constitutionalist*, p. 72.

18. Bain and Parris, *Convention Decisions*, p. 33.

19. JKP to Cave Johnson, May 15, 1844, JKP Papers, LOC.

20. JKP to S. H. Laughlin, Dec. 29, 1843, JKP Papers, LOC.

21. S. H. Laughlin to JKP, Dec. 29, 1843; GJP to JKP, Dec. 30, 1843, JKP Papers, LOC.

22. Bergeron, *Antebellum Politics in Tennessee*, p. 62.

23. S. H. Laughlin to JKP, Apr. 24, 1844, JKP Papers, LOC.

24. JKP to S. H. Laughlin, May 9, 1844, in Parks, "Letters from James K. Polk to Samuel H. Laughlin," p. 160; GJP to JKP, May 16, 1844, JKP Papers, LOC.

25. JKP to S. H. Laughlin, May 9, 1844, JKP Papers, LOC.

26. Holt, "The Democratic Party," p. 518; Binkley, *American Political Parties*, p. 87.

27. Garraty, *Silas Wright*, pp. 252–53.

28. GJP to JKP, May 22, 1844, JKP Papers, LOC; Shenton, *Walker*, p. 43.

29. Sellers, *Polk: Continentalist*, pp. 76–77, 82.

30. GJP to JKP, May 22, 1844, JKP Papers, LOC.

31. Paul, *Rift in the Democracy*, p. 142.

32. Sellers, *Polk: Continentalist*, p. 87.

33. Ibid., p. 81; GJP to JKP, May 24, 1844, JKP Papers, LOC.

34. S. H. Laughlin to JKP, May 23, 1844, JKP Papers, LOC.

35. Theisen, "Polk," p. 394.

36. GJP to JKP, May 22, 1844, JKP Papers, LOC.

37. Ibid.

38. Ibid.

39. Ibid.

40. GJP to JKP, May 24, 1844, JKP Papers, LOC.

41. Ibid.

42. Ibid.

43. Ibid.

44. A. V. Brown to JKP, Apr. 30, May 2, 1844, JKP Papers, LOC. Rumbles about Brown's hasty departure from Pulaski would come down through the years. In 1845 he married Cynthia Holland Pillow Saunders, Gideon Pillow's widowed sister, and became perhaps Pillow's closest political ally and friend.

45. Of course Wright, and probably Butler too, knew Wright could not win either. Sellers, *Polk: Continentalist*, p. 84; Washington *Globe*, June 6, 1844; Bain and Parris, *Convention Decisions*, p. 35; Wayne Cutler to author, Apr. 3, 1991.

46. Sellers, *Polk: Continentalist*, pp. 84–85.

47. Garraty, *Silas Wright*, pp. 264–67.

48. GJP to JKP, May 25, 1844, JKP Papers, LOC.

49. GJP to JKP, May 22, 25, 1844, JKP Papers, LOC.

50. Sellers, *Polk: Continentalist*, p. 88.

51. Ibid.

52. Ibid.; Shenton, *Walker*, p. 45; "Proceedings of the Democratic National Convention, Baltimore, May 27–30, 1844," in Schlesinger, Israel, and Hansen, *Presidential Elections*, 1:829–39; *Niles Weekly Register* 46 (June 1, 1844): 211, 213–15.

53. Cave Johnson to JKP, May 27, 1844, JKP Papers, LOC.

54. Sellers, *Polk: Continentalist*, p. 88; Shenton, *Walker*, p. 46; "Proceedings of the Democratic National Convention," pp. 829–39.

55. Sellers, *Polk: Continentalist*, pp. 90–91.

56. This delegate could have been Reah Frazer. Lambert, "Democratic Convention of 1844," p. 21.

57. Sellers, *Polk: Continentalist*, pp. 90–92; Howe, *Life and Letters of George Bancroft*, p. 253; Nye, *Bancroft*, pp. 131–32. His biography of Van Buren would not be completed for forty-five years. As might be expected, the work falls short of Bancroft's standard.

58. GJP to JKP, May 28, 1844, JKP Papers, LOC; Theisen, "Polk," p. 398.

59. GJP to JKP, May 28, 1844, JKP Papers, LOC.

60. GJP to JKP, May 30, 1844, JKP Papers, LOC; Paul, *Rift in the Democracy*, p. 160.

61. GJP to JKP, May 28, 1844, JKP Papers, LOC; Bain and Parris, *Convention Decisions*, pp. 34–35; Henry J. Seibert to his wife, May 29, 1844, Seibert Papers, DU.

62. Sellers, *Polk: Continentalist*, pp. 93–94; Nye, *Bancroft*, pp. 131–32; Howe, *Life and Letters of George Bancroft*, pp. 252–54, 99, 87; Paul, *Rift in the Democracy*, p. 160.

63. GJP to JKP, May 30, 1844, JKP Papers, LOC.

64. Ibid.

65. Paul, *Rift in the Democracy*, p. 161.

66. Sellers, *Polk: Continentalist*, pp. 96–97.

67. GJP to JKP, May 30, 1844, JKP Papers, LOC.

68. GJP to JKP, May 29, 1844, JKP Papers, LOC; Paul, *Rift in the Democracy*, p. 161; Howe, *Life and Letters of George Bancroft*, p. 254; Pillow, *Speech on Texas*; Lambert, "Democratic Convention of 1844," pp. 14, 21.

69. Sellers, *Polk: Continentalist*, p. 99.

70. George Bancroft to Isham G. Harris, Aug. 30, 1887, Bancroft Papers, MHS.

71. George Bancroft to JKP, July 6, 1844, in Howe, *Life and Letters of George Bancroft*, pp. 251–55.

72. GJP to JKP, May 30, 1844, JKP Papers, LOC.

73. Ibid.

74. S. H. Laughlin to JKP, May 31, 1844, JKP Papers, LOC.

75. A. J. Donelson to JKP, June 2, 1844; Henry Hicks to JKP, Sept. 6, 1844, JKP Papers, LOC.

76. GJP to JKP, June 2, 1844, JKP Papers, LOC.

77. Sellers, *Polk: Continentalist*, p. 119.

78. GJP to JKP, June 2, 1844, JKP Papers, LOC.

79. Ibid.

80. S. H. Laughlin to JKP, July 5, 1844, JKP Papers, LOC.

81. J. George Harris to JKP, June 28, 1844; GJP to JKP, July 2, 1844; Levin H. Coe to JKP, July 18, Oct. 1, 1844; Boling Gordon to JKP, Aug. 29, 1844; Moses Dawson to JKP, Oct. 9, 1844; GJP to R. Hoover, Nov. 12, 1844,

JKP Papers, LOC; GJP to G. Bancroft, July 22, 1844, Bancroft Papers, MHS; author's interview with Wayne Cutler, Nov. 30, 1990.

82. Washington *Globe*, June 6, 1844.

83. Nashville *Union*, Aug. 28, 1844.

84. Pillow, *Speech on Texas*; Everett, "James K. Polk and the Election of 1844 in Tennessee," pp. 10–19; Columbia *Tennessee Democrat*, July 24, Sept. 25, 1844; Nashville *American*, Nov. 3, 1878.

85. JKP to S. H. Laughlin, July 26, 1844, JKP Papers, LOC; Livingston, *Eminent American Lawyers*, p. 652.

86. GJP to Henry Horn and J. K. Kane, July 2, 1844, Bancroft Collection, New York Public Library.

87. L. H. Coe to JKP, July 18, 1844; George W. Rice to JKP, Oct. 3, 1844, JKP Papers, LOC.

88. GJP to Henry Horn and J. K. Kane, July 2, 1844, Pillow Letters, HSP; G. M. Dallas to JKP, July 6, 1844; J. George Harris to JKP, July 25, 1844; GJP to JKP, Oct. 26, 1844, JKP Papers, LOC.

89. John W. Goode et al. to JKP, Sept. 22, 1844, JKP Papers, LOC; author's interview with Wayne Cutler, Nov. 30, 1990.

90. Columbia *Tennessee Democrat*, Aug. 14, 1844; Little Rock *Arkansas Gazette and Democrat*, June 25, 1852.

91. GJP to E. Croswell, Oct. 1, 1844, JKP Papers, LOC; GJP to A. Jackson, Nov. 22, 1844, in possession of Douglas Schanz, Roanoke, Va.

92. JKP to A. J. Donelson, July 23, 1844; A. J. Donelson to JKP, July 29, 1844, JKP Papers, LOC; A. Jackson to JKP, July 26, 1844, in Bassett, *Correspondence of Jackson*, 6:303; Sellers, *Polk: Continentalist*, p. 136; Schlesinger, Israel, and Hansen, *American Presidential Elections*, 1:782–84.

93. Little Rock *Arkansas Gazette and Democrat*, June 25, 1852; W. B. Campbell to David Campbell, Oct. 18, 1844, Campbell Family Papers, DU.

94. P. M. Hamer, *Tennessee*, 1:308, 114; Bergeron, *Antebellum Politics*, p. 94; W. B. Campbell to David Campbell, Oct. 18, 1844, Campbell Family Papers, DU; Theisen, "Polk," p. 385; Tricamo, "Tennessee Politics," p. 20; Grant, "Cave Johnson and the Presidential Campaign of 1844," pp. 54–73.

95. William Moore to JKP, Nov. 6, 1844, JKP Papers, LOC.

96. GJP to R. Hoover, Nov. 12, 1844, JKP Papers, LOC.

CHAPTER THREE

1. JKP to GJP, Nov. 6, 1845, JKP Papers, LOC.

2. Pillow also wrote a mock-serious letter to Sarah Polk, telling her again how much he admired her husband's new address and thanking her for a present to Mary. GJP to Sara C. Polk, Jan. 8, 1846; Duff Green to JKP, Jan. 10, 1845, JKP Papers, LOC.

3. Holt, "The Democratic Party," p. 519; Lurie, *Party Politics*, pp. 71, 74; Duff Green to JKP, Jan. 20, 1845, JKP Papers, LOC.

4. McCormac, *Polk*, pp. 322–23, 339. Among Tennesseans, Cave Johnson

received the Post Office; A. J. Donelson, the ministry at Berlin; Sam Laughlin, the recordership of the General Land Office; and Romulus Sanders, the ministry at Madrid.

5. GJP to JKP, Jan. 22, 1846, JKP Papers, LOC.

6. JKP to GJP, Feb. 4, 1846, JKP Papers, LOC.

7. GJP to JKP, May 1, 1845, JKP Papers, LOC; GJP to Barkley Martin, May 10, 1845; Barkley Martin to George Bancroft, May 22, 1845; George Bancroft to Barkley Martin, May 22, 1845, Bancroft Papers, MHS.

8. GJP to JKP, Oct. 23, 1845, JKP Papers, LOC.

9. JKP to GJP, May 10, 1846, JKP Papers, LOC; Henry, *Story of the Mexican War*, pp. 47–48; Brooks, *History of the Mexican War*, pp. 158–59.

10. JKP to GJP, June 2, 1846, JKP Papers, LOC.

11. Cave Johnson to W. B. Campbell, June 27, 1846, Campbell Family Papers, DU.

12. JKP to GJP, July 7, 1846, JKP Papers, LOC.

13. JKP to GJP, June 29, July 2, 1846, JKP Papers, LOC; Cunliffe, *Soldiers and Civilians*, p. 308; Brooks, *History of the Mexican War*, pp. 162–63; Bauer, *Mexican War*, pp. 70–75; R. F. Nichols, *Stakes of Power*, p. 16; Quaife, *Diary of James K. Polk*, 1:395–401, 3:112–13; Sellers, *Polk: Continentalist*, pp. 434–37; J. H. Smith, *War with Mexico*, 1:546.

14. Although Polk disclaimed animosity toward regular officers and West Point, his Jacksonian sentiments were well known, and his hostility grew as the Mexican War progressed. Not only did he fill vacancies in the army with civilian officers, he overruled, interfered, and countermanded. Pillow, of course, felt exactly the same toward the Whiggish military establishment. Morrison, *"The Best School in the World,"* pp. 27–28.

15. Blaine, *Twenty Years of Congress*, 1:75; Milton A. Haynes to W. B. Campbell, July 10, 1846; David Campbell to W. B. Campbell, July 10, 1846, Campbell Family Papers, DU.

16. GJP to R. Jones, July 13, Aug. 1, 1846, Pillow Papers, RG 109, NARS; GJP to L. J. Cist, May 9, 1866, C. E. French Collection, MHS; notarized statement of GJP in Pillow Pension Application, RG 15, NARS.

17. Brooks, *History of the Mexican War*, p. 337.

18. GJP to MEP, July 19, 22, 1846, Pillow Papers, MOHS; Columbia *Tennessee Democrat*, July 30, 1846.

19. GJP to MEP, July 22, 1846, Pillow Papers, MOHS.

20. W. R. Caswell to Elizabeth Caswell, July 20, 21, 1846, Caswell Papers, SHC.

21. Columbia *Tennessee Democrat*, July 30, 1846, quoting *Nashville Union*, n.d.

22. Memphis *Daily Eagle*, July 15, 20, 1846.

23. William R. Caswell to Elizabeth Caswell, July 22, 27, 1846, Caswell Papers, SHC.

24. Ibid.; Claiborne, *Quitman*, 1:238.

25. GJP to MEP, Aug. 8, 1846, Pillow Letters, HSP; GJP to MEP, Aug. 8, 1846, Pillow Letters, BY; W. R. Caswell to Elizabeth Caswell, Aug. 7, 8,

1846, Caswell Papers, SHC; J. A. Quitman to Eliza Quitman, Aug. 14, 1846, Quitman Family Papers, SHC.

26. Pillow went ahead and visited Haskell's camp. Caswell recorded, "We have champagne, beef tongues, claret, limes, ham, tea, coffee and 'very many such comforts.'" They met the hero of Resaca de la Palma, Capt. Charles May, with his great black beard, and Haskell's fellow Whig, Col. Henry Clay, Jr., son of Polk's archenemy. W. R. Caswell to Elizabeth Caswell, Aug. 11, 1846, Caswell Papers, SHC; GJP to MEP, Aug. 8, 1846, Pillow Letters, HSP.

27. GJP to MEP, Aug. 16, 1846, Pillow Letters, HSP; GJP to W. B. Campbell, Aug. 24, 1846, Campbell Family Papers, DU; E. J. Nichols, *Zach Taylor's Little Army*, p. 128; Eisenhower, *So Far from God*, p. 54.

28. W. B. Campbell to David Campbell, Aug. 28, 1846, Campbell Family Papers, DU; Bauer, *Mexican War*, p. 88.

29. GJP to MEP, Aug. 16, 1846, Pillow Letters, HSP.

30. William M. Gardner Memoirs, Memphis State University Library, Mississippi Valley Collection, Memphis, Tenn.; "Pillow's Military Service," JRN; W. B. Campbell to Fanny Campbell, Aug. 8, 24, 1846; W. B. Campbell to David Campbell, Aug. 28, 1846, Campbell Family Papers, DU.

31. W. B. Campbell to David Campbell, Aug. 28, 1846, Campbell Family Papers, DU.

32. GJP to MEP, Aug. 16, 1846, Pillow Letters, HSP.

33. Ibid.

34. "Pillow's Military Service," JRN; Brooks, *History of the Mexican War*, pp. 162–66; *House Executive Document No. 60*, pp. 500–501; Special Orders No. 5, 2d Brig., 2d Div.; Special Orders No. 100, Army of Occupation, Campbell Family Papers, DU.

35. W. B. Campbell to David Campbell, Aug. 30, 1846, Campbell Family Papers, DU.

36. W. B. Campbell to GJP, Sept. 1, 1846, Campbell Family Papers, DU.

37. *House Executive Document No. 60*, pp. 500–501.

38. GJP to MEP, Sept. [?] 1846, Pillow Papers, MOHS.

39. W. B. Campbell to Fanny Campbell, Sept. 1, 5, 1846, Campbell Family Papers, DU.

40. GJP to MEP, Sept. 6, 1846, Pillow Letters, HSP; W. R. Caswell to Elizabeth Caswell, September 5, 1846, Caswell Papers, SHC; J. H. Smith, *War with Mexico*, 1:493.

41. Lawyer and attorney general, thirty-five-year-old Reynolds was a confidant of Polk's, having advised him for over ten years about political affairs in East Tennessee.

42. "Pillow's Military Service," JRN; W. R. Caswell to Elizabeth C. Caswell, Sept. 16, 1846, Caswell Papers, SHC; Special Orders No. 2, 3, 4, 2d Brig., 2d Div., Army of Occupation, Campbell Family Papers, DU; GJP to MEP, Sept. 6, 1846, Pillow Letters, HSP; Mary F. Caldwell, *Tennessee: The Dangerous Example*, p. 327; Conrad, *General Scott and His Staff*, p. 83.

43. W. R. Caswell to Elizabeth Caswell, Oct. 2, 1846, Caswell Papers, SHC.

44. Pillow found Jerome's brother-in-law, Thomas Dale, in the ranks and

brought him to brigade headquarters as orderly sergeant. W. R. Caswell to Elizabeth C. Caswell, Sept. 16, 1846, Caswell Papers, SHC; GJP to MEP, Sept. 6, 1846, Pillow Letters, HSP; Special Orders No. 6, 2d Brig., 2d Div., Army of Occupation, Campbell Family Papers, DU.

45. Memphis *Daily Eagle*, Sept. 20, 1846.

46. GJP to MEP, Sept. 6, 1846, Pillow Letters, HSP; Robertson, *Campaign in Mexico*, pp. 98, 197.

47. Columbia *Beacon*, Jan. 29, 1847, quoting *Nashville Whig*.

48. GJP to MEP, Sept. 20, 1846, Pillow Letters, HSP.

49. GJP to MEP, Oct. 27, Dec. 8, 1846, Pillow Letters, HSP; GJP to W. B. Campbell, Nov. 29, 1846, Campbell Family Papers, DU; GJP to unknown, Nov. 8, 1846, Pillow Papers, HUL; "Pillow's Military Service," JRN.

50. Lewis, *Captain Sam Grant*, p. 177; Furber, *Twelve Months Volunteer*, pp. 114–15; Henry, *Story of the Mexican War*, pp. 152–53; Bauer, *Mexican War*, pp. 92–99; J. H. Smith, *War with Mexico*, 1:234–37; GJP to men of the 1st Tennessee, Oct. 24, 1846, Campbell Family Papers, DU.

51. Memphis *Daily Appeal*, Oct. 3, 6, 1857; Vera Cruz *American Eagle*, May 5, 1847; Wilcox, *Mexican War*, pp. 113–14; *New York Times*, Aug. 24, 1872; Sears, *McClellan*, pp. 15–16; *CV* 1:355; New Orleans *Weekly Delta*, Mar. 18, 1850; New Orleans *Daily Picayune*, Apr. 23, 1847.

52. GJP to MEP, Oct. 27, 1846, Pillow Letters, HSP.

53. GJP to MEP, Dec. 8, 1846, Pillow Letters, HSP.

54. H. Hamilton, *Taylor: Soldier in the White House*, p. 48.

55. Z. Taylor to Dr. R. C. Wood, July 13, 1847, in Bixby, *Letters of Zachary Taylor*, pp. 112–13.

56. Nevins, *Polk: Diary of a President*, p. 150.

57. JKP to GJP, Sept. 22, 1846, JKP Papers, LOC; W. R. Caswell to Elizabeth Caswell, Oct. 10, 1846, Caswell Papers, SHC.

58. "Pillow's Military Service," JRN; Eisenhower, *So Far from God*, pp. 158–63; GJP to MEP, Oct. 27, 1846, Pillow Letters, HSP.

59. JKP to GJP, Oct. 22, 1846, JKP Papers, LOC.

60. *House Executive Document No. 60*, pp. 373–74.

61. W. B. Campbell to Fanny Campbell, Oct. 20, 1846, Campbell Family Papers, DU.

62. GJP to MEP, Dec. 8, 1846, Pillow Letters, HSP.

63. "Pillow's Military Service," JRN; GJP to W. B. Campbell, Nov. 29, 1846, Campbell Family Papers, DU; GJP to MEP, Dec. 14, 1846, Pillow Papers, MSPL; Livingston, *Eminent American Lawyers*, p. 652.

64. Columbia *Beacon*, Jan. 8, 1847; GJP to MEP, Dec. 8, 1846, Pillow Letters, HSP; Henry, *Story of the Mexican War*, p. 197; Myers, *Mexican War Diary of McClellan*, p. 35.

65. Campbell manuscript; W. B. Campbell to JKP, Feb. 19, 1847, Campbell Family Papers, DU.

66. GJP to MEP, Dec. 14, 1846, Pillow Papers, MSPL.

67. J. H. Smith, *War with Mexico*, 1:360–62; Cummings, *Yankee Quaker*, p. 107.

68. Myers, *Mexican War Diary of McClellan*, p. 35.

69. "Memoranda of Campaigns in Mexico," BY.

70. Furber, *Twelve Months Volunteer*, pp. 275–314; *House Executive Document No. 60*, pp. 383–84; Z. Taylor to Adj. Gen., Dec. 17, 1846, Records of the Adjutant General, Mexican War, Army of Occupation, Letters Sent, RG 94, NARS; May, *Quitman*, pp. 168–69; Robertson, *Campaign in Mexico*, p. 196.

71. W. B. Campbell to Fanny Campbell, Jan. 2, 14, 1846, Campbell Family Papers, DU.

72. Furber, *Twelve Months Volunteer*, p. 342.

73. Special Orders No. 54, Second Division, Army of Occupation, Campbell Family Papers, DU; "Memoranda of Campaigns in Mexico," BY.

74. Robertson, *Campaign in Mexico*, p. 199; Osteen, "Never a Good War," p. 37.

75. "Pillow's Military Service," JRN; Furber, *Twelve Months Volunteer*, pp. 346–47.

76. Caswell Diary, Jan. 16, 1847, Caswell Papers, SHC.

77. Ibid.; Columbia *Beacon*, Jan. 29, 1847.

78. O. F. Winship to W. B. Campbell, Jan. 19, 29, 1847; GJP to W. B. Campbell, Jan. 26, Mar. 30, 1847; W. B. Campbell to GJP, Mar. 30, 1847, Campbell Family Papers, DU; A. Heiman to Mrs. E. H. Foster, Feb. 28, 1847, Mexican War Letters, TSLA; Columbia *Beacon*, Apr. 30, May 4, 1847.

79. Lewis, *Captain Sam Grant*, pp. 164, 182, 189–91; John Vines Wright Speech, Apr. 13, 1907, Wright Scrapbook, SHC; J. H. Smith, *War with Mexico*, 1:543n.

80. "Pillow's Military Service," JRN; GJP to R. B. Hayes, May 28, 1877, Hayes Correspondence, Rutherford B. Hayes Library, Fremont, Ohio; J. T. Moore, "Pillow."

81. GJP to MEP, Jan. [?] 1847, Pillow Letters, HSP; W. B. Campbell to Fanny Campbell, Jan. 25, 1847; W. B. Campbell to JKP, Feb. 19, 1847, Campbell Family Papers, DU; May, *Quitman*, pp. 170–72.

82. Osteen, "Never a Good War," pp. 37–38; "Memoranda of Campaigns in Mexico," BY; R. B. Reynolds to A. R. Crozier, Crozier Letters, TSLA; W. B. Campbell to Fanny Campbell, Jan. 25, Feb. 3, 1847, Campbell Family Papers, DU.

83. W. H. T. Walker to Mary T. Walker, Feb. 1, 8, 16, 1847, Walker Papers, DU.

84. GJP to MEP, Feb. 14, 1847, Pillow Letters, HSP.

85. Furber, *Twelve Months Volunteer*, pp. 416–17, 423, 434; Caswell Diary, Feb. 12, 1847, Caswell Papers, SHC; W. B. Campbell to Fanny Campbell, Feb. 16, 1847, Campbell Family Papers, DU.

86. Osteen, "Never a Good War," p. 38; Furber, *Twelve Months Volunteer*, p. 434.

87. GJP to MEP, Feb. 23, 1847, Pillow Letters, HSP.

88. Pillow reluctantly told his cavalry that space on board was short. They had their choice of accompanying the brigade to fight on foot or remain-

ing behind at Tampico with their horses. All but one man elected to go on to Vera Cruz. They finally embarked on March 7. Special Orders No. 99, 2d Div., Army of Occupation, Campbell Family Papers, DU; Furber, *Twelve Months Volunteer*, pp. 435, 492–93.

89. Campbell manuscript, Campbell Family Papers, DU; Furber, *Twelve Months Volunteer*, pp. 434–35; Henry, *Story of the Mexican War*, pp. 202–58; Osteen, "Never a Good War," p. 38; "Memoranda of Campaigns in Mexico," BY; W. B. Campbell to Fanny Campbell, Feb. 22, 24, 1847; W. B. Campbell to David Campbell, Feb. 19, 21, 1847; Special Orders No. 69, 1st Brig., 2d Div., Army of Occupation; Special Orders No. 76, 2d Div., Army of Occupation, Campbell Family Papers, DU.

CHAPTER FOUR

1. W. B. Campbell to Fanny Campbell, Mar. 6, 1847, Campbell Family Papers, DU; D. H. Hill Diary, Mar. 5, 1847, SHC; Columbia *Beacon*, Mar. 12, 1847; John D. Wilkins Journal, BY; William Higgins to William Carter, Feb. 3, 1848, Wilkins Mexican War Collection, BY.

2. John D. Wilkins Journal, BY; "Memoranda of Campaigns," BY; E. K. Smith, *To Mexico with Scott*, p. 112; Elliott, *Winfield Scott*, pp. 451–52.

3. "Memoranda of Campaigns," BY; John D. Wilkins Journal, BY; Theodore O'Hara to J. M. McCalla, Mar. 28, 1847, McCalla Collection, DU; W. B. Campbell Diary, Campbell Family Papers, DU; Bauer, *Mexican War*, pp. 241–45; Eisenhower, *So Far from God*, pp. 257–59; Hill Diary, Mar. 7, 10, 1847, SHC; Williamson, *Historic Madison*, p. 453; F. R. Brown, *History of the Ninth Infantry*, p. 44.

4. Hill Diary, Mar. 10, 1847, SHC.

5. Vera Cruz *American Eagle*, May 5, 1847.

6. Fakes, "Memphis and the Mexican War," pp. 124–28; GJP to W. B. Campbell, Mar. [?] 1847, Campbell Family Papers, DU; Williamson, *Historic Madison*, p. 115; Robertson, *Campaign in Mexico*, pp. 222–23.

7. Williamson, *Historic Madison*, p. 115–16; Memphis *Daily Eagle*, Apr. 7, 1847; T. O'Hara to J. M. McCalla, Mar. 28, 1847, McCalla Collection, DU; Campbell Diary, Campbell Family Papers, DU; *Taylor and His Generals*, pp. 302–3; W. H. T. Walker to his wife, Mar. 11, 1847, Walker Papers, DU.

8. Bauer, *Mexican War*, p. 246; Quaife, *Diary of James K. Polk*, 2:469–70; Bill, *Rehearsal for Conflict*, p. 212; W. B. Campbell to Fanny Campbell, Apr. 21, 1847, Campbell Family Papers, DU; John D. Wilkins, "Expedition against Vera Cruz," Wilkins Mexican War Collection, BY; Hill Diary, Mar. 7, 13, 1847, SHC; *Senate Executive Document No. 1*, 1:216–17, 247–48; John D. Wilkins Journal, BY; S. R. Anderson to G. F. Crockett and A. R. Wynne, Mar. 18, 1847, quoted in Durham, "Mexican War Letters to Wynnewood," p. 402.

9. T. O'Hara to J. M. McCalla, Mar. 28, 1847, McCalla Collection, DU;

John D. Wilkins Journal, BY; S. R. Anderson to G. F. Crockett and A. R. Wynne, Mar. 18, 1847, quoted in Durham, "Mexican War Letters to Wynnewood," p. 402.

10. Campbell Diary; W. B. Campbell to Fanny Campbell, Mar. 15, 1847, Campbell Family Papers, DU; Durham, "Mexican War Letters to Wynnewood, p. 402.

11. Campbell Diary, Campbell Family Papers, DU; Hill Diary, Mar. 15, 1847, SHC.

12. Columbia *Beacon*, May 7, 1847.

13. Campbell Diary, Campbell Family Papers, DU.

14. T. O'Hara to J. M. McCalla, Mar. 28, 1847, McCalla Collection, DU; "Memoranda of Campaigns," BY; Elliot, *Winfield Scott*, pp. 458–59; Bauer, *Mexican War*, pp. 245–48; *Taylor and His Generals*, pp. 301–3; Campbell Diary, Campbell Family Papers, DU.

15. John D. Wilkins Journal, BY.

16. Brooks, *History of the Mexican War*, p. 303; Freeman, *Lee*, 1:230; *Taylor and His Generals*, pp. 301–6; Eisenhower, *So Far from God*, pp. 263, 263n.

17. John D. Wilkins Journal, BY; Campbell Diary, Campbell Family Papers, DU; Freeman, *Lee*, 1:229; Myers, *Mexican War Diary of McClellan*, pp. 63–64, 68; Vera Cruz *American Eagle*, May 5, 1847.

18. Campbell Diary, Campbell Family Papers, DU; John D. Wilkins Journal, BY; "Pillow's Military Service," JRN; Freeman, *Lee*, 1:230.

19. Campbell Diary, Campbell Family Papers, DU.

20. *Senate Executive Document No. 1*, pp. 251–52; Furber, *Mexico*, p. 543; N. C. Hughes, *Hardee*, p. 32; "Memoranda of Campaigns," BY; Campbell Diary, Campbell Family Papers, DU; Osteen, "Never a Good War," pp. 38–39.

21. Maj. Edmund Kirby to Gen. Joseph W. Brown, May 27, 1847, Wilkins Mexican War Collection, BY; Vera Cruz *American Eagle*, May 5, 1847.

22. W. B. Campbell to David Campbell, Mar. 29, 1847, Campbell Family Papers, DU; "Memoranda of Campaigns," BY; T. O'Hara to J. M. McCalla, Mar. 28, 1847, McCalla Correspondence, DU; Livingston, *Eminent American Lawyers*, p. 654.

23. *Life and Military Character of Maj. Gen. Scott*, pp. 35–36; *Senate Executive Document No. 1*, 1:229–30; John D. Wilkins Journal, BY; Columbia *Beacon*, Apr. 30, 1847.

24. This symbolic formation descended from the old Roman custom of marching a captured foe under the yoke of an arch.

25. Osteen, "Never a Good War," pp. 38–39; Henry Wilson Papers, BY; Special Orders No. 71, 1st Brig., 2d Div., Apr. 2, 1847, Campbell Family Papers, DU; Campbell Diary; W. B. Campbell to Fanny Campbell, Apr. 2, 1847, Campbell Family Papers, DU; W. H. T. Walker to his wife, Apr. 1, 1847, Walker Papers, DU.

26. Columbia *Beacon*, Apr. 16, 1847.

27. MEP to GJP, Apr. 11, 1847, Pillow Letters, HSP.

28. GJP to MEP, Apr. 9, 1847; MEP to GJP, Apr. 18, 1847, Pillow Papers, MOHS.

29. GJP to MEP, Apr. 9, 1847, Pillow Papers, MOHS. "Character" as used by Pillow, and by Polk for that matter, was defined in a nineteenth-century military or political context as reputation.

30. Eisenhower, *So Far from God*, pp. 288–90; Bauer, *Mexican War*, pp. 276n, 277n; David Campbell to W. B. Campbell, Mar. 4, 1847, Campbell Family Papers, DU.

31. GJP to Maj. R. B. Reynolds, Apr. 5, 1847, Reynolds Correspondence, NYHS.

32. Ibid.

33. John D. Wilkins Journal, BY; Bauer, *Mexican War*, pp. 259–61; J. H. Smith, *War with Mexico*, 2:47; GJP to MEP, Apr. 9, 1847, Pillow Papers, MOHS.

34. W. B. Campbell to Fanny Campbell, Apr. 18, 1847, Campbell Family Papers, DU; Lewis, *Captain Sam Grant*, p. 164; Bill, *Rehearsal for Conflict*, p. 222; Special Orders No. 1, Volunteer Division, Apr. 7, 1847, Campbell Family Papers, DU; Croffut, *Fifty Years in Camp and Field*, p. 249; John D. Wilkins Journal, BY; Furber, *Twelve Month Volunteer*, pp. 577–78; Brooks, *Mexican War*, p. 321; Oswandel, *Notes*, pp. 110–11.

35. W. R. Caswell to Elizabeth Caswell, Apr. 24, 1847, Caswell Papers, SHC; John D. Wilkins Journal, BY; *Senate Executive Document No. 1*, 1:293; Henry, *Story of the Mexican War*, p. 282; Bauer, *Mexican War*, p. 263.

36. J. H. Smith, *War with Mexico*, 2:50–52; Hill Diary, SHC; Freeman, *Lee*, 1:238–41; Henry, *Story of the Mexican War*, pp. 282–83; Eisenhower, *So Far from God*, pp. 272–79.

37. Gideon Pillow, Supplementary Report of Cerro Gordo, Apr. 29, 1847, Campbell Family Papers, DU; *Taylor and His Generals*, pp. 322–25; Columbia *Beacon*, June 25, 1847; Henry, *Story of the Mexican War*, p. 285; J. H. Smith, *War with Mexico*, 2:49–53; Eisenhower, *So Far from God*, pp. 276–80; Bauer, *Mexican War*, pp. 264–65; Sears, *McClellan*, p. 20; Lynchburg, Va., *Virginian*, June 19, 1847; Livingston, *Eminent American Lawyers*, p. 655.

38. Pillow, according to Scott staff officer Col. Ethan A. Hitchcock, seemed shaken by the responsibility of the attack. He gloomily told Scott that he considered it a "desperate undertaking." Scott tried to calm Pillow by telling him that the attack on the Mexican left "would distract the attention of the enemy and make an opening for him." Pillow answered that he "would go where ordered if he left his bones there" but noted that two of his regiments, the Pennsylvanians, were raw and without service. Scott said that even the regulars were "very much diluted with raw recruits, not so good as raw militia just from home," and, tiring of the conversation, made a remark about discipline and insisted that the attack be made.

Hitchcock's account should be discredited. His reminiscences are notoriously biased in favor of Scott and against Pillow. No other officer mentioned the incident. Furthermore, it contradicts Pillow's blind eagerness to lead his troops into battle. Colonel Campbell, certainly no Pillow apologist, wrote his uncle following the battle that Pillow "had sought" to have his brigade attack by this route. Croffut, *Fifty Years in Camp and Field*, pp. 250–51; W. B. Campbell to David Campbell, Apr. 18, 1847, Campbell Family Papers, DU.

39. General Order No. 111, Apr. 17, 1847, General and Special Orders, Army of Occupation, Office of the Adjutant General, RG 94, NARS; *Senate Executive Document No. 1*, 1:258–59; *Taylor and His Generals*, pp. 237–38, 319–21.

40. McClellan entertained no illusions about chaperoning "Gid Pillow & the Mohawks [as the regulars called the volunteers]. . . . The idea of being killed by or among a parcel of volunteers was anything but pleasant." Sears, *McClellan*, p. 20.

41. John D. Wilkins to his mother, May 7, 1847, John D. Wilkins Mexican War Collection, BY; Sears, *McClellan*, p. 20; Henry, *Story of the Mexican War*, p. 286.

42. Myers, *Mexican War Diary of McClellan*, pp. 80–82.

43. *Senate Executive Document No. 51*, 8:50.

44. Lynchburg, Va., *Virginian*, June 19, 1847; *Senate Executive Document No. 51*, 8:297; J. H. Smith, *War with Mexico*, 2:56–57; Bauer, *Mexican War*, p. 267; Semmes, *Service Afloat and Ashore*, p. 179; W. B. Campbell to Fanny Campbell, Apr. 24, 1847, Campbell Family Papers, DU; Livingston, *Eminent American Lawyers*, p. 655.

45. Lynchburg, Va., *Virginian*, June 19, 1847; *American Star*, Apr. 25, 1847; J. H. Smith, *War with Mexico*, 2:56–57; Oswandel, *Notes*, p. 124; Peskin, *Volunteers*, pp. 80–81.

46. Myers, *Mexican War Diary of McClellan*, p. 82; Lynchburg, Va., *Virginian*, June 19, 1847.

47. Pillow, Supplementary Report of Cerro Gordo, Apr. 29, 1847, Campbell Family Papers, DU; J. H. Smith, *War with Mexico*, 2:44; Eisenhower, *So Far from God*, pp. 280–82.

48. Myers, *Mexican War Diary of McClellan*, p. 83.

49. Pillow, Supplementary Report of Cerro Gordo, Apr. 29, 1847, Campbell Family Papers, DU; Robertson, *Campaign in Mexico*, p. 244.

50. John D. Wilkins to his mother, May 7, 1847, Wilkins Mexican War Collection, BY.

51. Williamson, *Historic Madison*, pp. 117–20; J. W. Caldwell, *Bench and Bar*, pp. 236–51; McBride, *Biographical Directory*, pp. 342–43.

52. Osteen, "Never a Good War," pp. 39–40; Robertson, *Campaign in Mexico*, p. 244.

53. After the battle Roberts reported to Pillow that his 2d Pennsylvania was slowed in going to Haskell's support by the "galling fire of grape and cannister" and the "denseness of the chaparral." *Senate Executive Document No. 51*, 8:52.

54. John D. Wilkins Journal, BY; Lynchburg, Va., *Virginian*, June 19, 1847; W. B. Campbell to Fanny Campbell, Apr. 18, 1847, Campbell Family Papers, DU; Wilcox, *Mexican War*, p. 257; Peskin, *Volunteers*, pp. 80–81; Myers, *Mexi-*

can War Diary of McClellan, p. 84; Jackson, Tenn., *Republican Extra*, May 7, 1847; Furber, *Twelve Month Volunteer*, pp. 592–93; Livingston, *Eminent American Lawyers*, pp. 655–56; Memphis *Daily Eagle*, May 18, 20, June 11, 1847; Columbia *Beacon*, June 25, 1847; Williamson, *Historic Madison*, pp. 117–20.

55. *Senate Executive Document No. 51*, 8:51.

56. In any event, D. H. Hill, as quick as any regular to denigrate volunteers, saw Wynkoop as "the coward who refused to charge at Cerro Gordo." Hill Diary, Mar. 1848, SHC; Pillow, Supplementary Report of Cerro Gordo, Apr. 29, 1847, Campbell Family Papers, DU.

57. Friends and foes made much of Pillow's wound. The *American Eagle* and other papers reported "his sword arm was nearly cut in two by a grape shot." Detractors pointed out that Pillow carried "the ball that hurt him in his breeches pocket." Pillow himself claimed he had been "disabled." Vera Cruz *American Eagle*, May 5, 1847; Columbia *Beacon*, May 14, 1847; *Senate Executive Document No. 51*, 8:52, 83; Lynchburg, Va., *Virginian*, June 19, 1847; Myers, *Mexican War Diary of McClellan*, p. 84; J. H. Smith, *War with Mexico*, 2:57; *Life of Maj. Gen. Scott*, p. 324; *Taylor and His Generals*, p. 238; Pillow, Supplementary Report of Cerro Gordo, Apr. 29, 1847, Campbell Family Papers, DU; GJP to L. J. Cist, May 9, 1866, C. E. French Collection, MHS; GJP Pension Application, RG 15, NARS; GJP to R. Jones, May 10, 1847, Pillow Papers, RG 109, NARS.

58. Pillow, Supplementary Report of Cerro Gordo, Apr. 29, 1847, Campbell Family Papers, DU; Myers, *Mexican War Diary of McClellan*, pp. 84–86.

59. *Senate Executive Document No. 51*, 8:51; Barclay Journal, Aug. 26, 1847, in Peskin, *Volunteers*, p. 179.

60. W. B. Campbell to editor of the *American Star*, Apr. 26, 1847, Campbell Family Papers, DU; Robertson, *Campaign in Mexico*, p. 244.

61. John D. Wilkins Journal, BY; Myers, *Mexican War Diary of McClellan*, pp. 86–87; J. H. Smith, *War with Mexico*, 2:57–58; Bauer, *Mexican War*, p. 267.

62. Semmes, *Service Afloat and Ashore*, p. 183.

63. John D. Wilkins Journal, BY; Robertson, *Campaign in Mexico*, p. 244; J. H. Smith, *War with Mexico*, 2:43, 58; Myers, *Mexican War Diary of McClellan*, pp. 86–87.

64. *Taylor and His Generals*, p. 324; *Senate Executive Document No. 1*, 1:257.

65. Grant, *Memoirs*, 1:64.

66. W. B. Campbell to D. Campbell, Apr. 18, 1847, Campbell Family Papers, DU.

67. W. H. T. Walker to his wife, Apr. 22, 1847, Walker Papers, DU.

68. Sears, *McClellan*, p. 20.

69. Hill Diary, SHC.

70. GJP to MEP, Apr. 9, 1847, Pillow Papers, MOHS; Pillow, Supplementary Report of Cerro Gordo, Apr. 29, 1847, Campbell Family Papers, DU.

71. W. B. Campbell to D. Campbell, Apr. 25, 1847, Campbell Family Papers, DU.

72. GJP to MEP, Apr. 2, 1847, Pillow Letters, HSP; John A. Quitman to his wife, Apr. 29, 1847, Quitman Family Papers, SHC; J. H. Smith, *War*

with Mexico, 2:59; W. B. Campbell to Fanny Campbell, May 3, 1847; Special Orders No. 9, 2d Volunteer Div., Apr. 29, 1847, Campbell Family Papers, DU.

73. Semmes, *Service Afloat and Ashore,* p. 165.

74. French, *Two Wars,* p. 87.

75. JKP to GJP, Apr. [?] 1847, JKP Papers, LOC; MEP to GJP, Apr. 11, 1847, Pillow Letters, HSP; Columbia *Beacon,* May 21, 28, 1847.

76. Memphis *Daily Eagle,* June 3, 1847.

77. Gilly, "Tennessee Opinion," pp. 23–24; Walton, "Triumph of Stability," pp. 21, 21n; Columbia *Beacon,* June 25, Aug. 20, 1847; Lynchburg, Va., *Virginian,* June 19, 1847; Knoxville *Whig,* June 16, 30, July 11, 1847; Memphis *Eagle,* June 7, 1847; Watters, "Harris," p. 19.

78. GJP to JKP, June 9, 1847, JKP Papers, LOC.

79. John L. Brown to R. B. Reynolds, Aug. 18, 1847; John P. Heise to Thomas Ritchie, Aug. 18, 1847, Ritchie-Harrison Papers, Earl Gregg Swem Library, College of William and Mary, Williamsburg, Va.

80. GJP to L. J. Cist, May 9, 1866, C. E. French Collection, MHS; Nashville *American,* Nov. 3, 1878; Livingston, *Eminent American Lawyers,* p. 657; JKP to GJP, May 25, 1847, JKP Papers, LOC; Joseph Davis to Jefferson Davis, May 13, 1847, in Woodworth, *Davis and His Generals,* p. 31.

81. J. K. Walker to GJP, May 26, 1847, JKP Papers, LOC; Schuster, "Nicholas P. Trist," pp. 8–9; Quaife, *Diary of James K. Polk,* 2:478; JKP to GJP, Apr. 18, 1847, JKP Papers, LOC; Pillow, *Letters from Pillow,* p. 5.

82. J. K. Walker to GJP, May 26, 1847; GJP to JKP, June 9, 14, 1847, JKP Papers, LOC; Fletcher, *Diplomacy of Annexation,* p. 505.

83. Reeves, *American Diplomacy under Tyler and Polk,* pp. 313–14.

84. Schuster, "Nicholas P. Trist," pp. 39–40, 57; W. Scott to N. P. Trist, May 29, 1847, Trist Papers, LOC; J. H. Smith, *War with Mexico,* 2:130; Callahan, *American Foreign Policy,* pp. 169–71, 186; Bailey, *Diplomatic History,* p. 261; Scott, *Memoirs,* 2:579; Fletcher, *Diplomacy of Annexation,* p. 505.

CHAPTER FIVE

1. J. H. Smith, *War with Mexico,* 2:76–77; Bauer, *Mexican War,* p. 273; Eisenhower, *So Far from God,* pp. 303–4.

2. GJP to unknown, June 19, 1847, Pillow Papers, RG 109, NARS; GJP to G. Cadwalader, June 28, 1847, Cadwalader Collection, HSP; Niles *Register,* July 10, 1847, quoted in Elliott, *Scott,* p. 489.

3. GJP to G. Cadwalader, June 28, 29, 1847, Cadwalader Collection, HSP; Nevins, *Polk: Diary of a President,* p. 249.

4. *House Executive Document No. 60,* p. 1012.

5. Barclay Journal, July 6, 1847, in Peskin, *Volunteers.*

6. Bill, *Rehearsal for Conflict,* pp. 258–59, 265; Henry, *Story of the Mexican War,* pp. 318–19; Croffut, *Fifty Years in Camp and Field,* p. 265; E. K. Smith, *To Mexico with Scott,* p. 181; Barclay Journal, July 8, 9, 1847, in Peskin, *Volunteers.*

7. GJP to JKP, Dec., 1847, JKP Papers, LOC; N. Trist to W. Scott, July 16, 1847, Trist Papers, LOC.

8. Essay by Nicholas Trist, 1848, Trist Papers, SHC; Bauer, *Mexican War*, p. 284; Schuster, "Nicholas P. Trist," pp. 73–75; Eisenhower, *So Far from God*, pp. 305–6; Claiborne, *Quitman*, 1:136.

9. Later, when he openly attacked Scott, Pillow would maintain that he protested against the bribe initially but "suspended my opposition" until after the council of general officers, and that when he made his sentiments known, Scott and Trist assured him that he "was right and that they would abandon the negotiations." This appears to be untrue. JKP to GJP, Dec. 19, 1847, JKP Papers, LOC; Bauer, *Mexican War*, p. 285; Eisenhower, *So Far from God*, p. 306; Croffut, *Fifty Years in Camp and Field*, pp. 266–68; W. Scott to N. Trist, July 17, 1847, Trist Papers, LOC; Bailey, *Diplomatic History*, p. 262; Pillow, *Letters from Pillow*, pp. 5–6.

10. Claiborne, *Quitman*, 1:317; Bauer, *Mexican War*, p. 285; Henry, *Story of the Mexican War*, p. 317; Freeman, *Lee*, 1:251; Bill, *Rehearsal for Conflict*, p. 264; Eisenhower, *So Far from God*, p. 307n; Hill Diary, Dec. 12, 1847, SHC; J. H. Smith, *War with Mexico*, 2:77–78, 391n; *House Executive Document No. 8*, p. 339.

11. Hooker previously served as staff officer for Brig. Gen. Persifor Smith. Tremain, *Two Days of War*, p. 300; Bauer, *Mexican War*, p. 274; F. R. Brown, *History of the Ninth Infantry*, p. 50; Hill Diary, Aug. 8–13, 1847, SHC; Barclay Journal, Aug. 8–13, 1847, in Peskin, *Volunteers*; Croffut, *Fifty Years in Camp and Field*, p. 273.

12. Henry, *Story of the Mexican War*, p. 324; Freeman, *Lee*, 1:252–53; W. J. Worth to J. Duncan, Mar. 31, 1848; W. J. Worth to W. S. Scott, Aug. 14, 1848, Duncan Letters, U.S. Military Academy Archives, West Point, N.Y.; Bauer, *Mexican War*, pp. 289–90.

13. Barclay Journal, Aug. 15–18, 1847, in Peskin, *Volunteers*.

14. Hill Diary, Aug. 17, 1847, SHC.

15. John D. Wilkins Journal, BY; Eisenhower, *So Far from God*, pp. 314–16.

16. Freeman, *Lee*, 1:256–62; *House Executive Document No. 8*, p. 304.

17. Eisenhower, *So Far from God*, p. 319; John D. Wilkins Journal, BY; Freeman, *Lee*, 1:258; *Senate Executive Document No. 65*, p. 182; May, *Quitman*, p. 183.

18. Ripley, *War with Mexico*, 2:214–15; Herbert, *Hooker*, p. 30.

19. Herbert, *Hooker*, p. 30.

20. Claiborne, Reminiscences of the Mexican War, SHC; Ripley, *War with Mexico*, 2:216–17.

21. Ripley, *War with Mexico*, 2:216–17.

22. Persifor Frazer Smith (1798–1858), conciliatory, well-educated, was a highly regarded soldier from Louisiana who had proved himself in the Seminole War and given distinguished service at Monterrey.

23. Active on Pillow's staff at this time was quartermaster Capt. Theodore O'Hara, a young Kentucky editor and passionate Democrat, who carried

instructions and helped position troops. He would win a brevet promotion for his performance that day. *House Executive Document No. 8*, pp. 323, 334; Henry, *Story of the Mexican War*, p. 330; Croffut, *Fifty Years in Camp and Field*, p. 276; Brackett, "Colonel Theodore O'Hara," p. 280; Freeman, *Lee*, 1:258; Pillow, *Defense*, p. 22.

24. John D. Wilkins Journal, BY; *House Executive Document No. 8*, p. 335.

25. Freeman, *Lee*, 1:259–60.

26. *House Executive Document No. 8*, p. 335; Barclay Journal, Aug. 20, 1847, in Peskin, *Volunteers*; John D. Wilkins Journal, BY; R. M. Hughes, *General Johnston*, p. 27; J. H. Smith, *War with Mexico*, 2:378; Henderson, *Jackson*, pp. 26–27.

27. John D. Wilkins Journal, BY.

28. Vandiver, *Mighty Stonewall*, pp. 34–35; Sears, *McClellan*, p. 22; Hill Diary, Aug. 23, 1847, SHC.

29. Peskin, *Volunteers*, pp. 143–46; Bauer, *Mexican War*, pp. 292–93; *Senate Executive Document No. 65*, pp. 99–100, 147, 182, 332; J. H. Smith, *War with Mexico*, 2:104–6.

30. O. A. Singletary, *Mexican War*, pp. 89–90.

31. *House Executive Document No. 8*, p. 335; Extracts from Reports of Pillow and Worth, Aug., 1847, Pillow Papers, HUL; R. F. Nichols, *Franklin Pierce*, pp. 161–63; J. H. Smith, *War with Mexico*, 2:104–5, 116; John D. Wilkins Journal, BY.

32. Scott later insisted that he, not Pillow, ordered Morgan to march. In the court of inquiry, however, this contention was not established. J. H. Smith, *War with Mexico*, 2:104–5, 378–80; *House Executive Document No. 8*, p. 305; *Senate Executive Document No. 65*, p. 247; Ripley, *War with Mexico*, 2:295–97; Bauer, *Mexican War*, p. 293; Bill, *Rehearsal for Conflict*, p. 274; Henry, *Story of the Mexican War*, p. 333; Pillow, *Defense*.

33. There was personal and political trouble between Santa Anna and Valencia that may have caused his hesitation. There was also a deep ravine that Santa Anna believed would block his approach. J. H. Smith, *War with Mexico*, 2:105–6.

34. Ibid.

35. *House Executive Document No. 8*, p. 335; Freeman, *Lee*, 1:263.

36. Ripley, *War with Mexico*, 2:293; John D. Wilkins Journal, BY.

37. Lee's crossing of the Pedregal in darkness thrilled the American army. "The greatest feat of physical and moral courage performed by any individual," Scott chose to say. Freeman, *Lee*, 1:272.

38. *House Executive Document No. 8*, p. 306; Freeman, *Lee*, 1:264–65; Memphis *Daily Appeal*, Oct. 6, 1857; Elliott, *Winfield Scott*, p. 510.

39. *House Executive Document No. 8*, pp. 307, 335–36; Peskin, *Volunteers*, pp. 144–49; John D. Wilkins Journal, BY; Livingston, *Eminent American Lawyers*, pp. 658–60; J. H. Smith, *War with Mexico*, 2:108–10; Hill Diary, Aug. 23, 1847, SHC.

40. Scott had anticipated him, however. He sent word back to Pillow by

messenger that he had already ordered Worth to attack San Antonio once Pillow and Twiggs appeared behind the town.

41. Memorandum by N. Trist, 1848, Nicholas P. Trist Papers, UVA; *House Executive Document No. 8*, pp. 308–9, 338; *Senate Executive Document No. 65*, p. 102.

42. Although painfully injured on the nineteenth, Franklin Pierce insisted on commanding his brigade; he fainted from the pain during this movement. Both Scott and Pillow complimented him highly.

43. J. H. Smith, *War with Mexico*, 2:112–13; Livingston, *Eminent American Lawyers*, pp. 660–61; Bauer, *Mexican War*, pp. 296–97; Eisenhower, *So Far from God*, pp. 324–25; *House Executive Document No. 8*, p. 310; Freeman, *Lee*, 1:267; Rodenbough and Haskins, *Army of the United States*, p. 439.

44. *House Executive Document No. 8*, p. 338.

45. J. H. Smith, *War with Mexico*, 2:111; R. Miller, *Shamrock and Sword*, p. 84; Ripley, *War with Mexico*, 2:257; Elliott, *Winfield Scott*, p. 517; Bauer, *Mexican War*, pp. 296–300.

46. *House Executive Document No. 8*, p. 310; Livingston, *Eminent American Lawyers*, p. 661; Ripley, *War with Mexico*, 2:267–68.

47. Ripley, *War with Mexico*, 2:269–70.

48. GJP to MEP, Aug. 27, 1847, Pillow Letters, BY.

49. Ripley, *War with Mexico*, 2:272; J. H. Smith, *War with Mexico*, 2:116; GJP to MEP, Oct. 18, 1847, Pillow Papers, HUL; Bill, *Rehearsal for Conflict*, p. 259.

50. F. R. Brown, *History of the Ninth Infantry*, p. 30.; William M. Gardner Memoirs, Memphis State University Library, Mississippi Valley Collection, Memphis, Tenn.; Livingston, *Eminent American Lawyers*, p. 662; R. Miller, *Shamrock and Sword*, pp. 84–86.

51. Romance and high-blown rhetoric and self-inflation aside, Pillow appears to have fired off a round at a Mexican officer. Several of them were advancing rapidly toward him, intending, he believed, either to attack him or to escape from the field. Pillow's staff was gone; only an orderly remained. When he fired, one of the officers fell from his horse—so much for the grand contest at arms. Mexico City *Daily American Star*, Oct. 23, 1847; *House Executive Document No. 8*, p. 311; *Senate Executive Document No. 65*, p. 331; Pillow, *Defense*.

52. Pillow maintained that he initiated the pursuit phase, throwing Capt. Phil Kearny with three troops of cavalry against the rear of the retreating column. Meanwhile, he claims, he reformed his and Worth's troops and set out in support; then Scott intervened and halted the pursuit. Pillow's claims, however, as set forth in Livingston, *Eminent American Lawyers*, p. 662, and the Nashville *American*, Nov. 3, 1878, are not substantiated by the official reports.

53. *Senate Executive Document No. 1*, p. 313.

54. *House Executive Document No. 8*, p. 321.

55. GJP to MEP, Aug. 27, 1847, Pillow Letters, BY.

56. J. H. Smith, *War with Mexico*, 2:120–21, 133.

57. Pillow, *Defense*; J. H. Smith, *War with Mexico*, 2:293–95; Bemis, *Diplo-*

matic History, p. 242; Nashville *American*, Nov. 3, 1878; Pillow, *Letters from Pillow*, pp. 6–8.

58. Henry, *Story of the Mexican War*, pp. 345, 351; Schuster, "Nicholas P. Trist," pp. 77, 79–97.

59. J. H. Smith, *War with Mexico*, 2:147.

60. Pillow, *Defense*, p. 42; Livingston, *Eminent American Lawyers*, p. 663.

61. The matter apparently did not die there. In 1854 Lt. T. J. Jackson, a professor at VMI, wrote Pillow asking him to provide a statement that would clear Hill's record of the arrest, so that Hill "shall be secure from such an interpretation as cowardice on his part." It seems Pillow did not reply. Pillow, *Defense*; Hill Diary, Sept. 9, 1847, SHC; T. J. Jackson to GJP, May 11, 1854, Dabney Papers, SHC; Bridges, *Hill*, pp. 20–21.

62. John D. Wilkins Journal, BY; Bauer, *Mexican War*, p. 311; Eisenhower, *So Far from God*, p. 332.

63. *Senate Executive Document No. 1*, p. 381.

64. J. H. Smith, *War with Mexico*, 2:149; John D. Wilkins Journal, BY; T. H. Williams, *Beauregard*, pp. 28–29; Freeman, *Lee*, 1:277.

65. John D. Wilkins Journal, BY.

66. Elliott, *Winfield Scott*, pp. 542–43; John D. Wilkins Journal, BY.

67. Hill Diary, Sept. 12, 1847, SHC.

68. John D. Wilkins Journal, BY.

69. Elliott, *Winfield Scott*, p. 543; Claiborne, *Quitman*, 1:380; John D. Wilkins Journal, BY.

70. May, *Quitman*, p. 158; J. H. Smith, *War with Mexico*, 2:153; *House Executive Document No. 8*, p. 401; Croffut, *Fifty Years in Camp and Field*, p. 302; Smith and Judah, *Chronicles of the Gringos*, p. 262; Pillow, *Defense*, p. 44.

71. Barclay Journal, Sept. 13, 1847, in Peskin, *Volunteers*.

72. John D. Wilkins Journal, BY; J. H. Smith, *War with Mexico*, 2:150–51; Bill, *Rehearsal for Conflict*, p. 293; Eisenhower, *So Far from God*, p. 339; Bauer, *Mexican War*, p. 313.

73. *House Executive Document No. 8*, pp. 401–2; Henry, *Story of the Mexican War*, pp. 359–60; P. G. T. Beauregard to GJP, Sept. 17, 1847, Civil War Collection, MOHS.

74. Barclay Journal, Sept. 13, 1847, in Peskin, *Volunteers*; John D. Wilkins Journal, BY; Livingston, *Eminent American Lawyers*, pp. 664–66.

75. E. S. Parker to Ike [?], Oct. 31, 1847, E. S. Parker Letters, HUL.

76. Pillow's boot, split down to the ankle, was recently discovered at Clifton. *House Executive Document No. 8*, pp. 378, 404; J. H. Smith, *War with Mexico*, 2:156; *Senate Executive Document No. 65*, p. 529; May, *Quitman*, p. 208; John D. Wilkins Journal, BY; GJP to L. J. Cist, May 9, 1866, C. E. French Collection, MHS; J. A. Quitman to his wife, Sept. 19, 1847, Quitman Family Papers, SHC; Pillow, *Defense*, pp. 47–51; *CV* 1:330; Pension Application of Mary Eliza Dickson Trigg Pillow, Dec. 10, 1887, Records Relating to Pension and Bounty Land Claims, 1773–1942, RG 15, NARS; conversation with Paul Cross, May 22, 1991.

77. J. H. Smith, *War with Mexico*, 2:155–56; F. R. Brown, *History of the Ninth*

Infantry, pp. 57–60; GJP to H. L. Scott, Jan. 3, 1848, Pillow Papers, MOHS.

78. J. H. Smith, *War with Mexico*, 2:156–57; *House Executive Document No. 8*, pp. 402–3, 412–13; John D. Wilkins Journal, BY; GJP to JKP, Oct. 4, 1847, JKP Papers, LOC; GJP to H. L. Scott, Jan. 3, 1848, Pillow Papers, MOHS; Livingston, *Eminent American Lawyers*, pp. 664–66; F. R. Brown, *History of the Ninth Infantry*, pp. 30, 35.

79. F. R. Brown, *History of the Ninth Infantry*, p. 35; Pillow, *Defense*, pp. 50–51; Barclay Journal, Sept. 13, 1847, in Peskin, *Volunteers*.

80. Jackson's biographer Henderson maintains that Pillow's decision "separating his section on the day of Chapultepec from his captain, had excited his abiding gratitude. . . . He loved him [Pillow] because he gave him an opportunity to win distinction." Henderson, *Jackson*, p. 35; Vandiver, *Rebel Brass*, p. 40.

81. *House Executive Document No. 8*, pp. 402–3, 413; J. H. Smith, *War with Mexico*, 2:163–64; Bauer, *Mexican War*, pp. 319–22; Eisenhower, *So Far from God*, pp. 340–42; Trousdale, "Trousdale," p. 127.

82. GJP to MEP, Oct. 18, 1847, Pillow Papers, HUL.

CHAPTER SIX

1. GJP to MEP, Oct. 18, Nov. 16, 1847, Feb. 1, 1848; GJP to Jerome Pillow, Mar. 5, 1848, Pillow Letters, HSP; William Preston Mexican War Journal, Special Collections, University of Kentucky Library, Lexington, Ky.; GJP to R. B. Reynolds, Oct. 28, 1847, Reynolds Correspondence, NYHS; GJP to MEP, Dec. 8, 1847, Washington Family Papers, UVA.

2. Pillow managed to find a source for good whiskey, buying five gallons for himself and five for his friend George Cadwalader. In his letters home, Pillow carefully included information about his servants Alfred and Ben, counting on Mary to relay news to their wives. GJP to George Cadwalader, Mar. 7, 1848, Cadwalader Collection, HSP; GJP to MEP, Dec. 8, 1847, Washington Family Papers, UVA; GJP to R. B. Reynolds, Oct. 28, Nov. 27, 1847, Reynolds Correspondence, NYHS.

3. Mexico City *Daily American Star*, Oct. 25, 1847.

4. Following the Civil War, James Walker was commissioned by Joseph Hooker for $20,000 to do a painting of the Battle of Lookout Mountain. It survives there in a museum, a magnificent thirty-foot-wide, thirteen-foot-high panorama featuring a decisive Hooker in the foreground. Hooker learned many lessons well from Pillow. GJP to JKP, Dec. 12, 1847, JKP Papers, LOC; GJP to MEP, Dec. 8, 1847, Washington Family Papers, UVA; Sandweiss, Stewart, and Huseman, *Eyewitness to War*, pp. 332–35, 334n; McNaughton, "James Walker," pp. 31–35; Tyler, "Mexican War," pp. 45–48.

5. *Senate Executive Document No. 1*, pp. 13–14; Stonesifer, "Pillow," p. 342; J. L. Freaner to GJP, Nov. 15, 1847 (a true copy signed by Capt. H. H. Sibley, 2d Dragoons), Trist Papers, UVA.

6. Croffut, *Fifty Years in Camp and Field*, p. 323; *Senate Executive Document*

No. 1, pp. 13–14, 61, 249–53; New Orleans *Daily Delta*, Sept. 10, 1847, reprinted in *Senate Executive Document No. 65*, pp. 385–89; Mexico City *Daily American Star*, Oct. 23, 1847; Memphis *Daily Appeal*, Oct. 3, 1857; J. H. Smith, *War with Mexico*, 2:435–37; Pillow, *Defense*.

7. Eisenhower, *So Far from God*, pp. 352, 352n; Stonesifer, "Pillow," p. 343.

8. *House Executive Document No. 60*, p. 1016.

9. Ibid., pp. 1016–17.

10. Essay by Nicholas Trist, Trist Papers, UVA; *House Executive Document No. 60*, pp. 1018–20; GJP to JKP, Dec. 12, 1847, JKP Papers, LOC; New York *Times*, Oct. 6, 1857.

11. Freeman, *Lee*, 1:287; John D. Wilkins to his mother, Nov. 1847, Wilkins Mexican War Collection, BY.

12. *Senate Executive Document No. 65*, p. 547.

13. Ibid., pp. 548–49; William J. Heady to MEP, Jan. 1, 1848, Dreer Collection, HSP.

14. GJP to W. Scott, Nov. 2, 1847; GJP to William Marcy, Nov. 15, 1847, JKP Papers, LOC; Memphis *Daily Appeal*, Oct. 3, 1857.

15. Although the Aztec Club has no record of Pillow's membership, his nephew J. G. Pillow of Atchison, Kansas, served in the club as his "successor." Conversation with Richard Sommers, U.S. Army Military History Institute, Carlisle, Pa., Sept. 16, 1991; conversation with Conway Hunt of Aztec Club, Sept. 4, 1991; Aztec Club, Membership Committee, *History of the Aztec Club*.

16. Aztec Club, Membership Committee, *History of the Aztec Club*; Eisenhower, *So Far from God*, p. 356; Bauer, *Mexican War*, pp. 327–28.

17. GJP to MEP, Oct. 18, 1847, Pillow Letters, HSP.

18. Eisenhower, *So Far from God*, p. 352.

19. *Senate Executive Document No. 65*, pp. 546, 550; GJP to W. Scott, Nov. 2, 1847, JKP Papers, LOC.

20. Edward Bradford to John Tazewell, Jan. 2, 1848, Wilkins Mexican War Collection, BY; Eisenhower, *So Far from God*, p. 352; Bill, *Rehearsal for Conflict*, p. 313; Elliott, *Winfield Scott*, p. 573; Hamlin, *Ewell*, p. 65.

21. GJP to MEP, Nov. 16, 1847, Pillow Letters, HSP.

22. Pillow and Trist seem to have been on fairly good terms as late as mid-August 1847. GJP to N. Trist, Aug. 26, 1847, Trist Papers, LOC; Trist essay, Trist Papers, SHC; *New York Times*, Oct. 6, 1857; McCormac, *Polk*, p. 526.

23. JKP to GJP, Dec. 19, 1847, JKP Papers, LOC; Quaife, *Diary of James K. Polk*, 3:245–46; Fletcher, *Diplomacy of Annexation*, p. 557.

24. *Senate Executive Document No. 65*, p. 546; GJP to JKP, Nov. 24, Dec. 12, 1847, JKP Papers, LOC.

25. W. Scott to GJP, Nov. 22, 1847, JKP Papers, LOC; Columbia *Beacon*, Jan. 14, 1848; Henry, *Story of the Mexican War*, p. 337; Benton, *Thirty Years View*, 2:711.

26. Freeman, *Lee*, 1:287.

27. *Senate Executive Document No. 65*, pp. 317–28.

28. H. L. Scott to J. Duncan, Nov. 18, 1847; Charges and Specifications Preferred Against Bvt. Lt. Col. Duncan, Nov. 28, 1847; GJP to J. Duncan,

Mar. 31, June 28, Sept. 30, 1848, Duncan Letters, U.S. Military Academy Archives, West Point, N.Y.; Henry, *Story of the Mexican War*, pp. 377–78; Elliott, *Winfield Scott*, pp. 571–72; Hill Diary, Nov. 25, 1847, SHC; Bill, *Rehearsal for Conflict*, pp. 311–12.

29. GJP to JKP, Nov. 24, 1847, JKP Papers, LOC; Sellers, *Polk: Continentalist*, p. 282.

30. Livingston, *Eminent American Lawyers*, p. 667; Pillow, *Letters from Pillow*, pp. 10–11; GJP to MEP, Nov. 25, 1847, Pillow Letters, HSP.

31. GJP to MEP, Nov. 25, 1847, Pillow Letters, HSP.

32. Ibid.

33. GJP to R. B. Reynolds, Nov. 27, 1847, Reynolds Correspondence, NYHS.

34. A. J. Coffee to A. D. Coffee, Jan. 15, 1848, Andrew J. Coffee Papers, Memphis State University Library, Mississippi Valley Collection, Memphis, Tenn.; Hill Diary, Nov. 25, 1847, SHC.

35. Quaife, *Diary of James K. Polk*, 3:261–62.

36. Ibid., p. 253.

37. JKP to GJP, Dec. 19, 1847, JKP Papers, LOC; Reeves, *American Diplomacy under Tyler and Polk*, pp. 318–19.

38. J. Knox Walker to GJP, Dec. 21, 1847, JKP Papers, LOC.

39. Nevins, *Polk: Diary of a President*, p. 288; Bauer, *Mexican War*, pp. 372–73.

40. Draft of W. L. Marcy to W. Scott, Jan. 13, 1848, Wilkins Mexican War Collection, BY; Scott, *Memoirs*, p. 584; Spencer, *Marcy*, p. 168; Eisenhower, *So Far from God*, p. 364; Bauer, *Mexican War*, p. 373.

41. Croffut, *Fifty Years in Camp and Field*, pp. 318, 320, 326–28; Edmund Bradford to John Tazewell, Jan. 2, Feb. 28, 1848, Wilkins Mexican War Collection, BY; Scammon, "A Chapter of the Mexican War," pp. 574–75; Hill Diary, Feb. [?] 1848, SHC; Helen B. Chapman to Emily W. Blair, Apr. 6, 1848, in Coker, *News from Brownsville*, p. 36.

42. GJP to MEP, Feb. 27, 1848, Pillow Letters, HSP.

43. GJP to JKP, Dec. 12, 1847, JKP Papers, LOC.

44. GJP to R. B. Reynolds, Jan. 13, 1848, Reynolds Correspondence, NYHS.

45. Mrs. Frances P. Butler to E. G. W. Butler, Jan. 27, 1848, Butler Family Papers, Historic New Orleans Collection, New Orleans, La.; Elliott, *Winfield Scott*, pp. 578–79; Draft of William L. Marcy to W. Scott, Jan. 13, 1848, Wilkins Mexican War Collection, BY; A. J. Coffee to A. D. Coffee, Jan. 15, 1848, Coffee Papers, Memphis State University Library, Mississippi Valley Collection, Memphis, Tenn.; General Order No. 2, Jan. 13, 1848, Adjutant General's Office, James A. Duncan Papers, U.S. Military Academy Archives, West Point, N.Y.

46. Fuess, *Caleb Cushing*, 2:75–76; Elliott, *Winfield Scott*, p. 580; GJP to MEP, Mar. 14, 1848, Pillow Letters, HSP.

47. R. E. Lee to Mary C. Lee, Mar. 24, 1848, Lee Family Papers, Virginia Historical Society, Richmond, Va.

48. Helen Chapman feared her friend Duncan had ruined himself with the army by involving himself with Pillow. Helen B. Chapman to Emily W. Blair, May 18, 1848, July 15, 1948, in Coker, *News from Brownsville*, pp. 44, 129.

49. In honor of Duncan, Pillow named his youngest daughter Alice Duncan Pillow. GJP to JKP, Jan. 2, 1849, JKP Papers, LOC; Nashville *American*, Nov. 3, 1878.

50. Pillow also wrote Polk that Burns, by his Leonidas testimony, "incurred the eternal displeasure of Scott—all his Friends & the Whigs everywhere." GJP to JKP, Nov. 2, 4, 1847; GJP to J. K. Walker, Feb. 18, 1849, JKP Papers, LOC; Basler, *Collected Works of Lincoln*, 4:413n.

51. J. H. Smith, *War with Mexico*, 2:185–86.

52. Ibid.; Johanssen, *To the Halls of the Montezumas*, p. 120; Hinds, "Mexican War Journal of Leander M. Cox," p. 55; GJP to MEP, Feb. 1, 1848, Pillow Papers, MOHS.

53. Henry, *Story of the Mexican War*, p. 383.

54. W. C. Davis, *Breckinridge*, p. 38; Fuess, *Caleb Cushing*, 2:75–76.

55. Pillow, *Defense*.

56. Sanborn, *Lee*, 1:193; Freeman, *Lee*, 1:290–91.

57. Freeman, *Lee*, 2:290–91; Bill, *Rehearsal for Conflict*, pp. 319–20.

58. GJP to MEP, Apr. 1, 8, 1848, Pillow Letters, HSP; R. E. Lee to Mrs. Anna M. Fitzhugh, Apr. 12, 1848, Lee Family Papers, Virginia Historical Society, Richmond, Va.; Pillow, *Defense*.

59. Pillow worried that he might "be thrown out of the service, before the proof in the U.S. can be taken, and the case brought to a close." GJP to C. Cushing, 1848 [exact date unknown], Cushing Papers, LOC; Nevins, *Polk: Diary of a President*, pp. 304–5; Elliott, *Winfield Scott*, p. 584; Bill, *Rehearsal for Conflict*, pp. 320–21; Fletcher, *Diplomacy of Annexation*, p. 557n.

60. Another daughter, Narcissa Cynthia, had been born April 11, 1848. Elliott, *Winfield Scott*, p. 588; Clark, "Nicholson," p. 61.

61. May, *Quitman*, pp. 208–9; Trist memorandum, Trist Papers, UVA; Croffut, *Fifty Years in Camp and Field*, pp. 326–28; Potter, *Impending Crisis*, pp. 3–4.

62. GJP to JKP, Nov. 2, 1848, JKP Papers, LOC.

63. The report of the court dated July 1 noted, "There is no direct evidence showing Gen. Pillow's connection with this article." This finding also struck down specifications 1, 7, and 8 of the second charge, all of which dealt in one way or the other with the Leonidas letter.

The eight specifications of the second charge—of conduct unbecoming an officer—dealt mainly with fine points of Pillow's reports of Padierna, Churubusco, and Chapultepec or comments that Pillow was said to have made.

Scott charged in subspecification 1 (of charge 2) that at Padierna he ordered the movement of Morgan's regiment and not Pillow. Pillow's witnesses on this point were formidable. Captain Hooker swore that Pillow gave the order for Morgan's advance and that he delivered it to Morgan. Colonel Morgan testified that he indeed received this order and placed his regiment in motion, and that as it moved off, Scott rode up. The court agreed with

Pillow, concluding that Pillow gave the order and Hooker delivered it, and that, with the arrival of Scott, the general-in-chief—not realizing that the order had been issued—repeated the order to Pillow, believing that it was his own.

Subspecification 2 dealt with a minor difference over the time of the arrival of Shields's brigade at Smith's position at San Gerónimo. Pillow, using the testimony of Shields, set the time of arrival at 1:00 A.M. The court's decision favored Scott's version and set the time in question at the earlier time of 10:00 P.M. It noted that Pillow's information was "inaccurate" but found "no intentional misstatement on his part."

Subspecification 3 dealt with Pierce's orders to support Twiggs in the assault across the Padierna ravine on the morning of August 20. The court correctly supported Scott's claim that he ordered Pierce's movement through Captain Lee but noted that Pillow assumed that Pierce's attack was part of his original attack plan.

In subspecification 4, Scott accused Pillow of attempting to take credit for Smith's flank attack on Valencia the morning of August 20 and for his pursuit of the enemy forces. The court noted that Pillow spent the night at San Augustin, arrived on the field of combat thirty minutes after Smith had carried the Mexican position, and then went to the head of the pursuit column.

In subspecification 5, Scott challenged Pillow's statement that he commanded all forces engaged at Padierna on August 19–20 except for Worth's division. The court passed over this specification, choosing to include its content in their decision on specification 3.

In subspecification 6, Scott attacked Pillow's assertion that "General Scott gave but one order on August 19 and 20, 1847 [Padierna and Churubusco] and that was to reinforce General Cadwalader's brigade." Scott bitterly added that the impression was that "Pillow was the general planner and director of all operations of the said two days." The court passed this on to specification 3.

Scott challenged Pillow's statement in subspecification 7 that read: "The general's [Pillow's] plan of battle [Padierna] and the disposition of his forces were most judicious and successful [and] General Scott was so perfectly well pleased with it that he could not interfere with it but left it to the gallant projector [Pillow] to carry into glorious and successful execution." Scott concluded that the plan of attack on the morning of August 20 was conceived and executed by Smith. The court deferred its judgment again to its decision on specification 3.

The eighth subspecification dealt with Pillow's assertion that in front of the tête de pont at Churubusco, he "had a long and severe conflict" with a Mexican officer and in the process disarmed and killed him. Scott's main witness who challenged Pillow's statement was Lt. James Longstreet. To counter Longstreet, Pillow's orderly, Private Ayers, stated that Pillow shot at a Mexican officer and that the officer fell from his horse. The court decided that Pillow did shoot at the Mexican, "who may have fallen by the shot, although it seems more probable that the officer fell in consequence of a musket shot or shots fired by others."

In specification 3, Scott again challenged Pillow's contention that he formulated and gave the plan of attack for Padierna. The court's decision was clearly and fairly drawn. It stated:

> On the afternoon of the 19th, Pillow was senior, and ordered first Colonel Riley's brigade across the pedregal to the left of Valencia's camp, then General Cadwalader's brigade to support Colonel Riley, and then Colonel Morgan's regiment to support General Cadwalader, before the arrival of General Scott on the ground; and the movement of these troops on the 19th was of great importance, in enabling our forces to occupy San Geronimo . . . , but it does not appear that any specific plan of battle was communicated by General Pillow either to Colonel Riley, General Cadwalader or Colonel Morgan; and although the idea of a simultaneous movement on two or more points of Valencia's camp seems, by the testimony, to have been entertained by General Pillow—as indicated by his suggestion to General Twiggs . . . the movement was planned and executed by Smith.

In specification 4, Scott attacked Pillow's statement that after the disaster at El Molino del Rey, the general-in-chief was "inert, indecisive or stunned." The court held that Pillow's opinion was erroneous "but were not satisfied that he made them with improper motive or purpose."

Scott charged in specification 5 that Pillow magnified his "zeal and heroism" at Chapultepec, and he challenged Pillow's statement "that although wounded, he had himself borne along in the face of enemy fire." The court noted that Pillow "was brought up [to the military academy] between 15–30 minutes after the storming party."

In specification 6, Scott charged that Pillow sent a letter to Marcy criticizing the armistice of August 23, 1847. The court found that the evidence did not support the specification. Specifications 7 and 8 dealt with the Leonidas letter and were struck down by the court's decision on charge 1. *Senate Executive Document No. 65*, pp. 324–33; Pillow, *Defense*.

64. Pillow, *Defense*; Elliott, *Winfield Scott*, p. 589.

65. Elliott, *Winfield Scott*, p. 589; *Senate Executive Document No. 65*, p. 335; Fuess, *Caleb Cushing*, 2:77.

66. Scott, *Memoirs*, p. 583n; Quaife, *Diary of James K. Polk*, 3:434.

67. Elliott, *Winfield Scott*, p. 589; Polk's Review of Court of Inquiry of Gideon J. Pillow, July 7, 1848, JKP Papers, LOC; Quaife, *Diary of James K. Polk*, 3:507, 4:7.

68. Claxton, *Eighty-eight Years with Sarah Polk*, p. 195; Quaife, *Diary of James K. Polk*, 3:503–7.

69. Quaife, *Diary of James K. Polk*, 4:5–6; GJP to L. J. Cist, May 9, 1866, C. E. French Collection, MHS; R. B. Reynolds to JKP, Dec. 21, 1847, Reynolds Correspondence, NYHS; GJP to George Cadwalader, June 19, July 1, 1848, Cadwalader Collection, HSP.

70. Quaife, *Diary of James K. Polk*, 4:12–13.

71. GJP to J. Duncan, May 15, 1849; GJP to J. K. Polk, Jan. 21, 1849, Duncan Letters, U.S. Military Academy Archives, West Point, N.Y.

72. GJP to George Cadwalader, July 28, Aug. 1, 10, 1848, Cadwalader Collection, HSP; GJP to JKP, July 30, 1848, JKP Papers, LOC.

73. Columbia, Tenn., *Maury Intelligencer*, May 10, 1849; Columbia, Tenn., *Maury Democrat*, Apr. 6, 1911.

74. JKP to GJP, Sept. 29, 1848; S. H. Laughlin to GJP, Oct. 5, 1848, JKP Papers, LOC; C. Johnson to GJP, Oct. 10, 1848, Dreer Collection, HSP.

75. The Pillows entertained neglected friends, and Clifton once again became noted for its "warm hospitality." Mary L. Polk, who dined there, observed that Mary Pillow "was very clever & officiated with ease & dignity." GJP to JKP, Oct. 4, 1848; M. L. Polk to Mrs. James K. Polk, Oct. 8, 1848, JKP Papers, LOC; GJP to J. Duncan, Sept. 30, 1848, Duncan Papers, U.S. Military Academy Archives, West Point, N.Y.

CHAPTER SEVEN

1. Cooper also did a portrait of Anne (Annie) Payne Pillow at the time he did her son's. Morrissey, *Portraits in Tennessee*, pp. 98–99; Cirker, *Dictionary of American Portraits*, p. 489.

2. Roswell Ripley to GJP, Mar. 8, 1849, Pillow Letters, University of California at Los Angeles; GJP to J. Knox Walker, Feb. 18, 1849, JKP Papers, LOC.

3. Pillow refers to W. F. P. Napier's classic six-volume history of the Napoleonic wars in Spain and Portugal published during the 1830s. GJP to G. Cadwalader, Apr. 28, 1849, Cadwalader Collection, HSP; GJP to J. Duncan, June 4, 1849, Duncan Letters, U.S. Military Academy Archives, West Point, N.Y.

4. Single-story wings opening on the rear portico were also constructed during Pillow's absence. Conversation with Linda Neal, Paul Cross, and Wallace Hebert, May 22, 1991; Cross, *Clifton Place Plantation*.

5. McCormac, *Polk*, p. 720; Columbia, Tenn., *Maury Intelligencer*, Apr. 5, 12, 1849; New Orleans *Daily Delta*, July 6, 1849; Columbia *Weekly Recorder*, Aug. 24, 1849; GJP to R. B. Reynolds, Aug. 18, 1849, Reynolds Correspondence, NYHS; Parker, Cross, and Hebert, *Friendship*, pp. 15–17.

6. Roswell Ripley to GJP, Mar. 8, 1849, Pillow Letters, University of California at Los Angeles; GJP to R. B. Reynolds, Aug. 18, 1849, Reynolds Correspondence, NYHS; Joseph Hooker to GJP, Apr. 9, 1849, Pillow Letters, HSP; GJP to J. Duncan, May 15, June 4, 1849, Duncan Letters, U.S. Military Academy Archives, West Point, N.Y.; Sioussat, "Tennessee and National Political Parties," pp. 248–49; Bergeron, *Antebellum Politics in Tennessee*, p. 84; P. M. Hamer, *Tennessee*, 1:472–73; A. V. Brown to A. O. P. Nicholson, Apr. 5, 1849, Nicholson Papers, NYHS; Nashville *Daily Union*, Apr. 9, 1849.

7. In 1853 the *Union* and the *American* combined into the Nashville *Union and American*. Elbridge Gerry Eastman (1813–59) was a New Englander Polk

had invited to Tennessee in 1839 to establish the Knoxville *Argus*. After holding a post in Washington during the Polk administration, Eastman moved to Nashville and took over the Democratic *Union*. Pillow's faithful ally, John C. Burch, would become editor at Eastman's death.

8. A. O. P. Nicholson to E. G. Eastman, Apr. 11, 1852, Nicholson Papers, NYHS; A. V. Brown to GJP, June 18, 1850, Pillow Letters, HSP; Wayne County, Tennessee, Deed Book G, pp. 126, 129; A. V. Brown to GJP, Dec. 18, 1849, Dearborn Collection, HLH.

9. Wiltse, *Calhoun*, pp. 288–89, 303–7, 460–65, 475; Strode, *Jefferson Davis*, 1:218–21.

10. N. Beverley Tucker to James H. Hammond, Dec. 14, 1849, Tucker Letters, DU.

11. Jennings, *Nashville Convention*, pp. 5–6; Bergeron, *Antebellum Politics in Tennessee*, pp. 104–5; Joel Ward to Lewis Ward, May 5, 1850, Ward Family Papers, DU; Henry B. Holcombe to M. B. Lamar, May 4, 1850, Lamar Papers, Texas State Library and Archives, Austin, Tex.; N. B. Tucker to J. H. Hammond, Feb. 8, 1850, Tucker Papers, DU; M. E. R. Campbell, *Attitude of Tennesseans*, pp. 60–61.

12. Bergeron, *Antebellum Politics in Tennessee*, pp. 104–5; Tricamo, "Tennessee Politics," p. 76; Jennings, *Nashville Convention*, pp. 130–33.

13. Pillow's brother-in-law West Humphreys also served as a delegate. Nashville *Union*, July 24, 1850; Sioussat, "Tennessee, the Compromise of 1850, and the Nashville Convention," pp. 331–32; Conyngham, *Sunny South*, pp. 131–35; Little Rock *Arkansas Gazette and Democrat*, June 14, 1850; Newberry, "Nashville Convention," pp. 120–21; Jennings, *Nashville Convention*, pp. 136–37.

14. Conyngham, *Sunny South*, p. 138.

15. Ibid., pp. 131–35; Sioussat, "Tennessee, the Compromise of 1850, and the Nashville Convention," pp. 340–42.

16. Sioussat, "Tennessee, the Compromise of 1850, and the Nashville Convention," p. 337; P. M. Hamer, *Tennessee*, 1:476–78; Jennings, *Nashville Convention*, pp. 145–53.

17. Livingston, *Eminent American Lawyers*, p. 669; H. Hamilton, *Taylor: Soldier in the White House*, pp. 372–73; Jennings, *Nashville Convention*, pp. 164–66.

18. GJP to C. Cushing, Aug. 23, 1850, Cushing Papers, LOC.

19. P. M. Hamer, *Tennessee*, 1:478–79; Sioussat, "Tennessee and National Political Parties," p. 253; Sioussat, "Tennessee, the Compromise of 1850, and the Nashville Convention," pp. 340–44.

20. Jennings, "Tennessee and the Nashville Convention of 1850," pp. 80–81; Bergeron, *Antebellum Politics in Tennessee*, pp. 104–5; Jennings, *Nashville Convention*, p. 191.

21. M. E. R. Campbell, *Attitude of Tennesseans*, pp. 60–61; Newberry, "Nashville Convention," p. 120; Jennings, "Tennessee and the Nashville Convention of 1850," pp. 80–81.

22. Jennings, *Nashville Convention*, p. 193.

23. Sioussat, "Tennessee, the Compromise of 1850, and the Nashville Convention," pp. 344n, 345n; A. V. Brown, *Speeches*, pp. 319–22.

24. M. E. R. Campbell, *Attitude of Tennesseans*, pp. 60–61; Sioussat, "Tennessee and National Political Parties," p. 253; Sioussat, "Tennessee, the Compromise of 1850, and the Nashville Convention," pp. 344n, 345n; Nashville *Union*, Nov. 16, 1850; Jennings, "Tennessee and the Nashville Convention of 1850," pp. 80–81.

25. Nashville *Union*, Nov. 19, 1850; Jennings, *Nashville Convention*, p. 197; P. M. Hamer, *Tennessee*, 1:478–79.

26. Sioussat, "Tennessee and National Political Parties," p. 253; M. E. R. Campbell, *Attitude of Tennesseans*, pp. 60–63; Bergeron, *Antebellum Tennessee Politics*, pp. 104–5.

27. Nashville *Union*, Nov. 20, 1850.

28. M. E. R. Campbell, *Attitude of Tennesseans*, p. 60; *Brownlow's Knoxville Whig and Independent Journal*, Nov. 30, 1850.

29. Fuess, *Caleb Cushing*, 2:113.

30. A. O. P. Nicholson to John P. Heiss, Nov. 30, 1851, in Sioussat, "Papers of Major John P. Heiss," p. 227.

31. Ibid.

32. An open admirer of Pillow over the years was the influential New Orleans editor J. D. B. DeBow. J. D. B. DeBow to GJP, Apr. 5, 1852, Miscellaneous Manuscript Collection, TSLA.

33. Garrett, "General Pillow"; R. F. Nichols, *Democratic Machine*, pp. 71, 113, 124–26; Andrew Johnson to A. O. P. Nicholson, Dec. 13, 1851, in Graf, Haskins, and Bergeron, *Papers of Andrew Johnson*, 1:630; Bergeron, *Antebellum Politics in Tennessee*, p. 136; Alfred Balch to A. J. Donelson, Dec. 28, 1851, in Sioussat, "Selected Letters, 1846–1856, from the Donelson Papers," pp. 283n, 283–84; W. L. Marcy to James Buchanan, Nov. 24, 1851, James Buchanan Papers, LOC; Cave Johnson to W. L. Marcy, Dec. 5, 1851, Jan. 14, 1852, William L. Marcy Papers, LOC; Washington *Union*, Jan. 25, 1853; Kent, *Democratic Party*, p. 165.

34. Pillow, in his hatred of Winfield Scott, sought opportunities to taunt him. He picked at Scott with inquiries about supplemental battle reports which he and Scott knew he intended to have published in the United States. Lt. Col. H. L. Scott to GJP, Feb. 3, 1852, Albert Tracy Papers, NYPL.

35. Bergeron, *Antebellum Politics in Tennessee*, p. 136.

36. GJP to C. Cushing, Aug. 25, 1851, Cushing Papers, LOC; R. F. Nichols, *Stakes of Power*, p. 45; T. R. Hay to author, Sept. 21, 1965.

37. Baltimore *Sun*, Apr. 12, 1852; GJP to C. Cushing, Mar. 3, 1852, Cushing Papers, LOC; GJP to E. Burke, Sept. 4, 1852, Burke Papers, LOC; R. F. Nichols, *Stakes of Power*, pp. 44–45; R. F. Nichols, *Franklin Pierce*, pp. 195–96.

38. R. F. Nichols, *Democratic Machine*, p. 125.

39. Boutwell, *Reminiscences*, pp. 121–22; R. F. Nichols, *Franklin Pierce*, p. 199.

40. Fuess, *Caleb Cushing*, 2:117–18; R. F. Nichols, *Franklin Pierce*, p. 199.

41. Fuess, *Caleb Cushing*, 2:117; R. F. Nichols, *Franklin Pierce*, p. 199.

42. *New York Herald*, May 8, 1852.

43. GJP to unknown, May 2, 1852, Pillow Papers, MSPL; R. F. Nichols, *Democratic Machine*, pp. 124–25; G. Cadwalader to James Buchanan, May 20, 1852, Buchanan Papers, LOC; Washington *Union*, May 15, 1852; R. F. Nichols, *Democratic Machine*, pp. 125–28; Fuess, *Caleb Cushing*, 2:118; Kent, *Democratic Party*, p. 167; Bain, *Convention Decisions*, p. 44.

44. R. F. Nichols, *Democratic Machine*, pp. 133–35; Fuess, *Caleb Cushing*, 2:119; R. F. Nichols, *Franklin Pierce*, p. 203.

45. Sioussat, "Tennessee, the Compromise of 1850, and the Nashville Convention," p. 313n; Chester, *Guide to Political Platforms*, p. 63; Tricamo, "Tennessee Politics," p. 103.

46. Fuess, *Caleb Cushing*, 2:120–21; R. F. Nichols, *Franklin Pierce*, p. 200.

47. R. F. Nichols, *Democratic Machine*, pp. 136–37.

48. Fuess, *Caleb Cushing*, 2:121.

49. Kent, *Democratic Party*, p. 169; Bain, *Convention Decisions*, pp. 44–45; R. F. Nichols, *Franklin Pierce*, p. 204.

50. Fuess, *Caleb Cushing*, 2:121–24; R. F. Nichols, *Democratic Machine*, pp. 139–40.

51. E. Burke to F. Pierce, June 6, 1852, in Pierce Papers, LOC.

52. GJP to F. Pierce, June 10, 1852, Pierce Papers, New Hampshire Historical Society, Concord, N.H.; GJP to C. Cushing, June 10, 1852, Cushing Papers, LOC; Ross, *Arkansas Gazette*, p. 289; Phelan, *Making of a State*, p. 445; *Proceedings of the National Democratic Convention, 1852*, p. 40; R. F. Nichols, *Stakes of Power*, p. 45; Schlesinger, Israel, and Hansen, *History of American Presidential Elections*, 2:963; Bergeron, *Antebellum Politics in Tennessee*, p. 137; A. Johnson to Sam Milligan, July 20, 1852, in Graf, Haskins, and Bergeron, *Papers of Andrew Johnson*, 2:67–70; W. E. Smith, *Francis Preston Blair Family*, 1:277; A. V. Brown to R. B. Reynolds, Jan. 22, 1853, Reynolds Correspondence, NYHS.

53. Nashville *Union*, July 13, 1852; Little Rock *Arkansas Gazette and Democrat*, Aug. 13, 1852; GJP to A. Tracy, Aug. 10, 1852, Albert Tracy Papers, NYPL; Louisville *Times*, Mar. 4, 20, 1853.

54. GJP to C. Cushing, Mar. 8, 1853, Cushing Papers, LOC; GJP to F. Pierce, Feb. 26, 1853, Pierce Papers, New Hampshire Historical Society, Concord, N.H.; R. F. Nichols, *Franklin Pierce*, pp. 216, 247–58; Tricamo, "Tennessee Politics," p. 104; Sioussat, "Tennessee, the Compromise of 1850, and the Nashville Convention," p. 313n; A. V. Brown to R. B. Reynolds, Jan. 22, 1853, Reynolds Correspondence, NYHS.

55. No evidence has been discovered linking Pillow with the secret Cuba schemes being carried out at this time. Theodore O'Hara and John A. Quitman were deeply involved, as were many individuals across the South, including many friends of Pillow. It seems likely that he took part, however, giving financial support if nothing else. Certainly he sympathized.

56. New York *Daily Times*, Sept. 15, 1853; A. O. P. Nicholson to C. Cushing, Apr. 19, 1853, Cushing Papers, LOC.

57. Pillow had sent Gideon, Jr., to Polk's college, the University of North Carolina. George would enroll there also after completing two years at the University of Nashville. Cummings, *Yankee Quaker*, pp. 140–44; Pillow, *"The Purpose of Life, etc."*; Cummings, "Forgotten Man at Fort Donelson," p. 383; GJP to unknown, Sept. 15, 1853, Pillow Papers, MOHS; individual alumni records, University of North Carolina, Chapel Hill, N.C.

58. Gower and Allen, *Pen and Sword*, p. 374.

59. Columbia *Democratic Herald*, July 21, 1855.

60. Pillow, *Address*, p. 20.

CHAPTER EIGHT

1. GJP to R. B. Reynolds, Mar. 4, 1853, Reynolds Correspondence, NYHS; Helena *Democratic Star*, Nov. 29, 1855; Purdue, *Cleburne*, pp. 45, 48; Nash, *Cleburne*, pp. 59–60.

2. GJP to R. B. Reynolds, Aug. 18, 1849, July 27, 1853, Jan. 18, 1854, Reynolds Correspondence, NYHS; Bergeron, *Antebellum Politics in Tennessee*, p. 84; Pillow v. Wade, 31 Ark. 678; GJP to William E. Woodruff, Oct. 16, 23, 1852, Nov. 5, Dec. 7, 1853, Jan. 4, 1854, July 12, Aug. 3, 1855, July 21, Nov. 7, 1856, May 21, June 13, Aug. 17, 28, Dec. 3, 1860, Woodruff Papers, Arkansas History Commission, Little Rock, Ark.; GJP to G. Cadwalader, June 29, 1855, Cadwalader Collection, HSP; S. S. Dawson to GJP, June 4, 1864, Pillow Papers, RG 109, NARS.

3. It is probable that Pillow owned land in West Tennessee and Mississippi as well. G. H. Thompson, *Arkansas and Reconstruction*, p. 188; Erickson, "Hunting for Cotton in Dixie," p. 497, July 27, 1862, entry.

4. O. Taylor, *Negro Slavery in Arkansas*, pp. 60, 98, 147–48; Fuller Journal, Apr. 20, 1857, UMI; Fogel and Engerman, *Time on the Cross*, pp. 93–94; Tax Assessment List, Phillips County, Ark., 1855, 1859; Census of Phillips County, Ark., 1860; Lewis, "Economic Conditions in Antebellum Arkansas," pp. 264–68; legal brief, John A. Pointer v. GJP, Pillow Correspondence, NYHS; Tricamo, "Tennessee Politics," p. 194; Columbia *Herald*, Mar. 31, 1871.

5. W. K. Scarborough to author, Jan. 3, 1993; 1860 Tennessee and Arkansas Slave Censuses.

6. Bancroft, *Slave Trading in the Old South*, pp. 146–48; Fuller Journal, Apr. 20, 1857, UMI; Fogel and Engerman, *Time on the Cross*, 1:115.

7. GJP to G. Cadwalader, June 29, 1855, Cadwalader Collection, HSP; J. Thompson to unknown, Apr. 30, 1857; A. V. Brown to C. Cushing, Apr. 30, 1859, William Selden Papers, Virginia Historical Society, Richmond, Va.

8. Pillow paid close attention to every detail of Clifton. In his annual trips east he kept an eye on the "latest trends in decorative arts" for his and his brothers' homes. He returned to Maury with "ideas as well as materials, such as silver-plated door locks and fine wallpapers which he used in updating and embellishing his plantation home." GJP to R. B. Reynolds, Mar. 4,

1853, Reynolds Correspondence, NYHS; Cross, *Clifton Place Plantation*; R. S. Ripley to GJP, Mar. 8, 1849, Pillow Letters, University of California at Los Angeles; GJP to Mr. Waldo, Nov. 1, 1854; GJP Bounty Land Warrant Application, Nov. 1, 1854, RG 15, NARS; GJP to G. Cadwalader, June 17, 1855, Cadwalader Collection, HSP.

9. A. V. Brown to C. Cushing, Apr. 30, 1859, Selden Papers, Virginia Historical Society, Richmond, Va.

10. Patterson, *Negro in Tennessee*, pp. 65–67.

11. Census of Maury County, Tenn., 1850, 1860; Garrett, "General Pillow."

12. Columbia, Tenn., *Maury Democrat*, Sept. 30, 1897.

13. Pillow, *Address*; Maury County Agricultural and Mechanical Association *Report*; *Commercial Review of the South and Southwest*, 11:679–80.

14. *Commercial Review of the South and Southwest*, 11:679–80.

15. Columbia *Herald*, Dec. 20, 1872; Agricultural Census of Maury County, Tenn., 1850, 1860.

16. Music appears to have made him happy, but probably because it, like dancing, was festive, exciting, and eminently social. Conversation with Linda Neal, May 22, 1991; Nashville *American*, Nov. 3, 1878.

17. P. M. Hamer, "Pillow," p. 604; A. Johnson to William M. Lowry, Dec. 22, 1855, in Graf, Haskins, and Bergeron, *Papers of Andrew Johnson*, 2:350–51; Bergeron, *Antebellum Politics in Tennessee*, p. 138; GJP to R. B. Reynolds, Mar. 31, 1856, Reynolds Correspondence, NYHS; GJP to W. E. Woodruff, June 9, 1856, Woodruff Papers, Arkansas History Commission, Little Rock, Ark.; GJP to A. V. Brown, Feb. 28, 1857, A. V. Brown Letters, Dickinson College Library, Carlisle, Pa.

18. Garrett, "General Pillow"; R. G. Russell, "Prelude to the Presidency," pp. 149, 153, 156–57; A. Johnson to Robert Johnson, Jan. 23, 1858, in Graf, Haskins, and Bergeron, *Papers of Andrew Johnson*, 3:7; Tricamo, "Tennessee Politics," pp. 111, 141; A. Johnson to William M. Lowry, June 26, 1856, in Graf, Haskins, and Bergeron, *Papers of Andrew Johnson*, 2:386; Bergeron, *Antebellum Politics in Tennessee*, p. 114.

19. M. Carroll Walsh to G. Cadwalader, Oct. 20, 1857, Cadwalader Collection, HSP; June 30, 1857, entry, Gower and Allen, *Pen and Sword*, p. 420; Clarksville, Tenn., *Weekly Chronicle*, Oct. 9, 1857; Stickles, *Buckner*, pp. 40–41.

20. July 30, 1857, entry, Gower and Allen, *Pen and Sword*, p. 425; GJP letter to the Democrats of Lawrence County, June 1857, JRN.

21. Aug. 10, 1857, entry, Gower and Allen, *Pen and Sword*, p. 427; R. G. Russell, "Prelude to the Presidency," pp. 170–75; Bergeron, *Antebellum Politics in Tennessee*, pp. 114–15; Clark, "Nicholson," pp. 102–3.

22. Memphis *Daily Appeal*, Oct. 3, 6, 7, 20, 1857; Oct. 2, 1857, entry, Gower and Allen, *Pen and Sword*, p. 434.

23. W. B. Campbell to David Campbell, Oct. 27, 1857, Campbell Family Papers, DU.

24. Gohmann, *Political Nativism in Tennessee*, p. 147; Russell, "Prelude to the Presidency," p. 174; Oct. 26, 1857, entry, Gower and Allen, *Pen and Sword*, p. 438; Clark, "Nicholson," p. 103.

25. Andrew Johnson to William M. Lowry, Aug. 16, 1857, in Rosenburg, "A Rare Letter from Andrew Johnson," pp. 70–71.

26. Ibid., Bergeron, *Antebellum Politics in Tennessee*, p. 115; *Memphis Avalanche*, Oct. 13, 1878; Temple, *Notable Men of Tennessee*, p. 391.

27. Thomas D. Eldridge to S. B. Buckner, Feb. 14, 1908, Buckner Papers, HUL.

28. Clarksville, Tenn., *Weekly Chronicle*, Oct. 30, 1857.

29. Nashville *Republican Banner*, Oct. 28, 31, 1857, Feb. 23, 1858; Oct. 28, 31, 1857, entries, Gower and Allen, *Pen and Sword*, pp. 438, 455; Stickles, *Buckner*, pp. 40–41.

30. The tragedy created a further bond between the grieving Pillow and Isham G. Harris. Harris's brother, Judge W. R. Harris, had been killed in a boiler explosion aboard the steamboat *Pennsylvania* the year before. Keating, *Memphis*, 1:420. Young Gideon had caused the family great distress two years earlier when he shot and killed a slave at Clifton. The slave "had resisted the authority of the overseer." GJP to Mr. Riggs, Dec. 27, 1858, Pillow Papers, MSPL; Apr. 26, 1859, entry, Gower and Allen, *Pen and Sword*, p. 517; L. H. Mangum to Martha P. Mangum, May 20, 1859, in Shanks, *Papers of Willie P. Mangum*, 5:363–64; Memphis *Daily Appeal*, Apr. 27, 1859; L. J. Polk to Mary B. Polk, Jan. 14, 1857, JKP Papers, LOC.

31. GJP to S. A. Douglas, Apr. 3, 1861, Douglas Papers, University of Chicago Library, Chicago, Ill.; Tricamo, "Tennessee Politics," pp. 205–7.

32. Milton, *Eve of Conflict*, p. 403; GJP to S. A. Douglas, Apr. 3, 1861, Douglas Papers, University of Chicago Library, Chicago, Ill.; Tricamo, "Tennessee Politics," pp. 210–13.

33. GJP to S. A. Douglas, Apr. 3, 1861, Douglas Papers, University of Chicago Library, Chicago, Ill.

34. Milton, *Eve of Conflict*, p. 403; GJP to S. A. Douglas, Apr. 3, 1860, Douglas Papers, University of Chicago Library, Chicago, Ill.; Tricamo, "Tennessee Politics," pp. 128–29, 205.

35. Graf, Haskins, and Bergeron, *Papers of Andrew Johnson*, 3:426–27; GJP to S. A. Douglas, Apr. 3, 1860, Douglas Papers, University of Chicago Library, Chicago, Ill.; Nevins, *Emergence of Lincoln*, 2:210.

36. Tricamo, "Tennessee Politics," pp. 209–11; Proceedings of the Charleston and Baltimore National Democratic Convention of 1860, George Petrie Papers, Auburn University Library, Auburn, Ala.

37. Graf, Haskins, and Bergeron, *Papers of Andrew Johnson*, 3:615n, 616n; Nashville *Union and American*, June 8, 1860.

38. Folmsbee, Corlew, and Mitchell, *Tennessee*, pp. 314–15; Tricamo, "Tennessee Politics," pp. 211–13.

39. Caldwell, *Bench and Bar*, pp. 314–19; Clayton, *History of Davidson County*, p. 407; Graf, Haskins, and Bergeron, *Papers of Andrew Johnson*, 3:204n.; Tricamo, "Tennessee Politics," pp. 219–24; M. B. Hamer, "Presidential Campaign of 1860," pp. 15–16; Crofts, *Reluctant Confederates*, pp. 63–64, 81–87; P. M. Hamer, *Tennessee*, 1:518.

40. P. M. Hamer, *Tennessee*, 1:522; C. M. Polk, *Colonial Families*, p. 122.

CHAPTER NINE

1. Crofts, *Reluctant Confederates*, pp. 265, 325–26; Lufkin, "Secession and Coercion," pp. 98–99; Connelly, *Army of the Heartland*, pp. 28, 33.

2. GJP to the President of the Congress of the Seceded States, Jan. 30, 1861, JRN.

3. George Dixon to W. B. Campbell, Apr. 26, 1861, Campbell Family Papers, DU; GJP to C. F. Hamer, Mar. 16, 1861, Lincoln Collection, Brown University Library, Providence, R.I.

4. John L. T. Sneed to GJP, Mar. 30, 1861, Dearborn Collection, HLH.

5. W. S. Walker to J. Davis, Mar. 17, 1861, Dearborn Collection, HLH; Phineas T. Scruggs to J. Davis, June 1, 1861, in Crist, McIntosh, and Monroe, *Papers of Jefferson Davis*, 7:183.

6. Memphis *Daily Appeal*, Apr. 17, 1861.

7. W. G. Coulter, *Brownlow*, pp. 143–44.

8. J. B. Clements to A. Johnson, Mar. 1, 1861, in Graf, Haskins, and Bergeron, *Papers of Andrew Johnson*, 4:350.

9. GJP to L. P. Walker, Apr. 24, 1861, in Hall, *Andrew Johnson*, p. 7.

10. GJP to W. B. Campbell, Apr. 22, 1861, Campbell Family Papers, DU.

11. E. B. Pickett to W. B. Campbell, May 25, 1861; Rolfe S. Saunders to W. B. Campbell, May 31, 1861, Campbell Family Papers, DU.

12. *OR*, 52(2):58–59.

13. Ibid., pp. 58–59, 68–69; Leslie Coombs to Benson J. Lossing, Nov. 22, 1861, Miscellaneous Collection, UMI.

14. Wills, *Forrest*, pp. 46–47; McIlwaine, *Memphis*, pp. 113–14.

15. *OR*, 52(2):56–59.

16. The previous day, April 18, Pillow had issued an address to the "Freemen of Tennessee," imploring them to organize immediately and follow the lead of Harris and Frank Cheatham. Unidentified letter, Apr. 19, 1861, Civil War Collection, Memphis State University Library, Mississippi Valley Collection, Memphis, Tenn.; Lossing, *Pictorial History*, pp. 349–51; Goodspeed, *History of Tennessee*, p. 518.

17. Lossing, *Pictorial History*, p. 340; *OR*, 52(2):58–59.

18. McIlwaine, *Memphis*, pp. 113–14.

19. *OR*, 52(2):63–64, 68–69, 72–73.

20. GJP to P. Smith, May 1, 1861, Pillow Papers, RG 109, NARS; Wright, *Diary*, p. 3, 3n; Durham, "Civil War Letters to Wynnewood," pp. 33, 35; *OR*, 52(2):72–73, 80–81.

21. The *General Pillow* would suffer the inglorious fate of being captured and transferred to the U.S. Navy. J. L. Nichols, *Confederate Engineers*, pp. 21, 54–55; Purdue, *Cleburne*, pp. 80–84; J. L. T. Sneed to GJP, Gratz Collection, HSP; Senate Doc. No. 63, 38th Cong., 1st sess., p. 41; Mainfort, "Notes and Documents," p. 74; Horn, *Army of Tennessee*, p. 48; *OR*, ser. 3, 5:478.

22. *OR*, 52(2):90–91; DeBerry, *Confederate Tennessee*, pp. 106–27; Horn, *Army of Tennessee*, p. 48; Connelly, *Army of the Heartland*, pp. 27–31; McMurry, *Two Great Rebel Armies*, pp. 79, 83–84.

23. Lunsford P. Yandell, Jr., to L. P. Yandell, Sr., May 10, 1861, Yandell Family Papers, Filson Club, Louisville, Ky.

24. Losson, *Tennessee's Forgotten Warriors*, p. 28; Horn, *Army of Tennessee*, pp. 43, 48; I. G. Harris to Jefferson Davis, July 2, 1861, Harris Papers, TSLA.

25. Other members of the board were former governor Neill S. Brown, Whig James E. Bailey, and the very wealthy and powerful Nashvillian, William G. Harding. Jacobs, "Outfitting the Provisional Army of Tennessee," pp. 257–59.

26. GJP to the Military and Financial Board, May 11, 1861; GJP to W. G. Harding, May 29, 1861, Pillow Papers, MSPL.

27. GJP to Military and Financial Board, June 19, 1861; GJP to Legislature of Tennessee, June 20, 1861; GJP to I. G. Harris, June 20, 1861, Pillow Papers, MSPL; Columbia *Herald*, Mar. 31, 1871; GJP to L. P. Walker, Aug. 1861, Pillow Papers, HUL.

28. GJP to Military and Financial Board, June 16, 19, 1861; GJP to Legislature of Tennessee, June 20, 1861; GJP to IGH, June 20, 21, 1861; GJP to J. E. Bailey, Pillow Papers, MSPL; General Orders No. 18, June 18, 1861, and No. 22, June 23, 1861, Pillow Order Book, RG 109, NARS.

29. GJP to Military and Financial Board, June 19, 24, 1861, Pillow Papers, MSPL; GJP to I. G. Harris, June 23, 1861, Pillow Letters, DU; Jacobs, "Outfitting the Provisional Army of Tennessee," pp. 268–69.

30. I. G. Harris to GJP, June 30, 1861, Dreer Collection, HSP. Pillow's accounts with the military board were still being settled as late as October. On the third, he paid a check for $35,000 to the Memphis branch of the Bank of Tennessee. GJP to Mr. Hale, Oct. 3, 1861, Pillow Order Book, Civil War Miscellany, Western Reserve Historical Society, Cleveland, Ohio.

31. General Order No. 20, June 21, 1861, Pillow Order Book, RG 109, NARS; GJP to I. G. Harris, June 21, 1861, Pillow Papers, MSPL.

32. Clarksville *Weekly Chronicle*, June 21, 1861.

33. I. G. Harris to GJP, June 18, 1861, Dreer Collection, HSP; Evans, *Confederate Military History*, 10:292.

34. I. G. Harris to GJP, June 30, 1861, Dreer Collection, HSP.

35. GJP to S. R. Anderson, June 1, 1861; GJP to Judge Swayne, June 1861, Pillow Papers, MSPL; Pillow Order Book, RG 109, NARS.

36. Russell, *My Diary North and South*, p. 162.

37. *OR*, 52(2):96; Watters, "Harris," p. 84; GJP to Military and Financial Board, June 19, 1861, Pillow Papers, MSPL; Connelly, *Army of the Heartland*, pp. 28–29, 35–36.

38. R. P. Neely to GJP, July 10, 1861, Pillow Letters, DU; GJP to I. G. Harris, May 15, 1861, Miscellaneous Collection, UMI; Sam Tate to GJP, May 21, 1861, Pillow Letters, DU; I. G. Harris to GJP, May 24, 28, 1861, Harris Letter Book, TSLA.

39. GJP to I. G. Harris, May 25, 1861, Special Collections, University of Kentucky Library, Lexington, Ky.; GJP to I. G. Harris, June 6, 1861, Dreer Collection, HSP; GJP to Jefferson Davis, June 11, 1861, Society Collection, HSP; Charles Clark to GJP, Dearborn Collection, HLH.

40. GJP to I. G. Harris, May 16, 1861; GJP to T. H. Allen, June 21, 1861; GJP to E. M. Ivers, June 27, 1861; GJP to Military and Financial Board, July 1, 1861, Pillow Papers, MSPL; T. H. and J. M. Allen to GJP, June 21, 1861, JRN; Daniel, "Quinby and Robinson Cannon Foundry," p. 18, 20.

41. GJP to J. L. T. Sneed, May 28, 1861, Dearborn Collection, HLH; GJP to S. R. Anderson, June 11, 1861; GJP to S. R. Mallory, June 4, 1861, Dreer Collection, HSP; Jacobs, "Outfitting the Provisional Army of Tennessee," pp. 260–62; Daniel, *Cannoneers in Gray*, p. 3; Connelly, *Army of the Heartland*, p. 36.

42. *New York Times*, Mar. 6, 1876; Ornelas-Struve, *Memphis*, 2:30; *CV* 34:12–13; J. T. Moore, *Tennessee*, 1:473; Daniel, "Quinby and Robinson Cannon Foundry," p. 18.

43. GJP to W. L. Harper, June 1, 1861, Dreer Collection, HSP; GJP to N. T. Martin, May 31, 1861; GJP to Walter Goodman, May 31, 1861; GJP to Milton Brown, May 31, 1861; GJP to Mr. Sampson, May 31, 1861; J. C. Atkins to GJP, June 24, 1861, Pillow Papers, MSPL.

44. J. L. T. Sneed to GJP, July 7, 1861, Dreer Collection, HSP.

45. P. Robbins, "Pinkerton's Southern Assignment," pp. 7–8, 10–11, 44–45.

46. Pillow Order Book, May 10, 1861, RG 109, NARS; DeBerry, *Confederate Tennessee*, pp. 117–18; Cummings, *Yankee Quaker*, pp. 170–71.

47. Connelly, *Army of the Heartland*, pp. 39–41; McMurry, *Two Great Rebel Armies*, pp. 83–84.

48. DeBerry, *Confederate Tennessee*, p. 119; *OR*, 52(2):90–91.

49. GJP to B. Magoffin, May 13, 1861, Snyder Collection, University of Missouri–Kansas City, Western Historical Collection, Kansas City, Mo.

50. I. G. Harris to GJP, May 7, 1861, Dreer Collection, HSP; *OR*, 52(2):100–101.

51. Lunsford P. Yandell, Jr., to L. P. Yandell, Sr., May 10, 1861, Yandell Family Papers, Filson Club, Louisville, Ky.

52. I. G. Harris to R. G. Fain, May 29, 1861, Pillow Letters, HSP; W. E. Butler to GJP, June 3, 1861, Confederate Collection, Barker Texas History Center, University of Texas, Austin, Tex.; Cummings, *Yankee Quaker*, pp. 170–71; Russell, *My Diary North and South*, pp. 168–70; GJP to J. H. McMahon, May 30, 1861, Pillow Papers, MSPL; Ornelas-Struve, *Memphis*, 2:41; Hubbard, *Notes of a Private*, pp. 13–14.

53. GJP to L. P. Walker, May 15, 1861, Pillow Papers, MSPL; GJP to J. J. Pettus, May 17, 1861, Special Collections, Boston Public Library, Boston, Mass.; GJP to W. L. Harper, June 1, 1861; J. H. Nelson to GJP, June 16, 1861, Pillow Papers, MSPL; GJP to W. L. Harper, June 1, 1861, Pillow Papers, HSP; GJP to I. G. Harris, May 16, 1861, Pillow Papers, MSPL; *OR*, 52(2):107, 111; Dubay, *Pettus*, p. 106.

54. GJP to B. Magoffin, May 13, 1861; GJP to J. J. Pettus, May 16, 1861, Snyder Collection, University of Missouri–Kansas City, Western Historical Collection, Kansas City, Mo.; GJP to J. J. Pettus, May 21, 1861; GJP to Captain Upshur, May 16, 1861, Pillow Papers, MSPL.

55. D. C. Govan to Mary O. Govan, July 4, 1861, Daniel Chevilette Govan Papers, SHC; John D. Martin to W. J. Hardee, Dreer Collection, HSP; W. J. Hardee to S. Cooper, July 3, 1861, Office of the Adjutant General, Letters Received, RG 109, NARS; Milton, *Abraham Lincoln and the Fifth Column*, p. 35; DeBerry, *Confederate Tennessee*, pp. 117–18; *OR*, 52(2):117; B. F. Cheatham to GJP, June 20, 1861, Breckinridge Collection, Chicago Historical Society, Chicago, Ill.; Lindsley, *Annals*, p. 600; B. F. Cheatham to GJP, June 7, 20, 30, July 18, 1861, Dreer Collection, HSP.

56. GJP to P. R. Cleburne, June 1, 1861, Pillow Papers, MSPL.

57. B. F. Cheatham to GJP, May 23, 1861, in possession of Douglas Schanz, Roanoke, Va.; F. K. Zollicoffer to GJP, May 25, 1861, Dreer Collection, HSP.

58. B. F. Cheatham to GJP, May 28, 1861, Dreer Collection, HSP; GJP to W. C. Pope, May 29, 1861; GJP to J. H. McMahon, May 30, 1861; GJP to M. T. Polk, May 31, 1861, Pillow Papers, MSPL.

59. GJP to Milton Brown, May 24, 1861, Harrisburg Civil War Roundtable Collection, USMH; GJP to W. E. Travis, May 26, 1861; GJP to Marshall T. Polk, May 25, 1861, Pillow Papers, MSPL; GJP to W. H. Carroll, June 6, 1861; GJP to R. M. Russell, June 5, 1861, Pillow Correspondence, Barker Texas History Center, University of Texas, Austin, Tex.

60. GJP to L. P. Walker, May 15, 1861; GJP to J. L. T. Sneed, May 15, 1861, Pillow Letters, MSPL; J. L. T. Sneed to GJP, June 7, 1861, Gratz Collection; *OR*, 52(2):99–100; Russell, *My Diary North and South*, pp. 166–67; Val W. Wynne to Alfred R. Wynne, June 2, 1861, in Durham, "Civil War Letters to Wynnewood," p. 35.

61. GJP to Philip Stockton, May 28, 1861, Pillow Papers, MSPL; *OR*, 52(2):112–13.

62. The *New York Times*, with slightly more charity, reported: "His cotton-bale street-fortifications made the locomotion of the citizens impossible and his earthworks on the esplanade will long furnish a subject of wonder to the curious traveler." *New York Times*, Jan. 11, 1863; Memphis *Daily Post*, Dec. 28, 1866.

63. Russell, *My Diary North and South*, pp. 162–63.

64. Ibid., p. 165; Law, "Diary of the Rev. J. G. Law," *SHSP* 10:565.

65. GJP to P. Smith, July 19, 1861, Pillow Papers, RG 109, NARS; *OR*, 52(2):112–13; GJP to J. L. T. Sneed, May 29, 1861, Pillow Papers, HUL; J. L. T. Sneed to GJP, July 9, 1861, Miscellaneous Collection, UMI.

66. GJP to Colonel Smith, July 18, 1861, Pillow Papers, MSPL; D. S. Donelson to GJP, May 31, 1861, Dearborn Collection, HLH; Neill S. Brown to Jefferson Davis, Sept. 22, 1861, Confederate States of America Papers, DU; F. K. Zollicoffer to GJP, July 18, 1861; S. R. Anderson to GJP, June 12, 20, 1861; GJP to S. R. Anderson, June 14, 1861, Dreer Collection, HSP.

67. B. W. Sharp to GJP, May 27, 1861; GJP to T. R. Bradley, May 24, 1861, Dearborn Collection, HLH; GJP to I. G. Harris, June 1, 1861, Harrisburg Civil War Roundtable Collection, USMH.

68. B. F. Cheatham to GJP, June 7, 1861, Dreer Collection, HSP.

69. F. Moore, *Civil War in Song and Story*, p. 261.

70. I. G. Harris to Jefferson Davis, July 2, 1861, Harris Letter Book, TSLA.

71. I. G. Harris to Jefferson Davis, July 13, 1861, Harris Letter Book, TSLA; *OR*, ser. 4, 1:527–28.

72. *OR*, ser. 4, 1:527–28; I. G. Harris to GJP, July 12, 1861, Dreer Collection, HSP.

73. *OR*, 52(2):119–20.

74. Pillow's appointment was confirmed August 29, 1861.

75. J. B. Jones, *Rebel War Clerk's Diary*, 1:53–54.

76. GJP to I. G. Harris, July 14, 1861, Harris Papers, TSLA; Connelly, *Army of the Heartland*, p. 32.

CHAPTER TEN

1. Parks, *Polk*, pp. 1–167; Lindsley, *Annals*, p. 24.

2. GJP to I. G. Harris, June 23, 1861, Pillow Letters, DU; I. G. Harris to GJP, June 30, 1861, Dreer Collection, HSP; GJP to L. P. Walker, July 2, 1861, in possession of Douglas Schanz, Roanoke, Va.; Parks, *Polk*, p. 171.

3. This edict reached only so far. Missourians in the 13th Arkansas stationed at Fort Pillow were never given the opportunity to enlist with Thompson. Stephenson, "My War Autobiography," Louisiana State University Libraries, Louisiana and Lower Mississippi Valley Collections, Baton Rouge, La.

4. Although Thompson had brought telegrams from Lt. Gov. T. C. Reynolds, the latter claimed in August that the attack on Missouri from Memphis had "been resolved on without my advice & against my expressed judgment." B. F. Cheatham to GJP, June 20, 1861, Dreer Collection, HSP; M. Jeff Thompson to GJP, June 15, 1861, Pillow Letters, DU; M. Jeff Thompson Reminiscences, SHC; T. C. Reynolds to W. J. Hardee, Aug. 25, 1861, Hardee Papers, HUL; GJP to Military and Financial Board, n.d., Pillow Papers, MSPL; B. F. Cheatham to GJP, July 2, 1861, Dearborn Collection, HLH.

5. *OR*, ser. 4, 1:376–78.

6. *OR*, 52(2):112–13; GJP to S. R. Anderson, June 20, 1861, Gratz Collection, HSP.

7. GJP to I. G. Harris, June 20, 1861, Dreer Collection, HSP.

8. Ibid.

9. I. G. Harris to GJP, June 20, 1861, Harris Letter Book, TSLA; GJP to IGH, June 23, 1861, Pillow Letters, DU.

10. GJP to S. R. Mallory, July 4, 1861, Pillow Papers, MSPL.

11. *OR*, 4:368–69, 371.

12. GJP to Military and Financial Board, July 3, 1861, Pillow Letters, MSPL; Sam Tate to L. Polk, Leonidas Polk Papers, SHC; *OR*, 3:612; D. C. Govan to his wife, July 28, 1861, Daniel Chevilette Govan Papers, SHC.

13. Connelly, *Army of the Heartland*, p. 48.

14. Horn, *Army of Tennessee*, pp. 25–27; *OR*, 3:612–15.

15. *OR*, 3:616, 618–19; Castel, *Sterling Price*, pp. 32–33; Connelly, *Army of the Heartland*, p. 49; Parks, *Polk*, pp. 174–75.

16. Law, "Diary of the Rev. J. G. Law," *SHSP*, 10:267–68, 568, 596.

17. Ibid., pp. 568, 596; L. P. Yandell to Sally Yandell, Aug. 10, 1861, Yandell Family Papers, Filson Club, Louisville, Ky.; Wright, *Diary*, pp. 3–5; *OR*, 3:612–13; *New York Times*, Aug. 5, 1861.

18. Stevenson, *Thirteen Months*, p. 63.

19. Durham, "Civil War Letters to Wynnewood," p. 36; L. P. Yandell to Sally Yandell, Aug. 10, 1861, Yandell Family Papers, Filson Club, Louisville, Ky.

20. Thompson Reminiscences, SHC.

21. Stanton, Berquist, and Bowers, *Reminiscences of Thompson*, p. 69; Hubbard, *Notes of a Private*, pp. 15–16.

22. Stanton, Berquist and Bowers, *Reminiscences of Thompson*, p. 73.

23. *OR*, 3:407.

24. Ibid., p. 617.

25. Ibid., p. 616.

26. Ibid., pp. 619–20.

27. Ibid., p. 624; W. J. Hardee to GJP, July 30, 1861, Hardee Letters, HSP.

28. *OR*, 3:621, 625–26.

29. Ibid., p. 626.

30. Ibid., pp. 626–27.

31. L. Polk to GJP, Aug. 3, 1861, Pillow Letters, DU.

32. W. J. Hardee to GJP, Aug. 4, 1861, Pillow Letters, HSP; Purdue, *Cleburne*, pp. 85–86; N. C. Hughes, *Hardee*, pp. 37–40; W. J. Hardee to Mrs. F. Shover, Shover Letters, LOC; *OR*, 3:684–85.

33. GJP to L. Polk, Aug. 5, 1861, Snyder Collection, University of Missouri–Kansas City, Western Historical Collection, Kansas City, Mo.

34. GJP to W. J. Hardee, Aug. 5, 1861, Miscellaneous Collection, UMI.

35. W. J. Hardee to GJP, Aug. 7, 1861, Confederate Collection, Barker Texas History Center, University of Texas, Austin, Tex.

36. *OR*, 3:635.

37. Ibid., pp. 725–26.

38. L. Polk to GJP, Aug. 10, 1861, Davis Collection, Howard Tilton Memorial Library, Tulane University, New Orleans, La.; G. A. Henry, Jr., to G. A. Henry, Aug. 12, 1861, Henry Papers, SHC; *OR*, 53:725–26.

39. *OR*, 3:643.

40. Ibid., p. 642.

41. Ibid., pp. 642–43, 53:723, 725; M. J. Thompson to W. J. Hardee, Aug. 13, 1861, 1st Division, Missouri State Guard Papers, RG 109, NARS.

42. W. J. Hardee to GJP, Aug. 11, 1861, Gratz Collection, HSP; *OR*, 3:644–45; Stanton, Berquist, and Bowers, *Reminiscences of Thompson*, pp. 76–77.

43. *OR*, 53:722–23, 725, 3:642.

44. L. Polk to GJP, Aug. 13, 1861, Pillow Letters, DU.

45. M. Jeff Thompson to GJP, Aug. 19, 1861, Dalton Collection, DU; Stan-

ton, Berquist, and Bowers, *Reminiscences of Thompson*, pp. 76–84; Wright, *Diary*, pp. 3–4; Edenton Diary, Aug. 15–Sept. 2, 1861, TSLA; *OR*, 3:659–66.

46. *OR*, 3:650–54.

47. Ibid., pp. 650–51.

48. Ibid., pp. 652–54.

49. Ibid., pp. 654–55, 659.

50. Knox Walker and his Irishmen always knew how to put on a show. The good citizens of New Madrid—and the other regiments, for that matter—marveled at the brilliant red dinner jackets lined in green worn by Walker's officers.

51. L. Polk to GJP, Aug. 17, 1861, Confederate Miscellany, Emory University, Robert W. Woodruff Library, Atlanta, Ga.; Lewis G. DeRussy to GJP, Aug. 17, 1861, Pillow Papers, MOHS.

52. *OR*, 3:660.

53. Ibid., p. 662; Cummings, "Strahl," p. 346.

54. *OR*, 3:662–63.

55. Ibid., pp. 664–66.

56. GJP to L. P. Walker, Pillow Papers, HUL; *OR*, 3:666–67.

57. Connelly, *Army of the Heartland*, p. 69; *OR*, 3:668, 670.

58. *OR*, 53:730–31.

59. Ibid., p. 664.

60. Ibid., pp. 370–71.

61. Ibid., pp. 676–77.

62. Ibid., 4:396.

63. T. C. Reynolds to J. Davis, Dearborn Collection, HLH.

64. *OR*, 3:677–79.

65. T. C. Reynolds, to W. J. Hardee, Aug. 25, 1861, Hardee Papers, HUL.

66. Looking back after the war, Thompson felt it would have been "very difficult" for Hardee and Pillow to have cooperated because of the terrain. "Neither of the officers commanding were acquainted with the peculiarities of the country." Probably "personal jealousy which has so often injured our cause may have had something to do with it." *OR*, 3:680; Thompson Reminiscences, SHC.

67. W. J. Hardee to GJP, Aug. 27, 1861, Bradley Papers, USMHI.

68. *OR*, 3:684.

69. Ibid., p. 685.

70. For a discussion of the abortive Missouri expedition from Hardee's standpoint, see N. C. Hughes, *Hardee*, pp. 45–55; *OR*, 3:686–87.

71. GJP to L. P. Walker, Sept. 1, 1861, Walker Letters, DU.

72. Twenty-four-year-old John Flournoy Henry, son of Pillow's old Whig rival, Gustavus A. Henry, was a graduate of the University of Virginia and Lebanon Law School. He remained on Pillow's staff until Donelson and later fought at Shiloh, where he received a mortal wound.

73. J. F. Henry to G. A. Henry, Aug. 31, 1861, Henry Papers, SHC.

74. T. C. Reynolds to GJP, Oct. 10, 1861, Pillow Correspondence, NYHS.

75. GJP to L. P. Walker, Sept. 1, 1861, Walker Papers, DU; GJP to W. H. L.

Wallace, Aug. 28, 31, 1861, PMSR; *OR*, ser. 2, 1:504–10; L. Polk to GJP, Oct. 12, 1861, Dreer Collection, HSP; Miller, *Photographic History of the Civil War*, 7:98.

76. *OR*, 3:688, 691.

CHAPTER ELEVEN

1. *OR*, 3:685–86; N. C. Hughes, *Belmont*, pp. 1, 222n.

2. *CV* 31:34; *OR*, 3:151, 4:181; N. C. Hughes, *Belmont*, pp. 4, 222, 223n; Solomon Scrapbook, p. 350, DU; E. G. W. Butler, Jr., to Frances Butler, Sept. 27, 1861, in Butler Family Papers, Historic New Orleans Collection, New Orleans, La.; W. M. Polk, *Polk*, 2:19; Edenton Diary, Sept. 5, 1861, TSLA; Woodworth, *Davis and His Generals*, pp. 35–39; Harrison, *Civil War in Kentucky*, p. 12.

3. Historian Steven Woodworth argues that Polk, not Pillow, bears immediate responsibility for the seizure of Columbus. In a reanalysis of communications between Davis, Polk, Harris, and L. P. Walker, Woodworth concludes that Polk "had been dishonest," "even more manipulative and duplicitous than heretofore." "He did not want any direction from his commander in chief [Davis]" and determined to keep "the president in ignorance." Such an interpretation, though carefully reasoned and researched, defies the long accepted, indeed unquestioned, understanding of Polk's character and loyalty to Davis and seems to overlook the provocative and dangerous Federal incursion at Belmont on September 2. It was Polk, not Davis, who was "obviously irresolute." Woodworth, "Indeterminate Quantities," pp. 289–97.

4. I. G. Harris to GJP, Sept. 4, 1861, Harris Letter Book, TSLA; *OR*, 4:197–200; J. B. Jones, *Rebel War Clerk's Diary*, 1:79, Sept. 12, 1861, entry; Harris, *Walker*, pp. 110–11; Connelly, *Army of the Heartland*, p. 53; Cooling, *Forts Henry and Donelson*, p. 11.

5. GJP to B. F. Cheatham, Sept. 13, 1861; Special Order, Pillow's Division, Sept. 7, 1861, Confederate Collection, Barker Texas History Center, University of Texas, Austin, Tex.

6. J. F. Henry to Mrs. Marion Henry, Sept. 12, 1861, Henry Papers, SHC; M. Jeff Thompson to GJP, Sept. 22, 1861, Dreer Collection, HSP.

7. Edenton Diary, Sept. 19, 1861, TSLA.

8. Eventually, however, "Pillow's Trot Line," as irreverent soldiers dubbed it, was swept away. Today a few giant links remain, exhibited like great dinosaur bones, in the Kentucky state park that oversees the site of what was the town of Columbus.

9. Special Order, Pillow's Division, Sept. 7, 1861; J. T. Shirley to GJP, Oct. 5, 1861; Charges and Specifications against Capt. Thomas Stokes, Oct. 31, 1861, Confederate Collection, Barker Texas History Center, University of Texas, Austin, Tex.; Special Orders No. 225–364, Oct. 1–Nov. 13, 1861, Department of the West, Civil War Miscellany, Western Reserve Historical Society, Cleveland, Ohio; J. M. Smith to GJP, Oct. 17, 1861, Palmer Collec-

tion, Western Reserve Historical Society, Cleveland, Ohio; Stevenson, *Thirteen Months*, pp. 59, 66; Simon, *Papers of Ulysses S. Grant*, 3:55; *CV* 34:221; Allen, *Center of Conflict*, p. 19.

10. He asked to be relieved of his ordnance responsibilities if Polk did not cease letting Thompson's Missouri troops have so much powder and ammunition.

11. GJP to E. D. Blake, Sept. 30, 1861, Confederate Collection, Barker Texas History Center, University of Texas, Austin, Tex.; J. F. Henry to Mrs. Marion Henry, Oct. 31, 1861, Henry Papers, SHC; *Battlefields of the South*, p. 121.

12. *OR*, 3:730, 723.

13. Ibid., 4:513–14, 554; Connelly, *Army of the Heartland*, pp. 69–72; Parks, *Polk*, p. 189.

14. Fielder Diary and Firth Diary, Nov. 6, 1861, entries, TSLA; *OR*, 3:306.

15. GJP to L. Polk, Nov. 6, 1861; W. W. Mackall to L. Polk, Nov. 4, 1861, Leonidas Polk Papers, RG 109, NARS; *CV* 16:345–46; Fielder Diary, Nov. 7, 1861, TSLA; D. Singletary, "Belmont," p. 507; Ray Reminiscences, University of Arkansas Libraries, Fayetteville, Ark.; Carnes, "Belmont," p. 369.

16. N. C. Hughes, *Belmont*, pp. 73–74.

17. *OR*, 3:355, 360; Stephenson, "My War Autobiography," Louisiana State University Libraries, Louisiana and Lower Mississippi Valley Collections, Baton Rouge, La.

18. *OR*, 3:325; Fielder Diary, Nov. 7, 1861, TSLA.

19. Kennison manuscript, H. L. Kennison Papers, SHC; *OR*, 3:358; Bell Report, Southern Illinois University, Morris Library, Carbondale, Ill.; Memphis *Daily Appeal*, Nov. 10, 1861.

20. *OR*, 3:360; Memphis *Daily Appeal*, Nov. 14, 1861; Columbus, Ky., *Daily Confederate News*, Nov. 12, 1861; R. H. Wood to Mary Wood, Nov. 10, 1861, Wood Letters, TSLA; Kennison manuscript, Kennison Papers, SHC.

21. N. C. Hughes, *Belmont*, p. 75; Vaughan, *Thirteenth Regiment*, pp. 12–14; *OR*, 3:333–35.

22. N. C. Hughes, *Belmont*, p. 77; *OR*, 3:341.

23. *OR*, 3:341–42; Wright, "Belmont," p. 73; N. C. Hughes, *Belmont*, pp. 77, 240n.·

24. For a discussion of the ammunition shortage at Belmont and the controversy that developed between Pillow and Polk concerning it, see N. C. Hughes, *Belmont*, p. 248n.

25. *OR*, 3:358; Stephenson, "My War Autobiography," Louisiana State University Libraries, Louisiana and Lower Mississippi Valley Collections, Baton Rouge, La.

26. Pillow maintains in his report that he ordered a number of bayonet charges. This is not borne out by the reports of subordinates or in other sources. *OR*, 3:337, 339, 358; Stephenson, "My War Autobiography," Louisiana State University Libraries, Louisiana and Lower Mississippi Valley Collections, Baton Rouge, La.; *Nashville Banner*, Nov. 12, 1861; Lindsley, *Annals*, p. 315; Memphis *Daily Appeal*, Nov. 10, 1861; Frazer Letter, Nov. 9, 1861, in

personal collection of Thomas P. Sweeney, Springfield, Mo.; R. H. Wood to Mary Wood, Nov. 10, 1861, Wood Letters, TSLA.

27. New Orleans *Daily Picayune*, Nov. 15, 1861; G. A. Henry, Jr., to G. A. Henry, Sr., Nov. 11, 1861, Henry Papers, SHC; Estvan, *War Pictures*, p. 184; GJP to MEP, Nov. 8, 1861, *CV* 5:210; *NOR*, 1, 22:416.

28. *OR*, 3:340.

29. R. H. Wood to Mary Wood, Nov. 10, 1861, Wood Letters, TSLA.

30. Twain, *Life on the Mississippi*, p. 205; Estvan, *War Pictures*, pp. 181–82; *OR*, 3:326.

31. *OR*, 3:334; Columbus, Ky., *Daily Confederate News*, Nov. 12, 1861; Rosser, "Battle," p. 38; Stevenson, *Thirteen Months*, pp. 72–73; Vaughan, *Thirteenth Regiment*, p. 51; Conger, *Rise of U. S. Grant*, p. 93; Force, *Fort Henry to Corinth*, pp. 21–22.

32. *Memphis Avalanche*, n.d., quoted in *Daily Nashville Patriot*, Nov. 12, 1861; *OR*, 3:326; J. Davis, *Rise and Fall*, 1:404; Carnes, "Belmont," p. 369; Twain, *Life on the Mississippi*, p. 206; Durham, "Civil War Letters to Wynnewood," p. 41; Schwartz Report, Chicago Historical Society, Chicago, Ill.; Nashville *Union and American*, Nov. 14, 1861; New Orleans *Daily Crescent*, Nov. 11, 1861; D. B. Frierson to unidentified correspondent, Nov. 11, 1861, Cooper Family Papers, TSLA; Seaton, "Belmont," p. 313; Byers, *Iowa*, p. 85; R. H. Wood to Mary Wood, Nov. 10, 1861, Wood Letters, TSLA; Evans, *Confederate Military History*, 10:62; J. F. Henry to G. A. Henry, Sr., Nov. 8, 1861, Confederate Collection, TSLA; Fielder Diary, Nov. 7, 1861, TSLA.

33. Private Trueman to Elizabeth Simpson, Nov. 11, 1861, Simpson Letters, Illinois State Historical Library, Springfield, Ill.; H. I. Smith, *Seventh Iowa*, p. 260.

34. William Montgomery Austin Diary, Illinois State Historical Library, Springfield, Ill.; Squier, *Leslie's Pictorial History*, 1:195.

35. Simon, "Grant at Belmont," p. 164; *OR*, 3:315, 326, 328.

36. *OR*, 3:307, 363; New Orleans *Daily Picayune*, Nov. 14, 1861.

37. *NOR*, 1, 22:406; N. C. Hughes, *Belmont*, pp. 137–39.

38. N. C. Hughes, *Belmont*, p. 158.

39. *OR*, 3:308.

40. N. C. Hughes, *Belmont*, pp. 141–43.

41. Brinton, *Memoirs*, p. 78; H. I. Smith, *Seventh Iowa*, p. 16; D. C. Smith to Carrie Pieper, Nov. 14, 1861, Smith Letters, Illinois State Historical Library, Springfield, Ill.; *OR*, 3:298; Ingersoll, *Iowa*, p. 134; Chicago *Daily Tribune*, Nov. 15, 1861; Stuart, *Iowa Colonels*, p. 172.

42. *OR*, 3:327, 308, 344, 346, 348; Wright, "Belmont," pp. 78, 82.

43. *OR*, 3:327; N. C. Hughes, *Belmont*, pp. 164–74, 265n.

44. GJP to MEP, Nov. 7, 1861, in *New York Times*, Nov. 19, 1861; *OR*, 3:315.

45. Mary Chesnut added perspective: "Pillow has had a victory—way off somewhere. First he lost, then he was being reinforced. Faraway news—I care not for it." *OR*, 3:312; Richardson, *Papers of the Confederacy*, 1:168; Gosnell, *Guns on Western Waters*, p. 32; Woodward, *Mary Chesnut's Civil War*, p. 233, Nov. 8, 1861, entry.

46. GJP to J. J. Pettus, Nov. 12, 1861; GJP to L. S. Dixon, Nov. 17, 1861; GJP to I. G. Harris, Nov. 17, 1861, PMSR; *OR*, 4:560–61, 7:684–85, 691; Connelly, *Army of the Heartland*, p. 104; *NOR*, 2, 1:647.

47. Historian Thomas Connelly contends Pillow saw his opportunity to resist the transfer and used the supposed threat against Columbus as "a clever scheme . . . to keep his men and also obtain additional troops" for the independent offensive campaign he had wanted so long. Connelly, *Army of the Heartland*, p. 104.

48. R. H. Wood to Mary Wood, Nov. 28, 1861, Wood Letters, TSLA; C. J. Johnson to Lou Johnson, Nov. 15, 17, 1861, Johnson Letters, Louisiana State University Libraries, Louisiana and Lower Mississippi Valley Collections, Baton Rouge, La.; D. T. Massey to his father, Civil War Collection, MOHS.

49. *OR*, 7:691.

50. Ibid., 52(2):222.

51. General Orders No. 25, Dec. 4, 1861, Pillow Order Book, RG 109, NARS; *OR*, 7:731, 52(2):223–26.

52. *OR*, 3:318.

53. L. P. Yandell, Jr., to L. P. Yandell, Sr., Dec. 29, 1861, Yandell Family Papers, Filson Club, Louisville, Ky.

54. Louisville *Daily Courier*, Jan. 4, 1862; Stickles, *Buckner*, p. 120; Lexington, Ky., *Observer and Reporter*, Feb. 5, 1862.

55. In his rebuttal to Pillow, Polk, who did not respond to Pillow's charges until July 22, 1862, solicited testimony from regimental commanders and staff officers. Their statements form the most valuable block of information about Belmont. Unfortunately for Pillow, the evidence contained considerable criticism of his conduct of the battle. Pillow's main charge—that Polk did not come to his assistance rapidly enough—was brushed aside. *OR*, 3:317–24; GJP to J. P. Benjamin, Jan. 16, 1862, PMSR.

56. When Pillow returned to Clifton, his staff scattered. Burch interested himself in the plight of prominent East Tennessee Unionists and, through court appearances and a direct appeal to the secretary of war, secured the release from prison of about sixteen prominent citizens. He thereby won the "undying" appreciation of many "uncompromising Union men" in that area. *OR*, 3:313–16; Hurlbut, *Bradley County*, pp. 115–18.

57. One might argue that the resignation was yet another stratagem to have Polk removed and Pillow himself reinstated in command at Columbus, or perhaps a ploy to force the desired promotion to major general. *OR*, 3:316; GJP to J. P. Benjamin, Jan. 16, 1862, PMSR.

58. *OR*, 3:318.

CHAPTER TWELVE

1. Durham, "Civil War Letters to Wynnewood," p. 41; J. J. Neely to F. W. Neely, Jan. 9, 1862, Miscellaneous Papers, Filson Club, Louisville, Ky.; Los-

son, *Tennessee's Forgotten Warriors*, p. 41; Lexington, Ky., *Observer and Reporter*, Feb. 5, 1862.

2. L. P. Yandell, Jr., to Willy Yandell, Feb. 4, 1862, Yandell Family Papers, Filson Club, Louisville, Ky.; William Sylvester Dillon Diary, Feb. 2, 1862, in possession of Mrs. N. E. Ward, Prescott, Ark.; J. F. Henry to G. A. Henry, Jan. 22, 1862, Henry Papers, SHC; *OR*, 52(2):256–57.

3. Stonesifer, "Forts Henry-Heiman and Donelson," pp. 183–84; Cooling, *Forts Henry and Donelson*, pp. 81–119.

4. G. A. Henry to GJP, May 6, 1862, Pillow Papers, RG 109, NARS.

5. Clarksville, Tenn., *Weekly Chronicle*, Feb. 7, 1862; GJP to W. D. Pickett, Feb. 6, 1862, Pillow Papers, RG 109, NARS; Connelly, *Army of the Heartland*, pp. 126–27; *OR*, 7:859–60; GJP to W. P. Johnston, Mar. 28, 1877, Davis Collection, Howard Tilton Memorial Library, Tulane University, New Orleans, La.

6. W. J. Hardee to J. B. Floyd, Feb. 6, 1862; W. W. Mackall to J. B. Floyd, Feb. 6, 1862, Floyd Papers, DU; J. Hamilton, *Battle of Fort Donelson*, pp. 32–33.

7. W. G. Kirby to GJP, Feb. 8, 1862; B. H. Egan to GJP, Feb 8, 1862, Floyd Papers, DU; Cooling, *Forts Henry and Donelson*, p. 127.

8. GJP to W. W. Mackall, Feb. 6, 7, 1862; GJP to A. S. Johnston, Feb. 7, 1862; C. Clark to W. J. Hardee, Feb. 5, 1862, Albert S. Johnston's Command, Telegrams Received, RG 109, NARS.

9. Roland, *Johnston*, p. 291; Cooling, *Forts Henry and Donelson*, p. 128; Connelly, *Army of the Heartland*, p. 113.

10. Cummings, "Forgotten Man at Fort Donelson," p. 382; B. R. Johnson to C. Shaaff, Feb. 7, 1862; W. J. Hardee to J. B. Floyd, Feb. 5, 1862; GJP to J. B. Floyd, Feb. 8, 1862, Floyd Papers, DU; J. Hamilton, *Battle of Fort Donelson*, pp. 44–45; Cooling, *Forts Henry and Donelson*, pp. 128–29; Cummings, *Yankee Quaker*, pp. 188–90, 380–81.

11. *CV* 37:301.

12. Surg. R. A. Felton to Pauline Kirkpatrick, Feb. 10, 1862, Kirkpatrick Papers, DU; *CV* 25:163; *OR*, 7:867–68; GJP to J. B. Floyd, Feb. 9, 1862, Floyd Papers, DU; Cummings, "Forgotten Man at Donelson," p. 382; Haskins, "War Seen through a Teen-ager's Eyes," p. 177; Feb. 9, 1862, entry, Gower and Allen, *Pen and Sword*, p. 589; Special Orders No. 1, Feb. 9, 1862, Pillow Special Order Book, RG 109, NARS; N. F. Cheairs to Jennie Cheairs, Apr. 22, 1862, Cheairs-Hughes Family Papers, TSLA.

13. J. F. Gilmer to his wife, Feb. 22, 1862, Gilmer Papers, SHC; Connelly, *Army of the Heartland*, p. 114.

14. J. Hamilton, *Battle of Fort Donelson*, pp. 48–51; Cheairs, "Notes on Donelson," in possession of author; Jordan and Pryor, *Campaigns of Forrest*, p. 60; Cooling, *Forts Henry and Donelson*, pp. 130–32.

15. *OR*, 7:383.

16. Gower and Allen, *Pen and Sword*, p. 589; N. F. Cheairs to Jennie Cheairs, Apr. 22, 1862, Cheairs-Hughes Family Papers, TSLA.

17. *CV* 4:393. Captain Ross and his company, after returning from cap-

tivity, would spend the war as heavy artillerists and never see their light field pieces again. J. T. Moore, "Pillow"; *NOR*, 1, 22:605.

18. Henry, *"First with the Most,"* pp. 52–53; *OR*, 7:868, 278, 328; Cooling, *Forts Henry and Donelson*, pp. 132–33.

19. Gower and Allen, *Pen and Sword*, p. 589; W. P. Johnston, *Life of Johnston*, pp. 437, 481–82; Henry, *"First with the Most,"* pp. 52–53; *OR*, 7:328–29; Sword, *Shiloh*, p. 55; Connelly, *Army of the Heartland*, p. 115.

20. GJP to J. B. Floyd, Feb. 12, 1862, Floyd Papers, DU; Cooling, *Forts Henry and Donelson*, pp. 133–34; Roland, *Johnston*, p. 291; Sword, *Shiloh*, p. 55.

21. Cummings, *Yankee Quaker*, p. 194; Lytle, *Forrest*, p. 66.

22. GJP to J. B. Floyd, Feb. 12, 1862, Floyd Papers, DU; Cheairs, "Notes on Donelson," in possession of author; Sword, *Shiloh*, p. 55; *CV* 5:283.

23. *OR*, 52(2):269, 271–72; Cooling, *Forts Henry and Donelson*, pp. 133–34; Stonesifer, "Forts Henry-Heiman and Donelson," pp. 217–18.

24. Grant, *Memoirs*, 1:298; *CV* 12:64.

25. *OR*, 7:260, 267, 271, 330; Stonesifer, "Forts Henry-Heiman and Donelson," pp. 218–20; J. Hamilton, *Battle of Fort Donelson*, pp. 83–84; J. McCausland to J. B. Floyd, Feb. 23, 1862, Special Collections, Boston Public Library, Boston, Mass.; Roland, *Johnston*, p. 291.

26. Bearss, "Fighting on February 13," pp. 3–4; J. McCausland to J. B. Floyd, Feb. 23, 1862, Special Collections, Boston Public Library, Boston, Mass.

27. *OR*, 7:343, 352; J. Hamilton, *Battle of Fort Donelson*, pp. 83–84.

28. Johnson and Buel, *Battles and Leaders*, 1:431; Ross manuscript, Buckner Papers, HUL; *OR*, 7:389; J. Hamilton, *Battle of Fort Donelson*, pp. 87–90, 95–98; J. McCausland to J. B. Floyd, Feb. 23, 1862, Special Collections, Boston Public Library, Boston, Mass.; Porter Diary, Feb. 14, 1862, SHC; *CV* 37:302; J. T. Moore, "Pillow."

29. J. Hamilton, *Battle of Fort Donelson*, pp. 88–89, 105–10; *OR*, 7:172–73, 368, 878; Cooling, *Forts Henry and Donelson*, pp. 143–45; Bearss, "Fighting on February 13," pp. 1–35.

30. *CV* 37:301–2; A. J. Campbell, *Civil War Diary*, Feb. 14, 1862, entry.

31. Cooling, *Forts Henry and Donelson*, p. 148.

32. Ibid., p. 149; *OR*, 7:330.

33. Dawn would bring downriver the last of the Confederate units, Col. John M. Lillard's 26th Tennessee. R. M. Saffell to J. Bogle, Feb. 18, 1862, Saffell Letters, Special Collections, University of Tennessee Library, Knoxville, Tenn.; Porter Diary, Feb. 15, 1862, SHC; Westrate, *Those Fatal Generals*, pp. 173–74; *OR*, 7:268, 330, 338, 379.

34. *CV* 37:301–3; Gower and Allen, *Pen and Sword*, p. 591.

35. Walke, "The Western Flotilla at Fort Donelson," pp. 433–35; J. Hamilton, *Battle of Fort Donelson*, pp. 132–49; Ross manuscript, Buckner Papers, HUL; Cooling, *Forts Henry and Donelson*, pp. 151–59; J. T. Moore, "Pillow"; J. McCausland to J. B. Floyd, Feb. 23, 1862, Special Collections, Boston Public Library, Boston, Mass.; Porter Diary, Feb. 14, 1862, SHC.

36. Johnston, through Nathan Wickliffe, his assistant adjutant general, for-warded the message to Polk at Columbus without comment. *NOR*, 1, 22:613; *CV* 4:393; *OR*, 7:880.

37. *OR*, 7:263, 880; Roland, *Johnston*, p. 291.

38. *OR*, 7:268, 330, 365.

39. Cooling, *Forts Henry and Donelson*, pp. 163–65; *OR*, 7:281–82, 365, 267–68, 369; J. Hamilton, *Battle of Fort Donelson*, pp. 157–62.

40. *OR*, 7:317–18, 323.

41. Ibid., pp. 328–36, 350, 353.

42. Westrake, *Those Fatal Generals*, pp. 173–74; *OR*, 7:286; Porter Diary, Feb. 15, 1862, SHC; A. J. Campbell, *Civil War Diary*, Feb. 14, 1862, entry; Cummings, "Forgotten Man at Fort Donelson," p. 387; Jordan and Pryor, *Campaigns of Forrest*, p. 74.

43. Davidson would not recover. Exposure on the trip from Donelson to Fort Warren, Massachusetts, aggravated his condition and he died in prison April 29, 1862. N. F. Cheairs to Susan P. Cheairs, Apr. 30, 1862, Cheairs-Hughes Papers, in possession of author. Cummings, "Forgotten Man at Fort Donelson," p. 387; Porter Diary, Feb. 15, 1862, SHC; J. McCausland to J. B. Floyd, Feb. 23, 1862, Floyd Papers, DU.

44. Bearss, "Confederate Breakout," pp. 3–8; J. McCausland to J. B. Floyd, Feb. 23, 1862, Floyd Papers, DU; *CV* 38:19.

45. *OR*, 7:339, 175, 218, 371–72; J. Hamilton, *Battle of Fort Donelson*, pp. 171–77.

46. *SHSP* 19:373; Bearss, *Confederate Breakout*, pp. 3–8; Cooling, "Gee's Fifteenth Arkansas," pp. 329, 342.

47. Cooling, *Forts Henry and Donelson*, pp. 166–70.

48. *CV* 38:19–20.

49. *OR*, 7:175, 243; J. Hamilton, *Battle of Fort Donelson*, pp. 195–97.

50. But not Lt. Dick Saffell, 26th Tennessee. Writing with the postsur-render bitterness of February 18, Saffell maintained that "Gen. Pillow is a damned white livered coward, he sold us to save his own carcas & hid behind a big poplar tree. We could have cut our way out, but Pillow was too much of a coward to lead us." R. M. Saffell to J. Bogle, Feb. 18, 1862, Saffell Letters, Special Collections, University of Tennessee Library, Knoxville, Tenn.; Cooling, *Forts Henry and Donelson*, p. 174.

51. Memphis *Daily Appeal*, Nov. 1, 1877; Jordan and Pryor, *Campaigns of Forrest*, pp. 81–83.

52. Daniel, *Cannoneers in Gray*, p. 24; Riddell, "Goochland Light Artillery," p. 319.

53. *OR*, 7:186–87, 195; S. C. Bishop to his mother, Mar. 8, 1862, Bishop Papers, Indiana State Historical Library, Indianapolis, Ind.; Cooling, *Forts Henry and Donelson*, pp. 173–74.

54. Stickles, *Buckner*, p. 142.

55. *OR*, 7:288, 300.

56. Wyeth, *That Devil Forrest*, p. 52.

57. U.S. Government, General Service Schools, *Fort Henry and Fort Donelson Campaigns*, pp. 1353–54; Westrate, *Those Fatal Generals*, pp. 174–75.

58. *OR*, 7:297.

59. Ibid., p. 334.

60. Ibid., pp. 334, 298

61. Ibid., pp. 297, 294, 300; W. C. Davis, *Orphan Brigade*, p. 67; Henry, *"First with the Most,"* p. 55.

62. Cummings, "Forgotten Man at Fort Donelson," p. 388; Jordan and Pryor, *Campaigns of Forrest*, p. 74; Cummings, *Yankee Quaker*, pp. 380–81; Lytle, *Forrest*, p. 66.

63. Maness, *Untutored Genius*, pp. 44–45; Robertson and McMurry, *Rank and File*, p. 41.

64. Cooling, *Forts Henry and Donelson*, pp. 178–80.

65. *OR*, 7:283, 332; *NOR*, 1, 22:607.

66. *CV* 37:303; Cooling, *Forts Henry and Donelson*, pp. 181, 304n.

67. GJP to W. P. Johnston, Mar. 28, 1877, Davis Collection, Howard Tilton Memorial Library, Tulane University, New Orleans, La.; Cooling, *Forts Henry and Donelson*, p. 181; *OR*, 7:269; J. Hamilton, *Battle of Fort Donelson*, p. 258.

68. *OR*, 7:318, 332; GJP to J. A. Sedden, Feb. 16, 1863; GJP to J. Davis, Feb. 15, 1863, Pillow Papers, RG 109, NARS; Sword, *Shiloh*, p. 56; Porter Diary, Feb. 15, 1862, SHC.

69. *CV* 38:20.

70. Selden Spencer Diary, MOHS.

71. Later Pillow would contend Grant's "army was rolled back—like a map rolled up." He had tossed McClernand back on C. F. Smith and then "broken the head" of Smith's column. GJP to W. P. Johnston, Mar. 28, 1877, Davis Collection, Howard Tilton Memorial Library, Tulane University, New Orleans, La.

72. *OR*, 7:167–69, 318; W. P. Johnston, *Life of Johnston*, p. 464.

73. Floyd's staff officer, Maj. Peter Otey, related a conversation he had with Pillow that afternoon as they rode back to Dover after the fighting. "He told me we could never have gone out and the works would have been carried all along the line had he not returned. He was convinced that we could not withdraw. In other words, the enemy were still too near Wynne's Ferry Road." This version is highly contradictory and should be viewed with suspicion. *CV* 37:303.

74. *CV* 38:19; Spencer Diary, MOHS; Casseday, "Surrender of Ft. Donelson," pp. 694–97; Cheairs, "Notes on Donelson"; *OR*, 7:253, 333, 350, 229.

75. Gower and Allen, *Pen and Sword*, p. 592.

76. Curiously, Pillow gave instructions to the captain of one of the steamers that left about 8:30 P.M. to drop off his staff officer, Lt. Col. Nathan Brandon, at his residence some five miles from Dover. H. C. Burnett to J. B. Floyd, Mar. 1, 1862, Floyd Papers, DU.

77. *OR*, 7:287, 269.

78. Ibid., 287, 269, 349, 293; Jordan and Pryor, *Campaigns of Forrest*, p. 88; Cooling, *Forts Henry and Donelson*, p. 201.

79. Statements of Henry, Nicholson, and Haynes in Pillow Letterbook, RG 109, NARS; Stickles, *Buckner*, pp. 132–42.

80. Historian Thomas Connelly believes Buckner "mentally went to pieces"; Frank Cooling agrees that "Buckner had obviously lost his grip." Connelly, *Army of the Heartland*, p. 124; Cooling, *Forts Henry and Donelson*, p. 202; Nashville *American*, Nov. 3, 1878.

81. *OR*, 7:293–300, 333–35, 386; Wyeth, *That Devil Forrest*, pp. 50, 581; Stickles, *Buckner*, pp. 154–58; Cooling, *Forts Henry and Donelson*, pp. 200–204.

82. Nashville *American*, Nov. 3, 1878; *OR*, 7:334.

83. John Hinson lived within two miles of Dover. Later that morning of the sixteenth, after dawn, he passed out up the bottom and found the extreme east or right of the Union line to be on the Wynn's Ferry road. Two hours of daylight passed before he met enemy returning to reoccupy their positions on the other side of the road. *OR*, 7:295, 386; Wyeth, *That Devil Forrest*, p. 50; sworn statements of John Hinson and Dr. J. W. Smith, Pillow Papers, RG 109, NARS; GJP to W. P. Johnston, Mar. 28, 1877, Davis Collection, Howard Tilton Memorial Library, Tulane University, New Orleans, La.; GJP to B. Bragg, Feb. 16, 1863, copy in possession of JRN; Maness, *Untutored Genius*, pp. 46–47.

84. Floyd, it seems well established, feared trial and hanging for his deeds as secretary of war.

85. *OR*, 7:293–300; J. F. Gilmer to his wife, Feb. 22, 1862, Gilmer Papers, SHC; Cooling, *Forts Henry and Donelson*, pp. 202–5; *Southern Bivouac*, 2:695; unidentified correspondent to S. B. Buckner, Apr. 27, 1902, Buckner Papers, HUL; Stickles, *Buckner*, pp. 156–63; New Orleans *Picayune* correspondent writing on March 15, 1862, quoted in McKee, *Great Panic*, p. 19; J. Davis, *Rise and Fall*, 1:34; U.S. Government, General Service Schools, *Fort Henry and Fort Donelson Campaigns*, pp. 1353–54; J. Hamilton, *Battle of Fort Donelson*, pp. 289–303; H. C. Lockhart to C. E. Lockhart, Mar. 9, 1862, Lockhart Papers, SHC; Spot F. Terrell Journal, Feb. 1862, Fort Donelson National Military Park, Dover, Tenn.; D. S. M. Bodenhamer, "The Battle of Fort Donelson," Confederate Collection, TSLA.

86. Wills, *Forrest*, p. 62; *OR*, 7:295.

87. Pillow Letterbook, RG 109, NARS; *OR*, 7:300.

88. *OR*, 7:300.

89. Veteran's Questionnaire of William E. McElwee, TSLA.

90. Nashville *American*, Nov. 3, 1878; *OR*, 7:302.

91. It is unclear whether the recruits were Tennesseans or Mississippians. *OR*, 7:275, 302, 306; *CV* 7:10–12; Porter Diary, Feb. 16, 1862, SHC; A. J. Campbell, *Civil War Diary*, Feb. 16, 1862, entry; Rowland, *Davis*, 8:486–87; J. F. Gilmer to his wife, Feb. 22, 1862, Gilmer Papers, SHC.

92. *OR*, 7:302; J. F. Gilmer to his wife, Feb. 22, 1862, Gilmer Papers, SHC; Riddell, "Goochland Light Artillery," p. 320.

93. *CV* 5:283; Mott, "War Journal," p. 240; McKee, *Great Panic*, pp. 12, 19, 255; Lynchburg *Republican*, n.d., quoted in Solomon Scrapbook, DU; Horn, *Tennessee's War*, pp. 61–63.

94. McKee, *Great Panic*, pp. 19, 254–55; Solomon Scrapbook, DU; H. C. Burnett to J. B. Floyd, Mar. 1, 1862, Floyd Papers, DU.

CHAPTER THIRTEEN

1. GJP to W. J. Hardee, Feb. 19, 1862, Floyd Papers, DU; Stickles, *Buckner*, p. 169n; Andrews, *South Reports the Civil War*, pp. 130–31.

2. Johnston expressed his high opinion of Pillow as a soldier to Judge James Love of Texas at Decatur, "a short time before the Battle of Shiloh." GJP to W. J. Hardee, Feb. 20, 1862; W. J. Hardee to GJP, Feb. 23, 1862, Pillow Papers, RG 109, NARS; Roland, *Johnston*, pp. 301–2; Ridley, *Battles*, p. 68; G. A. Henry to GJP, Pillow Papers, RG 109, NARS.

3. On March 6 Pillow wrote Johnston's chief of staff, Mackall, explaining why he had published the report: "I felt it was a duty" to lay the facts before the public. "If the President had been present & understood the public mind he would approve my course." *OR*, 7:312; Memphis *Daily Appeal*, Feb. 15, 1862; W. J. Hardee to GJP, Feb. 28, 1862, Pillow Papers, RG 109, NARS; GJP to W. W. Mackall, Mar. 6, 1862, Pillow Letterbook, RG 109, NARS.

4. GJP to J. P. Benjamin, Feb. 26, 1862, Special Collections, Boston Public Library, Boston, Mass.

5. Andrews, *South Reports the Civil War*, p. 131n; Memphis *Daily Appeal*, Feb. 26, 1862; H. C. Burnett to J. B. Floyd, Mar. 1, 1862, Floyd Papers, DU.

6. McIlwaine, *Memphis*, pp. 115–16.

7. *New York Times*, Mar. 8, 1862.

8. GJP to J. P. Benjamin, Feb. 26, 1862, Special Collections, Boston Public Library, Boston, Mass.

9. GJP to W. J. Hardee, Feb. 20, 1862, PMSR.

10. GJP to W. W. Mackall, Mar. 8, 1862, PMSR.

11. Nuermberger, *Clays of Alabama*, p. 211; Evans, *Confederate Military History*, 10:652; GJP to W. W. Mackall, Mar. 8, 1862, PMSR; GJP to W. P. Johnston, Mar. 28, 1877, Davis Collection, Howard Tilton Memorial Library, Tulane University, New Orleans, La.

12. Extract from Western Department Special Orders No. 47, Mar. 16, 1862, PMSR; J. Davis to J. P. Benjamin, Mar. 11, 1862, in Rowland, *Davis*, 5:214; Nashville *American*, Nov. 3, 1878.

13. Roland, *Johnston*, p. 343. Johnston disagreed with the War Department about disciplining Pillow and Floyd. Second-guessing commanders bothered him; he had been a victim of such himself. A sense of justice, he said, dictated that one "look at events as they appeared at the time and not alone by the light of subsequent information." He had assigned Floyd and Pillow to new duties immediately after Donelson, "for I still felt confidence in their gallantry, their energy, and their devotion to the Confederacy," and he removed them from command reluctantly. J. F. Gilmer to his wife, Feb. 22, 1862, Gilmer Papers, SHC; J. T. Mudd to Captain Dunlap, Aug. 20, 1862, Union Provost Marshal's file, RG 393, NARS.

14. Legal brief, John A. Pointer v. GJP, Pillow Correspondence, NYHS.

15. During the occupation that spring of 1862, one of the Pillows, probably Granville, charged out of his house at Union soldiers using his spring and cursed them, saying "if he were younger he would fight against the Yankees until the last man of them was killed or driven home." For his abuse and interfering ways, Pillow was put under arrest by a young lieutenant. This lieutenant's colonel, however, turned out to be a great admirer of a Pillow niece in Nashville, and as a result of her intercession, he released the prisoner, apologized, and arrested the young lieutenant instead. Hannaford, *Story of a Regiment*, p. 233; Garrett, "General Pillow"; Donald, *Inside Lincoln's Cabinet*, pp. 163–64.

16. N. B. Buford to J. B. Pillow, Nov. 4, 1863, Union Provost Marshal's File, RG 393, NARS; *OR*, 16(2):107, 183; M. Wilkins, "Some Papers," p. 338.

17. Unfortunately for the Pillow brothers, vigilant Yankees stopped Sol as he entered Tennessee, discovered the letter, and confiscated it. S. M. R. Trotter to Cynthia Carter, May 30, 1862, Pope-Carter Papers, DU; GJP to J. B. Pillow, July 20, 1862, PMSR; Nashville *Union and American*, Sept. 4, 1862.

18. Atlanta *Southern Confederacy*, Aug. 7, 1862; Knox, *Campfire*, pp. 226–27, 311; Carmichael, "Federal Experiments," pp. 106–7; Thomas, *Arkansas*, p. 365; *New York Times*, Jan. 11, 1863; GJP to S. P. Walker, Aug. 2, 1862, in *OR*, 17(2):171–72, 52(2):332.

19. J. Davis to GJP, July 31, 1862, in Rowland, *Davis*, 5:304.

20. *OR*, 17(2):172.

21. Confederate General Citizens File, M-346, NARS; Nashville *Dispatch*, Mar. 26, 1863; Durham, *Nashville*, pp. 150–51.

22. Northern papers happily joined in as well. The *New York Times* reported, "This military peacock has been in disgrace ever since the night of his shameful sneaking flight from Fort Donelson. . . . Since then he has been like Cain, a fugitive and a vagabond." Augusta, Ga., *Daily Constitutionalist*, Mar. 7, 1862; *Memphis Avalanche*, Feb. 27, 1862; *New York Times*, Jan. 11, 1863.

23.   Pillow and Floyd, two Generals of might
     Came to Donelson the Yankees to fight.
     Pillow said he is a Hero
     And would drive them back to Cairo,
     The Cumberland and Tennessee
     From Hessians I will free—
     In fact I am the man for the crisis
     If you only follow my advices—
     With Johnson on my left, and Buckner on my right
     I shall give them a Devil of a fight—
     Gideon, said Floyd, I'll make you understand
     That these troops here are under my command,
     Besides you are too big for your britches,
     This you have shown by your ditches—
     Ah! cried Pillow, do you mean at Camargo
     On this unkind hint I shall lay an Embargo—

But let this pass, we must have no contentions now,
Or we will not gain fresh laurels for our Brow.
With pick, shovel, and spade
Lines of rifle pits were made.
And a consultation was held of Cols & Gens wise
On the 15th of Feb by daylight in the morning
The Rebels gave them a *Hell* of a storming,
They were driven back from their position
And our affairs were thought to be in the best condition—
Now our Generals put together their wits
And ordered the troops back to their rifle pits—
Said it was no use to hold out any longer,
The enemy is by great odds the stronger—
They will cut off our communications
And that will be followed by starvation.
Gideon, said Floyd, I cannot, I will not surrender
And he felt his neck and pulled his suspender—
Ah Ha! said Pillow, you are afraid of the halter—
Now did you ever know me to falter—
But like yourself, surrender I will not,
Let us try and fix up a great plot—
Give the command over to Buckner and let us be smart,
Let him surrender while we depart—
And so they did
With kin and kith
And during the night
They took to flight
Said now all is over
We are the Heroes of Dover.

Gower and Allen, *Pen and Sword*, p. 617.

24. J. C. Brown to J. B. Palmer, July 20, 1862, in Neff, "Best and Bravest," p. 152.

25. When Tilghman was exchanged in September, he made Pillow answer for accusations about the former's inept defense of Fort Henry. Pillow lamely responded that he had been misinformed. Gower and Allen, *Pen and Sword*, p. 673; L. Tilghman to GJP, Sept. 21, 1862; GJP to L. Tilghman, Sept. 21, 1862, Pillow Papers, RG 109, NARS.

26. Garrett, "General Pillow"; Columbia *Herald*, Feb. 16, 1874.

27. McFeely, *Grant*, p. 617.

28. Ambrose, "Fort Donelson," p. 47; N. F. Cheairs to Nancy C. Perkins, May 7, 1862, Cheairs-Hughes Family Papers, TSLA.

29. Historians, almost without exception, have echoed similar sentiments. Frank Vandiver reports objectively:

The Southern people, the Confederate government itself, required a scapegoat. To choose Pillow was a most seductive temptation. He was noisy, insubordinate, difficult, pompous, and made enemies as fast as he made friends. So blatantly partisan was he by nature that he had lost credibility over the years. As a military man he could never free himself from the image he brought back from Mexico, an image carefully polished and re-polished by the professional military establishment. No matter the bravery and initiative and energy and sound battlefield leadership he had displayed at Donelson itself, he remained the foolish ditch-digger of Camargo.

30. Pillow Letterbook, RG 109, NARS; *OR*, 7:285–306.

31. Pillow attacked Davis in an unsigned letter to the Jackson *Daily Mississippian*, June 17, 1862, Pillow Papers, JRN.

32. *OR*, 32(2):543.

33. The Confederate House of Representatives appointed a special committee to investigate the Donelson disaster on March 31, 1862, headed by Pillow's friend, Henry S. Foote of Tennessee. The committee made its report April 18, 1862, refusing to place the responsibility on any officer. Yearns, *Confederate Congress*, p. 142.

34. *OR*, 7:308–9.

35. Ibid., p. 309.

36. Ibid., p. 310.

37. Davis had been under heavy pressure from most of the Tennessee congressional delegation, notably Henry S. Foote and Gustavus A. Henry. When Foote informed Pillow the suspension had been lifted, the general "burst into tears." Bragg to GJP, Aug. 26, 1862, Pillow Papers, RG 109, NARS; *OR*, 7:313; Nashville *Daily American*, Nov. 3, 1878.

38. *OR*, 7:313.

39. Nashville *Daily American*, Nov. 3, 1878. It is the belief of the authors that this nine-page biographical sketch of Pillow, which appeared less than a month after his death, is his own work.

40. *OR*, 17(2):691, 7:316–20.

41. Pillow executed a mortgage to Jerome on his real and personal estate in Maury County on October 27, 1862. It was to cover debts to Jerome of $50,000, to the Planters Bank of Tennessee, $45,000, and to his wards, John E. and Narcissa P. Saunders, and their mother, Cynthia Saunders, about $35,000. *OR*, 7:319–20; Merchants Bank v. Pillow, 1865, Davidson County Chancery Court Records, Nashville, Tenn.; Planters Bank of Nashville v. Pillow, June 5, 1866, Dempsey Weaver Papers, TSLA.

42. *OR*, 52(2):396, 7:320–24; GJP to J. A. Sedden, Feb. 16, 1863, typed copy in Garrett, "General Pillow."

43. *OR*, 7:325.

44. Ibid., pp. 325–26.

45. Jackson *Daily Mississippian*, Sept. 12, 1862.

46. *OR*, 17(2):716, 7:320–21.

47. He thrilled some of his old soldiers in the 13th Tennessee by saluting them as they marched past him. Rogers, "Memorandum Book," p. 75.

48. *OR*, 20(2):449.

49. Charles Spearman, Stones River National Military Park Historian, to N. C. Hughes, Nov. 2, 1991.

50. Breckinridge had five brigades at the time, but John K. Jackson's did not participate in the attack on the right.

51. McDonough, *Stones River*, pp. 177; Cozzens, *No Better Place*, p. 182; Neff, "Best and Bravest," p. 97; Connelly, *Autumn of Glory*, pp. 62–64.

52. McWhiney, *Braxton Bragg*, pp. 368–69; Losson, *Tennessee's Forgotten Warriors*, p. 56; Neff, "Best and Bravest," p. 97.

53. Neff, "Best and Bravest," pp. 97–98; Cummings, *Yankee Quaker*, pp. 310–11; Cozzens, *No Better Place*, pp. 181–83.

54. Col. Ed C. Cook's 32d was not present during the attack. The alignment of the participating regiments other than Palmer's 18th has not been determined. *OR*, 20(1):675, 659.

55. The brigade numbered 1,599 on January 19, 1863. *OR*, 20(1):807–9.

56. Ibid., pp. 805, 807.

57. Bearss, "Union Artillery and Breckinridge's Attack," 2:1; Pickett, "Reminiscences of Murfreesboro," *CV* 16:452–53; Cozzens, *No Better Place*, p. 181; GJP to T. O'Hara, Jan. 11, 1863, Ryder Collection, Tufts University Library, Medford, Mass.; *OR*, 20(1):785, 969; Connelly, *Autumn of Glory*, p. 64; H. B. Clay, "On the Right at Murfreesboro," p. 588; G. W. Brent to B. Bragg, Mar. 15, 1863, Palmer Collection, Western Reserve Historical Society, Cleveland, Ohio.

58. *OR*, 20(1):786; W. C. Davis, *Breckinridge*, p. 243; L. D. Young, *Reminiscences*, p. 49; Pickett, "Reminiscence of Murfreesboro," pp. 452–53.

59. The episode also is mentioned in a letter from a soldier named Worley to his mother cited in W. C. Davis, *Breckinridge*, pp. 343, 343n. Davis believes, however, that the citation is mistaken and that the Worley letter does not refer to the Pillow episode. W. C. Davis to N. C. Hughes, Dec. 5, 1991; Rice E. Graves, Charges and specifications of charges against Brig. Gen. G. J. Pillow, n.d., in Breckinridge Collection, Chicago Historical Society, Chicago, Ill.; McDonough, *Stones River*, p. 185; Cozzens, *No Better Place*, p. 186.

60. Breckinridge contended Col. Theodore O'Hara of his own staff, not Pillow, discovered the enemy on the right and took corrective action.

61. *OR*, 20(1):786, 826, 808, 823; Bearss, "Union Artillery and Breckinridge's Attack," 2:5–6.

62. *OR*, 20(1):786, 827; GJP to T. O'Hara, Jan. 11, 1863, Ryder Collection, Tufts University Library, Medford, Mass.; Pillow Letterbook, RG 109, NARS.

63. Johnson and Buel, *Battles and Leaders*, 3:630; Bearss, "Troop Movement Map, Jan. 2, 1863." Bearss's list of Union guns includes fifty-seven pieces. According to Ron Gibbs, Stones River National Park historian, Capt. John Mendenhall tended to confuse the sizes and refused to acknowledge loss of four twelve-pound Napoleons. Lt. C. C. Parsons's battery also received a replacement for a damaged gun. This extra cannon would bring the total to fifty-eight.

64. Johnson and Buel, *Battles and Leaders*, 3:633.

65. *OR*, 20(1):808; Pickett, "Reminiscence of Murfreesboro," pp. 452–53; Cozzens, *No Better Place*, pp. 190–92; Horn, *Army of Tennessee*, p. 208; Jamison, *Letters*, p. 158; Neff, "Best and Bravest," pp. 97–99.

66. Connelly, *Autumn of Glory*, p. 65; Neff, "Best and Bravest," p. 99; *OR*, 20(1):675.

CHAPTER FOURTEEN

1. Breckinridge appears to have been badly misled about Pillow's sympathies, probably counting on the solid relationship between his acting chief of staff, O'Hara, and Pillow. Breckinridge wrote Bragg on January 12 that Pillow and his three other brigade commanders concurred that "you do not possess the confidence of the Army to an extent which will enable you to be useful as its commander." Breckinridge took great liberties. Pillow contradicted this testimony and came to Bragg's defense, as did Col. Robert P. Trabue, who had taken command of Hanson's brigade. J. C. Breckinridge to B. Bragg, Jan. 12, 1863, Breckinridge Collection, NYHS; Connelly, *Autumn of Glory*, p. 83; Davis, *Orphan Brigade*, p. 164; Cozzens, *No Better Place*, p. 214; GJP to W. Clare, Mar. 9, 1863, Bragg Papers, William P. Palmer Collection, WRH.

2. *OR*, 20(2):498; GJP to B. Bragg, Jan. 12, 1863, Pillow Papers, RG 109, NARS.

3. General Orders No. 6, Army of Tennessee, Jan. 14, 1863, PMSR; *OR*, 20(2):498; *OR*, ser. 4, 2:305–6; Circular Order, Jan. 16, 1863, Pillow Order Book, RG 109, NARS; Purcell, "Military Conscription," p. 94; Rogers, "Memorandum Book," p. 79.

4. *OR*, 23(2):642.

5. Ibid., 20(2):498; *OR*, ser. 4, 2:362; Circular, Jan. 17, 1863, Pillow Order Book, RG 109, NARS.

6. Bell, "Pillow," p. 18; GJP to Lt. E. F. Cooper, Jan. 17, 1863, PMSR.

7. Pillow intended to sweep Tennessee counties like Bedford, closest to enemy lines, and then fall back to a secondary tier of counties where men could not flee so easily. *OR*, ser. 4, 2:361–62, 387; GJP to B. Bragg, Jan. 21, 1863, Pillow Letterbook, RG 109, NARS.

8. GJP to B. Bragg, Jan. 29, 1863, Pillow Letterbook, RG 109, NARS; A. B. Moore, *Conscription and Conflict*, p. 192.

9. *OR*, ser. 4, 2:361–62, 371, 374.

10. "If any officer otherwise appointed is styling himself an officer of conscripts, or acting as such, the confusion thus created should be immediately ended." *OR*, ser. 4, 2:431; Purcell, "Military Conscription," p. 95.

11. General Orders No. 6, Feb. 16, 1863, Pillow Order Book, RG 94, NARS; *OR*, ser. 4, 2:433–34.

12. Pillow knew well the games played in Richmond. His virulent congressional ally, Henry S. Foote of Tennessee, burned Secretary of War Seddon's

backside by having Pillow's ideas and criticisms of conscription—as practiced by the Richmond bureau—placed before the House Committee on Military Affairs. *OR*, ser. 4, 2:403; *SHSP* 48:175.

13. General Order No. 2, Jan. 27, 1863, Pillow Order Book, RG 94, NARS.

14. Bell, "Pillow," p. 18; Purcell, "Military Conscription," pp. 96–97; *OR*, ser. 4, 2:440–44.

15. A. B. Moore, *Conscription and Conflict*, p. 94; *OR*, 24(3):560, 562; *OR*, ser. 4, 2:433, 437–38; A. W. Bell to Z. B. Vance, Feb. 23, 1863, in possession of Richard Melvin, Franklin, N.C.

16. GJP to G. W. Brent (B. Bragg), Jan. 29, 1863, Pillow Letterbook, RG 109, NARS.

17. General Orders No. 12, Mar. 16, 1863, Pillow Order Book, RG 94, NARS.

18. A. B. Moore, *Conscription and Conflict*, pp. 12–18, 141–52, 155, 191–93, 202; E. M. Coulter, *Confederate States of America*, p. 327; Yearns, *Confederate Congress*, p. 82.

19. *OR*, 52(2):426.

20. Pillow had set up and staffed most of these in March 1863, so, in effect, he reactivated them. Special Orders No. 146, 195–901, Mar. 5, 18, 1863, Pillow Order Book, RG 109, NARS; *OR*, ser. 4, 2:819–22.

21. Knoxville *Register*, Sept. 24, 1863; *OR*, ser. 4, 2:805.

22. Pillow's black teamsters were not welcomed, however. Most, to his astonishment and distress, returned quickly to their owners. Some were given forged papers by white teamsters whose jobs they threatened. "Others were paid to leave, others persuaded, others threatened," Pillow informed Bragg, requesting an investigation; otherwise, he would abandon the effort. Special Orders No. 222, Apr. 12, 1863, Pillow Order Book, RG 94, NARS; *OR*, 23(2):624–25, 628–29; Rogers, "Memorandum Book," p. 91; Jamison, *Letters*, pp. 44–46; Teamster contract, Feb. 6, 1863, Pope-Carter Papers, DU; Special Order No. 56, Feb. 10, 1863, Pillow Order Book, RG 94, NARS; GJP to H. Nicholson, Feb. 10, 1863, Pillow Letterbook, RG 109, NARS; *New York Times*, Mar. 21, 1863; GJP vouchers and receipts, Jan. 16, 1863–Dec. 31, 1863, Confederate Citizens File, RG 109, NARS; GJP to L. Polk, Apr. 15, 1863; GJP to K. Falconer, Mar. 16, 1863, PMSR; B. F. Carter to Cynthia Carter, Mar. 29, 1863, Pope-Carter Papers, DU.

23. I. G. Harris to J. A. Seddon, Feb. 13, 1863, PMSR; GJP to B. Bragg, Feb. 16, 1863, with supporting testimony, Pillow Papers, JRN.

24. Proclamations to planters of Morgan, Lawrence, Lauderdale, and Franklin counties, Tenn., Mar. 6, 1863, Pillow Letterbook, RG 109, NARS; *New York Times*, Mar. 21, 1863.

25. *New York Times*, Mar. 21, 1863.

26. Hamlin, *Ewell*, p. 120.

27. *OR*, 23(2):758; Govan and Livingood, *A Different Valor*, p. 187; Connelly, *Autumn of Glory*, p. 109.

28. *OR*, ser. 4, 2:456, 473, 482, 749, 432; A. B. Moore, *Conscription and Conflict*, pp. 191–97.

29. *OR*, ser. 4, 2:415–16; General Orders No. 13, Mar. 19, 1863, Pillow Order Book, RG 94, NARS.

30. *OR*, ser. 4, 2:444–45; A. B. Moore, *Conscription and Conflict*, pp. 194–95.

31. *OR*, ser. 4, 2:432, 726–28.

32. Ibid., pp. 449–50.

33. A. B. Moore, *Conscription and Conflict*, pp. 194–95; *OR*, ser. 4, 2:431, 450; Purcell, "Military Conscription," pp. 100–101.

34. *OR*, 23(2):758; A. B. Moore, *Conscription and Conflict*, pp. 195–96; Purcell, "Military Conscription," pp. 97–98.

35. Pillow also kept the Donelson stove hot. As late as May 9, 1863, he continued to send to the War Department depositions from officers he ran across willing to testify on his behalf. GJP to B. Bragg, Apr. 3, 1863, Pillow Letterbook, RG 109, NARS; GJP to L. Polk, Apr. 15, 1863, PMSR; GJP to W. W. Mackall, July 20, 1863, William Whann Mackall Papers, SHC; *OR*, 23(2):817, 827.

36. *OR*, 23(1):219, 23(2):532–38, 827–28, 844, 24(1):515; Henry, *Forrest*, p. 160.

37. Purcell, "Military Conscription," pp. 98; A. B. Moore, *Conscription and Conflict*, p. 214; *OR*, ser. 4, 2:797, 868.

38. General Orders No. 21, July 15, 1863, PMSR; Purcell, "Military Conscription," pp. 98–99; *OR*, ser. 4, 2:869, 830; *OR*, 23(2):912–13; Speer, *Sketches of Prominent Tennesseans*, p. 343; Bell, "Pillow," p. 19; E. M. Coulter, *Confederate States of America*, p. 324.

39. *OR*, ser. 4, 2:636.

40. Ibid., p. 638; *OR*, 23(2):912–13; General Orders No. 1, No. 2, July 27, 1863, Pillow Orders and Letters, 1861–63, RG 109, NARS.

41. Hoole, *Alabama Tories*, pp. 5–6; *OR*, 32(3):681–82; *OR*, ser. 4, 2:638; Melton, "Disloyal Confederates," pp. 13–16; J. W. Estes to L. Polk, Apr. 28, 1864, Pillow Letterbook, RG 109, NARS.

42. Pillow adjusted this figure in September to "not less than 6,000 to 8,000 . . . eking out a precarious existence by a system of robbery." *OR*, ser. 4, 2:680–81; Lonn, *Desertion*, pp. 71, 81.

43. *OR*, ser. 4, 3:252; GJP to W. W. Mackall, Apr. 30, 1863, Pillow Letterbook, RG 109, NARS; Purcell, "Military Conscription," p. 101.

44. McMillan, *Disintegration of a Confederate State*, p. 59; Talladega, Ala., *Democratic Watchtower*, Dec. 16, 1863; Circular, Oct. 8, 1863, Lockhart Papers, SHC.

45. *OR*, 23(2):921.

46. *OR*, ser. 4, 2:741–43; N. C. Hughes, *Hardee*, pp. 158–62; S. T. Murray to E. B. Murray, Aug. 22, 1863, Murray Papers, DU; Dubay, *Pettus*, pp. 190–91; Bell, "Pillow," p. 18.

47. Martin, *Desertion of Alabama Troops*, p. 20; *OR*, ser. 4, 3:102.

48. A. B. Moore, *Conscription and Conflict*, pp. 210–11.

49. Purcell, "Military Conscription," p. 101; Special Orders, July 15, 1863, Pillow Order Book, RG 109, NARS.

50. *OR*, ser. 4, 2:276.

51. Ibid., pp. 782, 794, 707; A. B. Moore, *Conscription and Conflict*, pp. 214–15.

52. Unfortunately, Col. Alexander Campbell, bearing documents, was captured on a mission into West Tennessee, thus compromising the recruiting plans of Harris and Pillow. *OR*, ser. 4, 2:819–22; *OR*, 30(2):788, 24(3):560, 562, 31(3):708.

53. Candler, *Confederate Records of Georgia*, 3:389–91; Parks, *Joseph E. Brown*, p. 246.

54. J. B. Jones, *Rebel War Clerk's Diary*, 2:25.

55. *OR*, ser. 4, 2:748–49, 751–54; A. B. Moore, *Conscription and Conflict*, pp. 208–9.

56. A. B. Moore, *Conscription and Conflict*, pp. 212, 212n; *OR*, ser. 4, 3:8, 2:805.

57. *OR*, ser. 4, 2:859, 963, 916–18; A. B. Moore, *Conscription and Conflict*, p. 214; E. M. Coulter, *Confederate States of America*, p. 324.

58. *OR*, ser. 4, 2:707.

59. Ibid., p. 693.

60. Ibid., pp. 728, 682; *OR*, 31(3):713.

61. Purcell, "Military Conscription," p. 106.

62. Pillow cooperated with Seddon's request that cattle drivers and clerks for commissary officers be exempted. *OR*, ser. 4, 2:847–49; *OR*, 32(2):526–27.

63. *OR*, ser. 4, 2:859.

64. Ibid., pp. 847–48.

65. Ibid., pp. 867, 873; A. B. Moore, *Conscription and Conflict*, pp. 212–13; Purcell, "Military Conscription," p. 104.

66. *OR*, ser. 4, 2:884.

67. Ibid., pp. 1019–20.

68. *OR*, 31(3):836, 844, 854; Purcell, "Military Conscription," p. 105.

69. *OR*, ser. 4, 2:1063–64.

70. *OR*, 31(3):876, 32(3):574.

71. *OR*, ser. 4, 3:1123.

72. Proceedings of the First Confederate Congress, 4th sess., in *SHSP*, 50:127, 230–31.

73. B. Bragg to S. Cooper, Oct. 4, 1863; J. E. Johnston to S. Cooper, Oct. 21, 28, 1863, PMSR; *OR*, 23(2):921; B. F. Cheatham to J. A. Seddon, Oct. 10, 1863, PMSR.

74. *OR*, 32(3):645.

75. Recent scholarship deemphasizes the importance of manpower and stresses the Confederates' "maldistribution of equipment, supplies in connection with available manpower." Certainly the success of the Union war effort depended to a great extent upon magnificent utilization of its economic resources and modes of transportation and distribution. The point remains, however, that without the men Pillow pumped into the Army of Tennessee, the effectiveness of that army would have suffered and defeat come more

quickly. Another 50,000 Confederate troops in 1863 might not have reversed the war's outcome but would have been dreaded as much, if not more, by Grant as they would have been welcomed by Bragg.

CHAPTER FIFTEEN

1. B. Bragg to GJP, Jan. 10, 1864, Pillow Papers, RG 109, NARS.

2. Connelly, *Autumn of Glory*, pp. 281–89; Parks, *Polk*, pp. 354–58; Hattaway, "Lee," p. 173; *OR*, 32(2):518.

3. F. D. Polk to her daughter, Jan. 21, 1864, Polk Papers, University of the South, DuPont Library, Sewanee, Tenn.

4. *OR*, 32(2):556, 571–72, 561–62, 599, 638.

5. Special Orders No. 32, Army of Tennessee, PMSR; *OR*, 32(2):638; Gorgas, *Civil War Diary*, Jan. 30, 1864, entry.

6. J. B. Jones, *Rebel War Clerk's Diary*, 2:140; S. Cooper to GJP, Feb. 5, 1864, Pillow PMSR.

7. GJP to J. Johnston, Feb. 9, 1864; GJP to L. Polk, Feb. 9, 1864, PMSR.

8. J. I. Herrick (Chaplain and Superintendent of Freedmen) to T. C. Callicot, Jan. 22, Mar. 16, 1864; G. W. Perry to T. C. Callicot, Jan. 8, 1864; Memorial from Loyal Citizens of the United States to Supervising Special Agent, Treasury Department, Feb. 1864; Lease for Swan Lake Plantation, Feb. 16, 1864, U.S. Treasury Department Records, Helena District, RG 56, NARS; Carmichael, "Federal Experiments," p. 107.

9. J. H. Watts to L. Polk, Mar. 3, 1864; Special Orders No. 43, Mar. 18, 1864; GJP to S. M. Haskell, Mar. 16, 1864; L. D. Hatch to J. C. Burch, Apr. 1, 1864; L. D. Steele to GJP, Mar. 18, 1864; C. C. Henderson to GJP, Apr. 14, 1864, Pillow Papers, RG 109, NARS; *CV* 24:208, 17:350; *OR*, 35(2):388, 32(3):589, 52(2):683–84; GJP to J. E. Johnston, Feb. 6, 1864, PMSR.

10. *OR*, 52(2):683–84, 35(2):388; *OR*, ser. 4, 3:252–53.

11. *OR*, 32(3):620, 683; L. D. Hatch to J. C. Burch, Apr. 1, 1864; J. H. Watts to GJP, Mar. 8, 1864, Pillow Papers, RG 109, NARS.

12. *OR*, 32(3):683.

13. GJP to B. Bragg, Apr. 5, 1864, Pillow Papers, RG 109, NARS. Pillow's mother, Annie Payne Pillow, died in early April and was buried in Columbia. According to Jerome Pillow's postwar testimony, Gideon Pillow at this time used his brother's good offices with the Federals to see if he might be allowed to return home if he took the loyalty oath.

14. *OR*, 32(3):585.

15. Ibid., pp. 822–26, 858–59, 38(4):654–55; Special Orders No. 116, Apr. 25, 1864, Department of Alabama, Mississippi, East Louisiana, RG 109, NARS.

16. S. G. Spann to GJP, Apr. 27, 1864, Pillow Papers, RG 109, NARS; *OR*, 38(4):708–9, 39(2):593; Bearss, *Forrest at Brice's Cross Roads*, p. 21.

17. *OR*, 38(4):740, 737, 727, 752, 39(2):612–13, 621; S. D. Lee to GJP, May [?], 24, 1864, Pillow Papers, RG 109, NARS.

18. Hattaway, "Lee," p. 179; *OR*, 38(4):740–41, 39(2):635–37, 645–48, 78:645–48; Henry, *First with the Most*, p. 311.

19. *OR*, 38(4):772.

20. Ibid., (3):995; Van Horne, *Army of the Cumberland*, 2:95.

21. Tennessee Civil War Commission, *Tennesseans in the Civil War*, 1:85.

22. Joy, "Stampede at LaFayette," p. 474; Lindsley, *Military Annals of Tennessee*, p. 730.

23. Lee could not comply. Every man was needed in Mississippi to meet a threat from Memphis. Wheeler was active in the area, however, which took the enemy's attention. W. Elliott to GJP, June 23, 1864, Pillow Papers, RG 109, NARS; *OR*, 38(4):788, 38(3):1004–5; Dodson, *Wheeler*, p. 193.

24. *OR*, 38(3):1004, 995, 38(4):783–84, 794; Joy, "Stampede at LaFayette," p. 474.

25. *OR*, 38(3):995, 1004–5.

26. John Johnston, "Civil War Reminiscences," p. 342; *OR*, 38(2):795–96; Kelly, "Brush with Pillow," p. 324; Speer, *Sketches of Prominent Tennesseans*, p. 343; Sartain, *History of Walker County*, p. 113.

27. *OR*, 38(3):995.

28. Henry, "Battle of LaFayette"; John Johnston, "Civil War Reminiscences," p. 342; *OR*, 38(3):998, 1005.

29. *OR*, 38(3):995.

30. A company of Federals also were out scouting toward Summerville on the twenty-third but returned to LaFayette that evening "without seeing anything." Kelly, "Brush with Pillow," p. 324.

31. Ibid., pp. 330–31.

32. Watkins (1833–68), a native of Florida, educated in Washington, D.C., was the son-in-law of Gen. Lovell H. Rousseau, who would become the good friend of Jerome Pillow and later benefactor of Mary E. Pillow.

33. Henry, "Battle of LaFayette"; *OR*, 38(2):795–800; Kelly, "Brush with Pillow," pp. 323–24.

34. Henry, "Battle of LaFayette"; *OR*, 38(3):998.

35. "Col. Armistead had been shot in some of his fingers," reported Pvt. John Johnston, "and was standing near the road as we passed him, with his hand raised in the air, shouting out lustily that he had been shot and calling for help. This impressed me as being rather ludicrous and childish conduct for the commander of a brigade." *OR*, 38(3):998–1004, 1009–10; John Johnston, "Civil War Reminiscences," p. 342; Sartain, *History of Walker County*, p. 114.

36. Pvt. John Johnston remembered they sat or lay waiting—"another hour of long waiting." John Johnston, "Civil War Reminiscences," p. 342.

37. *OR*, 38(3):1005; Lindsley, *Military Annals of Tennessee*, p. 730; John Johnston, "Civil War Reminiscences," pp. 342–43; F. M. Stewart to E. S. Hammond, June 28, 1864, Confederate Collection, TSLA.

38. Kelly, "Brush with Pillow," p. 326.

39. *OR*, 38(2):795–96, 38(4):794; Kelly, "Brush with Pillow," p. 328; Henry, "Battle of LaFayette."

40. Kelly, "Brush with Pillow," p. 326; *OR*, 38(3):998–1010.

41. Joy, "Stampede at LaFayette," p. 474; *OR*, 52(1):102–4, 38(3):794, 1008, 38(2):777–78; Henry, "Battle of LaFayette"; Kelly, "Brush with Pillow," p. 324; Union Soldiers, *Union Regiments of Kentucky*, pp. 152, 173, 186–87; Sartain, *History of Walker County*, pp. 231–32.

42. John Johnston, "Civil War Reminiscences," p. 345.

43. F. M. Stewart to E. S. Hammond, June 28, 1864, Confederate Collection, TSLA; *OR*, 38(3):996, 1007; Speer, *Sketches of Prominent Tennesseans*, p. 343.

44. *OR*, 38(4):601, 794, 996–97, 38(2):494–95, 795–96, 38(3):1000–1010; Kelly, "Brush with Pillow," pp. 321–22.

45. *OR*, 38(3):996–97, 38(2):494–95, 777–78, 795–96; Van Horne, *Army of the Cumberland*, 2:95; Kelly, "Brush with Pillow," p. 330; *The Union Army*, 6:546.

46. *OR*, 38(3):996.

47. John Johnston, "Civil War Reminiscences," pp. 345–46.

48. *OR*, 38(5):112, 38(4):633.

49. Poor Pillow. Bards were bad enough, but one admiring editor, describing him as "battle-scarred," saw to his horror the typesetter had transposed letters, transforming Pillow into "bottle-scarred." Jones, "Babel of the Types," Jones Papers, DU; F. Moore, *Civil War in Song and Story*," p. 261.

50. *OR*, 38(3):994, 39(2):673; Lindsley, *Military Annals of Tennessee*, p. 730.

51. *OR*, 39(2):685, 689–90.

52. Ibid., 38(5):82, 884, 887, 38(3):978.

53. Rousseau's Alabama raid never received the attention, nor the admiration, it merited. With no pretense of being a cavalry commander, he managed to pull off one of the most successful Union cavalry strikes of the war. *OR*, 38(5):82, 52(2):708, 38(3):975, 39(2):714; McMillan, *Alabama Confederate Reader*, pp. 261–71.

54. *OR*, 39(2):709.

55. Ibid., pp. 723–24; Speer, *Sketches of Prominent Tennesseans*, p. 343.

56. GJP to G. A. Trenholm, July 31, 1864, PMSR; Roark, *Masters without Slaves*, p. 41.

57. Pillow may have attached himself to Jackson in north Alabama for a while but apparently did not take part in field operations. H. Bryan to G. W. Brent, Nov. 1, 1864, Brent Papers, DU; Graber, *A Terry Texas Ranger*, pp. 201–2; *OR*, 39(3):639.

58. His agreement, like the one governing Pillow's Swan Lake Plantation in Arkansas, called for Bean to pay the government two cents per pound on all cotton raised and a proportionate amount on other crops.

59. The Pillow family and other Confederate sympathizers in Maury were also threatened by the Unionist W. H. Pillow, Gideon's cousin and a man quick to report individuals to Federal authorities. H. G. Smith to L. H. Rousseau, Oct. 17, 1864, Register of Letters Received, Army of the Cumberland, RG 393, NARS; Provost Marshal's file, Nov. 9, 1864, entry; Provost Marshal's Register Book "B," Nov. 20, 1864, entry, RG 393, NARS; Maj. Gen.

Grenville M. Dodge Ledgerbook, n.d., RG 366, NARS; GJP to Commander of Federal Forces, Columbia, Tenn., Oct. 14, 1864; GJP to L. H. Rousseau, Oct. 17, 1864, Pillow Letters, HSP; Porter Diary, June 5, 1864, SHC.

60. *OR*, 39(3):639–40, 650.

61. MEP to L. H. Rousseau, Nov. 3, 1864, Dreer Collection, HSP.

62. They would be married the following May. Nashville *Union*, Apr. 14, 1864, May 30, 1865.

63. GJP to J. L. Monroe, Oct. [?] 1864, Pillow Papers, JRN.

64. *OR*, 45(1):1222–23.

65. Willie Smith Diary, Nov. 24, 1864, in possession of William L. McDonald, Florence, Ala.; Garrett, "General Pillow"; Athens, Ala., *Valley Featurette*, Nov. 13, 1970.

66. Willie Smith Diary, Nov. 22–27, 1864, in possession of William L. McDonald, Florence, Ala.; Garrett, "General Pillow."

67. *OR*, 45(2):689–90; J. C. Burch to G. W. Brent, Dec. 22, 1864, Brent Papers, DU; Porter Diary, Dec. 16, 1864, SHC.

68. *CV* 29:355.

69. This may have been the result of Pillow's association with Charles Quintard. To have come back through the lines without an escort took courage on Pillow's part. Bushwhackers and thieves roamed the roads. Pillow's son-in-law to be, Daniel F. Wade, was badly wounded in such an encounter. In March 1864 Confederate guerrillas had come to Clifton and made off with twenty-two horses and helped themselves to all the farm machinery they could carry. Federal soldiers appear to have taken no notice. In Arkansas other roaming Confederates made off with some of the few slaves still under Pillow's control. Nashville *Union*, Jan. 11, 1865; Sistler, *Battle Statistics*, 2:179; Porter Diary, Mar. 31, 1865, SHC; GJP to J. C. Breckinridge, Mar. 28, 1865, Letters Received, Office of the Secretary of War, RG 109, NARS.

70. General Orders No. 6, Adj. and Inspect. Gen. Office, Feb. 14, 1865, Confederate Papers, Florida State University, R. M. Strozier Library, Tallahassee, Fla.; *OR*, ser. 4, 3:1082; *OR*, 47(2):1174, 1202; Blakey, *Winder*, pp. 196–99, 211; Hesseltine, *Civil War Prisons*, p. 171; Nashville *Union*, Feb. 21, 1865; Futch, *History of Andersonville Prison*, pp. 119–20.

71. *SHSP* 1:189, 193.

72. *OR*, ser. 2, 8:421.

73. *OR*, 49(2):704; *SHSP* 1:189, 193.

74. GJP to E. P. Scammon, Mar. 24, 1865, Andersonville Prison Collection, UVA.

75. GJP to Colonel Gibbs, Mar. 22, 1865, Pillow Papers, RG 109, NARS; *SHSP* 1:192–95; GJP to E. P. Scammon, Mar. 24, 1865; undated R. G. H. Kean memorandum, Andersonville Prison Collection, UVA.

76. GJP to U.S. Commissary of Prisoners, Mar. 26, 1865, Pillow Papers, RG 109, NARS; *OR*, ser. 2, 8:471, 433–35.

77. *SHSP* 1:194–95; GJP to J. C. Rutherford, Mar. 22, 1865, Pillow Papers, RG 109, NARS; *OR*, ser. 2, 8:445, 426.

78. *OR*, ser. 2, 8:465, 487.

79. *OR*, ser. 4, 3:1177; *OR*, 47(3):712.

80. Special Orders No. 48, Feb. 27, 1865, Office of the Adjutant and In-spector General, RG 109, NARS; *OR*, ser. 2, 8:205, 224.

81. *Journal of the Congress of the Confederate States of America*, 7:685; *SHSP* 52:429.

82. *CV* 29:355.

83. One report had Pillow making a speech in Americus, Georgia, and then riding with Jefferson Davis in a closed carriage, attempting to outrun Union pursuers. Although Pillow's movements cannot be established day by day during this chaotic period, it is believed that he remained near Mont-gomery. *OR*, 49(2):704.

84. Pillow's train should not be confused with a Confederate wagon train captured a week later, hidden in the woods and laden with valuables and sev-eral million dollars in currency and coin. Thompson, "Personal Narrative," p. 30; *OR*, 49(1):306, 551, 49(2):562, 49(3):569–70; *New York Times*, May 20, 1865, Aug. 4, 1873.

85. Fike Diary, May 5, 1865, University of Missouri–Columbia Library, Columbia, Mo.; Parole of GJP, May 5, 1865, PMSR.

86. Nashville *Union and American*, May 28, 1865.

CHAPTER SIXTEEN

1. GJP to H. McCulloch, June 8, 1865; H. McCulloch to GJP, June 17, 1865, Secretary of the Treasury, Correspondence, NARS.

2. Pillow v. Bean and Watkins, Chancery Court Records, Maury County, Tenn.; GJP to C. B. Fisk, Dec. 6, 1868, E. P. Hotchkiss Notebook, Freedmen's Bureau Papers, RG 105, NARS.

3. Pillow v. Bean and Watkins, Chancery Court Records, Maury County, Tenn.

4. *New York Times*, July 4, 1865.

5. The court found for Bean, however, despite Pillow's stack of depositions testifying to mismanagement and failure to fulfill payments. G. M. Pillow to C. B. Fisk, Dec. 6, 1868, Letters Received, Bureau of Refugees, Freed-men, and Abandoned Lands, RG 105, NARS; Pillow v. Bean and Watkins, Chancery Court Records, Maury County, Tenn.

6. *CV* 1:330; GJP to W. G. Brownlow, June 12, 1865; GJP to G. H. Thomas, July 7, 1865; Mrs. A. V. Brown to W. G. Brownlow, June 30, 1865; GJP Loy-alty Oath, June 29, 1865; GJP to A. Johnson, June 29, 1865; J. B. Pillow to Capt. T. C. Williams, June 8, 1865; J. B. Pillow to A. Johnson, June 12, 1865, Amnesty Papers, RG 94, NARS; Dorris, *Pardon*, p. 176.

7. Porter Diary, July 31–Aug. 26, 1865, SHC.

8. Pillow v. Wade, 31 Ark. 678; legal brief, John A. Pointer v. GJP, NYHS.

9. GJP to O. O. Howard, Sept. 19, 1865, Howard Papers, Bowdoin College Library, Bowdoin, Maine; GJP to C. B. Fisk, Sept. 20, 1865, Letters Received, Bureau of Refugees, Freedmen, and Abandoned Lands, RG 105, NARS.

10. Always the promoter, Pillow was quoted by the Augusta *Weekly Constitutionalist* a week earlier as saying he had 400 freedmen working for him now and "could get 1,000 if he wanted them." Wilkins, "Papers of the American Cotton Planters Association," pp. 342–43; Coulter, *South during Reconstruction*, p. 78.

11. Brown and his brother William L., nephews of Aaron V. Brown, owned four plantations, including one of 4,000 acres in Phillips County, Arkansas.

12. Wilkins, "Papers of the American Cotton Planters Association," pp. 335–37, 342–43, 348–50, 352–55, 358, 50–54, 58.

13. GJP to Capt. N. B. Kirk, Oct. 27, 1865, Pillow Papers, JRN.

14. Memphis *Bulletin*, Nov. 26, 1865; Dorris, *Pardon*, p. 176; GJP to U. S. Grant, Oct. 26, 1867, Letters Received, Office of the Secretary of War, RG 107, NARS.

15. Evidently nothing came of this venture. GJP to O. O. Howard, Dec. 22, 1865, Letters Received, Commissioner of Bureau of Refugees, Freedmen, and Abandoned Lands, RG 105, NARS; *Memphis Avalanche*, Jan. 3, 1866.

16. *New York Times*, Jan. 10, 1866.

17. Pillow appears to have dropped this idea, although the treasury authorities had "no objection to the proposed bank." H. P. Coolidge statement, June 10, 1867; E. M. Apperson to GJP, Dec. 21, 1866; S. Innerman to GJP, Aug. 10, 1866, Pillow Papers, JRN; Porter Diary, Sept. 4, 1865, SHC; Wilkins, "Papers of the American Cotton Planters Association," p. 351.

18. Hamer, *Tennessee*, 2:608–9; Porter Diary, Dec. 31, 1866, SHC; C. F. Johnson to A. S. Brown, June 8, 1866, Letters Received, Freedmen's Bureau, RG 105, NARS; Trefousse, *Johnson*, p. 221.

19. Little attention seems to have been paid as the steamer *General Pillow* was sold at Cairo on February 7 for $1,900.

20. GJP to L. J. Cist, May 9, 1866, C. E. French Collection, MHS; Planters Bank v. Pillow, Dempsey Weaver Papers, TSLA.

21. Haynes's son, Landon C., Jr., would marry Pillow's next-to-youngest daughter, Gertrude, April 4, 1876, at Pillow's home in Memphis.

22. *CV* 1:330; Evans, *Confederate History*, 10:327; Riddle, Coleman & Co. v. GJP, U.S. 6th Judicial Circuit, District of West Tennessee, JRN; *New York Times*, Mar. 6, 1876; Nashville *American*, Nov. 3, 1878; Memphis *Press Scimitar*, Mar. 11, 1927.

23. Yearns, *Confederate Governors*, p. 194; Memphis *Daily Appeal*, Apr. 9, 1868; Watters, "Harris," p. 32; Jackson, Tenn., *Whig and Tribune*, Dec. 7, 1876.

24. Chandler et al., *South in the Building of the Nation*, 2:285; Cummings, *Yankee Quaker*, p. 344; J. M. Larkin to GJP, May 23, 1867, Pillow Papers, JRN; A. Sweeney to GJP, May 15, 1867, Freedmen's Bureau Correspondence, RG 105, NARS; Helena *Weekly Clarion*, Aug. 31, 1869; GJP to J. D. Mitchell, Jan. 4, Apr. 12, May 27, Dec. 2, 1868, Mitchell Papers, JRN; Memphis *Daily Appeal*, Oct. 14, 1878; Nashville *American*, Nov. 3, 1878.

25. When Grant was secretary of war in 1867, Pillow immediately appealed to him "as a personal favour" regarding his lost mules. Grant referred the

request to Judge Advocate Joseph Holt, who demurred. Let Pillow send a claim to Congress, Holt advised—but Pillow knew better. Little Rock *Arkansas Gazette*, June 11, 1867; *Memphis Avalanche*, Feb. 14, 1866; GJP to U. S. Grant, Oct. 26, 1867, Letters Received, Office of the Secretary of War, RG 107, NARS.

26. Pillow would join his fellow Confederates again in September with a letter to Gen. W. S. Rosecrans strongly approving of the conciliatory sentiments expressed by him and Gen. R. E. Lee in their correspondence that summer. W. G. Coulter, *Brownlow*, pp. 360–61; Cummings, *Yankee Quaker*, pp. 345–46; Hamer, *Tennessee*, 2:638; *Acts of Tennessee*, 35th General Assembly, Extra Session, 1868, pp. 19ff; Knoxville *Whig*, Mar. 25, Aug. 12, 1868; *Harper's Magazine* 37 (June–Nov. 1868): 835; Patton, *Unionism and Reconstruction in Tennessee*, pp. 183, 185–86, 190–94; Wills, *Forrest*, pp. 348–49; Losson, *Tennessee's Forgotten Warriors*, p. 257; I. G. Harris, GJP, and others to W. S. Rosecrans, Sept. 21, 1868, William S. Rosecrans Papers, University of California at Los Angeles.

27. The forever pragmatic Pillow had strenuously opposed "foreign pauper labor" and "convict labor" in 1855. *Acts of Tennessee*, 36th General Assembly, 1st sess., p. 188; Hesseltine, "Tennessee's Invitation to Carpet-Baggers," p. 115; Cribbs, "Memphis Chinese Labor Convention," p. 78; Wills, *Forrest*, pp. 351–52; Belissary, "Tennessee and Immigration," pp. 231, 234–35, 235n; Pillow, *Address*.

28. GJP to P. Clayton, Jan. 25, 1869, Governor's Letters Received, Arkansas History Commission, Little Rock, Ark.; Trelease, *White Terror*, pp. 169–70.

29. *CV* 1:330; Mathes, *Old Guard*, p. 274; GJP to E. G. W. Butler, Sr., Feb. 27, 1872, Butler Family Papers, Historic New Orleans Collection, New Orleans, La.; GJP to M. J. Wright, July 12, 1878, Wright Papers, SHC; GJP to M. J. Wright, Aug. 10, 1878, Miscellaneous Collection, UMI; GJP to W. P. Johnston, June 2, 1876, Mar. 22, 28, 1877, Davis Collection, Howard Tilton Memorial Library, Tulane University, New Orleans, La.; Memphis *Daily Appeal*, Apr. 29, 1870.

30. Davies-Rodgers, *The Great Book*, pp. 261–66; Memphis *Daily Public Ledger*, Apr. 12, 1871.

31. St. John's, Ashwood, the dream and work of Leonidas Polk, remains another irony in the life of Gideon Pillow.

32. Mary's death was attributed to a stroke. GJP to Mrs. Narcissa P. Mitchell, Jan. 7, 1869, Mitchell Papers, JRN; T. Barnett to D. Weaver, Jan. 28, 1869, Weaver Papers, TSLA; Columbia *Herald*, Oct. 8, Nov. 5, 1869; Nicholson, "Reminiscences," SHC.

33. Earlier that year Pillow and some of his children had served, as had Davis and Harris, as part of the large escort for the body of Gen. Patrick R. Cleburne when it was moved from St. John's to Memphis to Helena for reburial. Garrett, "St. John's," p. 19; Columbia *Herald*, Apr. 28, 1871; Purdue, *Cleburne*, pp. 434–35.

34. GJP to U. S. Grant, Apr. [?], 1870, Palmer Collection, WRH.

35. J. Davis to GJP, Dec. 20, 1870; GJP to J. Davis, Dec. 20, 1870, Pillow Papers, JRN.

36. GJP to J. D. Mitchell, Jan. 10, 1869, Mitchell Papers, JRN.

37. Pillow had many interesting clients, among them Hardee's confidante and friend, Mrs. Felicia Lee Cary Thornton Shover. GJP to F. Shover, Feb. 18, 1876, Thornton Family Papers, Virginia Historical Society, Richmond, Va.

38. Nashville *Republican Banner*, Feb. 25, 1871; Columbia *Herald*, June 10, 1870; GJP to U. S. Grant, May 31, 1873, Civil War Documents Collection, Southern Illinois University, Morris Library, Carbondale, Ill.; Pillow, *Opinion*; Herndon, *Centennial History of Arkansas*, 1:497; Hempstead, *Historical Review of Arkansas*, 1:265.

39. Columbia *Herald*, July 19, 1872; GJP to U. S. Grant, July 26, 1872 (typed copy), JRN; *New York Times*, Aug. 24, Sept. 9, 1872, Mar. 6, 1876.

40. GJP to W. E. Woodruff, Mar. 17, July 8, Aug. 31, Oct. 4, 1870, Woodruff Papers, Arkansas History Commission, Little Rock, Ark.; GJP to J. D. Mitchell, Feb. 11, 1871, May 29, Sept. 8, 29, 1871, Mitchell Papers, JRN; GJP to unidentified judge, June 7, 1871, Pillow Papers, JRN; Nashville *Republican Banner*, June 25, 1868; GJP to J. D. Mitchell, Oct. 21, 1871, Gratz Collection, HSP.

41. G. M. Pillow to J. D. Mitchell, Feb. 14, 1872; R. G. Pillow to J. D. Mitchell, July 2, 1872, Mitchell Papers, JRN; GJP to W. E. Woodruff, Nov. 13, 1872, Woodruff Papers, Arkansas History Commission, Little Rock, Ark.; Columbia *Herald*, Aug. 30, 1872.

42. He purchased the home from a merchant, James M. McCombs, who moved to St. Louis. The home still stands in 1993, on the southeast corner of Adams and Orleans streets. Columbia *Herald*, Aug. 30, 1872; Memphis *Commercial Appeal*, May 20, 1851, June 26, 1982.

43. Mary Eliza Pillow was born November 13, 1849, in East Feliciana Parish, Louisiana, and married Trigg in June 1863. Cotton and Captured Abandoned Property Case File No. 7151, RG 105, NARS.

44. Mary Eliza Dickson Trigg, aided by attorney Pillow, filed claim to a tract of 800 acres in Tipton County, Tennessee, deeded by will to her husband by his father, John Trigg. Col. H. Clay King represented Martha Trigg, John Trigg's second wife and a Union sympathizer. Nelson v. Trigg, 3 Tenn Cas 733 at 735, 72 Tenn 701 at 702; Cotton and Captured Abandoned Property Case File No. 7151, RG 105, NARS.

45. Pension Application of Mary E. D. Pillow, Dec. 10, 1887, Records Relating to Pension and Bounty Land Claims, 1773–1942, RG 15, NARS; Jackson, Tenn., *Whig and Tribune*, Dec. 7, 1872; Columbia *Herald*, Dec. 6, 1872, Mar. 13, 1891; Memphis *Press-Scimitar*, July 13, 1981; GJP to J. Goforth, Aug. 13, 1874, Pillow Papers, HUL.

46. Mary Eliza was also called Marie.

47. Prenuptial Marriage Contract between GJP and Mary E. Pillow, undated, Pillow Papers, MSPL; Will Book, Lee County, Ark., Probate Court Records, p. 40.

48. Columbia *Herald*, Jan. 24, 1873; GJP to U. S. Grant, Mar. 21, 1873,

Special Collections, University of Tennessee Library, Knoxville, Tenn.

49. GJP to U. S. Grant, Mar. 21, 1873, Special Collections, University of Tennessee Library, Knoxville, Tenn.

50. Mary Eliza Pillow was a determined woman. After Pillow's death, she prevailed upon an Arkansas congressman, Poindexter Dunn of Forrest City, to introduce bills in Congress for the restitution of her lost cotton property. He did so in 1881 and 1882 but met with no success. She continued to fight on, however, and the records of the Treasury Department in 1900 reveal inquiries by Mrs. Pillow's attorney in regard to the ancient claims. GJP to John Goforth, Oct. 18, 1874, Battles and Leaders Collection, Sterling Library, Yale University; GJP to J. Goforth, Aug. 13, 1874, Pillow Papers, HUL; Cotton and Captured Abandoned Property Case File No. 7151, RG 105, NARS.

51. Of particular note is a magnificent lavender and cream dress, with bodice and skirt designed by Charles Frederick Worth, a leading Paris dress designer in 1869. This dress, passed down through the family, has caused confusion, as it was long believed to have been that of Mary Martin Pillow worn at Polk's inauguration. It is on display at the Pink Palace in Memphis.

52. Case No. 1348, Bankruptcy Records, District of West Tennessee, RG 21, NARS; Memphis *Press-Scimitar*, July 13, 1981; Margaret H. Witt to N. C. Hughes, Jr., June 28, 1991; Ornelas-Struve, *Memphis*, 3:41, 55.

53. Nelson v. Trigg, 3 Tenn Cas 733 at 735.

54. GJP to W. F. Cooper, 1875 [exact date unknown], Cooper Family Papers; A. M. Hughes Diary, June 5, 1875, TSLA; *New York Times*, June 4, 1875.

55. *New York Times*, July 9, 1875; Tucker, "Black Politics," pp. 17–18; Memphis *Commercial Appeal*, July 25, 1875; Buck, *Road to Reunion*, p. 120.

56. Harris would find new Memphis law partners in Louis D. McKissack and T. B. Turley. Williams v. Whitmore, 77 Tenn 269.

57. Case No. 1396, Bankruptcy Records, District of West Tennessee, RG 21, NARS; Planters Bank v. Pillow, Merchants Bank of Kentucky v. Pillow, in Chancery Court Records, Davidson County, Tenn.; *CV* 1:329–30.

58. When Pillow was unwell at Mound Plantation in May 1866, Mrs. King wrote letters for him and apparently nursed him. Case No. 1396, Bankruptcy Records, District of West Tennessee, RG 21, NARS; *New York Times*, Mar. 16, 1876; Columbia *Herald and Mail*, Mar. 26, 31, 1876; *SHSP* 22:65; King, *Letter to His Friends*, pp. 3–4; M. Williams to J. D. Mitchell, Feb. 1, 1876, Mitchell Papers, JRN; GJP to L. J. Cist, May 9, 1866, C. E. French Collection, MHS.

59. GJP to New York *Tribune*, Feb. 24, 1876, Miscellaneous Collection, NYPL.

60. Pillow v. Wade, 31 Ark 678; GJP v. J. D. Mitchell and N. P. Mitchell, Oct. 7, 1875, Mitchell Papers, JRN.

61. History acted as a sharp-edged boomerang for Pillow. His grandson Gideon would marry a descendant of Winfield Scott. GJP to Mrs. N. P. Mitchell, Mar. 24, 1876, Mitchell Papers, JRN; Will of GJP, Apr. 1, 1876, Will Book, Lee County, Ark., Probate Court Records, p. 40; Mary Lou Pillow to author, July 16, 1991; author's interview with Paul Cross, May 22, 1991.

62. Marszalek, *Sherman*, p. 473; GJP to R. B. Hayes, Mar. 19, 1877, Hayes Correspondence, Rutherford B. Hayes Library, Fremont, Ohio.

63. GJP to Editor, New York *Sun*, May 24, 1877, Hayes Correspondence, Rutherford B. Hayes Library, Fremont, Ohio.

64. GJP to R. B. Hayes, May 28, June 2, 1877, Hayes Correspondence, Rutherford B. Hayes Library, Fremont, Ohio.

65. GJP to J. Black, June 13, 1878, Gratz Collection, HSP.

66. Daughter Annie Payne, in her appeal for money twenty years later, would contend Pillow died from the reopening of his Chapultepec wound. A. P. Pillow, *The Great Seal*; Memphis *Daily Appeal*, Oct. 13, 1878; *Memphis Avalanche*, Oct. 13, 1878; Memphis *Commercial Appeal*, Oct. 31, 1878.

67. *New York Times*, Oct. 10, 1878.

68. Pillow's body was reinterred at Elmwood, February 14, 1884. King, *Letter to His Friends*, p. 4; Memphis *Commercial Appeal*, Oct. 30, 1988; Elmwood Cemetery Records.

EPILOGUE

1. Will of GJP, Apr. 1, 1876 (probated Jan. 30, 1879), Will Book, Lee County, Ark., Probate Court Records, p. 40.

2. Scott, *Memoirs*, 2:416.

Bibliography

MANUSCRIPT COLLECTIONS

Ann Arbor, Mich.
  University of Michigan, William L. Clements Library
    Cooke Collection
    Corydon Fuller Journal
    Haskell Collection
    Miscellaneous Collection
    Schoff Collection
Atlanta, Ga.
  Emory University, Robert W. Woodruff Library
    Confederate Miscellany
    Frank Richardson Letters, Bell I. Wiley Papers
Auburn, Ala.
  Auburn University Library
    George Petrie Papers
Austin, Tex.
  Texas State Library and Archives
    Mirabeau B. Lamar Papers
  University of Texas, Eugene C. Barker Texas History Center
    Confederate States of America Records Collection
    Correspondence of General Gideon J. Pillow
Baton Rouge, La.
  Louisiana State University Libraries, Louisiana and Lower Mississippi
  Valley Collections
    Edward George Washington Butler Letters
    Samuel W. Ferguson Papers
    Charles James Johnson and Family Letters
    Philip D. Stephenson, "My War Autobiography"
Berkeley, Calif.
  University of California, Bancroft Library
    E. O. C. Ord Collection
Bloomington, Ind.
  Indiana University, Lilly Library
    U.S. History Manuscripts
Boston, Mass.
  Boston Athenaeum Library
    Special Collections

Boston Public Library
  Special Collections
Massachusetts Historical Society
  George Bancroft Papers
  John B. Floyd Letters
  C. E. French Collection
  Gideon Johnson Pillow Letters
Bowling Green, Ky.
  Western Kentucky University Library
  Stickles Collection
Brunswick, Maine
  Bowdoin College Library
  Oliver Otis Howard Papers
Cambridge, Mass.
  Harvard University, Houghton Library
  Dearborn Collection
Carbondale, Ill.
  Southern Illinois University, Morris Library
  Tyree H. Bell Report of the Battle of Belmont
  Civil War Documents Collection
Carlisle, Pa.
  Dickinson College Library
  A. V. Brown Letters
  U.S. Army Military History Institute
  Bradley Papers
  L. B. Claiborne Memoirs, *Civil War Times Illustrated* Collection
  Stuart Goldman Collection
  Aaron C. Harper Diary
  Harrisburg Civil War Roundtable Collection
Chapel Hill, N.C.
  University of North Carolina, Southern Historical Collection
  William R. Caswell Papers
  Thomas Claiborne, Reminiscences of the Mexican War
  Robert L. Dabney Papers
  Jeremy Francis Gilmer Papers
  Daniel Chevilette Govan Papers
  Gustavus A. Henry Papers
  Daniel Harvey Hill Diary
  H. L. Kennison Papers
  H. C. Lockhart Papers
  William Whann Mackall Papers
  Alfred Osborn Pope Nicholson Papers
  Mrs. A. O. P. Nicholson, "Reminiscences of an Octogenarian"
  Leonidas Polk Papers (microfilm copies)
  Nimrod Porter Diary and Notes

Quitman Family Papers
Kenneth Rayner Papers
M. Jeff Thompson Reminiscences (typed copy)
Nicholas Trist Papers
John Vines Wright Scrapbooks
Marcus Joseph Wright Papers
Charlottesville, Va.
  University of Virginia, Alderman Library
    Andersonville Prison Collection
    John Buchanan Floyd Papers
    Kean Family Papers
    Thomas G. Pollock Papers
    Nicholas P. Trist Papers
    Washington Family Papers
Chattanooga, Tenn.
  In possession of author
    N. F. Cheairs, "Notes on Donelson"
    Cheairs-Hughes Papers
Chicago, Ill.
  Chicago Historical Society
    Mason Brayman Papers
    John Cabell Breckinridge Collection
    John A. McClernand, Autobiography
    Gideon J. Pillow Collection
    Adolphus Schwartz, Report of Battle of Belmont
  University of Chicago Library
    Stephen A. Douglas Papers
Cleveland, Ohio
  Western Reserve Historical Society
    Civil War Miscellany
    William P. Palmer Collection
Columbia, Mo.
  State Historical Society of Missouri
    Meriwether Jeff Thompson Papers
  University of Missouri–Columbia Library
    Richard W. Burt Papers
    Lyman C. Draper Collection (microfilm copies)
    Henry C. Fike Diaries
    A. W. Reese Personal Recollections
    M. Jeff Thompson Papers
Columbia, Tenn.
  In possession of Jill K. Garrett
    Robert M. McBride, "The Gideon J. Pillow Everybody Knows"
    Nathan Vaught, "Youth and Old Age"
  In possession of John R. Neal

John D. Mitchell Papers
"Gen. G. J. Pillow's Military Service in the Mexican War"
Gideon Johnson Pillow Papers
Concord, N.H.
New Hampshire Historical Society
Franklin Pierce Papers
Detroit, Mich.
Detroit Public Library
Lewis Cass Papers
Dover, Tenn.
Fort Donelson National Military Park
Ben Bounds, Civil War Memoirs
R. Hill Diary
Spot F. Terrell Journal
Durham, N.C.
Duke University, William R. Perkins Library
George W. Brent Papers
Edward George Washington Butler Papers
Campbell Family Papers
Confederate States of America Papers
Dalton Collection
Flowers Collection
John Buchanan Floyd Papers
Charles C. Jones Papers
Kirkpatrick Papers
John M. McCalla Collection
John Euclid Magee Diary
E. B. Murray Papers
Gideon J. Pillow Letters
Pope-Carter Papers
Henry J. Seibert Papers
Solomon Scrapbook
Nathaniel Beverley Tucker Letters
Leroy Pope Walker Letters
William Henry Talbot Walker Papers
Ward Family Papers
Fayetteville, Ark.
University of Arkansas Libraries
William Stephen Ray Reminiscences
Florence, Ala.
In possession of William L. McDonald
Willie Smith Diary
Franklin, N.C.
In possession of Richard Melvin
A. W. Bell Letter

Fremont, Ohio
  Rutherford B. Hayes Presidential Center
    Rutherford B. Hayes Correspondence
Indianapolis, Indiana
  Indiana State Historical Library
    Sylvester C. Bishop Papers
Kansas City, Mo.
  University of Missouri–Kansas City, Western Historical Collection
    Robert M. Snyder, Jr., Collection
Knoxville, Tenn.
  University of Tennessee at Knoxville Library
    Special Collections
Lexington, Ky.
  University of Kentucky Library
    Special Collections
Little Rock, Ark.
  Arkansas History Commission
    Governor's Letters Received
    William E. Woodruff Papers
Los Angeles, Calif.
  In possession of Harry G. Shepherd, Jr.
    Hazen Churchill Ladd Diary
  University of California at Los Angeles
    Gideon J. Pillow Letters
    William S. Rosecrans Papers
Louisville, Ky.
  Filson Club
    Miscellaneous Papers
    Yandell Family Papers
Medford, Mass.
  Tufts University Library
    Ryder Collection of Confederate Archives
Memphis, Tenn.
  Memphis–Shelby County Public Library
    Goodman Collection
    Gideon Johnson Pillow Papers
  Memphis State University Library, Mississippi Valley Collection
    Civil War Collection
    Andrew J. Coffee Papers
    William M. Gardner Memoirs
Nashville, Tenn.
  Tennessee State Library and Archives
    Sally Walker Boone, "After the Battle of Belmont"
    Aaron V. Brown Papers
    Carroll Papers

Civil War Collection
Nathaniel Francis Cheairs, "Personal Experiences in the War Between
  the States"
Cheairs-Hughes Family Papers
Cheatham Family Papers
Civil War Veterans Questionnaires
Confederate Collection (John Trotwood Moore)
Cooper Family Papers
Arthur R. Crozier Letters
James Caswell Edenton Diary, Civil War Collection
Alfred Tyler Fielder Diary
Thomas Firth Diary
Gov. Isham Green Harris Letter Book
Gov. Isham Green Harris Papers
Archelaus M. Hughes Diary
William Hicks Jackson Papers
John Johnston, "Civil War Reminiscences," Civil War Collection
Samuel R. Latta Papers
John B. Lindsley Diaries
Robert M. McBride Papers
McLaughlin Family Papers
Mexican War Letters
Miscellaneous Manuscript Collection
St. Peter's Parish Records, Columbia, Tenn.
William Trousdale Papers
Tennessee Civil War Veterans Questionnaires
University of Nashville Records
Dempsey Weaver Papers
Robert Hancock Wood Letters, Bills Family Papers
New Haven, Conn.
  Yale University, Beinecke Rare Book Library
    William L. Marcy, Drafts of Dispatches to Winfield Scott
    Gideon J. Pillow Letters
    Unidentified author, "Memoranda of Campaigns in Mexico"
    John D. Wilkins Mexican War Collection
    John D. Wilkins Journal
    John D. Wilkins Letters
    Henry Wilson Papers
  Yale University, Sterling Library
    Battles and Leaders Collection
    Civil War Manuscript Collection
    Leonidas Polk Family Papers
New Orleans, La.
  Historic New Orleans Collection
    Butler Family Papers
  Tulane University, Howard Tilton Memorial Library

George H. and Katherine M. Davis Collection
Albert Sidney Johnston Headquarters Book
Albert Sidney Johnston Letters
New York, N.Y.
New-York Historical Society
John Cabell Breckinridge Collection
Alfred O. P. Nicholson Papers
Gideon Johnson Pillow Correspondence
Robert B. Reynolds Correspondence
Benjamin H. Streeter Papers
New York Public Library
Bancroft Collection
Miscellaneous Collection
Albert Tracy Papers
Newark, N.J.
New Jersey Historical Society
Edmund J. Cleveland Collection
Norman, Okla.
University of Oklahoma Libraries
Dr. Fayette Copeland Collection
George Kendall Wilkins, "The War Between the United States and
Mexico"
Philadelphia, Pa.
Historical Society of Pennsylvania
George Cadwalader Collection
Ferdinand J. Dreer Collection
Gratz Collection
William J. Hardee Letters
Gideon Johnson Pillow Letters
Society Collection
Prescott, Ark.
In possession of Mrs. N. E. Ward
William Sylvester Dillon Diary
Princeton, N.J.
Princeton University Library
deCoppet Collection
Providence, R.I.
Brown University Library
Lincoln Collection
Raleigh, N.C.
North Carolina State Archives
Daniel Harvey Hill Papers
Richmond, Va.
Virginia Historical Society
Lee Family Papers
William Selden Papers

Thornton Family Papers
Beverley R. Wellford Papers
Roanoke, Va.
In possession of Douglas Schanz
Gideon J. Pillow Letters
St. Louis, Mo.
Missouri Historical Society
Civil War Collection
Hitchcock Papers
Gideon Johnson Pillow Papers
Selden Spencer Diary
Sweringen Papers
Thompson-Pillow-Polk Papers
St. Paul, Minn.
Minnesota Historical Society
Allyn Kellogg Ford Collection
San Marino, Cal.
Henry E. Huntington Library and Art Gallery
Simon Bolivar Buckner Papers
William J. Hardee Papers
E. S. Parker Letters
Franklin Pierce Mexican War Diary
Gideon J. Pillow Papers
Searcy, Ark.
In possession of Brig. Gen. and Mrs. William P. Campbell
"The Birth, Parentage, Family and Ancestry of General Gideon J.
Pillow, His Early Life, Education and Selection of a Profession"
Sewanee, Tenn.
University of the South, DuPont Library
Cheatham Family Papers
Leonidas Polk Papers
Springfield, Ill.
Illinois State Historical Library
Lemuel Adams, "Memoirs of Lemuel Adams"
William Montgomery Austin Diary (typed copies)
Lewis F. Lake, "My War Service as a Member of 'Taylor's Battery,'
Company B, First Illinois Light Artillery"
John Alexander McClernand Papers
Addison Odum, "Reminiscences about the Battle of Belmont"
Elizabeth Simpson Letters
Dietrich C. Smith Letters
Joseph Wallace Papers
Springfield, Mo.
In possession of Thomas P. Sweeney, M.D.
Capt. C. W. Frazer Letter and Map

Tallahassee, Fla.
  Florida State University, R. M. Strozier Library
    Confederate Papers
Washington, D.C.
  Library of Congress
    James Buchanan Papers
    Edmund Burke Papers
    Caleb Cushing Papers
    Ulysses S. Grant Papers
    Andrew Jackson Papers
    William L. Marcy Papers
    Franklin Pierce Papers
    James K. Polk Papers
    Leonidas Polk Papers
    Felicia Shover Letters
    Nicholas Trist Papers
    Martin Van Buren Papers
    Robert J. Walker Papers
  National Archives and Record Service
    Amnesty Papers (RG 94)
    Army of the Cumberland, Register of Letters Received (RG 393)
    Bureau of Refugees, Freedmen, and Abandoned Lands, Letters
      Received (RG 105)
    Confederate General Citizens File (M-346)
    Cotton and Captured Abandoned Property Case Files (RG 105)
    Courts of Inquiry Proceedings (RG 153)
    Dispatches from United States Counsels in Vera Cruz (RG 59)
    District of Southeast Missouri, Letters Received (RG 393)
    District of West Tennessee, Bankruptcy Papers (RG 21)
    Maj. Gen. Grenville M. Dodge Ledgerbook (RG 366)
    First Division, Missouri State Guard Papers (RG 109)
    General and Special Orders, Army of Occupation, Office of the
      Adjutant General (RG 94)
    General and Special Orders, 1845–48, Office of the Adjutant
      General (RG 94)
    Albert S. Johnston's Command, Letters Sent, Telegrams Sent and
      Received (RG 109)
    Letters Received, 1845–48, Office of the Secretary of War
      (RG 107)
    Letters Received, Office of the Adjutant General (RG 109)
    Letters Received, Office of the Secretary of War (RG 109)
    Letters Sent, Army of Occupation, Office of the Adjutant General
      (RG 94)
    Letters Sent, 1845–48, Office of the Secretary of War (RG 107)
    Letters Sent, 1846–47, Office of the Adjutant General
      (RG 94)

Brig. Gen. Gideon J. Pillow, Commanding Conscript Bureau, Army of
Tennessee, Orders (RG 109)
Maj. Gen. G. J. Pillow, Order Book (RG 94)
Gideon Johnson Pillow Military Service Record (RG 109)
Gideon J. Pillow Papers (RG 109)
Gideon J. Pillow Papers, 1861–64 (RG 109)
Gen. Gideon J. Pillow's Command, Letterbook (RG 109)
Gen. Gideon J. Pillow's Command, Orders and Letters, 1861–63
(RG 109)
Brig. Gen. Gideon J. Pillow's Command, Special Order Book (RG 109)
Leonidas Polk Military Service Record (RG 109)
Leonidas Polk Papers (RG 109)
Provost Marshal's File (RG 393)
Records of the Secretary of War, Confidential and Unofficial Letters
Sent (RG 107)
Records Relating to Pension and Bounty Land Claims, 1773–1942
(RG 15)
Second Special Agency, Treasury Department (RG 56)
Special Orders, Office of the Adjutant and Inspector General (RG 109)
United States Private Citizens File (RG 109)
Western Department, First Division, General Orders (RG 109)
Western Department, Letters Received (RG 393)
Western Department (Dept. 2), Records (RG 109)
Western Department, Telegrams (RG 393)
West Point, N.Y.
United States Military Academy Archives
James Duncan Letters
Williamsburg, Va.
College of William and Mary, Earl Gregg Swem Library
Ritchie-Harrison Papers

INTERVIEWS

Author's interview with Paul Cross, Wallace Hebert, Linda and John R.
Neal, May 22, June 20, 1991, January 28, 1993.
Author's interview with Wayne Cutler, November 30, 1990.
Author's interview with Thomas R. Hay, November 30–December 1, 1956,
November 1–2, 1958, in Locust Valley, N.Y.
Author's interview with Stanley F. Horn, August 12, 26, 1957, in Nash-
ville, Tenn.
Frank H. Smith's interview with Maj. N. F. Cheairs, June 15, 1904, Spring
Hill, Tenn.

NEWSPAPERS

Athens, Ala., *Valley Featurette*
Baltimore, Md., *Niles Weekly Register*
Chicago, Ill., *Daily Tribune*
Clarksville, Tenn., *Weekly Chronicle*
Columbia, Tenn., *Beacon*
Columbia, Tenn., *Democratic Herald*
Columbia, Tenn., *Herald and Mail*
Columbia, Tenn., *Maury Democrat*
Columbia, Tenn., *Maury Intelligencer*
Columbia, Tenn., *Observer*
Columbia, Tenn., *Southern Cultivator and Journal of Science and General Improvement*
Columbia, Tenn., *Tennessee Democrat*
Columbia, Tenn., *Weekly Recorder*
Columbia, Tenn., *Western Mercury*
Columbus, Ky., *Daily Confederate News*
Frank Leslie's Illustrated Newspaper
Helena, Ark., *Weekly Clarion*
Jackson, Tenn., *Whig and Tribune*
Lexington, Ky., *Kentucky Statesman*
Lexington, Ky., *Observer and Reporter*
Little Rock, Ark., *Daily Arkansas Gazette*
Louisville, Ky., *Daily Courier*
Lynchburg, Va., *Virginian*
Memphis, Tenn., *Daily Appeal*
Memphis, Tenn., *Daily Eagle*
Memphis, Tenn., *Press Scimitar*
Memphis Argus
Memphis Avalanche
Mexico City *Daily American Star*
Nashville, Tenn., *Agriculturist*
Nashville, Tenn., *Clarion*
Nashville, Tenn., *Daily Gazette*
Nashville, Tenn., *Daily Nashville Patriot*
Nashville, Tenn., *Republican Banner*
Nashville, Tenn., *Union and American*
New Orleans, La., *Commercial Bulletin*
New Orleans, La., *Daily Crescent*
New Orleans, La., *Daily Picayune*
New Orleans, La., *DeBow's Southern and Western Review*
New Orleans, La., *Daily Delta*
New York Herald
New York Times

Vera Cruz *American Eagle*
Washington, D.C., *Globe*

GOVERNMENT DOCUMENTS

Arkansas State Historical Commission. Tax Assessment Lists, Phillips
County, Arkansas, 1855, 1859.

Arkansas Supreme Court. *Revised Edition of Pillow's Brief in Supreme Court of
Arkansas: John C. Brown and Miriam Childers, Executors of John H. Pointer,
Appellee. Gideon J. Pillow and H. P. Coolidge, Appellants.* In Pillow Corre-
spondence, New-York Historical Society.

Candler, Allen D. *The Confederate Records of the State of Georgia.* 6 vols.
Atlanta, 1910.

Davidson County, Tennessee. Chancery Court Records.

Haywood, John, and Robert L. Cobbs. *The Statute Laws of the State of Tennessee.* 2 vols. (Vol. 2, *Land Laws of Tennessee*). Knoxville, 1831.

Journal of the Congress of the Confederate States of America. 7 vols. Washington,
1904–5.

Lee County, Arkansas. Probate Court Records.

Maury County, Tennessee. Chancery Court Records.

———. Circuit Court Minute Book.

———. County Court Summons, State v. A. J. Donelson and G. J. Pillow,
Aug. 1, 1855.

———. Deed Book A.

———. State Docket Book, 1828–37.

United States Government. *Biographical Directory of the American Congress,
1774–1949.* Washington, 1950.

———. Census of Giles County, Tennessee, 1820.

———. Census of Maury County, Tennessee, 1840–70.

———. Census of Phillips County, Arkansas, 1850–60.

———. Census of St. Francis County, Arkansas, 1850–60.

———. General Service Schools. *Fort Henry and Fort Donelson Campaigns,
February, 1862.* Fort Leavenworth, 1923.

———. *House Miscellaneous Document 179.* 44th Cong., 1st sess.

———. *House of Representatives Executive Document No. 8.* 30th Cong., 1st sess.

———. *House of Representatives Executive Document No. 60. Messages of the
President of the United States and the Correspondence, therewith Communicated,
Between the Secretary of War and Other Officers of the Government: The Mexican
War.* 30th Cong., 1st sess. Washington, 1848.

———. *The Medical and Surgical History of the War of the Rebellion, 1861–1865.*
3 vols. in 6 pts. Washington, 1870–88.

———. Office of War Information. File 20517.

———. *Official Records of the Union and Confederate Navies in the War of the
Rebellion.* 31 vols. Washington, 1894–1919.

———. *Senate Executive Document No. 1.* 30th Cong., 1st sess.

———. *Senate Executive Document No. 51.* 32d Cong., 1st sess.
———. *Senate Executive Document No. 63.* 38th Cong., 1st sess.
———. *Senate Executive Document No. 65.* 30th Cong., 1st sess.
———. *War of the Rebellion: A Compilation of the Official Records of the Union and Confederate Armies.* 128 vols. Washington, 1880–1901.

COURT CASES

Nelson v. Trigg, 3 Tenn Cas 733 at 735; 72 Tenn 701 at 702; 75 Tenn 69.
Pillow v. Wade, 31 Ark 678.
Williams v. Whitmore, 77 Tenn 269; 1 Tenn Cas 239.

COLLECTED WORKS, MEMOIRS, LETTERS, DIARIES, AND REMINISCENCES

Bailey, L. J. "Escape from Fort Donelson." *Confederate Veteran* 12 (December 1913): 64.
Baird, Nancy D. "There Is No Sunday in the Army: Civil War Letters of Lunsford P. Yandell, 1861–62." *Filson Club Historical Quarterly* 53 (July 1979): 317–27.
Basler, Roy P., ed. *Collected Works of Abraham Lincoln.* 9 vols. New Brunswick, N.J., 1953–55.
Bassett, John Spencer, ed. *Correspondence of Andrew Jackson.* 7 vols. Washington, 1926–35.
Battlefields of the South, from Bull Run to Fredericksburgh; with Sketches of Confederate Commanders, and Gossip of the Camps. By an English Combatant, Lieutenant of Artillery in the Field Staff. New York, 1864.
Benton, Thomas Hart. *Thirty Years View; or, A History of the Working of the American Government for Thirty Years, from 1820 to 1850.* New York, 1864.
Bixby, William. *Letters of Zachary Taylor.* Rochester, N.Y., 1908.
Blaine, James G. *Twenty Years of Congress.* 2 vols. Norwich, Conn., 1884–86.
Bounds, Ben H. *Civil War Memoirs.* Greenville, Tex., 1911.
Boutwell, George S. *Reminiscences of Sixty Years in Public Affairs.* 2 vols. New York, 1902.
Brinton, John H. *Personal Memoirs.* New York, 1914.
Brown, Aaron V. *Speeches, Congressional and Political, and Other Writings.* Nashville, 1854.
Brown, Lucy E., comp. *Civil War Letters of John Knight, First Lieutenant, 7th Iowa Infantry, July 30, 1861–May 31, 1865.* Oak Park, Ill., 1951.
Burr, Barbara, "Letters from Two Wars." *Journal of the Illinois State Historical Society* 30 (April 1937): 135–58.
Campbell, Andrew J. *Civil War Diary of Andrew Jackson Campbell.* Edited by Jill K. Garrett. Columbia, Tenn., 1965.
Campbell, William B. "Mexican War Letters of Col. Wm. B. Campbell to

Gov. David Campbell of Va." *Tennessee Historical Magazine* 1 (June 1915): 129–67.

Carnes, W. W. "In the Battle of Belmont." *Confederate Veteran* 39:369–70.

Casseday, Morton M. "The Surrender of Fort Donelson." *Southern Bivouac* 2:694–97.

Chetlain, Augustus Lewis. *Recollections of Seventy Years*. Galena, Ill., 1899.

Claiborne, J. F. H. *Life and Correspondence of John A. Quitman, Major-General, U.S.A., and Governor of the State of Mississippi*. 2 vols. New York, 1860.

Claxton, Jimmie Lou Sparkman. *Eighty-eight Years with Sarah Polk*. New York, 1972.

Clay, Mrs. C. C. *A Belle of the Fifties*. New York, 1905.

Clay, H. B. "On the Right at Murfreesboro." *Confederate Veteran* 21 (December 1913): 588–89

Coffin, Charles Carleton. *Four Years of Fighting*. Boston, 1866.

Coker, Caleb, ed. *The News from Brownsville: Helen Chapman's Letters from the Texas Military Frontier, 1848–1852*. Austin, Tex., 1992.

Conyngham, Kate. *The Sunny South; or, The Southerner at Home, Embracing Five Years Experience of a Northern Governess in the Land of Sugar and the Cotton*. Edited by J. H. Ingraham. Philadelphia, 1860.

Crist, Lynda L., James T. McIntosh, and Haskell M. Monroe, Jr., eds. *Papers of Jefferson Davis*. 7 vols. Baton Rouge, 1971–.

Crittenden, Thomas L. "The Union Left at Stones River." In *Battles and Leaders of the Civil War*, 4 vols., edited by Robert Underwood Johnson and Clarence Clough Buel, 3:632–34. New York, 1887.

Croffut, W. A., ed. *Fifty Years in Camp and Field: Diary of Major-General Ethan Allen Hitchcock, U.S.A.* New York, 1910.

Davis, George T. *Autobiography*. New York, 1891.

Davis, Jefferson. *The Rise and Fall of the Confederate Government*. 2 vols. New York, 1881.

Donald, David, ed. *Inside Lincoln's Cabinet: The Civil War Diaries of Salmon P. Chase*. New York, 1954.

Duncan, T. D. *Recollections*. Nashville, 1922.

Durham, Walter T. "Civil War Letters to Wynnewood." *Tennessee Historical Quarterly* 34:32–47.

———. "Mexican War Letters to Wynnewood." *Tennessee Historical Quarterly* 33:389–409.

Erickson, Edgar L., ed. "Hunting for Cotton in Dixie: From the Civil War Diary of Captain Charles E. Wilcox." *Journal of Southern History* 4 (November 1938): 493–514.

Everett, Robert B. "James K. Polk and the Election of 1844 in Tennessee." *West Tennessee Historical Society Papers* 16 (1962): 5–28.

Folmar, John Kent, ed. *From That Terrible Field: Civil War Letters of James M. Williams, Twenty-first Alabama Infantry Volunteers*. University, Ala., 1981.

Force, Manning F. *From Fort Henry to Corinth*. New York, 1881.

Forney, John W. *Anecdotes of Public Men*. New York, 1873–81.

French, Samuel G. *Two Wars: An Autobiography*. Nashville, 1901.

Furber, George C. *The Twelve Months Volunteer; or, Journal of a Private in the Tennessee Regiment of Cavalry, in the Campaign in Mexico, 1846–7.* Cincinnati, 1857.

Gorgas, Josiah. *Civil War Diary.* Edited by Frank Vandiver. Tuscaloosa, Ala., 1947.

Gower, Herschel, and Jack Allen, eds. *Pen and Sword: The Life and Journals of Randall McGavock.* Nashville, 1959.

Graber, H. W. *A Terry Texas Ranger.* Austin, 1987.

Graf, LeRoy A., Ralph W. Haskins, and Paul H. Bergeron, eds. *The Papers of Andrew Johnson.* 8 vols. to date. Knoxville, 1967–89.

Grainger, Gervis D. *Four Years with the Boys in Gray.* Franklin, Ky., 1902.

Grant, Ulysses Simpson. *Personal Memoirs of U. S. Grant.* 2 vols. New York, 1885–86.

Greenawalt, John. "A Charge at Fort Donelson, Feb. 15, 1862." In *War Papers*, no. 41, Loyal Legion, Commandery of the District of Columbia, pp. 9–12. Washington, 1887–1916.

Guild, Josephus C. *Old Times in Tennessee.* Nashville, 1878.

Hannaford, Ebenezer. *The Story of a Regiment.* Cincinnati, 1868.

Harwell, Richard, and Philip N. Racine, eds. *The Fiery Trail: A Union Officer's Account of Sherman's Last Campaign.* Knoxville, 1986.

Haskins, Nannie E. "War Seen through a Teen-ager's Eyes." Edited by Betsy S. Underwood. *Tennessee Historical Quarterly* 20:177–87.

Hinds, Charles F., ed. "Mexican War Journal of Leander M. Cox." *Register of the Kentucky Historical Society* 55 (January 1957): 29–52, (July 1957): 213–36, and 56 (January 1958): 47–70.

Howe, A. D. *The Life and Letters of George Bancroft.* New York, 1908.

Hubbard, John M. *Notes of a Private.* Bolivar, Tenn., 1973.

Jamison, Henry D., Jr., ed. *Letters and Recollections of a Confederate Soldier, 1860–1865.* Nashville, 1964.

Johnson, Robert Underwood, and Clarence Clough Buel, eds. *Battles and Leaders of the Civil War.* 4 vols. New York, 1887.

Johnston, John. "Civil War Reminiscences." *Tennessee Historical Quarterly* 13:65–82, 156–78, 329–54.

Johnston, Joseph E. *Narrative of Military Operations.* New York, 1874.

Johnston, R. M. *To Mexico with Scott.* Cambridge, Mass., 1917.

Jones, J. B. *A Rebel War Clerk's Diary.* 2 vols. New York, 1935.

Jones, Nat W. *A History of Mount Pleasant.* Nashville, 1903.

Joy, Charles G. "The Stampede at LaFayette, Ga." *Confederate Veteran* 20:473–77.

Kelly, R. M. "A Brush with Pillow." In *Ohio Commandery of the Military Order of the Loyal Legion of the U.S. Sketches of War History*, 9 vols., 3:319–32. Cincinnati, 1888–1908.

King, H. Clay. *Col. King's Letter to His Friends throughout the United States of America.* Nashville, 1893.

Knox, Thomas W. *Camp-fire and Cotton-field: Southern Adventure in Time of War.* New York, 1969.

Law, Reverend J. G. "Diary of the Rev. J. G. Law." *Southern Historical Society Papers* 11:175–81, 297–304, 460–65, 12:538–43.

Lossing, Benson, Jr. *Pictorial History of the Civil War.* Philadelphia, 1866.

McBride, Robert M. "The 'Confederate Sins' of Major Cheairs." *Tennessee Historical Quarterly* 23:121–35.

McKee, John M. *The Great Panic.* Nashville, 1977.

McMillan, Malcolm C. *Alabama Confederate Reader.* Tuscaloosa, 1963.

Maury County Agricultural and Mechanical Association. *Report of the Maury County Agricultural and Mechanical Association to E. G. Eastman, Secretary of the State Agricultural Bureau.* Columbia, Tenn., 1855.

Moore, Frank, ed. *Anecdotes, Poetry and Incidents of the War: North and South. 1860–1865.* New York, 1867.

————, comp. *The Civil War in Song and Story.* New York, 1889.

————. *Rebellion Record: A Diary of American Events, with Documents, Narratives, Illustrative Incidents, Poetry etc.* 10 vols. New York, 1861–63.

Moore, John Bassett, ed. *Works of James Buchanan.* Philadelphia, 1908–10.

Mott, Charles R., Jr. "War Journal of a Confederate Officer." *Tennessee Historical Quarterly* 5:234–48.

Myers, William S., ed. *The Mexican War Diary of George B. McClellan.* Princeton, 1917.

Nevins, Allan, ed. *Polk: The Diary of a President, 1845–49.* London, 1929.

Nevins, Allan, and Milton H. Thomas, eds. *The Diary of George Templeton Strong.* 4 vols. New York, 1952.

Noll, Arthur H. *Doctor Quintard, Chaplain, C.S.A., and Second Bishop of Tennessee.* Sewanee, Tenn., 1905.

Osborn, George C. "Stephen Washington Holladay's Civil War Letters." *Tennessee Historical Quarterly* 4:256–64.

Osteen, Neal. "Never a Good War." *Tennessee Alumnus* 71 (Winter 1991): 35–40.

Oswandel, J. J. *Notes of the Mexican War.* Philadelphia, 1885.

Otey, Peter J. "Why Fort Donelson Was Surrendered." *Confederate Veteran* 37:301–3.

Parks, Joseph H. "Letters from James K. Polk to Samuel H. Laughlin, 1835–1844." *East Tennessee Historical Society Publications* 18 (1946): 147–67.

Peskin, Allan. *Volunteers: The Mexican War Journals of Private Richard Coulter and Sergeant Thomas Barclay, Company B, Second Pennsylvania Infantry.* Kent, Ohio, 1991.

Pickett, William D. "A Reminiscence of Murfreesboro." Nashville *Union and American*, November 10, 1907. Reprint. *Confederate Veteran* 16:325–26, 452–53.

Pillow, Annie Payne. *The Great Seal.* Washington, 1911.

Pillow, Gideon J. *Address Delivered Before the Maury Agricultural and Mechanical Society, at the Annual Fair, October 24, 1855.* Columbia, Tenn., 1855.

————. *Defensese of Maj. Gen. Pillow Before the Court of Inquiry at Frederick, Maryland, Against the Charges Preferred Against Him by Maj. Gen. Winfield Scott.* N.p., 1848.

———. *Letter from Gen. Gideon J. Pillow on the Politics of the Day, Addressed to a Committee of Democrats of Lawrence County.* Nashville, 1857.
———. *Letters from Gen. Gid. J. Pillow, to the People of Tennessee, and in Reply to Gen'l Hitchcock.* Nashville, 1857.
———. *Opinion of Gen. Pillow Upon the Constitutionality of Arkansas Levee Tax Law of 1871.* Memphis, 1871.
———. *"The Purpose of Life, etc.,"* an Address Delivered before the Agatheridan and Erosophian Societies of the University of Nashville. Nashville, 1856.
———. *Speech of Gen. Gideon J. Pillow, Delivered at the Mass Meeting of the Democracy, Near Columbia, Tenn. On the 13th of July, 1844, on the Annexation of Texas.* Columbia, Tenn., 1844.
Pinkerton, Allan. *The Spy of the Rebellion.* New York, 1883.
Proceedings of the National Democratic Convention, 1852. Washington, 1852.
Quaife, Milo Milton. *Diary of James K. Polk during His Presidency, 1845 to 1849.* 4 vols. Chicago, 1910.
Reeves, Jesse S., ed. "Letters of Gideon J. Pillow to James K. Polk, 1844." *American Historical Review* 11 (July 1906): 832–43.
Reunions of Taylor's Battery, 18th Anniversary of the Battle of Fort Donelson, Feb. 14, 1880, 25th Anniversary of the Battle of Belmont, Nov. 6, 1886. Chicago, 1890.
Richardson, James D. *The Messages and Papers of Jefferson Davis and the Confederacy, Including Diplomatic Correspondence, 1861–1865.* New York, 1966.
Riddell, Thomas J. "The Goochland Light Artillery." *Southern Historical Society Papers* 24:316–23.
Ridley, Bromfield Lewis. *Battles and Sketches of the Army of Tennessee.* Mexico, Mo., 1906.
Robertson, J. B. *Reminiscences of a Campaign in Mexico.* Nashville, 1849.
Rogers, William J. "William J. Roger's Memorandum Book." *West Tennessee Historical Quarterly* 9 (1955): 59–92.
Rosenburg, R. B. "A Rare Letter from Andrew Johnson." *Journal of the East Tennessee Historical Society* 64 (1992): 68–73.
Rosser, R. W., ed. "The Battle of Belmont: Pvt. John Bell Battle's Eyewitness Account." *Confederate Chronicles of Tennessee* 2 (1987): 21–54.
Rowland, Dunbar, ed. *Jefferson Davis, Constitutionalist: His Letters, Papers and Speeches.* 10 vols. Jackson, Miss., 1923.
Russell, William H. *My Diary North and South.* New York, 1954.
Scammon, E. Parker. "A Chapter of the Mexican War." *Magazine of American History* 14 (1885): 562–99.
Scott, Winfield. *Memoirs.* 2 vols. New York, 1864.
Seaton, John. "The Battle of Belmont." In Military Order of the Loyal Legion of the United States, Kansas Commandery, *War Talks in Kansas.* Kansas City, 1906.
Semmes, Raphael. *Service Afloat and Ashore during the Mexican War.* Cincinnati, 1851.
Shanks, Henry T. *The Papers of Willie Person Mangum.* 5 vols. Raleigh, N.C., 1950–56.

Sherman, William T. *Personal Memoirs of William T. Sherman*. New York, 1892.

Silver, James W., ed. *A Life for the Confederacy as Recorded in the Pocket Diaries of Pvt. Robert A. Moore*. Jackson, Tenn., 1959.

Simon, John Y., ed. *The Papers of Ulysses S. Grant*. 14 vols. Carbondale, Ill., 1967–.

Singletary, Don. "The Day of the Battle of Belmont." *Hickman County Gazette*, September 30, 1971.

Sioussat, St. George L., ed. "Diaries of S. H. Laughlin, of Tennessee, 1840, 1843." *Tennessee Historical Magazine* 2 (March 1916): 43–85.

———. "Papers of Major John P. Heiss." *Tennessee Historical Magazine* 2 (September 1916): 208–30.

———. "Polk-Johnson Letters." *Tennessee Historical Magazine* 1 (June 1915): 209–56.

———. "Selected Letters, 1846–1856, from the Donelson Papers." *Tennessee Historical Magazine* 3 (1917): 257–91.

Smith, Ephriam Kirby. *To Mexico with Scott: Letters of Captain E. Kirby Smith to His Wife*. Cambridge, Mass., 1917.

Smith, Henry I. *History of the Seventh Iowa Veteran Volunteer Infantry*. Mason City, Iowa, 1903.

Smith, Robert D. *Confederate Diary of Robert D. Smith*. Edited by Jill K. Garrett. Columbia, Tenn., 1975.

Smith, Mrs. Susan. "The Soldier's Friend." *Confederate Veteran* 7:444–46.

Squier, Ephriam George, ed. *Frank Leslie's Pictorial History of the American Civil War*. 2 vols. New York, 1861–62.

Stanton, Donald J., Goodwin F. Berquist, and Paul C. Bowers, eds. *The Civil War Reminiscences of General M. Jeff Thompson*. Dayton, Ohio, 1988.

Stevenson, William G. *Thirteen Months in the Rebel Army*. New York, 1862.

Thompson, William W. "Personal Narrative of Experiences in the Civil War, 1861–1865." *Civil War Times Illustrated* 12 (August–December 1973): 12–21, 13–23, 28–39, 25–33.

Twain, Mark. *Life on the Mississippi*. New York, 1883.

Vaughan, Alfred J. *Personal Record of the Thirteenth Regiment Tennessee Infantry*. Memphis, 1897.

Walker, T. J. "Reminiscences of the Civil War." *Confederate Chronicles of Tennessee* 1 (June 1986): 37–94.

Wallace, Lew. *An Autobiography*. 2 vols. New York, 1906.

———. "The Capture of Ft. Donelson." In *Battles and Leaders of the Civil War*, 4 vols., edited by Robert Underwood Johnson and Clarence Clough Buel, 1:398–428. New York, 1887.

Weaver, Herbert, Paul Bergeron, James P. Cooper, Jr., Wayne Cutler, Earl J. Smith, and Carese M. Parker, eds. *Correspondence of James K. Polk*. 7 vols. Nashville and Knoxville, 1969–.

Wilkins, Mary, ed. "Some Papers of the American Cotton Planters Association, 1865–1866." *Tennessee Historical Quarterly* 7:335–61, 8:49–62.

Woodward, C. Vann. *Mary Chesnut's Civil War*. London, 1981.

Wright, Marcus Joseph. "The Battle of Belmont." *Southern Historical Society Papers* 16:69–82.

———. *Diary of Brigadier-General Marcus J. Wright, C.S.A.* N.p., 1935.

Young, Jesse. *What a Boy Saw in the Army.* New York, 1894.

Young, Lot D. *Reminiscences of a Soldier in the Orphan Brigade.* Louisville, 1918.

BOOKS

Abernathy, Thomas P. *From Frontier to Plantation in Tennessee: A Study in Frontier Democracy.* Chapel Hill, 1932.

Alexander, Thomas B. *Political Reconstruction in Tennessee.* Nashville, 1950.

Allen, Hall. *Center of Conflict: A Factual Story of the War between the States in Western Kentucky and Tennessee.* Paducah, Ky., 1961.

Ambrose, Stephen. *Duty, Honor, Country: A History of West Point.* Baltimore, 1966.

Andrews, J. Cutler. *The South Reports the Civil War.* Princeton, 1979.

Aztec Club, Membership Committee. *History of the Aztec Club: Founded in the City of Mexico, 1847.* 1898.

Bailey, Thomas A. *A Diplomatic History of the American People.* 6th ed. New York, 1958.

Bain, Richard C., and Judith H. Parris. *Convention Decisions and Voting Records.* Washington, 1973.

Bakeless, John. *Background to Glory: The Life of George Rogers Clark.* Philadelphia, 1957.

Bancroft, Frederic. *Slave Trading in the Old South.* Baltimore, 1931.

Barton, George. *Angels of the Battlefield.* Philadelphia, 1898.

Bassett, John S. *The Life of Andrew Jackson.* 2 vols. New York, 1925.

Bauer, Karl Jack. *The Mexican War, 1846–1848.* New York, 1974.

———. *Zachary Taylor: Soldier, Planter, Statesman of the Old Southwest.* Baton Rouge, 1985.

Bearss, Edwin C. *Forrest at Brice's Cross Roads and in North Mississippi in 1864.* Dayton, Ohio, 1979.

Belohlavek, John M. *George Mifflin Dallas: Jacksonian Patrician.* University Park, Pa., 1977.

Bemis, Samuel F. *A Diplomatic History of the United States.* 4th ed. New York, 1955.

Bergeron, Paul. *Antebellum Politics in Tennessee.* Lexington, Ky., 1982.

———. *The Presidency of James K. Polk.* Lawrence, Kans., 1987.

Bill, Alfred H. *Rehearsal for Conflict: The War with Mexico, 1846–1848.* New York, 1947.

Binkley, Wilfred E. *American Political Parties: Their Natural History.* New York, 1962.

Black, Robert, III. *The Railroads of the Confederacy.* Chapel Hill, 1952.

Blakey, Arch F. *General John H. Winder, C.S.A.* Gainesville, Fla., 1990.

Brandau, Roberta S. *History of Homes and Gardens of Tennessee*. Nashville, 1936.

Bridges, Hal. *Lee's Maverick General: Daniel Harvey Hill*. New York, 1961.

Brooks, Nathan C. *A Complete History of the Mexican War, 1846–1848*. Chicago, 1849.

Brown, Dee Alexander. *Grierson's Raid*. Urbana, Ill., 1954.

Brown, Fred R. *History of the Ninth U.S. Infantry, 1799–1909*. Chicago, 1909.

Brown, Leonard. *American Patriotism*. Des Moines, 1869.

Bryan, Grace M. *Southern Kinsmen*. New Orleans, 1977.

Buck, Paul H. *Road to Reunion, 1865 to 1900*. New York, 1959.

Burt, Nathaniel. *The Perennial Philadelphian*. Boston, 1963.

Byers, Samuel H. M. *Iowa in War Times*. Des Moines, 1888.

Caldwell, Joshua William. *Sketches of the Bench and Bar of Tennessee*. Knoxville, 1898.

Caldwell, Mary F. *Tennessee: The Dangerous Example*. Nashville, 1974.

Callahan, James M. *American Foreign Policy in Mexican Relations*. New York, 1932.

Campbell, Mary E. R. *The Attitude of Tennesseans toward the Union, 1847–1861*. New York, 1961.

Carter, Samuel, III. *The Final Fortress: The Campaign for Vicksburg, 1862–1863*. New York, 1980.

Castel, Albert. *General Sterling Price and the Civil War in the West*. Baton Rouge, 1968.

Catton, Bruce. *Grant Moves South*. Boston, 1960.

———. *Never Call Retreat*. Garden City, N.Y., 1965.

———. *Terrible Swift Sword*. Garden City, N.Y., 1963.

———. *This Hallowed Ground: The Story of the Union Side of the Civil War*. Garden City, N.Y., 1956.

———. *U. S. Grant and the American Military Tradition*. Boston, 1954.

Chandler, Julian A. C., et al., eds. *The South in the Building of the Nation*. 12 vols. Richmond, 1909.

Chester, Edward W. *A Guide to Political Platforms*. Hamden, Conn., 1977.

Cirker, Hayward. *Dictionary of American Portraits*. New York, 1967.

Clayton, W. Woodford. *History of Davidson County, Tenn*. Philadelphia: 1880.

Coatesworth, Stella S. *The Loyal People of the North-west*. Chicago, 1869.

Coggins, Jack. *Arms and Equipment of the Civil War*. Garden City, N.Y., 1962.

Cole, Donald B. *Martin Van Buren and the American Political System*. Princeton, 1984.

Conger, A. L. *The Rise of U. S. Grant*. New York, 1931.

Connelly, Thomas Lawrence. *Army of the Heartland: The Army of Tennessee, 1861–1862*. Baton Rouge, 1967.

———. *Autumn of Glory*. Baton Rouge, 1971.

Conrad, Robert Taylor. *General Scott and His Staff*. Philadelphia, 1848.

Cooling, Benjamin Franklin. *Forts Henry and Donelson: The Key to the Confederate Heartland*. Knoxville, 1987.

Coulter, E. Merton. *The Confederate States of America, 1861–1865*. Baton Rouge, 1950.

——. *The South during Reconstruction, 1865–77*. Baton Rouge, 1947.

Coulter, William G. *Brownlow: Fighting Parson of the Southern Highlands*. Chapel Hill, 1937.

Cozzens, Peter. *No Better Place to Die: The Battle of Stones River*. Urbana, Ill., 1990.

Crew, H. W. *History of Nashville, Tennessee*. Nashville, 1890.

Crofts, Daniel W. *Reluctant Confederates: Upper South Unionists in the Secession Crisis*. Chapel Hill, 1989.

Cross, Paul. *Clifton Place Plantation*. Columbia, Tenn., 1985.

Cullom, George W. *Biographical Register of the Officers and Graduates of the U.S. Military Academy*. 6 vols. New York, 1879–1920.

Cummings, Charles M. *Yankee Quaker and Confederate General: The Curious Career of Bushrod Rust Johnson*. Rutherford, N.J., 1971.

Cunliffe, Marcus. *Soldiers and Civilians*. Boston, 1968.

Curtis, George T. *Life of James Buchanan*. New York, 1883.

Daniel, Larry J. *Cannoneers in Gray: The Field Artillery of the Army of Tennessee, 1861–1865*. University, Ala., 1984.

Davies-Rodgers, Ellen. *The Great Book: Calvary Protestant Episcopal Church, 1832–1972*. Memphis, 1973.

Davis, William C. *Breckinridge: Statesman, Soldier, Symbol*. Baton Rouge, 1974.

——. *Jefferson Davis: The Man and His Hour*. New York, 1991.

——. *The Orphan Brigade: The Kentucky Confederates Who Couldn't Go Home*. Garden City, N.Y., 1980.

Dodson, W. C. *Campaigns of Wheeler and His Cavalry, 1862–1865*. Atlanta, 1899.

Dorris, Jonathan T. *Pardon and Amnesty under Lincoln and Johnson: The Restoration of the Confederates to Their Rights and Privileges, 1861–1868*. Chapel Hill, 1953.

Drake, Edwin L., ed. *Annals of the Army of Tennessee*. Nashville, 1878.

Dubay, Robert W. *John Jones Pettus*. Jackson, Miss., 1975.

Dufow, Charles L. *The Mexican War*. New York, 1968.

Durham, Walter T. *Nashville, the Occupied City*. Nashville, 1985.

Dyer, Brainerd. *Zachary Taylor*. Baton Rouge, 1946.

Eaton, Clement. *Henry Clay and the Art of American Politics*. Boston, 1957.

——. *A History of the Confederacy*. New York, 1954.

Eisenhower, John S. D. *So Far from God: The U.S. War with Mexico*. New York, 1989.

Eliot, Ellsworth, Jr. *West Point in the Confederacy*. New York, 1941.

Elliott, Charles Winslow. *Winfield Scott: The Soldier and the Man*. New York, 1937.

Estvan, Bela. *War Pictures from the South*. New York, 1863.

Evans, Clement Anselm. *Confederate Military History*. 12 vols. Atlanta, 1899.

Fertig, James Walker. *The Secession and Reconstruction of Tennessee*. Chicago, 1898.

Fiske, John. *The Mississippi Valley in the Civil War*. New York, 1902.

Fletcher, David M. *The Diplomacy of Annexation: Texas, Oregon, and the Mexican War*. Columbia, Mo., 1973.

Fogel, Robert, and Stanley Engerman. *Time on the Cross*. Boston, 1974.

Folmsbee, Stanley J. *Sectionalism and Internal Improvements in Tennessee, 1796–1845*. Knoxville, 1939.

Folmsbee, Stanley J., Robert E. Corlew, and Enoch L. Mitchell. *Tennessee: A Short History*. Knoxville, 1969.

Foreman, Grant. *Indian Removal*. Norman, Okla., 1932.

Fox, William F. *Regimental Losses in the American Civil War, 1861–1865*. Albany, N.Y., 1889.

Franklin, John Hope. *From Slavery to Freedom*. New York, 1967.

Freeman, Douglas S. *R. E. Lee*. 4 vols. New York, 1934–35.

Frost, John. *The Mexican War: Its Warriors*. New York, 1848.

Fuess, Claude. *The Life of Caleb Cushing*. 2 vols. New York, 1923.

Futch, Ovid L. *History of Andersonville Prison*. Gainesville, Fla., 1968.

Garraty, John. *Silas Wright*. New York, 1949.

Gohmann, Sister Mary de Lourdes. *Political Nativism in Tennessee to 1860*. Washington, 1938.

Goodspeed, Weston A., ed. *History of Tennessee*. Nashville, 1887.

Gosnell, Harpur Allan. *Guns on Western Waters: The Story of River Gunboats in the Civil War*. Baton Rouge, 1949.

Govan, Gilbert E., and James W. Livingood. *A Different Valor*. New York, 1956.

Greeley, Horace. *The American Conflict: A History of the Great Rebellion in the United States of America, 1860–1864*. 2 vols. Hartford, Conn., 1865.

Green, William Mercer. *Memoir of Rt. Rev. James Hervey Otey*. New York, 1885.

Hall, Clifton R. *Andrew Johnson: Military Governor of Tennessee*. Princeton, 1916.

Hallum, John. *Biographical and Pictorial History of Arkansas*. Albany, N.Y., 1887.

Halpin, T. M. *Memphis City Directory, 1867–68*. Memphis, 1867.

Hamer, Philip M. *Tennessee: A History, 1673–1932*. 2 vols. New York, 1933.

Hamilton, Holman. *Zachary Taylor: Soldier in the White House*. New York, 1951.

———. *Zachary Taylor: Soldier of the Republic*. Indianapolis, 1941.

Hamilton, James. *The Battle of Fort Donelson*. New York, 1968.

Hamlin, Percy G. *"Old Bald Head" (General R. S. Ewell): The Portrait of a Soldier and the Making of a Soldier: Letters of General R. S. Ewell*. Gaithersburg, Md., 1988.

Hanlin, Lilian. *George Bancroft: The Intellectual as Democrat*. New York, 1984.

Harris, William C. *Leroy Pope Walker: Confederate Secretary of War*. Tuscaloosa, Ala., 1962.

Harrison, Lowell H. *The Civil War in Kentucky*. Lexington, Ky., 1975.

Heitman, Francis B. *Historical Register and Dictionary of the United States Army.* 2 vols. Washington, 1903.

Hempstead, Fay. *Historical Review of Arkansas: Its Commerce, Industry and Modern Affairs.* Chicago, 1911.

Henderson, G. F. R. *Stonewall Jackson and the American Civil War.* New York, 1955.

Henry, Robert S. *"First with the Most" Forrest.* Indianapolis, 1944.

————. *The Story of the Mexican War.* Indianapolis, 1950.

Herbert, Walter H. *Fighting Joe Hooker.* Indianapolis, 1944.

Herndon, Dallas T. *Centennial History of Arkansas.* Little Rock, 1922.

Hesseltine, William B. *Civil War Prisons.* Columbus, Ohio, 1930.

Hodgson, Sister M. Michael Catherine. *Caleb Cushing: Attorney General of the United States, 1853–1857.* Washington, 1955.

Hofstadter, Richard. *Anti-Intellectualism in American Life.* New York, 1966.

Hoole, William S. *Alabama Tories.* Tuscaloosa, Ala., 1960.

Horn, Stanley Fitzgerald. *The Army of Tennessee.* Norman, Okla., 1941.

Howe, M. A. DeWolfe. *The Life and Letters of George Bancroft.* 2 vols. New York, 1908.

Hughes, Nathaniel Cheairs, Jr. *The Battle of Belmont: Grant Strikes South.* Chapel Hill, 1991.

————. *General William J. Hardee: Old Reliable.* Baton Rouge, 1965.

Hughes, Robert M. *General Johnston.* New York, 1893.

Hurlburt, J. S. *History of the Rebellion in Bradley County, East Tennessee.* Indianapolis, 1866.

Ingersoll, Lurton Dunham. *Iowa and the Rebellion.* Philadelphia, 1866.

James, Marquis. *Andrew Jackson: The Border Captain.* New York, 1933.

Jennings, Thelma. *The Nashville Convention: Southern Movement for Unity, 1848–1851.* Memphis, 1980.

Johanssen, Robert W. *Stephen A. Douglas.* New York, 1973.

————. *To the Halls of the Montezumas: The Mexican War in the American Imagination.* New York, 1985.

Johnson, Allen, and Dumas Malone, eds. *Dictionary of American Biography.* 21 vols. New York, 1928–37.

Johnston, William Preston. *Life of General Albert Sidney Johnston.* New York, 1878.

Jones, Archer. *Confederate Strategy: From Shiloh to Vicksburg.* Baton Rouge, 1961.

Jones, Nat W. *A History of Mount Pleasant.* Nashville, 1903.

Jordan, Thomas, and J. P. Pryor. *The Campaigns of Lieut.-Gen. N. B. Forrest, and of Forrest's Cavalry.* New Orleans, 1868.

Keasler, Suzy. "General Gideon Pillow, C.S.A." In Lee County Sesquicentennial Committee, *History of Lee County, Arkansas.* Dallas, Tex., 1987.

Keating, J. M. *History of the City of Memphis and Shelby County, Tennessee.* 2 vols. Syracuse, N.Y., 1888.

Kelley, Sarah F. *Children of Nashville.* Nashville, 1973.

Kent, Frank R. *The Democratic Party: A History*. New York, 1928.

Klein, Philip S. *President James Buchanan: A Biography*. University Park, Pa., 1962.

Lewis, Lloyd. *Captain Sam Grant*. Boston, 1950.

Liddell Hart, Basil Henry. *Sherman: Soldier, Realist, American*. New York, 1929.

Life and Military Character of Maj. Gen. Scott. New York, 1847.

Linderman, Gerald P. *Embattled Courage: The Experience of Combat in the American Civil War*. New York, 1987.

Lindsley, John Berrien, ed. *The Military Annals of Tennessee*. Nashville, 1896.

Livermore, Thomas Leonard. *Numbers and Losses in the Civil War in America, 1861–1865*. New York, 1901.

Livingston, John. *Biographical Sketches of Eminent American Lawyers, Now Living*. New York, 1852.

————. *Portraits of Eminent Americans*. 2 vols. New York, 1853.

Lonn, Ella. *Desertion during the Civil War*. New York, 1928.

Losson, Christopher. *Tennessee's Forgotten Warriors: Frank Cheatham and His Confederate Division*. Knoxville, 1990.

Lurie, Leonard. *Party Politics: Why We Have Poor Presidents*. New York, 1980.

Lytle, Andrew. *Bedford Forrest and His Critter Company*. New York, 1960.

McBride, Robert M., and Daniel M. Robison, eds. *Biographical Directory of the Tennessee General Assembly*. 2 vols. Nashville, 1975.

McCallum, James. *A Brief Sketch of the Settlement and Early History of Giles County, Tennessee*. Pulaski, Tenn., 1976.

McCormac, Eugene Irving. *James K. Polk: A Political Biography*. Berkeley, Calif., 1922.

McCoy, Charles A. *Polk and the Presidency*. Austin, Tex., 1961.

McDonough, James Lee. *Stones River: Bloody Winter in Tennessee*. Knoxville, 1980.

McFeely, William S. *Grant: A Biography*. New York, 1981.

McIlwaine, Shields. *Memphis Down in Dixie*. New York, 1948.

McLaughlin, Andrew C. *Life of Lewis Cass*. Boston, 1891.

McMillan, Malcolm C. *The Disintegration of a Confederate State*. Macon, Ga., 1986.

McMurry, Richard M. *Two Great Rebel Armies: An Essay in Confederate Military History*. Chapel Hill, 1989.

McPherson, James M. *Battle Cry of Freedom: The Civil War Era*. New York, 1988.

McWhiney, Grady. *Braxton Bragg and Confederate Defeat*. New York, 1969.

Maness, Lonnie E. *An Untutored Genius*. Oxford, Miss., 1990.

Marszalek, John F. *Sherman: A Soldier's Passion for Order*. New York, 1993.

Martin, Bessie. *Desertion of Alabama Troops from the Confederate Army: A Study in Sectionalism*. New York, 1932.

Mathes, James Harvey. *The Old Guard in Gray*. Memphis, 1897.

May, Robert E. *John A. Quitman: Old South Crusader*. Baton Rouge, 1985.

The Mexican War and Its Heroes: Being a Complete History of the Mexican War.
2 vols. in 1. Philadelphia, 1850.

Miller, Francis T., ed. *The Photographic History of the Civil War.* 10 vols. New York, 1911.

Miller, Robert. *Shamrock and Sword: The San Patricio Battalion in the Mexican War.* Norman, Okla., 1989.

Milton, George Fort. *Abraham Lincoln and the Fifth Column.* New York, 1942.

———. *The Eve of Conflict: Stephen A. Douglas and the Needless War.* Boston, 1934.

Monaghan, Jay. *Swamp Fox of the Confederacy: The Life and Military Services of M. Jeff Thompson.* Tuscaloosa, Ala., 1957.

Moore, Albert Burton. *Conscription and Conflict in the Confederacy.* New York, 1963.

Moore, John Trotwood. *Tennessee, the Volunteer State, 1769–1923.* Nashville, 1923.

Morrison, James L., Jr. *"The Best School in the World," West Point, the Pre–Civil War Years, 1833–1866.* Kent, Ohio, 1986.

Morrissey, Eleanor F. *Portraits in Tennessee Painted before 1866.* Nashville, 1964.

Mushkat, Jerome. *Tammany: The Evolution of a Political Machine, 1789–1865.* Syracuse, N.Y., 1971.

Nash, Charles E. *Biographical Sketches of Gen. Pat Cleburne and Gen. T. C. Hindman.* Little Rock, 1898.

Nevins, Allan. *Emergence of Lincoln.* 2 vols. New York, 1950.

———. *Fremont: Pathmaker of the West.* 2 vols. New York, 1939.

Nichols, Edward J. *Zach Taylor's Little Army.* Garden City, N.Y., 1963.

Nichols, James L. *Confederate Engineers.* Tuscaloosa, Ala., 1957.

Nichols, Roy Franklin. *The Democratic Machine, 1850–1859.* Garden City, N.Y., 1923.

———. *Franklin Pierce: Young Hickory of the Granite Hills.* Philadelphia, 1931.

———. *The Stakes of Power, 1845–1877.* New York, 1961.

Niven, John. *Martin Van Buren.* New York, 1983.

Nuermberger, Ruth Ketring. *The Clays of Alabama: A Planter-Lawyer-Politician Family.* Lexington, Ky., 1958.

Nye, Russell B. *George Bancroft: Brahmin Rebel.* New York, 1945.

Ornelas-Struve, Carole. *Memphis, 1800–1900.* 3 vols. New York, 1982.

Parker, Carese, Paul Cross, and Wallace Hebert. *The Friendship of James Knox Polk and Gideon Johnson Pillow.* Columbia, Tenn., 1986.

Parks, Joseph H. *Felix Grundy, Champion of Democracy.* University, La., 1940.

———. *General Leonidas Polk, C.S.A.* Baton Rouge, 1962.

———. *Joseph E. Brown of Georgia.* Baton Rouge, 1977.

Patrick, James. *Architecture in Tennessee, 1786–1897.* Knoxville, 1981.

Patterson, Caleb P. *The Negro in Tennessee, 1790–1865.* Austin, Tex., 1922.

Patton, James W. *Unionism and Reconstruction in Tennessee, 1860–1869.* Chapel Hill, 1934.

Paul, James C. N. *Rift in the Democracy*. Philadelphia, 1951.

Perman, Michael. *Reunion without Compromise: The South and Reconstruction, 1865–1868*. Cambridge, Mass., 1973.

Phelan, James. *The Making of a State*. Boston, 1889.

Polk, Cynthia M. *Some Old Colonial Families*. Memphis, 1915.

Polk, William Mecklenburg. *Leonidas Polk, Bishop and General*. 2d ed. 2 vols. New York, 1915.

Pollard, Edward A. *The First Year of the War*. Richmond, Va., 1862.

Pollard, James E. *The President and the Press*. New York, 1973.

Potter, David M. *The Impending Crisis, 1848–1861*. New York, 1963.

Purdue, Howell, and Elizabeth Purdue. *Pat Cleburne, Confederate General*. Hillsboro, Tex., 1973.

Ramsey, James G. M. *The Annals of Tennessee*. Charleston, S.C., 1853.

Reeves, Jesse S. *American Diplomacy under Tyler and Polk*. Gloucester, Mass., 1967.

Richardson, Albert D. *A Personal History of Ulysses S. Grant*. Chicago, 1868.

Richmond, Douglas W., ed. *Essays on the Mexican War*. College Station, Tex., 1986.

Ridley, Bromfield L. *Battles and Sketches of the Army of Tennessee*. Mexico, Mo., 1906.

Ripley, Roswell S. *The War with Mexico*. 2 vols. New York, 1849.

Roark, James. *Masters without Slaves*. New York, 1977.

Robertson, James I., and Richard McMurry. *Rank and File*. San Rafael, Calif., 1976.

Robinson, William Morrison. *Justice in Grey: History of the Judicial System of the Confederate States of America*. Cambridge, Mass., 1941.

Rodenbough, Theodore F., and William L. Haskins, eds. *The Army of the United States*. New York, 1896.

Roland, Charles P. *Albert Sidney Johnston*. Austin, Tex., 1964.

Roman, Alfred. *The Military Operations of General Beauregard*. New York, 1884.

Ross, Margaret. *Arkansas Gazette: The Early Years, 1819–1866*. Little Rock, 1969.

Sanborn, Margaret. *Robert E. Lee*. 2 vols. Philadelphia, 1966–67.

Sandburg, Carl. *Abraham Lincoln: The War Years*. 4 vols. New York, 1939.

Sandweiss, Martha A., Rick Stewart, and Ben H. Huseman. *Eyewitness to War: Prints and Daguerreotypes of the Mexican War, 1846–1848*. Fort Worth, 1989.

Sartain, James A. *History of Walker County Georgia*. 2 vols. Dalton, Ga., 1932.

Schlesinger, Arthur M., Jr., Fred L. Israel, and William P. Hansen, eds. *History of American Presidential Elections, 1789–1968*. 4 vols. New York, 1971.

Schroder, John. *Mr. Polk's War*. Madison, Wis., 1973.

Sears, Stephen W. *George B. McClellan: The Young Napoleon*. New York, 1988.

Sellers, Charles. *James K. Polk: Continentalist*. Princeton, 1966.

———. *James K. Polk: Jacksonian, 1795–1843*. Princeton, 1957.

Semmes, Raphael. *Campaigns of Scott in the Valley of Mexico*. Cincinnati, 1852.

Shenton, James P. *Robert John Walker: A Politician from Jackson to Lincoln*. New York, 1961.

Singletary, Byron. *Vital Statistics from 19th Century Tennessee Church Records*. Nashville, 1979.

Singletary, Otis A. *The Mexican War*. Chicago, 1960.

Sistler, Byron. *Battle Statistics from 19th Century Church Records*. 2 vols. Nashville, 1979.

Smith, A. D. H. *Old Fuss and Feathers*. New York, 1937.

Smith, Edward. *The Borderland in the Civil War*. New York, 1927.

Smith, Frank H. *History of Maury County*. Columbia, Tenn., 1969.

Smith, George W., and Charles Judah. *Chronicles of the Gringos: The U.S. Army in the Mexican War, 1846–1848*. Albuquerque, 1968.

Smith, John T. *History of the Thirty-first Regiment of Indiana Volunteer Infantry*. Cincinnati, 1900.

Smith, Justin H. *The War with Mexico*. 2 vols. New York, 1929.

Smith, Reid. *Majestic Middle Tennessee*. Prattsville, Ala., 1975.

Smith, William E. *The Francis Preston Blair Family in Politics*. 2 vols. New York, 1933.

Speer, William S. *Sketches of Prominent Tennesseans*. Nashville, 1888.

Spencer, Ivor Debenham. *The Victor and the Spoils: A Life of William L. Marcy*. Providence, R.I., 1959.

Stephens, Isaac I. *Campaigns of the Rio Grande and of Mexico*. New York, 1851.

Stevenson, Alexander F. *The Battle of Stone's River*. Boston, 1884.

Stickles, Arndt M. *Simon Bolivar Buckner*. Chapel Hill, 1940.

Strode, Hudson. *Jefferson Davis, 1801–1861*. 3 vols. New York, 1955–64.

Stuart, Addison A. *Iowa Colonels and Regiments: Being a History of Iowa Regiments in the War of the Rebellion*. Des Moines, 1865.

Sword, Wiley. *Shiloh: Bloody April*. New York, 1974.

Symonds, Craig L. *Joseph E. Johnston: A Civil War Biography*. New York, 1992.

Taylor and His Generals. A Biography of Major General Zachary Taylor; Sketches of the Lives of Generals Worth, Wool, and Twiggs; with a Full Account of the Various Actions of Their Divisions in Mexico up to the Present Time; Together with a History of the Bombardment of Vera Cruz, and a Sketch of the Life of Major General Winfield Scott. Philadelphia, 1847.

Taylor, Orville. *Negro Slavery in Arkansas*. Durham, N.C., 1958.

Tebbel, John. *The Compact History of the Indian Wars*. New York, 1966.

Temple, Oliver. *Notable Men of Tennessee*. New York, 1912.

Tennessee Civil War Commission. *Tennesseans in the Civil War*. 2 vols. Nashville, 1964–65.

Thomas, David Y. *Arkansas and Its People*. 4 vols. New York, 1930.

Thompson, George H. *Arkansas and Reconstruction*. London, 1976.

Trefousse, Hans L. *Andrew Johnson: A Biography*. New York, 1989.

Trelease, Allen W. *White Terror: The Ku Klux Klan Conspiracy and Southern Reconstruction*. New York, 1971.

Tremain, Henry E. *Two Days of War*. New York, 1905.

Turner, George. *Victory Rode the Rails*. Indianapolis, 1953.

Turner, W. B. *History of Maury County.* Nashville, 1955.

Tutorow, Norman E. *The Mexican-American War: An Annotated Bibliography.* Westport, Conn., 1981.

Tyler, Ronnie C. *The Mexican War: A Lithographic Record.* Austin, Tex., 1973.

The Union Army: A History of Military Affairs in the Loyal States, 1861–65. 8 vols. Madison, Wis., 1908.

Union Soldiers and Sailors Monument Association, Louisville. *Union Regiments of Kentucky.* Louisville, 1897.

Van Deusen, G. G. *The Life of Henry Clay.* Boston, 1937.

Vandiver, Frank. *Basic History of the Confederacy.* Princeton, 1962.

———. *Mighty Stonewall.* New York, 1957.

———. *Rebel Brass: The Confederate Command System.* Baton Rouge, 1956.

Van Horne, Thomas B. *History of the Army of the Cumberland.* 3 vols. Cincinnati, 1875.

Wakelyn, Jon L. *Biographical Directory of the Confederacy.* Edited by Frank Vandiver. Westover, Conn., 1977.

Walker County Historical Commission. *Walker County, Georgia, 1833–1983.* Dallas, 1984.

Wallace, Edward S. *General William Jenkins Worth, Monterrey's Forgotten Hero.* Dallas, 1953.

Warner, Ezra J. *Generals in Blue: Lives of the Union Commanders.* Baton Rouge, 1964.

———. *Generals in Gray: Lives of the Confederate Commanders.* Baton Rouge, 1959.

Westrate, Edwin V. *Those Fatal Generals.* New York, 1936.

Wilcox, Cadmus M. *History of the Mexican War.* Washington, 1892.

Williams, Kenneth P. *Lincoln Finds a General.* 5 vols. New York, 1949–59.

Williams, Thomas H. *P. G. T. Beauregard: Napoleon in Gray.* Baton Rouge, 1954.

Williamson, Emma J. *Historic Madison: The Story of Jackson and Madison County, Tennessee.* Jackson, Tenn., 1946.

Wills, Brian Steel. *A Battle from the Start: The Life of Nathan Bedford Forrest.* New York, 1992.

Wiltse, Charles. *John C. Calhoun: Sectionalist, 1840–1850.* New York, 1951.

Wingfield, Marshall. *Literary Memphis: A Survey of Its Writers and Writings.* Memphis, 1942.

Wood, D. W. *History of the Twentieth Ohio Veteran Volunteer Infantry.* Columbus, Ohio, 1876.

Woodward, Grace S. *The Cherokees.* Norman, Okla., 1963.

Woodward, William E. *Meet General Grant.* New York, 1928.

Woodworth, Stephen G. *Jefferson Davis and His Generals: The Failure of Confederate Command in the West.* Lawrence, Kans., 1990.

Wright, Marcus Joseph. *Tennessee in the War, 1861–1865.* New York, 1908.

Wyeth, John. *That Devil Forrest: Life of Nathan Bedford Forrest.* New York, 1959.

Yearns, Wilfred. *The Confederate Congress.* Athens, Ga., 1960.

————, ed. *The Confederate Governors.* Athens, Ga., 1985.

Young, J. P. *The Seventh Cavalry.* Nashville, 1890.

————. *Standard History of Memphis, Tennessee.* Knoxville, 1912.

ARTICLES

Ambrose, Stephen. "Fort Donelson, a Disastrous Blow to the South." *Civil War Times Illustrated* 5 (June 1966): 8–13, 42–47.

Barnwell, Robert W. "Fort Donelson—by Official Record." *Confederate Veteran* 38:16–20.

Bearss, Edwin C. "Unconditional Surrender: The Fall of Fort Donelson." Pamphlet reprinted from *Tennessee Historical Quarterly* 21:47–65, 140–61.

————. "The Union Artillery and Breckinridge's Attack." Research Project No. 2, Stones River National Military Park, July 1959.

Bedford, H. L. "Fight between the Batteries and Gunboats at Fort Donelson." *Southern Historical Society Papers* 13:165–73.

Belissary, C. G. "Tennessee and Immigration, 1865–1880." *Tennessee Historical Quarterly* 7:229–48.

Bell, Patricia. "Gideon Pillow: A Personality Profile." *Civil War Times Illustrated* 6 (June 1967): 12–19.

Bergeron, Paul H. "All in the Family: President Polk in the White House." *Tennessee Historical Quarterly* 46:10–20.

Brackett, Albert G. "Colonel Theodore O'Hara." *Southern Historical Society Papers* 19:275–81.

Carmichael, Maude. "Federal Experiments with Negro Labor on Abandoned Plantations in Arkansas: 1862–1865." *Phillips County (Arkansas) Historical Quarterly* 1 (June 1942): 101–16.

Collins, William H. "Biographical Sketch of Maj. Gen. James D. Morgan." *Transactions of the Illinois State Historical Society* 11:274–85.

Cooling, B. Franklin. "Gee's Fifteenth Arkansas Infantry in the Forts Henry and Donelson Campaigns." *Arkansas Historical Quarterly* 23:324–42.

————. "Gideon Johnson Pillow." In *Dictionary of American Military Biography*, 3 vols., edited by Roger J. Spiller, 3:861–65. Westport, Conn., 1985.

————. "Lew Wallace and Gideon Pillow: Enigmas and Variations on an American Military Theme." *Lincoln Herald*, Summer 1964.

Cribbs, Lennie A. "The Memphis Chinese Labor Convention, 1869." *West Tennessee Historical Society Papers* 37:74–81.

Cummings, Charles M. "Forgotten Man at Fort Donelson: Bushrod Rust Johnson." *Tennessee Historical Quarterly* 27:380–97.

————. "Otho French Strahl." *Tennessee Historical Quarterly* 24:341–55.

Cunningham, Sumner A. "Career of Gen. Gideon J. Pillow." *Confederate Veteran* 1:329–30.

————. "Tyree H. Bell." *Confederate Veteran* 6:529.

Daniel, Larry. "The Quinby and Robinson Cannon Foundry at Memphis." *West Tennessee Historical Society Papers* 27 (1973): 18–32.

Everett, Robert B. "James K. Polk and the Election of 1844 in Tennessee." *West Tennessee Historical Society Papers* 16 (1962): 10–19.

Fakes, Turner J., Jr. "Memphis and the Mexican War." *West Tennessee Historical Society Papers* 11 (1948): 119–44.

Garrett, Jill K. "St. John's Church, Ashwood." *Tennessee Historical Quarterly* 29:2–23.

Gilly, Billy H. "Tennessee Opinion of the Mexican War as Reflected in the State Press." *East Tennessee Historical Society Publications* 26 (1954): 7–26.

Golden, Gabriel H. "William Carroll and His Administration." *Tennessee Historical Magazine* 9 (April 1925): 9–30.

Graebner, Norman A. "Party Politics and the Trist Mission." *Journal of Southern History* 19 (May 1953): 140–42.

Grant, C. L. "Cave Johnson and the Presidential Campaign of 1844." *East Tennessee Historical Society Publications* 25 (1953): 54–73.

————. "The Politics Behind a Presidential Nomination as Shown in Letters from Cave Johnson to James K. Polk." *Tennessee Historical Quarterly* 12:152–81.

————. "The Public Career of Cave Johnson." *Tennessee Historical Quarterly* 10:195–223.

Hall, Kermit L. "West Humphreys and the Crisis of the Union." *Tennessee Historical Quarterly* 34:48–69.

Hamer, Marquerite B. "The Presidential Campaign of 1860 in Tennessee." *East Tennessee Historical Society Publications* 3 (January 1931): 102–15.

Hamer, Philip M. "Gideon Johnson Pillow." *Dictionary of American Biography* 14:603–4.

Henry, J. M. "Detailed and Authentic History of the Battle of LaFayette, June 24, 1864." *Walker County Messenger* (LaFayette, Ga.), July 29, 1927.

Hesseltine, W. B. "Tennessee's Invitation to Carpet-Baggers." *East Tennessee Historical Society Publications* 4 (January 1932): 102–15.

Highsaw, Mary W. "A History of Zion Community in Maury County, 1806–1860." *Tennessee Historical Quarterly* 5:3–34, 111–40.

Hogan, Don L. "General Pillow's Body Rests in Lonely Grave." Memphis *Press Scimitar*, March 11, 1927.

Holt, Michael F. "The Democratic Party: 1828–1860." In *History of U.S. Political Parties*, 4 vols., by Arthur M. Schlesinger, Jr., 1:495–536. New York, 1973.

Jacobs, Dillard. "Outfitting the Provisional Army of Tennessee: A Report on New Source Material." *Tennessee Historical Quarterly* 40:257–71.

Jennings, Thelma. "Tennessee and the Nashville Convention of 1850." *Tennessee Historical Quarterly* 30:70–82.

Johnson, John. "Gen. Gideon Pillow of Maury County." Columbia, Tenn., *Maury Democrat*, August 4, 1927.

Johnson, Timothy D. "Benjamin Franklin Cheatham: The Early Years." *Tennessee Historical Quarterly* 42:269–75.

————."Benjamin Franklin Cheatham at Belmont." *Missouri Historical Review* 81 (1986–87): 159–72.

Jones, John M. "General Gideon J. Pillow." Memphis and Shelby County Library, 1983.

Jones, Joseph. "Medical History of the Southern Confederacy." *Southern Historical Society Papers* 20:121–32.

Kniffen, Gilbert C. "The Battle of Stone's River." In *Battles and Leaders of the Civil War*, 4 vols., edited by Robert Underwood Johnson and Clarence Clough Buel, 3:613–32. New York, 1887.

Lambert, Robert S. "The Democratic National Convention of 1844." *Tennessee Historical Quarterly* 14:3–23.

Lewis, Elsie M. "Economic Conditions in Antebellum Arkansas, 1850–1861." *Arkansas Historical Quarterly* 6:256–74.

Lufkin, Charles L. "Divided Loyalties: Sectionalism in Civil War McNairy County, Tennessee." *Tennessee Historical Quarterly* 47:169–77.

―――. "Secession and Coercion in Tennessee, the Spring of 1861." *Tennessee Historical Quarterly* 50:98–109.

McIlvaine, Charles Pettit. "Leonidas Polk." *Southern Historical Society Papers* 18:371–81.

McNaughton, Maria R. "James Walker—Combat Artist of Two American Wars." *Military Collector and Historian* 9:31–35.

Mainfort, Robert C., Jr. "Notes and Documents." *West Tennessee Historical Society Papers* 40 (1986): 72–81.

Melton, Maurice. "Disloyal Confederates." *Civil War Times Illustrated* 16 (August 1977): 12–19.

Moore, John Trotwood. "General Gideon J. Pillow." Unidentified newspaper clipping in possession of James C. Cole, Memphis, Tenn.

Morton, M. B. "General Simon Bolivar Buckner Tells the Story of the Fall of Fort Donelson." *Nashville Banner*, December 11, 1909.

Neff, Robert O. "The Best and the Bravest." *Confederate Chronicles of Tennessee* 2 (1987): 81–142.

Newberry, Farrar. "The Nashville Convention of 1850." *Confederate Veteran* 23:120–21.

Northrup, Jack. "Nicholas Trist's Mission to Mexico: A Reinterpretation." *Southwest Historical Quarterly* 71 (January 1968): 321–46.

Nye, W. S. "The Battle of LaFayette." *Civil War Times Illustrated* 6 (June 1966): 34–40.

Polk, William Mecklenburg. "General Polk and the Battle of Belmont." In *Battles and Leaders of the Civil War*, 4 vols., edited by Robert Underwood Johnson and Clarence Clough Buel, 1:348–57. New York, 1887.

Porter, James Davis. "A Sketch of the Life and Services of Gen. B. F. Cheatham." *Southern Bivouac* 2 (1883–84): 145–50.

Purcell, Douglas C. "Military Conscription in Alabama during the Civil War." *Alabama Review* 34 (April 1981): 94–106.

Quintard, Rt. Rev. Charles. "B. F. Cheatham, C.S.A." *Southern Historical Society Papers* 16:349–54.

Riley, Harris D., and Amos Christie. "Deaths and Disabilities in the Provisional Army of Tennessee." *Tennessee Historical Quarterly* 43:132–54.

Robbins, Charles D., and Johnny D. Walker. "General Gideon Is Most Controversial of Pillows." Paris, Tenn., *Post-Intelligencer*, April 23, 30, 1982.

Robbins, Peggy. "Allan Pinkerton's Southern Assignment." *Civil War Times Illustrated* 15 (January 1977): 6–47.

Russell, Robert G. "Prelude to the Presidency: The Election of Andrew Johnson to the Senate." *Tennessee Historical Quarterly* 26:148–76.

Sears, Louis M. "Nicholas P. Trist, a Diplomat with Ideals." *Mississippi Valley Historical Review* 11 (June 1924): 85–92.

Simon, John Y. "Grant at Belmont." *Military Affairs* 45 (December 1981): 161–66.

Sioussat, St. George L. "Tennessee and National Political Parties, 1850–1860." *Annual Report of the American Historical Association* (1914), 2:245–58.

———. "Tennessee, the Compromise of 1850, and the Nashville Convention." *Mississippi Valley Historical Review* 2 (December 1915): 313–47.

Smith, William F. "Operations before Fort Donelson." *Magazine of American History* 15 (January 1886): 21–43.

Spence, Philip B. "Leonidas Polk." *Confederate Veteran* 8:373.

Stonesifer, Roy P., Jr. "Gideon J. Pillow: A Study in Egotism." *Tennessee Historical Quarterly* 25:340–50.

Taylor, Jesse. "The Defense of Fort Henry." In *Battles and Leaders of the Civil War*, 4 vols., edited by Robert Underwood Johnson and Clarence Clough Buel, 1:368–72. New York, 1887.

Theisen, Lee S. "James K. Polk: Not So Dark a Horse." *Tennessee Historical Quarterly* 30:383–401.

Treichel, James A. "Lew Wallace at Fort Donelson." *Indiana Magazine of History* 49 (March 1963): 3–18.

Trousdale, J. A. "A History of the Life of William Trousdale." *Tennessee Historical Magazine* 2 (June 1916): 119–36.

Tucker, David M. "Black Politics in Memphis, 1865–1875." *West Tennessee Historical Society Papers* 26 (1972): 13–19.

Tyler, Ronnie C. "The Mexican War: A Lithographic Record." *Southwestern Historical Quarterly* 77:1–84.

Walke, Henry. "The Western Flotilla at Fort Donelson, Island Number Ten, Fort Pillow, and Memphis." In *Battles and Leaders of the Civil War*, 4 vols., edited by Robert Underwood Johnson and Clarence Clough Buel, 1:430–52. New York, 1887.

Walker, Peter Franklin. "Building a Tennessee Army: Autumn, 1861." *Tennessee Historical Quarterly* 16:99–116.

———. "Command Failure: The Fall of Forts Henry and Donelson." *Tennessee Historical Quarterly* 16:335–60.

———. "Holding the Tennessee Line: Winter, 1861–1862." *Tennessee Historical Quarterly* 16:228–49.

Walton, Brian G. "A Triumph of Political Stability: The Elections of 1847 in Tennessee." *East Tennessee Historical Society Publications* 40 (1967): 3–27.

Watson, Elbert L. "James Walker of Columbia, Polk's Critic and Compatriot." *Tennessee Historical Quarterly* 23:24–37.

Weller, Jac. "Combat Usefulness of Shotguns." *The American Rifleman* 112 (November 1964): 17–19.

Williams, Frank B., Jr. "Samuel Hervey Laughlin, Polk's Political Handyman." *Tennessee Historical Quarterly* 24:356–92.

Woodworth, Steven E. "The Indeterminate Quantities: Jefferson Davis, Leonidas Polk, and the End of Kentucky Neutrality, September, 1861." *Civil War History* 38 (December 1992): 289–97.

UNPUBLISHED STUDIES

Bearss, Edwin C. "Confederate Breakout." Fort Donelson National Military Park, February 1960.

———. "The Fighting on February 13—The Assault on Maney's Battery." Fort Donelson National Military Park, August 1959.

———. "The Fortifications at Fort Donelson." Fort Donelson National Military Park, May 1959.

———. "General C. F. Smith's Attack on the Rebel Right." Fort Donelson National Military Park, December 1959.

———. "Troop Movement Map, Jan. 2, 1863." Stones River National Military Park.

Brent, Robert A. "Nicholas Philip Trist: Biography of a Disobedient Diplomat." Ph.D. dissertation, University of Virginia, 1950.

Clark, Patricia P. "A. O. P. Nicholson of Tennessee: Editor, Statesman and Jurist." Master's thesis, University of Tennessee, 1965.

DeBerry, John H. "Confederate Tennessee." Ph.D. dissertation, University of Kentucky, 1967.

Garrett, Jill K. "General Gideon J. Pillow and the Pillow Family." In possession of Jill K. Garrett, Columbia, Tenn.

Hattaway, Herman M. "Stephen Dill Lee: A Biography." Ph.D. dissertation, Louisiana State University, 1969.

Johnson, Clarence L., Lonnie G. McPherson, and Ronald G. Hayhoe. "The Significance of Forts Henry and Donelson in the Western Campaign, 1862." Fort Donelson National Military Park, 1934.

Looney, John T. "Isham G. Harris of Tennessee: Bourbon Senator, 1877–1897." Master's thesis, University of Tennessee, 1970.

Schuster, Alice K. "Nicholas Philip Trist: Peace Mission to Mexico." Ph.D. dissertation, University of Pittsburgh, 1947.

Stonesifer, Roy P., Jr. "The Forts Henry-Heiman and Fort Donelson Campaigns: A Study of Confederate Command." Ph.D. dissertation, Pennsylvania State University, 1965.

Tricamo, John E. "Tennessee Politics, 1845–1861." Ph.D. dissertation, Columbia University, 1965.

Watters, George W. "Isham Green Harris, Civil War Governor and Senator from Tennessee, 1818–1897." Ph.D. dissertation, Florida State University, 1977.

Index

Smith, C. F., 91, 220, 231, 234, 386 (n. 71)

Smith, H. G., 292

Smith, Dr. J. W., 233–34

Smith, Justin, 116

Smith, Persifor Frazer, 83, 86, 88–89, 93, 95, 98, 108, 355 (nn. 11, 22), 363 (n. 63)

Smith, Preston, 52, 189, 204

Sneed, John L. T., 157, 162–63, 166–67, 170, 173

Sol (slave of GJP), 244, 389 (n. 17)

Southern Commercial Convention, 150

Sparrow, Edward, 274

Stanton, Edwin M., 305

Stanton, Fred P., 138

Steedman, James B., 282

Steele, Frederick, 299

Stephens, Alexander, 120

Stephens, William H., 170

Stephenson, Philip D., 197

Steptoe, Edward J., 54, 57

Stewart, Francis M., 286

Stone's River, 251, 253, 256

Strahl, Otho F., 186

Stuart, James E. B., 47

Summerville, Ga., 284, 288, 290

Swan Lake Plantation, 279, 312, 399 (n. 58)

Tacubaya, Mex., 95, 98

Talladega, Ala., 268, 277, 288

Talladega, Battle of, 3

Talladega *Democratic Watchtower*, 269

Tallushatchee, Battle of, 3

Tampico, Mex., 49–50, 53, 54, 349 (n. 88)

"Tampico Letter," 112

Tappan, James C., 197–98, 201, 203, 205

Tate, Sam, 165, 188–89, 206, 263, 304

Tatnall, Josiah, 57

Taylor, Gov. John, 24, 31

Taylor, Richard, 295, 297

Taylor, Zachary, 41–42, 44–45, 48–51, 77, 121, 126, 325

Tennessee Agriculturist, 19

Terry, Nathaniel, 37

Texas: annexation issue, 25, 36–37

Thayer, John M., 221, 229

Thomas, Benjamin, 313

Thomas, George H., 309

Thomas, Jonas E., 42

Thomas, Samuel, 317

Thompson, Jacob, 141

Thompson, M. Jeff, 175, 179–85, 188, 190, 192, 195, 376 (n. 3), 378 (n. 66), 380 (n. 10)

Thornton, Edward, 79

Tilden, Samuel J., 321

Tilghman, Lloyd, 246, 251, 390 (n. 25)

Totten, Joseph G., 58–59, 62, 117

Totten, Mrs. Joseph G., 117

Tower, Zealous B., 67–68, 70, 88, 97

Towson, Nathan, 115, 119

Travis, William E., 170, 196

Trenholm, George A., 292

Trigg, James B., 314, 317, 404 (n. 44)

Trigg, John, 404 (n. 44)

Trigg, Martha, 404 (n. 44)

Trist, Nicholas P., 76–77, 79–80, 95–96, 108, 111, 115, 118, 251, 331

Trousdale, Gov. William, 41, 100–101, 124, 132–33

Tucker, Beverley, 126, 130

Tullahoma, Tenn., 263

Tupelo, Miss., 248, 291

Turney, Hopkins L., 38, 41

Tuscaloosa, Ala., 277, 291

Tuscumbia, Ala., 277, 292

Twiggs, David E., 52, 58, 65–67, 70, 72, 80–83, 88–91, 93, 95, 97–98, 101, 110, 326, 357 (n. 40), 364 (n. 63)

Tyler, John, 24, 37–38, 149

Union and Planters Bank, 164

Union City, Tenn., 167–70, 172, 185, 190, 193, 194

Union Springs, Ala., 299
University of Alabama, 279
University of Georgia, 331
University of Nashville, 4
University of North Carolina, 152, 174, 369 (n. 57)

Valencia, Gabriel, 82–89, 356 (n. 33)
Van Buren, Martin, 13–15, 21–35 passim, 112, 325, 341 (n. 14), 343 (n. 57)
Vandiver, Frank, 390 (n. 29)
Van Dorn, Earl, 250–51, 266
Vaught, Nathan, 18, 21
Vera Cruz, Mex., 44, 49, 53, 54–60, 62, 77
"Veritas," 111–12
Vicksburg, Siege of, 269
Victoria, Mex., 50
Virginia, 54

Wade, Daniel Fountain, 312, 400 (n. 69)
Wade, Margaret Anne "Annie" Pillow, 312, 320
Waldron, W. M., 321
Walker, J. Knox, 7, 76–77, 114, 123, 131, 135, 153, 173, 181, 185–86, 196, 201–3, 245, 319, 332, 337 (n. 18), 378 (n. 50)
Walker, James, 17
Walker, James C., 102, 106, 325, 359 (n. 4)
Walker, Jimmie, 332
Walker, Leroy Pope, 158, 160, 165, 168, 171, 176, 187, 191, 379 (n. 3)
Walker, Marcus M., 304
Walker, Sen. Robert J., 27, 31–32, 34–35, 38
Walker, Sam P., 245, 332
Walker, William H. T., 53, 58, 74
Walker, William S., 157
Wallace, Lew, 221, 226, 229, 231
Wallace, W. H. L., 191, 226–27, 229
Warwick, Washington, 279
War with Mexico, The, 122–23

Washington, Martha Dandridge Custis, 336 (n. 2)
Washington, D.C., 26, 107, 120, 132, 135, 331
Washington *Union*, 115, 117, 330
Watkins, Louis D., 285–87, 398 (n. 32)
Watson Battery, 197–99, 201
Watterson, Henry, 155
Watts, Gov. Thomas H., 278, 280, 299
Watts, Given and Company, 304, 306
Wayne County, Tenn., 17
Welker, George, 117
Wells, R. C., 144–46
Welsh, Mr., 109
Werth, Alexander, 107
Western Military Institute, 138
West Point, 174, 345 (n. 14)
Wharton, Gabriel C., 225, 238
Wharton, John A., 254–55
Wheeler, Joseph, 266, 270, 398 (n. 23)
Whig party, 13, 16, 22, 37–38, 41, 65, 113, 116, 119–21, 126, 131–37, 148–51, 162, 172
White, Judge Hugh Lawson, 4, 13–15
White, R. R., 286
Whiteside, James A., 9
Whitthorne, Washington C., 140
Wickliffe, Nathan, 385 (n. 36)
Wilkins, John D., 109
Williams, Charles J., 47
Williams, Melville, 307, 314, 319, 320, 329
Williams, Sallie Polk Pillow, 314, 320, 329
Williams, Thomas C., 293
Williams v. Whitmore, 319
Wilmot Proviso, 124
Wilson, James H., 298–99
Wilson's Creek, Battle of, 183, 185
Winder, John H., 296
Winship, Oscar F., 46, 332
Winslow, Henry, 199
Winston County, Ala., 268
Wise, Henry A., 136

Wood, Sterling A. M., 241
Woodbury, Levi, 24
Woodruff, William E., 314
Woodson, Frederick, 304
Woodward Academy, 3, 337 (n. 10)
Woodworth, Steven, 379 (n. 3)
Wool, John E., 43
Worth, Charles F., 405 (n. 51)
Worth, William J., 56, 62, 80–83,
    89–93, 95–96, 98–101, 106, 108,
    110–14, 123, 357 (n. 40)
Wright, Hendrick B., 31–32
Wright, John V., 52, 173, 189, 198–99
Wright, Marcus J., 160
Wright, Silas, 28, 31, 33, 342 (n. 45)

Wurttenburg Academy, 3
Wynkoop, Francis M., 57, 70–73, 353
    (n. 56)
Wynne, Val, 179, 209

Yandell, Lunsford P., Jr., 162, 207, 210
Yeatman, Henry C., 277
Young, Evan, 17
"Young America," 131

Zacatepec, 82–86
Zion Church (Columbia), 12
Zollicoffer, Felix K., 146, 162, 167,
    170, 173, 175, 210